KATE GOSSELIN:
HOW SHE FOOLED THE WORLD
The Rise And Fall Of A Reality TV Queen

By Robert Hoffman

To Alexis, Leah, Hannah, Joel, Aaden, Collin,
Cara and Mady.
Remember that, no matter what,
you will always have each other.
Stay close to one another.
There is nothing more important than family.

"Children are the magic dreams that we all once were, filling the air with laughter and sunshine. Carefree, beautiful little gifts from God, children are our students, yet they teach us so much. Through the eyes of children we see life as a path of adventure, with caves to explore, secrets to keep, and a lifetime of experiences just waiting to be discovered."

– *Author Unknown*

"…And I wish I could remember what we ate, and what we talked about, and how they sounded, and how they looked when they slept that night. I wish I had not been in such a hurry to get on to the next thing: dinner, bath, book, and bed. I wish I had treasured the doing a little more, and the getting it done a little less."

– *Anna Quindlen, Author*

TABLE OF CONTENTS

PREFACE

WARNING: For those of you who love Kate Gosselin and support her unconditionally, and think that every bad thing ever said or written about her is a lie, then this book probably isn't for you.

> "Do not judge, or you too will be judged.
> For in the same way you judge others, you will be judged,
> and with the measure you use, it will be measured to you."
>
> *– Matthew 7:1*

That passage is for me. I am a "Gosselin Insider." My intention in writing this "book," for lack of a better word, was not to judge Kate Gosselin, but rather to present information that I learned in the past several years that might hopefully, somehow, help eight of the most beautiful children I have ever met.

I'm not a professional writer, obviously, and I have no ambitions of becoming a writer or anything of the kind. I'm just a mediocre guy from small-town Pennsylvania; a simple father of three. My involvement in this story and in the lives of the Gosselins happened by chance, and perhaps by fate.

This book is an unpolished look at the real Kate Gosselin; a collection of my observations, experiences and findings. It's a little bit rough around the edges, and I like it that way. I'd rather you read my exact thoughts and not the thoughts of high-priced editors who altered the text according to their own line of thinking.

I started writing this book while working professionally covering Jon and Kate, but then ended the project all together when the massive story died down. I had mistakenly thought that the exploitation of the Gosselin children would end once they were no longer being forced to film a television show for the world's entertainment. I was wrong.

This story started for me in the summer of 2009. I had lost one of my two full-time jobs and was working from home as an art director for two record companies, one of my two careers for the past 15 years. Money was very tight for my wife and me, as it was for many people. With the economy tanking, and with three small children of our own, I was getting desperate for work.

I was in my home office one morning when my phone rang. It was my wife, Dana, calling from her office at the *Reading Eagle*, the local newspaper where I had also once worked for 21 years as a graphic designer and web designer. Dana told me she had just gotten a call and that she might have some freelance work for me if I was interested. Before she even finished her sentence I said, "I'll take it! I don't care what it is. We need the money!"

Dana's phone call was from *US Weekly*, and they were looking for someone local to cover the Jon and Kate Gosselin story. They had contacted Dana because she was the first person on record to publicly question Kate Gosselin's parenting methods, and to write about Kate and the Gosselin saga, before it even was. Several years ago, Dana had a very successful online blog on the paper's website, and one of the hot topics for her at the time, and that generated the most heated discussion, was Kate Gosselin, back before she was a household name.

Dana had to pass on the *US Weekly* offer because she worked at the paper and wouldn't be available for the full-time reporting that *US Weekly* was looking for. She recommended me for the job, and after a single phone call and a couple of emails I started reporting for *US Weekly* the next day. The job was only supposed to last a week or two, and I thought it would be fun.

I knew Jon and Kate lived nearby, about 10 minutes away, but I had no idea exactly where. I had never happened across either of them in town, even though I'm a regular at many of the stores that Kate frequents, and I shop at the same grocery store as Kate.

I had never seen their reality TV show, primarily because we didn't have cable in our house – for the sake of our own children – and I had never so much as picked up a tabloid to read. Really. I certainly don't consider myself to be above that sort of thing, I just really don't care about other people's problems since I have enough of my own.

I had heard all of the negative comments about Kate Gosselin from Dana and her fellow bloggers years before, but I went into this job completely open minded, unbiased and with no real pre-conceived ideas about Jon or Kate. I certainly had no intention of judging either of them. Being a flawed person myself, I'm the last person to judge anyone. My job for *US Weekly* was simply to report what I saw.

As the father of three beautiful children, whom my world revolves around, I went into my assignment with a parent's perspective, and I paid very close attention to the kids – how they behaved and how they were treated.

Throngs of media and paparazzi had already been stalking this family for two months before I arrived at the Gosselin home on Heffner Road in Lower Heidelberg Township, PA. Up until then, they had basically resigned themselves to staring at the house from behind a fence a football field away, looking at the family through long lenses and following them on their everyday travels.

As a tabloid reporter, I was paid to be at the Gosselin house every day, taking notes on EVERYTHING I saw and heard, no matter how minor, right down to what Kate was wearing and what she bought at the grocery store. Each night I would type up my notes and email them to my editor at the magazine. Those notes were kept on file for the next week's magazine, for possible use in a story.

"What did Kate buy at the grocery store?" was a very big story back then for the person who had worked the local Gosselin beat for *US Weekly* before me.

That all changed in a New York minute.

When I got to the Gosselin house that first day, Jon had, just two days prior, hired a "management team" from New York City and was starting to take control of his own image. If only he could go back and have a do-over on that decision. That was the real beginning of the end for him.

Jon's new philosophy worked in my favor for longevity on the job though, because now he was talking more to people at the house, and an hour into my first day at the fence I was face to face with him having a one-on-one conversation. Jon and I clicked instantly, I think, because I was local; I was a father of three kids the same ages as his, who were going to the same school as he did when he was younger; and I had been through a failed marriage of my own. At first, we just talked about nothing. He could see that I really didn't care about who he was and what his problems were and that I was just there doing a job to support my family.

I like Jon Gosselin - a lot. He's my friend. I like Jon Gosselin's family as well. Hanging out with Jon is like hanging out with any of your friends. It's relaxed and usually uneventful, and we both like it that way. Except for time spent with my children, I lead a very boring life, and I have fun when I'm with Jon. I've traveled with him and partied with him and have been with him through his highest highs and his lowest lows. Jon is a regular guy who has gotten himself into a very bad situation. He tasted fame for a few minutes and it got the best of him. Like most people, Jon is flawed.

No matter what he's done or what people have written about him, I have never once seen Jon act in a rude manner to anyone, or act like he was better than anyone, even when he was being treated like a rock star and on top of the world in Las Vegas hosting a celebrity pool party at the MGM Grand's Wet Republic. I was there with him, "working" for *US Weekly*. Jon has always acted like a regular guy, and he has always treated me, and every other media person, fairly – even when I was helping to destroy his life by reporting his every move to my employer.

It made me sick to my stomach at times, doing this job, but Jon knew my family and our financial situation, and he understood that I needed to work to feed my kids as well. All he ever asked of me was that I tell the truth about what I saw.

All that being said, none of it is why this book is mainly about Kate. There just really aren't too many more things that can be written about Jon. The tabloids, mine included, and countless media outlets and bloggers have dragged him over the coals and through the mud and back, while a lot of the time giving Kate a free pass.

Did Jon deserve a lot or most of the criticism and mudslinging that he received? Of course he did. He's received a lot of very bad advice from unscrupulous people, and he's made one bad decision after another since I've known him. He got caught up in the excitement of being a "celebrity." Jon got into bed with the wrong people, perhaps literally and figuratively, and he's paying a heavy price even today. I believe Jon when he says that he was acting out after his behind-closed-doors split with Kate because he got married and took on so much responsibility when he was just 22. He was trying to get back some of what he missed out on. This doesn't excuse his behavior, but it does explain it.

Meanwhile, Kate Gosselin continued to be immune from criticism. She strutted around like a peacock with her head held high – with her bodyguards, her handlers and public relations team, her media trainer, her team of lawyers, and her protective Network family feeding her a script of talking points for the week – pretending to be mother-of-the-year, and fooling millions of people while pursuing her Hollywood lifestyle on the backs of her eight beautiful children.

I don't like that last part.

So why have I written this book? Some people insist it is for the money. It is not. With the size of the book running through Amazon's self-publishing division, I would have to pay them for each copy sold. I did the math. A book half this size would gross me $2.00 per book after Amazon's cut.

If anything, I'll be sued by one or more parties before this is over, so the thought of any profit from this project is not even a consideration.

I have received "cease and desist" letters from Williams & Connolly LLP, the law firm that represents Discovery Communications, Inc. TLC and Discovery Talent Services, Inc. ("Discovery"), and from Lavely & Singer, the firm representing Kate. The letter on behalf of Discovery expressed concern that my book contained Discovery's trade secrets and other confidential information protected by law. The letter from Kate's attorney was more heavy handed and threatening. But it is very telling that neither firm accused me of writing untruths or disputed the facts I have presented. Even Kate, who takes to Twitter to attack anyone who even hints at criticizing her, has not denied any of what I have written. She can't deny it because many of the words that form this book are her own.

I am not trying to ruin Kate or destroy her life. I wish her a long and successful career at whatever she ends up doing – but I would love it if she would leave her kids out of her quest to retain her celebrity and give them back what's left of their childhoods, while they still have a chance to be young and innocent.

I would also love for this book to cause people to question why TLC and Discovery kept filming this family for five seasons knowing full well that Kate Gosselin was abusing her children. I have been told that there is much footage of this that obviously never saw, and will never see, the light of day.

It will be simple, if necessary, for me to prove that I had intended to write a book on my experiences as a tabloid reporter in 2009, in partnership with a colleague of mine. We had met with a publisher in Manhattan who was interested in backing the book, and I came home excited that I had a new project. But a short time later, after getting to know the Gosselin kids, I decided that I didn't want anything to do with a book that could potentially cause them even more harm. I also wasn't happy with my partner's tactics and the direction in which he was taking the book. My decision to not continue with him also cost me a friendship.

So no, I did not write this book for money. I wrote it for the Gosselin kids.

My experiences with the Gosselin children, especially Collin, are priceless to me.

Even though every embarrassing moment of their lives up to this point has been documented for all the world to see, first by Jon and Kate and a film crew, then by Kate and a film crew, Kate continues to exploit her children today. She tweets about them, and blogs about them, and complains about them, and posts photos of them on her personal website and on Twitter. Photos of the children in their bathing suits and photos of the children in bed. I personally find that disgusting.

I mention the children as little as possible in this book, to respect what's left of their privacy. But since they are the reason this book was necessary, I will share a personal story.

One day, back in 2009, knowing how strict Kate is with the kids about them not eating anything even remotely fun, I brought them two big boxes of Dunkin Donuts. Their eyes lit up like Christmas morning, and they dug into them and couldn't eat them fast enough. (I had checked with Jon first to make sure that nobody had a peanut allergy or anything of the sort.) After a few minutes, Collin had icing all over his face and a donut in each hand. There was one donut left in the box, and he said to me in his precious little voice, "Robert, will you hold that donut for me until I finish these two? I really want it, but I can't carry it."

Then one of the little girls reprimanded me in a stern voice, saying "Mommy doesn't let us eat sweets!" and I acted surprised and said, "Oh, I'm sorry. I won't bring anymore donuts to the house, I promise." And she said in a quieter voice, "Oh no, Robert, you bring us more donuts."

And my heart melted.

Whenever I was with the kids, or my kids were playing with them and it was time for us to go, Collin would ALWAYS make sure to come and give us big hugs and kisses and say goodbye. Always. And when I'd look back as I was walking away, he'd still be waving to us. He has so much love to give and his heart is so big.

In 2010, two of these sweet kids, Collin being one of them, were EXPELLED from KINDERGARTEN for acts of violence and for using foul language. When I saw Kate go on television to deny they had been expelled and to blame Jon and the stress of the divorce as the reason they were acting out, I knew I had to at least tell what I know, and what I've seen. I hope that maybe, just maybe, someone will step in to help them. I don't know whom, and I don't know how, but something needs to be done – for the sake of the children.

This book contains information I have come to learn, both personally and through exhaustive research, while reporting for *US Weekly* and in the days since. I have had no official conversations at all with any of the Gosselin extremists – the bloggers. Also, I have not interviewed Aunt Jodi and Uncle Kevin or anyone connected with them, as they have been accused by Kate and her supporters of having their own personal agenda.

I have, however, spoken to and interviewed hundreds of people along the way, including Gosselin friends, family members, nannies, babysitters (both former and present), "helpers," restaurant owners, wait staff, anonymous TLC/Discovery employees, physicians, nurses, fertility specialists, childhood friends, etc. Not much is from a single source. Wherever possible, I have verified my information through separate sources independently. Contrary to what has been reported in some articles, Jon has never given me a personal interview for *US Weekly* or for this book, which he didn't even know I was writing until I went public with it in June of 2012. Again, the only thing he ever asked was that I report the truth.

For the record, I have had exactly one face-to-face conversation with Kate Gosselin. It lasted about a minute on a day when she had no choice but to exchange a few brief words with me because she had let the dogs get out of her property and drove away, leaving them scared and roaming on a busy road in front of her house. You will read more about this later. I have tried to speak to Kate to get her side of the story, but I have never even come close to getting a civil response from her. Just an angry, hateful glare.

I have, however, been in rooms and in cars, and I've overheard conversations with Kate Gosselin, so I have heard some things directly from the horse's mouth.

In leaving no stone unturned in researching this book, I came across a treasure trove of Kate Gosselin's personal documents and information. Among those documents was Kate's personal, very detailed daily journal from 2005-2007, chronicling the Gosselin's day-to-day lives – the good, and the very bad – in Kate's own words.

In the interest of full disclosure, I found Kate's journal while combing through documents and computer discs and files that she had thrown in the trash the day after she threw Jon out of the apartment above the garage for good.

Many, many negative stories have been written online and in the tabloids about Kate Gosselin. Some stories are similar to what I have written here, but they can't be proven, so Kate Gosselin has been allowed to continue on with business as usual. I would never have dreamed of publishing a book filled with my own opinions about Kate Gosselin. It would have been laughed off by Kate and everyone affiliated with her, as a pack of lies made up by a "hater." She is incredibly insulated by her handlers.

Kate's journal is what finally convinced me to move ahead with this book and kept me motivated while writing. The journal, once and for all, gives us a glimpse into what happened behind closed doors, in Kate's own words, and provides hard evidence that cannot be disputed.

This book may be difficult to read. It isn't easy to see Kate's words describing how she routinely spanked her children so hard that she had to pray to God to help her stop. It isn't easy to read how she lied and misrepresented herself and her family's situation so she could get good, caring people to generously hand over their money, time and lots and lots of gifts to her.

I have no regrets about the kids someday reading this book because they are living this nightmare, and I'm sure their reality has been far, far worse than I, or anyone outside of that house, will ever know or could possibly imagine.

I've used many quotes throughout this book – quotes that I feel capture the essence of what I'm trying to convey. I use quotes because Kate uses them throughout her life and in her writings, and I wanted to keep this book in that same spirit.

My professional opinion and diagnosis as a graphic designer and photographer is that Kate Gosselin is mentally ill and very sick on several different levels. She needs to get professional help before she seriously injures one or all of her children…or worse. I hope that the truths in this book will push her to get that help because, despite all her lies and the physical, verbal, emotional and psychological abuses she has heaped upon her children, she is still their mother, and I would guess that they love her. Because that is what children do, until they one day realize that their "normal" is really not normal at all.

(Disclaimer: In paraphrasing Kate's words, I left her misspellings as written.)

"I tell you, on the day of judgment,
people will give account
for every careless word they speak,
for by your words you will be justified,
and by your words you will be condemned."
– *Matthew 12:36-37*

ONCE UPON A TIME ...

... there lived a beautiful little girl named Katie Irene. She grew up in a beautiful house in the country, with a barn and a big yard for her to run around and play in. She had everything a little girl could ever want or need.

Katie had a loving family, which included a nurturing and doting father, who was also an associate pastor at the local church; a protective and supportive mother, who baked cookies and pies and would do anything to see her little Katie smile; and a house full of siblings to play with, and to share in all of her dreams.

Like most little girls, Katie played with her dolls and dreamed of one day becoming a mother herself. She watched her parents closely and learned a lifetime's worth of parenting skills that would guide her on her way to motherhood.

Katie was raised as a Christian and practiced her faith daily. She was wholesome and shy around boys and, growing up, never really went on dates or spent much time with them. She stayed focused on her schoolwork and her career instead, and worked very hard to achieve all of her goals.

Katie loved people so much, especially little children, and she knew from an early age that she would one day become a pediatric nurse, so that she could take care of as many children as she possibly could. Her heart was filled with so much faith and love, and she wanted to share it.

She knew that one day, her prince would come riding up on his big white horse and sweep her off her feet, and they would get married and have a house full of children of their own, to pamper and nurture and to grow old loving. She dreamed that very same dream every night until, at last, it finally came true.

Katie met her knight in shining armor, and soon after, they married and had that giant house full of happy children of their own. All of Katie's dreams had come true, just like she had planned from the time she was a little girl.

And they all lived happily ever after.

~

I wish I could say that's how this story goes, and that little Katie's life was filled with butterflies and lollipops and tender, cherished, heartfelt moments. Unfortunately, the reality is very different.

THE FORMATIVE YEARS

This is not a happy story. Rather, it is the sad tale of a greedy and selfish woman, so consumed by the desire for fame and monetary riches, that she sold her children's privacy, dignity and childhoods; discarded their loving father; drove away family and friends; scammed a generous public; displayed unspeakable cruelty to humans and animals alike; and behaved in the most deceitful, rude, nasty and unappreciative ways imaginable. Something must have gone terribly wrong in nature or nurture, or a combination of the two, for such a person to be created.

Katie Irene Kreider was born in Hershey, PA, on March 28, 1975. She is one of five children born to parents Charlene and Kenton Kreider. Her father, Kenton, is a church pastor.

For those who have followed Kate's public life closely, you will already know that her words and actions show her to be an emotionally disturbed woman. She displays all the traits of a textbook narcissist and has been officially diagnosed with bipolar disorder, according to two members of her family. She would never, ever admit to being a narcissist – what narcissist would? – And she chooses not to take medication for her bipolar disorder, dismissing the doctor's diagnosis as nonsense. For those who know little about this woman, you will come to understand more as you read further.

Kate reportedly suffered a violent and abusive childhood, which may have triggered her severe narcissistic behavior. In her words, she was "very overly disciplined." Several people close to Kate, including a sibling, told me that her childhood behind closed doors was a house of horrors for her. I have also been told that, in addition to being regularly beaten by her father, Kenton, she was also "sexually abused by a family member."

While in high school, Kate became pregnant. This will probably be surprising news to everyone who bought her oft-repeated story that she could not conceive naturally. It was just one of many very public lies she told to solidify her carefully crafted image. The sad truth is that Kate's father forced her to secretly abort the baby, which left her empty and hollow inside, and very angry. She left home at the request of her father, who could no longer tolerate her rebellious behavior and sexual promiscuity.

Kate didn't have any marketable skills or a work ethic, but she was driven by hate and resentment toward her father. While still in high school, Kate decided that she would become a nurse so she could marry a wealthy doctor and have children of her own, and would never have to work again. This was her original master plan, and anyone who knows Kate Gosselin knows that, once she gets an idea in her head, there is nothing that is going to stand in her way.

Patience was not one of Kate's strong points, however, and she couldn't wait to get started. She was still in high school, but she was resourceful enough to start her plan in motion, and began EMS training.

After graduating from Mount Calvary Christian School in Elizabethtown, PA, Kate tried her hand at college, but gave up quickly after realizing that four years of schooling was just too much of her valuable time to waste. She attended Harrisburg Area Community College from June to August of 1994.

Kate decided to expedite the process of becoming a nurse and applied to the diploma program at the Reading Hospital and Medical Center School of Nursing in West Reading, PA. She attended that school from August 1994 to June 1997, earning her diploma in three years.

In Kate's first book, *Multiple Blessings*, she paints a very romantic picture of herself as a wholesome, God-fearing individual. She quotes from Proverbs and talks about how, as a little girl, she dreamed of meeting her husband, having children and settling down "to live a happily-ever-after kind of life."

Unfortunately for Kate, two of her former lovers spoke out to the tabloids to share a few of their own personal experiences with a young Katie Irene Kreider.

Kate's one-time fiancé, Adam Miller, said that **Kate pressured him into marriage, but he broke up with her after he caught her cheating on him** – at her 21st birthday party – **with a guy who had even more money** to offer her. He had a Corvette! Adam also shared that "Kate was always chasing the money. I spoiled Kate with gifts, like a diamond bracelet and a gold locket, and she loved that. **I think one of the main reasons she liked me is that I had so much money flowing.**" He said, **"My friends didn't like her."** Adam also said that sweet little Katie Irene, from a church pastor's home and upbringing was a **"sex kitten,"** and that she became **"very possessive."**

So it appeared that Katie had found a great guy in Adam, who showered her with money and gifts, moved her into his family's home, and was going to marry her, like she wanted. So what did she do? She cheated on him. She tried to trade up for bigger and better, with a guy who had a Corvette. Remember, Kate wanted a doctor at this point, but until she found one she would settle for anybody with money.

After Katie realized that all Corvette guy wanted was sex from a younger girl, and nothing more – no wife, no babies, no future – Kate ran back to Adam, who now wanted absolutely nothing to do with her. So Kate devised a complicated plan to get Adam back: she would date one of his friends to make him jealous.

Kate started dating a guy named Jason Lentz, who just happened to know Adam. According to Jason, "Kate brought up marriage and kids three months into their relationship."

Jason added "Kate was spending weekends at the home that he shared with his mother. Kate did not pay for a thing, and his mom waited on Kate hand and foot. **She expected people to take care of her.**"

So after three months of Kate's games, and her pressuring him into marriage and children already, Jason learned that Kate had been calling Adam to get back together. He said, "Adam confided she was calling him. She wanted to get back together. I wasn't surprised. I had a feeling Kate was seeing me to stay close to him." Kate then dumped Jason and moved on in search of her next victim.

After Adam and Jason, "Kate bounced from guy to guy, at one point even living with two guys at the same time."

In June of 1997, Kate graduated from nursing school and was very concerned that she hadn't yet landed that doctor. She was now going to have to actually go to work as a nurse. She got a job as a registered nurse in labor and delivery at The Reading Hospital and Medical Center.

Kate didn't enjoy being a nurse, and she wasn't particularly good at it. Kate believed she was better than the other nurses who were content with just being nurses. In her mind, she was already in that place where she had always envisioned herself – a wealthy doctor's wife – and she treated her fellow nurses with contempt and disrespect, as if she thought she was so much better than "those people."

Kate was very much disliked by her co-workers. "Nobody could understand why she wanted to become a nurse in the first place. It was obvious that she didn't like people and had no interest in helping them. She cringed at the thought of touching sick people," a fellow nurse who worked with Kate told me. "She thought she was better and smarter than everyone else, even though clearly she wasn't."

It isn't hard to believe that Kate wasn't cut out for nursing. Besides lacking in empathy, Kate is a self-described manic germophobe and always has been. It is hard to imagine Kate Gosselin wanting to be around germs and sickness all day, every day. After she had children, she was repulsed by her own babies' poop and pee and germs of any kind. On the "Sextuplets Turn Three" episode of *Jon & Kate Plus Ei8ht*, Kate basically said her own children were Petri dishes. She and Jon talked on the interview couch about never eating anything the kids make, and they went through the motions of showing the audience how filthy their kids are.

During the "RV Trip" episode of *Kate Plus Ei8ht*, Kate screamed in disgust because her daughter handed a slice of pizza to Steve Neild, Kate's bodyguard, with her bare hands. Those were her own children that "disgusted" her. It is inconceivable that she would ever subject herself to sick, germy strangers.

No, Kate didn't, and doesn't, like people. She especially didn't like sick people, which is a bit of a problem for anyone who is a nurse. Unfortunately for Kate, the eligible doctors noticed this about her as well. A former nurse who went to nursing school with Kate said, "Even during nursing school, Kate threw herself at every doctor she could find, even the ugly ones, but was rejected every time. That made her mad."

Unable to snare a doctor, Kate had to alter her life plan, which was not easy for her to do. She never wanted to give up, but Kate was still a "lowly" nurse, and she knew she'd have to make a change.

Although Kate didn't have anything close to a good bedside manner, she did have a couple of other powerful things going for her. She had drive and determination and she loved to "mastermind," as she would repeatedly say in the following years. So it wasn't long before she set her new plan in motion.

The first thing she desperately needed, though, was a husband. Well, technically, she didn't really NEED a husband, but one was required because she wanted her "brand" to be wholesome to make sure it would sell.

WHEN KATIE MET JONNY

WITH ALL MY LOVE
Ever since the day we met, I've known you were the one for me.
No one else has ever made me feel as happy, as content,
as full of smiles as you do. Wherever I am, you are there also,
even if only in thought, and I know that if we hadn't met and
fallen in love, I'd still be looking for happiness.
Love at Thanksgiving and Always
– Love, Kate – 11/26/98

Katie Irene Kreider was on the prowl for a man with money, and her friends knew it. But Kate didn't give Jonathan Keith Gosselin a second glance at the company picnic they were both attending – not until one of Kate's friends mentioned to her that Jon came from a "rich family" that is. "His father is a big doctor in Wyomissing," the friend said to Kate.

Having had zero luck in finding an actual doctor to force into marriage, Kate did the next best thing she could think of – she went after a doctor's son. Kate quickly learned that Jon lived on the "best street" in affluent Wyomissing, PA, and her blood started pumping. Kate also learned that Jon had a girlfriend. "Not for long!" Kate told her friend.

This is the story of how Jon and Kate met. It is "their story," in Kate's own words, as it was written on Jon and Kate's earliest website:

"It all started when Jon and I met on October 5, 1997 at a picnic. I never believed in "love at first sight", but this came really close. Jon was walking across the grass and I saw him and was instantly intrigued! Our eyes met and continued to meet from across the way all afternoon. Finally, I arranged for someone to introduce us…and the rest is history!

This is how Kate described that initial meeting with Jon in her first book.

Kate said that she had been a planner her entire life and she took great pride when all of her plans worked out exactly as her detailed, scheduled list and calendar said it should.

When Jon, a twenty-year-old soccer player sauntered across the lawn in front of Kate, who sat under a pavilion chatting with her friends, Kate says she tried not to watch him for too long because she was at the picnic to be with her friend, not to find a date.

After she and Jon "danced around each other all afternoon, stealing glances and quickly turning away," she says that Jon was the one who walked over to her because he noticed Kate holding a baby bundled up in a soft pink blanket. Jon said, "Are you going to let anyone else have a turn holding that baby?"

Kate said that that was the moment that she knew she wanted to know more about this "cute, friendly, Asian guy who, like me, seemed to melt at the sight of a ten-pound package of sleepy promise."

That sounds simply beautiful, doesn't it? But in an early draft of *Multiple Blessings,* Kate described that very same moment at the picnic differently.

Kate said that she was "spurred on" by her eager matchmaking friends so she "devised a complicated plan to go talk to someone who knew someone else who just might know him and be able to introduce the two of us." Kate added that she wasn't usually wasn't so bold and that this was out of character for her but she was excited that it worked.

So let's recap. On her website version, Kate said that she arranged for a friend to introduce her and Jon. In *Multiple Blessings*, she said that she wasn't interested in finding a date and that Jon had nonchalantly walked over to her while she was holding a baby. And in the version that didn't make it into her book, she said she devised a complicated plan to enlist a couple of someones to introduce them. It is all clear as mud, and leads to some obvious questions.

Where the heck did the baby come from? Was it a prop in her "complicated plan" to meet Jon? It certainly wouldn't be surprising to learn that she was exploiting a baby for her personal gain even back then. Talk about foreshadowing. And was it really the "baby" moment that made her want to know more about the "cute, friendly Asian guy," or was it the moment her friend told her that Jon's father was a big doctor in Wyomissing?

In the first line of Chapter 1 of *Multiple Blessings*, from one of Kate's earlier drafts, she says that it's strange how the moment when you meet someone special is forever engraved in your memory.

What's more strange is that this very special moment that was "forever engraved" in Kate's memory changed throughout three different drafts of the same story. As you will soon see, nothing is ever what it seems with Kate Gosselin.

It's hard to know if Kate ever really wanted love from Jon, or if she was just looking for someone with money to fill the role of a father in her master plan. At any rate, Katie and Jonny started dating.

Jon didn't want to get married right away. Not to Kate or anyone else. He wanted to enjoy his youth. Back then Jon was a very good-looking guy. I was surprised when he showed me his pictures from high school and all of the very attractive girls who were interested in him. My first experience in seeing Jon was watching him getting beaten down by Kate on *Jon & Kate Plus Ei8ht* during the divorce episodes. I had always just assumed he was a nerdy guy with no other options. Well, I saw evidence of many better options, but Kate pressured him enough that he finally went along on her journey.

Jon and Kate got married on June 12, 1999, at a friend's home in Wyomissing. Kate said it was "A perfect garden wedding with equally perfect weather," and that "It was truly a beautiful thing!"

Kate did pretty well for herself in marrying Jon because his father was extremely generous. He paid for their wedding, bought them their first house in Wyomissing, and quietly supported them financially, giving them a large check each month. He gave them a lot of support and a lot of money, and Kate LOVED that about him. OK. The self-proclaimed planner found herself a husband, check. What was next on the list?

THE ACTION PLAN

"I'm the plan maker and you're the plan follower."
– Kate Gosselin

By the time Kate and Jon married, Kate had become fascinated and completely obsessed with something that was going on in Carlisle, Iowa. A woman named Bobbi McCaughey had given birth in 1997 to septuplets – seven babies at one time. Kate initially thought of her as a "freak show," until she started reading about her…and reading some more.

Kate read every word written about this miraculous story – a woman giving birth to seven babies at one time – but she could only focus on two things: the massive amount of media attention Bobbi McCaughey was receiving, and the money and gifts being heaped upon her by her adoring public.

This was it. Kate found her new life's mission. She wanted what Bobbi McCaughey was getting, and a whole lot more. Just for having a bunch of babies, Bobbi McCaughey was showered with a huge assortment of gifts, including seven years of free cable TV, college scholarships for all of her children, ten years of portrait photos, a lifetime supply of Pampers diapers, a 15-passenger van, and … a new and very large house.

In addition to those gifts, she also received free meals, babysitting, housecleaning, laundry service and personal transportation. Her community turned out in full force to volunteer their services in doing anything and everything the family needed. Local banks opened up accounts for the donations that were already pouring in. President Clinton even phoned to congratulate Bobbi and told her, "You know, when those kids all go off to school, you will be the best-organized manager in the U.S."

And there it was! That last thing was what sparked the idea that led to Kate creating her "Supermom" persona. It was going to be her "brand." Her master plan was to have two sets of Higher Order Multiples and build an empire bigger than Martha Stewart's because, in addition to all of Martha's skills, Kate would also be a "Supermom." She would be everything Martha Stewart was, only with a house full of babies to take care of as well. Every mother in America would look up to her; mothers of the world would adore her!!

With her idea fully formed, Kate just needed to figure out how she was going to conceive Higher Order Multiples naturally. The first major problem Kate encountered in achieving her master plan of having multiples was a sticky one. She didn't have a fertility problem, having already become pregnant by accident a few years earlier. But that certainly wasn't going to stop Kate Gosselin though. She was a nurse, and she did her research and concocted a good story that she told Jon, and later the world.

She said that she had wanted to have children as soon as they got married but Jon wasn't ready. She had a nagging feeling since she was a child that she would have a difficult time getting pregnant so she got herself tested right away and found out that she had PCOS, which is Polycystic Ovarian Syndrome. So according to Kate, they decided to check out fertility doctors "just in case" in would take a long time to get pregnant.

Of course it didn't take long. On only their second cycle of treatment, they were pregnant with twins and Kate was "ecstatic!!!!!!!!"

First of all, the notion that Kate had a "nagging feeling" that she wouldn't be able to become pregnant from as far back as when she was a child sounds preposterous. It is not something a child would even think about, much less be worried about. Kate would also have us believe that, as a young and healthy 23-year-old girl, she had a hunch and nagging thoughts that she would not be able to get pregnant. (This subject was later used to promote her first television special.) It all sounds very unique, indeed. Unique and suspicious.

When leading into the subject of getting pregnant in *Multiple Blessings*, Kate writes, "We were young, healthy and ambitious, and it wasn't long before baby fever set in."

She certainly picked a strange choice of words. Healthy? Why would she mention being healthy unless she wanted to add drama by trying to convince people that she really did have PCOS, but she just didn't know it? And what is the connection between being ambitious and having "baby fever?" Ambition generally relates to having a desire for success or achievement; it is not usually a term used in connection with wanting to have a baby. In looking at how things turned out, however, maybe "ambitious" was the correct word after all.

The next sentences in the book also sound suspicious. Kate said that she always longed to be a mom, she still had the perennial dark question of "What if I can't?" accompanied her dream.

Kate was 25 when she had her twins. So according to Kate, even as a teenager dreaming of becoming a mother, she had "the perennial dark question, what if I can't?" It seems she conveniently forgot about that "accidental" pregnancy from when she was younger.

But those pesky details didn't matter. All that mattered was that Kate had her public reason to seek infertility treatment: Polycystic Ovarian Syndrome (PCOS). Oddly enough though, she never exhibited one single symptom of PCOS. According to WebMD, the most common symptoms of PCOS are:

- Acne.
- Weight gain and trouble losing weight.
- Extra hair on the face and body. Often women get thicker and darker facial hair and more hair on the chest, belly, and back.
- Thinning hair on the scalp.
- Irregular periods. Often women with PCOS have fewer than nine periods a year. Some women have no periods. Others have very heavy bleeding.

- Fertility problems. Many women who have PCOS have trouble getting pregnant (infertility).
- Depression.

I've done two years' worth of research on PCOS and have spoken to many, many women who suffer from the disease. There are no absolutes and generalizations that apply to every woman with PCOS.

Ten out of ten mothers I spoke to said that the thought that they might not be able to get pregnant had never even occurred to them beforehand. One said, "That's something that would come after several failed attempts at getting pregnant." PCOS seems to run in families, so your chances of having it are higher if other women in your family have PCOS, irregular periods, or diabetes. PCOS can be passed down from either your mother's side or your father's side. PCOS did not run in Kate's family, as the Kreider clan was full of children.

Kate had none of the symptoms of PCOS, but she stuck with her story. At the time, there was no reason for anybody to even think twice about it, much less be suspicious of her intentions. But her PCOS claim was hugely important because it gave Kate her reason to seek infertility treatments.

(Writer's note: I asked Jon several times over the years about Kate having PCOS, and he swore she does indeed have it and displayed at least one symptom. With so much evidence to the contrary, I don't believe that Kate does or ever did have PCOS.)

Kate didn't want to waste another minute and started shopping for infertility doctors right away. The standard in the industry for someone as young as Kate is to try to get pregnant on your own for at least a year before turning to infertility treatments. This made Kate furious that she would have to wait.

Her persistence paid off and she finally found a doctor who would begin treating her, undiagnosed, after only six months of marriage – given Kate's lie to her that she and Jon had been trying to conceive for over a year – and Kate began her journey into the world of infertility. It's not uncommon for an infertility doctor to treat a woman without first diagnosing her problem, especially if she's as convincing as Kate was. The business of infertility is extremely competitive among doctors, and the way to get more business is to have more success stories. I spent a lot of time on online chat boards talking to women about this subject, and I heard many stories of doctors treating patients without diagnosing them. They would take their patients at their word. It's a business.

And after all, who in their right mind would ever make up something like having PCOS and put themselves through the costly and painful process of infertility treatment if it weren't really necessary?

That's a rhetorical question. Who, indeed?

Even though Kate was young and healthy, really healthy, and even without actually having PCOS and with taking infertility medication, she still failed to become pregnant the first time around.

The second cycle was a good one, and Kate became pregnant – with twins. Most people going through a similar situation would be thrilled at that news. Kate was disappointed, though, and angry again. "Just twins?" she said in a dejected voice.

Kate said that they had prayed for twins because Jon was as "baby crazy" as she was that they decided that they would fight over just one baby. She also said that she and Jon joked about that since they were dating.

Cara and Mady Gosselin were born that October.

Although Kate says that she was thrilled, the reality was that she was upset because she was hoping for at least triplets. Higher Order Multiples was her ultimate goal.

Kate had done the research and knew that having twins wasn't going to get her the attention she desired. Even women not taking infertility drugs can have twins. Twins are no big deal.

In 2000, when Kate's twin daughters were born, there were more twins walking around than you could shake a home pregnancy stick at. These are the statistics about multiples that Kate had tucked away in a file:

```
The number of births in twin deliveries rose 6 percent for 1999-
2000 to 110,670 births - the largest single year rise in several
decades.

The number of Triplet Births climbed to 6919, a rise of 13
percent.

Births in quadruplet deliveries increased from 510 to 627 between
1999 and 2000.

The number of quintuplet and other higher order multiples were
unchanged at 79.

Since 1980 twin births have risen 62 percent and other higher
order multiples births have jumped 470 percent.
```

This was not good news for Kate, and she knew it. Now she was stuck with "just" twins, like more than 100,000 other parents that year alone.

She did her best to make the most of her situation though. She tried to market her girls from the time they were babies. At less than one year old, she paraded Mady and Cara Gosselin down Main Street USA (Wyomissing Boulevard, actually) in a decorated "float" during the annual Fourth of July parade and celebration in her new hometown of Wyomissing, PA. Kate, their controlling and masterminding mother, had already put a label on them. They weren't Mady and Cara Gosselin. They were "The Gosselin Twins!" and "Little Miss Americas!"

The Gosselin name at that time meant as much as the Hoffman name in this area, which was absolutely nothing. So the idea of Kate making a spectacle of herself and her family was laughable to the affluent neighbors she passed by in the parade. But Kate held her daughters up and put them on display. Here they are world ... "The Gosselin Twins!" The locals didn't know what to make of Kate Gosselin, even then.

Kate had headshots taken of the girls, contacted modeling agencies and tried to get them commercial jobs and anything else on television, but there were no takers. "There just was nothing special about a set of twins," she was told by a local photographer she had contacted.

Even though Kate did not get the Higher Order Multiples she wanted, she would not give up on her plan. These are Kate's words from Jon and Kate's earliest website:

```
The girls turned one and I started thinking about more children….
After all, the girls had been pure fun and I wanted to do it again!
But, Jon wasn't convinced. I prayed for a long time that God would
change his mind. It took a long time and a rough experience for both
of us for that to happen…In May 2003, we had the opportunity to adopt
a newborn in kind of a rare circumstance. Things were moving really
fast and we prayed about it and felt that this was not meant to be.
Jon and I came to a joint decision that we were not ready to take on
such a responsibility at the time. We felt God leading us that way.
Jon was amazed that I so willingly "turned down a baby". It hurt so
badly, but I knew we were doing the right thing. I mourned for the
better part of a month and it was then that Jon agreed to let us
return to try and have another baby. He saw just how badly I wanted
to be a mommy again.
```

This was "not meant to be" because Kate did not want just one more baby. There was more masterminding to be done.

JUST ONE MORE

"We were so thrilled we decided to try for just one more,
And ended up with six."
– *Kate Gosselin*

This chapter took me more than two years to research and write. I had read the wild speculation about Kate intentionally trying to become pregnant with multiples by an "anonymous blogger" and on several of the "anti-Kate" blogs when I first began my job reporting on the Gosselins, so I started looking for a big story for *US Weekly*. I had no evidence at the time, and *US Weekly* would never have printed this anyway.

As it turned out, I did find evidence that told a story, and it pointed to Kate's biggest lie of all. You hear it so lovingly spoken in the intro to *Jon & Kate Plus Ei8ht*. "We wanted **Just one** more and got six."

The truth is, Kate never wanted "Just one more" baby. In fact, "she's disappointed in only having eight."

In studying Kate Gosselin's entire body of work – her television shows, print and television interviews, her books, etc. – along with having first-person information about her and having personally watched her in action nearly every day for two years, it is quite clear that she is most definitely not a good actress. Kate delivers the same scripted talking points, over and over, almost verbatim.

But even after all that time watching Kate and listening to her, I was not prepared at all to find out everything I did about Kate's capacity to deceive, and about how far she would go to achieve her grand plan. What I discovered is that Kate Gosselin deliberately and intentionally got pregnant with two sets of multiples in order to seek fame and fortune.

In the early days of the Gosselin mania, Kate Gosselin repeated, over and over – in interviews, in her books and on her television shows – that she wanted "JUST ONE MORE" baby. "Just" one more. It was always those exact same words, over and over again. "Just one more." But logic, common sense and evidence make Kate's claim that she wanted "just one more" baby difficult to believe.

Ask yourself if this makes sense. If you were a young woman, as Kate was at the time, and you easily got pregnant with twins the first time around using Intrauterine Insemination (IUI), and you really, really only wanted JUST ONE MORE baby, why would you go against your doctor's recommendation to switch to In Vitro Fertilization (IVF)? Why would you go out and find a different doctor who had no problem with giving you IUI again, even though you KNEW the risk of having multiples was much, much greater using this method?

Being so young and having already had twins via IUI, the logical thing to do, if Kate truly wanted JUST ONE MORE baby, would have been to follow her first infertility doctor's recommendation to use IVF with a single embryo transfer. There would have been no real chance of twins, triplets, or even worse – Higher Order Multiples. If successful, Kate would have gotten JUST ONE MORE baby. Kate wasn't a naive, 17-year-old girl who was ignorant about fertility issues. She was a registered labor and delivery nurse with plenty of experience. She was also, by her own admission, a type A planner, scheduler and list maker – and masterminder. Kate knew exactly what she was doing. She didn't take her first doctor's advice, because JUST ONE MORE baby was exactly what Kate Gosselin did *NOT* want. So she left that doctor behind. That doctor was no longer on board with Kate's plan, and Kate wanted nothing more to do with her.

Someone who worked with Kate's first infertility doctor said that "Kate Gosselin was told by Doctor X to use IVF, and that made her angry. 'Who is she to tell me what I can and can't do with my body,' Kate demanded."

I've met with that person, and a second individual from that doctor's office, several times in the course of writing this book. In wanting to protect their careers and their own families, they have chosen to remain anonymous.

In Kate's early drafts of *Multiple Blessings*, she gives the names of her infertility doctors. Strangely, they were omitted from the final version of the book. There is a very logical reason for that: Kate didn't want people asking questions.

But that's jumping ahead. Let's go back to the beginning where this story gets a whole lot worse.

ON THE JOB TRAINING

Kate asked a lot of strange "what-iffy" kind of questions while working briefly as a nurse. "She seemed to have an agenda, but at the time, we had no idea what she was up to," a former co-worker of Kate's told me. "Looking back, it makes a lot more sense now. The questions she was asking had nothing to do with her job at the time. She talked about the McCaughey septuplets a lot and how dangerous it must have been for the mother." "Kate was also very interested in the many different fertility medications that were out there, and what each one did, even though we weren't a fertility clinic. It just seemed strange. She already knew everything there was to know about infertility by the sound of her, but she seemed to be looking for reinforcement and first-hand stories."

So, how did Kate end up with six babies when she wanted **just one more**? Here is the answer: she found a doctor who didn't ask questions, and she manipulated the entire infertility process to get the results she wanted. In *Multiple Blessings*, Kate tells us that Jon "finally" agreed to do fertility treatments again so Kate dove for the phone and made an appointment with a new fertility doctor closer to home, in Wyomissing, PA. She told us that she drove an hour each way with the first fertility doctor and of course it was a very successful experience, but she felt that the convenience of seeing a doctor closer to home made much more sense now, because she had two two-year-olds at home.

That paragraph is loaded with "Kate speak" and deception. Kate Gosselin is a creature of habit, almost obsessive-compulsively, and she had great success with her first infertility doctor in Allentown, PA, who gave her perfectly healthy twin girls. So the thought of Kate not going back to this same doctor because it was an inconvenient drive is so over-the-top false that my head spun when I read it. Remember, I followed Kate seven days a week for close to two years. I know her habits. She's as hard to figure out as a third-grader. Kate drove an hour each way to get her hair styled in Harrisburg. She drove almost an hour each way to go to Whole Foods for a bag of groceries. She drove an hour each way to go shopping at the Park City Mall in Lancaster (all while her now EIGHT busy kids were at home with strangers), so the idea that she wouldn't drive an hour to see her infertility specialist, the most important person in the world to someone who was trying to get pregnant, and who gave Kate her beautiful twins, is absolutely, positively, preposterous. Period. Nothing could be further from the truth. Kate Gosselin would never do that in a million years.

Kate's second infertility doctor, from Wyomissing, PA, whose practice is less than one mile from my front door, was there when Kate originally went searching for doctors. Why then did Kate pass on him and drive all the way to Allentown in the first place? That's an easy one. She did so because she thought the Allentown doctor was a more respected and reputable doctor.

Kate did the research. The reason Kate settled on her Wyomissing doctor the second time around was because the Allentown specialist rejected Kate when she returned and wanted that doctor to do IUI again. Her first doctor instructed Kate that it would be irresponsible for her to use IUI again, given her still young age and the fact that she had gotten pregnant so easily the first time around – with twins. She wanted Kate to do IVF with a single embryo transfer to start, and informed her that if this didn't work, she would agree to IUI. Kate became irate and left the office – for good.

Kate had masterminded her entire plan, and IVF and the thought of having just one more baby was not a part of it. So she ended up settling for the Wyomissing doctor.

Kate realized that the infertility doctor is just a minor player in the whole baby-producing process. Dr. Botti, her maternity doctor, was the real brain of the operation and someone Kate respects and speaks very highly of, very often. Why do you suppose that Kate never mentions the names of either of her infertility doctors who gave her perfect twins and sextuplets? After all, these doctors were the conduits between God and science, right?

In *Multiple Blessings*, the only mention of Dr. xxxxxxx is that he was her "African Doctor." I know his name. In fact, I've been to his office several times.

Wyomissing is a small town. It's hard to not know a friend of a friend who works anywhere around here, and nurses and staff at a local doctor's office are no exception. Anyway, Kate found herself a new doctor who would give IUI treatments for her undiagnosed case of PCOS.

Kate's doctor gave her injections of a drug called Human Chorionic Gonadotropin, or HCG, which is an ovulation inducer that would help Kate ovulate and release her eggs. Since Kate never really had PCOS in the first place, her eggs were released on their own, so adding injections of HCG to the mix would only serve to release even more eggs for possible fertilization. (For the men or other scientifically challenged: Ovulation occurs when a mature egg is released from the ovary, pushed down the fallopian tube, and is available to be fertilized.)

Her first cycle was a failure. At least that's what she claimed. Actually, she didn't try and fail with the first cycle. She lied about the first cycle to make the story of her not being able to get pregnant more believable.

The second cycle, according to Kate, was a "great cycle." When Kate went to see the infertility doctor for her scheduled ultrasound, she was told that it was a great cycle with three or four mature follicles. That would be an expected result for a healthy woman taking the controlled injections of HCG, and it would be a great cycle for someone with PCOS taking controlled injections of HCG. The doctor had no reason to be suspicious at this point.

Kate described that doctor's visit by saying that the doctor was thrilled that he had discovered three mature follicles and maybe even a fourth with the potential to still mature.

Then, to make herself look special while also covering the lie, Kate said that the doctor must have read their minds because he was quick to reassure them that statistically it would no be likely that all four or even three follicles would be fertilized. She went on to tell us that the doctor was "completely thorough in giving us an escape route if we so chose. We simply could discontinue the injections and repeat the process in two months, aiming for enough but not too many follicles."

Those sentences are also Kate-speak, to keep her doctor from blowing the whistle on the whole operation. She makes sure that we're aware that the doctor did everything humanly possible to ensure that there was no risk of Higher Order Multiples, and he did his job to his fullest capacity.

Now all of this begs a question. If Kate was, indeed, so adamant about wanting **"just one more"** baby, why didn't she just turn around and go home like her doctor suggested, and come back again in another two months to try again? It wasn't a money issue because Jon's dad was paying for everything. So why the big hurry?

If she had just listened to her doctor and tried again in a couple of months, she could have reduced the risk of fertilizing three, or possibly four, mature eggs, and would never have been subjected to the thought of "killing" any babies when her doctor suggested selective reduction. God would not have had a problem with Kate going home and trying again next time.

But Kate did come back, the very next day, and received her "one final injection of HCG" and then the IUI, and went home again to wait.

At least that's what she was *supposed* to do. What Kate doesn't mention in *Multiple Blessings*, or anywhere else for that matter, is what she *did* do during that "second cycle." What Kate actually did when she got home was to immediately give herself at least one more shot of HCG, which she had purchased online in a kit three months earlier. To keep the purchase a secret, she went outside the United States and purchased the drug overseas and had it shipped to her newly created post office box in Wyomissing. She used the name K. Kauffman when ordering. Perhaps the only mistake she made is not destroying the HCG packaging.

With the IUI, Jon's sperm were now swimming around inside of Kate's uterus among the three or four mature eggs that the doctor knew about. Kate wasn't looking for maybe two, or three, or even four babies this time around though, and she wasn't about to leave anything to chance either. She knew that by administering her own injection of HCG, even more mature eggs would drop down to join the others, unbeknownst to her "African doctor."

After injecting herself with HCG, something happened twelve days later that didn't go according to Kate's master plan. She experienced pain... severe pain, and she was rushed to the hospital where it was discovered that she had over-stimulated ovaries.

For fear of anyone finding out what she had done, Kate kept silent about the additional HCG shot she had given herself. She writes in *Multiple Blessings* that over-stimulated ovaries like she experienced "are only evident in approximately 2 percent of women undergoing similar infertility treatment." That's pretty rare indeed. Indeed.

So by my calculation, only two women out of 100 have this problem. And honest, wholesome, God-fearing Katie Irene Gosselin just happened to be one of them.

Take a look at what the Mayo Clinic has to say about the cause of Ovarian Hyper stimulation Syndrome (over-stimulated ovaries):

"Ovarian Hyper stimulation Syndrome is particularly associated with injection of a hormone called Human Chorionic Gonadotropin (HCG) which is used for triggering oocyte release. **The risk is further increased by multiple doses of HCG after ovulation and if the procedure results in pregnancy.**"

In an early, unedited version of *Multiple Blessings*, Kate wrote about her over-stimulated ovaries saying that neither she nor Jon even vaguely considered that the pain could possibly be related in any way to the HCG shot that she had gotten just a few weeks beforehand.
Kate changed this wording in the final version of *Multiple Blessings*, taking out any mention of the HCG shot and just referring broadly to fertility treatments. Even Kate knew that it would be best for her to mention HCG as little as possible so as not to arouse suspicion. In the printed book version Kate dropped the mention of the HCG shot and changed it to simply say 'fertility treatments.'
Kate had researched infertility to the point where she had become an "expert" in the field. So in her book when Kate says something like neither one of us at that point **even vaguely considered that this pain could possibly be related in any way to the HCG shot...** it is impossible to not be very, very suspicious, at the very least.
Weeks after Kate's hospitalization, she went back to see her doctor for the initial ultrasound. According to Kate, he was "in a trance," and "visibly shaken." It's no wonder he was visibly shaken. He was, no doubt, trying to figure out how three, possibly four, mature follicles had magically turned into seven.
In *Multiple Blessings,* Kate overstates her fear and horror and disappointment about the moment she learned she was pregnant with seven babies. She also makes sure to throw some statistics into the book so that readers would realize just how rare of an occurrence this was and, oh, of course, that it wasn't her fault.
She says that she was instantly in a state of denial and simply could not allow her brain to process what her eyes were telling it. She said the chill of reality washed over her as she watched Jon drop to his knees at the sound of five. According to Kate Jon was fear stricken and nauseous and he couldn't bear to look anymore. She said she and Jon sat in a stunned silence and that she was completely numb as she got dressed. She had an almost unbearable urge to run but the reality was that they had almost a better chance at winning the lottery she added.

While telling the world of her shock and stunned silence, Kate Gosselin did something else that would propel her into the hallowed halls of Christian heroism: she focused on the hot-button issue of selective reduction. Selective reduction is a procedure where the number of fetuses that result from infertility treatments like IUI is reduced to a safer number. When Kate portrayed herself as adamantly opposed to selective reduction, she immediately turned herself into an admirable Christian figure, thus ensuring a built-in audience of supporters and admirers. This would later serve her and her pocketbook very well. This is what she said on her and Jon's earliest website:

"I will never forget this day as long as I live. There were seven
sacs with four yolk sacs, or babies in four of them. At the count of
four, I was scared. At five I started crying and at six I was shaking
absolutely sobbing. Jon had turned form the screen, he couldn't look
anymore. I have never seen him so close to tears in my life! The
doctor "reassured" us by telling us we would talk about reduction. I
pulled myself together and stared right at him and said, "We're not
doing reduction!" After the ultrasound he called us into his office
and tried to convince us that reduction was the thing to do. Again,
we refused!"

In *Multiple Blessings* regarding selective reduction, Kate said that at every single
meeting with their doctor, she and Jon expressed serious reservations about the
possibility of multiples and made sure that he fully understood their unwavering
position on selective reduction. Kate said that selective reduction in her opinion is
the politically correct term for the process by which a fetus is injected with a lethal
dose of potassium chloride, which mercilessly silences its tiny heart forever. She
went on to say that being Christians, they firmly believed that every life whether
seconds old or a full forty-week life is designed and ordained from God. She said
that because of that, they would never consider choosing to end that life in any
way at any time. Period.

A standard topic in Kate's countless paid church speaking engagements around the
country was that she was absolutely dead set against selective reduction. That went
over HUGE with her Christian audience. It's what elevated Kate as a Christian
speaker. It was exactly what they wanted to hear…and she knew it. Kate was fully
aware of how powerful the issue was, so she overstated her conversations with her
doctor about selective reduction in *Multiple Blessings*:

So on that fateful day in November of 2003, in the doctor's office during the
ultrasound where seven babies were detected, after being told by Kate **"at every
single meeting"** with him that she was **against selective reduction, period**, why
then would the doctor state calmly (as Kate tells us on page 35 of *Multiple
Blessings*), "Kate, when you're done here, come into my office, and we will talk
about selective reduction."? Because Kate Gosselin lied about ever mentioning
selective reduction to him. She only brought it up for the first time *after* the seven
babies had been seen in the ultrasound.
Kate had gotten exactly what she had wanted and planned for; however, she said
that she didn't even know that words could describe that "horrible day." She said it
was "so horrible." She wanted nothing more than to be pregnant but now she was
pregnant with seven babies and "scared to death."

But the fact is, Friday, November 21, 2003, will forever go down as the happiest
day of Kate Gosselin's life. That's the day her plan unfolded exactly as her
detailed, scheduled list and calendar said it would. Kate Gosselin was pregnant
with seven babies.

"The lady doth protest too much, methinks."
– *William Shakespeare*

Kate's "just one more" lie was front and center during the *Jon & Kate Plus Ei8ht* television years. If you start at the very beginning, with the first television special on the Gosselin family, you'll see and hear Kate already on the defensive – before anyone even questioned her about whether or not she intentionally set out to have multiples. The thought that Kate had planned to have Higher Order Multiples would NEVER have crossed my mind had Kate not gone on and on about how she in fact, did *not* plan to have multiples. The lady most certainly doth protest too much.

On the first episode of Season 1, it was "…Then, when we decided to have **Just one more**, we got a little more than we bargained for. We got six."

By Season 5, it was "We were so thrilled, we decided to try for **Just one more** … and ended up with six."

This is from Season 3 of *Jon & Kate Plus Ei8ht's* Viewer Email FAQ episode on the interview couch. These FAQ episodes, as well as every other Gosselin episode, were very carefully scripted, with Kate having complete knowledge of every question that was to be asked of her. Most of the time, Kate and the producers wrote the questions themselves to push whatever agenda they were going for on any given week. Here are the fake questions from that episode.

Jon says, "Here's one for the record books. I got an email about a woman who wants to have sextuplets" and Kate says, "I don't think I remember this one. Is she feeling all right?"

Jon says, "She asks, did you have In Vitro fertilization or Intrauterine Insemination?" He answers with "Uh, we had, Kate had Intrauterine Insemination" and Kate quickly chimes in with "IUI, and no, we didn't desire multiples, but this is what God gave us and we love em."

Why was the last part of that answer from Kate even necessary? The question on the table was "Did you have In Vitro fertilization or Intrauterine Insemination?" It was a very simple and straightforward question, even if Kate hadn't made it up herself. No one asked if Kate "desired multiples." And no one asked if she loved them. Why would she not "love em"? She's their mother.

Here is Kate's attempt to pretend this all caught her by surprise. She says, "We get a lot of emails asking us what did we do fertility-wise, and I always say to Jon, why are they asking us? We're considered a fertility nightmare."

This exchange is from the very first Gosselin television special, *Surviving Sextuplets and Twins*:

Kate says that this whole thing started of course, when she wanted a third child and Jon was happy with two. That's the debate they always had according to Kate. "Two or three? Two or three? Then she whispers and looks down and says that she just wanted that third one… "And I bought one, got five free."

Jon said that life was great, and he missed the family of four and said that Kate wanted "Just one more" and he said no, no, no, no he's happy with the twins and said that everything is perfect. He said the whole world is designed for four people, and Kate added "Let's face it, infertility produces multiples. We all know that."

"We all know that." Kate said that she truly only wanted **Just one more**, and yet she knew that "infertility produces multiples" and she had made it clear that she was dead set against selective reduction. Period. So it makes no sense to think she really did want "just one more" child.

Jon said that anytime anyone decides to go ahead with infertility treatments that you should expect two or three and Kate responded, "we even agreed that going back, we had to be willing to accept twins or triplets."

This is from the second Gosselin television special, *Sextuplets And Twins: One Year Later.* Kate is already defending herself, even when nobody asked.

Kate says that she doesn't know anybody in the world who has walked into the fertility clinic and said "I've seen these people on TV and I really wanna know what sextuplets is like." Kate adds "You'd have to be nuts."

They really glossed over this part. A voiceover asked, "at this point, you might be wondering how this couple ended up with two sets of multiples and Kate jumped right in and said, "we did infertility and with the girls, uh, we succeeded, the second IUI. We were so happy with them and they were so much fun."

That's Kate speak again. She sounds like a robot reading from a script that she's bored with. Why wouldn't she be happy with her babies? Oh, that's right, she was upset and disappointed that they were only twins.

Kate said that when they were one actually, she started thinking about having another baby.

Jon said no because he liked the family of four and everything was easier.

Kate said she silently prayed, but we silently not argued and discussed.

Jon said that he caved and they went in and had her appointment and then we had an ultrasound and that's when he saw the satellites.

There they go again. They just went from silently discussing trying for "Just one more" to seeing the "satellites." I'd like Katie to tell the world the truth about what happened in between.

Kate laughed and said ...the planets. It was awful.

And Jon said yeah, it was very scary cause you don't go in expecting that.

Kate said the doctor looked at me and said; well we can talk about reduction.

And for some crazy reason, there is a close-up shot, obviously edited in, of Kate being wide-eyed and serious saying; I said we will not talk about reduction!

Jon said we knew we were gonna take it head on, regardless of what it was and Kate said we told them that from the very beginning.

Well there you have it. Kate said it, so it must be true. Even though nobody asked. Again, it was extremely important for Kate to reinforce to her Christian public that they never even considered reduction.
"We will not talk about reduction! We told them that, from the beginning."
Kate learned how important that was from doing her research on Bobbi McCaughey. Kate learned a lot more from researching the McCaughey septuplets. The similarities are eerie, if not extremely suspicious.

JON & KATE 101: HOW DID WE GET HERE?

"How did our quiet little existence in the suburbs of Pennsylvania somehow blossom (or maybe explode is a better word) into a "story" that someone wanted to tell on national television?"
– *Kate Gosselin*

Kate has often said that Figure 8 Films contacted them "out of the blue" about filming a reality show because of their website. Kate has also said that she didn't want news of her "unique" pregnancy to leak out. I know these things are not true. One of the first of many lies Kate told the public in her quest to exploit her unique situation was that the media contacted them. The fact is Kate worked very hard to make sure the media was aware of their situation, and she did everything she could to drum up interest in their story. She acted as if the media attention was unwelcome, when it was what she was seeking all along.

In Chapter 6, "Media Mayhem," of *Multiple Blessings*, Kate writes that it was "everyone's fear" that once she had been admitted to the hospital, "the news of our unusual adventure would leak to the media."

She also says that, when she was in the hospital, her doctor made Jon look him in the eye and promise to do everything in his power to shield her from the press "for the sake of our babies' well-being."

Now why would Kate's doctor have to tell them that do you suppose?

Kate said about the media attention that it was decided that when the time came, Jon would be the one to speak to the media for the both of them. She said that she and Jon had agreed to give their hometown newspaper, the *Reading Eagle*, an in-room exclusive interview only out of self-defense because of information that she had received several weeks earlier that someone who had worked with Kate at the Reading Hospital was threatening to talk to the press about them. Kate said it was an attempt to buy them a few more precious weeks that their doctor wanted. She said that they began to get calls for interviews and details about the pregnancy and that she was getting more and more physically uncomfortable and had no patience for the extra annoyance of media attention.

That was a big lie. Kate was the one who contacted the *Reading Eagle* to get as much publicity for herself as possible. In an editorial published on March 27, 2011, about famous citizens of Berks County, Harry Deitz, editor of the *Reading Eagle*, wrote the following:

`Harry Deitz: Lots of fame, some fortune in our county`

"… Another example is Kate Gosselin, whose delivery of sextuplets on May 10, 2004, (around the same time Taylor moved to Nashville) and twins three years earlier eventually gave rise to the TV show "*Jon & Kate Plus 8.*"

Before all that fame, **Kate called our newspaper and offered to allow a reporter to follow the delivery of the sextuplets.** It was a great story then, and it changed quickly. Enter the TLC television network, lots of fame and apparently lots of money."
(http://readingeagle.com/article.aspx?id=297419)

Harry Deitz has been at the *Eagle* since 1978. He was there when I started working there in 1986, so I have known him for more than 20 years. He is a straight shooter and has always stated the facts. Kate, not so much. Here is some of Kate's additional spin from *Multiple Blessings*:

"One day in August of 2005, Jon received an email he thought I should read. It was from a television production company that **had heard of our family** and was interested in doing a one-hour documentary of our story."
"Whoa," I said. "Seriously?"
"It was becoming more and more difficult to **duck into the shadows.** How did our quiet little existence in the suburbs of Pennsylvania somehow blossom (or maybe explode is a better word) into a "story" that someone wanted to tell on national television?"

The Gosselin's story did not reach Discovery Communications, Inc. and its TLC network by chance. The Gosselin's quiet existence in the suburbs of Pennsylvania blossomed into a story because Kate Gosselin marketed the story. She spent countless hours contacting media outlets and pitching reality shows and doing everything she could to draw attention to herself and her "unique" story. The last thing on Earth that Kate Gosselin wanted was to "duck into the shadows." This was part of her "masterminded" grand plan from day one, and she succeeded. Kate was making deals with media outlets before her babies were even born; before she knew if any of her babies would be sick, or disabled, or even survive. The risk factor was huge to bring these six babies into the world, but that didn't stop Kate from trying to use them to get the things she cared most about: money and publicity and fame.

A FAMILY UNDER (DISCOVERY'S) CONTROL

"... Family ... shall be subject to the instructions and direction of Company and its designated representatives ..."

I'm not an attorney, and I don't have a lot of experience with reading or signing television contracts, but after giving the Discovery/Gosselin family contracts a few reads, I found it alarming that Jon and Kate Gosselin would be so driven to cash in on their children, that they would turn over TOTAL control of their family, including family photos and videos, to a television network. Jon eventually came to his senses and realized what he had signed away. Unfortunately, his family was making so much money for Discovery and TLC, there was no way they were going to let him get his kids out without a battle.

I've read all of the contracts for *Jon & Kate Plus Ei8ht*. These include a copy of the signed contract as well as the rough draft of the original contract on which changes were made and final details were ironed out. The first contract is dated October 4, 2006. It is a 17-page document filled with all manner of legal-speak. Legal considerations prevent me from including the contracts in their entirety here, so I have summarized them instead.

These are some key provisions from the full contract. Read them and decide for yourself if this "reality" show sounds anywhere near real.

- The "Talent Agreement" defined the "Family" as parents Jonathan and Kate Gosselin and their children, Cara Nicole Gosselin, Madelyn Kate Gosselin, Aaden Jonathan Gosselin, Collin Thomas Gosselin, Hannah Joy Gosselin, Leah Hope Gosselin, Alexis Faith Gosselin, and Joel Kevin Gosselin.

- The "Company" was defined as Discovery Talent Services, LLC; and the "Program" was defined as the series of episodes up to one half-hour in length tentatively entitled, "Gosselins The Series."

- The Family agreed to render "Services" as themselves as "featured, On-Camera Personalities". They would be required to provide preproduction, production and postproduction "Services" that would include any necessary **rehearsals**; travel; auditions and pickups; on-camera shoot days; narration; voice overs; vignettes; on-air promos, "special" episodes; and "behind-the-scenes" programs.

- The Family was subject to the **instructions and direction** of Discovery and its designated representatives.

- The Company, Network and/or the Producer had "final and controlling" say in all matters concerning the performance of the Family's Services (including matters involving artistic taste, quality and judgment).

- The Family's principal photography would be performed in and around Elizabethtown, PA, and/or at other locations determined at the "sole discretion" of Discovery.

- When traveling, Discovery was responsible for providing and/or paying for airfare (coach class), ground transportation, car rental (intermediate size car), and hotel accommodations (2-star, based on the "Mobil Travel Guide").

- Discovery and/or a designee of Discovery had complete creative control over the Program. This included, but was not limited to, approval over the Family's **make-up, hairstyle and wardrobe**.

- It was stipulated that this was a non-union agreement, and that the Family's Services were not subject to the terms of any collective bargaining agreement such as SAG or AFTRA.

- The Family was allowed to appear as a guest on news programs, and on talk shows on broadcast networks and their local affiliates, as long as the Family coordinated the activities through the Network's press department.

- Kate gave her Parental Consent and signed on behalf of her minor children and she **fully and unconditionally guaranteed the performance of each of her children's obligations as set forth in the contract**.

Signed by Kate and Jon Gosselin

These are some of the standard terms and conditions contained in Exhibit A of the contract:

- The Family was contracted on a **"work-made-for-hire"** basis, specially ordered or commissioned by Discovery. Therefore, all results and proceeds from the Family's services, and all material connected with the program that was suggested, composed, written, performed or furnished by the Family, and all material owned or controlled by the Family that was used in the show or in connection with the show, was **"owned exclusively by Discovery in perpetuity and in all languages throughout the universe."**

- Discovery had the unlimited right to "**cut, edit, add to, subtract and omit from, adapt, change, arrange, rearrange, or otherwise modify the Results and Proceeds.**" This included, without limitation, doubling the Family or freely "dubbing" or subtitling the Results.

- The Family agreed to release Discovery from any claim or cause of action for workers' compensation benefits.

- Discovery had the right to secure "cast" insurance covering the Family, but the Family would have no right, title or interest in or to any such insurance.

- If Discovery determined that the Family was not able to fully render its services according to the terms of the Agreement because of any Family illness, injury or mental disability, or because of impairment of Family's voice, appearance and/or mobility, it was considered an event of "Family Incapacity."

- During the time of "Family Incapacity," Discovery would not be obligated to pay or credit the Family with any compensation and would have the right to suspend the Agreement during that period. Discovery could extend the Agreement by the length of any such suspension, but was not obligated to do so.

- Discovery had the right to terminate the Agreement due to any "Family Incapacity" that lasted at least seven (7) days. If any Family Incapacity caused Discovery to terminate the Agreement, Discovery would have no further obligation to the Family except to pay them for any services they had satisfactorily completed before the termination, as long as the Family was not in breach of the Agreement.

- Discovery had the right to terminate the Family's services **for any reason with or without cause**, at any time and without further obligations to the Family.

- **The Family was responsible for obtaining and maintaining any and all work permits or immigration clearances necessary at all times during the Service Term (and for any extensions).**

- The Parents agreed to fully and unconditionally guarantee the performance of each of the children's obligations.

- The Family agreed that Discovery would be entitled to seek injunctive and other equitable relief to stop or prevent any breach or threatened breach of any obligation by the Family.

- If Discovery incurred any damages as a result of the Family breaching the Agreement in any way, Discovery had the right to withhold and offset any payments they owed the Family under any agreement between the parties in an amount that would cover the Family's indemnity obligations or any damages incurred by Discovery.

- The Family would not accept any money, services or other valuable consideration, other than the Family's compensation, for the inclusion of any matter in the Program or for the endorsement of any company, product or service in the Program.

- The Family agreed that any information it learned about Discovery's, TLC's and/or any Producer's business operations, strategies, future plans, financial affairs, or any other information about the Program, Discovery, TLC, Producer and/or their parent, subsidiary and/or affiliated companies, including the terms and provisions of this Agreement, was confidential and proprietary. The Family agreed not to disclose any information with respect to the Confidential Information to any third party.

- The Family (and any representatives of the Family) was not allowed to bring or use any cameras or audiovisual recording devices to any of Discovery's and/or the Program's offices, sets, or locations without Discovery giving prior written consent. If Discovery gave written consent, the copyrights in all photographs and audiovisual recordings made by the Family (or any representative of the Family) at any of those locations belonged to Discovery alone, and the Family was not allowed to display, exhibit, or distribute, or authorize the display, exhibition, or distribution of, any such photographs or audiovisual recordings publicly for any purpose.

Jon and Kate said they weren't well represented when they signed this contract, so maybe they didn't fully understand what they were getting into. But even though the actual Agreement contains a lot of legalese, it should have been completely clear to anyone who can read that they were giving up their rights, and more importantly, their children's rights, to their privacy, their images, their actions, and their ability to control precious family photos and videos. They sold their children's privacy and childhoods. In the simplest of terms, Discovery owned the Gosselin family.

SAG/AFTRA

The Screen Actors Guild (SAG) and American Federation of Television and Radio Artists (AFTRA) unions were formed to protect the rights of actors. (The unions have since merged into SAG-AFTRA.) For child actors, the union requires some strict protections and accommodations, such as restricting the number of hours they can work in a day, and mandating studio teachers and education time on set. Hiding behind the argument that children on reality shows are not working actors, Discovery made it clear that neither SAG nor AFTRA would be a part of the Gosselin children's lives when they drew up the family's first contract. It is easy to see why.

The union regulations would have prevented the children from being filmed 24 hours a day. Here are the very specific rules about a child's working hours taken from the *Young Performers Handbook* on the SAG-AFTRA website (http://youngperformers.sagaftra.org/files/youngperformers/YPH_FNL3.pdf):

Work Day Rules

The SAG contract governs minor's work hours *everywhere in the United States unless stricter work hours are mandated by the state.*
Work day rules are as follows:
- Minors may not work before 5:30 a.m. or after 10:00 p.m. on evenings preceding a school day (work days must end by 12:30 a.m. on non-school days). The minor's final work day must be concluded at least twelve hours before the beginning of the minor's next regular school day.
- On a school day (determined by the calendar of the district where the child resides), school age minors must receive at least three hours of instruction. Maximum allowable hours and times of instruction vary by grade level.
- Minors through age 15 must be accompanied at all times by a parent or guardian. Minors age 16 or 17 may work without a parent or guardian but are entitled to have a parent or guardian present. The parent or guardian is entitled to be within sight and sound of the minor at all times.
- Minors who are high school graduates are exempt from the child labor laws and may work on the same basis as adults.

School Age Minors

On a school day, school age minors may work as follows:
- Ages 6 to 8 — four hours (maximum of eight and one half hours on the set).
- Ages 9 to 15 — five hours (maximum of nine and one half hours on the set).
- Ages 16 and 17 — six hours (maximum of ten and one half hours on the set).
- On days when school is not in session, school age minors may work an additional two hours a day.
- On all days, the minor must have at least one hour of rest and recreation and one half-hour meal break.
- By prior arrangement with the studio teacher, up to two hours of school may be banked (stored) to offset additional work hours on other days; there must be at least one hour of school on each day the minor's regular school is in session.

Pre-School Age Minors
Minors who are 6 months through 5 years do not attend school on the set, even though they may attend pre-school or kindergarten on a regular basis. Work hours are as follows:
• Ages 6 months to 2 years — two hours (maximum of four hours on the set).
• Ages 2 years through 5 years — three hours (maximum of four and one half hours on the set).
• Minors 6 months through 5 years must have at least one hour of rest and recreation.
• Minors 2 to 5 years may also have a half hour meal break.

Infants
In California, infants 15 days to 6 months of age may only be on the set between the hours of 9:30 a.m. to 11:30 a.m. or 1:30 p.m. to 3:30 p.m. No infant born prematurely may work until he/she would be at least 15 days old if born at full-term. SAG producers have agreed to observe these restrictions in other jurisdictions.
• Ages 15 days to 6 months — twenty minutes (maximum two hours on the set).

THE SKI TRIP AMENDMENT

When Jon took Cara to Park City, Utah, for a skiing/snowboarding vacation in January 2009, Discovery wanted to film it. They just didn't want to assume any financial risk or liability in case there was an accident. Discovery wanted to exploit the family for filming, but didn't want to be held responsible in case Jon or Cara was injured. The Discovery legal department drew up an Amendment to the Gosselin's contract that was in force at the time. The Amendment named Jonathan Gosselin and Cara Nicole Gosselin as the "Outing Participants." Here are the key points of the Amendment that the "Outing Participants" agreed to:

• They acknowledged that they were going to be participating in activities between January 1 through January 6, 2009 that were inherently dangerous, and they could be exposed to "foreseen and unforeseen" hazards and risks.

• They understood that participating in the Activity carried with it the potential for injury or loss, including but not limited to death, serious physical injury, extreme emotional distress, mental or physical illness and property loss, and other unforeseen losses.

• They acknowledged that they were voluntarily participating in the Activity with "full knowledge, appreciation and understanding of the dangers and personal risks involved," and they agreed to assume any and all risks associated with participating in the Activity.

- They represented that they were in excellent physical, emotional, psychological and mental health, and were physically and mentally capable of participating in the Activity.

- They said that they were voluntarily participating in the Activity with full knowledge, appreciation and understanding of the dangers and personal risks involved, and they agreed to assume any and all risks of participating in the Activity.

- They agreed that the "Released Parties" (Discovery/TLC/Producers and any subsidiaries, etc.) would not have any legal obligation to either or both of them or their family for any claim, loss, or injury that they or their family could blame on the Activity. They held the released parties harmless from liability, damages, claims, losses and expenses (including reasonable legal fees), arising out of, or resulting from, any filming and/or their participation in the Activity.

- Any and all footage of Jon and Cara's activities, and any services they performed in connection with the show, were owned exclusively by Discovery "in perpetuity in all languages throughout the universe."

KATE'S RATIONALIZATION

When faced with any kind of criticism about exploiting her children, Kate's standard response has always been to say that any one of us would have done the same thing if we were presented with the opportunity to film a reality show. I wouldn't bet on that.

The thought of having strangers around filming my family sounds repulsive and disgusting to me and would seem to be attractive only to someone seeking attention and fame. If my family were in dire need of money though, I would agree to take the meetings. However, after reading the terms in that first contract about Discovery having control over how my family dressed and acted and wore our hair, and how they would have total control over my family photos and videos, etc., that would have been the end of the conversation. I would have shown them the door without another word. As most normal, mediocre people trying to protect their family would do.

SIGN HERE – OR ELSE!!!

One of the great frustrations for people who are disgusted by Kate Gosselin's actions and lies, and who are concerned for her children, is that almost no one has ever gone on record to tell what they know. With all of the gossip and tabloid rumors coming out over the years about Kate's horrible behavior, and with accusations that she abused her children being reported in the tabloids and online, many are baffled as to why not a single person close to the Gosselin family, or a single member of the TLC crew, or any of Kate's present or former nannies, babysitters, cooks, cleaners, etc., would speak out to help the children.

It is difficult to understand how Kate could get away with all of the nasty and vicious things she has been accused of saying and doing without somebody spilling the beans. And yet, that is exactly what has happened. Kate continues to appear on television talk shows with her fake smile and her head held high, portraying herself as a victim and telling one lie after another, while blaming everyone but herself for everything bad that has been said about her, and every perceived wrong done to her. How is that possible?

The answer is really very simple. It is very likely that all those people who have witnessed her actions are afraid for their financial lives.

While the Gosselins were under contract with Discovery, anyone who had any contact at all with Jon and Kate, or came anywhere near their children – from lawn service technicians to their very own family and former friends – had to sign a Confidentiality and Nondisclosure Agreement. Anyone who signed this document agreed to not utter one word about anything they saw or heard while around the Gosselins.

While such agreements are standard entertainment industry practice, Kate Gosselin made sure to revise that legal document to make it better – for her. And she had the full legal muscle of Discovery Communications standing firmly behind her to enforce it.

So many people have disappeared from the Gosselin children's lives because they couldn't sit by any longer and watch Kate abuse and destroy their childhoods. But because they signed the Confidentiality Agreement, they couldn't legally tell anyone about anything they ever saw Kate do. To do so would have meant exposing themselves to severe penalties and risking possible financial ruin.

Armed with the power of the Confidentiality Agreement, Kate knew she could do anything she wanted and get away with it. She paid very special attention to the wording of the Agreement and wanted additional, stronger wording added to ensure that it would be completely clear to anyone reading and signing it that they couldn't talk about the Gosselin family. At all. EVER.

Even after at least one revision to the Confidentiality Agreement had already been made at Kate's insistence, Kate continued to have concerns about the wording in the document. An email exchange between Kate and Wendy Douglas of Discovery in May of 2008 confirmed this when Kate expressed her strong opinion that she wanted the Confidentiality Agreement to be clearer in regard to people discussing "the Gosselin family." Kate wrote to Wendy that she noticed the addition of the words "the Gosselin" family in a paragraph, but she still didn't think it was clear enough.

Kate told Wendy that she was satisfied that anyone reading the Agreement would understand they could not talk about their participation in "the shoot," and/or any plans for a particular TLC shoot; she also agreed that the Agreement made it clear that someone could not send out any press releases to benefit their own business. However, she was concerned that only a close reader would pick up on the fact that they were not permitted to discuss the family. Kate wanted to make absolutely certain that readers of the Agreement completely understood that they couldn't discuss the Gosselin family at all. She wanted more flagging and attention paid to the Gosselin part of it because she felt that people NEEDED to know they were not permitted to discuss her family.

Wendy Douglas assured Kate that their Legal team felt the language in the Agreement covered Kate's concerns, and that it applied to "all" information, not just "disparaging" information about the family. Through this Confidentiality Agreement, Discovery/TLC/Figure 8 Films and Kate threatened potential blabbermouths with massive lawsuits – in the millions of dollars – that would leave them homeless, according to Kate.

Some key points from the Confidentiality and Nondisclosure Agreement are summarized below. Anyone who signed this Agreement to be engaged by Figure 8 Films (the "Producer") "to render services in connection with the production of the television series entitled 'Jon & Kate Plus 8' (the 'Series')" agreed to the following and more:

- They would follow all of the Producer's security procedures, and maintain and preserve the confidentiality and secrecy of all information and materials concerning the Series (whether the information or materials were confidential or not).

- They would not participate in any publicity, press releases or press conferences, or speak with the press, about the Series or Confidential Information.

- They would not sell any stories or Confidential Information about the Series to any third party.

- They would reject any request from any third party (e.g., journalists, media representatives, book publishers or authors, or anyone who wrote for or published on the Internet) to disclose, confirm or deny any information covered by the Agreement. They were instructed to issue a "no comment" and immediately advise the Producer if they received any such request.

- They would not participate in any way in the preparation or production of any materials, including books, magazine articles, newspaper articles, television shows, Internet Websites and any other form of media, about the Series.

- They understood that any disclosure or misappropriation of any Confidential Information at any time was a violation of the Agreement and could cause the Producer and the Gosselin Family irreparable harm, and could adversely affect the reputation of the Gosselin Family, or the Series, or television ratings, and place the Producer and the Gosselin Family in breach of their respective agreements with third parties.

- They understood that any monetary damages might not be sufficient to compensate the Producer or the Gosselin Family for the unauthorized use or disclosure of the Confidential Information and that "injunctive or other equitable relief would be appropriate to prevent any improper actual or threatened use or disclosure of the Confidential Information or other breach of this Agreement." (In simple terms, they would get their pants sued off.)

- They would not give any interviews or disclose any Confidential Information or any other information relating to the subject matter of the Confidentiality and Nondisclosure Agreement.

- They would not give interviews or disclose information about their participation in the production of the Series without the prior written consent of Producer.

- They would not disclose any of the following during the time they were connected with the Series or any time after their involvement with the Series had ended, "in perpetuity": any non-public information about the Series; any information generally not known to the public that was developed by or disclosed to them by the Producer; any information the Producer told them not to disclose or confirm; and any information relating to the public or private lives of the Gosselins or of any of the Producer's employees (this included, but was not limited to, personal affairs and relationships, the names and addresses of personal friends, personal and business schedules and appointments or the location of them, or professional or personal activities).

- They understood that the provisions of the Agreement would survive even if their services in connection with the Series had expired or had been terminated.

- They could only disclose Confidential Information in response to a subpoena or other legal process, but they would have to give the

"Producer" written notice at least five business days before, specifying the Confidential Information to be disclosed.

- If they violated the Agreement they would be liable for damages sustained by the Producer or the Gosselin Family as a result of the disclosure or misappropriation of any Confidential Information.

To sum things up, anyone who signed this Agreement was put under a permanent gag order to not disclose anything, ever, to anyone about anything they had seen, heard or experienced in relation to the show, the Gosselin family, the Producer, or any of the Producer's employees, except if they were under subpoena to do so. If they violated the Agreement, they would be sued.

To underscore the seriousness of this Agreement, I can give a personal perspective. I have received a threatening letter from Kate's lawyers regarding the release of this book, and I have to admit, it was a pretty scary read. I have also received a Cease and Desist letter from Discovery's legal representation. These actions were taken without me ever signing a single Confidentiality Agreement in connection with the show. It is no wonder that those who did sign the Agreement have remained quiet.

All the threats appear to have worked, because there has been almost complete silence from all of the people who have mysteriously vanished from the Gosselin's lives.

KATE'S GOD COMPLEX

"Ours is a story that is encouraging to everyone who hears it! It is a story of God's hope, grace and love in a time when there was a lot of uncertainty, fear and doubt! Anyone who listens can apply these same lessons in their own lives!"
– *Kate Gosselin*

I have included in this chapter some of Kate's words from her books and journal. You will notice rather quickly that she refers to God and prayer extensively. For reasons that should be fairly apparent by now, Kate rarely, if ever, mentioned God during the actual filming of her reality shows. She does not mention Him now on her website or on Twitter. It is certainly an oddity considering how aggressively she cultivated her image of being so deeply devoted to her religion and God. Here are some of Kate's early thoughts on God. These were written at a time when she was still doing speaking engagements and asking for money from the Christian community, and successfully convincing the world that she was a devout Christian mother struggling financially to raise her family.

God brought this their way as part of His continual blessing of them.

She feels that God is using them to do the extraordinary.

God will take care her when she flies because He loves her and wants the best for her.

God will always provide for them and He has their best interests at heart.

God not only provides their needs but sometimes their wants like her tummy tuck surgery.

This is all God's will for them. Ask and you shall receive. You have not because you ask not.

God is challenging Kate to buy what they need and He will continue to provide for her. God comforts Kate while she's shopping.

Kate believes that God will answer her prayers and they will be able to do a television commercial.

God is sending income her way through the filming of her family.

God provided the TV series and the money so Kate could stay home with the children until they go to kindergarten.

Kate doesn't want to work and she feels God urging her to quit her job.

God asks Kate to do the things she does.

Kate prays to God to provide the necessary funds to continue their lifestyle.

Kate prays to God for advice on what they should do about redoing the girl's bedroom.

Kate prays to God to work out a scholarship for the kids to a private school.

Kate prays to God for Jon's complacency to leave him and for him to become a man of integrity.

Kate isn't shocked about getting a second season of the TV show but amazed at God's provisions and the way He decided to go about it.

Kate prays to God to send them the right house when He's ready.

Kate began to doubt God because she hadn't heard back about doing a TV commercial.

Free dentistry for eight kids was another miracle from the Lord.

The miracle of the week was that God made Tony from Alexia Foods call her and send her two cases of Julienne French fries and two cases of their crinkle fries.

Kate prayed to God about not having to go to work anymore. Just the thought was soooo amazing!

God sent Kate's sister to them with 250 cans of organic tomatoes and organic butter and He had her load them in the garage.

Kate prays to God for nice weather on a specific day so it's convenient for her. She asks for an exact temperature of 75 degrees.

Kate thanked God because the farmer is charging her half price for his strawberry seconds.

Kate begged the Lord to help her be a loving, caring and slow to anger mommy. She pleaded with Him to stop her from hurting her children and to be slow to anger. She asked God to help the kids **obey** her.

Wow. God helped Kate get Julienne fries, crinkle fries, organic tomatoes, organic butter, strawberries and 75-degree weather for filming! Helping her be a "loving caring kind and slow to anger mommy" must still be a work in progress.

Kate wasn't content to rely solely on her own personal prayers to accumulate a bounty of riches, so she began soliciting money from churches around the country, and putting the word out that she and Jon were available to come and "share their unique story." Kate was the one who did the soliciting; it was not the other way around as she tells it. She was the one with the plan, from the very beginning. The following is text taken from one of Kate's speaking engagement forms she used to get churches and organizations to cough up money for her. It is custom-tailored to exploit her reputation as a good Christian mother.

```
Ours is a story that is encouraging to everyone who hears it! It is a
story of God's hope, grace and love in a time when there was a lot of
uncertainty, fear and doubt! Anyone who listens can apply these same
lessons in their own lives!

We enjoy speaking but are still surprised at the demand! We know it
is what God is asking of us!!!!

Many people wonder why we do the show. We like to travel and tell the
story, our history to give a background and answer the question: why
we do what we do!

1. God is in control.
2. God is Gracious and Strong.
3. Trust in God.
4. God is love.
5. God will provide.
6. Give God the Glory and Praise.
```

Kate's references to God also showed up frequently in her journal when she wrote in detail about her morning sickness and how it wasn't fair that she should suffer more because she had already suffered enough trying to get pregnant. Here are more instances of Kate's extensive writings on praying to God, realizing God's intentions, and understanding God's lessons in every part of her life.

Kate marveled at the grade of God who was preparing them for something that would test their strength, endurance, tenacity and sanity.

Kate prayed about not wanting to jump ahead of God in her quest for another baby.

God sent an angel to Kate in the form of her daughter to deliver a message of reassurance.

Kate felt the peace of God wash over her. She would be treading on holy ground and needed that peace to sustain her life as He walked her through the minefield of surprises that awaited.

Kate had more than mother's intuition because she had already carried twins. She had "the voice of God."

Even though science and humans had given their best efforts, Kate's pregnancy rested in God's hands.

God was succeeding in teaching Kate life lessons. He told Kate that He was in control of Kate's children, not her. He loves them more than she does.

God was again teaching Kate lessons, this time that she needed to swallow her pride and ask for help.

Everyone around Kate felt the almighty hand of God working through her.

Kate was beaten, bedraggled and holding on by a thread, but because of God, she was adding life to the party.

Kate prayed to God to get her pregnant as she lay there looking at the ceiling.

God chose Kate to go on this journey.

God knew Kate's children by name before Kate did.

God and a social worker allowed Kate and Jon to move into the Ronald McDonald House.

Kate was the planner but God handled all the details.

God spoke to Kate while she was drying her hair.

God put people and businesses in Kate's path to remind her that he was still there. One was C.J. Pony Parts. They gave Kate and Jon gift cards to Target and Giant.

God sent more angels to Kate to show her His love.

God supplied Kate and Jon a new house.

Kate spoke to God often, questioning Him if He was sure about some of His decisions regarding her. She went through her list with God. Why did He only give her two hands and six babies? And the small house? Oh and Lord, Jon has no job. How will we provide for our children?

Kate knew that God would simply reach down, scoop her up and carry her. He's gracious and strong.

God is not only persistent but also tireless. He literally begged Kate to write a check, get a family's address and mail it to them immediately.

God taught Kate that she would never be able to out-give him.

God didn't only allow things to happen to Kate, He actually hoped to accomplish things *through* her.

God decided that Kate, with her direct, blunt and even dangerous mouth should now bring glory to Him by having Kate stand up in front of people and spread His word.

No wonder the whole world is so screwed up. God is spending all of His time taking care of Kate Gosselin.

Since Kate's writings featured God so heavily, it would be safe to assume that her personal website, *kateplusmy8.com*, which she launched in 2011, would be jam-packed with references and prayers to God, just like those writings in her journal entries above.

Well, you know what they say about assuming. There is not one mention of God, or anything remotely associated with God or Kate's belief in Him, on her website. The site has been up for close to two years, and there it is, right at the top: a tab called "Inspiration" where you would think she could post a biblical passage or two. But when you click on that tab, a page opens that says … "COMING SOON!" Below that, there is a picture of Kate and her children with country singer Taylor Swift.

Coming Soon! could mean that the page hasn't found a sponsor yet. Remember, Kate Gosselin only does things for money. Coming Soon! could also mean that she is just too lazy to look for inspirational sayings or bible verses because they are not important to her.

In case you haven't looked, Kate's website is loaded with everything that would interest a 13-year-old child, including many blog posts from Shoka the dog. Yes, you heard right. Kate has taken time out of her extraordinarily busy days to ghostwrite blogs from her dog, about what he's thinking and doing…and eating. Kate has written many entire blog entries from Shoka the dog, but she hasn't taken a moment to post any inspirational bible passages. Not one.

This is in stark contrast to Kate's original website, *sixgosselins.com*, which was up and running when she first started conning Christians out of their hard-earned money. This was on that site's home page, front and center:

"For you created my inmost being;
You knit me together in my mother's womb.
I praise you because I am fearfully and wonderfully made;
Your works are wonderful,
I know that full and well.
My frame was not hidden from you when I was made in the secret place,
When I was woven together in the depths of the Earth.
Your eye saw my unformed body;
All the days ordained for me were written in your book before one of them came to be.

Psalm 1 39: 13-16"

All these years later, into March of 2013, this quote appeared on the Home page of *kateplusmy8.com*, the "Official site for all things Kate Gosselin & Kids":

What's meant to be will be. It is better to be hated for who you are than loved for who you're not.
Don't let what others think define who you are. Be bold and courageous, when you look
back on your life you will regret the things you didn't do more than the things you did.
What appears to be the end is really a new beginning.
– Unknown

This is who she is today, according to her website:

News & Events
Ask Kate
Fitness
Fashion & Beauty
Just My 8 cents Worth
Lovable Products
Inspiration
Kate + Rumors
Words From Fans
Shoka Diaries
K8's Kids

So where did Kate's religion go? It's a completely fair question, especially since as of March of 2013 she had the following quote prominently displayed on her Home page:

"The question isn't who is going to let me; it's who is going to stop me."
– Ayn Rand via @ Share Awakening

Uh, oh. Does Kate even know who Ayn Rand was? I'm guessing not, because if she had done even the tiniest bit of research before choosing one of Rand's quotes for the front page of her website, she would have learned that Ayn Rand was an atheist who rejected all forms of faith and religion. It is inconceivable that this woman, who is supposedly so committed to God and religion, and who was so adamantly opposed to selective reduction, would *ever* choose to honor Rand by displaying her words on a website. These Frequently Asked Questions appear on the Ayn Rand Institute website:

What was Ayn Rand's view on abortion?
Excerpt from "Of Living Death" in The Objectivist, October 1968:

> "An embryo has no rights. Rights do not pertain to a potential, only to an actual being. A child cannot acquire any rights until it is born. The living take precedence over the not-yet-living (or the unborn).

"Abortion is a moral right—which should be left to the sole discretion of the woman involved; morally, nothing other than her wish in the matter is to be considered. Who can conceivably have the right to dictate to her what disposition she is to make of the functions of her own body?"

What was Ayn Rand's view on charity?
[From "Playboy's 1964 interview with Ayn Rand"]:

"My views on charity are very simple. I do not consider it a major virtue and, above all, I do not consider it a moral duty. There is nothing wrong in helping other people, if and when they are worthy of the help and you can afford to help them. I regard charity as a marginal issue. What I am fighting is the idea that charity is a moral duty and a primary virtue."

Given Kate's actions, can we surmise that she does, in fact, share Rand's beliefs, and that her carefully crafted image of Christian mom was just an elaborate façade to scam people? Or is it simply that Kate's laziness and stupidity caused her to include on her website a quote from a person many would find offensive and intolerable? You can draw your own conclusions.

(Note: In late March 2013, Kate removed all the quotes from her website's Home page and began using that space to promote her new [old] cookbook, *Love Is In The Mix: Making Meals Into Memories with 108+ Family-Friendly Recipes, Tips and Traditions*, due out in September of 2013.)

This is not the only example that runs counter to Kate's Christian image. In July of 2012, while being interviewed on local radio station Y-102 in Reading, PA, Kate was asked if she had read the book *Fifty Shades of Grey*, and she answered that, yes, she had, in fact, read it. *Fifty Shades of Grey* is notable for its explicitly erotic scenes featuring elements of sexual practices involving bondage/discipline, dominance/submission, and sadism and masochism (BDSM).

It is probably safe to say that this book did not make any of the Christian bestseller lists. It most certainly is not a book Zondervan, the Christian publisher of Kate's books, would ever touch.

I wonder if Kate would have admitted to reading a book like that a few years ago when she was fleecing kind, trusting church members out of their hard-earned money, all the while preaching the word of God with her hand out.

Kate will insist over and over on Twitter that she hasn't changed, though.

"Whoever claims to understand God is either arrogant or needs a psychiatrist. It contradicts the whole idea of God."
– *Father Karl, Stift Heiligenkreuz Abbey*

THE WORLD ACCORDING TO KATE

"Stand with me or stand against me!"
– *Kate Gosselin*

Kate Gosselin's world is a very unsettling place. Anyone who has ever crossed paths with Kate knows that she speaks, acts and believes that she is better than everyone else. She knows better than her ex-husband, Jon. She knows better than her eight children. She knows better than her parents; and her siblings; and her cousins, nieces and nephews. She knows better than doctors and lawyers and television executives, and she sure as Hell knows better than the people who watch her television shows and follow her on Twitter. This is Kate Gosselin's reality world.

Kate would like everyone to believe that she has many friends; however, despite her desperate tweeting to the contrary, she has no real friends at all. She has paid employees like her bodyguard Steve Neild, or paid friends like Jamie Cole Ayers. She likes it that way, though. She likes to be in control. She has said this herself numerous times throughout her television shows and during interviews.

Kate has banished everyone of any importance from her life, and the lives of her children, because they "had opinions of their own" about how to raise her children, or save her marriage, or anything really for that matter. Kate does not want to hear any opinion other than her own. Rather than hire an experienced, professional nanny with knowledge of how to raise and care for children properly, Kate hires high school and college-age girls who would be intimidated to volunteer any of their own thoughts on the children, let alone disagree with anything Kate has to say.

Kate does not tolerate anyone telling her anything that goes against what she wants. "Stand with me or stand against me!" she infamously told Jon during a filmed discussion in the family's garage.

Kate's parents; her siblings; Jon's family; Judy the nanny; Bob and Beth Carson: all gone. The children's father, grandparents, aunts, uncles, cousins, and their favorite caregiver: all gone from their daily lives. This 2012 tweet from Kate responding to one of her tweeties sums up all you need to know about why this is: Don't question my mothering – thanks!

The remainder of this chapter provides a small glimpse into the mind and world of Kate Gosselin. It gives examples of Kate's interactions with people, and clearly illustrates not only her extraordinary sense of entitlement and self-importance, but also her eagerness to paint herself as a victim.

KATE VERSUS THE STATE

In 2005, while fighting to retain a free, full-time nurse to care for her children, Kate Gosselin told the State of Pennsylvania in a letter that her children were disabled. Here is that letter:

To Whom It May Concern:

This letter is in reference to the adverse determination as described in PA number 0433410338. (Please see enclosed letter)

We are appealing the decision made and desire to continue services during the appeal process.

We have eight children four years old and under. Our six youngest are 11 months old. In a sense **our children (our six 11 month olds) are disabled.** They cannot feed themselves, transport themselves up and down stairs or at all, bathe themselves, get a drink when they are thirsty, go to the bathroom by themselves, put themselves to bed or dress themselves.

Furthermore, and extremely dangerously, they do not know right from wrong or safe from unsafe. They will put anything of choking hazard size in their mouths, climb up or fall down any of the 4 flights of stairs (if the gate has been left open by our 4 year olds), pinch their fingers in anything they touch and shouldn't, pull each other down, or poke each others eyes!

Any one person cannot safely care for and keep eight children from danger, 12 hours per day, 5 days per week!

Take for instance bath time…How does one person have "X" number of babies in the tub, monitor the ones still in the tub while diapering and going to retrieve the next baby? Safely, that's impossible!

How does one person take 3 babies to the doctor, with no one to help and find a third capable person to watch the five children I've left behind? Each doctor's appointment? Nearly Impossible!

How does one person care for my six 11 month olds while effectively meeting the needs of 2 dear 4 year olds whose needs have been "put aside" all day, day after day? They have been patiently waiting their turns…which never come because one person is busily scurrying around to care for the babies needs which supersede their own!

How does one person take 8 children for a walk? Two strollers and 2 walking 4 year olds? A "normal" thing for any child? Impossible! How does one person care for all 8 children while never leaving the house for things that are very important such as 320 diapers weekly, 13 cases of formula per month, 112 jars of baby food per week not to mention, all the "normal" necessities or preschool drop-offs or pickups! Completely impossible! Literally, we will be completely HOUSEBOUND!

How does one person effectively evacuate eight children from 4 different rooms in the case of a fire? Or how does one person care for an injured bleeding child while 7 others are left unattended? Absolutely unsafe!

And have we forgotten one thing? One stability in our constantly hectic, crazy lives? Continuity of care! "Community Resources"—a list of college students or high school students available "here and there" as their schedules allow, who when other things come up aren't afraid to cancel on us — thus leaving my children to wait for lunch or my 4 year olds home form preschool for lack of transportation. "Community Resources" — elderly ladies who cannot lift one 20 lbs. baby let alone 6 and who certainly cannot do stairs while carrying one or two babies! Baths are out of the question!

Where will I find this person to walk in, take over for minimal pay as a home health aide, who we as parents trust, who our children trust and love and who will be able to on a whim do what 9 months (with our nurse) of history has built? Exactly my point! By the time May 30 rolls around, a new person, will just be scratching the surface of learning our daily routine and handling the many time management challenges! That is all too exhausting and unworth it for me and my family!

The past 9 months have run very safely and smoothly because of our constant caregiver, Angie. Thanks to our approval through Medicaid. Thank you! We can't thank you enough for the amount of sanity in our crazy and unusual world, but we still need that same help now.

I am a very capable person and mother. I pride myself in organization, cleanliness and all American fun! However, at this stage in our lives, this task is bigger than even me!

I hate asking for help but for the safety of each of my precious children, I must ask, because I love them. I need the constant care of our nurse Angie to continue!

The previous scenarios are things I worry and pray about constantly. I am thankful that none of them have happened and pray that our care will continue to help ensure that they won't happen.

Please come and spend some time in our home so you can see that what I'm telling you is true!

If it is possible to hold our hearing in Reading, I would like to attend in person. However, I strongly desire a home visit so that a clear picture can be demonstrated.

Sincerely,

Kate and Jonathan Gosselin

First, it would do Kate some good to sit down at her computer and do some research on children with disabilities to find out what it's like for people who really have a disabled child.

Kate's words in this letter make her sound not just unbelievably stupid, but shockingly removed from reality. It would almost be amusing if it weren't so truly pathetic. What Kate describes as disabilities are the characteristics of being a baby. Any baby. Every baby. No, babies can't feed themselves or bathe themselves or dress themselves or go to the bathroom by themselves. They're babies. That's part of the package. Did that somehow come as a surprise to Kate? As a registered nurse, surely somewhere along the line someone must have mentioned to her that she would be responsible for taking care of those needs.

That letter also speaks to Kate's arrogance and sense of entitlement. It suggests that she had no intention of taking on the burden of caring for the children she actively set out to create, and expected others to do it for her.

Never one to take no for an answer, Kate went straight to the top of the local political scene, enlisting Senator Mike O'Pake to speak to the welfare department on her behalf, when her free nurse, Angie Krall, was taken away after 9 months of waiting on Kate and the kids.

```
Dear Secretary Richman:

    I have been contacted by Mr. and Mrs. Gosselin regarding their
    sextuplet's Medical Assistance benefits and need for in-home
    childcare.

    The Gosselin family is composed of Mr. and Mrs. Gosselin, a set
    of 4-year old twins and 9-month old sextuplets who were born on
    May 10, 2003. In October 2004 the Department of Public Welfare
    had informed the family that they would no longer be eligible for
    in home care. On appeal the decision was reversed and a special
    exemption was provided "due to the number of babies." Now the
    family has again been informed that in home services will be
    terminated, effective April 30, 2005. Since receiving
    notification, they have attempted to secure childcare through the
    Child Care Information Service of Berks County only to be
    informed that they are not eligible due to not meeting the work
    requirements. Mr. and Mrs. Gosselin find themselves in a
    quandary, as it is physically impossible for Mrs. Gosselin to be
    employed outside the home and care for her eight children.
    However, they are also unable to afford in home care on Mr.
    Gosselin's income.

    In light of the above noted information I would like to
    respectfully request that you personally review this case so that
    a compassionate and just result be obtained.

    Thank you for your prompt attention to this matter. I will wait
    to hear from you.

Sincerely,

Michael A. O'Pake
Senator — 11ᵗʰ District
```

Even back in 2005, some astute observers were not buying into Kate's sob story. In a May 2005 TRIBUNE-REVIEW article about the Gosselin family, Dimitri Vassilaros wrote of Kate's claims that the sextuplets were disabled; that volunteers helped, but nowhere near enough; and that one mom can't take care of six individuals. It would appear he had her number from the start. Here are excerpts from that article:

Eight is enough
By Dimitri Vassilaros, TRIBUNE-REVIEW
Sunday, May 15, 2005

Kate and Jonathan Gosselin want you to pretend that their sextuplets are disabled.

If you play along, they can keep the free nurse provided by Medicaid to help raise the six 1-year-olds and the Gosselins' 4-year-old twin daughters in their Berks County home. Mom and Dad will plead their case at a hearing on Thursday.

"Every morning I ask the Lord for the strength to try to remain calm," Kate said.

As a registered nurse, however, she knew the risks of fertility drugs. Gosselin did not regret the decision after she was told about her six babies. Nor for opposing the "selective reduction" that sometimes is performed in multi-fetal pregnancies to lessen potential risk to the mother and the surviving fetuses.

But if Kate had had a crystal ball, would she have taken the fertility drugs?

"If I could have looked into the future, I would not have done it," she admitted.

The two parents have more kids than they can handle. Volunteers have helped, some, but nowhere near enough, she said. The taxpayers are helping by providing health coverage, but the Gosselins want much more.

...But the need for special services such as a nurse is not based on income. The state's first question was whether the Gosselin children qualify *medically*. "The answer is 'no,' so you do not get it," Kate said.

The little ones' good health was her bad luck. Go figure.

"I am urging them to see us as a rare situation, which we are," she said. "And I am begging them to make a special exception. They are six individuals. One mom cannot take care of them.

"I might be able to meet their physical needs, but not the emotional needs. It is very difficult. I'm talking about time to talk about feelings, read books and the absolute bare necessities to get done. I cannot do it five days a week."

...keeping the free nurse is a priority.

"I understand that there is no medical necessity," Kate said. "But I hope they see my need. There is nothing set up for someone in our situation. I hope I can hang on to the person that I have."

The Gosselins called the day after my telephone interview with Kate. They asked to preview this column before publication. My editor declined their request. Kate then said she wanted to retract everything -- even though she admitted all of it was true.

"People are out to make us look bad," she said.

It is not surprising that Kate asked to preview the column before it was published. It is even less surprising that, after her request was denied, Kate wanted to retract everything, even though she admitted that it was all true. It is how Kate operates. She expects everyone to roll over and meet her demands.

This was the last time Kate would give an interview where she didn't have complete control. It was the last time she would handle an interview without a publicist there to guard her every word and control its direction. Future interviews with Kate Gosselin would be submitted to her publicist in writing. Most times, Kate wouldn't have the chance to answer her own questions. It would be too dangerous for her "career" if she were allowed to respond on her own.

For an interview in the *Hershey Chronicle*, the following questions were forwarded to Kate. She answered them and sent them back, but she still managed to mess it all up a bit and upset people with her begging.

Q: Do you have anyone helping you take care of the babies?

A: Currently yes, but we are losing her due to insurance denying our request to keep her (our nurse). She is our only "fulltime help"! We are currently praying for private funding to keep her! **We are desperate! I will have to do this alone otherwise!**

Q: What changes are you hoping for in the future?

A: **We are still hoping for a 15-passenger van to miraculously materialize! We are still praying.** The babies have been nowhere because we can't transport our whole family in even our 2 vehicles! We are hoping to keep our nurse Angie. She is why we're still sane and our family is doing as well as we are! We are frantically searching for a way to keep her for another year! However, **we cannot afford her salary!**

I have read stories, interviewed helpers, and seen photos of what it was like inside the Gosselin home during this period of time. There were more volunteers than Kate could possibly keep busy in a lifetime. While they did all the work, Kate laid around and gave orders or posted notes and lists that only served to upset people. She spent little to no time with her children, opting instead to position herself in her kitchen while her children were out of sight being looked after by complete strangers. Kate felt that it was more important to spend the entire day in the kitchen making formula and washing and labeling bottles than to bond with her babies. So for her to state that if she lost her only "fulltime help" she would have to "do this alone" is an outrageous lie.

And that 15-passenger van she was "hoping" and "praying" would miraculously materialize? Well, ever since she read that Bobbi McCaughey got one for free when she had her septuplets, Kate had been absolutely obsessed with getting herself one for free as well.

SHE AND BOBBI McC

Speaking of Bobbi McCaughey, this would be a good time to bring up some of the very strange coincidences between the Gosselin and McCaughey stories. In Kate's world, she was every bit as deserving of the same freebies that the McCaughey family had received.

Kate always needs to control everything. She says things like, "I had an action plan." "I had been a planner my whole life and took great pride when my plans unfolded exactly as my detailed, scheduled list and calendar said they should."

Was one of Kate's plans to commandeer Bobbi McCaughey's story for herself, making a few slight alterations here and there? Decide for yourself.

Kate Gosselin needed a public relations team to create her message. TLC wrote her blog, and the wording for her product endorsements was written for her as well. She has been accused of plagiarism in a cookbook filled with existing recipes taken from various sources. She couldn't even come up with an original title for her own book, and ended up pilfering *Multiple Blessings* from Betty Rothbart, who wrote about the same subject years earlier. Given these circumstances, all evidence suggests that Kate Gosselin lifted her story and her talking points directly from Bobbi McCaughey.

The McCaughey birth attracted significant media attention, including a feature in *Time* magazine in December 1997. Kate saved that issue among several other pieces of McCaughey memorabilia she had collected. Kate even spoke to Bobbi McCaughey on the phone after Kate had her sextuplets. Was she trying to get advice on how to make the most of her "miracle?"

Here are some eerie, and some downright creepy, similarities between Bobbi McCaughey and her septuplets and Kate Gosselin, whose sextuplets were born nearly 7 years later:

Bobbi McCaughey is a devout Christian and preacher's daughter.

Kate Gosselin came from a devout Christian family and is a preacher's daughter.

The McCaughey septuplets were conceived as a result of fertility drugs.

The Gosselin sextuplets were conceived as a result of fertility drugs.

OK. Nothing too unusual yet, but we're just getting started.

When Bobbi McCaughey found out she was carrying multiples, she declined selective reduction saying that they would "Put it in **God's hands**," and, "That just wasn't an option. We were trusting in the Lord for the outcome."

When Kate Gosselin found out she was carrying multiples, she declined selective reduction saying, "The results ultimately lay in **God's hands**," and "This truly is God's plan for us," and "Whatever God chose to give us, we would accept as a blessing."

Bobbi McCaughey came out strongly against selective reduction, thus making her a hero to Christians the world over. She was also quoted as saying, "Well, come to our house, and tell me which four I shouldn't have had!"

Kate Gosselin matched that quote, saying, "Tell me how I as a mother would go about "selecting" which beating heart to snuff out as if it were just a candle," and "Who lived and who died was not a decision that rested in our human hands."

Kate was very aware that denouncing selective reduction was the most important part of her plan to play to a Christian audience, and she took every opportunity to play that message up.

In *Multiple Blessings*, she wrote about discussing selective reduction with her doctor: "I resolutely sat in the sturdy cherry wood chair of the doctor's office. He and I went head to head as he offered facts and information, statistics and grim details of how my life would be at risk. ... The risks also for my seven babies were huge and could not be denied. Assuming that the medical field was capable of getting them to a viable gestational age, usually at least twenty four weeks, they still stood the risk of suffering premature lungs, blindness, cerebral palsy and mental retardation – just to name a few. I was not swayed."

She also said this: "Jon, even at the risk of losing me and raising Mady and Cara on his own, unconditionally agreed with me. Who would live and who would die was not a decision that rested in our human hands."

In addition to their views on selective reduction, here are some more similarities between Bobbi McCaughey and Kate Gosselin.

Bobbi McCaughey thought about becoming a nurse.

Kate Gosselin *did* become a nurse.

Bobbi McCaughey was the recipient of many generous donations, including a 5500-square-foot house, a 15-seat van, full college scholarships for her children to any state university, 2 years worth of diapers, nanny services, meal preparation, and transportation services, among other things.

Kate Gosselin focused on what Bobbi McCaughey received and immediately asked for the same big-ticket items. Kate wanted a larger house, but didn't initially receive one – she only got the free home makeover, which made her very angry.

Kate asked over and over and over for college money from the time her babies were born. She was always talking about college, trying to get a university to bite and give them full scholarships. She was angry that it wasn't donated right away like it was for Bobbi McCaughey.

Kate mentioned and begged for a 15-seat van on her website as soon as the sextuplets were born, and in every interview she did at the time. Additionally, her last words to the media after the well-orchestrated media event that was her sextuplets' 1st birthday party was, "And we still need a 15-seat van with lots of storage!"

Carters donated clothing to Bobbi McCaughey's septuplets for the first 5 years of their lives.

Kate tried to solicit the same deal from Carters, but they turned her down. She then approached Gymboree and found success with them.

Bobbi McCaughey's church turned out in full force to help.

Kate Gosselin had her father's church mobilize and had Jon alert their own church to make sure that an army of volunteers turned out in full force to help.

The McCaughey's spoke at pro-life events and continue to oppose selective reduction.

Kate Gosselin spoke at pro-life events and continues to oppose selective reduction. Kate sent out solicitations to huge numbers of church groups in the United States to hire her to come and speak.

As written in the *Time* magazine article in 1997, Bobbi McCaughey, upon seeing the ultrasound with seven babies said, "The words shock and disbelief come to mind. For a good length of time, I couldn't wrap my mind around this."

In *Multiple Blessings* in 2008, Kate Gosselin, upon seeing the ultrasound with seven babies said, "I was in a state of denial. I simply could not allow my brain to process what my eyes were telling it."

Kenny McCaughey said at the first news conference when his septuplets were born, "It just strikes me as a **miracle.**"

In a *Newsday* article in 1997, Bobbi McCaughey said, "The whole notion of the miracle, after all, hinges upon the acknowledgement that **the odds were extraordinarily slim for the infants' survival** in the first place."

Nobody mentioned a miracle regarding Kate Gosselin's story, so she mentioned the word "miracle" herself, over and over again in her books and in her church speaking engagements.

From *Time* magazine: All the McCaughey girls wear identical outfits, as do the boys.

All the Gosselin girls wear identical outfits, as do the boys.

Bobbi McCaughey said, "They're my children, and I **wanted** them."

Kate Gosselin said she needed them to know how much that they were **wanted**, loved and know it wasn't the plan they had (to have them). It was the plan God had for their family.

Bobbi McCaughey said, "**God gave us these kids.** He wants us to raise them."

Kate Gosselin said, "**God gave us these** exact **kids.**"

Bobbi McCaughey said, "Just to have the daily assurance that nothing's going to happen today that God hasn't already planned for me."

Kate Gosselin said that as a Christian she believed Psalm 139:16 which says that all of our days are fashioned for us before we've even lived one of them. God had already ordained exactly if, when, where and how Kate's baby would eventually come to be... The doctor Kate believed was simply put in her path to carry out what was already her God-given destiny.

Bobbi McCaughey's perinatologist said, "I attribute the success of the pregnancy to God **blessing** Bobbi McCaughey."

Kate Gosselin said she feels too that God brought this our way as part of His continual **blessing** of and whatever God chose to give us, we would accept as a **blessing.**

In fact, nearly every tenth word in *Multiple Blessings* is **blessing.**

Bobbi McCaughey said, "We can't do anything but **trust God.** So far, He has come through."

Regarding trusting God, Kate said that a lack of trust in God would always prevent them from receiving His best; She would continue to wait and trust God to send them the right house in His right timing; Kate, the complete planner and obsessive controller, finally absorbed the fact that she could trust God to see to all the details; Kate realized that God did not make a mistake when He gave her six instead of just one. This was the beginning of learning to trust God completely.

In 1997, the media dubbed the McCaughey septuplets, "The Magnificent seven." The media didn't make up any cool names for Kate Gosselin's children, so she did it herself. Kate dubbed her own children and family:

> The six
> The Gosselin six
> Sixgosselins.com (Original website)
> Ten Gosselins (Mailing labels)
> Kate Plus Nine (June 2008, when she and Jon were supposedly happily married)
> KatePlusMy8 (Email address and later her website)
> Katemomof8@ (Kate's early email address)
> Momofeight@ (Another of Kate's early email addresses)
> Sixymomma@ (Yet another of Kate's email addresses)
> Kateplusmy8.com (Post-divorce and current as of December 2012 website)

When discussing the naming of her sextuplets in her book, Kate Gosselin says that they just picked first names **randomly**. Bobbi McCaughey's first-born septuplet daughter was named Alexis, and her last-born septuplet son was named Joel. Kate Gosselin "randomly" named her first-born sextuplet daughter Alexis and her last-born sextuplet son Joel.
Read that part again.

IN HER OWN WORDS

These paraphrased excerpts from Kate's journal are examples of how Kate expresses herself when the cameras aren't rolling and Discovery isn't there to tell her what to say. The exclamation points are Kate's.

July 2006
Kate wrote that Betty Hayes from New Jersey called her to probe her about their specials with Discovery Health, asking for details about if and how much they were getting paid. Kate was like shocked and instantly irritated! Apparently Billy Hayes of Adv Med Prod called them again and asked them to do a special AGAIN!!! Kate said she is so mad! She then said the Betty asked her if anyone sent them gifts? Kate told her about the stroller and her surgery because she didn't want to lie. (What????) Kate didn't tell her about the twenty episodes or the amount they are getting because they were sworn to secrecy on that! Kate wrote that she is just so appalled at the competition that higher order multiples creates! Kate says that she's merely trying to provide for her family and rely on the Lord to do so! Kate HATES this competition pressure that she is forced to deal with! She called her producer as soon as she hung up with Betty to let her know that she is not going to compete with the Hayes family or anyone else!

August 2006
Kate wrote about kindergarten testing for the twins. She quickly got to how unimpressed with the teacher she was after her first conversation with one of the twins. She said that the teacher somewhat blandly tolerated her daughter's infamous blithering on and on and Kate didn't like that. She accused the teacher of not being interested in what the child was saying and only being interested in what she had to say next!!!! She made fun of the teacher's name writing, Mrs Shufflebottom (how's that for a name?) She also said she wasn't really reassured with a Mrs. Dolan either.

August 2006
Kate was very upset that they missed their connecting flight out of Detroit saying that it was the dumbest thing ever! Because nobody ever paged us!!!! Kate apparently wanted star treatment even back then. Kate was bothered because it made a longer day for her. The only saving grace was that there were shops in the airport and food, neither of which she had to pay for because it was a trip for filming!!!!
It was a trip to film for Sam's Club and Kate was promised an exciting gift card. Kate was angry when she found out that the card was only for $750 even though the trip was a paid filming trip, which included meals and shopping.

September 2006
The crew came to the house for filming and Kate was very annoyed with a really annoying sound guy. He was new and she didn't like him already. Kate called her kids boring because they didn't do anything interesting like the trained monkeys they usually behave like apparently. Jen the producer was bummed too.
Local people are now starting to drive Kate crazy because Kate feels that they are trying to be included in her limelight while filming. Someone came up to the girls when they got off the bus and offered to have the girls wait with her. Kate wrote Oh brother! And how annoying!
Kate ended by writing that the babies took their nap while she hung out with Jen and Scott while the annoying sound man went to the garage and did who know what!

___

September 2006
Kate and Beth and Bob Carson and all of their kids were having trouble being served at restaurants on a busy Saturday night and it was making Kate very angry. She said the people at her favorite restaurant Austin's were not nice to them even though Kate begged and begged. According to Kate they threw them the Wyomissing attitude so they left. Then they went to another restaurant and had to wait a long time…like an hour! Kate and Bob and the rest of the adults were on their last nerve when they were finally seated. The kids were surprisingly good she said, despite the 7 pm dinner!!!!!!

Apparently even back then, Kate felt that her party of about twenty people deserved to move past all of the other customers who were waiting patiently in line to eat.

January 2007
Kate was upset about getting another Discovery Health check in the mail today because it was left on the porch with another package flapping in the breeze! Lovely! No mention of how happy she was with the money she was being paid. Only the negative as usual.

January 2007
Kate says how happy she is for Jon because he's going to spend the weekend with her brother and five other guys in a cabin. She says he didn't ask. She gave him permission to go! She goes on to say that she hopes she and the kids are all alive and well when he gets back!

February 2007
Kate and Jon took the kids to the King of Prussia mall to a casting agent. Kate was instantly horrified because the office smelled of smoke and nobody acknowledged them and the woman snapped at Kate when Kate tried to talk to her daughter. Kate said they should have walked out of there and that it was a complete waste of time!
Next they moved on to a photographer who was a pompous jerk himself. He was extremely annoying but took good pictures according to Kate.

March 2007
Kate talks about her visit with Doctor Phil. The first guest was shockingly an exorcist or however you spell it…Kate said he was awful and she prayed that Satan would get out. He was sitting in the exact chair that Kate would have to sit in.
Next came a jealous girlfriend! Ugh she was so immature! Kate wrote. It was actually pathetic!
Kate said that the Gosselins were the breath of fresh air to the show. Everyone was clapping!

Bla, bla, bla Doctor Phil gave them a bunch of free stuff, there were more nuts on after us Kate wrote and Kate badgered everyone who worked there and told them that Doctor Phil said she could meet Robin so they got paraded around with all the nuts who were on with them.

April 2007
Kate writes about Poor little Joel and how he is so in love with his daddy and wants to be loved by her. She says she does love him but hates to say that his father like cluelessness makes her crazy!

June 2007
According to Kate, Jon had the nerve to lie to her about buying lunch in Philadelphia that day. Kate said she knew he was lying because his eyes were as big as saucers!!! He made the mistake of putting his lunch on the credit card!!!! That was apparently the absolute end to the most horrible day in history!!!! Kate wonders why she is so unloved that Jon has to continually lie to her. She wonders if she is that stupid? Is Jon that characterless? She decides that Jon must care more about his OWN fear or whatever that lying is okay! She asks if Jon really thought that she would never EVER find out, then says just be honest weak boy!!!!! Jon is not teaching his children any life lessons this day my friends. Now because of Jon buying himself lunch (while he's working to earn the family money while Kate stays home) they're going to have a house full of lying kids. This makes Kate completely sick!!!!!!!

Wow, so Kate just had the absolute most horrible day in history because Jon bought his own lunch and was so afraid to tell her about it that he lied?

She's not finished with this one. She now wishes that because of this, that Jon would crack the bible daily and really seek the Lord in this matter! She asks God to help Jon to become a man of integrity!!!!! Lord Please!!!!! Jon could be the perfect man if he could get these things under control and let God take control!!!!!

These journal entries show Kate keeping a very close eye on any potential competition to her reality show future. She is reveling in the misfortunes of another:

June 2007
Kate mentions a Stacy Bailey from Arizona being pregnant after her frozen transfer and says they are waiting to hear how many. She says she is nervous that Bailey is trying to come up with another TV show for herself.

July 2007
Kate checks in to celebrate the fact that Stacy Bailey is NOT pregnant saying she has two more embryos that she needs to use but they are of bad quality supposedly. She seems very happy about this sad news for the Bailey family.

RING MY BELL

Here is an example of Kate's grateful side. This was a sign posted on Kate's front door when she was being overwhelmed with support from the community that was helping to take care of her new babies. Help that she had begged for. There's nothing wrong with a family wanting their privacy, but there was no justification for her rudeness. A "Please" would have been in order. Kate named the actual computer file she used to make the sign "GO AWAY.doc". And while the lowly helpers were forbidden to ring the doorbell, any delivery services bringing packages were welcome to ring away.

```
Thanks for watching!
If you are here to offer your services of any
kind,
```
Do Not Ring the door bell
```
(This excludes package delivery services. Ex: FedEx, UPS, etc.)
```

BOMBINGS OR WHATEVER

Like the rest of the world, you would think that Kate must have been shattered, heartbroken and distraught over the events of September 11, 2001. Indeed. She displayed her caring, sensitive and empathetic nature when she entered her private thoughts about the 5th anniversary of the 9/11 tragedies into her daily journal.

On September 11, 2006, Kate Gosselin wrote that "today is the five year remembrance of the September 11th bombings or whatever."

You read that correctly. Kate Gosselin callously and inexcusably (and inaccurately, I might add) described the events of our September 11, 2001, national and world tragedy in her journal as "**bombings or whatever**." Aside from her stunning ignorance about the cause of the events that unfolded on that tragic day, she reveals herself to be completely devoid of any emotion about the loved ones and sense of security our nation lost.

Some will excuse her words as nothing more than a lapse in judgment, either because they do not understand, or simply refuse to believe, that it is completely in character for Kate to not care about anyone or anything if it doesn't benefit her personally.

As the years passed, there were some positive signs that Kate was becoming more aware and sensitive to the despair of others. On the 10-year anniversary of 9/11, Kate tweeted this:

Wish I could say GM 2day butthere'sstill so much hurt in the air-it's palpable! We will nvr 4get! Thx esp 2day2all who hav fought fear..&won!

I'm watching CNN- Time tribute to 9/11 &I still can't bear the accounts. We will NEVER forget! Survivors/ victims families u r in r hearts!

Maybe there was a ray of hope after all that Kate had actually learned something in the 6 years since the 5th anniversary of 9/11, when she wrote of "bombings or whatever." Maybe she wasn't now being phony in expressing concern for others. Maybe she was showing compassion. Then again, maybe not. At this point, Kate had been abandoned by the entertainment industry and was desperate for attention and even more desperate to change her negative image. Twitter was her only outlet.

In October of 2012, Kate reverted to form. Her inability to feel or express empathy for the plight of others was on full display when she took to Twitter to immortalize her thoughts about Hurricane Sandy. That devastating "superstorm" was responsible for more than 120 deaths in the US alone, thousands of people losing their homes and/or livelihoods, millions losing power for extended periods of time, and billions of dollars in damage. Despite all that, Kate stayed sheltered in her little cocoon of ignorance and tweeted these happy things:

> **Is it bad 2say that so far,we r having nothing but FUN w Sandy(or the lack of her)? HurricaneSandy**

> **Winding down now with some uber exciting Disney channel.. #SuperfunSandy**

Tragically, Superstorm Sandy wasn't "Superfun" at all.

THE GREAT COMMUNICATOR

Kate's communications with others tell a lot about her personality and reveal a distinct superiority complex. She is condescending and dismissive towards anyone who has nothing of value to offer her. Numerous examples of her disdain for others litter her email communications.

Since there might be possible legal issues with reprinting actual email texts in their entirety here, I have, instead, only provided the dates of the emails, and summarized and paraphrased the email text. Where necessary, I have included parts of actual quotes. I have in no way changed the meaning or intent of the email communications.

Kate frequently signed off in her emails with a "Thanks! Have a gr8t day!" The last line in her emails was often the tag "Sent from my PINK iPhone". I have set the separate email subjects apart from one another with spaces above and below. Thanks! Have a gr8t day!

On August 1, 2006, an Ohio University student sent an email to the info@sixgosselins.com address to suggest that Jon and Kate apply to be on *Extreme Makeover/Home Edition*. "Abby T" addressed her note "Dear Gosselins." She said she had watched their story and was "truly touched" by their family, love and strength. Abby went on to say that their children are "beautiful and so adorable" and that Jon and Kate are "amazing and funny as well!" She told them that they are "so deserving" and "so sweet that viewers would melt." Abby then provided the website address to the ABC casting department in case Jon and Kate wanted to apply.

This poor young woman's heart was in the right place. Little did she know, however, that her idea would fall victim to Kate's disdain. Jon got the email and forwarded it to Kate, who got a good laugh out of Abby T's sincere suggestion. When she replied to Jon, Kate mockingly said that the girl obviously doesn't understand the world of television. She followed that with a "Thanks but absolutely no thanks!!!!!!!" and a derisive "HAA HAA HEE HEE."

In an email dated Monday, November 27, 2006, a representative named Liz from the 32 Flavors Public Relations company forwarded an email to Kate from a book agent who wasn't interested in Kate's book proposal. The book agent, a woman named Laurie, thanked Liz for thinking of her, but said that after checking out Jon and Kate's website, she decided it wasn't quite right for her. Laurie said it was a good story, but it was "not particularly unique," and she had seen a lot of book proposals like theirs.

Liz apologized to Kate that it didn't work out, telling her, "geez I didn't think it would go this way." Kate brushed off the rejection saying, "Ha- she obviously doesn't know how rare we are!" The book was later reworked by Beth Carson into the Christian love story, *Multiple Blessings*, and the rest is history.

Still in November of 2006, Kate sent an angry email to Jon for, well, just being Jon, I guess. She told him she was "soooooooooooooooooo frustrated" with him, and that she "begs and pleads and begs some more" for him to do things around the house that she can't do. She asked him why he couldn't see that he had to help with more than just the daily stuff in order to keep the house running smoothly, because then everybody would win. Kate also told Jon not to take the "lazy approach," and informed him that if he helped more, she would be happy, which meant that everyone else would be happy as well, including him. She threatened that she was "not going away," so he could either do the stuff she asks or "live miserably!" and ended by saying, "You choose!" She signed it "me".

On December 31, 2006, Jon forwarded Kate an email that he had received the day before from the coordinator of something called the "MOST" forum. (MOST stands for Mothers of Supertwins.) The forum coordinator, "Patti T," asked Jon if he would post something to introduce himself and his family on the forum at http://www.mostonline.org/MostBB/viewtopic.php?t=92. It is not clear why Patti T's email annoyed Kate, but her curt response to Jon about it is offensive. Kate said, "**These people are retarded!**"

In March of 2008, Kate sent Jon a list of ways the kids should help at home. She also included a Gosselin Family Mission Statement and listed principles based on the statement. Kate did not preface her letter with a "Hi Jon," or even a small greeting. She simply greeted him with the dictatorial command, "Here's what I want." She instructed Jon to write out the items on her list and include a picture to describe the task next to each item. These are the **10 Ways To Help at Home** that Kate listed:

1. Clean up toys.
2. Sweep floor after meals.
3. Turn off lights when I leave a room.
4. Make my bed.
5. Brush my teeth.
6. Put things where they belong.
7. Put dirty laundry in hamper.
8. Put my shoes away and hang my coat.
9. Empty trash cans.
10. Straighten bathroom.

This is the **Gosselin Family Mission Statement**:

"We the people of the Gosselin Family
do dedicate ourselves to
telling others about God's love."

Kate said that two basic principles were established through the mission statement:

1. Love and honor God and others.
2. Be thankful for our blessings.

She then listed eight (of course) limits based on those principles:

1. Honor mom and dad by obeying them.
2. Trust God always and completely.
   3. Honor God by remembering their blessings and choosing to be thankful for each other
      and what they have.
4. Honor each other by choosing to love, be patient with, and help one another.
5. Honor the family by always choosing family first before other opportunities.
   6. Honor the family and God by choosing to speak positive and encouraging words even when they don't feel like it.
7. Love others by sharing what they have with those in need.
   8. Realize that God built their family with the exact members for His purpose! Enjoy their unique qualities individually and as a whole to contribute to their family!

Reading Kate's lists as they pertained to the Gosselin Family Mission Statement, it is glaringly obvious that the principles and limits she listed applied to everyone in her family except herself.

On May 26, 2008, Jon forwarded Kate an email from "Larry W," a fellow who was trying to be nice by offering the Gosselins information about a full-tuition scholarship opportunity in Arkansas. He told Jon that he and his wife were big fans of their show, and that he was a member of the El Dorado Promise Marketing Committee. He explained that "E.P." is a full-tuition scholarship funded by Murphy Oil Co., which is headquartered in El Dorado, and that any student who graduates from the El Dorado School District is eligible. Larry said he had heard Kate mention on the show about possibly being interested in relocating, and thought that free college tuition for eight kids would be a good reason to move to a great southern town that would welcome them with open arms. Larry W then provided contact information.

Kate could have replied to Jon about the email in any number of polite ways to indicate she wasn't interested. Instead, her words to Jon in dismissing the information were snide and uncalled for, and most certainly would have been hurtful to Larry W if he had heard them. Kate told Jon, "Yeah, ok. Let's become the Duggars neighbors-yeehaw!!!!!"

Not many people do "rude" quite as well as Kate does. (As an additional observation, in looking through all of Kate's emails and journal ramblings, she seemed to be very jealous of the Duggars and threatened by their wholesomeness.)

Kate had some very specific demands for accommodations and meals while traveling. These are some particular stipulations she submitted to Wendy Douglas from Discovery for their stay at the Essex House in New York City. Kate told Wendy they had security concerns and layout concerns at other hotels, but in the "spirit of partnership" they were "willing to do the Essex House again" as long as her stipulations were met. It is really nice that Kate was "willing" to stay at the exclusive Essex House at Central Park for free. (I invite you to check out the prices of rooms and suites at the Essex House for some perspective on this.) This is a list of Kate's stipulations:

- Accommodations: Kate asked for the same suite setup they had the last time they stayed, but with an additional king room "DIRECTLY NEXT DOOR" to the suite setup. Kate also specified a room number, and indicated it was the floor the spa was on. She adamantly stated, "A room down the hall even one room further will not work!!!!!" She also said she would need an additional rollaway bed in the suite.

- Meals: Kate said the room service menu selection for breakfast would be fine. She specified the following exact menu items for lunches for two days, and dinners for two or possibly three days:

  - Wednesday dinner: Kobe beef tips cooked medium to medium well; steamed broccoli; mashed potatoes; French fries; organic blueberries; and vanilla ice cream. Kate asked that a mixed green/grilled chicken salad option be provided for the adults. She listed these ingredients to be used in the salad: grilled chicken, cucumber, tomato, sliced strawberries or pears, feta cheese crumbles, pecans and a balsamic vinaigrette dressing.

– Thursday lunch: Homemade macaroni and cheese with mild white cheddar and small shell pasta; French fries with honey mustard sauce; carrots and celery sticks; apple slices; and chocolate chip cookies (with a mixed green/grilled chicken salad option for the adults).

– Thursday dinner: Hamburgers (sliders); cheeseburgers (sliders); hot dogs; chicken fingers with honey mustard sauce; French fries; onion rings; dill pickles and steamed seasoned green beans on the side; and vanilla cake with vanilla icing (with a mixed green/grilled chicken salad option for the adults).

– Friday lunch: Peanut butter and grape jelly on wheat bread (Kate specified whole grain bread with no "obvious" grain in it); potato chips; fruit salad with blueberries, bananas, apple, grapes, strawberries, kiwi, and pineapple; Monterey Jack cheese cubes; and oatmeal raisin cookies. (With a substitute for the adults of ham and cheese sandwiches on wheat with lettuce, tomato and onion and horseradish spread; and a mixed green/grilled chicken salad.)

– Friday dinner (if they were still there): Pizza - cheese, pepperoni, onion and green peppers in different configurations; French fries; steamed broccoli; and chocolate brownies (with a mixed green/grilled chicken salad option for the adults).

– Kate requested these additional specific items from Whole Foods in the main suite only:
10 Organic bananas; 4 boxes organic blueberries; 4 packages organic cheese sticks; 2 boxes organic "Ritz" crackers; 2 six packs Yo Kids (Stonyfield Farms) organic yogurt; 1 pack organic peanut butter cookies; 3 bottles organic lemonade; 1 gallon organic pulp-free orange juice; 2 gallons spring water; 2 packages of individually packaged cookies; 2 packages of individually packaged peanut butter crackers and/ or cheese crackers.

Kate then thanked Wendy and told her that having these things would alleviate some of the stress of traveling! She then very graciously told Wendy that, as always, "we really appreciate you!!!!! :)".

On June 9, 2008, some poor guy named Tony, who was the North American Sales Director for Cutco Logo Gifts and a paying advertiser on the Gosselin website, sent Jon and Kate an email simply requesting that they change his web address on their website. You know, so the money he was paying to advertise on their site might actually do him some good. He asked that they please change the website they had listed at the bottom of his ad from www.cutco.com to http://www.mycutcorep.com/TonyCxxxxxxx. Even though Tony asked politely and said "please" and "Thanks," his request irritated Kate. She commented to Jon "He's annoying me!" and told Jon, "But do it to get rid of him!"

On June 22, 2008, Kate sent an email to Wendy Douglas of Discovery, with copies to Jon, Julie Carson May (Kate's manager), and Jen Stocks (a producer/writer/director at Figure 8 Films, which was the company that filmed the Gosselins for TLC) to complain that Jon's name was misspelled on a TLC television promo. Jon's name certainly should not have been spelled incorrectly, but Kate went berserk over it. She shouted that Jon's name was "MISPELLED" as "John" on "a TLC promo … A TV promo!!!!" and said "Sorry but that is completely unacceptable!!!!" (Oh, what would Kate do without her beloved exclamation points?) She is like a bull in a china shop. She could have softened her approach just a bit when communicating with the network that was paying her salary and supporting her family.
Wendy thanked Kate for letting her know about the problem and told Kate she would tell TLC marketing right away so they could take care of the situation. Kate thanked Wendy for working on it. She said she always gets annoyed when fans use the "h" when writing the name of the show, and then "the dreaded happened..... I actually saw it misspelled on TLC…" In a postscript, Kate also thanked Wendy for having a "horrible fan pop site removed!!!!!!"

On June 26, 2008, Kate received an email from a gentleman named Michael expressing how excited he and his wife were when they spotted some toys they had sent to the Gosselin children in the background of an episode of *Jon & Kate Plus Ei8ht*. Michael said they were thrilled to see that the kids had received them and seemed to enjoy them. He then told Kate that he and his wife were celebrating the recent birth of their 3rd child "…same name as one of yours- Aaden." He gave Kate their phone number and said that if she ever had a spare moment, his wife would love to chat and introduce herself.
It is understandable that Kate should be extremely careful when dealing with strangers, but that certainly didn't stop her from accepting their gifts. Her greatest annoyance was that the gift-givers spelled their child's name the same way as one of Kate's boys. Kate complained, "These are the people that sent us the Christian toys..... notice they used our spelling of Aaden...how annoying...fans naming their kids our kids names!" Apparently, Kate thinks the names she chose for her children should have been retired, never to be used for another child again.

In August of 2008, Jon and Julie May exchanged emails to discuss letting a customer, Colleen, know about a change in advertising opportunities on the Gosselin family website. Kate was not happy about how Jon was handling the situation, so she got a tad bit testy. She scolded Jon, saying "You need to do this on your own and stop bothering Julie with stupidity!" Kate then gave Jon specific instructions to explain to the customer that their "new, updated site does not have the same opportunities or space for advertising at this time." She instructed Jon to let Colleen know that they would not bill her for June-August, but the site was going to switch over within the week. Kate then told Jon to write, "Thanks for your support. We have enjoyed working with you!"

On December 23, 2008, Julie May forwarded an email to Kate from Jeff Lanter, the new series producer. Jeff wanted to touch base with Julie to let her know that 100% of his attention would be focused on the series. He said his first priority was getting the production team in "the right mindset." He also said he understood that "Jon and Kate are celebrities," and that they are extremely busy and have a family to raise, so he would be looking for ways to make their lives easier regarding the production of the show.

Jeff assured Julie that anyone new who would be joining the team would have a history of working with him or their team over the last 15+ years, and they would all have the same mindset and commitment to the show. He also commented on his relationship with the network, stating that he didn't always see eye to eye with it. He said he agreed to take on the series producer role only if he could speak freely and not always feel the need to toe the party line.

Jeff also explained that there would be many situations when he would whole-heartedly agree with Jon and Kate, but there would also be times when they wouldn't see to eye to eye. He said that in cases where something wasn't working, they would simply find a way to change it.

Jeff informed Julie that he wanted to set up a dinner with Jon and Kate to discuss scheduling, communication, the crew, and what was and wasn't working from their standpoint. He also asked for her help with scheduling a time to "re-shoot" the "All You Wanted To Know" interview. (Author's note: Doesn't everybody "re-shoot" their lives like this in "reality"?) He closed by saying he was looking forward to working on the series in a new role.

After Kate read Jeff's email, she replied to Julie, saying that it sounded like Jeff really wanted to do a good job. But she was suspicious about how he could "suddenly surface and become so ever present?!" Kate said, "Don't trust them...Any of them. Period. A dinner AFTER their trial month... Maybe."

In a postscript to that email, Kate told Julie that some network amendment was signed, but Jon had forgotten to scan and send it before he went out with his friends. Kate said, "I'll nag again tomorrow about it!"

On December 29, 2008, Jon forwarded an email to Kate from a woman named "Phyllis M," who was the registrar for the Triplet Connection, which is an organization for parents of higher multiples (defined as triplets or more). She was inquiring about Jon and Kate's availability and rates for a possible speaking engagement at a convention in Philadelphia in July of 2010.

Phyllis introduced herself as the mother of "3NQuads," which means she had "3 children and wanted a fourth," but "oops we got 4 (now age 22) !!!!!" (I have to wonder aloud here whether there is some strange side-effect of birthing multiples that compels those moms to use multiple exclamation points as well.) Phyllis gave a brief history of the Triplet Connection and explained how she had become involved as a way to give back to the organization, which she believed gave her valuable information and help with her quadruplets.

This speaking opportunity sounds like just the kind of thing Kate would have jumped at, but for some reason, she was completely dismissive of it. In her usual polite manner, Kate replied to Jon with a "Blah blah blah… No thanks" and said it could get them in "biggg trouble!" It is unclear how this particular engagement could get them in "biggg trouble!" Maybe it's because the people attending the convention would have far greater knowledge and wisdom to impart about multiples than Kate could ever have.

Later that same day, December 29, 2008, Jon forwarded another email to Kate from a woman named "Joy R," who wrote that she had a friend in Columbia, South Carolina, who was expecting sextuplets. She said that her friend, Courtney, and Courtney's husband, Allen, were "grounded, solid Christians" who, like Jon and Kate, would not consider selective reduction. Joy explained that the couple was anxious and scared about the health of Courtney and the babies, but they knew God was in control and would "lead them through the tough days ahead." She then asked whether Jon and Kate would consider sending Courtney an email because she was a big fan of the show and she would be thrilled to get it.

Kate's reply to Jon once again showed off her sensitive, supportive, empathetic side. Kate made it clear that she viewed Courtney as a potential threat. She stated, "You realize…. She's only 8 wks along ……."

December 29, 2008, was a busy day for email. Julie May was on vacation, and Kate sent her an email telling her she missed her. Julie replied that she would call Kate the next day, and that she thought she would have a few things for her to sign. She told Kate that she missed her, too.

Kate then sent Julie another email telling her that she was looking forward to talking to her. Kate said, "I hate when the business world takes a vacation!!!! :)" and "Vacation is soon over.... Thank goodness!" Kate also needed to let Julie know that people were annoying her. She said, "I've emailed Angela and Karen numerous times now with very little action and it's annoying me! Will wait to hear tomorrow then may have to send you after them again! :) And the email from Jeff- ugh annoying! Your thoughts!?"

On December 30, 2008, Kate had a conversation with her publicist Laurie Goldberg at Discovery Communications. Laurie wanted to know if Kate would like to answer any questions from journalists who were looking to interview her. Kate wanted questions submitted to her via email to play it safe. When prodded a bit by Goldberg that some of the reporters actually wanted to speak to Kate, Kate asked if there was "anyone worth talking to?:)" Kate went on to say that "if it's worth it" she would do it, but only "if it isn't someone dumb!"

Pot meet Kettle.

Kate did manage to answer one tabloid reporter's question. The reporter wanted Kate to give some advice to Tom Cruise, who recently said in an interview that he wanted 10 kids with his wife Katie Holmes.

Kate's reply? "He's a Brad Pitt wanna be.....he's a jerk! But don't let them print any of that!"

THE WORLD ACCORDING TO KATE – PART 2

"… I need you to know, don't believe what you read
unless you hear it from that person."
– *Kate Gosselin*

As mentioned earlier, Kate was laser-focused on turning herself into a Martha Stewart-like character so she could cash in on as much as she possibly could. Her eight children were mere props – pawns in her game to accumulate as much wealth and notoriety as she could.

Kate loved the idea of becoming the "working mom's Martha Stewart," but she didn't like or respect Martha Stewart herself. Kate believed she was better than Martha Stewart even before she had her first set of babies. Kate's mind jumps to the last chapter without reading the book.

When Kate took the kids and Jon, along with Aunt Jodi, to New York City to appear on the Martha Stewart show, she was very disrespectful to, and unappreciative of, Martha. "Kate already thought she was better than Martha Stewart!" a source told me.

When I was going through the photos Kate took with her own camera during that trip, I didn't find a single photo of Kate with Martha Stewart. It seemed odd that Aunt Jodi wanted a picture with Martha, but Kate did not. "Kate wouldn't give Martha the satisfaction of asking to be in a picture with her," said my source.

When they were taping the show in Martha's studio, Kate made sure to stick Jon in the middle next to Martha. "Kate did not want a side-by-side comparison to Martha Stewart." Not yet anyway.

One of Kate's earlier entries into Martha Stewart's territory was a dismal failure. Kate's Christian book publisher, Zondervan, was going to release Kate's next big "bestseller," a cookbook called *Love Is In The Mix: Making Meals Into Memories*, but canceled it in its tracks. They didn't cancel it because the timing was bad (it was to be released around the time that the Gosselin marriage scandal was making headlines) – as it was widely reported – they canceled it because they discovered that the recipes in Kate's cookbook were not actually hers. They found out that she had taken recipes from various sources, changed the names, and tried to pass them off as her own.

This isn't such a shocking revelation when you consider that Kate Gosselin can't cook. "She's a nightmare in the kitchen. All she does is make a mess," a Gosselin *very* insider told me.

The public caught on to Kate's recipe "borrowing" right away and went crazy posting comments on every website and blog that gave the book a mention. Zondervan took notice, and Kate's cookbook was toast.

Another way in which Kate Gosselin wanted to be like Martha Stewart, yet be even more admired by America's moms, had to do with her self-proclaimed organizational skill. Kate has always said, and said on the RV episode of *Kate Plus Ei8ht*, "I'm the most organized person on the planet!"

On THE PLANET! Not, "In my house," but "On the planet!" She takes hyperbole to a whole new level, especially when she is singing her own praises. But of course, that's not an accident. Remember President Clinton's phone call to Bobby McCaughey? "You know, when those kids all go off to school, you will be the best-organized manager in the U.S."

Kate Gosselin is no Martha Stewart, and never could be, no matter how hard she and Julie Carson May/TLC/Discovery tried to create that image and shove it down the public's throats. Pretending to be organized and actually *being* organized are two entirely different things. And no matter how hard Kate tries to make it seem like she is multi-talented, she will always be far too lazy to succeed on her own without her children.

Kate and TLC liked to depict Jon as a lazy slob. They made it appear as if Kate was the one doing all the work and keeping everything tidy, but that was one big, fat lie. It was just one more deception intended to build the "Kate" brand.

I've been inside Kate's home, during the divorce when Jon still lived there. I've been in the apartment above the garage when Jon lived there after he was vanquished from the main part of the home. I was in Jon's luxury New York City apartment. I was in Jon's Wyomissing, Pennsylvania, apartment, and I've been in Jon's current house. I have also been in Jon's cars. Here's what I can tell you from first-hand experience.

Jon Gosselin is a neat freak – almost to the point of being compulsive. Every one of his living spaces I have seen has been very well organized and clean. His clothes are always folded and ironed and put away. His rugs are vacuumed daily. There are never dishes in the sink. He has drawer organizers, closet organizers, and cabinet organizers. His pantry is organized. His windows are clean. His car is always spotless, inside and out, and he always has a new air freshener in place. And guess who does all that cleaning and organizing? Jon does. I'm an artsy, metrosexual kind of guy, but next to Jon Gosselin, I'm a filthy pig. Since I've known Jon, he has had no help with his living spaces or with taking care of the kids, except from whichever girlfriend he happened to be with at the time. And there were no neat-freaks among them, believe me. Kate wanted that neat-freak, organized persona for herself, so she stole it from Jon.

I've seen some of Kate's personal areas, and I've looked in her cars, and they were nowhere near as organized or clean as anything I have ever seen of Jon's. She has piles of clothes on top of suitcases, and laundry in piles waiting for someone else to do it. She piles up her dishes until someone else does them. She feeds the kids on paper plates so she can just throw them away. So much for her being "green" nonsense.

If you are looking for proof of Kate's lack of domestic skills, and her foul temperament to boot, go back and watch the RV Trip episode of *Kate Plus Ei8ht*. Pay attention to the scene where Kate decides she is going to vacuum. It speaks volumes about Kate's relationship, or lack thereof, with a vacuum cleaner. I've watched Jon vacuum, many times. I, myself, have vacuumed hundreds of times. I know what it looks like when someone has actually handled a vacuum cleaner before. In that episode, you will see that Kate has absolutely no idea how to even handle the thing.

In the vacuuming scene from the episode, where they are talking inside the RV and Kate is standing in the background doing nothing, her paid best friend Jamie announces that she's going to vacuum the floors. Kate's eyes light up as she gets the idea that vacuuming is something she should be doing to maintain her brand of being the neat freak. Kate totally steals Jamie's moment for herself, but it's what happens next that is so funny – and so telling.

Kate storms around looking for the vacuum cleaner – you know – the vacuum cleaner that she told us in that very same episode that she has been using to clean all of the floors every day during the trip. This is supposedly day six of the trip, according to TLC, and yet Kate had no idea where the vacuum was. Once she finds it, she bangs her head and hurts herself, of course, because she's helpless. She then grabs the vacuum and drags it violently across the rock-covered ground, banging it all the way to the RV.

Besides a 6-year-old child, who would be physically incapable of lugging a vacuum, who in their right mind would ever do something like that? Whether the vacuum was yours personally, or whether it was part of the RV or TLC's property, who would ever drag a vacuum over rocks rather than carry it? Kate has been telling us for several years now about how much she exercises and works out, so it couldn't possibly be that she wasn't strong enough to lift the darn thing. My grandmother used to carry her vacuum up and down three flights of stairs. Surely Kate has picked up one or more of her children at some point and can lift the weight of a vacuum cleaner. Kate had no idea what to do with the vacuum cleaner, but she sure put on a show for the filming of her "most real" reality.

YOU WIN SOME; YOU LOSE SOME

In 2009, Julie May, the Gosselin's manager, was hard at work trying to secure lucrative endorsement deals for Jon and Kate with various companies. For a potential deal with Hershey and Kraft, Julie May worked with a representative from Burns Entertainment & Sports Marketing, Inc. She used an article from the *Baltimore Sun*, which talked about the return of the American family to network television, as a marketing tool. The article, written by David Zurawik, also known as Z on TV, was titled "Family Matters for TLC and its Viewers." Zurawik wrote "family fare is making a comeback in a big way on cable channel TLC (The Learning Channel) these days, particularly with young female viewers." He also said:

Jon & Kate Plus 8, a reality TV show that follows the everyday lives of Jon and Kate Gosselin and their eight children, is one of the highest-rated series on cable TV with an audience of 3.7 million viewers. It is the top show on advertiser-supported cable with young women, one of TV's most desired demographic groups. It beats out such series as TNT's *The Closer*.

The Gosselins have been on the cover of *Good Housekeeping* magazine and were featured last week on *The Oprah Winfrey Show*, a barometer of mass popularity if ever there was one. Their success has driven year-to-year, double-digit growth for the once-foundering Maryland-based operation - lifting TLC this year into the Top 10 basic cable channels.

Thinking this would be great, positive publicity, Julie May passed the article along on March 16, 2009, to "Marc I," the Burns Entertainment & Sports Marketing, Inc. representative who was working on the Hershey and Kraft deals. She told him she thought he might be interested in getting some viewership stats.

But things didn't work out the way Julie May and Kate had hoped. On the morning of March 19, 2009, Marc sent Julie an email informing her that Hershey and Kraft were probably going to pass on working with the Gosselins. Marc told Julie that "the recent round of news regarding Jon and Kate has caused the client to put this on hold, and it may no longer happen." He said they were concerned that the story would "dominate their media tour and take away from the S'mores messages." What this really meant was that Hershey and Kraft were smart enough to distance themselves from the Gosselin train wreck that was happening with the messy divorce and all the bad press.

That afternoon, Julie May gave Kate the bad news, saying that it was very frustrating. After hearing that the deal was dead, Kate forwarded the email to Jon and said: "Lost another $100,000...read below... wonderful!"

One piece of the "recent round of news" about Jon and Kate that portrayed them in a bad light was from a March 2009 article entitled, "Show Biz: Jon + Kate + 8 = $$$." Written by Jessica Remo and published in *Philadelphia* magazine, the article painted a very unflattering picture of the Gosselins, Kate in particular. Even more disturbing than the critical picture of Kate and the entire Gosselin drama was what the author had to say about the possible outcome for the children. This is what she wrote:

If Jon and Kate Gosselin have sold their children's privacy, we the viewers are the guilty buyers, even as we find it harder and harder to see the pair as the guileless, relatable-to, in-over-their-heads parents we once knew and adored. Looking ahead, the Gosselins' challenges are still real and many, though different: How will they teach their kids to be humble, and that normal people don't get to run the bases at Phillies games? That everything isn't free and yours when you want it? That fame is, by and large, capricious and fleeting? Only time will tell how their eight will deal with having grown up in a home studio, in front of cameras and fans, as the world watched.

"As their friend, as somebody who loves the kids, I was always the one saying [to Jon and Kate], 'Okay, be careful.' Because they're not just a commodity, they're people," says one of the kids' former babysitters. "And someday will come and … you know? Nothing comes free. Everything, everything, has a price. And because I love them, I don't want them to pay a price that's too dear."

Despite losing out on some endorsement deals, plenty of other companies continued to be interested in using the Gosselins to promote their products. In this next case, the product happened to be a new album by singer/songwriter Kenny Loggins.

On May 15, 2009, Julie May received an email from "Maria K," vice president of media relations at Walt Disney Records, who was aware that the Gosselin children had been dancing to Loggins' song, "Footloose," on an episode of *Jon & Kate Plus 8*, and that Jon had mentioned he loved Kenny and wished he could meet him one day. Maria said she was working with Loggins on a new album, called "All Join In," which was due out that summer. She also said he had a concert near Lancaster, PA, scheduled for July 17, and they would be open to arranging a meeting with the Gosselins "to be incorporated into the show somehow."

Julie May forwarded that email to Kate asking for her thoughts about a possible meet-and-greet with Loggins. Now, the chance to meet Kenny Loggins in and of itself would have been a thrill for most normal people, but Kate Gosselin isn't most people, and she certainly doesn't want to be treated as normal. Always thinking she is more important than she is, Kate had the nerve to request that Kenny Loggins give them a private outdoor concert at their home. She did say, however, "We will go to the concert if that is only option though..."

THE TERRIBLE TABLOID EXPLOITATION RUMOR

On May 21, 2009, Laurie Goldberg of Discovery sent Julie May an email informing Julie that *US Weekly* planned to publish a possibly damaging story about Jon and Kate exploiting their children. In Laurie Goldberg's email, which had the subject line "Terrible rumor I am hearing," she told Julie May she wanted to give her a heads up about the *US Weekly* cover piece tentatively titled "What About the Kids?" She said it had a big shot of the family as the main image and it alleged that Jon and Kate are terrible, exploitative parents who could legally be sued.

Julie May forwarded Kate the email, telling her that *US Weekly* was "stooping to new lows," and saying it was "Unbelievable." Kate didn't seem terribly concerned about the charges. In her reply, she said she wondered whether *US Weekly* was trolling "gwop" (Gosselins Without Pity website) for their topics, and made a comment about being tired of *US Weekly*. She then said that all *US Weekly* was doing was increasing their ratings at that point, and ended with a "Thank you US weekly!" It is interesting that Kate didn't say one word about being incensed that they were being portrayed inaccurately.

Kate couldn't blame all the bad press on just the tabloids. An article in *Vanity Fair* magazine entitled "The Unreal Rise of Jon and Kate Gosselin," (Google it) written by Nancy Jo Sales, a *Vanity Fair* contributing editor, was published on October 19, 2009, just a few months after I started writing and reporting for *US Weekly*. Jon and Kate Gosselin's marriage had been publicly unraveling for several months by that time, and Kate's star was on the rise. The Discovery/TLC/Kate-concocted smear campaign against John had reached full force. In the article, the author's observations provided an objective, eyewitness look at the demanding, annoyed and annoying, self-absorbed celebrity that is Kate Gosselin. The following are excerpts from that article.

"Nobu, Nobu, I want Nobu!" Kate Gosselin wants to go to Nobu. She's got a night away from her eight kids—also her co-stars on the hit reality series Jon & Kate Plus Eight—and a reporter is offering to take her out on the town. "I want sushi!" Kate says, leaning back in an armchair in her suite at the Essex House hotel overlooking Central Park, checking her BlackBerry, popping gum.

But Laurie Goldberg, senior vice president of communications at the Learning Channel, which airs Jon & Kate, doesn't think Nobu's such a great idea. Kate cried on the Today show this morning, answering questions about why she's still wearing her wedding ring ("for them," she said of her children, sniffling), and this afternoon she told People, "I am so emotionally spent" (from her husband's behavior, which has included philandering with the daughter of the plastic surgeon who gave Kate her tummy tuck), and so it might not look good for her to be out enjoying herself at a hot spot.

"You're like a prisoner," Kate says of her newfound fame, annoyed.

Kate says they have hounded her "every single single single single single single single day of my life. I hate it. I hate it so much." I say you can almost feel sympathy for the celebrities who lose their tempers around photographers.

"Who says I didn't lose it—or may not?" Kate asks archly.
"I'm waiting for the call," Goldberg says, laughing.
"I'm actually there to keep the paparazzi safe," Neild jokes.
"Shut up," Kate tells them sharply, frowning. "Now that's where I draw the line."

... A personal shopper, an older lady in a floral-print dress, is summoned to help Kate select toys for her brood. Kate sails along beside her, ignoring all the gawkers. The personal shopper shows her some hacky sacks: "Boys like these." "I'll take your word for it," Kate sniffs, moving past them. The personal shopper shows her some action figures: "This is the hottest stuff for boys." "I'd rather die," says Kate. "Moving right along!"

That article not only shined a light on Kate's obnoxious, entitled, rude self, it revealed a very interesting, but little-known fact. The author mentioned that Laurie Goldberg expressed concerned about Kate wanting to dine at Nobu after she had wailed about being emotionally spent on the *Today* show. Goldberg didn't think it would look good for Kate to be seen enjoying herself at a hot spot.

So why was Laurie Goldberg, Executive VP of Public Relations for Discovery and TLC, even present for that interview? The fact is, while under contract with Discovery, whenever Kate went anywhere in public, to speak or to make a television appearance, she was not alone. Yes, we already know that her shadow and bodyguard, Steve Neild, was always at her side, but someone else was in the room with Kate and Steve. That someone was Laurie Goldberg, Kate's personal public relations expert.

We never got to see her, but Laurie Goldberg or someone like her was always there, and her influence was powerful. She was the person who told Kate what to say and how to answer questions and how to spin things. She pretty much controlled the message coming out of Kate's mouth, and she performed that duty for years.

KATE LOVES HER FANS

At Thanksgiving of 2010, I was camped outside of Kate's front gate, working, when a lovely Mennonite woman drove up with a beautifully adorned gift bag for Kate. As a reporter, I needed to know what was inside, so I asked. The nice woman reluctantly showed me the contents. I could see she was disgusted by my presence, being the "paparazzi" and all, as she called me, but she was still gracious enough to remove the gift to show me what she had brought for Kate. The woman had hand-carved and painted three beautiful rectangular blocks of wood for Kate to put on a mantel, table or shelf. Each block had a single word. "Faith". "Family". "Friends".

The woman was from Hebron, KY, but she was visiting family members in nearby Ephrata, PA, so she drove out of her way to bring the gift to Kate. She rang the buzzer on the intercom for a few minutes, but got no response. Kate was at home, and there's a camera on the intercom box, so it's very possible that Kate saw the woman dressed in conservative Mennonite clothing, but chose not to respond, as was her right. The woman left the bag inside the front gate for Kate to pick up the next time she came down the driveway.

The next day, I was back at the house working, when I noticed in the trashcan out front, the very same gift bag that the lady left for Kate. I picked it out of the trash and wasn't surprised to see that the beautiful hand-carved blocks were still in the bag, along with a letter from the lady. The envelope was opened, and the letter was torn in half. This is what the letter that Kate tore in half and threw away said:

```
Dear Kate —

I made this gift not knowing who to give it to.
Then it came to me — You!
We all need these 3 in our life.

Friends — during times of trouble in one's life, this is a test
of who your real/true friends are.

Family — is next. Unfortunately, some have betrayed you. We can't
choose our family. We are born into one.

Faith — is at the top. Our friends will leave us, our family will
disappoint us but one thing for sure, God will never leave us or
forsake us.

Kate, Happy Thanksgiving. May the Lord be with you.
Take care & God Bless!

S.
```

Kate has gladly accepted many gifts of monetary value from fans and well-wishers. Some wooden blocks were obviously not worthy of her. So fans, in the future, please send Kate only things that she can really use. Cash, checks or gift cards are preferred, even if they're only to Starbucks.

As a postscript, I liked the blocks and the words on them, and the nice woman who had created them as a labor of love, so I brought them home and gave them to my mother. She doesn't know the backstory, and she keeps them proudly displayed on her piano for everyone to see.

MEDIOCRE

In September of 2011, Kate opened her mouth once again without thinking and set off yet another firestorm of controversy. While being interviewed on the *Today* show, Matt Lauer asked Kate about Jon's comments to *Radar Online*, in which he said that he was "very relieved" that his little ones would finally be out of the limelight since *Kate Plus Ei8ht* was canceled. Kate said that she holds herself to higher expectations as a provider than her ex-husband, and stated:

```
"It's a situation where Jon may be accepting of mediocre for
his kids and working a regular job…I want the best for my
kids and the best opportunities, not unlike every parent. I
think that to be a good parent is to work as hard as you can
and give them the best opportunities in life, and this has
provided that."
```

So to Kate, regular people who don't have jobs on television are simply mediocre. Yes, Kate pretty much told us all that we're simply mediocre for going to our pathetic 9-to-5 jobs every day to give our children a good life. Apparently, in Kate's world, you have to be on television making millions of dollars to provide a good life for your children.

In one brief moment, without her longtime publicist, Laurie Goldberg, putting words in her mouth on a daily basis, Kate managed to upset and alienate her core audience – the working moms. As usual, she had to immediately backpedal on her ignorant comment because of the negative backlash, so she took to Twitter to "set the record straight." The first tweet below was Kate's response to a fan who asked her about her "mediocre" comment. She followed that first tweet with a clarification tweet moments later. It would appear that Kate was given a talking point to address her unfortunate remark, because she basically copied and pasted her response … except for changing the "and" in her first tweet to "&" in her second tweet.

> **not what I meant.. – I meant this job is not a career acc 2 jon but tv is 4 me and is hard but will prov best opps 4 my kids vs nursing!**

> **2clarify re 'mediocre' – I meant this job is not a career acc 2 jon but tv is 4 me & is hard but will prov best opps 4 my kids vs nursing!**

I wonder where periodic blogging for a little-known coupon website would fall on Kate's list of mediocre jobs.

PAY NO ATTENTION TO THAT PREDATOR BEHIND THE COMPUTER

In October of 2011, there was more trouble in Gosselin/TLC paradise when it was revealed that an editor named Bill Blankinship, who worked for a company called Serious Robots, which does editing work for Figure 8 Films, was arrested and charged with ten counts of second-degree sexual exploitation of a minor (distribution of child pornography). Blankinship worked as an editor for *Jon & Kate Plus 8*,
17 Kids and Counting, and *Table for 12*, among other projects.
As usual, Kate was in her own little world and had no idea that anything was even going on until one of her tweeties alerted her. When informed about Blankinship, this was Kate's response on Twitter:

NEVER HEARD OF HIM!

Instead of expressing shock and outrage that someone who had access to film footage of her children was charged with this terrible crime, she acted oblivious to the gravity of the situation. But after a few days of ignoring the matter, and after hearing Jon's statement to *Star* magazine expressing his concern and outrage, Kate finally thought of a response. It was a lie, of course, but it was, nonetheless, a response. It was her way of trumping Jon's concern over the issue ... that Kate knew absolutely nothing about.

Re news issue at hand, I'm dealing w it properly. Serves 0 purpose2run2 tabs esp w/o all facts.not helpful 2 any1...other than 2 make quick $.

Kate then followed that up with this tweet in response to the hundreds of tweets she was receiving on the subject:

Just because you don't see and hear what I'm doing about it, doesn't mean I'm ignoring the issue... I'm not!

IT'S ALL THE KIDS' FAULT

In January of 2012, on the Dr. Drew television show, Kate pretty much blamed her children for being the reason she can't find another man.

```
Dr. Drew: How about you, do you have a love life?

Kate: "No, too busy, I think a lot of my friends who are being
       constructive, or trying, say gosh, who are you gonna meet
       that's um, gonna be able to deal with eight kids and my
       answer is always, if they can deal with eight kids in our
       situation, they probably will be the person. It'll sort of
       prove it."
```

Yes, Kate. Your eight wonderful children are the reason no man wants anything to do with you. It couldn't possibly be due to the fact that you are mean and nasty and that you very publicly humiliated, emasculated, disparaged and denigrated your first husband.

On the topic of finding a man, one of her followers sent this tweet:

> xxxxx @Kateplusmy8 My Mama always said it's nice to have a man, but also know how to stand...on your own.. :)

> **agreed! I won't know how to act if/when I ever don't have to stand totally on my own anymore....;)**

It's rather amusing that Katie Irene Gosselin wrote the words, "if/when I ever don't have to stand totally on my own anymore." Kate Gosselin went from being taken care of by her parents…

To being taken care of by her boyfriends and their parents…
To being taken care of by Jon and his wealthy father…
To being taken care of by TLC/Discovery Communications…
To being taken care of by her manager...
To being taken care of by her children.

Even today, she's still being directed and shuttled around by her road manager/bodyguard, Steve Neild, and she still has nannies and babysitters at home to take care of the kids for her, as well as people to clean her house and cook her family's meals. She does NOTHING on her own for her kids. And she never did.

EVERYBODY LOVES KATE

One of Kate's rabid, lunatic Twitter buddies tweeted that she needed some new haters because the "old ones are starting to like me. :)" Kate tweeted back:

> **lol. My same challenge. Meet me in person then try to hate me… Doesn't work! Real is real. Made up/hear say doesn't match ME!**

Well, I have met Kate in person, and I have read her personal thoughts, and I have seen what only a handful of people have ever seen. So I think I can say with some authority that Kate has made it very easy for people to find her unlikeable.

Since 2009, I have met and interviewed literally hundreds of people who have met or worked with Kate, or have known her in some capacity – not fans who only see her on television or read her tweets. I have yet to find **one person** to say one single nice thing about her. Not one single thing.

Everyone who was EVER a part of Kate Gosselin's life, except for her children who can't leave and the few people like Steve Neild who are still getting paid to be around her, ran far away because they absolutely, positively, couldn't stand being around her. How long will it be before her eight kids follow?

KATE AND THE FLOTUS

This will give you a bit of insight into just how delusional Kate Gosselin really is. Carrie Ann Inaba, one of the judges from *Dancing With The Stars*, nailed it perfectly when she commented that Kate has no self-awareness. It is hard to imagine anyone having less self-awareness than Kate Gosselin does.

On June 8, 2012, someone tweeted Kate the ridiculous idea that she should team up with First Lady Michelle Obama. Kate took it a step further, of course, and implied that the idea had already been put out there and was "circulating around."

> xxxxx @Kateplusmy8 I wish there was a way you could team up with Michelle Obama with the exercise for kids and healthy eating viewpoints

> **it's circulating around... I'd love to help M Obama in her quest... It's SO my passion :) for kids, moms& families as a whole!**

Michelle Obama is a hard-working, uber-educated, classy woman who, by the way, also happens to be the First Lady of the United States of America (FLOTUS). She graduated from arguably two of the most prestigious educational institutions in the country in Princeton University and Harvard Law School. Above all else, she is an involved mother who fiercely protects her daughters' privacy and puts their needs first.

Kate Gosselin is a scheming narcissist who exploits her children for wealth and fame; takes advantage of kind, unsuspecting people; flits from one project to the next trying to get on TV; shows no appreciation for anything or anyone; is intolerant of those she deems unworthy; has shown herself to be ignorant of anything regarding health and nutrition; and who tells mostly lies and says "um" a lot.

Yeah, it makes perfect sense that the idea of Kate Gosselin teaming up with Michelle Obama was being kicked around the White House. It sounds like a match made in Heaven.

THE HOUSE SALE

Kate sent an email to her attorney, Cheryl Young; Jon; and Jon's attorney, Charlie Meyer, to follow up on some information about the sale of Jon and Kate's old house that "we all received falsely from Charlie this morning." (I'm guessing what Kate meant to say was that it was false information.) Charlie must have written something about the deal on the house falling through, so Kate wanted to set the record straight.

Kate explained that the deal on their old house had "NOT" fallen through, and that the "perspective" buyers were still very interested, but had placed a contingency on the contract because they had to sell their house. Kate stated that after having conversations with Jon and their realtor, it was decided that they would not share any more information with their divorce attorneys about the sale or sales price of their property. In a rare instance of unity, Kate said that she and Jon were handling it together, and they both agreed that it needed to stay that way.

Kate also said that their goal was to move forward and "solve each issue peacefully" as it came up, and that they were both confident they could do this for their kids. She wrote that this was one situation where they both agreed (sale price and current sale agreement), and they didn't need any intervention.

RANDOM SITUATIONS

These are just a few extra, random examples of how Kate's mind works.

In the "Potty Training the Boys" episode of Season 3 of *Jon & Kate Plus Ei8ht*, Kate takes two of the little kids to an eye doctor she had never met before, and says to him, "I'm always in a hurry, didn't you learn that?" The man is a doctor, but somehow, Kate thought she was so famous he should have known everything about her and her petty issues.

During the "Dutch Wonderland" episode, after taking all of the kids to the bathroom at the park, Jon also needed to use the facilities. Instead of just waiting patiently for Jon for a few minutes, Kate disrespected him by saying, "Do you really have to go!? I just want to get going!"

Kate Gosselin was so passionate about filming her children, and she would have done ANYTHING to keep it going, that she was prepared to pack up her family and leave her home in Pennsylvania, her friends, her extended family and everything else behind, to move to North Carolina to be closer to Figure 8 Films, the production company that did the filming of *Jon & Kate Plus Ei8ht.*

Kate and Discovery put a refundable deposit of $10,000 on a nine and one-quarter acre property – through Standout Properties in Raleigh, NC – in a development oddly enough called "Windfall" Phase VI, in Chatham County, North Carolina, which was a mere 30-minute drive from Figure 8 headquarters.

US Weekly Reporting

The following excerpts from my reporting for *US Weekly* are examples of Kate's interactions with helpers, neighbors, and others whose duty it was to make her life easier.

Jon and Kate Gosselin PA Reporting
November 2009
(Source — Robert/former helper)

I spoke to a woman who helped Kate with the kids when the sextuplets were first born. She told me Kate was a horrible person to be around. She thought she was a celebrity even back then. She was always demanding things get done fast and would fire people for nothing — people that worked for free because they wanted to help. This woman was from the church where Kate used to go. She told me that Kate was fanatical about helpers not using the family refrigerator. One time this woman put a yogurt in there to keep it cold for her lunch and Kate found it and started screaming at her. She yelled "how dare you put your food in our refrigerator!" and she took out the yogurt and threw it in the trash in front of her. She threatened to fire her if she ever did anything like that again. The woman quit after about a month. She couldn't take it anymore. She couldn't understand how a person getting everything for free, including help with her kids, could be so mean-spirited.

Jon and Kate Gosselin PA Reporting
September 2009

I spoke to a nearby neighbor today and asked if she had any contact with Kate or Jon and she told me "They always say they live in Wernersville but they never even drive through town. Kate never comes near us. She always goes the other way down State Hill Road. That's more high society I guess. She calls Wernersville 'Ghettoville.' She thinks she's better than the rest of us."

Jon and Kate Gosselin PA Reporting
November 2009

Next we headed toward the house but got on the highway heading in an entirely new direction. Nobody had a guess as to where we were going. It was exciting. We went 75 mph in a 55 zone in the rain, in and out of traffic and ended up at St. Joseph's Hospital on Rt. 183. She pulled up to the front door and an employee came running out and handed her some files through the passenger window. I'm sure we could all get that same service at the hospital if we asked.

I WANT MY FAKE TV

"We're not scripted. You heard me. We are not scripted.
We're living.
The kids run in and out of the frame and they just live."
– Kate Gosselin

It should be no secret to anyone that "reality" television isn't anywhere near as real as networks would like us to believe. There does, however, seem to be a large contingent of people who believe that camera crews really do remain silent and in the background, just following the "reality stars" around and documenting them going about their normal, everyday lives while, oh by the way, filming them for a television show. I keep flashing back to the haunting words from the paragraph in the Gosselin's contract with Discovery Communications that stated "…Company and/or Company's designee shall have all creative control with respect to the Program including, but not limited to, approval over Family's make-up, hairstyle and wardrobe."

There is nothing about a company having "creative control" over the "Program" of a family's life, or dictating such things as "make-up, hairstyle and wardrobe" that is true to how a family really lives.

Kate Gosselin has been quoted many, many times proudly declaring that, "Our show is the most real reality show you'll ever see." If you are a person who believes her statement, and who wants to continue to believe her statement, stop reading now.

The true "reality" is that the Gosselin kids were told where to go, how to act, what to say, and what to do to fit each episode's pre-planned and "scripted" storyline. They were threatened and/or bribed before filming began to smile and look happy, and they lived in constant fear of being punished or hit by Kate for not performing up to her standards during filming. They were tricked, lied to and/or deprived of food and drink if they didn't perform to Kate's satisfaction.

The camera crew bribed the kids with candy and presents to get them to be happy during their couch interviews. Lollipops, jellybeans and M&Ms were the candies of choice. The kids' interviews were shot, and re-shot, over and over, until they got things right. A film crewmember told me "It all depends on which kids act the happiest as to who you see on the interview couch during an episode."

It was painful, but I watched all of the *Jon & Kate Plus Ei8ht* episodes, at least twice, after the fact, and after I knew what I knew about the show from my own personal experience. The first time around, I started with Season 3, Episode 1, because the kids were around the same age as they were in Kate's journal, and I wanted to compare that period first. Watching those episodes, I learned first-hand the ugly truth behind the edited, re-shot, carefully constructed "reality" show that was *Jon & Kate Plus Ei8ht.*

Kate's stock spiel to the world was that the kids "love filming" and their world would collapse if the filming stopped. She continually said that her children were being given opportunities to go on all kinds of "adventures" and were getting to have wonderful new experiences. But how much could a 3- or 4-year-old child possibly remember from a trip to, say, New Zealand? It was pure BS, but the public bought it.

The problem with all of these "family adventures" is that they were actually some of the worst kind of torture you could put a small child through. The kids were driven or flown long hours from home to a location where they were marched around and told what to say and what to do and how to act so they could be filmed like little actors and actresses. They couldn't just BE. They were never allowed to do what THEY wanted to do, and they were denied the chance to act naturally and spontaneously during filming. It would be incredibly frustrating for anyone, small child or otherwise, to be constantly instructed on how to feel or behave or react to life.

On one of their "adventures" to the beach on Bald Head Island in North Carolina, the TLC cameras were rolling to capture the children's reactions as they saw the ocean for the first time on the trip. The kids were so excited to run down to the water from their beach house and play and splash around like normal kids do when they hit the beach. Unfortunately, the "adventure" the Gosselin kids got to experience that day was 3 minutes of being filmed as they ran down to the water's edge. They were then ordered to immediately turn around and return to the house because they had more filming to do elsewhere. They were wrangled like cattle down to the water for a few minutes of filming, and then marched right back to the house and taken somewhere else. Just think about how disappointed and frustrated they must have felt when they weren't allowed to play on the beach after a 10-hour car ride.

In another high point of reality programming, the Gosselin children were misled about Christmas Day, that most magical of childhood holidays. Can you even begin to imagine how stressful it must have been for those small children to wake up on Christmas morning, with a TLC camera crew upon them, and lights and cameras in their faces, filming their every move for a Christmas episode? Can you understand how confused they must have felt when, after experiencing all the joy and excitement of their Christmas Day festivities, and opening their presents with wide-eyed anticipation, they found out later that it wasn't really Christmas Day at all? It just happened to be a convenient time for TLC to shoot their Christmas episode.

"Reality?" The only thing real was that this cruel deception actually occurred.

In another example of non-real reality, TLC filmed the kids' first day of school on September 12, 2006 – two weeks *after* the first day of school actually took place on August 31. The kids were told by Kate and the crew to act like it was their first day. This pretense was not something that was out of the ordinary. In fact, it was a common occurrence for Kate Gosselin, TLC and their film crew. The "powers that be" would set a schedule that was convenient for them, and then they let Kate know in advance what they would be filming, where they would be filming and, most importantly, what products would be featured in any given episode. It didn't matter how this deception would affect the kids. It also obviously didn't matter to the adults involved that they were teaching the children to lie.

This is part of an entry from Kate's journal where she talks about the first day of school filming:

September 2006
Kate said the big buzz of the day today was the principal called from the girl's school and was asking about Jen and the whole filming thing. Kate said the principal says that Jen wants to film Friday as if it was the first day of school and wanted to make sure that Kate was okay with it. Kate said the principal also wanted to make sure that she knew which amused Kate. She wrote (hello?!)

Obviously the school's principal found this to be an unusual request and wanted to alert the parents about the filming. She must not have understood how reality must be constructed for reality TV. This is just one instance of reality TV's standard operating procedure. Here's another example of how they deceived the viewers, as documented in this journal entry from Kate:

February 2007
Kate said that the film crew arrived early and they faked Janet being there while they 'were away'.

There is so much more. How about you're a kid, sitting around your house on Thanksgiving Day, not celebrating Thanksgiving like everyone else because your mommy is too tired to wake up and watch the staff cook the Thanksgiving meal because she got in too late the night before from filming in California? Then, how would you feel when you finally get to celebrate Thanksgiving the next day, on Black Friday, but you are forced to dress up in an Indian costume and be paraded out on your front lawn for the paparazzi to photograph you having a great time? That's how the Gosselin children spent their Thanksgiving in 2010. You may have seen the photos of poor Collin standing there in his little Indian dress. His classmates probably saw them as well.
On another trip, this time to Alaska, Mady couldn't take it anymore and called Jon the night before, begging him to come and get her and take her back to his apartment. She absolutely did not want to go away for more filming, and especially not as far away as Alaska. I know this because I went to Kate's house that night with Jon to pick up Mady, and I heard the discussion between Jon and Kate – through the intercom at the gate. Kate completely disregarded Jon's concerns about Mady and blew it off by saying that Mady was just tired and she didn't mean what she said. She, of course, managed to insult Jon several times during the exchange. This was at night, in the dark, with no paparazzi watching; it was just a loving father coming to get his unhappy daughter who had called him for help. Jon told Kate that he would be back in the morning to get Mady, and Kate told him that she would have the police at the house to arrest him if he tried. Mady went to Alaska.

While only a handful of people knew about the drama leading up to the Alaska trip, the family photo that TLC released to the media to promote the episode actually ended up giving away the fact that something was going on with Mady. Google it and look at the photo closely for yourself. You'll see a very smiley Kate with all the kids. But if you look at Mady, on the far right, you'll see how sad and miserable she is. She's crying in the publicity photo. That photo is all the proof anyone would ever need to see that she didn't want to be there. TLC couldn't come up with one single publicity "still" where Mady appeared even a little bit happy. Not one. That picture was worth a thousand words.

The last few seasons of *Jon & Kate Plus Ei8ht* and *Kate Plus Ei8ht* were nothing more than damage control. The couch interview sessions were always about answering the public criticism that they read online every day. They would deny that, but it's obvious to anyone who followed the Gosselin saga. Without fail, they always seemed to address, either on the interview couch, or with Kate giving a television interview somewhere else, the rumors and criticism that they were receiving in the public. It was tacky, and after people caught on a little bit more, it became blatantly obvious.

As an example, people were saying that Kate didn't do her own grocery shopping, so TLC filmed Kate grocery shopping at the supermarket with all eight kids to prove them wrong. The tactic must have worked, because the show continued on. Even with all evidence to the contrary, Kate continued to steadfastly deny that her show was fake and she was difficult. After some negative comments started circulating on the internet about her and *Jon & Kate Plus Ei8ht*, Kate posted the following message on the Gosselin family website:

> To our faithful fans who deserve an answer.
>
> In the recent days, we have been informed there are a lot of lies circulating about us. Just so you know we have worked hard to show you our real life and we have succeeded. Although it is not always easy we will continue to show you the good, the bad and the ugly on our show. Unfortunately, as with anyone who is on TV **there are jealous bystanders, family included, who for whatever reason insist upon telling hurtful untruths.** We will continue to love these family members. We will not retaliate. We will leave it alone out of respect for them. But as a reminder, **nothing that you read on the Internet or in print is true unless it is approved by us.** Thank you for watching as our family grows and develops. Our children have always been our priority, will continue to be our top priority and quite honestly nothing else matters to us.
>
> (This message has been personally written by Jon and Kate Gosselin)

This is a TLC producer's scripted question to Jon and Kate, during the Season 3 "Behind The Scenes" episode of *Jon & Kate Plus Ei8ht*. The "random" question, like most questions on the interview couch, was thrown in there to dispel any rumors that were floating around at the time. Kate spent hours rehearsing her responses to these questions, and it sometimes took that much time to shoot and re-shoot her answers to her satisfaction.

Q: Would you say that the show that we do is realistic?

Kate responded that Yes, the show is realistic. She said there is no scripting but there's a plan about what they wanna get and when they are gonna do it, when they are gonna talk about it and when, you know, how they are gonna accomplish it. Kate says that she's a very big stickler and if you say let's do this and this and she says that's not how they do things, then they don't film it because it annoys her and from the very beginning Kate has always said that she doesn't want to watch a show that was done a certain way for the sake of TV, because it will bug her so what you see is what you get.

She finished the thought by saying, "Our crew follows us whatever we do and how we do it."

In that very same episode of *Jon & Kate Plus Ei8ht*, we see shots of producer Jen Stocks holding a clapboard with "Take 4" written on it, and a cute little video montage of the clapboard clapping, signaling retakes aplenty. Just minutes later though, we see an interview clip of "Alex, the location sound guy" sharing his insight. Here's what "Alex, the location sound guy" said, just minutes after we saw the clapboard clapping:

Alex the sound guy said that the one thing about the show is that it's not your typical reality show where it's all fake and they're doing things two or three times and all this sorta nonsense. He said everything they do happens in real time and what you're seeing actually happens so he appreciates that his show is dealing with real people and not dealing with actors.

Really, Alex, the location sound guy? Were our eyes playing tricks on us when we saw the clapboard clapping away, with "Take 4" written on it? How can you say just moments later that retakes don't exist? How can you stand there and lie that "everything happens in real time"?

Kate, ever undaunted in her quest to "set the record straight," tweeted this long after most people had already caught on to the charade:

My show is real but ppl bel tabloids.i get2pt I don't care. ppl believe what they want.i live4my kids – that's all that matters.

IT IS WHAT IT IS . . . OR IS IT?

Talking about how real her reality show is Kate says that it's their life. It's them telling their story. She says it starts with an idea and they roll with it. Whether it's an event like they're going somewhere, or just, they're gonna do a day in the life or just hanging around the house, sometimes even then, once they start shooting it, it takes a change. Kate says they're not cast and they're not producers. They're filming their lives, and unless they're absolutely dead set against something in the show, it's too bad because once it's created, it is, and they don't really have a say, so basically, Kate says, when the crew walks in the door, what they get is the footage and they have permission to use it.

This is not true of course. Kate was given the opportunity to view the episodes and ask for changes before they were broadcast. I read emails where Kate requested that certain scenes be edited or cut completely because she didn't like how she was being portrayed. In one particular email, she said that "overall" it was a "good hour," but she wanted "a few things" changed:

- Kate noted that "there's a little too much crying in the hair braiding scene…" and she really didn't want all the nasty emails about it.

- She said that in the cake-decorating scene where she was referring to Collin wanting to help, Joel was shown.

- She followed that comment by saying "the way I am shown sending him away (what I am saying) is not good... Could we cut that out please?"

Kate then complained that the licensed song at the end "is plain hideous!!!!" and the lyrics were not appropriate for a Fourth of July episode where they were watching fireworks. She described the kazoo music used during the episode as "horrible!" and asked if it was possible to find a new music composer for the series because she wished she could hear "what good music would sound like!!!!" Kate said all this "as kindly as possible, of course!!!!" and signed off with her standard "Thanks! Have a gr8t day!"

After Kate sent her email with her change requests, Jen Stocks replied to Jon and Kate, assuring them that the changes Kate had requested were being made. She said they had also heard from Julie May about concerns Jon and Kate had about the FAQ episode, and she wanted to let them know they were making the changes they requested right away. Jen apologized that they had included shots and information that were upsetting to them.

Jen later sent another email with a link to view the revised FAQ episode. She said they had addressed Jon and Kate's notes, and Wendy's notes, but they should let her know by the next morning if they wanted anything else removed or revised.

In an email from September 25, 2008, Kate asked if her words "I don't want this in (the episode)" could be removed from a conversation between her and Jon without removing the rest of the conversation, which she liked. She said she wanted to make the episode "friendlier" so they wouldn't "get shot again."

Jen emailed Kate to thank her for her quick notes and to let her know that it was "no problem" for them to edit that out.

SCHEDULING REAL LIFE

The Gosselin's lives were very heavily scheduled. From the sound of things, it doesn't look like too much of real life was "just happening" on its own.
In June of 2008, Kate was becoming increasingly agitated about scheduling issues. When the issues over scheduling and operations came to a boiling point for Kate, Jen Stocks bore the brunt of Kate's wrath. A series of emails between Kate and Jen highlight the tensions.
In one of those emails, Kate gave Jen the following instructions:

–   Reschedule the yard sale.

–   Email a detailed plan to her for the week by the next day.

–   Provide them (Jon and Kate) with plans by three days before the next week's shoot. (Kate said, "The "disorganization is not working well.")

–   Let them know what was wanted from them on each day, then Kate would "pick the time slots that work best for us."

–   Verify whether the beach house was officially reserved, but "... NOT in our names" and let Kate know the exact dates it was reserved for.

–   Schedule a meeting with "production, Wendy, Steve and Julie to iron out the continuing oversights, lack of organization etc." (Kate said there were major issues every week and "Jon and I are MORE than frustrated!!!!! We are hoping everyone involved sees the importance of such a meeting.... We can't go on like this!")

–   Work out a plan that suited them all, kept them safe, and worked for them and not against them.

On June 16, 2008, at 8:30 AM, Jen Stocks replied to Kate to let her know the schedule for the week. I guess Kate needed advance notice of what she was going to be doing in her real life for the next week as well. Jen told Kate that she had tried "many times last week to get the plans for this week confirmed with you, and I am still waiting on you to tell me if we can do interviews on Friday. I emailed you this week's schedule, as it existed last week, on Thursday. And that is when you decided that you wanted to make changes."

Jen sounded perplexed when she wrote that she wasn't sure "when we have ever done anything at a time that did not suit you." She reminded Kate that "you are the one who always chooses the times, we work around your schedule, always." Jen then started talking about work and assured Kate that the beach house had been booked "under Deanie's name from June 29th-July 13th." She then listed a very detailed schedule for the week, which included the family's activity, day and time.

Even with Jen spelling out each day's activities, Kate was still aggravated with the disorganization of her real life schedule. She took exception to Jen telling her that she had tried to get Kate's input when Kate was in NYC. Kate said, "Unfortunately, I could never be expected to confirm a schedule while in NYC (without my calendar) with my 8 kids, doing three appearances and two additional shoots for the show, one of which was a disorganized mess!" Kate told Jen that she had to wait until she got home to think it through, but her point was that they should not be waiting until days before that week.

Kate also told Jen that they should be "finalizing the schedule for TWO weeks from now.... Not this weeks schedule." She said "Trust me, the results will be better!!! I don't work well last minute!" Kate then let Jen know that they would leave for the Thomas the Train visit at 9:30, and that she wasn't sure which other activities they would be doing because it depended on "crowds, moods etc." Kate said she would know when they got there and saw the setup.

Given all the tension, Jen was ready to walk out. On June 17, 2008, Kate sent Jen a "heart-to-heart" email to explain herself and to apologize. Kate said she knew Jen was hurt and wanted to let Jen know that, despite being very frustrated with operations, it was nothing personal. Kate told Jen, "You are the 'front line' person and you receive the brunt of the explosion" even though "most times" the problem is "something that is not your direct doing." Kate then uttered words rarely heard from her. She said: "For handing you those explosions of frustration, I am sorry! For any rude/unacceptable comments or behavior I am sorry as well."

Kate went on to explain to Jen what a tough position they were in because they have eight children who "in a million years" they could "never spend the amount of time with each that we want." She talked about how well the show was doing in the ratings and how, with that and all their other commitments, they had "TONS to do and no time to complete it all." Kate also mentioned security issues that were escalating daily, and how everything was causing her and Jon to be very stressed out, overworked and short-fused. She said, "It is more of a daily thing to be stressed out beyond belief as the pressure cooker continues to cook." Kate then spelled out to Jen things she would appreciate:

- Having a schedule a full week or more in advance.

- Organization (location, addresses, who they were going to meet with and at what time, etc.).

- Having a say about WHO came to their house as part of the crew.

- A crew without opinions.

- Respect for their privacy and property.

- Crewmembers who were informed about recent security issues and would watch out for them.

- Crewmembers who would respect their home (i.e., always putting things in the exact locations requested; cleaning up equipment, trash, and toys that were moved for interviews).

- A crew that would consider ALL that they were doing (marketing/media shoots, speaking engagements) and understood when they were frazzled.

Kate also told Jen "honestly, if you aren't here producing in our house, I don't want to do this anymore." She pleaded with Jen to stay on, saying "you have been here with us since the beginning, our kids know and love you and we want YOU to continue to do this job!" Kate then suggested that Jen go ahead and take a break, but then come back to them because no one could replace her .... "Honestly."

The next day, Jen sent Kate an email thanking her for the apology and kind words, saying she really appreciated it. Kate forwarded Jen's response to Wendy Douglas of Discovery, thanking Wendy for her "honesty in alerting us to a problem..." The logical assumption is that Jen must have told Wendy about the problems she was having with Kate.

After Jen thanked Kate, she immediately switched back to work mode, talking about getting a schedule made up for the next week and shooting the family's preparation and packing for their beach trip. She asked Kate if they could squeeze in one interview, but said she knew they had music video stuff to get done so it might not work out. Jen signed off by saying she would talk to Kate soon.

In reviewing the content of these emails, and the escalating tension, one exceptionally disturbing fact stands out above the rest. It is the fact that the entire family was under a tremendous amount of stress. Reading Kate's words about the "pressure cooker" they were in, and "explosions of frustration," it would be ridiculous for anyone to try to argue that the kids weren't feeling a significant amount of stress as well. They were required to participate in all the filming, and in marketing and interviews and photo shoots. Also, Jon and Kate would not have been able to hide all the tension they were feeling from the children, so the children would have felt that as well.

The schedules sound like they were exhausting. It is hard to imagine adults handling such pressures well, much less thinking that kids would be able to handle the relentless filming and instructions and direction, and all the extras they had to participate in.

And for someone who raved in interviews about the wonderful crew being like family members, Kate certainly had a lot of complaints about them in that list of things she told Jen she would appreciate.

Kate's words to Jen, above all else, expose the reality of filming a reality TV show. They reveal the toll such filming takes on a family, and should be taken as a warning to all those who would agree to open their life to the world in such a way. If TLC were, in fact, filming a family just running around doing their normal, everyday business, as Kate has always argued, there would never have been such high and such constant levels of stress.

As a final point, Jen Stocks ultimately did leave the show and was replaced by another producer. But the show continued merrily along. Kate must have forgotten that she didn't want to "do this" anymore if Jen wasn't producing their show.

EPISODES OF LIFE

Kate was being a big helper by providing ideas for episodes, while also working in as many new freebies as possible at the same time. In an email to "all", Kate said she would love to add the trainer episode where she would be doing weight training, but that would have to be filmed at the end of the month because she couldn't weight train following surgery until April 30th. Other ideas she suggested were building a dog house, which would go with the wireless fence training; showing the passport process for the kids (with applications and photos); updating the Sam's club or grocery store visit where the "(kids scramble to help put stuff away-- SO cute!)"; installation of the crooked houses; the birthday party for the "little kids"; mothers day; and the southern leg of her book tour which was beginning in North Carolina. Kate said it would be great if they could get those items scheduled in April around her "ridiculously busy schedule".

Kate also made suggestions about what to do for "the little kids birthday party". She said that the kids wanted a bouncy house party and they could do that at a park and "invite preschool friends who are willing to sign NDAs and agree to be on camera ONLY." She said: "We can forbid all cameras at the party and make area secure according to Steve who obviously would orchestrate all security." Kate also noted that the party should be held as close to May 10th as possible.

On April 3, 2009, at 8:13 AM, Jeff, the series producer, wrote to Julie May about scheduling some more episodes of the Gosselin family's life:

April 9 - Cabinets
April 22 - Invisible Fence training

On Monday, May 25, 2009, Wendy Douglas sent Jon and Kate the following schedule for their real and unscripted life for the week:

Tuesday - arrive Gosselin Home @ 9:30 AM
1. Shoot Beach + Cabinet Set-up + Slice of Life   9:30 -11:00
2. Status of Cabinets/kitchen will no cabinets - Jon/Kate   11:00-11:30
3. American Chopper Interviews 1:00 - 2:00
4. Kate packing for beach 3:00 -4:00

Wednesday - arrive Gosselin House @ 8:00 AM - 5:00PM
1. Merilatt crew begins install - Jon

Wednesday - Kate & Kids @ Beach - 8:00 AM - 6:00 PM
1. Arriving to house
2. Beach
3. Dinner

Thursday - arrive @ Gosselin House - 8:00 AM
1. B-roll/status of cabinets - NO JON

Thursday - Kate & Kids @ Beach - 8:00 AM - 6:00 PM
1. Slice of Life beach

Friday - arrive @ Gosselin House @ 1:00 PM - 5:00 PM
1. Jon checking in on cabinet construction

PLAY CHEESE FOR THE CAMERAS, KIDS

In September 2008, Wendy Douglas sent an email to Jon and Kate and the series producers to provide them with information about working some paid product placement from Hasbro into the show. She explained that Hasbro toys had to be integrated into two separate episodes. The toys were the Tonka Bounce Back Racers (8 of them) and the Dreamtown Cherry Blossom Market (2 of them). The market included the following accessories that are sold separately to the mediocre: the Cherry Blossom Produce Stand, the Scoop & Smile Set, and the Fruit & Cheese Plate.
Wendy said the goal was to see the sextuplets "playing with the games naturally" and to make it look "as organic as possible." She suggested that they shoot the Bounce Back Racers the next morning because "they are smaller and easier to get out", and then shoot the Cherry Blossom Market episode on Saturday October 4th because the market needed some assembly.
Wendy then told producers Jen and Jeff that Kate said it would be okay for a production assistant or someone to arrive earlier than 8 AM the next day so they could take out the racers and set them up for the kids. She also instructed Jen and Jeff to have someone get batteries for the remote controls ahead of time. Doesn't everyone in real life have people come to their home to set up toys for their children to play with and to make sure there are plenty of batteries?
It should come as no surprise by now that Wendy wanted the sextuplets to look fake natural while they were fake playing with their free toys.

MEDIA TRAINING

Kate was freaked out after word got out that there was trouble in the Gosselin marriage. The tabloids got wind of it and were requesting interviews. Kate certainly didn't know what to say or do, so she waited for Discovery to give her the approved "messaging" that they "could all live with."

On April 29, 2009, at 10:48 AM, Laurie Goldberg wrote to Kate that she had talked to Steve Gray, Kate's media trainer, and wanted to get him on the phone with them ASAP to go over how to handle the mess and come up with messaging they could all live with and help them move forward.

Laurie told Kate that Vicki from *People* magazine wanted to talk to her. She said they wouldn't do it right away, but they would have to cooperate because *People* had been good to them, even if it was in a week or two after the ugliness had died down somewhat.

SEND IN THE PRODUCTION ASSISTANTS

In the yard sale episode of *Jon & Kate Plus Ei8ht*, Kate and Jon appear to be doing everything themselves. There is absolutely no sign of them getting any help from production assistants (PAs) or anyone on the crew, but an email from Maggie of Figure 8 Films gave away what really went on during the day's shoot. Kate must have really been exhausted typing her instructions for the "pa's."

Maggie wrote that they had gotten official confirmation from the Community Fellowship Church that the yard sale could be held there on Saturday, September 20th. She said they could arrive at any time to start the setup outside, and someone would open the church from 8-12 so they could use the facilities. She also said that if the weather was bad, they could hold the sale inside the church, and someone would be there to open the door earlier than 8 to accommodate the setup.

Maggie explained that the church did not have any tables that could be brought outside for the sale, so they would look into renting some. She said that if the sale was held inside due to bad weather, however, there were 10 round tables they could use.

Kate replied to Maggie to give her the following instructions. She first told Maggie to include the words "rain or shine" in the newspaper ad for the sale. She said they should rent 12 tables that are 8 feet long, but if only 6-foot-long tables were available, to rent more. Kate said, "We have SOOO much stuff it is unbelievable." She then asked Maggie if she could also rent a "medium to large U-Haul/ Penske/ whatever brand moving truck to transport the stuff." Kate said she thought it would work best if the "pa's" that day went to get the truck, then went to get the yard sale stuff from the storage unit, and then came to their house to load what was in the garage.

Kate told Maggie that she wanted to be at the church at 6 AM to set up, so the production assistants would have to be at her house at 5 AM. She said "they better get lots of sleep the night before!!!! :)". She then pondered what they would do with any stuff that was left over. She told Maggie "It is not at all junk so we should think of what to do in the way of getting rid of it because it is NOT coming back here!!!"

Finally, Kate asked Maggie to have Kinkos make signs reading "Proceeds to benefit Pediatric Cancer Research" and told her that she would have Mady and Cara make their own sign for their juice box/soda/ water stand.

NANNY-GATE

When the Gosselins appeared on the *Dr. Phil* show, they were offered free nanny service from a company called Nannies 4 Hire. In a Season 3 episode called "Kate Hires a Nanny," Kate was supposed to select a nanny from candidates chosen by Candi Wingate, the owner of Nannies 4 Hire. It turns out that the nanny Kate ended up hiring didn't work for Nannies 4 Hire, but they had to pretend she did. The nanny that was hired even had to wear the Nannies 4 Hire T-shirt on camera during the episode, despite the fact that she was not found through Nannies 4 Hire. Kate must not have been happy when Candi Wingate apparently used the episode to promote her business, and a little brouhaha ensued. On Tuesday, May 19, 2009, at 2:10 PM, Maggie from Figure 8 Films wrote to Kirk Streb, also of Figure 8 Films, to give him information about Candi Wingate.

Maggie told Kirk that Candi Wingate had participated in a shoot for the Season 3 episode "Kate Hires a Nanny" on Saturday September 22, 2007. She explained that the Gosselins had won free nanny service from Candi's company on Dr. Phil, and the episode was about Kate selecting a nanny from a small pool of candidates chosen by Candi. Maggie recalled that, in the episode, Kate watched Candi interview the girls on closed circuit TV in the next room. She told Kirk she was going to watch the episode and let him know if she saw "anything about it that comes up as a red flag."

Maggie then told Kirk the name of Candi Wingate's husband, and said she attached her release and "a picture (just for kicks).

About 16 minutes later, at 2:26 PM, Maggie sent another email to Kirk telling him she had glanced through the episode. She remembered that the babysitter the family ended up hiring did not come from Nannies 4 Hire.

On May 19, 2009, at 3:39 PM, Laurie Goldberg of Discovery jumped into the fray and sent an email to Kate to let her know that Candi Wingate had said "lovely things about you guys and your parenting" and that her sources told her it was a very positive "(and probably very self-promoting)" piece.

In a great example of the pot calling the kettle black, Kate chimed in to personally attack the woman. She said, "she is such such such a publicity whore.... good things said, great but her need to promote her business is appalling..."

GHOST WRITER

If anyone reading here actually thinks Kate Gosselin created her own loving, nurturing, inspiring, well-written blog on the TLC website, what you read next may come as an unpleasant surprise to you. This is an excerpt from Julie May's notes to Discovery while she was renegotiating the Gosselin contract:

- For the blog, Ed Sabin said that TLC would have a ghostwriter prepare it.

Some of Kate's fans on Twitter actually questioned whether Kate was writing her own material. She assured them in tweets that she would never allow anyone to choose her words, on "twitter or otherwise".

xxxxx @Kateplusmy8 Some of your crazy AntiFans say it isn't you twittering but a TLC intern. What do you say? Should I be ready to LOL? ;-)

It's totally me. I wouldn't ever allow TLC to assign someone to 'be me' and if that was the case, I wouldn't be verified.

xxxxx @Kateplusmy8 is this actually kate tweeting her self? JW :LX

yes. What would you like to know? :) (I'd never ever allow anyone else to choose my words – twitter or otherwise :)

xxxxx @Kateplusmy8 she says thanks so much!! :)) I told her its really you who tweets (she thinks you hire sum1 to do it!) lol I hope not!!!!

tell her NO ONE gets to speak for me! I don't know who I'd trust to 'be me'! Lol

Someone needs to break the news to these poor, deluded fans that Kate will most certainly allow others to put words in her mouth as long as she is getting the credit and being paid for pretending to do the work.
Not only were TLC and Discovery making things up and passing them off as Kate's, sometimes they were not really even making them up. They were stealing them from online websites – *familydoctor.org* and *familiesonlinemagazine.com*. It makes you wonder when and if Kate was ever even involved in "Kate's tips." I have the documents where notes were made and sent back and forth to Kate. There are underlined parts of the text that are the notes from the TV executives who put this together for Kate. Does this count as "realist reality"?

Finding out about this kind of pokes holes in Kate's answer to the following question on Twitter:

xxxxx @Kateplusmy8 I have a family recipe, but you're not going to publish them on your blog as your own are you?

sounds sarcastic... I'm not into plagiarism, no... But thanks for asking.

FIRST-HAND OBSERVATIONS

These are excerpts from my reporting for *US Weekly*.

Jon and Kate Gosselin PA Reporting
August 2009
    Kate told the Today show that Jon & Kate plus 8 is the most
real reality show you'll ever see. I've been watching tapings etc.
for two weeks now and I can assure you that it's the most fake,
scripted, sad thing I've ever seen. Kate acts like a devoted parent
while the cameras are rolling but the moment the cameras stop, she
completely ignores the kids and at times seems bothered by their
wanting attention. The nannies and babysitter are expected to
immediately corral the kids in between takes so Kate can do her own
thing.

Jon and Kate Gosselin PA Reporting
September 2009
    I went to the dance supply store in Reading today to back
report the TLC filming yesterday. I've been going in there for years
getting my daughter's dance supplies so I know the owner well enough
to ask questions. She signed a confidentiality agreement for TLC
which said she couldn't talk to anybody about anything that she saw,
but she told me off the record that "Kate was very polite and
courteous while the crew was filming, but as soon as they stopped,
she lost her smile and became very bossy to the camera guys, telling
them which angles to shoot her from and when to and not to shoot the
kids. She yelled at the kids to behave several times when the cameras
were off but laughed off their behavior when they were taping. Seemed
to treat the kids like props rather than little people. She talks to
them with disdain, like they're a burden to her. The kids didn't seem
to mind though. They looked very happy and the nanny was there to
take care of them. She would take them to the bathroom and be there
to control them for Kate. I lost some business yesterday because the
TLC crew wouldn't let any of my customers inside the store. At least
four people were turned away while they were here for over an hour
and I had to explain to them over the phone what was happening. It
was fun though. It was nice to see the kids. They tried on shoes and
leotards and bought some clothing for gymnastics and ballet.

Jon and Kate Gosselin PA Reporting
September 2009
    Paps told me that Kate drove to the Toyota dealership this
morning to drop her car off to have some work done. The employees
chased the paps off the property so they didn't have many details to
give me. Luke the bodyguard picked her up and drove her back home.
    No outside activity at the house for the rest of the morning
into early afternoon.

2:30 pm - The TLC crew is there again filming. Kate and the sextuplets and the crew walked down the driveway and out of the gate and walked in the street down the road to a neighbor's house where a tractor and hay wagon was waiting to load them up and take them for a ride. The walk was a little over a quarter mile and it seemed very dangerous to me to have them walking in the right lane of traffic on their winding country road. Luke the bodyguard was there today keeping the paparazzi under control and watching over them as they made their journey. The main nanny was along for the walk as well. With the cameras rolling the entire way, **Kate was just the perfect mother. She was laughing and talking to the kids and smiling and having a great time. In stark contrast to how she acts when she's not being filmed. Her normal behavior is to ignore everyone including the kids except when she's telling them what to do like a drill sergeant.**

After the ten-minute walk, they got to the neighbor's house and loaded everyone onto the wagon filled with hay bails. It was a traditional hayride and the kids loved it. A woman in a car is slowly following them down the road taking pictures on her cell phone. She stops on the road in front of the house where they're loading and yells "You're beautiful Kate!" Luke the bodyguard moves her on so the tractor and wagon can back out of the yard onto the road. Two paparazzi are taking photos and video as they move.

A short five-minute ride on the road and they enter the Spring Creek Farms — Organic milk and fresh hamburgers. Luke the bodyguard points to the 'no trespassing' signs and says "I know I don't even have to say it, right?" Kate yells "run Luke run" and Luke goes up the road after them.

The property is HUGE and they drive up a country hill into the field beyond our view. We drove around the outside of the property and could see them briefly from about a half-mile away in the field with cows nearby. Couldn't see what exactly they were doing though.

After two long hours, the wagon came back down the hill and drove the half-mile back up to the Gosselin house. It's a very big hill so they didn't make them walk back up. The wagon backed into the Gosselin driveway and slowly unloaded the kids and adults. Mady and Cara were home from school now and they were at the gate to great them. Mady had a brief conversation with Kate and then they all walked up the driveway to the house.

The one thing that struck me about this trip was how absolutely wonderful Kate behaves when the cameras are rolling. She smiles all the time and talks lovingly to the kids and is animated with her gestures and is just the polar opposite of the Kate I see when the cameras aren't there.

The media left when they went inside to get ready for dinner. They usually stay inside once they're home.

Jon and Kate Gosselin PA Reporting
August 2010
Kate has blogged about being sad when the kids all go to school full time, really playing up the "I'll miss my kids so much" angle, when in reality she feels burdened by having to deal with the kids for only a few hours a day and she can't wait until next week when they're gone all day and she has the house to herself. "She's such a phony and it makes me sick to think that she's happy to get rid of her kids."

"Kate walks around acting exhausted like she actually takes care of eight kids. She's just a supervisor and observes and oversees her nannies and 'helpers' doing all the work." "If the world could only see how little this woman does around her own house, her popularity would end. She has no idea what it takes to raise a family. All she's concerned with is making herself famous."

NOT JUST JON & KATE PLUS EI8HT WAS FAKE

It appears that everywhere Kate went in the early days, her manager had everyone on board to build the fake "Kate Gosselin is a Supermom" brand. This even included Rachel Ray.

In May of 2009, Kate made an appearance on the Rachel Ray television show to spread her magic to a huge new audience. It was a great brand builder set up by Julie Carson May, and it was a great platform for Kate to show the world her abilities as a "Supermom."

Rachel herself used that word: "Supermom." She also called Kate "Kate The Great" and "Double New York Times Best Seller." Rachel even went so far as to call Kate "super smart" after Kate demonstrated her superior supermom skills by making ice cream in a Ziploc bag. It was awesome…even though most people had seen this done 20 years ago. But maybe Rachel Ray had never seen the old ice cream in a bag phenomenon and she was just overcome with excitement when she told Kate, "You are super smart."

In addition to teaching viewers how to magically create their own ice cream in a Ziploc bag, Kate also showed them her crafting ability by using a TV dinner plastic tray, some glue and a popsicle stick to make a little boat for the kids to play with, or for the kids to build at home.

Kate Gosselin IS super smart! Or is she?

In looking at Kate's Healthtex itinerary for her four-day appearance trip to New York City, the details of her May 6th visit (pre-recorded; the show actually aired on May 12) to the Rachel Ray studios paint a slightly different picture of Kate as a "Supermom" who is "super smart."

Kate's talking points were written out for her in advance, so all she had to do was memorize them and parrot them back as her own, but this part of the Healthtex itinerary was a bit more interesting:

It says that in addition to Kate and Rachel doing the interview, they will head to the kitchen to make some fun crafts for kids. On the next page are three ideas that the producers presented to Kate. They said they would discuss with Kate later, which ideas she likes so they can have the materials on set for the show.

At 11:00 AM, Kate had a "Producer briefing and show run through," at which time they told her what to say and gave her a choice of three craft ideas to pass off as her own. Here are the three ideas the producers gave Kate. Do any of these look familiar?

SAND SCULPTURE:
Now kids can craft a permanent sand sculpture just by using sand, water and cornstarch.

MAKING ICE CREAM IN A BAGGIE:
Put in a sandwich-size Zip[Loc bag and "zip" closed: 1 tablespoon sugar ½ cup milk or half & half ¼ teaspoon vanilla.
Put in a gallon-size Zip-Loc bag and zip closed: 2 t. rock salt (baking aisle in grocery) the filled and zipped sandwich bag from above ice cubes to fill bag about ¾ full. Shake and roll filled bag over and over until frozen (about 15-20 min.) YUMMY!!

HOLD A BOAT RACE
You will need:
Large paper flag for each boat (design your own or use some of our scrapbook paper)
Popsicle stick
Sticky tape
Plastic tray (the sort pre-packaged vegetables come in)
Stick your flag to the popsicle stick with tape. Use lots of tape to make the stick stand upright in the center of your boat. To sail pop into a paddling pool and blow into the sail!

All Kate had to do was show up, take the gum out of her mouth, and learn how to make ice cream in a baggie and a little boat out of a plastic tray and a popsicle stick.
Kate Gosselin is SUPER SMART!

PHILADELPHIA

Kate was keeping the money train rolling down the tracks – without Jon as part of the show – by filming episodes of *Kate Plus 8*. To further speak to the subject of scripted or fake filming, this piece was filed by NBC TV in Philadelphia on Monday, January 3, 2011. Read it and decide for yourself if this was a family out for a leisurely day simply being followed around by a camera crew or if it was, perhaps, something else entirely.

Philly reporter: Kate 'miserable' and 'distant' on shoot

A Philadelphia entertainment reporter gave more details of Kate and the kids' working vacation to Philadelphia that he observed in December (just before they took off for an even bigger business trip to Australia).
The first stop of the trip was Starbucks.
Confidentiality agreements were required wherever they went.
The nanny tended to the children at lunch at Waterworks and Kate was "off to the side."
Steve (Neild, the bodyguard) tried to block the photos and the reporter just shot around him.
Then finally Steve said fine.
Collin fell on the Rocky steps and Kate didn't even acknowledge him.
The kids looked happy but Kate appeared "miserable" and "distant."

Also, an eyewitness to the Philadelphia filming had this to say:

> "Oh, I was at the Phila Art Museum when the kids had to run and then re-run up the steps the right way. Kate was on her phone. The kids were falling because the steps are very wide. She had them repeat and redo scenes where she talked to the kids. The camera was behind her and **she was mouthing the words so the kids would remember their lines.**"

Isn't this the way all kids just live their real lives?

SAD, SAD, SAD, SAD, SAD ☺

On the final episode of *Kate Plus Ei8ht*, the kids were put on the interview couch to speak their minds. Unfortunately, they were forced to speak Kate's mind instead.

Interviewer Question to Alexis and Joel: The show is ending. How do you guys feel about that?

Alexis and Joel: "Sad." "Sad" (as they're laughing). "We're sad."

Hannah and Collin also said they're "sad."

Mady said she was sad as she was smiling. She had to make a frowny face and point to it to try to convince us that she really was sad.

FEAR FACTOR

For years, Kate used fear as a weapon to get her children to perform on cue in front of the cameras. In later years of the show, Kate told her kids, even her then 6-year-olds, that if they didn't say what they were told to say on the interview couch, they would lose their TV show, which would mean they would have to move back into a tiny house with one bathroom, and they would be taken out of their private school and sent to public school where they would never see their friends again. Listen to what Kate said on the Wendy Williams show in September of 2011:

Williams: "How are the kids reacting to the cancellation of the show?"

Kate: "They, sigh, you know, for them, it's um, we're gonna miss
       the crew, but what about the trips? And, um, surprisingly,
       when I told them, it, it, moments later, it was, are, are
       we gonna, are we gonna be able to afford to stay in our
       house and go to our school? And I was like, I wasn't
       prepared for that, I mean, how sweet of them? I wasn't
       prepared for them and I just told them I'll work my
       fingers to the bone to continue what they deserve which is
       the best."

Young children would not know to worry about things such as being able to afford
to stay in their house and having to leave their school if someone had not put those
thoughts into their heads. Who do you suppose would be cruel enough to put those
fears into a 6-year-old child?

THE GOSSELIN GIVE-BACK?

"God had just taught me something big.
He proved to me that I would never be able to out-give Him."
– *Kate Gosselin*

Kate Gosselin and Discovery/TLC made a big show out of Kate Gosselin "giving back" at least twice in the early shows. They filmed a trip to St. Jude Children's Research Hospital in Memphis, TN, for Kate to "give back" to children with pediatric cancer, and they created a yard sale episode where Kate sold their belongings to raise money for pediatric cancer research. The actual name of the St. Jude episode was "Giving Back."

Those episodes were, no doubt, intended to lead viewers and the public into believing that Kate Gosselin is a charitable woman who cares about people, children in particular, who are less fortunate than herself. But there is an ugly truth you may not know about Kate's charitable side.

By 2009, Kate Gosselin had already made several million dollars from a combination of earnings from her television show, her Christian books, speaking engagements, and endorsement deals, plus whatever other money-making ventures she had going on that we don't know about. There is no disputing the fact that Kate was very well off financially.

In addition, all, or most of, the clothing that Kate and her children wore on the show was given to them, either by sponsors of the show or from individual endorsement deals put together by Kate or her manager. The Gymboree, GAP, Peace Love World, etc., clothing you saw the kids wearing was all free.

Kate had also received an enormous outpouring of support, both financially and in the form of clothing for her children, from her community and from people all across the country in the early days – when she was supposedly struggling to make ends meet for her family. So, it would be reasonable to think that this self-proclaimed Christian woman who had been on the receiving end of such generosity from others would be eager to "give back," even just a little bit, to show how much she appreciated all she had been given. You would be wrong.

In 2009, I watched as UPS employees loaded cases and cases of free Nestle Juicy Juice into Kate's car. I learned by reading her contracts and endorsement deals that Nestle had donated a "lifetime supply of Juicy Juice" to Kate and the kids. As a millionaire who could afford to buy Juicy Juice, it would have been nice to see Kate donate at least some of that juice to the local food bank, or have Nestle send it directly there in her kids' names.

Also in 2009, when it was time for Kate to clean out some of the kid's clothing that she could no longer use, I followed her, several times, to a consignment shop in Shillington, PA, where she carried in piles of children's clothing, to RESELL. Kate Gosselin, a millionaire, was selling clothes she didn't even pay for in the first place to those truly in need. There is no disputing this because I watched her and photographed her doing this, and the paparazzi photographed her doing this. I also spoke to the consignment shop owner after Kate had left. This particular shop is 3 miles from my house, and I had been there many times before.

The worst part of this story is that, on the way to that consignment shop from her house, Kate had to drive by – in her $69,000 Toyota Land Cruiser – a giant Goodwill Industries distribution center and retail store, where she could have donated the items and gotten a tax write off in the process…and saved a lot of time if she was in a hurry. Kate was a millionaire getting everything for free, and she was reselling her children's free clothing, rather than donating it to the needy.

That was nothing new for Kate, though. As far back as when the sextuplets were babies, Kate was begging for help and handouts of any kind. It would have been easier and more honest if she had just come right out and told her community up front that what she was really looking for was cold, hard cash. Even then, Kate was accepting bag after bag of gently used clothing at her house in Wyomissing, only to then take it all directly to the local consignment shop where she would turn it into cash. Kate only wanted, and felt she deserved, brand new designer clothes for her brood. To that end, she was contacting stores every day soliciting freebies. Kate's aversion to donating is not confined to clothing alone. This is a partial excerpt from my reporting for *US Weekly*:

```
Jon and Kate Gosselin PA Reporting
December 2009
        Kate cleaned out many of the kid's old toys that they don't
use anymore and filled three giant trashcans and made a pile next to
them with some things that wouldn't fit in cans. There was a full-
size electric keyboard sticking out of one of the trash cans with a
pile of small, plastic chairs broken up and pushed all around it. On
the ground next to the cans was a Buzz Lightyear stationary bicycle
and a large, plush hobbyhorse on springs that a child can ride on and
bounce up and down. The toys outside the trashcan looked in very
clean/new condition and I'm wondering why they were thrown away
rather than being given or sold to a thrift store or charity.
```

So, you are reading all this, and you may be thinking right about now that, surely, Kate does "give back" though, right? Well I am happy to report that Kate is not completely greedy and cold-hearted after all. Here's the proof – in her own paraphrased words from her journal – that Kate really does, or at least did at one point, "give back."

June 2007
Kate was excited about their second yard sale of the season because they had so much to sell. She couldn't believe the full garage of stuff considering that they just had a yard sale two months ago!!!! They sold six cribs for $300 and six car seats and a lot of other stuff for a profit of $760. Kate was proud to be giving God His ten percent of the proceeds.

We don't know whether God eventually ever did see His share of those yard sale profits, but we'll give Kate the benefit of the doubt here. So let's see, 10 percent of $760-something is, hold on, carry the ..., um, is $76-something. So in 2007, Discovery paid Kate $109,186.90 in show salary alone, plus bonuses, plus they filled her home with free merchandise as far as the eye could see, and she gave God $76. Not bad for God.

In December of 2008, Kate Gosselin, accompanied by her children, a camera crew, Steve Neild, babysitters, and Discovery's own public relations expert, Laurie Goldberg, traveled to Memphis to film the episode of *Jon & Kate plus Ei8ht* called "Giving Back".

The stated purpose of the show was a good one. It was to bring awareness to the needs of families with children suffering from cancer. They decided to go to St. Jude Hospital because, as Kate said during the show, it was the closest one to her house in Pennsylvania. (There are actually several children's pediatric cancer research hospitals in Pennsylvania, but I digress.) But no matter, the point was they were going out of the goodness of their hearts to help sick children.

In the episode, there were a couple of cute scenes where the family first went to a local Kmart to buy presents for the children at St. Jude, and then they returned to their hotel to wrap them. But then, inexplicably, and completely out of character for Kate Gosselin, they broke into a warm and tender, 1-minute and 41-second scene where Kate read her kids a book before bedtime, while they were all cuddled around her on the bed. It was a warm and touching scene straight out of a Disney movie. It was certainly a scene that the Gosselin children didn't experience with Kate at home.

In this heartwarming scene, Kate said, "We're gonna read the *Tales of Despereaux*. It's an adorable story about a little mouse that's a movie, and we have the book, and I'm slowly but surely reading it to them." The camera pulled in close on Kate as she read the book aloud, and the kids all had Despereaux mouse stuffed dolls, which were prominently displayed.

When she finished the story, Kate said, "They liked it. It's a cute little story. He's a cute little guy, and of course, it helped that they each had a little Despereaux, and they are hysterical to hear them say, where's my Despereaux? It's a neat little story."

The kids were shown carrying their Despereaux dolls throughout the entire episode.

When Kate and the crew arrived at the hospital to see the sick children, they pulled in wagons filled with Kate's book, *Multiple Blessings*; *Jon & Kate Plus Ei8ht* DVDs; and, you guessed it, a big stack of *The Tale of Despereaux* coloring books to hand out to all. Inside the hospital, they showed a close-up of a Despereaux doll while one of the girls sat coloring at a table. Kate made a point of mentioning the "Despereaux coloring/sticker books, which are adorable."

After visiting with many sick children and talking to their families, and handing out the books and DVD sets, Kate ended the episode by telling the viewing audience, "This was **strictly** a trip to raise awareness for this wonderful cause." And we viewers ate it up and believed every word of it, and felt warm and fuzzy thinking that it was such a generous thing for Kate to do. I know I felt like that. I had tears in my eyes thinking about the suffering those families were dealing with on a daily basis with their sick children.

But then, my Kate Gosselin/TLC bullshit sensor went off, and my once-photographic memory flashed back to one of the Gosselin/Discovery contract amendments I had read a few months before. And I got a terrible, queasy feeling in my stomach.

So I dug through my Gosselin archives and found an amendment to the Talent Agreement for the Gosselin family for Jon & Kate + 8 dated October 22, 2008. The amendment gave permission for the Gosselin family to participate in a third-party promotion for, yes, "The Tales of Despereaux". The promotion coincided with Universal Pictures' theatrical release of the movie.

Wording from Paragraph 13, Third Party Promotional Uses of Name and Likeness, stated that the family granted the Company permission to create custom marketing spots, which incorporated footage from the show and featured one or more family members, to be used for a tie-in with the Program and was intended to be telecast somewhere around December 15, 2008. The Amendment stated that the family was to be paid $10,000 for its participation in connection with the Despereaux marketing spots.

There is no way to sugarcoat this. The "Giving Back" episode of *Jon & Kate Plus Ei8ht*, which Kate made a point of telling us was "strictly a trip to raise awareness for this wonderful cause," had nothing to do with Kate or the Gosselin family giving anything back to anyone. There was nothing altruistic about it on Kate's part. It was a business arrangement and an elaborate lie, plain and simple; nothing more than a paid commercial for a movie. For her part in the deception, Kate was paid an additional $10,000, on top of the $22,500, plus expenses, that she was already getting paid just to film the episode. It is not out of bounds to wonder if Kate would have even agreed to go on this trip to "give back" if she had not been paid to do so. I hope the episode at least did some good in bringing attention to St. Jude Children's Research Hospital.

So in light of the St. Jude "Giving Back" episode, and Kate's less than charitable behavior with the yard sales and consignment shop visits, how could Discovery/TLC possibly expect anyone to buy into their new, 2011, second season promotion of *Kate Plus Ei8ht*, where they visited a food bank, curiously enough, also in Tennessee, and hinted at changes in the show's format that season, where they were going to be doing more on Kate "giving back?"

Ron Bonacci, Food City vice president of marketing, said "Gosselin's visit is part of an initiative she plans to spell out in an upcoming season of the show, where she will go to different parts of the country volunteering her time for charities." Kate said the kids were on spring break from school and the visit to the food bank was the **"beginning of the Gosselin give back."** She said the kids had experienced so many things through the show that it was "time we take the chance to help others." These are excerpts from Kate's interview at the Second Harvest Food Bank in Tennessee.

"Um, to be very honest, we've had a few days where we've you know, learned about **things that we didn't know about, you know, food banks and feeding people at homeless shelters**, and so today we're here collecting food, and just, you know, here to greet people and the kids are lining up downstairs and they're taking their turns collecting the food and putting it in the boxes behind us, and they are having a great time, like, we make a game of it, and it's really exciting to see, um, you know, the Gosselin family being able to pull together, to help, um, different communities and we're really glad to be here.

"… beyond that, it's helping, giving back and being aware, **I am guilty of hearing that food banks are collecting food and you kind of, let it go in one ear and out the other**, and, um, we're here, um, not to show, you know, oh look what the Gosselins did, you know, good deeds on TV, that's not our aim, our aim is to bring awareness, and to help other people to think, oh, food bank, people need food, there are kids who don't have breakfast, lunch or dinner, and so we need to give.

"Well, I told the kids this is our first, you know, we, we did a St. Jude's episode and a whole learning experience, um, uh, for St. Jude's a few years ago, here in Tennessee actually, and it's funny that we're back here again, but the thing is, I said to the kids, this is oooonly the beginning for us, so, um, it's gonna be the beginning of the Gosselin give back, I mean, it's, it was interesting and very exciting for me to see that they can form an assembly line and truly help, I mean, it wasn't like, you know, we were, you know, changing anything to, to make them able to help, they're downstairs collecting food and, and they did the, the serving food and the, um, assembly line for the kids backpacks, so they're able to make a difference and um, **I told em, this is only the beginning.**"

By this time, Kate's public image, as well as her show's ratings, were taking a beating, and she was most certainly not TLC's star anymore. So Discovery went into full damage-control mode, trying desperately to rehab Kate's tarnished image. The last few seasons of *Jon & Kate Plus Ei8ht*, and then her new show, *Kate Plus Ei8ht*, had turned into nothing but damage control. Their couch interview sessions were always about answering the public criticism that they read online every day. They will deny that, of course, but it was obvious to anyone who had been following the Gosselin saga online. Without fail, they always seemed to address, either on the interview couch or with Kate giving a television interview somewhere else, the rumors and criticism that they were receiving in the public. It's tacky, and once people caught on a little bit more, it became blatantly obvious. When people began saying Kate doesn't do her own grocery shopping, TLC would film Kate at the supermarket with all eight kids to prove them wrong, etc.

It's funny how Kate now equates her show, not to the kids living their normal lives at home and the camera crew filming, but to "um, the traveling the world and seeing the sights." She doesn't even realize that that's a big reason people stopped watching; because the show was no longer about a normal family struggling to raise eight children. It had turned into the escapades of a rich, spoiled brat of a woman, being chauffeured first-class around the globe, staying at four-star hotels and resorts, living the high life – during a recession – all at the expense of her eight children. The public just couldn't relate anymore.

Undaunted in my search to find some sign of Kate's charitable, giving nature; I pressed on looking for evidence. In December of 2011, right after Christmas, I was looking through some of the personal belongings Kate had discarded, and I came across some paperwork from her children's school – you know, the very expensive private school that gave her kids an almost free ride on the huge tuition bill. The paperwork included applications and invitations for events where she or family members could have become involved in school activities with or for her kids, and things she could have done to help raise funds for her children's school.

But even the school was not worthy of Kate Gosselin's charity. She simply threw these things in the garbage with the rest of the "junk mail." These are some of the things I found in Kate's trash:

THE EXCELLENCE FUND
Kid's school holiday fundraiser.

Opened and thrown in the trash, complete with pledge card and envelope.

RUN FOR FITNESS APPLICATION
Opened and thrown in the trash, application form untouched.

The Run for Fitness was a chance for Kate to be with Cara for a school RUNNING event on September 30, 2011 at the school. It was a ½ mile run. Kate tells us all the time via Twitter that Cara is a runner and they run together. What could be more perfect than the two of them running together to help their own school raise money?

GRANDPARENT'S DAY

"Dear Lower School Families,
Grandparent/Grandfriend's Day was one of the most successful lower school events last year. This special day provides grandparents the opportunity to spend some time with their grandchild(ren) at school. This year G Day has been set for Tuesday, November 22, 2011."

Opened and thrown in the trash, complete with the invitation to send to the kids' grandparents.

FLOWER POWER FUNDRAISING
Order and Payment collection envelope, and order form and product catalog, with the Gosselin kids' names on them, thrown in the trash without any writing on them. Never used.

So scratch involvement with the school off the giveback list.

But wait! It turns out Kate did give something back to you, the viewers, for all your years of support and your contributions to her show's ratings. When a fan tweeted her in September of 2011 after her last *People* magazine cover hit the newsstands, she responded:

Yay! Enjoy! Did cover of people so u all would have something to keep to remember! :)

Oh, how very generous of her. Another tweeter asked if Kate had approved the *People* article:

> xxxxx @Kateplusmy8 I hope all is going well with you & that you're getting the support you need, Is 'People' article approved by you? XO

Yes. People does interviews and NO they don't pay for them!

The tweeter simply asked Kate if she had approved the *People* article. There was no need for Kate to blurt out that *People* doesn't pay for interviews. But once again, this is Kate Gosselin doing what she does best. She's lying, while sort of telling the truth. Kate was correct in saying that *People* magazine does not pay for interviews. *US Weekly* does not pay for interviews, either. But do you know what they do pay very big money for? Photos. They pay for photos to go along with the interview. Kate did a photo shoot for *People* magazine that included an interview and was paid, by my guestimate, between $50,000 and $75,000. And she did it all for you.

Thanks for giving back, Kate.

"Be careful not to do your 'acts of righteousness' before men, to be seen by them. If you do, you will have no reward from your Father in heaven. So when you give to the needy, do not announce it with trumpets, as the hypocrites do in the synagogues and on the streets, to be honored by men. I tell you the truth; they have received their reward in full.
But when you give to the needy, do not let your left hand know what your right hand is doing, so that your giving may be in secret.
Then your Father, who sees what is done in secret, will reward you."
– Matthew 6:1-4

I DREAMED A DREAM

If you go back and watch episodes of *Jon & Kate Plus Ei8ht* or *Kate Plus Ei8ht*, or listen to Kate's interviews, or read her words on Twitter, you will notice that Kate says over and over that "it was always a 'dream' of mine," about everything. Every trip; every job. "A dream."

"I have always dreamed of taking the kids on an RV trip to see this country."

"I wanted to go to Australia because it was a lifelong dream."

Just like the Hawaii dream, and the New Zealand dream, and on and on and on. Kate seems to start every conversation about one of her exotic trips or new "career" choices with the words "It has always been a dream of mine."

Whenever fans tweet suggestions, ideas or hopes for shows or projects they think she should do, Kate's standard reply, no matter what the suggestion, is that it is, or has always been, a "dream" of hers. Here are just a few of the many examples of this (Kate's tweets here and in following sections are in bold type):

xxxxx @Kateplusmy8 The fans are hoping for perhaps a fitness show for 2012? Maybe something where you can also teach your healthy eating to fans?

a fitness show would be a dream come true- not for me only but a way to reach ALL moms who desire fitness but don't know how!

@xxxxx @Kateplusmy8 Lol, @sesamestreet Shud have u on to do No. 8. w/Super Grover or Cookie Monster #Canyoutellmehowtoget?

at 1 time @sesamestreet @pbs **was on the schedule...I dream of doing it...counting my kids would b SO much fun! Such a great show!**

RT @xxxx I think @Kateplusmy8 should host @nbcsnl. **I'D WATCH THAT! HOSTING SNL IS A DREAM OF MINE!**

There are many additional examples of Kate's "dreams," but you get the idea. In Kate's world, a "dream" is code for "I want it, so get it for me now, Julie Carson May/TLC/Discovery."

The idea of the "dream" appears to have come about from Kirk Streb, producer/director/editor for *Jon & Kate Plus Ei8ht*, during a meeting he had with Jon and Kate. On September 9, 2007, Kirk sent an email to Kate, Jon, and Jen Stocks to review what was discussed at that meeting. In his "Thanks and Thoughts" email, Streb warmly greeted his "fellow diners and limo riders!" saying what a "blast" he had at their meeting with "Great company ... great food ... great ideas for the upcoming season." He wanted to review what they had discussed "before the brandy and benedicting (sic) fogged memories" slipped permanently from his brain.

During that meeting, they discussed the hope that they could find "a brilliant blend of 'big ideas' and 'easy/quick to tape ideas' to help make the taping process more manageable AND more fun." To achieve that, they divided ideas into "piles" they called Fast Dreams, Helpful Dreams, and Big Dreams. In other words, they were manufacturing "reality" for the *Jon & Kate Plus Ei8ht* reality show.

Here are a few brief excerpts of how Kirk Streb summarized their ideas for those big piles of dreams.

FAST DREAMS:

Fast dreams would be developing short segments that they could use to fill out episodes that didn't have enough footage, like mailbag segments which would be Q&A answering viewer's questions. They would focus on simple, manageable parts of the Gosselin's lives that happen with our without cameras like doing laundry, clothes shopping, grocery shopping, dinner, house cleaning, taking the kids to school, going to church etc.

HELPFUL DREAMS:

These are ideas that would be worth filming and things that are designed to make the Gosselin's lives less stressful. Ideas like buying Blackberry's, getting a personal chef to prepare organic meals that are frozen to help reduce stress of shoot days or busy days etc.

BIG DREAMS:

Big dreams are ideas that will provide big opportunities for filming full episodes, in some cases, many episodes and would also give the family either great experiences or great additions to their daily life like finding a way for the family to afford to move into a house with long-term appeal. This is the top big dream according to Streb. He tells them that nothing is impossible with the right energy put towards finding in-kind help, sponsor deals etc., that would make building a house more affordable.

Another big dream would be helping the Gosselins go to Hawaii, European travel, further renovations of existing house, in-home consultation with a family expert. Streb suggested having Doctor Phil actually come to the Gosselin house, thinking his eyes would bug out of his head if he stood there for thirty minutes.

Discovery certainly did everything possible to make all of Kate's dreams come true, even those she never thought to have herself.

"ENTERING THE PROMISED LAND"

"Kate thought they were owed stuff. The money factor was huge."
– Angela Krall

Kate's former nurse whom Kate loved and fought to keep by her side.

Kate kept a file on her computer with photos of the throngs of media waiting for them as they arrived at their Wyomissing home, which had just been remodeled and enlarged for them, free of charge. The file was called "Entering the promised land."

"Money DID fall from the sky!!!!"
– Kate Gosselin

2. Manna From Heaven - a sudden happening that brings good fortune (as a sudden opportunity to make money.)

Once Jon and Kate brought the sextuplets home from the hospital, the money started pouring in. It was Kate's "Manna from Heaven." But after a short time, something strange happened. Kate stopped going to church on a regular basis, and then she stopped going at all. She began happily working on Sunday and was frustrated by people who didn't. In an email from Kate to her manager, Julie May, speaking for herself and bodyguard Steve Neild, Kate said they are both dying to dig into work because they are both thinking and working on a Sunday!

Kate had discovered a new god, and its name was DISCOVERY. And she worshiped her new god very hard and very often.

MARKETING YOUR BABIES – 101

"… if there is a way my children could be a help in marketing your clothing lines, we're all for it!"
– Kate Gosselin

Even before the sextuplets were born, back when it was just Jon and Kate plus two, Kate's mind was already in full gear, working to label and market her children. Before the babies took their first breaths, Kate had directed Jon to get a website up and running to start spreading the word nationally, and more importantly, to tell the world how they could help, and to solicit donations, including a 15-passenger van.

And from the moment the news that Kate Gosselin was pregnant with six babies hit the headlines during that first press conference in April 2004 at the Hershey Medical Center in Hershey, PA, the Gosselin sextuplets were marketed to the world like a new product.

The remainder of this chapter provides details about some of Kate's numerous requests, schemes, demands and opportunities to make money off her babies.

THE BIRTHDAY KIDS NEED A VAN!

To celebrate the first birthday of her sextuplets, Kate sent out this party invitation to some of her "closest" friends. That's some guest list of "friends" below.

FOR IMMEDIATE RELEASE:
April 15, 2005

Jonathan & Kate Gosselin
610-374-0179
info@sixgosselins.com

MEDIA ADVISORY

For Planning Purposes Only

HAPPY BIRTHDAY GOSSELIN SIX!!!

LOCATION: INN AT READING

EVENT:
The Gosselin Sextuplets (Born at Hershey Medical Center on May 10, 2004) are celebrating their 1st Birthday. All Media are welcome to a press availability beginning at 10:30am.

DATE:
Saturday, May 7, 2005

TIME:
11am

LOCATION:
1040 Park Road, Wyomissing, PA 19610 USA
(800) 383-9713 (610) 372-7811
www.innatreading.com

MEDIA ADVISORY RECIPENTS (Guest List)
citydesk@patriot-news.com
editor@hersheychron.com
juniatanews@prodigy.net
jferguson@lnpnews.com
pmekeel@lnpnews.com

```
citydesk@ldnews.com
sentinel@lewistownsentinal.com
news@thewgalchannel.com
newsdesk@whptv.com
news@abc27.com
fox43assignment@tribune.com
news@mcall.com
news@theallentowntimes.com
kevindonahue@cable.comcast.com
newsdesk@kyw.com
news@readingeagle.com
wcaudesk@nbc.com
news@wfmz.com
info@wlvt.org
wb17newsdesk@tribune.com
mike.neilon@abc.com
foxphiladelphia@hotmail.com
TFacc245@Fox.com
news@altoonamirror.com
```

A reporter who attended the Gosselin sextuplet's first birthday party said this:

> "After the Gosselins first birthday party, a final comment from
> Kate to the media was, "We need transportation! A 15-Passenger
> van, with plenty of storage!"

GIFT CARDS GLADLY ACCEPTED

Kate posted this polite little note on the family's website informing fans about what the family needs:

> Thank you for inquiring about sending our kids a gift. Due to
> space constraints it would help us best if you would send them a
> Target gift card.
> Thank you for your kindness to our family.
>
> Sincerely,
> The Gosselin Family

THE FLOOD GATES OPEN

These are some brief, paraphrased excerpts from Kate's journal that document her getting a taste of things to come, and show how she began dabbling into asking for freebies. These are the "unsolicited" freebies, as Kate likes to tell people.

July 2006
Adv Med Prod called Kate and she said it sounded like they are going to pay for their train tickets, lunch and show tickets too!!!!!!

July 2006

Kate said that Jen told them that money is involved for them and that they would be paid $1,000 for each of their 20 new episodes!!!! Kate was also told that Discovery would pay for everything whenever they went anywhere with them as an added benefit!

July 2006

Kate learned from Jen Stocks that they would be filming at the Giant grocery store and that their entire shopping trip would be donated by Giant and Kate's lost salary for the day would also be covered!!!!!!

September 2006

Kate finds out that Discovery will be for the girl's bedroom renovation because they'll be filming it.

September 2006

Kate and Jen Stocks discuss episode ideas, which will include an assortment of paid excursions including having the twins head shots taken for possible acting commercial deals. They'll also get free Christmas shopping, beds for the kid's rooms, Valentines Day dinner at a fancy restaurant, a trip to California, Carnival-themed birthday party for the little kids, new carpet, a Disney vacation among many other things.

Kate was excited to talk about doing a product commercial saying that would get them started because Jen told her that the Gosselin family is the total package.

September 2006

Kate discusses the big business news of the day. The head of Discovery Network talent search called Kate to discuss the financial future of her family but he called at a bad time and Kate told him she'd have to call him back later. Jen stocks had previously advised Kate to ask for $1,400 per episode in hopes of getting $1,200 but Kate rounded up to $1,500. Kate was shocked and thrilled to find out that they were offering $2,000 per episode right off the bat with no negotiation. If she only knew that if she had a manager at that time she could have probably gotten more than $10,000 per episode.

Kate was so proud of herself because after this big money offer, she responded with a simple 'OK'. She said he paused for her reaction but she didn't give him one. She's very thankful to God for sending the offer. Kate finds it mind boggling that the will be paid for each episode and receive the many fringe benefits!!!!! She ended it with Lord, how great thou art!!!!!

November 2006

Kate reveals that her best friend Beth Carson told her that sometimes God provides and it is right in front of us and we don't see it! Beth also told Kate that God provided the show and money so that Kate could quit work and stay home with the kids until they went to school. That thought very much excited Kate. She said that just thinking that she wouldn't have to go to work is sooo amazing!

After all of that good news, Kate got a check in the mail for $800 from a lady Kate had been emailing with because of the show.

November 2006
Kate describes the beginning of the church speaking engagements and how she became addicted to the fame and money. After the spoke they were immediately bombarded with people handing them cash and checks. Someone told Kate that this is a 'Pilot' performance! Kate said that was good because that is where she'd like to head! She talks about wanting to book a monthly family weekend to speak at a church and said that would be her dream!

December 2006
Kate finds out that Discovery will pay for their trip to Florida but is outraged when she learns that they want to go to 'a place called Discovery Cove' but are not interested in paying for Disney World. How lovely! Kate writes. Kate says she wants Jen to get at least Magic Kingdom included. Period.

January 2007
This month Kate will hire a cleaning lady and feels that she will be comped by the network.

January 2007
Kate takes charge saying she made Jon talk to Jen about the beds, saying I made him tell her that if Discovery wasn't paying for the room, then they wouldn't be filming in it. She says push has come to shove! The birth of Kate Gosselin as we know her.

February 2007
Kate got an email about possibly going on Dr. Phil! She was excited. So much so that the first thing she thought to do was write out a list of logistics for them so that there would be accommodated well. She wanted two helpers of her choice, one stop flight etc.

March 2007
Kate discusses many events and opportunities and proudly states that she has a feeling that this would be the beginning of lots of weeks like this to come!!

April 2007
Kate's AWESOME news of the day is that the girls are getting $12,000 each of the $13,500 tuition for their school paid by scholarship...for first grade!!!!!

May 2007
Kate and Jon got a $5,000 bonus from Discovery, an offer to stay at a resort in Park City Utah with ski lessons for the kids and spa trips for Kate.

MULTIPLE BLESSINGS

On December 10, 2007, Paul J. Datte of the law firm Cerullo, Datte & Wallbillich, P.C, who represented Kate Gosselin and Beth Carson, sent a letter to Zondervan regarding Zondervan's proposal to publish Kate and Beth's book, *Multiple Blessings*. The letter included specific comments about the proposal and mentioned financial arrangements, performance and merchandising rights, royalty rates on net sales, and cover price. The letter stated that the first-time authors would require an advance of $100,000. It also covered the following:

- Kate and Beth will require a royalty rate of 24% of net sales for 1 to 20,000 books sold; 27% for 2.001 to 40,000 books sold; and 30% for all books sold in excess of 40,000.

- Kate and Beth will require a cover price of $21.99 rather than the $19.99 price reflected in your proposal.

GOING ROGUE

This is a good example of Kate taking matters into her own hands and going outside of Discovery's Advertising Sales department to get her own product placement/endorsement deals. This violated the terms of their agreement with Discovery. An email from Kate to Wendy Douglas of Discovery showed that Kate very much wanted to do a publicity campaign for Frigidaire. This was Kate in action, 3 months before she hired a manager to handle the dirty work for her. On January 25, 2008, Kate sent an email to Wendy Douglas of Discovery to let her know about a long conversation she had with "Brandon," who was a representative from Burns Entertainment. She said Brandon was representing Frigidaire and their "new, largest available to date double oven" and he had chosen her to do the campaign. Kate told Wendy the campaign would involve her doing a media tour sometime in the spring "(preferably during our filming break)," morning shows, radio, and interviews.

Kate further explained that Frigidaire had offered to supply "ALL appliances in the quantity that we desire for our new house that we badly need and desire in the form of product placement." She said that Brandon had requested Wendy's information and she was sure he would be in contact with her soon. She told Wendy, "This is really exciting for me. Talking about a kitchen appliance is wonderful and very comfortable for me. However, I also see this as a big way to advertise 'Jon & Kate plus 8' in a way that we haven't yet had the chance! I am hopeful that we can all work together to make this happen!"

Kate then forwarded that email to Kirk Streb, a producer on *Jon & Kate Plus Ei8ht*, telling him of the "(deeply desired) opportunity I have to work with Frigidaire!!!!" (On an unrelated note, Kate also wrote to Kirk in that email, "PS my carpet is beyond dandy and I am in love. Scott has footage of me rolling on it! Imagine!!!!!")

Imagine.

Kirk replied to Kate and told her that he thought it was a cool offer and "outstanding!" But he gave her this caution: "The only thing that might get in the way is if the network has some deal with some other manufacturer... but, then wouldn't they have to match it anyway?" He told her he was "Glad the carpet is groovy."

Kate was not happy to hear that there was a possibility that Discovery wouldn't let her make a deal to get lots of free appliances from Frigidaire. She wrote to Kirk asking him to find out more about which company the network might have other deals with. She told him "I will be thoroughly annoyed if I cannot do this. This has **(don't mention at this point to the network)** a pretty decent sized monetary price tag on it for me personally so to our family this is big!!!! **I am really tired of them sucking the life out of any other opp to do anything to help secure our future!** Who will help to push this for me????? This is the first of many of these to come our way and this is a perfect fit!!!!"

(It's funny that Kate didn't say anything about that pesky Discovery "sucking the life" out of her when the network was making plans to build a new house for her family.)

Kirk then very diplomatically took Kate to task. He told Kate that he wasn't saying that he knew for sure that there was definitely WAS another manufacturer, just that it would only be a bump in the road that might possibly, by some remote chance, come up. He sheepishly added that he had NO reason to believe that it would. Kurt sounded scared to death of Kate Gosselin.

He asked Kate to please not assume that the network was going to "suck the life" out of any opportunity, and told her that other opportunities were rolling in and getting bigger and better in part because a lot of people were working very hard to make the show a hit by promoting it and getting it into the press, etc.

Kirk told Kate that in meetings he had at the network that week he had started to understand that "they look at ad deals and even the building of a house in a MUCH BIGGER way than we do... which is good." He said, "With the proper alliances, through the ad sales people and the deals the network has in place, etc.— there's almost no limit to what could be comped in the building of the house."

Kirk also said that while he and Kate might look at "birds in hands", the network was "focusing on a whole flock!", and he thought it was to her benefit to "at least imagine that they have the ability to pull off deals that would impress you in ways you've yet to be impressed- by far."

Kirk closed out his email by saying, "Above all, please remember- we truly do want to help you secure your future (I mean Figure 8 specifically). We all regard you as family, as trite as that may sound. I want every possible good thing for you and your family and that's the truth." He told Kate that when she gives them background information on deals like this, it helps them with their "endless behind the scenes 'nudging and maneuvering' that has benefitted you in ways you'll never know."

Duly chastised, Kate changed her tune and apologized to Kirk, telling him how very grateful they were to everyone who was working hard for the same goals. Pretending to be aware of more than she was, she said, "Oh, okay. Thanks for clearing that up. I already knew that the snag would be other appliance companies that stand in the way."

Kate then made an excuse to Kirk that she had spoken with Wendy once about it and Wendy had not mentioned anything that would compete. Kate said she realized that ad sales handled that more than Wendy did, but initially, she got minimal but slightly somewhat positive feedback.

She apologized, saying "Sorry, if I am going beyond being 'Kate' in the show, but I also want to secure a 'foreverness' for our family (house, college etc) that goes beyond our show so that when I look back when I am old and gray **(and probably STILL filming- ha ha)** I know without a doubt that we did the right thing."

In her closing paragraph, Kate did a little brown nosing. She told Kirk that they are MORE than grateful for AMP/Figure 8. She added that they have all proven that they are on her side and are working with her goals in mind, while they were busily keeping the network happy! She thanked them for their tireless work and told Kurt that she has really come to enjoy working together and she loves them all.

Before signing off, Kate repeated that she was EXTREMELY excited to work with Frigidaire not only for the obvious benefits, but because she felt it was a "big ad sales/ exposure opp for all of us- us personally and our show!!!!"

PLUGOLA/PAYOLA

Jim Ford, director of Talent Business Affairs for Discovery, sent a letter to Paul J. Datte, Jon and Kate's attorney at the time, to inform him about a couple of issues: 1) compensation for Seasons 4 and 5, and 2) a contract issue dealing with "Plugola/Payola". It appears that Kate may have been trying to take advantage of financial opportunities outside the provisions of her Discovery contract. Jim Ford told Paul Datte that they needed to make sure that the Gosselins fully understood the standard plugola/payola provision in their agreement, and that it was very important for a number of reasons.

In his response to Jim Ford, Paul Datte first addressed the compensation issue. He played a little bit of hardball with the network by letting them know that the Gosselins were "aware of the immense success" of their show. Datte told Ford that the episodic fee for the fourth and fifth seasons of their show had been the subject of significant discussion and consideration by the Gosselins, and that the compensation for those seasons would have to be adequate. He said that the Gosselins would need to be paid $9,000 per half-hour episode for the fourth season and $13,000 per half-hour episode for the fifth season. Datte also said that while he recognized that the final negotiation process for the contract addendum had been laborious, the Gosselins needed to wrap things up that week. Otherwise, they would need to review their options.

Datte then addressed the plugola/payola issue. He wrote that the Gosselins were aware of the plugola/payola provisions and their implications in the contract, and they had done nothing to violate those provisions. He denied any impropriety on their part and said they had directed any potential endorsement or advertising opportunities to Discovery.

He explained that if Discovery's concern was related to a very recent opportunity the Gosselins had referred to Discovery, they recognized the obligation to address the opportunity within the bounds of the agreement, but viewed the opportunity to be significant. He said they would like to arrive at a mutually acceptable arrangement in that regard.

THE NEW HOUSE

In a not-so-subtle way, Kate hinted to Discovery that she needed a new house, and fast! OK. There was no hinting. She bypassed that and went straight to outright begging. Here are some things she wrote about needing a new house and more privacy:

- "What do we do????????!!"

- "Okay, I am about to move to the south of France with Brangelina..."

- "On a regular basis, without asking or knocking or whatever, in the middle of the day, people pull into our driveway, drop off all manner of who knows what for the kids, hang out for awhile hoping we emerge, and leave...."

- "Meanwhile, we are all sequestered in our room with the shades drawn waiting to come out of hiding when they leave!!!"

- "I can't take it ANYMORE!!!!! Leave us alone, world... We give you our whole lives on TV....isn't that ENOUGH?!!!????"

- "Really, what can we do because we have had enough!!!!!!! Someone, anyone?!!!!!!!"

- "I plan on putting our house on the market next week.... So that we can rent somewhere more private...... Hope it doesnt throw off our filming plans!!!! Hope the house plans work out so that we can move 'for real' SOON!!!"

If she hadn't put her children out to the world like a product to be consumed, and worked so hard to keep them and herself there, this problem would probably have been far more manageable.

This is a wish list that Kate had written, in preparation for her new house.

```
Driveway to pool house / guesthouse.
Home monitoring security system w/surround sound — centralized
system.
Gated entrance with keypad and sliding or swinging gate.
Fenced in property.
```

Centrally located wiring closet in office.
Barn (rumble room) for kids and storage.
Tray ceilings of production lighting.
Home theatre for Friday night movie nights.

PROCTER & GAMBLE INITIATIVE

In February 2008, Kate signed a contract to participate in Procter & Gamble's initiative to provide clean drinking water to children around the world. Here is a description of the program from Procter & Gamble's website:

> Four thousand children die each day from poor water around the world. In order to assist in efforts for providing children with clean drinking water, P&G has created an initiative to help. For every coupon used from P&G's brandSAVER this March and April, P&G will donate a bottle of PUR clean drinking water to children in developing worlds.

In exchange for the right to use her approved image and voice to endorse the program, Procter & Gamble Distributing LLC paid Kate the tidy sum of $25,000. Here are some key points from the contract, which was effective from February 15, 2008, through May 31, 2008. Kate is the "TALENT," and P&G is the "CLIENT." Kate (the TALENT) agreed to participate in the following activities:

- MEDIA TRAINING, tentatively scheduled for February or March 2008, which would entail one (1) in-person media training session, not to exceed four (4) consecutive hours, with the CLIENT to review the PROGRAM messaging and services. The CLIENT may travel to location convenient to TALENT.

- MEDIA DAYS, tentatively scheduled for March or April 2008, which would be three (3) non-consecutive days, each not to exceed eight (8) consecutive hours exclusive of hair, makeup and travel. The Media days could take place in New York, NY; Los Angeles, CA; or Chicago, IL. (The final location would be determined at the discretion of the Client and would be based on the TALENT'S professional and personal schedule.)

- The TALENT would be expected to deliver pre-approved branded P&G Brand Saver/PUR Charity Program Key Messages (to be provided by Client and Agency) during each media interview.

For Kate's participation in the program, she was to be paid $25,000, which included all agent and TALENT fees. She would receive 50% of the payment within thirty (30) business days of full execution of the agreement, and 50% upon the completion of the second MEDIA DAY, but no later than April 30, 2008. The CLIENT agreed to provide and pay for the following:

- Round-trip airfare for two (if destination is Chicago or Los Angeles) or chartered bus for the family (if destination is New York) for all media-related activities;

- First-class hotel accommodations for up to two (2) nights for all media-related activities (for TALENT and two suites for entire family plus two handlers if needed);

- Hair and make-up stylists not to exceed $500 total per day for all on-camera activities;

- A per diem of $150 per day, not including travel days;

- Security by TALENT's preferred security company for all media activities;

So for very little effort, Kate was rewarded with a huge payday. Kate didn't even have to write her own material for her Procter & Gamble endorsement; her management did it for her.

Now, companies use celebrities to endorse their products, services or programs all the time. They try to choose people who will inspire others to donate or to just drum up publicity. Ideally, the company will get a return on their initial investment far in excess of what they paid the celebrity. A lot of celebrities do charitable endorsements for free. Kate does nothing for free, unless there is something in it for her to gain.

I don't have information about whether Kate's participation was worth the $25,000, plus expenses, that P&G paid her. However, based on statistics from P&G's Children's Safe Drinking Water website (http://www.csdw.org/csdw/donate.shtml), which states that "$30 gives a family clean water for a year," that $25,000 P&G gave Kate could have provided clean drinking water to about 833 families for an entire year.

THE GOSSELIN FAMILY HARDSHIPS

Kate's sister-in-law, Aunt Jodi, and her brother, Kevin, were as close to Jon and Kate back in the early days as anyone, so they were privy to personal details that no one else knew at the time. Aunt Jodi's sister, Julie, posted this on a blog about Jon and Kate in 2008:

> "When the sextuplets were about 6 months old, an email was going around from them, asking for financial help. They were telling a tale of having absolutely no money, and not knowing how they were going to survive. I received the email, and it had very detailed information about how to contact the utilities and mortgage company to pay their bills.

"There was also a fund set up through their church. There was a huge outpouring of generosity from their community. Family and friends stepped up and gave money, offered time, tried to help in every way imaginable.

"Disbelief set in a few months later. We found out (by their own admission) that all along, they had a rather large sum of money in their savings account. Let's just say it was more than I made in a year working full time when I came out of nursing school. They had been giving everyone this story of being financially destitute, when all along, a very wealthy family member was supporting them, and they were sitting on a large sum of money. When they were questioned, their response was along the lines that they shouldn't have to use their own money to support their family. It was society's obligation. "We have 8 kids!!"

"I actually hadn't even thought about any of that until I heard the story they were telling at the churches. The story wasn't even entirely true; I know that from my own experience. I tried to understand why they would tell such a story and lead people to believe that was still the way they were living. Had they run that story over in their minds so much that they began to believe it? I also knew there were college funds set up for the kids. Were they lying about that too?
"To top it all off, I knew that part of their contract with the network included being paid for every 'appearance.' Let's just say for about 3-4 'appearances,' they could make as much as the average person makes in a year. Did they let anyone at the churches know that? So I picture kind, generous people, sitting in a church, listening to tales of financial hardship. Led to believe it's still this way, offering plates being passed and people (who really can't afford it) digging deep into their pockets, giving money to a family who probably makes well more than twice as much money as they do — just for the show. I'm not even including the freebies and all of the money they get from product endorsements and appearances. I find that disturbing!

"Why mislead good people? Speak at the churches, collect your money from the network, promote your show, but don't be dishonest. Don't tell people your kids don't have a college fund, and don't continue to tell tales of being financially destitute. I can hear it now, 'who am I to say no?' It's my opinion that it's their obligation to tell the truth and stop collecting love offerings."

Jon and Kate put it another way on their website:

"We ask others to please pray for us as we go through terrible financial and family hardships. It is hard to let people into our personal lives but we are praying that people could walk in our shoes for one day and understand that God has given us these children and we are responsible to raise them the best we can. Please pray that Kate and I can do this with help of all our awesome volunteers that God has provided us. Amen."

THE COLLEGE FUNDS

Kate had many scheduled speaking engagements at churches in 2008, where she told the same story of hardship over and over again while asking for "Love Offerings" for her children's college funds, which she said didn't exist. The Gosselin family website, *sixgosselins.com*, also said there were no college funds set up for their kids.

But Pennsylvania Lt. Governor Katherine Baker Knoll had attended and spoken at the Gosselin sextuplet's first birthday party held at the Inn at Reading in Wyomissing, PA. She was there in person to announce that the state had made college funding available for the Gosselin kids.

This press release from that first birthday party in 2005 tells a story much different from Kate's about college funds:

> "If you would like to make a contribution to the Gosselin Family's TAP account, you can do so by making your check payable to "TAP 529," writing "Gosselin" in the memo portion of the check, and sending your contributions to: Gosselin Sextuplets and Twins Accounts, TAP Bureau, 218 Finance Building, Harrisburg, PA 17120. More information on the Tuition Account Program can be obtained by calling 1-800-440-4000 or by visiting the Treasury website and clicking on Tuition Account Program."

It's funny how Kate conveniently never mentioned that TAP account while the "Love Offering" plate was being passed around the churches for her.

UNDER NEW
MANAGEMENT

"All mine. All mine as far as the eye can see."
– *Kate Gosselin*

There has been a great deal of speculation about how much money the Gosselins, first both Jon and Kate, and later just Kate, made by exploiting their children. The media has reported many different figures for how much Discovery was paying Kate and Jon per episode for filming *Jon & Kate Plus Ei8ht*. When I first began digging for this information, I had heard all of the same figures from sources I thought were reliable.

Originally, reports surfaced that the family was being paid $75,000 per episode for Season 5, which was the season being filmed when I started reporting about the family.

An online search for the actual amount of compensation turned up the following dizzying array of figures:

```
"Jon Gosselin confirmed the family was paid $22,500 per episode
    of Jon & Kate Plus 8."
"CNN reports that the Gosselins are paid approximately $50,000-
    $75,000 per episode."
"Matt Lauer of the Today show reported the family is paid
    $25,000-$50,000 per episode."
"The Gosselins make up to $75,000 per episode on their TLC hit."
"$70,000 per episode."
"The correct answer is $75,000 per episode."
"They make appearances on TV shows and talk shows for about
    $1,000-$2,000."
"Depending on the show, anywhere from $5,000-$40,000 per
    episode."
"$60,000-$90,000 per show."
"They make $45,000-$65,000 per season."
"$65,000 an episode."
"Some sources have said $5,000-$65,000 per episode.""
"The Gosselins make $75,000 per episode. So that figures between
    three million and four million per season."
"In previous seasons, Jon and Kate were paid $40,000 per episode
    or about $1.48 million per season (about $3 million per
    year)."
"It is estimated between $25,000 and $50,000 per episode."
```

It turns out the Gosselins were not making as much as a lot of people thought – at least not from just filming the show. After investigating further, I was told that the figure was actually about $22,000 per episode, much lower than the $75,000 amount originally reported.

In reading all of the contracts between the Gosselin family and Discovery Communications, as well as the Gosselin tax documents, the reports were way off base on how much money was changing hands.

According to a 1099-MISC that I obtained, Discovery paid Jon and Kate a total of $109,186.90 in 2007. Here is the breakdown of their earnings from their 2007 1099-MISC:

1/4/07 - $6,000 – 20 days of shooting
3/7/07 - $6,000 – 20 days of shooting
4/25/07 – $250 - Appearance Fee $125 x 2
5/9/07 - $5,000 – Service Recognition Add'l Payment
7/25/07 - $6,000 – 20 days of shooting
8/8/07 - $6,000 – 20 days of shooting
8/29/07 - $14,285 – Jon & Kate season 2
9/26/07 - $6,000 – Seasons 1 & 2 20 days of shooting
9/26/07 - $1,500 – Missed work pay for publicity appearances
10/3/07 - $2,246 – Shed site season 1 & 2 remove from 1099
11/7/07 - $25,952.50 – Season 3
11/7/07 - $2,000 – Seasons 1 & 2 on camera services all programs
11/14/07 - $2,000 – Season 1 & 2 contract amend for last 12 episodes
11/20/07 - $25,952 – Season 3
Adjusted 1099 - $109,186.90

The following is a breakdown of how much money the Gosselins were paid per episode for each season. According to the Gosselin/Discovery contracts, these figures do not include such things as bonuses, travel expenses, or per diems.

Season 1:
$2,000 per episode x 9 episodes = $18,000

Season 2:
$5,000 per ½-hour episode x 9 episodes = $45,000
(3) 1 hour episodes=$15,000 extra
Season 2 Total=$60,000

Season 3:
$5,000 per ½-hour episode x 32 episodes = $160,000
(4) 1 hour episodes=$20,000 extra
Season 3 Total=$180,000

Season 4:
$9,000 per ½-hour episode x 41 episodes = $369,000
(8) 1 hour episodes=$72,000 extra
Season 4 Total=$441,000

Season 4 was renegotiated to $22,500 per ½-hour episode x 41 episodes = $922,500
(8) 1 hour episodes=$180,000 extra
Season 4 Total=$1,102,500

Season 5: $$22,500 per ½-hour episode x 24 episodes = $540,000

(7) 1 hour episodes = $157,500 extra
Season 5 Total=$697,500

These numbers confirm that Jon was telling the truth when he said they were being paid $22,500 per episode. Now $22,500 is a lot of money, but it is a far cry from $75,000 per episode. Maybe that's the real reason Kate felt she had to be out there working so hard. She wasn't really shaking up the world financially with just filming alone, although it looked like she enjoyed having people think she was. It's decent money, but not when you consider what the family had to give up for it.

JULIE CARSON MAY

On April 14, 2008, just in time for contract negotiations for Season 4 of the show, Kate hired her new manager, Julie Carson May. This was Kate's best move to date. That day, Kate and Jon, both individually and on behalf of their minor children Cara Nicole Gosselin, Madelyn Kate Gosselin, Aaden Jonathan Gosselin, Collin Thomas Gosselin, Hannah Joy Gosselin, Leah Hope Gosselin, Alexis Faith Gosselin and Joel Kevin Gosselin, entered into an agreement with Media Motion International, LLC, (MMI) to represent and advise them in the "entertainment/parenting" industry. Some of the terms of the agreement with MMI are summarized below.

- The Gosselins engaged MMI (the Manager) to be the sole and exclusive personal manager, representative and advisor for the Gosselins in all facets of their career in the entertainment/parenting industry, with the exception of the items listed in Exhibit A.

- The Manager agreed to advise and counsel the Gosselins regarding their career in the entertainment/parenting industry and to use its good faith efforts to promote, develop and advance their career, including negotiating applicable contracts.

- The Manager agreed to assign Julie Carson May as the primary individual responsible for providing and/or coordinating the services to be rendered by MMI.

- The initial term of the agreement was for a period of one (1) year from the date it was first written.

- The Manager would not have the option of renewing and extending the term of the agreement for the first option period unless gross compensation of $350,000 (not including any revenues related to Exhibit A) had been paid to the Gosselins during the initial term.

- For each additional option period, the Manager would not have the option to renew and extend the term unless gross compensation of $300,000 (not including any revenues related to Exhibit A) had been paid to the Gosselins in the previous 1-year term.

- Gross compensation included, without limitation, all forms of income, consideration and compensation relating to the Gosselin's endeavors in the entertainment/parenting industry (excluding compensation from Exhibit A). This included salaries, advances, earnings, fees, royalties, sponsorship fees, commercial fees, product licensing fees, partnership interests, shares of stock, bonuses, shares of profits, shares of receipts, and any other considerations earned or received directly or indirectly by the Gosselins.

- Commission on all gross compensation related to any book projects or pre-existing projects that the Gosselins chose to have the manager work to expand would be fifteen percent (15%).

- Commission for licensing, endorsements, sponsorships, DVD, CD, training programs/licensing, new product lines/extensions, television, radio, speaking, voiceover and internet/online and wireless would be fifteen percent (15%) (excluding Exhibit A).

EXHIBIT A listed the following things that were or would be excluded from the MMI/Jon and Kate Gosselin Management Agreement dated April 14, 2008:

1. Book projects/literary projects
2. All current aspects/revenues from the existing Discovery deal for *Jon & Kate Plus 8* were excluded entirely. Only improvements to the deal would be subject to commission.
3. The contract with Procter & Gamble Distributing LLC in conjunction with the P & G brands Save/PUR Charity Program.
4. The Gosselin's website advertising that had been procured or developed on behalf of the Gosselins, unless originated by the manager with the consent and agreement of the Gosselins.

To illustrate the impact Julie May had on the Gosselin financial picture, a paragraph from the original Season 4 and Season 5 contract negotiation, before she was hired shows that the Gosselins asked for $9,000 per half-hour episode for Season 4, and $13,000 per episode for Season 5.

Julie May earned her money immediately and took the family from $180,000 to $441,000 in her first contract negotiation for Season 4. The Season 5 contract and amendment makes no mention of a pay raise per episode, so $22,500 appears to be the maximum earned per episode. They would have earned more for Season 5 if it had not been cut short by 16 episodes, due to Jon's shutting down the filming because he stated that he didn't want the kids to film anymore.

The figures that were originally being thrown around for how much Kate was making per episode for her newest show, *Kate Plus Ei8ht* were staggering. *TV Guide* reported that she made $250,000 per episode. At the height of her fame on *Jon & Kate Plus Ei8ht*, the entire family was only making $22,500 per episode, so the $250,000 figure per episode is very hard to believe.

But all the compensation that was being discussed was for the television show alone. Julie May was just getting warmed up. She jumped head-first into everything Gosselin and, before long, the offers were pouring in. Speaking engagements. Product endorsements. You name it, they asked for it, and usually got it. The sky was the limit.

When a tweeter asked Kate if the "5 million" figure was true, she quickly shot down the figure, tweeting the following reply:

I can absolutely say EVERY figure is way way way high. Only published 3 books too... All crap, but wish was true ;(

Given Kate's track record for lying, it is possible that the actual figure was higher.

OUTER BANKS FILMING

On June 4, 2008, an email exchange shows Kate talking about "reality" when trying to justify having Discovery pay for her vacation to the Outer Banks, when Discovery wanted to film in Chapel Hill, NC, instead. Deanie from Figure 8 Films informed Kate and "Everyone" that they couldn't book the house at the Outer Banks without first considering what would be shot and how many episodes they could cover.

Deanie said she had previously mentioned that the Outer Banks is many hours away from the Chapel Hill area and from the Myrtle Beach area, where Ripley's Aquarium is located. She also reminded everyone that their original intention months ago when they were offered the OB location was that they would be able to shoot a minimum of four episodes over the course of two weeks. Deanie said that since that had dwindled to one episode on looking for property in North Carolina, they could not justify the expense. She then wrote that if they couldn't figure out a way to cover more episodes, she didn't think the beach outing would be a possibility.

Kate replied to "All" telling them that there was "TONS" of things to shoot near the house. She made it clear that visiting the aquarium was not mandatory because there were plenty of other aquariums for other times. She suggested wild horse tours they had always wanted to do and a lighthouse they could tour; she also mentioned the Wright Brothers Visitors Center. Kate said these were "All things we would normally do in REALITY!!!!!"

Kate also asked, "What happened to swim lessons". She said she had not enrolled the kids in their usual swim lesson program because she was told they would do the swimming that week. It also sounded like there may have been an issue with filming the house because Kate argued that "(we don't need to show the house and as for permission to shoot there, we could LAST MINUTE get a conf form signed)." She ended by saying, "Its time to think outside the box" and consider "what is reality for us!!!!"

"SPA-ING"

In an email from July 31, 2008, Wendy Douglas of Discovery gave everyone a friendly reminder that their weekly call was scheduled for 2:00 PM the next day. But Kate had other plans. She decided to skip the weekly phone meeting with Discovery – you know, the company that was paying her millions of dollars – to go to the spa instead. She said that she "may or may not be able to be on this call today" because she was going to be "spa-ing….for some wonderful stress relief!" She assured Wendy that Jon would be on the call.

T-SHIRT LINE

On top of everything else, a new Gosselin T-Shirt line was being designed. Julie May wrote to Jon and Kate to tell them "Good news—they are getting a T-shirt line going!" She sent them a first set of designs for their approval and comments. Julie told them that some of the designs were fun and good in her "humble" opinion, but there were some she thought they should nix for one reason or another. She asked Kate and Jon to take a look because she wanted to get them feedback as soon as possible because they needed to get revisions done by the end of the week.

KMART HOLIDAY CAMPAIGN

On September 15, 2008, Kate signed a contract to participate in a holiday campaign for Kmart. The Gosselins were paid $158,000 for up to 24 hours of "work."

FREE HOME FURNISHINGS

When the Gosselins moved into their new million-dollar home in October 2008, you might have noticed that it was devoid of furniture for several weeks (episodes). There is a reason for that. Discovery was still working on getting a deal in place with Ethan Allen, to film Jon and Kate picking out furniture. Of course, anyone watching the episode would naturally think that the Gosselins were actually at the furniture stores buying their furniture with their own money, and the cameras just happened to be along that day filming them living their lives.
On September 23, 2008, a letter was sent to formalize an agreement between Jon and Kate, and Chandler Ehrlich LLC on behalf of Lane Home Furnishings, for Jon and Kate to serve as "celebrities for Lane Home Furnishings Home Theater Initiative from October 2008-October 2009." Here are some specifics from the agreement with Lane:

- Jon and Kate would be paid a fee of $30,000 ($15,000 due at signing and $15,000 due when the video shoot is completed).

- Jon and Kate would receive up to $30,000 (msrp) in Lane Furniture (which was to be delivered after they moved into their new home).

- Lane agreed to pay taxes on the furniture (including paying the Gosselins for any other taxes that would be due as a result of Lane providing furniture. Lane also agreed to provide a gross up payment to Jon and Kate to cover these taxes and any taxes due that would result from 1099).

- Jon and Kate would provide a high-quality picture of themselves together to be used inside the truck only and for Market public relations activities. Jon and Kate would also provide a high-quality family picture with the children for use inside the truck only (an 11x14 photo to be displayed above the truck sofa).

- Jon and Kate would have approval over all usage of their name/likeness and video usage.

Julie May emailed Jon and Kate to let them know she had talked to "Laura" at Lane, and Laura said she "LOVED" meeting them and was really happy with the film footage. Julie told Jon and Kate that Laura was going to send their second check out that week.
Julie asked them to get her the name and city of the furniture store they had in mind to go, and she would get the information to Laura so she could call the store and set up the "shopping spree 'credit'!" Julie told them to let her know if they needed her to get store options.
Julie also explained that Laura would take some photos of the "new collection" when she saw it in about 2 weeks, and said it was up to them if they wanted to wait on that. Julie said, "You may want to shop now and then pick up some more pieces down the line? Whatever works best for you!"

In an email dated November 13, 2008, Wendy Douglas of Discovery informed Jon and Kate that they were working hard on a plan for the "Ethan Allan" shoot, and to please give her possible dates to go to the Ethan Allan store at King of Prussia and a date for a consultant to go to their house to give them advice for furniture. She stated that once they had dates, they could confirm the shoot and "get you some furniture!!! Gorgeous furniture from Ethan Allan!"

THE BOOK SERIES

In their ongoing and unrelenting efforts to squeeze every last drop of usefulness out of the kids, Kate and Julie May tried to pimp out Mady and Cara, two 8-year-old girls, to write a SERIES of children's books. They had this "right" built into an amended Discovery contract." Julie May sent the amendment that would give Cara and Mady the right to do children's books (including any sequels, which could be a series) to Kate on December 26, 2008. Julie told Kate if she could please sign, scan and email, she would get the documents back for signature and set up the "Cara/Mady project" in early 2009.

THE GOSSELIN GAME

There had been talk about exploiting the Gosselin children in a new and exciting way by developing an iPhone game about them. This is a partial description of the game.

Jon & Kate Plus 8 Game

> In the game, the object is to make your way through the day while keeping all 8 of the kids entertained, fed, and organized until bedtime so you can finally get some rest.

> The game would start with the player taking on the roll of Kate on Monday morning. The player needs to get through 7 day/night cycles to win the games first level. Each level will not only be separated by days, but each day will also be separated in sections like breakfast, lunch and dinner time, with bedtime being the goal the player needs to reach each day.

> Week one is about basic daily life in the Gosselin house, with getting the twins ready for school and getting the sextuplets awake and ready for breakfast and to start their day. Each of the Gosselin kids will have their own timer, where they will get antsy, start crying and even have a full blown tantrum if they're left alone for too long without getting what they need.

There will also be special actions that will have to be managed or prepared for, i.e. getting the children ready to go to the park, go to school or be picked up by the nanny, or hooking up a new television for the children to watch.

Jon and Kate will act as a tag team, where on alternate days the player (either Jon or Kate) will only be able to get the others help for a limited amount of time. When both of them are taking care of the kids, the player gets a time bonus, as there will be less running around to do.

Kate could barely contain her excitement over the possibility of this game. She exclaimed, "Sounds fun! Do it!!!!" to Julie May and Jon.

FREEBIES

"All mine. All mine as far as the eye can see."
– Kate Gosselin

I could write page after page about Kate asking for and getting everything for free, but my words would be written off by Kate and Discovery as more lies. So instead of simply listing and describing all the freebies that were showered upon Kate and the Gosselins, I will provide specific details straight from the sources so you don't have to take my word for it.

This is my reporting entry for *US Weekly* detailing just one occurrence of Kate expecting and demanding goods for free. Her words and actions paint a very clear picture of how she views herself.

A clerk at a local department store had an amusing experience with 'Kate the celebrity' as she put it to me in 2009. She was working the makeup counter and Kate was there for almost an hour testing products and asking for free samples of everything. Then, when the clerk totaled up her bill, Kate demanded to see the store manager to ask why she was being charged so much. When the manager told Kate that that's what the items cost, Kate laughed and told them that she was Kate Gosselin and she's on television and she's not used to paying for things.

Kate stormed off telling them that she would never shop there again. This was a store that, years before donated thousands of dollars worth of clothing and furniture to Kate, when she may have actually needed it for her kids.

The remainder of this chapter summarizes numerous emails to and from Kate, and occasionally Jon, about goods and services that were offered to, and almost always accepted by, the Gosselins. I have copies of every email I have summarized here, but due to legal concerns, I have not reprinted all of them in their entirety. I have included dates of the emails, the names of senders (in some cases, I have included only first names and a last initial), and pertinent text, along with responses from Kate. I have not included email addresses from private citizens not associated with a company.

Pay close attention to the dates of the offers, then read "The Lies and Times of Kate Gosselin" to see how the dates coincide with the times she was crying poor during her church speaking engagements.

HAIR PLUGS

Kate received an email from Dr. Jae Pak of the New Hair Institute offering to donate his services for free hair plugs for Jon. She sounded very excited when she forwarded the email to producer Jen Stocks. She said "YEAH!!!!!!! Ye-HAW!!!!!!!" and asked Jen when they could schedule it. She wanted to know if they were doing it on their own or filming it, but either way there were going to do it.

CONDOS

On June 24, 2008, Jon forwarded an email to Kate from a fan that was offering Jon and Kate the use of two condos on the beach in the Caribbean. Jon asked Kate, "After Hawaii how about this place for a winter retreat."

In her email, "Lois F" explained that she and her husband loved *Jon & Kate Plus Ei8ht*. She said they had recently purchased a condo in the Caribbean on an island called Isla Mujeres off the coast of Cancun. She described it as a three-bedroom condo right on the beach with beautiful views from every room. Lois F said her sister had also purchased a condo on the same floor as hers, and Lois thought it would be a wonderful place to film a show of Jon and Kate and the children on vacation. She said that between the two condos there were six bedrooms and four bathrooms and that they were the only condos on the third floor so they would have the entire floor to themselves.

Lois then described some possible opportunities for filming the children, including a small turtle farm, a dolphin discovery program, and a small and very colorful town. Sheesh. Even perfect strangers were coming up ideas for filming the crap out of the kids.

After learning of the offer, Kate gave Jon her standard response to all things free: "Yes please!!!!!"

SAGGY BAGGIES

Kate was THIS close to ditching Dr. Glassman's magic touch to get her "saggy baggies" done for an all-expense-paid trip to San Diego to have the surgery. Could it be possible that she just didn't want the procedure filmed?

On June 24, 2008, Jon sent along an email to Kate from "Tricia," patient care coordinator at Brucker Plastic Surgery in San Diego. The subject line in Tricia's email was "Breast lift surgery". Tricia explained that she was a fan of their show and their "beautiful children!" and she had seen the tummy tuck episode where the surgeon had dismissed Kate's request for a mastopexy (breast lift). She said she had spoken to her employer, Dr. Michael Brucker, who was one of the "premier plastic surgeons in La Jolla", about Kate's situation. She wrote that if Kate was still considering a "mastopexy and/or augmentation procedure" and she wouldn't mind a portion being filmed, Dr. Brucker would be more than happy to offer his services at no charge to complete her "mommy make-over." Tricia also said that if Jon were considering any cosmetic procedure, it would be their pleasure to extend their services to him at no charge. She said they would also cover Kate's (or Jon and Kate's) stay at The Hideaway, which is a retreat for patients recovering from cosmetic surgery.

Kate responded to Jon that she had just been obsessing about "my saggy baggies!!!!!" She said, "Wanna go..... Or stick to Dr Glassman and NOT film!????"

LANDSCAPING AND FENCING

This email exchange between Kate's bodyguard, Steve Neild, and her manager, Julie May, is interesting because it shows that Steve was involved in getting landscaping and fencing estimates for Kate in October 2008. This was around the same time that Jon said that Kate told him their marriage was over. It also shows that Discovery was paying for everything, as usual.

On October 6, 2008, Steve sent Julie May a quote for fencing from Amity Fencing. He told her there was a choice of either three plank or four plank horse style fencing. He said he had also gotten a quote for "just the area across the front to the driveway entrance and then down the horse driveway to the barn" and additional fencing if they wanted to fence the rest of the road frontage. Steve said it was not necessary to do that if they could create the smaller secure area. He thought it might be a good concession to make to DCL, to show they were prepared to save them some money.

Steve told Julie that this was their first quote so they might be able to go back to the fencing company and ask for a better price. He also explained to Julie that the price did not include the cost for Jon and Kate's contractor to build stone pillars around the steel post gate supports, or additional wiring out to the gate if required. Julie replied to Steve thanking him for the information. She told him she would get it to Discovery, but she would love to get them the quotes all at once, including the landscaping related to security.

MAKEUP OF THE RICH AND "GEORGOUS"

A series of emails between Kate and the president/creator of Mally Beauty sounded like an over-the-top meeting of a mutual admiration society. It was mutual as long as "Mally R" continued to shower Kate with free beauty products, that is.

On December 8, 2008, at 12:34 PM, Kate checked in with Mally to see if she had mailed Kate her latest shipment of beauty in a box. She said that she was "so so low on supply" and that it was scary because "I NEED to be beautiful, as you know!" Kate also said that if the shipment had not been sent yet, she could use some more of the light pink natural eye shadow called "natural2knockout".

At 1:12 PM that same day, Mally R wrote to Kate that her shipment was on the way. She told Kate, "P.s. you are already beautiful!!!!!!!!!!!!!!!!"

Kate replied to Mally at 1:17 PM, telling her "You are marvelous.... And georgous indeed!". She said she had run into some PR people who had met Mally, and "they all say you are SO georgous! :)".

On December 29, 2008, Mally sent Kate a note wishing her "Merry Christmas, Beautiful!" and asked if she had gotten her stuff. She told Kate she had some new things to send her as well.

Kate thanked Mally and said she had received the shipment. She then asked if Mally could include lots of medium foundation/powder in the shipment of new stuff she was going to send. Kate told her that she loved the holiday colored lip gloss she had received. She signed off telling Mally, "you're.... Georgous as usual! :)".

(Note to Kate: It's gorgeous; not georgous. Don't blame spell-check. You misspell it always and everywhere.)

ANN TAYLOR

The Devil wears Ann Taylor, but only if the clothing is free. On Wednesday, December 17, 2008, Kate sent an email to Kate Foster, an Ann Taylor representative, to tell her how much she enjoyed her recent "shopping jaunt" to the Loft. Kate said that she had sadly spent the entire gift card quickly and had made appearances at Lofts in "Louisianna, New York City and Lansing, Michigan!!!!" Kate said that the store employees "are never shocked to see me seeing as they ALL know that all I wear is the Loft!!! :)". She then wondered if there was "a card refill on the horizon?" and said that she loved wearing a new outfit for each book signing.

Kate gushed that she was "shocked and amazed at the skinny jeans you sent in a size 27. Can't find them around here and LOVE the skinny fit!!!!"

Kate Foster said that she would be happy to keep the cards coming. She said, "Let's make a deal...I'd love to do a press segment...perhaps you shopping with an entertainment or morning show at LOFT with our designer?" She then asked Kate if she had a publicist or producer that she should discuss this with, or if Kate made those decisions. She told Kate she could send out a card next week, and wanted to know what Kate thought she would need on an ongoing basis.

Kate sent Julie May the response from Kate Foster and asked if they could do this because she wanted that "supply to keep coming!!!!" She told Julie she wanted to do "whatever it takes... I obviously love their stuff **and spend AT LEAST $500 per week there**."

GYMBOREE

On Wednesday, December 31, 2008, at 4:23 AM on **New Year's Eve,** Kate sent a last-minute request to Juliet Montague of Gymboree requesting free stuff. Kate said she knew it was New Year's Eve, but she was hoping Juliet would be willing to call in a gift card number to the Wyomissing Gymboree so she could pick up "some fresh stuff for our resume of filming" on Friday. Kate said they had been off for the "last three weeks- yeah!" She also told Juliet that she needed some things for Cara for her ski trip to Utah, which was also being filmed. Kate thanked Juliet and said she hoped to hear from her soon before the stores close.

Juliet replied to Kate telling her she would definitely call in the gift card for her. Kate emailed Juliet again the next day wishing her a happy 2009. She thanked her for "fixing yesterday's issues!" and then continued on to tell Juliet that she had a handful of items on hold at the Park City Mall in Lancaster, PA. Kate was far too busy to go pick up the freebies herself, so she said she was going to send a film crewmember to pick up the things she needed the next day for the next day's shoot. Kate said that she also had an item on hold at the Berkshire Mall in Wyomissing, and the crewmember would be picking that up as well. Kate told Juliet that the total of items was less than 10, and asked if it would be possible for her to supply those stores with a gift card number. She told Juliet that the crewmember would probably get to Lancaster around 11:15 Pennsylvania time, and to the Wyomissing store some time after that.

On yet another occasion, Kate desperately cried to the Gymboree representative that she needed more money on her card. She said, "I'm over my gift card amount....help! Please call the shoppes To tell them what to do?!"

CREST WHITESTRIPS

There was nothing too big or too small for Kate to try to get for FREE. In this case, she had received some Crest Whitestrips and needed more. She raved to her contact, "Katie," about how wonderful and "amazing" the dry whitestrips are and told her that all the types she sent her were "more than wonderful." She told "Katie" that whenever anyone asks her about her white teeth she tells them about how great the Crest Whitestrips are. She then told "Katie" that "any more supply" along with those "amazing Olay daily facials" would "always be much appreciated!" Kate cheerily signed off with a "Thanks again! Have a white (teeth) day! :)".

FREEBIES, FREEBIES EVERYWHERE!

So much free merchandise was rolling into the Gosselin house that Kate couldn't keep track of it all. On January 20, 2009, at 11:34 AM, "Amanda B" from Media Motion International sent an email asking Kate if they had received the "Honest Tea merchandise?"
Kate replied that she thought so because she saw some in their cabinets. She then asked Jon if they had received it. Kate also said that she would "love all that they would send" because "We love love love their stuff!"

NIAGARA FALLS

On February 6, 2009, Julie May wrote to Kate about an offer for a "trip situation" to "Niagra" Falls. Julie told Kate that it might be a possibility for the summer since Kate had mentioned "Niagra" Falls as a fun destination. Julie said she was keeping a "stack of possible things" so she wanted to pass it along.
Kate responded, as usual, with a "Yes please!" and suggested that they go in early June right after school got out.

ELECTRIC FENCE

On March 17, 2009, an offer came in from a company in Reading, PA, who wanted to donate invisible fencing for the new puppies at the Gosselin's million-dollar compound. Kate accepted immediately, saying, "yes... asap! They ran three miles away the other day!!!"

LASIK SURGERY

On April 3, 2009, Julie May forwarded Kate an email that had originated on March 27, 2009, from "Liana M" on behalf of Dr. Robert Maloney, a "world-renown" ophthalmologist. Liana said that Dr. Maloney had followed Jon and Kate's story and noticed that Jon struggled with glasses. She said the doctor wanted to talk to Jon about LASIK surgery, and if Jon were a candidate, he would fly him to Los Angeles and do the surgery for free. Julie May forwarded the information to Kate on April 3, 2009.

This offer for free LASIK surgery came in for Jon only, but Kate hijacked it for herself as well. She replied to Julie with a "yes please for both." Kate then said she had always wanted LASIK and she could get it done on one of her trips to Los Angeles.

TOILET PAPER

On April 14, 2009, "Joni S" from Discovery sent some good news about free toilet paper. Who wouldn't want that? She said that Ad Sales had just sent a bunch of Charmin their way, and asked them to confirm that they received it at their Sinking Spring address.

Kate didn't know if they had received the Charmin, so she replied, "I have not . . . Jon have you?"

CAMPING EQUIPMENT

On May 20, 2009, at 2:04 PM, good old Joni from Discovery sent an email telling Jon and Kate to be on the lookout for free camping equipment that was being delivered to their home for filming of the backyard campout episode. Joni said she wanted to give them a heads up that the camping equipment was headed their way via their Sinking Spring address.

DIVORCE, REALITY STYLE

"Jonathan – I am so very thankful for you.
Thanks for taking care of me, loving me and for
brightening my day each & every day. And especially thanks
for helping me and working together with me so we can be
a successful team ... at least until we're 100! :)
Thanks (ahead of time) for taking me to Hawaii and marrying me! :)
I love you so much!"
– Me

In looking at Kate's writings, it would appear that Kate at one time really did love Jon, and Jon really did love Kate. Kate was still speaking lovingly about Jon in her journal as late as July 2007. Kate has said repeatedly that the filming of her family for the television show had nothing to do with their marriage falling apart, and ultimately ending, but it seems that the love stopped right around the time that the filming started.

In Kate's journal she wrote that Sidney Portiere quoted his father as saying that "the measure of a man is how well he takes care of his children' and that made her think of Jon!

Kate said about Jon in *Multiple Blessings* that it struck her as very impressive how he was capable of bathing, feeding, swaddling, diapering, dressing and entertaining to infants all day long and then going to work all night.

In *Eight Little Faces*, Kate wrote about Jon that he is her balance, her strength and her stability.

So what happened that got them to this point, when Kate said this to Jon? "I am not going away so you can either do the stuff I ask or live miserably!

As soon as Jon finally stood up to Kate and refused to participate in taking money from well-meaning people at church speaking engagements, the marriage was over. The moment he wanted the filming to stop, Kate no longer had a need for him. She came to view him as an enemy who threatened to destroy the rich dream world she had so carefully built.

THE MARRIAGE CONTRACT

Back in late 2007 to mid 2008, Jon went to Kate and said he wouldn't be going along on any more speaking engagements at churches or conferences because he just couldn't do it anymore. His conscience was eating at him (believe it or not). That's when Kate told him that their marriage was over and that she wanted to live separate lives, except for filming the show. Kate gave Jon Carte blanche to see other women and do whatever he wanted, as long as he was present and on time for filming. She told Jon that he could date whomever he wanted and do whatever he wanted on non-filming days, as long as he was in front of those cameras when the crew came to town. She used the words "open marriage" to Jon.

Kate's brother and sister-in-law spoke about this arrangement and a "marriage contract" during interviews, but they were ridiculed and criticized as trying to cash in on Kate's fame. I have never spoken to either of them, but here is what they said in their interviews.

> "All we know is what Jon told us, that Kate came to him with a contract saying he could have girlfriends and that he can do his own thing. In exchange, Jon needs to show up for filming. But otherwise he has the freedom, certain days, to do whatever he wants."

The actual "marriage contract" is a document that I would obviously love to get my hands on, but as of now, I haven't seen it, so I can't say for certain if it even exists at all. Jon told me about it as well, and described it to me, but again, I haven't seen it. I'll keep looking.

Kate wanted to continue to deceive the world by pretending that they were still one big happy family. Jon didn't want that, and he begged Kate to go to marriage counseling, but in true Kate fashion, she told Jon that she didn't want or need counseling of any kind. Jon told me on countless occasions that every time he suggested counseling to Kate, she told him "no." She said, "If something is wrong with you, you should go and fix it." Jon did go to counseling and therapy to try to "fix" himself. He spent a small fortune on it. I can prove this because I have copies of the invoices from the counseling sessions.

The marriage of Jon and Kate was over well before they ever moved into their new $1.3 million dollar house on Heffner Road. The house appealed to them because of the apartment above the garage. Jon's apartment. Jon never even got to sleep in the master bedroom.

It is impossible to know how long this scheme to deceive the viewers would have continued had it not been for the *US Weekly* cover of Jon and Deanna Hummel. Kate and Discovery were prepared to ride this wave of lies all the way to the bank for as long as they possibly could.

DISCOVERY BACKED KATE FROM DAY ONE

There were 34 different T-shirt ideas designed to promote *Jon & Kate Plus Ei8ht.* One pictured Kate's glowing, smiling face with the tagline "Kate Is My Role Model".

That slogan sounds about right coming from the company that brought us such heart-warming characters as Lori, who sleeps with her blow dryer; Kesha, who eats toilet paper; Rhonda, the thumb sucker; Crystal, who eats household cleanser; Tempesst, who eats detergent and soap; Haley, who pulls out her own hair and eats the follicles; Lauren, who runs around wearing a fur rabbit suit; Davecat, who has a silicon wife; Rachel, the compulsive scab picker; Nathaniel, who has sex with his car; and my favorite, Adele, who eats couch cushions.

TLC: The Learning Channel. TLC: the network that brought us toddlers wearing Madonna-like cone bras, polygamists, midgets, circus freaks, hoarders, and yes – Kate Gosselin.

So out of 34 T-shirt designs, you would think that, if there were several for Kate alone, there would be at least one shirt devoted solely to Jon. This would not be the case, of course, if Discovery knew from the beginning that Kate was their girl and Jon was just a fringe necessity.

The first sign that Discovery was hooking their wagon to Kate dates back to the very first Discovery contract signed by Jon and Kate for the first season of *Jon & Kate Plus Ei8ht*. It's an early "red line" version of the contract; the one where they make changes. Kate has always been in control of the family "business," and she was the negotiator for the family during this first contract signing.

Clause 3 dealing with "Compensation" on the rough draft says that all compensation payable to the Gosselin family for their services shall be made payable to ~~Jon and~~ Kate Gosselin.

It is very interesting and telling that Jon's name was scratched out on the compensation part of the contract, leaving Kate to control the family fortune. Was this just a minor detail, or was it something that foretold things to come between Kate Gosselin and Discovery Talent Services, LLC?

Clause 8, Representations and Warranties; Indemnity, of Exhibit A, STANDARD TERMS AND CONDITIONS, of the contract, read "Company hereby agrees to at all times defend and indemnify **Family** from any and all claims, damages, or other liabilities ..." It would have been more accurate if the name "Kate Gosselin" rather than "Family" had been inserted there instead.

In 2009, once Kate and Discovery decided Jon was a "liability," they went into a full-court press to "defend and indemnify" Kate from Jon's claims, as well as those from the media and viewing public.

Jon wanted the show to stop to save his children, or for whatever other reason he may have had in his head at the time. It was well within his right as a parent to stop the filming; that had been agreed upon from the very beginning. Even Kate confirmed this many times. She said, "If either parent wants the filming to stop, then the filming would stop. Period."

Still, Jon went along with Kate's plan for a while, as he had done so many times before. He laid low for a few months, but he couldn't deal with the kids filming anymore. That's when it hit him. "It's right there in the contract," he thought, under the heading "Termination." Jon would get the show stopped indirectly, by his actions. The Termination clause of the contract included wording that said that Discovery could terminate his contract for making disparaging remarks about the program, insubordination, dishonesty, intoxication or failure to perform services or for failure to conduct himself with due regard to social conventions or public morals or decency, or for actions that bring family into public disrepute, contempt, scandal or ridicule.

Reading that one clause, it would appear that Jon had clearly violated the terms of the Agreement. Jon had made disparaging remarks about the Program, Company and/or Producer. He was insubordinate in that he didn't show up to film his interviews when he was scheduled to do so. He was at times dishonest and intoxicated. He didn't always conduct himself with "due regard to social conventions or public morals or decency" (whatever that even means).

It would appear that Jon did everything he could to get this show stopped long before he tweeted the following in October 2010 about the show doing harm to his children:

> "Due to the overwhelming amount of questions, statements, false statements in the media, I would like to clarify a few things.
>
> "First and foremost, for people who did not watch *Jon & Kate Plus Ei8ht*, I stated years ago, and on television, that I no longer wanted to film and wanted my privacy back. This is not a decision I made lightly or without weighing all the factors involved.
>
> "The negative effects on my family was my greatest concern and far outweigh any monetary gain we received. Today, my children are much older than when we first started. They are acutely aware their life is markedly different from their peers.
>
> "They are six, and ten, and have to deal with paparazzi! They can't visit a public place without a crowd gathering or people snapping pictures with cell phones.
>
> "Whether the children want to film or not is completely irrelevant.
>
> "Children rely on the guidance of the adults to ensure their best interest. Left to their own most children would not eat properly, visit the dentist, or complete homework. Do you think a child would choose a day on the beach instead of school?
>
> "Is this the best thing for them? Is it the child's decision to make? Of course not.
>
> "I am acutely aware of the mistakes I made in 2009 and I am ashamed of the choices I made. I have apologized to Kate, my family, and to my friends. Through counseling I have learned to own my actions. My goal is to move forward in a positive direction.

"Lastly, my children have experienced a lot of life changes in a short period of time; new home, new school, parents divorced, increased media attention, and much more.

"Obviously it would be inaccurate and short-sighted to declare that all of their current struggles are attributed to one factor. These multiple changes are exactly why I feel they need privacy, stability, and security.

"Filming and displaying their private lives at this time is not in their best interest."

Given that Jon had so clearly violated many of the conditions in the Termination clause, why didn't Discovery terminate the contract, or at least let Jon and the kids walk away? Knowing what they knew about what was going on behind the scenes with the Gosselin family, why did Discovery continue to keep them under contract and film them like they were a normal, happy, albeit dysfunctional, family? Why did they continue this very public lie and take them to Hawaii, to film, of all things, a renewal of their marriage vows when they knew that Jon and Kate were quietly at war behind the scenes about keeping their marriage and the show going? Why did they continue filming if they knew it was all a big lie?

So many questions. And the answer to each one of them is easy. Money.

Discovery and TLC were making millions and millions of dollars off of this family and this show, and there was nothing in the world that was going to stop them from continuing to do so; certainly not Jon Gosselin.

After all, Kate was their girl, and she was ready and willing to allow them to continue to film the kids as much as they wanted. So Discovery formulated a plan to spin and lie and manipulate audience perception through the editing of the show. They gave Kate her scripts of talking points to steer the story through the media in the direction that they (Discovery) wanted, to keep things moving in the direction that they wanted, and to keep the money pouring in. They fed stories to the media to damage Jon and to make Kate look like an innocent victim, all the while knowing that they were lying.

The final episode of *Jon & Kate Plus Ei8ht* was so blatantly edited to show Jon in a bad light, while making Kate look like the loving, innocent victim of Jon's bad behavior, that it would have been laughable had it not been so sad and damaging for Jon. When I watched it for the first time – after being involved with this story and having firsthand knowledge of what was really going on – I saw that it was clearly intended to make it look like "Jon is mean to the twins and Kate is soft and gentle."

TLC has hours and hours of footage of Kate behaving the exact same way as Jon did in that episode; far worse, they have footage of her being cruel to the children. But they chose to bury Jon for his defiant behavior and canonize Kate because they knew that Kate alone wanted the show to go on, and the filming to continue – without Jon, and they wanted to milk that for all it was worth. They needed the public to support Kate and follow her to TLC's next show, *Kate Plus Ei8ht*, so that the money would keep flowing.

Discovery wasn't about to give up on their biggest cash cow, Kate Gosselin, so once it was clear that filming *Jon & Kate Plus Ei8ht* with Jon was no longer an option, they hunkered down, regrouped and hatched the plan to make Jon the bad guy and to make Kate look like the scared, hurt little victim, wondering how she was going to take care of her children all by herself … all alone, with no money. In their quest to paint Kate as a sympathetic figure, the biggest lie of all in the divorce proceedings was still to come.

THE SPIN

Discovery controlled EVERY aspect of Jon and Kate Gosselin's divorce "storyline." After Jon exposed the lies of their "happy marriage" by being seen out and about with women other than his loving wife, Discovery went into full damage control mode. If they weren't already completely behind Kate as their bread-winning star, they sure were at this point.

On May 4, 2009, Jennifer E. Williams, Director of Talent Relations Business and Legal Affairs for Discovery, sent Julie May a certified letter regarding their "outrage" at Jon's behavior. She copied Eileen O'Neill, President and General Manager of TLC; Edward Sabin, COO of TLC; and Laurie Goldberg, Senior Vice President, Communications of TLC.

Discovery decided what Kate was going to say regarding the divorce, and everything else, and when she was going to say it. Their first order of business was to convince the world that Jon was having affairs and stealing money, and that Kate had no choice but to file for divorce from him, "to protect her children." They did this even though they knew that Jon and Kate were no longer happily married, and hadn't been for some time.

The next step was for Discovery to exploit this tragic family situation to garner huge ratings and, thus, profit for themselves. Discovery wanted Jon and Kate to sit down in front of a television camera and answer painful questions about their most private troubles, for the entire world to see. Surely, any couple that is hostile to one another and about to go into a huge public divorce would want to do that first, right? Kate was completely on board with the idea, of course, but Jon wanted nothing to do with it.

It didn't matter what Jon did or did not want. On June 14, 2009, Julie May sent an email listing Discovery's 20 possible interview questions for Jon. That same evening, Jon informed his attorney that he told Julie he wasn't going to answer any of the questions. He said, "The network is glorifying my divorce!!!"

These are some of the interview questions Discovery wanted Jon and Kate to answer:

How did you tell the kids?
How are they doing?
How will this change your day to day with the kids?
Where will the kids live?
Will you move from the house that you just bought?

Where are you living?

Have you already been separate? Was it earlier than reported in the press?

You renewed your vows in Hawaii. Was that real?

Did you consider marriage counseling or therapy?

Will your series continue and how?

Will you be stronger and happier apart than together?

What are your arrangements moving forward?

Will you be stronger and happier apart?

What would you have changed looking back?

Do you blame anyone?

Is there anything you would like to discuss or clear the air about?

For any normal person, the idea of sitting down in front of millions of people and answering these very personal questions would be humiliating. Jon wanted nothing to do with it, but that didn't really matter to Discovery because Jon was under contract to do everything they asked him to do.

Even their manager, Julie May, thought it would be a bad idea to film Jon or Kate answering questions about their divorce so soon, but Discovery was determined that they would do just that. Julie May wrote to Jon that she had made it "VERY" clear that she didn't think he and Kate were ready to sit down and do an interview together. She added, "but they are indicating that they would still like you to do so."

If you were a fan of the show, or just an interested observer at that time, you already know that Discovery won that battle. Jon and Kate did, in fact, sit down together to answer questions on camera. And that episode of *Jon & Kate Plus Ei8ht* became their highest rated ever. Approximately 10 million viewers tuned in to see the Gosselin divorce disaster unfold.

When it came time for the actual filing of the divorce, Discovery really began manipulating the situation behind the scenes, in favor of Kate over Jon. This was war, and the party with the biggest guns (lawyers) was going to win in a landslide. Kate had the full muscle of Discovery's legal department and Public Relations team standing behind her, and Jon, well, he didn't. He never stood a chance.

As the following series of emails demonstrates, Discovery's lawyers changed the rules of the game, on the fly, leaving Jon's lawyer shaking his head and feeling foolish. It's no wonder he got out.

Jon's attorney, Charlie Meyer, sent an email to one of Kate's attorneys, Cheryl Young, to let her know he had drafted a rough statement that would need to be released at the same time as the filing of the divorce complaint. He said if Kate approved of the statement, there might still have to be some minor tweaks. He then told Cheryl that they wanted the statement released by TLC. Charlie actually thought he would be dictating something regarding this divorce process to Discovery. Sorry, Charlie. This is Charlie's rough draft of the statement:

"**Jon and Kate have mutually decided** to move forward with their lives.
In Pennsylvania, one of the parties has to be the one to file for divorce and it was decided that Jon would do so.

> The allegations in the divorce complaint filed by Jon merely are
> a formality, and Kate has or shortly will be filing an answer
> admitting those allegations.
>
> The parties will continue to do everything they can to be good
> parents to the children, to put the children's well-being above
> everything else, and to support the other party as the parent to
> their children."

Charlie also sent Julie May this same statement he had prepared for the media regarding the divorce, changing the word "allegations" to "statements", and asked her to let him know what she thought of it. At this point, **Jon and Kate had mutually decided that Jon would be the one to actually file for divorce**, because it is a requirement in Pennsylvania that one of the parties has to be the one to file.

On Thursday, June 18, 2009, Julie May sent an email to the attorneys for both sides to pass along the news that the network was concerned that the timing of the divorce filing was messing up their already-finished episodes of *Jon & Kate Plus Ei8ht*. Julie said the network was worried that the announcement on the show wouldn't match the press reports about the filing and the show would be outdated when the news broke. She said the network suggested that if the plan was to file on Monday, they wanted Jon and Kate to do a brief "pick up" interview or maybe some voiceover lines they could add to cover the new information. They even suggested delaying the filing of the divorce papers so they could incorporate it into future episodes.

That same day, Cheryl Young replied to Julie May and Charlie, telling them that Kate wanted the filing to occur on Monday. She told them she would double-check that with her based on concerns from the network.

You can imagine Charlie's surprise, then, when he received a network-approved statement that had been prepared for Jon. As you can see, it is a bit different from Charlie's original draft. This is what Discovery wanted, and this is what Discovery got.

> "This afternoon, **Kate filed for divorce.** Our kids are still my
> number one priority. I love them and want to make sure they stay
> happy, healthy and safe. My job is being the best, most
> supportive and loving father that I can be to my kids, and not
> being married to Kate doesn't change that. This will be a
> difficult transition for all of us, but Kate and I will work out
> a schedule that enables our kids to have plenty of quality time
> with both of us at home in Pennsylvania. In terms of my marriage,
> it's no secret that the past six months or so have been very
> difficult for Kate and me. We are no different than other couples
> and parents who are facing a crossroads in their marriage. I am
> of course deeply saddened that we are divorcing."

Charlie was then caught off guard by Kate and Discovery, who had gone to their favorite media outlet, *People* magazine, and released their own story. It was a Discovery-generated spin fest. Remember, Jon and Kate both originally agreed that, as a formality, Jon would be the one to actually file for divorce. But Discovery stepped in and created a complete fabrication to further their own agenda.

On Monday, June 22, 2009, at 10:22 PM, Charlie sent the link to the *People* article to his associates and Jon (http://www.people.com/people/article/0,,20286839,00.html).

Charlie said, "I didn't think she was going to make a statement."

Charlie also emailed Cheryl Young that same night at 10:23 PM about Kate's statement and included the *People* link (http://www.people.com/people/article/0,,20286839,00.html.) He said, "I thought the statement was coming from you. That wasn't very vague."

It became apparent that Discovery was controlling the situation and standing by Kate. Charlie told Cheryl that it was interesting that the network had changed Kate's statement based on the fact that Jon was going to make a statement. He also said that Kate's statement was stronger than he was told it was going to be.

Cheryl replied to Charlie on June 22, 2009, at 10:25 PM, saying, "I thought so, too". She explained that the network changed Kate's statement because of Jon's statement. She told Charlie she would discuss it with him the next day.

That same evening, at 10:27 PM, Charlie's associate, Kimberly Kress, sent out an email to Charlie, Jon and some others involved with the case to keep them abreast of the changing situation. Kimberly said she thought it was good that they had put out the official statement from Jon first. She also said that even though this was Jon's official statement, she didn't think anyone (meaning TLC) should be issuing it to other press outlets on his behalf. Kimberly predicted that the TLC public relation's phone would be "ringing off the hook tomorrow with press requests."

As if things weren't convoluted enough, another attorney for Jon, Richard Hofstetter of the firm Frankfurt Kurnit Klein & Selz PC, joined the party. He said he was unhappy that TLC was not keeping them informed about major decisions such as the show's hiatus. He said he spoke to Edward Sabin and told him very clearly that it was unacceptable and disrespectful that they learned about the show's hiatus from a general press release instead of being told in advance by TLC. Sabin blamed it on a last-minute "broadcast pattern situation".

Discovery was clearly the big player in this game, and they were dictating everything, including having the right to "approve" or not, Jon's statements to the press.

Here is an excerpt from the *People* magazine article:

Kate Gosselin on Divorce: 'Jon Left Me No Choice'
Update Tuesday June 23, 2009 09:20 AM EDT

> **"Over the course of this weekend, Jon's activities have left me no choice but to file legal procedures in order to protect myself and our children," Kate said in a statement Monday night. "While there are reasons why it was appropriate and necessary for me to initiate this proceeding,** I do not wish to discuss those reasons at this time, in the hope that all issues will be resolved amicably between Jon and myself. As always, my first priority remains our children."

So, to recap, in reality, the divorce was going to be a mutual decision made by Jon and Kate, with both of them deciding together, as a formality, that Jon would be the one to file the papers. When Discovery got wind of that plan they immediately put a stop to it because, of course, it wouldn't portray Kate in a light that would allow TLC's biggest star to move forward and into their next money-making venture – *Kate Plus Ei8ht*.

So Discovery did an end-around and released their spin through *People* magazine, who always seemed to be the one to break the big Kate Gosselin news and to "set the record straight," according to Kate and Discovery. Discovery also forced Jon to sit by as Kate announced the big lie to the *Jon & Kate Plus Ei8ht* viewing audience. Discovery gave Kate her prepared statement and she memorized it, worked on it with her "media trainer" and, in less than four takes on the interview couch, delivered the big lie.

If any further proof is needed to support the claim that Jon was originally supposed to be the one filing for divorce from Kate, the Divorce petition confirms it. Here is the original Divorce petition, with some private information redacted.

ELLIOTT GREENLEAF & SIEDZIKOWSKI, P.e.
By: CHARLES J. MEYER, ESQUIRE
Identification No. 58484
925 Harvest Drive, Suite 300
Blue Bell, P A 19422
Telephone: (215) 977-1041
Telecopy: (215) 977-1099

JONATHAN GOSSELIN
298 Heffner Road
Wernersville, PA 19565
Plaintiff,

vs.

KATE GOSSELIN
298 Heffner Road
Wernersville, PA 19565
Defendant.

Attorneys for Plaintiff
COURT OF COMMON PLEAS
MONTGOMERY COUNTY
PENNSYLVANIA
NO.
IN DIVORCE

COMPLAINT IN DIVORCE
Jonathan Gosselin, by his attorneys, Charles J. Meyer, Esquire, and Elliott
Greenleaf & Siedzikowski, P.C., respectfully represents:

1. Plaintiff is Jonathan Gosselin, who currently resides at 298 Heffner Road
in Wernersville, County of Berks, Pennsylvania.

2. Defendant is Kate, who currently resides at 298 Heffner Road in

Wernersville, County of Berks, Pennsylvania.

3. Plaintiff and Defendant are sui juris and both have been bona fide
residents of the Commonwealth of Pennsylvania for a period of more than six (6) months
immediately preceding the filing of this Complaint.

4. The parties were married on _____ , In _____ _

5. Neither Plaintiff nor Defendant is in the military or naval service of the United States or its allies within the provisions of the Soldiers' and Sailors' Civil Relief Act of the Congress of 1940 and its amendments.

6. There has been no prior action for divorce or annulment instituted by
either of the parties in this or any other jurisdiction.

7. The parties have agreed to submit to the jurisdiction and venue of this matter in the Court of Common Pleas of Montgomery County, Pennsylvania.

8. Plaintiff has been advised of the availability of counseling and of the right to request that the Court require the parties to participate in counseling.

COUNT I

REQUEST FOR A NO-FAULT DIVORCE
UNDER SECTION 3301(c) OF THE DIVORCE CODE

9. The prior paragraphs of this Complaint are incorporated herein by
reference as though set forth in full.

10. The marriage of the parties is irretrievably broken.
WHEREFORE, if both parties file affidavits consenting to a divorce after ninety (90) days have elapsed from the date of the filing of this Complaint, Plaintiff respectfully requests that the Court enter a decree of divorce pursuant to Section 3301 (c) of the Divorce Code, 23 Pa.C.S.A.

COUNT II

REQUEST FOR A NO-FAULT DIVORCE
UNDER SECTION 3301(d) OF THE DIVORCE CODE

11. The prior paragraphs of this Complaint are incorporated herein by
reference as though set forth in full.

12. The marriage of the parties is irretrievably broken.

13. **At the time of the hearing, Plaintiff will submit an affidavit alleging that**
the parties have lived separate and apart for at least two (2) years.
WHEREFORE, Plaintiff respectfully requests that the Court enter a decree of

divorce pursuant to Section 3301(d) of the Divorce Code, 23
Pa.C.S.A.

COUNT III

**REQUEST FOR EQUITABLE DISTRIBUTION OF
MARITAL PROPERTY UNDER
SECTION 3502 OF THE DIVORCE CODE**

14. The prior paragraphs of this Complaint are incorporated
herein by
reference as though set forth in full.

15. Plaintiff and Defendant have acquired marital property as
defined by the Divorce Code, which is subject to equitable
distribution pursuant to Section 3502 of the Divorce Code.

16. Plaintiff and Defendant have been unable to agree as to the
equitable
division of said property, as of the date of the filing of this
Complaint.

17. Plaintiff requests that the Court equitably divide,
distribute or assign the
marital property between the parties.

WHEREFORE, Plaintiff respectfully requests that the Court enter
an order of
equitable distribution of marital property pursuant to Section
3502 of the Divorce Code, 23 Pa.C.S.A.

-3-

COUNT IV
**REQUEST FOR APPROVAL OF ANY SETTLEMENT
AGREEMENT AND INCORPORATION THEREOF IN
DIVORCE DECREE UNDER SECTIONS 3104(a)(I) and (3),
AND 3323(b) OF THE DIVORCE CODE AND FOR OTHER RELIEF**

18. The prior paragraphs of this Complaint are incorporated
herein by
reference as though set forth in full.

19. While no settlement has been reached as of the date of the
filing of this
Complaint, Plaintiff is and has always been willing to negotiate
a fair and reasonable settlement of all matters with Defendant.

20. Although no written settlement agreement has been entered
into between
the parties as of the date of the filing of this Complaint, in
the event that a written settlement agreement is entered prior to
the final disposition of this action, Plaintiff desires that such
written settlement agreement be approved by the Court and
incorporated in any divorce decree which may be entered
dissolving the marriage between the parties.

WHEREFORE, if a written settlement agreement is reached between
the parties

On June 26, 2009, Laurie Goldberg of Discovery sent an email to Julie May, with a copy to Eileen O'Neil, passing along the official "agreed upon" statement that Jon and Kate would be releasing regarding their divorce. That's right. The network wrote Jon and Kate's official statement for them. You would think that something so personal, especially your divorce, would be handled by, you know, the people it's about. Laurie Goldberg asked Julie May to alert her when the statement had been posted onto Jon and Kate's website, and they would then post it on TLC's website. Laurie said they "would love to move as quickly as possible on this". Here is the statement about the divorce:

"During this very difficult time we will be working to focus solely
on the needs of our family. This includes no longer commenting
publicly or reacting to media stories and speculation. Our goal is to
do the very best for our children and that will be done as privately
as possible. We appreciate the understanding, support and well wishes
from so many. Thank you".

Once the media circus surrounding their divorce was in full swing, Kate went from interview to interview, telling the same big lie and drumming up more support for herself, while continuing to make Jon look like the bad guy. This must have been particularly painful to Jon since it was Kate who ended the marriage in the first place, at least a full year before it became public fodder. Using every available opportunity and resource in their campaign to discredit Jon, Discovery continued to use *People* magazine as a mouthpiece to spout their lies about the divorce.

People magazine deputy managing editor Peter Castro told "Good
Morning America" that the situation is "the portrait of an
American family crumbling." "They don't hate each other," he
said, but **"Jon did not want any part of counseling; he wanted out
of this marriage."**

Now, any reasonable person would have to ask this question: **How in the Hell would Peter Castro from *People* magazine know the first thing about what Jon Gosselin did or did not want?** He was simply regurgitating the untruths that had been fed to him by a "source." Count Mr. Castro as just another pawn under Discovery's control.

Discovery's handling and control of Jon and Kate's divorce was the deciding factor as to why Kate Gosselin is a millionaire and living in a mansion today, and Jon Gosselin is broke and struggling to make ends meet.

"MOMMY'S JOURNAL"

"… I need you to know, don't believe what you read
unless you hear it from that person."
– *Kate Gosselin*

Kate's journal is her collection of notes that she used to write her books, *Multiple Blessings* and *I Just Want You To Know – Letters To My Kids On Love, Faith, and Family*. I know this because I read every word in her journal over a two-day period. In doing research for this book, I also read her published works.

As I mentioned previously, I found Kate's journal while looking at information burned onto computer discs she had thrown in the trash. I fully understand and expect that some will question the authenticity of these journal entries. I can assure you they are genuine and will tell you that these same computer discs hold close to 5,000 Gosselin family photos and many, many personal documents and mementos, including tax and business records and personal and business contracts, all created, dated and burned to disc years before I ever heard the name Kate Gosselin.

For those who question whether her journal exists at all, Kate mentions it herself in this interview with *Cupcake MAG*, whose tagline seems very appropriate for a Kate Gosselin interview: "All things sugar coated & the sweet desire of fashion."

> "I Just Want You To Know was the combining of my journal I kept nearly daily while still married and before (Jon &) Kate plus 8 was a household name. It describes my struggles of that time with 8 young kids…"

Kate also describes her journal on page 176 of *I Just Want You To Know*:

Reading *I Just Want You To Know* was like reading her journal, in the same order, except that the published book was edited and polished by an editor who was skilled enough to make Kate sound like a decent human being. Now a word of caution: some of Kate's thoughts and writings are very disturbing, especially when she talks about harming her children. What shocked me the most as a parent was the fact that Kate would be foolish enough to actually document the beatings and humiliation she inflicted upon her children and husband – as if it were normal behavior – even in a place she thought was private. Surely she would have to consider that someday, someone beside herself might find her journal and read it. Unfortunately for the Gosselin children, this is their *normal*, as Kate reminds us over and over again.

Some might find Kate's actions to be normal parenting. It's up to you to decide. Keep in mind that the sextuplets were two years old at that point in time. My personal view on corporal punishment is that it should never be used to teach or discipline a child. Parenting is hard work, no doubt about it, but there are a hundred ways to teach discipline without becoming physical. I do believe, however, that Kate has the right to discipline her children in any way she sees fit, as long as that discipline does not cause them physical or emotional harm. But I don't believe she has the right to lie and blame Jon and the divorce for the kids' anger issues. The kids are angry and violent because that is how they were raised – with Kate's anger and violence imprinted upon them.

Kate's words are "an intimate look at the heart of a mother."

July 2006
Kate wrote that she was less than patient with her kids today. She gets so tired that her fuse is almost non-existent according to her. She knows that it's not fair to her children to have an impatient mother and she is aware of what she is doing when she is doing it. She wishes that she could stop and become patient.

July 2006
In detailing a trip, Kate writes that they had a great time. She said that the kids, with the exception of one of the twins who received a spanking when they got home for her behavior, were all well behaved and had fun!

July 2006
Kate said that little Alexis got injured and Collin brought her a drink without being asked to. She thought it was nice of him and she praised him because according to her he gets more negative attention than positive. She said he is so naughty and she really doesn't know how to handle him!!!!! She says that she needs to show him more love!!!!!

July 2006
Kate is sad because one of the twins commented to Jon and her separately about why Kate doesn't play with them. She made a sad face in her journal. ☹

July 2006
A memorable Sunday in the Gosselin house today according Kate. They didn't go to church of course but they cleaned the house and she and Jon didn't argue at all!!!!!

July 2006
The family went shopping at Target and got the usual stares. Most of the kids were very good except for one of the twins who was grouchy so she received a few spankings with something Kate calls 'the spanker' that has been added to the family van's emergency supply stash!!!! The spanked girl eventually happied up according to Kate.

July 2006
Kate used many exclamation points when discussing getting a glass of wine with dinner!!!!!

(Tummy tuck operation at Dr. Glassman's in New York)

August 2006
Kate and Jon stayed at hotel. She said the hotel is okay but seems very busy and the staff is not very nice. She can't complain though because they don't have to foot the bill. This is just another gracious gift from the Lord!

August 2006
Kate was grouchy because she didn't have breakfast or coffee. Nothing was written about her receiving a spanking though.
Kate realized that she and Jon rarely ever kiss because Jen the producer was excited about them filming their first on camera kiss like it was a milestone.

August 2006
Kate writes about the twins going off to kindergarten and that she'll feel sad and lonely and she is upset that this is a control issue that she can't control. She's excited to have her afternoons to herself now that the girls will be gone. She talks about how the kids love Jon and how much Jon loves his kids. More praying to God about asking for things and receiving them. "You have not because you ask not."

September 2006
Kate admits that she was a horrible mommy today and that she failed all the way. She was absolutely awful to Collin because apparently he was awful to her. She says that he does things just to irritate her. He's only two years old and Kate is beside herself because she can't 'control' him. She told him to sit in the corner a million times and he disregarded her. She admits to being to rough with him in front of the girls. She says she feels guilty for treating him like that and will try to be a better mommy tomorrow.
She says she can't explain it but she needs to pray for her relationship with Collin. She does love him but she doesn't understand him. She can't understand or explain his frustration and she doesn't know what he wants. He just starts shrieking and she ignores him a lot. She admits that Collin is a sweet, cute and smart boy but she just doesn't understand him! She prays to the Lord for her to be able to understand him and to feel only love for him. She asks the Lord to help her to be slow to wrath with him. She also prays for help to be able to take time to play with her children.

September 2006
Kate talks about her bliss-less childhood and adult life and how much she loved her grandparents.

September 11, 2006
Kate takes time out of her busy schedule on the five-year anniversary of 9/11 to
remember "the Sept 11 bombings or whatever."

September 2006
(The first day of school was really two weeks before.)
Kate discusses the fake filming of the twins first day of school which was actually
two weeks prior. She also is frustrated that the twins are too smart for the class that
they're in right now.

September 2006
God is comforting Kate throughout the grocery store when she shops, telling Kate
to buy what she needs in the quantities that she needs. He'll take care of
everything. This makes Kate feel at peace so that's good for the kids.

September 2006
Kate writes about getting another free dinner from their best friends the Carsons
and that she doesn't want to steal their joy so she lets them pay.

September 2006
Uh oh. Another official horrible mother day for Kate. She yelled at the kids all day
and said things to them that she regrets. She thinks the kids think that she's a
terrible witch and she feels like she is as well. Once again, she'll try to be better
tomorrow because she realizes that her children are a gift to her. She asks the Lord
again to be a patient and loving mother and not to be so mean and a yelling, crazy
mother. She asks the Lord to remind her when she gets out of line.

September 2006
This was a strange entry in the journal. Kate went from being sad and emotional
because she didn't visit her grandma in the last few days of her life, to getting the
phone call from Jon that she had passed away, to wanting to skip going to a parade
with the kids and instead going shopping for and getting some 'retail therapy' by
buying some new jeans and pants at Old Navy. She goes on talk about how skinny
she looks in them and how Jon panted at the sight of her.

October 2006
Kate and Jon and the twins were in NYC heading to the American Girls store
when they were inconvenienced by a Hispanic parade near the store. Then a big
black bodyguard told them they would have to wait in line like everyone else in
the store. He shares the joy of being waved in front of all the other families to the
front of the line so they could be seated first. She wished that she could see the
look on the black man's face.

October 2006
Another very ugly day today. Kate screamed at Jon in the hallway at church and a
lady was shocked at her behavior. The pastor gave a good message about
marriages and Kate realized that she cannot talk ugly to Jon and that she must love
him. It was a really good message!

___
168

Went to Target after church and yelled at the kids for spilling their popcorn and drinks.

Got home to a wreck of a house that Kate had to clean up and things spiraled quickly into a big ugly argument (Just a few hours after the good message about not talking ugly to your spouse). Kate feels like she and Jon are the worst parents in the whole world and their kids will grow up scarred about what they have heard them say in front of them when they fight. Kate asks the Lord to deliver her from herself and Jon from himself. Kate actually asks the Lord to help her to keep her mouth shut when she's tired and irritable.

October 2006
Another two-year-old rough day! Before the official start of nap the kids stripped again and got spankings. Then the kids acted like two-year-olds do and Kate got out of control with Collin again but luckily she sent him to his room until Kate could settle. Kate hates this two-year-old stuff!

October 2006
Kate worked a double shift and can feel God urging her to quit and live fully on faith instead of down and living on less. She prays to the Lord to be able to let go and let Him handle her finances totally.

November 2006
Today is going to be the worst day of Kate's life. Teacher conferences in the morning and Mrs. Dolan just blew smoke up Kate's butt about the twins. Kate said "No duh!" to herself when she was told how well the girls are doing in school. Kate also got mad at the builders because they left dust even after Kate showed them exactly how she wanted it to be cleaned up as they were working.

November 2006
Kate snapped at the pastor at a church tonight because he made the mistake of asking her if her babies were natural. This is a question that Kate HATES. Kate responded that she had a good answer for him. She told him that it was written in God's history book so yes, they are natural.

November 2006
God has been urging and urging Kate to quit her job and she finally said yes. She is sure that she will be amazed at how God provides for them now that she won't be earning a paycheck.

Kate says that she has been hard on Joel the last few days because he (a two-year-old) says no too often. She says that she must work that out of him.

November 2006
Some big wigs from Discovery Health were coming to visit Kate at home today. A Wendy Douglas, who was an executive producer from Discovery and a Reenie Kuhlman. Kate got showered and the house was in order and she had eaten lunch before they arrived. She was proud that she was actually under control when they got there. The visit went well. They told Kate that Discovery people were obsessed with her and the family, especially someone named Eileen. Kate said, whatever!

Kate expresses her disgust that friends are starting to come out of the woodwork to visit. She says that people are making her want to move to an island!

December 2006
Money fell from the sky and the house was filled with a sea of Christmas presents for the kids. Kate listed the amount of money each of her friends gave her.

January 2007
Kids are sick and Kate is having a difficult time getting an appointment with the 'obnoxious pediatrician.' Kate writes that she knows what she's talking about and the pediatrician office is driving her nuts! Kate says she can't stand this area's lack of intelligence and calls the local pediatrician a retarded practice.
Kate wants to mention in her journal yet another stress melt down today.
The kids were outside playing and Collin poured some beans on the floor and was sent inside. He didn't like that so he knocked down some highchairs in the kitchen and that set Kate off.
Kate said that she was instantly so SO angry that she grabbed him and spanked him as hard as she could and thought that she may seriously injure him so she sent him to his crib and whipped him into it very hard! Kate Gosselin said that for the first time she thought she might really lose it and she was glad that she left him in his crib until Jon came home from work. Kate wrote today was the day that she felt like she may really seriously injure a child!
Kate goes on to pontificate about Collin saying she doesn't understand him. She says he's usually kind and caring and tender and nice until his (two-year-old) temper flairs. Kate says she doesn't like that little Collin doesn't know how to handle his frustration and anger, but apparently beating him and screaming at him is her way of trying to calm him down and make him understand. Kate then laments that she didn't even get the chance to have Collin apologize to her because she had other things to do.
Kate feels like a horrible mom after this day. She feels like a mean awful mommy and asks the Lord to make her kind and loving and patient and caring. The Lord should also help the Gosselin kids to know that everything Kate does is for them.

January 2007
Another bad day at the Gosselin house. Kate discusses all of the infractions that the children committed and her meltdown that went along with it all while the film crew was documenting everything. Kate gave the toddlers a lecture, on and on in her words about the importance of staying in their cribs and how happy it would make her and how she would hug and kiss them if they stayed in. Kate has learned that spanking toddlers in diapers for climbing out of their cribs doesn't work so now she makes the offenders stay in their cribs for at least a half an hour while everyone else goes down stairs. That makes the kids in cribs quiet upset according to Kate.

January 2007

Kate thinks using pull-ups is a bad parenting method but she gave in to avoid the stream of pee she would have to deal with while potty training. Her stress level has decreased since using pull ups! Kate's reward system for successful potty use is one mini M&M for pee and two mini M&Ms for a poop.

Leah fell out of her crib since the side has been removed for them to get out and go pee and because of that, Kate announced the start of another horrible day.

January 2007

Kate thought that she might seriously lose her mind after the week she's had. She's praying that God works out a scholarship for the girls to attend a new school.

February 2007

Kate got a phone call from the twin's school and she knew something was wrong. One of the girls had a bloody nose and was hysterical and incoherent and the teacher said she wanted to come home immediately. Kate told her that she would come to get her asap. After Kate hung up the phone she ran to the mirror and scared herself and she discovered that a shower was in order before she could go to her hysterical child at school.

That same day of great mothering found little Leah telling Kate that her belly hurt. Kate said she only half listened to Leah's cries because she was concentrating on her dinner. Kate finally turned around to see her young daughter lying on the floor in front of the kitchen sink vomiting continuously and profusely!!!!!! Amazingly, Kate stayed calm and sent children for a towel, a new outfit and a bucket.

March 2007

Kate apparently spoke freely during an interview for Chicken Soup for the Soul magazine and was labeled a 'radical' by her television network. She said they were listening in to the interview and got a call afterwards where they treated her like a high school kid receiving a detention! She didn't appreciate any of their message and now knows that she can't say any 'hot button' words and can only say approved phrases and words governed by others. Kate is exhausted by this ugly turnout.

When Kate came upstairs to reprimand the little kids for not being in their beds and lying down, poor little Leah told Kate that big girls don't want a spanking so Kate lovingly told her to lie down and she won't get a spanking.

April 2007

Great day today in Gosselin Land. The first episode of JK+8 aired to great ratings and the twins got almost a full scholarship to attend first grade at their new private school.

Discipline is the Gosselin children's normal. They get their daily spankings and apparently they love it. Kate went from describing an adorable moment with little Aaden in one sentence right into describing her disciplining him at night before bed. While she was 'disciplining' him she included "and I love you" and she said he looked up at her immediately and said "I love you too." Kate said that totally melted her, hearing his little small voice saying I love you as she's beating him.

May 2007
Kate said that the kids were actually naughtier than normal. Two-year-olds Collin and Aaden continue to try Kate's patience. She thinks they might actually set out to do exactly what she asks them not to do. She is sooo frustrated and she knows that she's not as patient as she should be. She goes on to say that not only is she not patient with the boys, she is plain rough with them in response to their constant disobedience!!!

May 2007
Today, Kate thinks she may have crossed the line with the little kids. Alexis and Joel trashed their room twice according to Kate and she spanked them both times plus they were made to stay in their beds for a long time. Once she finally allowed them to come downstairs, they got right into the M&Ms for potty training with Collin and that's when Kate REALLY lost it and pulled Collin up by the hair and spanked them all so hard!!! Kate says she loves them but she was so very angry with them for eating mini M&Ms that were obviously left out where toddlers can get their little fingers on them.
Kate says that she put them back into their beds for their own safety. Kate saw her father in herself today and she says that really scares her. She is once again begging the Lord to help her to become a slow to anger mommy. She asks the Lord to please somehow stop her from hurting her children. Help them Lord to obey me Kate asks the Lord. Help them to not get into trouble!!!!! Kate ends her thought by saying Please Lord, amen!!!!

June 2007
Kate writes how she heard gleeful laughing and giggling in the laundry room but she was exhausted which she adds is not a good thing. Kate discovered to Aaden and Alexis splashing and playing in a bucket of Oxiclean water, which some irresponsible parent must have left on the floor with the door open. The babies splashed water all over the floor and Aaden had it in his hair and on his face. She added that the Oxiclean water was STRONG!!!! So Kate lost it. She wrote that she absolutely melted down!!!! While she was cleaning the floor she called Jon thankfully to tell him ALL of the news. She said she was crying so hard he couldn't understand. She told Jon that she felt like she may hurt his children because of this. Thankfully, Kate says that she knows to send them to their beds when they act like toddlers and are naughty. Once they are out of Kate's sight, she knows that they are safe from her. So now Kate is cleaning the water from the floor and sobbing and she decided to lie down on the wet towels and continue to cry. She describes the scene saying that she was sobbing for some to please help her...won't someone please come and help her, when she says she heard a little voice say mommy I will help you. Leah had been standing there and witnessed the whole meltdown and she and Hannah offered to help.

Aaden had a few more potty accidents that night so Kate gave up and put him back into diapers because she can't take the accidents.

June 2007
Kate once again prays to the Lord to take away their ugly parenting and replace it with LOVE!!!!!

July 2007
Kate is thrilled to hear the news that their dearest friends the Carsons are looking into buying a house for them.

Kate says that Bob Carson offered Jon a job. According to Kate, Beth Carson told her that Bob knew Jon was brilliant but didn't know he was this brilliant!!!!! Kate says she has know thins for a long time and she prayed that someone else would pick up on it and make Jon successful!

Kate got an email from a national convention asking for her speaking rates. She didn't know so she said she was going to pray about it!

July 2007
Another rough day today according to Kate. She says she's being horrible to the kids but they have also been horrible.

While talking on the phone, Kate noticed a HUGE centipede on the wall near the coffee pot. She said she almost died and was sweating. Rather than handling the harmless bug, Kate taped a plastic cup over it against the wall so Jon can kill it when he comes home from working.

Kate says she was awful to the kids and they were awful back to her. A man doing work on their house apparently couldn't take being around Kate anymore because he asked Kate for Jon's number and QUIT!!!!!! He just packed up his things and left without a word to Kate.

Kate prays again to not take her stress out on the kids.

Kate prays to the Lord to not let Satan win the battle when he throws rough things Kate's way.

Kate feels that Satan is gaining ground with her and Jon and she doesn't want that to happen.

"What lies behind us and what lies before us are tiny matters compared to what lies within us."
– *Ralph Waldo Emerson*

CHILD ABUSE?

"I was very, very, over disciplined.
Jon was very, very, under disciplined.
So imagine us finding a common ground then. It's hard."
– Kate Gosselin

"It's not important how it LOOKS,
only how I LIVE & care for my kids! Thx tho!"
– Kate Gosselin

There are four kinds of child abuse: physical, emotional, neglect and sexual. Kate demonstrated "emotional" abuse on just about every episode of *Jon & Kate Plus Ei8ht* and *Kate Plus Ei8ht*. Kate admitted to and documented her "physical abuse" as well as her "neglect" of her children in her journal.

I witnessed instances of Kate neglecting her children for nearly 2 years while I was assigned to report on the family for *US Weekly*. Three separate sources close to the Gosselin family told me that Kate was abused as a child. Remember, too, that a family member close to Kate disclosed to me that Kate had also been sexually abused by a family member.

There is evidence that abused children are more likely to repeat the cycle of abuse as adults, unconsciously repeating what they experienced as children. But many adult survivors of child abuse have a strong motivation to protect their own children against what they went through as children, and they become excellent parents.

Some people will argue that they have the right to discipline their children in any way they see fit. Some of these same people seem to be incapable of making the distinction between discipline and abuse.

Physical abuse vs. Discipline
In physical abuse, unlike physical forms of discipline, the following elements are present:

Unpredictability: The child never knows what is going to set the parent off. There are no clear boundaries or rules. The child is constantly walking on eggshells, never sure what behavior will trigger a physical assault. (See the "Katie Dearest" chapter for examples of this.)

Lashing out in anger: Physically abusive parents act out of anger and the desire to assert **control**, not the motivation to lovingly teach the child. The angrier the parent, the more intense the abuse.

Using fear to control behavior: Parents who are physically abusive may believe that their children need to fear them in order to behave, so they use physical abuse to "keep their child in line." However, what children are really learning is how to avoid being hit, not how to behave or grow as individuals. (Read "Mommy's Journal" for examples of this.)

The following text was taken from an article that was published in *The National Enquirer* on June 22, 2009. Kate Gosselin, her Network family, and her followers dismissed it as a crazy pack of lies from a disgruntled, former Gosselin employee, just as they always dismissed every negative story that any tabloid ever wrote about Kate.

"An ex-staffer of Kate Gosselin, who worked for the Gosselins for more than a year before recently resigning, claims they have witnessed Kate using corporal punishment on the couple's 8-year-old twins and 5-year-old sextuplets.

"When one of the boys closed a door on another one once, Kate got in their faces and yelled, "You tell me the truth about what happened!"

"The children just stood there terrified. **Then she dragged one of the boys into the bathroom and spanked him five or six times with a large plastic spoon.**"

"**You could hear Kate forcefully whacking the child and the child screaming at the top of his lungs. People told me it happened more than once, but it was off-camera because Kate didn't want it in the show.**"

Now read this quote from Kate Gosselin about how "real" her show is, and how they don't hide anything from you – the viewer:

"We know we're doing the best for our family, and I'm sorry if you're unhappy. How about that? I'm not always happy with what you see (on the show), nor is Jon. But we are certainly not going to hide our imperfections."

- Kate Gosselin

The problem with Kate's statement is that she did, indeed, make every effort possible to hide the forceful spanking and physical "disciplining" of her children. I don't recall ever seeing Kate smacking any of her children around on her TV shows, but her writings tell us it most definitely happened.

You just read for yourself how Kate Gosselin describes, **in her own words** from her personal journal, how she treated her children, and you can decide if you think the former staffer was lying or telling the truth. You decide if Kate was hiding anything from you as you were tuning in to watch her wholesome "reality" show. And you decide if this is an appropriate way of disciplining children of this age, or any age. The sextuplets were **2 years old** and in diapers at the time of these incidents, as recorded by Kate in her journal. Here are a few more.

September 2006
Joel had gotten out of his crib at naptime, I guess because he wasn't tired anymore. Kate heard him getting into drawers so she went upstairs and spanked him and put him back in his crib. After the designated naptime was officially over, Kate made Joel stay in his crib while everyone else got to go downstairs. She wants him to know how serious she is about naptime and that she will not tolerate crib climbing!!!!! She says she hopes he got the message but isn't sure because of the glazy look in his eyes when she talks to him!!!!!

October 2006
Four little toddlers in diapers got into the tissue box on Grandma's desk AGAIN. Kate says they did it yesterday as well and she spanked all six of them and put them in the corner.

May 2007
Kate talks about Aaden's fifth day of potty training. He had an accident and pooped on the floor. Kate said she screamed at the top of her lungs as she picked him up. She spanked him after the clean up because, as she says, they are not dogs and Kate felt that five days was more than enough time for a two-year-old boy to become potty trained.

Think about these words from Kate's journal:

"I spanked them so hard!!!!"
"I felt like I may hurt his children."
"I grabbed him and spanked him as hard as I could and thought I may seriously injure him."
"I was out of control."

Now read them again, and picture six tiny children in nothing but diapers, being brutally spanked by their enraged and clearly out-of-control mother. That is not a loving parent disciplining her children. That is violence and abuse. And remember – these are the things that Kate was comfortable documenting in her journal as source material for possible inclusion in her book, *I Just Want You To Know – Letters To My Kids On Love, Faith, and Family.* These are normal, everyday occurrences in the Gosselin children's lives. These are things that Kate was prepared to share with the world if an editor at Zondervan hadn't gotten his or her hands on them first.

Reading about this harsh reality, it begs the question: **What were the things that even Kate Gosselin knew better than to put into writing?**

We'll never know ... not until one of the kids gives their first interview in a few years.

This physical abuse is the Gosselin children's "normal," as Kate would say. Being smacked is their normal. To a child who is beaten every day, or burned every day, that is their normal, too. It doesn't mean it is ever acceptable or should be allowed to continue.

In hindsight, the clues were there for all of us to see, right out in the open on the TLC episodes of *Jon & Kate Plus Ei8ht*. During the second episode of Season 1, Kate cutely says to the camera, "They're always biting, hitting, pulling hair, slugging, wrestling. They even beat up on the girls. I wonder where they learned that?"

There really is no need to wonder. These children were displaying these behaviors as babies, still in diapers and still in their cribs. They were the same age as when Kate was writing about her physical and verbal ragings against them. Children learn what they live.

Watch the clip of that episode. It's from "Sextuplets and Twins: One Year Later," when Kate returns home from her tummy tuck surgery. It's chilling to watch, knowing now about how Kate was beating these tiny angels at the time.

Kate had been gone for a week and the kids were at home and very happy. Pay attention to what happens when Kate arrives back home and goes to greet them in their cribs. Poor little Alexis is instantly frightened and starts crying, only to be subdued by Kate's "soothing" voice. Kate explains it away on the show saying that she looked different and that's why the kids were afraid.

Kate has held this moment up on several occasions as her favorite moment ever of her children on the show.

THE "DISCIPLINE" EPISODE

"If there was no discipline, there would be chaos 24/7."
– Kate Gosselin

During Season 3 of *Jon & Kate Plus Ei8ht*, Discovery/TLC created an entire episode about discipline, which aired in June 2008. The sole purpose of this episode appeared to be an attempt to whitewash any potential rumors about Kate being abusive to the children – before any such rumors were even widely circulating. They knew what they saw, and were aware of what was happening to the children while they were at the house filming.

When watching the "Discipline" episode, I thought I would finally get to see and hear Kate Gosselin explain her views on corporal punishment. I was wrong. This episode appeared to be carefully scripted and focused on showing the world that Kate is a strict disciplinarian, who DOES NOT spank her children. There was absolutely no mention whatsoever of spanking in this entire episode about discipline; not even a setup question thrown at Kate from her crew interviewer/producer who crafted the episode. Wouldn't that be a normal question to at least throw out there during an episode about discipline?

Here's one of Kate's quotes from the "Discipline" episode: "The struggles that we face are being consistent. Because discipline for us is about a 24 hour a day job." Consistent.

They even made a point of showing one of the sextuplets hitting another child, which happened all the time during these episodes (they used the footage to get laughs) and showing Kate saying loudly, **"Oh no, we don't hit!"**

Later, in this same "Discipline" episode, Jon told the viewing audience, "The most common offense in the house is hitting."

Where do you suppose the kids learned to hit each other?

During the Season 3 episode of *Jon & Kate Plus Ei8ht* entitled "A Day In The Life" from January 2008, Alexis hit Collin and Kate yelled, "Go sit in time out! **We don't touch other people! We keep our hands to ourselves!"** Kate does many, many things to confuse and frustrate her children, and then she wonders why they act out.

So how does Kate Gosselin discipline her children, according to the TLC show? "Usually they go to time out and they sit in the corner," Kate tells us.

I certainly don't doubt that they do go and sit in the corner … when the camera crew is in the house filming. It's what happens to them when the crew goes home that concerns me most.

The part that sickens me in this episode is TLC putting all of the sextuplets on the interview couch and showing us an obviously scripted, three-second clip of the kids answering a simple question from the TLC interviewer.

"What happens when you're naughty?"

The six kids look like this is probably the fourth or fifth take of answering this question, and in very unrealistic form for six children that young, they all answer EXACTLY the same, and somewhat robotically.

"Go in the corner."

"Go in the corner."

"Go in the corner."

Having three young children of my own and having been around children for years at the kids' schools, I can tell you from experience that that would never happen. It is far more believable to think that in an earlier take, Collin yelled out "Mommy spanks us!!!" and the crew and parents quickly yelled, "cut! cut! cut!" "Take two. Take three. Take four." Get out the jellybeans to bribe the kids! "We need to get this right!!!"

Later, on the interview couch, when it's just Jon and Kate together, Jon says this about discipline, "I give very stern looks to my kids."

Kate couldn't even give Jon that. She had to turn it back to herself, saying in her smug, condescending way, "You do? I don't know if I ever see them."

In a different Season 3 episode about discipline, Kate lectured Jon on the interview couch, saying, "Don't scream at him. If you're too upset to discipline him quietly and explain what he did wrong, and help him to learn to do better, than don't deal with it. Deal with it when you're calmed down."

In that same episode, after Jon yelled at Collin, Kate said to Collin sympathetically, "Collin, I'm sorry. It's fine. Ignore Daddy. He's mean." This from the same woman who wrote about really losing it, pulling Collin up by the hair, and spanking them so hard.

"The bottom line is you have to be responsible for your own actions,
And if your actions get out of control, there's consequences.
That's the bottom line."
– Kate Gosselin

EYEWITNESS ACCOUNTS

Kate's bad temper wasn't much of a secret. This is an excerpt from my *US Weekly* reporting where some sources recounted seeing Kate in action:

```
Jon and Kate Gosselin PA Reporting
September 2009
        My xxxxx source told me about Kate's terrible temper and how
she spanks the kids all the time for little things. "When they don't
listen to her just once, she would snap out and spank them. Kate
would get crazy when the kids wouldn't pick their toys up and didn't
give them a second chance.
```
She once kicked a Lego building the boys made into a million pieces because they didn't put it away the first time she asked them too. Then she made them clean up the mess she had made, all the time yelling at them to put their toys away.
```
The kids
are afraid of Kate. All she has to do is look at them and they get
scared of her because they know what she'll do to them. She's
completely different from what you see on TLC. She's always yelling
at them and that's one of the reasons they split up. Jon was always
the fun parent while Kate was the mean one. Jon would let them have
fun and make a mess while Kate wanted everything to be neat and tidy.
She would get mad at them for getting out their toys to play with."
        Another former neighbor that I spoke to several weeks ago
told me that Kate was always screaming at the kids, even when they
were very small. "She would run the house like a military base,
expecting the kids to jump whenever she yelled for them. I saw Kate
spank the kids many times. She believed in old-school discipline. If
she said something and they didn't listen, they'd get spanked. It got
to the point that the kids would cower when she yelled at them
because they didn't know if they were going to get hit or not."
```

BULLY, BULLY

Kate Gosselin has bullied, and continues to bully, EVERYONE who has ever been a part of her life. You can simply watch any episode of either of her television shows to see proof of this. But reading her tweets from April 2012, Kate has the nerve to chime in on the topic of bullying. Her reply tweets are in bold:

xxxxx @Kateplusmy8 Since bullying is such an important and relevant topic these days, do you talk to your kids about it?

I talk to my kids about bullying ALL THE TIME! No 'mean girls' allowed here! There's psych why people do it & view/attitude change can help it!

xxxxx @Kateplusmy8 No wonder why cyberbullying/bullying is at an all time high. Parents are teaching their children that its ok.

I know! I talk about bullying with friends often! How can kids not bully at school when the parents are doing it online??!

I'd love to be the national spokesperson for cyber bullying. I cannot believe it is tolerated & mostly ignored! BULLYING MUST STOP!!!

Kate Gosselin, the woman who wrote that she grabbed her toddler son and spanked him as hard as she could to the point that she thought she would seriously injure him, had the nerve to actually say that she would "love to be the national spokesperson 4 cyber bullying." This is a woman who is a champion at mocking and criticizing and threatening others.

In March of 2012, Kate Gosselin, non-bully, tweeted these happy thoughts:

Good day! Busy Sunday here! Church, C&M baked two birthday cakes, now family weeding project outside! Then dinner to make etc. Are you tired? Yeah, me too!:)

But on that day, the reality was that Kate was screaming at her little children as they worked all day doing yard work for her ... while she jogged around the driveway and sat in the shade. She was visibly mean as she was screaming at the children to stay away from her car and to move faster and to stop fooling around. The kids were crying, but they were not allowed to stop working. Kate wasn't just yelling at them, she was being cruel and degrading, and treating them with complete disrespect. She should have been more careful about who was standing nearby watching her abusive behavior.

THE WHEELS ON THE BUS GO 'ROUND AND 'ROUND – ALL OVER JON

Kate not only physically abuses her children; she emotionally abuses them as well. She criticizes Jon publicly at every chance she gets – in interviews and on TV. This is the father they love, but she can't put aside her hate for him to try to take care of their emotional well being. One can only imagine the terrible things she says about him directly to the kids.

None of that matters to Kate, however, as long as she continues to have the kind of support like this on Twitter, where her followers bad-mouth Jon right along with her:

xxxxx @Kateplusmy8 watched last ep with John in it on Sat.He was horrid to the kids very bitter and twisted!You never took your pain out on them

No parent should punish innocent kids for the way things turned out. Extra love is needed...Kids/I thriving now so all is good!

Once again, instead of asking the tweeter to stop criticizing the father of her children, Kate eagerly joined in and threw Jon under the bus yet again. She accused him of "punishing" the kids, while in her mind she was busy giving them "extra love."

THE BUCK STOPS HERE

Many adults have come and gone from the Gosselin children's lives over the years. Some may have even witnessed abuse, but chose to remain silent about it. This begs the question: Who should have reported the obvious abuse of the Gosselin children at the hands of their mother? The answer is, well, everyone who knew about it.

People who report abuse are protected by law. Even that very restrictive and threatening Confidentiality and Nondisclosure Agreement pertaining to the Gosselins had to include wording that the Confidential Information could be disclosed "in response to a subpoena or other legal process."

The *Pennsylvania Code*, which is an official publication of the Commonwealth of Pennsylvania, sets forth regulations regarding child abuse and explains who is a mandatory reporter. A key clause in the *Code* states that to protect children from abuse, reporting requirements take precedence over any ethical principles or professional standard that might otherwise apply. This pertains even to those people who signed Kate's super-special Confidentiality Agreement. Here is the text concerning child abuse taken directly from the *Pennsylvania Code*:

Subchapter G. MINIMUM STANDARDS OF PRACTICE—CHILD ABUSE REPORTING

http://www.pacode.com/secure/data/049/chapter16/subchapGtoc.html

§ 16.102. Suspected child abuse—mandated reporting requirements.

(a) *General rule.* Under 23 Pa.C.S. § 6311 (relating to persons required to report suspected child abuse), Board regulated practitioners who, in the course of their employment, occupation or practice of their profession, come into contact with children shall report or cause a report to be made to the Department of Public Welfare when the Board regulated practitioners have reasonable cause to suspect on the basis of their professional or other training or experience, that a child coming before them in their professional or official capacity is a victim of child abuse.

(b) *Staff members of public or private agencies, institutions and facilities.* Board regulated practitioners who are staff members of a medical or other public or private institution, school, facility or agency, and who, in the course of their employment, occupation or practice of their profession, come into contact with children shall immediately notify the person in charge of the institution, school, facility or agency or the designated agent of the person in charge when they have reasonable cause to suspect on the basis of their professional or other training or experience, that a child coming before them in their professional or official capacity is a victim of child abuse. Upon notification by the Board regulated practitioner, the person in charge or the designated agent shall assume the responsibility and have the legal obligation to report or cause a report to be made in accordance with subsections (a), (c) and (d).

§ 16.106. Confidentiality—waived.

To protect children from abuse, the reporting requirements of § § 16.102—16.104 (relating to suspected child abuse—mandated reporting requirements; photographs, medical tests and X-rays of child subject to report; and suspected death as a result of child abuse— mandated reporting requirement) **take precedence over any ethical principles or professional standard that might otherwise apply.**

Every producer, crewmember or person employed by Discovery/TLC/Figure 8 Films who witnessed any abuse of the Gosselin children bears some responsibility for allowing it to continue and for not reporting it. Every executive who knew about the abuse is responsible. Everyone who turned a blind eye to the abuse bears some blame. It is probably safe to say that no damning, un-aired Gosselin film where Kate is screaming at, threatening and spanking her children will ever see the light of day. That unseen film is proof that all the adults who witnessed the abuse, or saw signs that made them strongly suspect abuse, and who could have and should have done something to protect those children, failed them – all because there was a boatload of money to be made off of them. The Gosselin children were nothing more than collateral damage in a business driven by greed, where profit trumps the safety and well being of our most innocent. The welfare of those children was everybody's business.

THE THREAT

The question most people will be asking right about now is: Why hasn't Jon Gosselin spoken up about the abuse? I can't answer that. Only Jon can answer that. I don't know that he hasn't reported it, and I don't know what conversations or arguments he's had with Kate about it. I don't even know if he was ever present for the physical abuse.

I do know that Jon had to sign Discovery's agreements not to talk about it, and the contract he signed forbids him from talking about it. But that piece of paper should never have been anyone's excuse for not intervening if they saw or knew about the abuse happening. Fully understanding this, Kate took it a step further than just threatening Jon with the repercussions of him violating the Nondisclosure Agreement. Kate told Jon that if he ever breathed a word about her abusing the kids, Discovery would sue him for every cent he'd ever make, and she would make sure he never saw or had any contact with his children ever again. Probably the most complicating factor in reporting child abuse is that it can be very hard to prove, since it is open to interpretation, especially in a state like Pennsylvania, which allows parents to use force "for the purpose of safeguarding or promoting the welfare" of a minor. *The Pennsylvania Code* states:

> Parents can use reasonable supervision and control when raising their children. 23 § 6302. [Civil Code] Parent/guardian/person responsible for general care and supervision/ person acting at request of the above **may use force** for the purpose of safeguarding or promoting welfare of minor including the prevention or punishment of his misconduct, if the force is not designed to cause or known to create a substantial risk of causing death, serious bodily injury, disfigurement, extreme pain, mental distress, or gross degradation. 18 § 509. [Criminal Code]

> Howard Stern said it best in 2014. "You're beating your children for your incompetence as a parent. If you've gotta spank your kids, something's really wrong with you, not the kids."

ALL YOU NEED IS LOVE

All you need is love. Those words appear on the screen, with calming, happy music playing as the "Discipline" episode of *Jon & Kate Plus Ei8ht* comes to a close. And then Kate gives her final thoughts for the TLC viewing audience: "Our positive words and our positive reinforcement is the best thing you could ever give them."

"You know, love is the best discipline of all."
– Kate Gosselin

END CREDITS.

There is an INF paparazzi video online, taken in August 2010, of Jon bringing the kids back to Kate's house after his custody time. The kids are in hysterics, screaming and crying about having to go back inside to Kate. They are inconsolable, despite Jon's efforts to calm them.
This was one of the saddest things I had ever seen happening with these children.

I had spoken to Jon on the phone that day, just before he left his apartment with the kids. He told me he was having trouble getting the kids to go back home. He ended up being almost an hour late bringing them home because they didn't want to leave him and go back to whatever awaited them at home.

The video is easy to find. Just Google "Gosselin kids screaming," or anything similar, and you'll see it for yourself. It is painful and gut wrenching.

Watch it until the end when Jon gets into the car to leave. That's me driving him. I was there, and I saw and heard the terrified cries of the children for myself. I didn't read about it online, or speculate about what might have happened, or make assumptions about what was causing their distress. I was there. Eight little children were terrified of going home to their mother.

"I Wish…that there would be peace on earth and only love –
no abuse, hurt, gossip, strife or struggles for anyone!"
– *Kate Gosselin*
9.19.11 Kateplusmy8.com

It is truly heartbreaking to think about the many times the Gosselin children also must have wished that there would be no abuse and hurt.

KATIE DEAREST

"They're crying which means they haven't been abducted
and they're not dead, so that's a good thing, right?"
– *Kate Gosselin*

There are people in this world that should not be blessed with having children. I'm not talking about people who make a conscious decision to not have children – those people are actually the least selfish of us all because they are aware that having kids is not a commitment they are prepared to make. No, the people who don't deserve to have children include those who would harm them in any way, those who would disrespect them, those who would view them as possessions, those who would ignore them, those who would treat them as a means to get rich, those who are not prepared to teach them well, those who have a constant need to dominate and control, and those who would view them as mere extensions of themselves instead of as separate and unique beings. It is no surprise that Kate Gosselin meets every one of these criteria for someone who should never have children.

Kate may have always wanted lots of kids, but years of watching her behavior on TV and seeing how she treats her children make it very apparent that she completely lacks the mental and emotional maturity to nurture and raise children, and to understand, respect and relate to them. Her behavior often resembles that of a 13-year-old child who is old enough to believe she knows everything, but too young to understand she knows almost nothing.

Everything Kate says and does relative to her children seems to come from some angry, impatient place; this almost always manifests itself as constant irritation with them. Any words of praise she has uttered about them sound hollow and insincere, especially since she has been so publicly critical of them so often. It is heartbreaking to hear her mock and ridicule her beautiful children. It must be terrible for them to be caught in the constant vortex of turmoil created by their mother, the person who is supposed to be their safe port in a storm.

THE MOTHER'S DAY TRADITION

For years, Kate Gosselin has been trying to sell herself as the finest example of motherhood that ever existed, but her actions scream the exact opposite. Let's do a little comparison. The following paraphrased excerpts are from blogs that Kate wrote for Mother's Day 2012. They represent the kind of mother Kate Gosselin has tried to fool the world into believing she is.

Mother's Day at the Gosselins
Posted on May 7th, 2012 by Kate G

Kate writes that her twins and sextuplets have all been plotting and thinking for weeks about what to make her for breakfast on Mother's Day. They've even asked for a list of foods that Kate will eat according to her, because they know how routine and boring her food choices can be...

Kate says that her kids are excited to pull off their Mother's Day tradition of breakfast in bed. They may even let her take a nap and have a relaxing day for Mommy...

After breakfast in bed and a nap, Kate says the kids usually sneak in extra surprises like home cards telling her how much they love and appreciate her, and sometimes they create coupons for back massages for when she's the most stressed out. Then she adds, Um, is there one for, like, every day? Wink wink.

Kate looks down the road to when she has teenagers and she envisions a spa day for all of the girls with pedicures in side by side chairs, chatting and laughing and spending time together. She adds an insult to her yucky boys that they may even leave the boys home to make them dinner. Lol!

Kate wants her kids and us to know that a loving mother is the most important part of any child's life. She feels underappreciated and thinks that she, like most moms feels taken for granted and stressed out sometimes.

Kate tells us that the greatest gift we could give is to show mom that she's not forgotten and that she's really important and that we're really thankful for her.

And remember everyone, being a mom is the most difficult of any job ever, but it's by far, the most rewarding. Kate tells us that mothers are not only caring for their own children, but they are also educating and forming the future citizens of our world...and mothers have just one shot to do it right!

My Mother's Day Plans + coupons for Moms
May 9, 2012

Kate says that one of her favorite traditions in her house is breakfast in bed on Mother's Day! She says that all the kids have been planning the big meal for weeks! And we should check out her latest coupon blog for more Mother's Day deals.

> One of my favorite **traditions** in our house is breakfast in bed on Mother's Day! All the kids have been planning the big meal for weeks now. Check out my latest CouponCabin blog for more of our plans and make sure to see below for some great Mother's Day deals!

Reading those posts, Kate would have us believe that her children, including the six who were 7 years old at the time she wrote those blogs, were "plotting and thinking" about her Mother's Day celebration for weeks. Not likely, unless she was mentioning it to them every day for weeks. Kids pretty much live in the here and now, and just one week can seem like an eternity to them. Kids will think ahead to the biggest, most exciting holidays of the year and to their birthdays, which are all about them, but Mother's Day would barely register as a blip on their radar until it was almost upon them.

Let's take a moment to review some more of Kate's words in these posts. Kate says the "greatest gift" is to show your mom "that she's not forgotten," that "she's really important," and that "you're really thankful for her." That's such beautiful sentiment. Coming from Kate, it is sheer hypocrisy. Her words must only apply to HER being showered with appreciation and gratitude; because Kate is certainly not showing that same respect to her own mother, who she has conspicuously cut from her and her children's lives.

Kate also uses that word "tradition" again. There are absolutely zero "traditions" in the Gosselin children's lives. There are a lot of manufactured events that she wants the public to believe are traditions. A "tradition" to Kate Gosselin means that TLC filmed her doing something with or for the kids one time, and she wants you to believe it happens that way year after year.

INDIFFERENCE

I have heard Kate say some incredibly hurtful things to Jon and her children. Here is a look at their daily reality through some of Kate's actual words:

"You're costing me even MORE money!!!
"We're late because of you!!!
"Shut up. Go away. Don't bother me!"

If you were to go through every episode of *Jon & Kate Plus Ei8ht*, you could fill several pages with statements just like those that Kate has made to her children. The scariest part about this is that she spoke to them like that while television cameras were filming. Most people being filmed would be acutely aware of their actions and would hold back from doing anything ugly and mean. They would put their best face forward for the world to see. If what Kate showed us is her best face, just imagine what life is like for the Gosselin children inside of that house with no cameras rolling.

At the time of their divorce, when Kate was splitting time at the house with Jon, she would always leave a list for Jon of things she wanted him to take care of at home when he had the kids. These were things that she was just too "busy" to do. Like doctor's appointments, clothes shopping, filling the gas tank on the big blue bus, etc. Kate *always* left a list for Jon.

I remember when little Lexi had been sick and complained about it to Kate for four days, but Kate put off helping her until Jon had custody. She left him a note telling him to take her to the doctor. It turned out that Lexi had strep and had been suffering with an infected throat and a fever for days. But Kate felt it could wait a few more days until Jon had custody. Caring for her sick child just wasn't a priority for her. During those days, I followed Kate as she went to the tanning salon numerous times, got her nails done, and made countless trips to the Target shopping center, all without any children along to bother her. It was all about Kate - all day, every day. She had time for herself, but not for her sick child.

Kate's indifference to the needs of her children is astonishing. A perfect example of this was highlighted by something I learned secondhand and from reading Kate's journal and emails. Several years ago, when Jon and Kate were out to dinner doing a magazine interview, they received a call from their manager, who was back at their house watching the kids. One of the little girls had accidentally slammed one of the boy's fingers in the bathroom door and nearly cut the end of his finger off. He was left with a fracture that required stitches. Such news would have sent most parents flying out of the restaurant and home to care for their child, but not Kate. She told Jon to go and handle it while she stayed at dinner to continue the interview. This is the type of scenario that plays out with Kate Gosselin every day, like clockwork.

Instead of being at home with her kids, Kate always manages to fill her day running errands by herself while the kids stay behind with a babysitter or nanny. If she truly enjoyed spending time with her children, and it was important to her, wouldn't it be better to have her paid assistants do the menial tasks and errands so she could spend time mothering her kids?

If not for a reality television show, how was Kate planning to support her large family, back in the very beginning, when she decided to undergo fertility treatments in the first place?

"All faith was in God to deliver?"

Did God want Kate to treat the kids this way?

To leave them with strangers?

To beat them?

To emotionally and physically abuse them?

If not for television, how was she going to support her family?

CLEAR AS MUD

Children need structure and consistency to help them learn appropriate behavior and to develop self-confidence. Kate does many, many things to confuse and frustrate her children, and then she wonders why they might not be perfect like she wants them to be. She's inconsistent on a daily basis in how she teaches and disciplines them, and they act accordingly.

While doing research for this book, I watched Kate with the kids, over many months. I also bought and watched every episode of *Jon & Kate Plus Ei8ht*. As a loving parent, it was painful to sit through the shows. There are many examples of Kate sending contradictory and conflicting messages to her children. For instance, what kind of mother would say this to her 4-year-old children when showing them their new house for the first time?

```
"Do you see this room? Honestly, you will never open this door and
come in here again. No one will be found in here. If you do, severe
punishment! Mommy and daddy need their privacy and we haven't had any
for a good four years now. Excuse me! I'm talking! Come in here! Now
Jon, you can help by standing in here instead of wandering. Let's
have you talk. Speak!!
"Excuse me, severe punishment if you come in here. We need privacy.
You may knock on our door. You will never open our door and walk in.
That's rude. Understand?"
```

Never mind that the only reason Kate was able to move into her giant house was because her beautiful children worked to put her there. That fact always seems to escape Kate's notice. She thinks it's all about her.

So now, on what was supposed to be an incredibly happy day, when Kate was showing her children their new $1.3 million dollar home in the country, she turned it into an opportunity to threaten them about something that could have and should have been handled in a much less stressful way.

If you had the stomach for it, you could go through each episode, one at a time, and document Kate's words and actions, identifying the behavior she exhibited that might have led to her children's own behavioral problems, and that certainly led to marriage problems between Kate and Jon.

Kate has no emotional connection with any of her children. It is obvious from viewing her interactions with them that there was never any bonding between Kate and her kids. She always had Jon and many other people bathing them, feeding them, and doing everything for them, while she made lists and barked orders and sat back and watched.

Even to this day, Kate treats her children not as individuals, but as groups. It is the "twins" and the "little kids" or the "littles." They must dress alike and do everything together. There is absolutely zero individuality promoted by Kate.

The "little kids" all wake up at different times, but are forced to stay in their rooms until they are all awake before they can come downstairs. They're told to put a DVD in the player and entertain themselves, sometimes for several hours until they are all up, dressed and ready to come downstairs. I've known about this for several years, but recently Kate was silly enough to reveal this fact to the world during a local radio interview on Berks County's Y102.

During the "Day In The Life" episode of Season 3, poor little Aaden was sick and trying to throw up. This should have been a private moment for any person. Kate should have closed the door and taken care of and comforted her son with no one watching or filming. Instead, she held the throw-up bucket for him and allowed the camera to get right in his face with the sound boom mic hanging just overhead. As a parent watching that, it was embarrassing and disgusting. Kate thought it would make great TV.

Kate talks about being "consistent" with the children regarding discipline, but she doesn't practice what she preaches. In that same "Day In The Life" episode, Kate throws a dirty diaper at Jen Stocks, who was the show's writer/director/producer at the time, right in front of the kids. Kate and Jen both laugh about it and have a great time. The kids see this behavior from Kate, so they would obviously conclude that it is OK to disrespect someone like that. How is a child supposed to understand what they can and cannot do when they get spanked or put in time out for small infractions like talking when they're not supposed to, but they see their mother laughing about throwing a diaper filled with pee and poop at another person?

"THE SEXTUPLETS TURN 4"

For the sextuplet's third birthday, Kate and TLC threw them an elaborate, carnival-themed party in the front and back yards of their house, complete with clowns, pony rides, games, cotton candy, and friends and family. But one year later, according to Kate, "They didn't want a repeat of the fun-filled day, opting instead to do something small."

Offering my opinion as just an objective parent, that alone sounds far-fetched. Offering my opinion as someone who knows the Gosselin kids personally as I do, it is completely untrue.

I can just imagine how that discussion would play out at my house, with my kids being the same age as the sextuplets:

Me: "Kids, would you rather have a carnival in the back yard, with all your friends and games and pony rides and popcorn and cotton candy, or would you rather have a small family day?"

Kids: "What, are you kidding me? CARNIVAL!! CARNIVAL!!!"

During the show, Kate's exact words were, "They wanted a family day. They did not want a carnival again. Much to my dismay..."

Right at that moment, one of the little girls, hearing Kate's obvious crapola, says "Mommyyyyyy!" and Kate says, "We'll do a carnival next year, right?"

Well, the next year came and went and there was no carnival. Big surprise.

Kate went on to say, "So the little kids recently turned four, and, um, as opposed to a big party this year, we decided to decorate cupcakes at a bakery."

"We actually did something small this year because they requested it. I was going to redo a carnival, but they said they just wanted a family day."

Even though two separate people close to Kate told me that Kate absolutely did not want to go through the "hassle" of repeating the carnival-themed party, for the sake of argument, let's take her at her word on this one. Surely this would be a great family day if it were going to replace a carnival with pony rides and clowns for 4-year-olds.

In the kitchen during the episode, Kate says to Leah, "Yeah, they know they're going to decorate a cupcake, don't you Leah?"

Leah nods yes.

"And then what do you do after you decorate it?" Kate asks.

"Eeeeaaat it!" Leah responds happily.

"That's right!" adds Kate.

So after a battle to get the kids dressed and out the door, off they go to a bakery, with the sextuplets filled with excitement at what was going to be a day better than last year's backyard carnival.

Once at the bakery, one of the workers explains to Kate what fun they will be having with the kids, and asks, "Is that OK?"

Kate responds, "Yeah, just so it doesn't get messy."

Uh, oh.

On the interview couch, Kate says, "We'll I'm always concerned about the mess."

And Jon says, "And I was just kind of, let them have fun, here's your bibs."

To which Kate says, "I know but they were in church clothes which I didn't feel like changing them either. That would be a hassle."

Heaven forbid Kate should be hassled by having to change her children's clothes so they could enjoy their birthday.

Meanwhile, back at the bakery, Kate tells Collin, in her nurturing passive-aggressive way, "I love your dirty nails Collin. It's such a nice feature. Remind me not to eat anything you bake."

Then the bakery woman explains to Kate, "I was gonna do one for them to eat here and one to take home, or do you wanna just do one each?"

Kate quickly says, "Uh, let's just take one home."

Remember, this day was replacing clowns, cotton candy and pony rides.

Jon says, "It's better to change them and let them have fun then sit there and monitor every single thing they're doing."

While Kate is yelling, "Don't touch! Don't touch. We're not eating them here. We're not eating them here!"

Jon says, "Kate!"

Kate says, "No, not in these dresses, sorry!"

Back on the interview couch, Kate says, "I didn't want to let them eat them there because they would be messy, and it was getting closer to dinner time so I wanted to use that as their dessert."

Jon says, "Didn't Cara and Mady eat theirs?"

And Kate says, "Yeah, I let them eat theirs."

Voiceover: "So we were gonna go home and eat dinner and eat our cupcakes for dessert."

Kate says, "But this day was no different than any other day. You had to eat your dinner to get your dessert."

Except that this day *was* different from any other day. It was the celebration of the sextuplets' 4th birthday. It was their special day. The episode was called, "Sextuplets Turn 4," not, "This day was no different than any other day."

Back home in the kitchen, Kate says, "Dinner, dessert, bath and bed. I was thinking on the way home, it's a lot of hours 'til bedtime. I'm exhausted. I must be getting old."

"I'm gonna make dinner. Then after dinner they can eat their special surprises."

Now comes the trouble. Some of the little kids didn't eat their dinner according to Kate's standards. And we see Hannah in front of a full plate of food asking, "Do I get my cupcake?"

On the interview couch, Kate says of Hannah, "She made a good dent. Again, they don't have to clean their plates to get their dessert, but she did make a good dent, whereas the boys weren't even into trying."

"Collin didn't try. Aaden barely tried. And Joel certainly didn't try," says Kate. The boys are all crying at this point.

Kate says, "Dessert is a treat. Not a mandatory course."

Poor little Aaden looks up and says, "I don't get my cupcake??!" And starts wailing and sobbing.

Collin is crying and saying, "I want my cuuupcaaaake!"

Kate says, "We'll save it for tomorrow night and then you can eat it tomorrow night for dessert."

Back on the couch, the producer, trying to egg Kate on, says, "The boys were really sad that they didn't get their cupcake."

To which Jon says, "But guess what? They had no clue the next day."

Kate takes his cue and jumps in, happily chirping, "They didn't even ask for them. They never even missed them."

Meanwhile, back at the table, Kate lets the girls eat their cupcakes in front of the boys as they watch, and cry.

Happy 4th birthday, kids.

WATER-GATE

In early 2009, Kate and the kids were waiting to tape an interview for Access Hollywood, and the kids, especially Mady, were thirsty.

"I want a drink. I haven't had a drink all day," Mady complained, placing her hand on her head. Kate ignored her, and Mady said, "I'm going to get dehydrated!"

Kate then announced, "Yes, me too," and asked if someone could throw her a bottle of water.

Kate was given the bottle of water, unscrewed the cap, and took a sip. She then put the bottle down on the floor next to her chair without offering any to a clearly distressed Mady.

Mady pleaded, "I need a drink now." Kate told her to "Be quiet." Mady then said, "You're really, really mean! You drank it right in front of my face."

Good call, Mady.

But as is always the case, Kate alters reality to paint herself as a caring, nurturing mom who always puts the needs of her children first. During an interview on *Jon & Kate plus Ei8ht*, Kate proudly tells the viewing audience:

"I think that Jon does well, he listens, especially to Cara and Mady, He's a good listener and he hears them out and hears their stories and he sees all the little things that are important to them, um, and I sometimes probably overlook those things."

Kate then says this to and about Jon: "I think you have trouble hearing past their whining. That so bothers him. He just says, Oh, just go away, and all somebody was saying was, Daddy, **I want a drink (in a child's voice), and I always say, honey, are you listening to her, do you hear what she asked for? That I think I usually am pretty good about**, is hearing them, not the long drawn out heart to heart conversations, Jon tends to have with Cara and Mady, but the little kids, like the immediate needs, I think I'm probably better at hearing."

A very thirsty Mady would probably beg to differ.

WHO GETS THE BROKEN LOLLIPOP?

In the summer of 2010, Kate and the kids and the film crew were in New York City, filming for *Kate Plus Ei8ht*. This particular situation was left out of the actual episode that aired, but for some peculiar reason, TLC included it on their website as a "webisode" called "Lollipops."

In the webisode, Kate and the kids get a bunch lollipops shaped like the Statue of Liberty to eat. Lollipops are the treat of choice to bribe the kids during filming, so that's not so strange. But Kate showed the viewing audience her deeply selfish side as she was handing out the lollipops. While she was violently and not-so-carefully unwrapping them, she broke off Lady Liberty's torch arm on one of the lollipops. So rather than keeping the broken one for herself, like any normal, loving, considerate, unselfish mother would do, she instead handed the broken lollipop to 6-year-old Joel, while she kept a perfect one for herself.

I guess Kate felt she deserved an unbroken lollipop. After all, the show is all about Kate. She's the star. What does she care if her little boy gets a broken – and pink – lollipop, as long as hers is "perfect"?

CRIB CLIMBING – GOOD OR EVIL?

I discovered something while cross-referencing Kate's journals, TV shows and books, etc. It's some of Kate's worst behavior of all, in my opinion, because it involves physical violence against 2-year-olds, for acting like ... 2-year-olds. How she treats the kids all depends on the day, Kate's mood, and who's watching ... or filming.

On *Jon & Kate Plus Ei8ht*, Season 1, Episode 3, "Shopping For Ten," Kate is getting ready to go to the grocery store. But before leaving, she wants to put the kids down for a nap. So far, so good.

With the cameras rolling, Kate watches in amazement, eyes wide and mouth open, as Aaden climbs up into his crib on his own. Kate cheers Aaden on, even giving him a little boost under his diaper to help him climb. Kate says to Aaden, in a very excited and happy tone, "Wow!!! That's a big boy!!!"

Then she looks at the cameraman and the audience and says, "He like scaled it like a monkey!!!!"

Then she looks back at Aaden and says proudly and lovingly, "You got in!!! Good job!!!!!!"

In my house, that accomplishment would be cause for celebration as well. It's exciting when your
2-year-old takes on new challenges. A lot of parents, me included, have videotaped such milestones for posterity.

But in reading Kate's journal, I began to get a sense of why the kids might be anxious, and scared, and especially confused. Here are a few of Kate's paraphrased journal entries regarding crib climbing. See if you can spot any inconsistencies in her parenting.

July 2006
Kate describes the scene after the kid's nap, Hannah was tattling on Collin because HE WAS IN AADEN'S CRIB WITH HIM!!!!!! Kate says that Collin had climbed into his crib and he did it again after she had removed him!!!!! She told him NO MORE!!!!

September 2006
Again, at naptime Kate heard a thud and she knew what it was. This time Joel had climbed out of his crib!!! Kate let him go for a little while until she heard him getting into drawers. That's when she went up and spanked him and put him back in his crib. Kate yelled at him that she's serious and she will not tolerate crib climbing!!!!! She hopes he got the message but she can't be sure because of his glazy stare when she talks.

But then, in an entry a month later, Kate wrote this:

October 2006
Kate said apparently at naptime, the girls have a 'new thing.' Hannah and Leah like to climb up the outside of the boys' cribs and kiss them!!!! Kate says it is sooooooo cute and she let's them do it.

January 2007
Kate likes crib climbing so much now that she alerted the film crew to set up a camera in the nursery to catch the climbers.

So for filming, crib climbing is happily cheered and celebrated.
Crib climbing is "sooooooo cute" when the girls do it.

Sometimes, though, crib climbing will get you spanked and punished. Two-year-olds in diapers should be able to figure that out, right? It's no wonder Joel has a "glazy look in his eyes" when Kate talks.

This is not a circumstance that can be excused away by saying that Kate doesn't understand child development (even though most of the time she doesn't). Kate fully understands that they're only 2 though, and should act like 2-year-olds. In the "Sextuplets Turn 3!" episode of *Jon & Kate Plus Ei8ht*, Mady yanks a doll out of the hands of one of the little girls and Kate yells at Mady and tells her to give it back. Mady yells at Kate and says this about the little girl: "She's mean." Kate tells Mady, "No, she's not mean. She's two!"

It sounds like Kate does understand age-appropriate behavior on some level, so why the spankings for equally age-appropriate behavior in crib climbing? Spanking a 2-year-old child in diapers for climbing into and out of a crib, especially after praising the child previously for the exact same thing, is just sick.

> "The struggles that we face are being consistent.
> Because discipline for us is about a 24 hour a day job."
> – *Kate Gosselin*

POTTY TRAINING

It's been very well documented that Jon and Kate allowed the television cameras and the world to watch their children being potty trained on several episodes of their reality show. The kids were shown partially naked and sitting on the potty countless times throughout the Season 3 episodes. At one point, the boys were sitting on their potty chairs outside in the driveway, because "boys are messy," according to Kate. There is so much dignity in that.

One potty training event in particular bothered me greatly. It happened, once again, to poor little Collin. He was trying to go to the potty, and Kate left him sitting in a room by himself. Well, he was by himself except for the strange man who was pointing a video camera at him. For the viewing audience, Kate and the crew had a timer on him, to further the humiliation. After more than 30 minutes of Collin sitting, trying to go potty, Kate turns the light out on Collin, leaving him alone to sit in the dark on the potty, and telling him, "Don't get up 'til there's pee in there. Understand?"

Then Kate passive-aggressively taunts Collin by singing "Aaden's a big boy, Aaden's a big boy!" because he managed to pee in the potty.

Aaden peed in the potty because he was scared to death to not pee in the potty, Kate.

Kate's reward to the kids for peeing in the potty is one mini M&M.

That's right. One. Mini. M&M.

For pooping in the potty, the children were rewarded with two MINI M&Ms.

KATE JUSTIFIES HER APPEARANCE AS AN EXAMPLE TO HER KIDS

In Kate's book, *I Just Want You To Know*, Kate talks of how her mommy transformation played out very publicly and tells us that it's important that mothers not lose track of who they are. She goes on to say that looking nice sets a good example for our kids. Kate says that looking nice improves self-confidence, which she can pass along to her daughters.

This sounds surprisingly logical, but Kate's words do not fit the reality of her actions. The reality is that through her actions and words, Kate is passing along a dangerous message to her five beautiful, impressionable daughters that how they look naturally isn't good enough. She is modeling the unhealthy example that the only way they can feel good about themselves is with fake breasts (I know she got breast augmentation because I've seen the paperwork from the doctor), Botox treatments, fake tan, fake teeth, hair extensions, fake nails and tinted contact lenses.
Instead of teaching her daughters to be proud of who they are, and not to be consumed by false images of what they "should" look like, she is setting them up for some potential body image issues.

QUEEN BEE

During the "Twins In Charge" episode of *Jon & Kate Plus Ei8ht*, Kate yells at Jon, "It's not all about you all the time!" Kate then says to the camera, "Man, he makes me mad."
Then, rather than play with her children, she moans about the clutter, saying, "Someday I'll have a house that we fit in. I don't know what size that is gonna be, but I know we don't fit here."
Jon, having had enough, yells "Who cares Kate? Just shut your mouth and stop cleaning and play!"
And Kate responds, "I can't play before the work is done."
Jon fires back, "You don't play with your kids!!!"
And Kate answers with, "You're right. I'm busy doing your work."
Jon says, "You're busy sitting in a chair!"
Mady finally chimes in, telling the camera, "Mommy's making lunch. She just sat in the chair and gave orders to daddy. That's really all she did. She's like queen bee."
Indeed, Mady. Indeed.

DISGUSTING, DIRTY BOYS

The Gosselin boys are afraid of Kate. Actually, they're scared to death of what she might do to them for breaking one of her biggest rules…getting dirty. I've seen it in how they act when they're outside. I've heard it from them. And I've seen it very subtly many times during the *Jon & Kate Plus Ei8ht* episodes. The boys are afraid of their mother, and they are afraid to get dirty.

It is just so sad to see little boys afraid of getting dirty because they have been threatened with punishment by their mother.

In the Season 4 episode of *Jon & Kate Plus Ei8ht* called "Boys Day Out," Kate says, "Boys, they're just dirty. I'm telling you boys are just dirt, they're just dirty!"

Poor little Aaden is seen scratching his behind, like any male of any species does on occasion, and Kate berates him by saying, "It's disgusting Aaden." She also goes on to tell Aaden, "You're nails are horrendous child."

Then she tells us, "They can be boys but why do they have to be dirty?"

BECAUSE THEY'RE BOYS, KATE! READ A PARENTING BOOK!

Kate says: "The girls are definitely more verbal. Girls have feelings and emotions and outbursts."

So she is basically stating outright that boys don't have feelings or emotions.

Here's where a trained eye picked up on the problem though.

At the golf course during the episode, the boys are sitting in the golf cart and Collin says angrily and nervously to Joel: "Stop it Joel, you're getting me dirty! You're getting me dirty Joel!"

And Jon says to Collin: "Stop. Who cares? Look everyone's dirty. Calm down. I don't care. Your mother has got you brain-warped, thinking you have to be a clean boy all the time. Who cares? I don't."

Jon sure wins that parenting battle, and this was years ago.

The Gosselin boys have lived their whole lives without knowing the joys of crawling around in the dirt playing with Tonka trucks or making mud pies or sliding into home plate or rolling down a grassy hill and getting grass stains and not having a care in the world…because Kate tells them they can't. Even worse, she spanks them and screams at them if they get their clothes dirty.

BUSTED AT THE BUS STOP

On October 4, 2011, Kate posted a blog on her website called "Just Another Day in Mommy Paradise." She described a typical day in her life, and one of the things she mentioned is her morning bus stop procedure.

"I hug and kiss each one – not once – but twice and send them off for another day of brain filling instruction! Knowledge is power, after all!"

I've been at the bus stop watching the morning drop off somewhere around 40 times since 2009. I have NEVER, not one single time, witnessed a loving moment from Kate toward her kids. Not once. If she ever says anything nice to them before school, she must say it in the van on the way to the bus stop, because the only thing I have seen and heard on a regular basis is Kate yelling at and rushing her kids onto the bus. There's always something that one or more of them have done wrong to incur Kate's wrath in the morning...before a 45-minute ride to school. So the last thing they hear and see each morning before boarding the school bus is their mother screaming at them for something meaningless. She even climbs onto the bus with them and yells at them to get in their "Kate-assigned" seats on the bus.

Just a few weeks after Kate's blog about being all huggy/kissy at the bus stop, she got busted by the paps. Kate hadn't been photographed by the paparazzi in months, so her guard was down and she felt free to be herself and be nasty to her children in public.

On October 25, 2011, a few paps passing through town on their way to Philadelphia shot Kate at the bus stop at 6:45 AM, as she was yelling at her children while sending them off to school. Realizing the paps were there, Kate launched a preemptive strike. She knew the paps had caught her red-handed verbally abusing her kids, so she wanted to get out in front of the story before it hit the Internet. She tweeted this:

Seriously? Paparazzi at busstop before 7 am? Inhumane! Glad I remembered to wipe yesterdays melted eyeliner off! Pictures of difficult school morning. We all have them though, right?

Every parent, guardian or caregiver has probably experienced a difficult school morning at one time or another. But most parents, guardians or caregivers would never resort to screaming and yelling at their kids at the bus stop. Personally, even on "difficult" mornings, I hug and kiss each of my children and tell them how much I love them and how much I'll miss them each day while they're at school. I also give them encouragement to work hard and have a great day. But hey, that's just me (and every single other good, loving parent in the world). Kate ended up on Twitter defending and excusing her actions, as usual. Kate's responses are in bold.

xxxxx @Kateplusmy8 That's ridiculous! Do the media hounds ever give you some peace? Try and have a great day.

Not sure what was up with those clowns this morning?! Tried to hide but I hear those clicks from miles away.

xxxxx @Kateplusmy8 you always look hot Kate

Thanks for kind words but not this morning (or any for that matter) before 7 am!

xxxxx @Kateplusmy8 must be a slow news week. They need to leave your kids alone

They wouldn't have pictures of me 'yelling at my kids' then...Ugh

Agreed! How is that news? I do it every morning! Don't we all?

xxxxx @Kateplusmy8 I swear the paparazzi are going to extreme levels right now!!! Just keep you're head held high and forget them Kate <3

Just sick of instructing like a mom and getting pics taken with scowl face... Then they say 'Kate yelling at her kids' uh...

First of all, why is it impossible for Kate to be "instructing like a mom" without scowling at her children? Secondly, Kate was yelling at her kids as she was sending them off to school. What should the tabloids say? Here's a tweet from Kate about the bus from a different day:

They ride for 45 minutes..say it's the best part of the day! So I no longer feel bad. Have ridden since pre k! Overall goes well!

I wonder why Kate can't figure out the mystery of why the kids say the bus ride is the best part of their day. Could it possibly be that the long bus ride is the only time they can relax and be themselves, without having someone barking at them?

VOMIT-FEST, GOSSELIN STYLE

During the "A Rough Ride" episode of *Kate Plus Ei8ht*, Kate and about 20 people took the Gosselin kids to Bald Head Island to film a series of episodes about their summer vacation. This episode showed the world how ill-equipped, uncaring and unloving a "mother" Kate Gosselin really is. She can't use her tired excuse that what was aired was all the result of bad editing because she had final approval over every bit of it; that means she must have been proud of her work. I recommend that you watch it on YouTube to get the full effect of Kate's horrible parenting and exploitation of her children … for money and fame.
Here are a few of the lowlights.
Inside their beach house on Bald Head Island, Kate is preparing to take the twins surfing while the little kids go to the beach with Ashley the babysitter. When Kate is leaving and the kids come to hug and kiss her goodbye, the editing shows only the actual hug, not the yelling leading up to it. They cut out the part where Kate yells at the kids to "Get over here now and give me hugs for the camera so we can leave!!!"
Mady and Cara learn to surf while Kate, of course, is standing over Mady telling her what to do. Two professional surf instructors are there, but Kate feels the need to hover over Mady and chime in because of her vast surfing experience. Mady screams at Kate "Don't yell at me!" and eventually quits and storms off. Just one more positive life experience ruined by Kate's need to control everything.
In another of the many, many examples of Kate believing that everyone is beneath her, she makes this comment about her surf instructor:

"My little instructor man said, when I knew I was falling I should concentrate on not screaming and closing my mouth so I didn't drink half the ocean."

I think he was only interested in her closing her mouth.

Later in the episode, they decide it would be a good idea to take the kids deep-sea fishing.

Watch how sad poor Cara is and Mady didn't even go along. Neither of the twins wanted to be there. They wanted to be back playing on the beach like normal children.

On the deep-sea fishing boat, things get very ugly as all of the kids start feeling sick. They are all laying around, getting ready to start throwing up, and Kate, with all her wisdom as a nurse, decides to hand out animal crackers and juice! Eating and drinking is exactly what anyone would want to think about in the seconds before they begin vomiting.

And the vomiting begins. And Kate just barks orders rather than trying to comfort her sick children and help them through a horrible situation. She commands other people to take care of her children. She is a nurse, yet it would appear that she has absolutely no idea what to do during this "emergency."

Kate screams, "I need something for vomiting now!" Steve the bodyguard comes running to the rescue with chum buckets. Chum buckets! Buckets that already stink from having chopped up rotted fish inside that are used to lure the sharks and other fish they hope to catch. Good idea, Steve, you jackass.

On the interview couch at home, Kate proudly says, "It was a vomit fest Gosselin style."

What the Hell is that? A vomit-fest Gosselin style?

Cut back to the boat. Cara is now crying. All the kids are crying and sick.

Collin is wailing "I want to gooooo baaaaack."

And Kate says in her loving and nurturing way, "Well you can't go back. What's wrong!?"

What's wrong? All your kids are seasick, dumbass. That's what's wrong. Anyone who has ever experienced being seasick will tell you that it is complete and utter misery.

Kate says, "Crew members were holding buckets and security people were holding buckets and PAs were holding buckets."

Guess who *wasn't* holding a bucket though? Kate Gosselin, the children's mother. Surprise.

So Kate, "the most organized person on the planet," and a nurse no less, did not bring one thing along for the kids on a deep-sea fishing trip, just on the outside chance that one or more of them might get seasick. No Dramamine. No extra clothes. No meds of any kind.

No clue.

Thinking that the vomit-fest was television gold, we are exposed to even more of the children's suffering. Steve holds Aaden over a bucket as Aaden throws up all over himself – with a TLC camera right in his face, of course. In the background you hear drill sergeant Kate yelling "Aaden's throwing up!!!"

Kate's firm grasp of the obvious is impressive. Don't worry though, the cameras are already there documenting it.

Back home on the interview couch, Kate says, "It was a vomit fest Gosselin style! It was disgusting!"

Back on the boat Kate screams in a panic, "OK, oh crap, oh man!!" as Steve wipes vomit off of Aaden's face.

Then Kate dramatically screams for the camera, "Oh my gosh look at him!!!" while pointing to the cameraman who zooms in for a close up of Aaden and Steve walking away to clean up. "Look at the back of him!!" And the camera zooms in for a close-up of vomit on Aaden's back.

What an example of wonderful mothering. And then Kate wonders why people accuse her of treating her children like props and commodities. There wasn't a single second of film during that entire episode showing Kate comforting her sick children. It appeared that the idea never even crossed her mind.

Kate makes a big deal out of a genius camera guy who brought along an extra shirt to wrap one of the girls in. The camera guy was smart enough to bring a clean shirt. Kate the nurse, best mother ever and "most organized person on the planet" brought nothing.

Cut back to the boat and Kate is barking orders at the production assistant. "Scoop it right into that bucket!! You want me to do it? It's my kid's puke!"

She says that, but doesn't actually do anything. Another surprise.

Then back on the interview couch, after all that we've just witnessed, Kate has the absolute nerve to say, "I guess that's probably why I held it together so well. Cause I knew it was like a boat ride, it was a small period of time where this was gonna occur and then it would kinda be over."

"But I mean uh, I was really grateful for the pockets of time that no one was throwing up, like really grateful, like that I got to sit down and like sit there for a minute. Um, I was grateful that the kids, you know did their throwing up and then a lot of them fell asleep and got away from the torture."

She actually said that.

Thank God kids are resilient and they came around and at least got to have some fun fishing.

Once back on land, Kate says, "We were going to fish and I was going to grill them."

Since the catching fish part of the plan clearly didn't work out, they end up buying fish at a market. Kate is shown wildly dumping some kind of oil on the already-prepared-for-her fish and she's complaining, as usual, and mumbling to herself "We should've gone out to dinner, I don't know what …(Inaudible)."

Flash to Kate carrying the fish inside the house and throwing out paper plates on the counter like she doesn't want to be there. Then she has the nerve to say, "I'm gonna start grilling fish more often. That's like easy as pie."

That was like easy as pie because Katie didn't do it. A production assistant did. Flash forward to March 6, 2012. Kate is responding to a Twitter fan regarding the televised "vomit fest." It appears Kate is rewriting history, even though the ugly history of that day is forever recorded on DVD and YouTube for all the world to see.

After the Hell the kids went through on that boat trip, it is mind-boggling that Kate said she felt the worst for the film crew and her security guards. Not her suffering children.

xxxxx @Kateplusmy8 I'm still feeling sick after watching the film crew puke as well on the boat! U have a very strong stomach.

Yep; nursing background helps! Was a marathon & certainly required 'all hands on deck' – no pun intended! Felt worst for film crew/security!

"All hands on deck."

No pun intended. Yet she put the pun in quotes.

To wrap up the show, Kate says "I believe that the kids will look forward to it every year, waiting to go down there because it's a place where we find peace and happiness and rest and relaxation."

Oh, yeah. It sure looked like those poor kids were incredibly peaceful and relaxed as they puked their guts up on a made-up reality fishing trip.

Cut to the kids about to eat and Ashley the babysitter, not Kate the religious mother, leading a lunch prayer for the kids.

Back on the couch Kate tells us, "Last year it felt weird taking the kids on my first vacation, just me, and this year it felt normal, it felt good, and um, wow, it's a great place."

By "just me," Kate means just her and two bodyguards, two production assistants, five TLC crewmembers and Ashley the babysitter…at the very least.

The "traditional" trips to Bald Head Island stopped after TLC stopped filming. Kate only created traditions for her children when someone else was footing the bill.

On April 16, 2012, Twitter photos showing one of the Gosselin boys looking very thin, even gaunt, were circulating. The bloggers pointed to them as evidence that Kate doesn't feed the kids enough food, as they had been claiming for many months. Kate, ever the protective mother, got wind of the photos and leaped into action to make sure that NOBODY would be exploiting any of her children. Here is a Twitter exchange about the photos:

> xxxxx @Kateplusmy8 Kate, you have fans/nonfans posting half naked pictures of your kids on Twitter. Improper.
>
> **Where? Please send me links. I'll take care of it... Fast!**

As it turned out, the joke was on Kate. The improper pictures of her "half-naked" kids that were posted on Twitter – the ones she was so prepared to take care of – were actually screen captures from the TLC "Vomit Fest" episode of *Kate Plus Ei8ht*. Sorry Kate, but you're the only one showing us half-naked pictures of your kids.

AN EXHAUSTING LIFE

The Gosselin kids wake up at 5:30 AM and are out the door at 6:30 AM to get to the bus stop in time for a 6:45 AM pickup. By my calculations, that amounts to a whopping 1 hour of time that Kate has to "deal" with her kids each morning before she spends the next 8 hours and 45 minutes alone in her big house with nothing to do except nap and tweet. Oh, did I mention…there is always a "helper" there in the morning to do most of the work for Kate and sometimes even to drive the kids to the bus stop while Kate stays behind being "exhausted." So was this unsolicited tweet from Kate really necessary?

> **..Some mornings it's a miracle if I can get away for five seconds to go to the bathroom..'wait, mommy' 'hey mommy!' 'mommy where are you?**

And did she really need to imply that her children are animals?

> xxxxx @Kateplusmy8 happy birthday to you, you live in a zoo. Im sure u know the rest lol that's what my kids sang to me! Have a good one:)
>
> **Doesn't even have to be my birthday.... I always live in a zoo! Lol! :) I say to people 'welcome to my zoo' all the time! :)**

This is a woman who is home alone – without her kids – for NINE hours every school day, while most REAL moms are working one, sometimes two jobs to support their children. But Kate wants everyone to believe that she is the most exhausted person on Earth. She tans, she jogs, she gets her nails done, she travels to New York City to get her hair done, she goes to Starbucks, she shops, and she tweets. Over and over and over again. Doing all of that for herself can get very exhausting.

TWIT-MOMMY DEAREST

Anyone who is interested in learning about the real Kate Gosselin and finding out what kind of a mother she is should simply follow her comments on Twitter. All day, most every day, except when she is traveling or doing things for herself, you too can have the pleasure of reading about how burdensome her children are. They're nothing more to her than a means to make her rich and famous.

> **Good morning all..Doing the school morning grind here...Another day, same routine..Have a great day! Who's running today? How far? I just want to know! :)**

Anything having to do with the kids is always a burden to Kate, or in this case, a "grind."

At dinner table, twins talking in code to figure out winner of their quiet game??! It's amazing..& I don't get it?! Dinners here are entertaining!

Kate can't even make it through a meal spending quality time with her children without taking time out to ignore them while tweeting. When she is alone or with Steve, she rarely tweets, but when she's with the kids, she tweets non-stop so she doesn't have to interact with them. She tells them she's working to provide for them.

Here she is again, not spending quality time with her kids while she spends quality time telling the Twitterverse that she's spending quality time with her kids:

Mady and Cara are hanging out in my room & we are riveted by the latest issue of Natl Geographic Kids..Such neat facts! Thanks to the sender ;)!

THE GLOBE INQUISITION

The following tweets and blog from Kate's website provide a disturbing snapshot of Kate's idea of conflict resolution. They also left a lot of people, fans and haters alike, shaking their heads at the madness of it. It left me wondering, once again, if Kate Gosselin is insane.

A globe taught us all an important lesson! Go to: http//t.co/J4Q4wUXz **to read about it...**

Moms especially, please go to: http//t.co/J4Q4wUXz **today to read an emotional parenting story! I'll never forget our GLOBE experience!**

It is impossible to appreciate the sadness and cruelty of this situation without reading Kate's blog in its entirety. Credit, or blame to be more accurate, goes to Kate Gosselin for posting this on her website, *kateplusmy8.com.*
Please take the time to read the entire post:

Lessons Learned from the Gosselin Globe
(http://www.kateplusmy8.com/lessons-learned-from-the-gosselin-globe/)
MARCH 15, 2012

What mother in their right mind would post something like that? Those poor Gosselin children are subjected to this kind of treatment every day, but on a much more severe scale.
Kate related this incident with the globe with such pride; you would have thought her method of resolving this conflict was worthy of the Nobel Peace prize. It sounded like Kate actually thought she was a genius, and that her handling of the situation would be an example to mediocre moms everywhere on how to handle such terrible crises.

There are so many things wrong, on so many levels, with what Kate recounted here. To start with, Kate allowed her son Joel to be vilified and humiliated by the rest of his family. Then, after finding out he had been unjustly accused in her kangaroo court, Kate decided not to tell the other children who the guilty party was, thus leaving Joel to remain the scapegoat. I have a feeling that poor, little Joel will "remember the globe" for a very, very long time to come.

To make matters worse, all this drama happened at dinner time, which should have been a calm, pleasant time where the family could have bonded sharing stories of the day. But while the children were sitting at the table, trying to eat their dinner after a full day at school, Kate was giving them the third degree. Instead of dinner being a safe and happy time for family discussion, Kate turned it into an opportunity to interrogate her children and terrify them with her global warning. Talk about law and disorder. The damaged object was a simple globe from Target that costs around $14, and Kate used it to traumatize her children and get them to turn on each other in "Gosselin court" because they were desperate to save themselves from suffering the "consequence!"

In this charming story, Kate also informed us that, with her eight children in the house, she was holed up in her bedroom with the door closed "finishing some work." She has all day long to be alone and away from her children to finish her work, and only a few short hours to spend with them after school until bedtime, but she vanishes to her room to get away from them.

Continuing with the absurdity, Kate felt compelled to mix in her "wonderful" dinner and dessert menu (with a side of sick and twisted) in this blog about a life lesson. She must have been trying to convince her groupies and tweeties that, despite the horror she had endured with the unlawful peeling of the equator, she's still able to be a great mother. It was also a not-so-thinly veiled reminder for them to continue to beg her to put out a cookbook.

Let's not forget another surreal part of her blog. Kate had the nerve to write:

"I am very clear with them about respecting our own belongings and especially others belongings. It's an important lesson and I have taught it well, or so I thought..."

Kate has been filmed throwing her children's toys down the stairs. She has admitted to throwing her kids' toys, stuffed animals and school projects in the trash. She kicks the boys' Lego buildings into a million pieces if they don't put them away the minute she tells them to. She mistreats and mishandles everything that doesn't belong to her, including Jon's two German Shepherds (now only one), ... all in front of her children. Is that her definition of respecting others' belongings?

The globe blog offered even more proof of the depth of Kate's delusions:

"I was frustrated and disappointed at this point because I felt like I had a group of lying kids on my hands – something I have always harped against!!!! How could this be happening?"

First of all, if the children do lie, it is probably for self-preservation, and because they learned to do so from their mother. For Kate, lying is like breathing. She even lied in her blog when she said that lying is something she has "always harped against." Maybe she meant that she has always harped against having "a group of lying kids" on her hands, but it is perfectly OK for her to lie.

After her weeping and gnashing of teeth about the lying kids, she had the nerve to ask the question, **"How could this be happening?"**

It's happening because eight beautiful little children were terrified of what their mother would do to them if they were found to be the one who damaged her precious, piece-of-crap globe.

SELF-INCRIMINATION

You have already read some of these excerpts from Kate's journal in the MOMMY'S JOURNAL chapter. Here's one more.

July 2007

After naptime Kate went into the kid's room and found a tall dresser had been knocked over, a lamp knocked down with it's bulb shattered, leaving shards of glass everywhere, a two foot by one foot section of the wall was peeled down to the inside of the drywall leaving those pieces thrown everywhere in the room. The locked box of lotions was opened and all over the floor and smeared everywhere!!!!!!!!!!!!!!!!!!!!!!!!!! Kate said this had all happened while she was downstairs listening on the baby monitor and thinking the kids were playing nicely.

Anybody who has ever used baby monitors knows that they are so sensitive you can hear a baby breathing. That's kind of the point of them. So Kate was downstairs listening to her children through the baby monitor, and she did nothing about what must have sounded like World War III upstairs. How could anyone hear a dresser being toppled and a light bulb shattering and think, "They are playing nicely"?

LUNCH MONEY

Kate is in control of the Gosselin operation 24/7, including when she is traveling. She makes time for every infinitesimal business detail that comes along and is constantly monitoring her emails and talking on her cell phone. Yet, somehow, she failed to handle the minor little detail of paying for her kids' lunches at school, and managed to make it look like it was Jon's fault in the process.

In an email from April 24, 2009, Beth Stine from the children's school informed Kate that lunch money accounts for Mady and Cara were overdrawn. She told Kate that "Madelyn's" account was overdrawn by $234.65, and Cara's account was overdrawn by $187.60. She asked Kate to please send in a check made out to LCDS for $422.25 to cover the amount currently owed, and to please send in a little extra to cover their cafeteria purchases through the end of the school year. She explained to Kate that if there was any money left in their accounts at the end of the year she could carry it over to the next year.

In her response to Beth, Kate managed to show her ignorance, provide excuses, and blame Jon for the situation all in one fell swoop of just four short sentences. Kate told Beth that Mady and Cara were obviously "buying lunch a lot more than I realized!!!!" She explained that she would be away until the next week, but would mail her a check as soon as possible. Kate then apologized, and told Beth that she travels a lot and "Jon must not be packing lunch as I had thought! :)"

I have never seen Kate Gosselin EVER put her children's needs ahead of hers, whether those needs are for lunches or anything else. And, of course, it was all Jon's fault anyway.

AND THE WINNER IS …

What kind of mother, not just a loving mother, but any kind of mother, would do this?

In Season 4, on the "Legos & Safaris" episode of *Jon & Kate Plus Ei8ht*, while racing on a small pond in little paddle boats with the kids, Kate races ahead of her small children so she can beat them in the race. Then, back on the interview couch discussing the incident, Kate enthusiastically tells us, "…and I ended up passing everyone and winning!!!"

Most mothers go out of their way to let their little ones win races or games until they get to an age where they are capable of learning how to handle defeat. A grown woman racing against her 5-year-old children…and taking delight in beating them…and then bragging about it to the world, is a perfect example of someone who is sick, emotionally vacant, and narcissistic. I think I gave her too much credit when I compared her to a 13-year-old child. In this instance, she seems to not have made it beyond 8 years old in the maturation process.

On that same trip to San Diego, Kate again showed her lack of maturity and reason by punishing Mady and making her miss out on seeing some wildlife that the kids were all looking forward to.

"Mady was having a meltdown and I opted that if she has meltdowns she needs to skip out on the fun. She was very angry with us but we made her stay back cause I just didn't want her ugliness to rub off on everybody else, I wanted them to have a good time and I was excited to show them these fish so she stayed back with Jenny."

Kate didn't want Mady's "ugliness" to rub off on everybody else, but she sure wasn't worried about her own ugliness ruining their good time. While feeding the fish, Kate says to Joel, "Um yeah, you're dripping it on yourself! You're gonna stink! That was wonderful, Joel! Now you're gonna stink like a fish but we can't change you!"

I'd like to ask poor little Joel if he had a good time being scolded and ridiculed by his mother. Any possible "ugliness" from Mady would have paled in comparison to that shown by Kate.

POST-SPLIT REPORTING

The following are excerpts from my daily reporting for *US Weekly*.

Jon & Kate Gosselin PA Reporting
August 2009
        …Jon got a basketball from the garage and shot around for a few minutes with Cara. The other kids are playing. They're thrilled that Jon is home because Kate rarely lets them outside and I never hear them yelling and playing while she's here. They're going crazy running around now and having fun.

Jon and Kate Gosselin PA Reporting
September 2009
        5:30 pm — Kate was supposed to come home to relieve Jon but she was waiting for him to leave the house and Jon didn't want to leave the house and let the kids alone without her being there, so we had a three hour stalemate. Kate went to the tanning salon and the UPS store the paps told me and then to the Giant where she bought groceries. She then sat in her Land Cruiser in the Giant parking lot for over an hour while Jon waited at the house for her to get home. He was getting pissed at her for acting like this.
        Jon told me that it was exhausting taking care of eight kids alone in response to my question. I have a couple little ones and I can't imagine what it must be like to have eight. He said he just did dinner, dessert, played, and bathed them all while Mady and Cara packed their own lunches for school tomorrow. He told me that with the little girls, you have to shampoo, condition and brush their hair as well. He loves doing it all. He always smiles when talking about the kids.
        7 pm — Kate finally came home and she was dressed to kill in a bright pink dress and heels. She looked stunning. When she first pulled in I could hear just a brief but heated exchange but that was because of the kids. All the kids were excited to see her. I could hear "Mommyyyyyyyyy" from the road and they were giving her big hugs etc. Mady and Cara and most of the little ones helped with the groceries and Kate's bags. There was just one pap and me there at this point and she didn't seem happy about it. She did her best to keep herself hidden behind the car and trees, parking right by the front door again.

Jon & Kate Gosselin PA Reporting
September 2009
	…Another neighbor from Elizabethtown that I spoke to several weeks ago told me that Kate was always screaming at the kids, even when they were very small. She would run the house like a military base, expecting the kids to jump whenever she yelled for them. "I saw Kate spank the kids many times. She believed in old-school discipline. If she said something and they didn't listen, they'd get spanked. It got to the point that the kids would cover up when she yelled at them because they didn't know if they were going to get hit or not."

Jon & Kate Gosselin PA Reporting
September 2009
	After leaving the Target shopping center, she drove in the opposite direction of home and I wasn't sure where she was headed but she ended up at the kid's orthodontist in Wyomissing. The TLC crew was there waiting for her outside in the back where she parked. She pulled into their very small lot and a pap pulled in right next to her and she yelled to TLC "They can't park here! They can't park here!!" and the TLC guys told him he had to leave. I had parked past there and ran back to see her get out of the car. Kate yelled at Mady, "Move! We're late because of you!"

Jon & Kate Gosselin PA Reporting
September 2009
	I went to the filming location from yesterday to back report on what happened inside during the shoot.
I've been going in there for years getting my daughter's dance supplies so I know the owner well enough to ask questions. She told me off the record that "Kate was very polite and courteous while the crew was filming, but as soon as they stopped, she lost her smile and became very bossy to the camera guys, telling them which angles to shoot her from and when to and not to shoot the kids. She yelled at the kids to behave several times when the cameras were off but laughed off their behavior when they were filming. She seemed to treat the kids like props rather than little people. She talks to them with disdain, like they're a burden to her. The kids didn't seem to mind though. They looked very happy and the nanny was there to take care of them. She would take them to the bathroom and be there to control them for Kate."

Jon & Kate Gosselin PA Reporting
October 2009
	…Back at the house, the kids are very tense and easily upset. They're fighting constantly and are acting out at school. Kate doesn't spend any real, quality time with them so they're on their own to figure things out for themselves. Mady and Cara are getting upset at little things and yelling back at the babysitters. They don't have a mother in their lives to give them discipline right now while Kate is off giving interviews, etc. They talk back to the nannies too now and the nannies are yelling back at them.

Jon & Kate Gosselin PA Reporting
October 2009

...I waited at the bus stop this afternoon for Kate to show up but there was nobody there from the Gosselin camp. The bus pulled in on schedule but Kate wasn't there yet. A few minutes later, Kate came speeding into the parking lot and pulled up to the bus. Mady and Cara were already out of the bus and Mady was standing there with her arms out at her side as if to say, "where were you??" Kate stayed in the car and they started getting in but then she got out and helped them with their bags. A single paparazzo was following her and he told me that Kate was in the bank just before racing to the bus stop.

Jon & Kate Gosselin PA Reporting
October 2009

I spoke to xxxxxx today and she told me that Kate went crazy last week after reading the US Weekly story. She knows that somebody that works for her is talking and she's threatening to fire everyone and hire new people to watch the kids. She said if she finds out that one of the babysitters is talking to anybody about her family, she's going to "fire their asses and sue them." After that, she's been completely quiet around the babysitters. She was on the phone yelling at Jaime Ayers about the photo of her yelling at the kids. She said "how could you be so stupid to do that in front of the paparazzi??!!"

Jon & Kate Gosselin PA Reporting
October 2009

Kate is off again doing TV interviews to gain the public's sympathy. I wish just one time an actual tear would come out of her eye as she's pretending to cry and wipe away imaginary tears. It would be so much more convincing. Kate's busy doing interviews and book signings and speaking engagements and taping a pilot for a new TV show, all while her eight children are home with paid staffers. She says it's all for the children but the children are the ones suffering. They're growing up without parents and the lesson they're learning here is that money is more important than love. Kate is so consumed with fortune and fame that she's lost sight of what should be most important. The future and well being of her children.

Jon & Kate Gosselin PA Reporting
December 2009

The nanny took all eight kids to the bus stop this morning while Kate stayed inside. She left the house at 8:30 and lost the paps on the country roads and disappeared for the rest of the day. The nanny came to the house at 3:30 to get the van to go and pick the kids up. The bus pulled in and the kids jumped out and she gave them big hugs and gathered them up and made their way back toward home. On my way back home, I drove past one of Kate's hot spots just to check and sure enough, there was her car sitting right out front. She was at the tanning salon, two minutes from the bus stop! I guess keeping that healthy glow is more important than picking your kids up from school.

Jon & Kate Gosselin PA Reporting
December 2009

...Jon approached Kate to try to discuss his TLC situation. He was hoping to convince her to talk TLC into dropping the injunction against him and releasing him from his contract so he could take jobs and make some money to pay his bills and child support. Jon said to Kate, "there's no way I can pay that much child support if I'm not on TV," and Kate responded, "I guess you're going to jail then."

Jon and Kate Gosselin PA Reporting
December 2009

   The bus pulled in and Judy the nanny got out and went to the door to welcome the kids home. I could hear them yelling "Judyyyyyy!" They love her. She gave them hugs and gathered them up and they made their way to the van. It took close to fifteen minutes to get them all settled and strapped in. Judy took them straight back to the house and they went inside. The kids were laughing and having a good time on the way in. On the way back home, I passed Kate in her Land Cruiser but by the time I got myself turned around, she was out of sight. At the spot that I passed her, the only place she could have been is the tanning salon. She's a creature of habit and the tanning place is the only place that she goes near where I saw her.

Jon & Kate Gosselin PA Reporting
January 2010

   Even though Kate was at the house ten minutes away, she arrived at the bus stop ten minutes late to get the kids. The bus driver had to sit and wait for her to get there while the kids just sat on the bus and wondered where their mommy was. They were sitting there looking out the window. When Kate finally arrived, she jumped out of the van and went to the bus and was confronted by paparazzi. She was clearly angry as they ere firing questions at her in front of the kids.

Jon & Kate Gosselin PA Reporting
February 2010

   Kate is away from the kids again, leaving them with a college-age babysitter. She's been gone since early on Saturday morning and Jon is still in Hawaii. The sextuplets seem fine as always but Mady and Cara really seem to notice the absence of a parent. They seem depressed and mopey, rarely smiling, like when they're with Jon or Kate. Five days is a long time for a 9-year-old to be away from both parents.

Jon & Kate Gosselin PA Reporting
February 2010

   The Gosselin kids are growing up without the presence of either parent for the majority of the time. The TV show makes it appear that Kate is a great mother, always cooking or organizing or taking the kids places, but having had a glimpse behind the scenes for several months of filming the show, it's just not the case. When the cameras were rolling, Kate smiled and laughed and cooked and cleaned and traveled with the children. What you didn't see, if you could have panned back a little bit behind the TLC crew, was the nanny(s) standing by to take the kids the moment the cameras stopped rolling. When the cameras stopped, so did Kate's pleasant demeanor. The smile went away instantly and she either yelled at the kids for messing up the shot, or yelled at someone on the crew for something else. Nothing is ever good enough for Kate. She has a vision in her head of how she wants things to go, and if anyone deviates from her plan, even a little bit, it sends her into a rage. Kate acted like a monster sometimes when the cameras were rolling. Just imagine how she acted when she didn't think the audience was watching. "She's a total control freak and if anybody messes with that, she explodes," said a *former Gosselin nanny.*

Kate puts her career ahead of her children's needs. She has herself so convinced that she needs to have a career on TV "to take care of the kids," that she overlooks the fact that what the kids really need is a mother that loves them and shows them she loves them and doesn't put work ahead of them. The Gosselin kids are treated like pets when a family is on vacation. They're left in the care of someone else while their mother goes off for days and sometimes weeks at a time.

Mady and Cara are having a hard time dealing with their parent's split and the surrounding media attention. They've always taken on Kate's dramatic personality and thrown tantrums and had emotional issues, but lately they've been acting out even more. They ask often "when is mommy coming home?" and seem sad and depressed that she's not around. They feel lost when Kate's gone and sometimes they take it out on the little kids. They become very bossy and mean and try to take on Kate's roll as the mother.

The sextuplets are happy but have no parental direction most of the time with Kate away. The nanny's job is just to make sure they're safe and well taken care of but she's no substitute for a mother when it comes to having talks with the kids or teaching them right and wrong. "That's Kate's job. I'm not their mother."

The sextuplets seem to be very happy and well-adjusted kids but they're too young to understand much of what's going with their family. As far as they know, this is how every child grows up. They do well in school and are smart and play together, but they don't have that bond really with Kate. They talk back and generally just do what they want until it gets too bad and Kate snaps and starts screaming. Then the kids end up running to their rooms crying.

The Gosselin kids are very spoiled, with TLC providing them with gifts and experiences that most kids will never have. First of all, they live in a palatial 8,000 square-foot house with a pool and 24 acres of yard to run around in. They've pretty much been given every toy you could possibly imagine and when TLC filming was going strong, there would be a constant flow of new toys and gadgets and equipment coming into the house on a daily basis. When they wanted to film the family camping, bang a Coleman truck shows up with tents and grills and chairs and everything else in their product line. When they wanted to film Jon playing water games in the yard with the kids, bang, the crew shows up with and hands out balloons and guns and water rockets. The kids get to go places that normal kids can't go, wherever they go because of their celebrity. Floor seats to the Harlem Globetrotters, meet and greet backstage with the team, team shirts with their name on the back and many other gifts from the Globetrotters. You want to go to a Phillies game? The Gosselin kids got to sit in the owner's box and meat the general manager and had a personal meeting with the Philly Phanatic and a trip through the souvenir stand to grab anything they wanted — all courtesy of TLC. They have no concept of working for things and paying for things as everything has always been given to them for free.

The Gosselin kids are growing up thinking their parent's lives are normal so they'll strive to act the same way. Kids take after their parents and want to be like them. What they learn from Kate is how to be demanding and stubborn and again, how to put your own needs ahead of your kids'. She says she's doing what's best for her kids, but the reality is that she's doing the opposite.

———

212

Kate has been away from home since Saturday and just returned to the house a few minutes before 3 pm today. She unloaded her suitcases and travel bags from the Land Cruiser and went in the house for a few minutes before coming out and getting the Sprinter van to go and pick up the kids at the bus stop. She wasn't wearing a hat when she came home but made sure to put one on before going out to face the paparazzi at the bus.

Kate drove the van straight to the bus stop and waited. The parking lot where the bus drops the kids off is still under four inches of snow with only a small area for waiting parents to park, but that didn't stop Kate from parking the huge van sideways across six parking spaces. She's got style and her own way of doing things.

Kate jumped out of the van and went to the bus door before it opened and one by one talked to the kids on the last step before directing them to the van. When a few of the kids were at the van they noticed a pap taking their picture and Colin yelled to Kate, "he's taking our picture!!" Kate yelled back "don't look at him and get in the van!!" After the last of the tups was off the bus and at the van, Kate talked to the driver for a few minutes and then went back to load the kids into their seats. She took their backpacks one by one as they got off the bus and was left holding three colorful packs in each hand. She loaded them into the very back of the van and then jumped inside the side door and closed it behind her so she couldn't be photographed. I was twenty feet away from them as everything went down and I didn't see or hear anything emotional come from Kate or any of the kids. It didn't look like a mother who hasn't seen her kids in a week. Mady and Cara weren't on the bus which means they had an after-school activity and would be coming on the late bus at 6 pm.

After bus pickup, Kate ran a few errands with the kids before heading home. The first stop was a coffee run at the Starbucks drive-thru. Nothing for the little kids this time around though. Kate just got a single cup for herself. With Coffee in hand, she drove the kids to the UPS store to pick up her mail. She parked the van illegally as always, facing the wrong direction at the curb, right under the 'No parking fire lane' sign. Kate left the kids in the car as she went inside for her packages and letters. She was in there for twelve minutes while the kids waited alone in the van with only the paparazzi watching them. Kate made two trips out to the van, carrying several packages the first time and then her letters. She was smiling and talking to the kids through the back of the van as she loaded up. They were yelling and laughing inside, keeping themselves occupied.

After UPS she drove into West Reading to her dry cleaner and again went through the drive-thru and picked up her freshly laundered clothing. After this, she got back on State Hill Road and headed home. Once parked by the front door, they were out of sight as they entered the house but it was very quiet. Once inside, they stayed there until dark. There was only a single set of tracks in the snow where the kids usually play. The nanny was instructed by Kate to keep them out of sight of the paps so they were only allowed to play behind the house.

Jon & Kate Gosselin PA Reporting
February 2010
        Kate is away from home for the third straight day today,
leaving the kids with Judy and several other sitters and nannies. She
disappeared at lunchtime on Saturday and hasn't been seen since. The
kids were off from school today and spent some time outside playing
in the snow, going sledding and just running around having fun,
throwing snow at each other. It usually turns into the boys against
the girls and today was no exception. The girls were the aggressors
today, throwing the first snowball when Lexi threw snow in Colin's
face. That got Joel and Aaden into the war and the rest of the girls
quickly came to Lexi's defense. They were laughing and having fun
though and nobody got hurt and nobody ended up crying for a change.

Jon & Kate Gosselin PA Reporting
March 2010
        Kate told Jon earlier this week that she was going to be on
the new season of Dancing With The Stars for sure. She's been in
California for more than a week. "He's angry because this will keep
her away from the kids for an extended period of time and nannies
will watch the kids instead of Jon. Kate won't let Jon have any extra
custody days. When it's his time to be at the house, he's there or he
isn't — his choice. Other than that, the kids are Kate's
responsibility and she thinks they're better off with a nanny than
Jon."

Jon & Kate Gosselin PA Reporting
March 2010
        Kate hasn't seen her kids since Saturday, February 20th. She
left the house at 6 am on Sunday morning. Jon took over custody at
7:30 am that day. Jon left the house and kids on Sunday, February 28th
so the kids have been without either parent all week. They've been
with a nanny and various babysitters and helpers.
        "Mady and Cara are mopey and being very dramatic and whiny —
more than usual. They feel like they've been abandoned by both
parents. They're excited that Kate will be on DWTS but miss having
her at the house." They love the nanny but she thinks they get scared
sometimes not having either parent around.
        Mady and Cara have learned to deal with Kate being away by
pretending to be in charge of the little kids and taking turns being
'mommy.' That works well for them but the little kids don't like
being bossed around by them and yell at and fight with them. This
just makes Mady and Cara yell and fight back and all out wars break
out that have to be settled by the nanny.

Jon & Kate Gosselin PA Reporting
April 2010
        Kate has been away from home and the kids since last Saturday
afternoon and she got home sometime overnight last night but didn't
take them to the bus stop this morning, which means she probably
slept in and didn't see them this morning. The nanny took the kids to
the bus stop. So after six days away from the kids, you'd think that
Kate would be anxious to see them and do anything to be with them,
right? Well at the very same time that the nanny was waiting at the
bus stop to pick up the kids this afternoon, Kate opted instead to ……
GO TANNING! She and Tony jumped in his Porsche SUV and went to Kate's
salon for a thirty-minute session. Tony didn't tan today. He just
waited patiently in the lobby for her while she went in the back for
a spray tan.

Jon & Kate Gosselin PA Reporting
April 2010

Carla brought the kids outside to play at 9:30 and parked herself in a chair up by the garage while the kids rode their bikes, scooters and just generally ran around. The kids were having a great time playing but Carla got too cold and ended playtime after only fifteen minutes. The kids were visibly upset and yelling that they wanted to stay outside but she made them go in. Cries of "we want to stay outside!" could be heard down at the fence.

In the short time that they were outside, Carla sat in a chair reading Kate's new book. She made sure it was visible to the paparazzi. Every moment of these people's lives are carefully orchestrated for maximum media exposure. It's all an illusion.

Jon & Kate Gosselin PA Reporting
April 2010

Despite what Kate says to the contrary, and despite her efforts to make the kids afraid of the paparazzi, the kids love them. It's pretty much the same people every day and Jon says that since they grew up with cameras in their faces, it's a natural part of their lives. I play with the kids all the time and they love it. They know us as their daddy's friends and they feel at ease around us. It's sad that Kate scares them and yells at them to the point that when she's with them and they see us nearby, they're afraid to even look in our direction. Colin is such a sweet little boy and he smiled and waved to one of the paps in the parking lot at the bus stop a few weeks back and that turned into the infamous photo of Kate slapping him and covering his mouth. She's a horrible mother.

Jon & Kate Gosselin PA Reporting
April 2010

Jon is extremely upset with Kate because she threw him out of the house in front of Mady and Cara when she got home. She came in the house and walked over to him and said, "I'm home, get out." He's also pissed because she wouldn't let him stay in the garage apartment one last night. His custody starts again at 6 am on Sunday but she made him leave the house and forced him to get all of his things out of the apartment at night, in the rain and cold, alone.

Jon & Kate Gosselin PA Reporting
August 2010

Jon had custody of the kids and when it was time to go back home to Kate, things got a little sad. When Jon called for them to start packing up, the kids started crying and told him that they didn't want to go back to Kate's house because she's hardly ever home and they don't want to film anymore. They refused to pick up their toys and sleeping bags and sat themselves down on the sofa with their arms folded and said they weren't going.

When they finally arrived at the gate the kids were crying for Jon to take them back to his apartment and not make them go back with Kate. When they saw the nanny approaching, they started freaking out, getting hysterical and wailing and sobbing uncontrollably. Jon got out of the van and came around to give them hugs goodbye and to try and calm them down but that made it worse and they were crying even louder. Then Jon gave last hugs and got into my car to go back home.

(Source — A Gosselin Insider — I wasn't in Alaska)
The kids are having a miserable time in Alaska and have been saying things like "I don't want to film today. Can we just go home now!" They're being pushed around and guided physically by the crew because they don't want to be there. There's a lot of foot-stomping by the little kids and Mady and Cara are just generally moping and whining that they want to go home. Kate doesn't seem to care at all about their feelings. She just tells them to be quiet and keep moving.

The kids were crying and wanting to come home after only the second day in Alaska. They want to be at home in their pool enjoying their summer. They asked Jon to come and get them and bring them home. Mady is so sad and even threatened to run away. Kate told her if she did, a bear would eat her.

Kate scares the kids into filming. Kate said to the kids previously "you have to keep working or we'll lose everything we have!" Kate told them they'd lose the house and have to live in a shack, that they wouldn't be able to go to their school anymore and that they wouldn't have nice clothes and good food to eat.

TLC, Kate and the kids filmed an episode on Friday afternoon on Penn Avenue in West Reading, two blocks from Jon's apartment. Kate took the kids to get their haircut and to Wendy's for fast food of all places. Kate doesn't allow Jon to give them anything but organic but now she's the one giving them junk food. Could this be a bid to win some affection from the kids who obviously have had enough of her parenting skills? TLC also filmed Kate getting her dry cleaning at a nearby cleaners.

The boys were grumbling about having to wear matching shirts when the girls didn't have to. The girls have already been complaining to Kate about this and it looks like she gave in to them but not to the boys. When the kids are with Jon they pick out their own outfits.

IT'S NOT RAINING MEN

Does Kate ever have anything nice to say about her children? Everything is always about how difficult or messy or expensive they are. Now she has added scaring men away to that list of complaints. Kate Gosselin claims that she hasn't met a new man, or even dated, because of her children. In April of 2011, she told Matt Lauer on *Today* that she's only been on "half a date" since her split from Jon.

Kate shoulders the bulk of parental duties and also soldiers on solo with the show. In between, she has made a cottage industry of her fame – writing two books, competing on Dancing With The Stars and guest-hosting on The View. But she told Lauer that none of that is why she's only been on "half a date" since her split with Jon – it's tending to her two 10-year-olds and six 5-year-olds that's to blame. And she fears her love life might be hopeless.

Then, in January of 2012, Kate sat down with Dr. Drew (Pinsky) to discuss, among other things, how her children are keeping her from finding love.

```
Dr Drew: How about you, do you have a love life?

Kate:  "No, too busy. I think a lot of my friends who are
        being constructive, or trying, say gosh, who are
        you gonna meet that's um, gonna be able to deal
        with eight kids? And my answer is always, if they
        can deal with eight kids in our situation, they
        probably will be the person. It'll sort of prove
        it.
```

Having eight kids hasn't prevented Kate's ex-husband from dating and having other relationships. Maybe Kate's lack of dating has more to do with the fact that she is unpleasant, mean and so self-absorbed than with her having eight kids. I have spent time with Jon and Kate's eight children, and they couldn't be any more delightful. They're inquisitive, funny, and eager to learn and play and be children. When I look into their precious eyes though, all I can think of is the torture that Kate has put them through.

POETRY

One of the twins is an aspiring poet. One day in 2011, she read me every poem in her poetry journal that she carried with her. She seemed shocked that an adult would take the time to sit quietly with her, or even be interested in what she had written. She said her mom never sits down with her and listens to her poetry. She was starving for parental attention and didn't want it to end.

MOVIE NIGHT

This woman is her own worst enemy and a PR person's worst nightmare. Luckily for Laurie Goldberg, PR guru at Discovery Communications, Kate Gosselin is no longer her problem.
On one particular Friday and half of the Saturday after, all eight Gosselin kids were with their father. That Saturday night when her kids returned home to Kate, what do you think was the first thing this loving mother who missed her children would be anxious to do? Escape to Twitter, of course!

Kate went straight to Twitter to tell her followers that they were having a "family movie night!" at home. She tweeted a picture of the movie they were going to watch, along with photos of the kids all lined up and evenly spaced out on "the stripe" (otherwise known as the edge) of the rug on the floor in front of the TV. The kids must sit along "the stripe" so Kate doesn't have to worry about any popcorn spilling on her rug. While the kids are made to sit in that oh-so-comfortable configuration, Kate lounges on a cushiony sofa behind them, drinking wine…and tweeting. Kate tweeted 114 tweets during that particular "family movie night."

In her Twitter frenzy, she stupidly became engaged in a back and forth about why she doesn't take the kids out to the movie theater instead of staying at home. She opened up this particular can of worms when she wrote about movies being expensive, and then got defensive and angry when a tweetie continued to question her. This was the start of the great Twitter movie war:

> xxxxx @Kateplusmy8 Just saw The Lorax!!!! Will be buying the DVD!! Cried like a baby at the end!! Such a HUGE message so beautifully done!!

> I'll put in on my list to get when out on DVD. Movie theater is $$$ and hard to do for us!:) Thanks for review!

> xxxxx @Kateplusmy8 Great movie! Sounds like fun nght planned. But I don't get why u don't take kids to movie theatre? U have money.

> **…We all have money. It's in our personal choices on how to spend it that counts… Have a good day!**

Why did Kate even engage in this conversation in the first place? Because she is just too stupid to know any better. She never thinks about the possible consequences of her words before she says them. This is a very wide-open window into the amount of influence Discovery had in controlling the message that came out of her mouth for the years she was under contract with them. When the Discovery contract expired, Kate was on her own with little oversight, and she became totally unplugged.

Kate's personal choice on how to spend the money her kids made for her is to treat herself like a first-class Hollywood starlet, sparing no expense on anything that's for her. Kate sits in her mansion with her $200,000 in cars parked in the driveway and garage, enjoys her glamorous, first-class trips around the world and her millions of dollars in investments tucked away in her many accounts, and her $800-a-day personal bodyguard, etc., but she can't take her children to see a movie in a theater because it's too expensive.

AND THE TWEET GOES ON

Here are some of Kate's Twitter thoughts where she criticizes other mothers and crows about her own great, personal accomplishments:

xxxxx @Kateplusmy8 How does Kate deal every day???

A mom's gotta do what a mom's gotta do. Love motivates me to do my best no matter how I feel :)

xxxxx @Kateplusmy8 Would you ever sign them up to dance ? Could you be a "dance mom?" LOL! Happy Sunday!

Um dance.. Yes. Um those horrible Dance moms? Never ever ever!

xxxxx @Kateplusmy8 it's amazing what you have done for your kids some people may judge u but u wouldn't be able to provide half as much as a nurse

Correct! Thanks for recognizing that I am doing BEST I can for my kids. They have a wonderful life..It's my greatest accomplishment!:)

Then there is this gem where Kate strays from her script that she is the perfect, most organized mother on the planet:

xxxxx @Kateplusmy8 Morning Kate! Are you recouped from the baking frenzy? LOL working here today but back at it tomorrow. Have a gr8 day!

Yes, I slept so well last night I forgot to set my alarm clock. Two days alarm clock's name was Leah :) Thank goodness for conscientious child.

Two days in a row Kate had to be awakened by a first-grader…on school days. And she proudly announced this online to the world. No worries. Kate knows that her fans will make excuses for her.

"It was truly the sweetest thing I had ever witnessed…"

Kate Gosselin has eight children. You've probably picked up on that by now. She's been a mother since 2000, so it's probably safe to assume that she has seen and experienced countless sweet and precious moments from and with her kids. Someday, when her children read her writings and see the above quote from her, they might be a little taken aback to learn that the sweetest thing their mommy ever witnessed had nothing to do with any one of them; instead, it was about an animal in another country.

That quote came from Kate's blog, "Dear Honey," which she posted on November 18, 2011. Kate was referring to the time she was moved to tears as she held Honey, the koala bear, while filming for the Australia episode. It was very touching. She showed a lot of emotion toward that little bear; more than she has ever shown toward any of her children at any time during seven seasons of filming a reality show.

We could simply chalk the statement up to Kate's overblown hyperbole. Unfortunately, her kids have to live without any of the warm, genuine affection their mom gave to a bear.

UNDER THE BBBUS

On November 3, 2001, radaronline.com posted the following story about Kate Gosselin.
Kate Gosselin Slammed By Child Safety Group After Her Son Is Seen Playing Under her Van
http://radaronline.com/exclusives/2011/11/kate-gosselin-son-plays-under-wheels-her-van-danger-child-safety-group-photos/

Not only did Kate stay in the van as one of her boys crawled underneath to retrieve something with his head right behind the front wheel, but the engine was running the entire time. A mishap could have resulted in death for her child but she stayed in the van texting.

NO GUIDANCE

Kate Gosselin keeps her children as isolated from the world around them as she possibly can. She wants people to only know about her children what she tells them and nothing more. I learned that the Gosselin children are not permitted to meet with their school's guidance counselor, at all, for any reason. Kate is afraid they will be asked questions about their home life that she absolutely does not want answered.

A SAD TRUTH

In a child's first 5 to 7 years of life, 80% of their personality, morals, values and self-identity are formed. Given this statistic, how does Kate Gosselin rate as a parent instilling morals, values and self-identity in her impressionable, young children? Based on the following tips on personality development found through online research, not very well. Not very well at all. She fails at all twelve bullet points:

Tips on personality development of the child
- Do not scold the child all the time for minor failures.
- Do not trouble the child constantly.
- Avoid frequent use of bitter or harsh remarks.

- Avoid the practice of preferring one child over the other and thereby neglecting the other.
- Do not denigrate or disparage the child.
- Avoid prolonged separation of the child.
- Constant friction with the child or between the parents should not be expressed in front of the child.
- Never discourage the child.
- Do not praise your child always.
- Excessive discipline is also harmful.
- Repetitive or severe punishment should be avoided. The child should be given a chance to rectify him/herself, and punishment should be the last resort.
- Parents should not be over-ambitious regarding their children, and they should not set goals for a child which are not in harmony with his or her intellectual endowment, capabilities, achievements and interests.

Kate forces her children to make her cards and presents and she tells them what to do to celebrate her, be it a birthday, Mother's Day or any one of her hobbies of the week, like when she ran in a marathon on the other side of the country in Las Vegas. In that case she told the world via Twitter and on her blog that her kids made signs to encourage her and stood outside watching and cheering her on as she ran around in her driveway. She had a cake made for them to have a 'Go Mommy' party while they sat at home with a babysitter while their mommy was away for a week with her married bodyguard. She makes the children her own personal cheerleaders while doing nothing to encourage their growth by allowing them to participate in their own activities outside of their house.

Given her failures as a parent, it may very well be best for the Gosselin children's mother to be absent from them as much as possible. It is not my imagination that Kate looks and acts her happiest when she is away from her kids. It definitely appears as if Kate doesn't enjoy interacting with her children. All photographic, video and Twitter evidence shows this beyond any doubt. Take her recent *Celebrity Wife Swap* appearance. With a film crew in her house and cameras rolling for the entire world to see, you would think that Kate or any sane person would be on their best behavior to show what a loving mother she is. Not Kate Gosselin. She actually yelled at her twin daughters in front of the cameras for coming down to the kitchen a few minutes early, before their scheduled 6:03 morning kitchen entrance time. The poor girls looked dejected and beat down as they were belittled and sent away…for the television audience's viewing enjoyment.

Her M.O. has always been to hide in the kitchen while volunteers and paid 'helpers' took care of her children. In the early days, the twins would get off the school bus alone and come inside the house to find Kate 'busy' in the kitchen while their six brothers and sisters were caged in by the front window entertaining themselves. She couldn't take the five or ten minutes like a normal mother and come outside to greet her children as they arrived home from school. Kate invents reasons to have to be in the kitchen so she can spend as little time with them as possible. She is an awful cook, baker and even dishwasher but the kitchen has always been her escape from the reality that is being a mother.

If you look at photos or video of Kate when she is with her children, she always looks angry, sullen, disapproving and mean. When you see photos of her when she is away from her kids, either on one of her "business" jaunts or for any other reason, she is always smiling broadly and is positively beaming. Whenever she is with her kids, she tweets like there is no tomorrow. When she is not with her kids, she barely tweets at all.

In a related sense, Kate's idea of fun is anything that doesn't involve her children. Everything we have seen of her actions indicates that she is fulfilled only when she is the center of attention and when others are complimenting her or gushing about how wonderful she is.

Maybe this is because she resents the fact that it is her children who made her famous. But time and time again, she is slapped with the reality that exposing her children's private lives to the world is the only reason anyone outside her immediate circle of life even knows she exists, and the only reason anyone has ever been, or will ever be, interested in her. She has traveled numerous paths to try to find fame on her own, but try as she might, she just doesn't have the talent, personality, intelligence or likeability to succeed in celebrity endeavors on her own. Since she can't shake those cute little albatrosses from around her neck, she must continue to wring every last drop of moneymaking usefulness out of them as she can.

> "I need to look at, 'what's best for the kids?
> What's best for the kids?'
> That is what I say to myself constantly."
> – *Kate Gosselin*

DADDY'S LITTLE GIRL

"Their protectivity of me is so dear!
I honestly loved how they took such protective care of me!"
– *Kate Gosselin*

That's beautiful, right? The way Kate talked about her parents in the above quote? Only Kate wasn't talking about her parents when she said that. Kate hates her parents, especially her father, Kenton Kreider. That quote was taken from one of Kate's journal entries in which she was discussing spending time with Dr. and Mrs. Glassman during her tummy tuck surgery back in 2006. Here's how Kate described it in her journal:

August 2006
Kate said that she felt like they were her parents and it felt so good! She said that she never had that as a kid and she enjoyed the feeling.

There are only four entries in Kate's journal where she mentions her parents or her childhood. That isn't much considering she wrote down every minute detail of what was happening in her life during this period. These are the first three paraphrased entries:

September 2006
Kate remembers her grandmother and all of the pure bliss that she and Kate's grandfather tried to create in Kate's bliss-less life as a kid and actually as an adult too.

October 2006
Kate talks about her grandmother's funeral and how it's so hard to believe that she's gone. She was the perfect example of unconditional love. Kate said that her own mother tried to preach to her and her brother and sisters through her tribute to her grandmother and none of the kids appreciated it!!!

December 2006
Kate said that her parents were being crazy as usual but doesn't disclose any details.

The final entry is from May 2007, when she wrote about pulling Collin up by the hair. She said that she saw her dad in herself today and that really scared her!!!!!

When Kate was making the rounds during her great church scamming tour, she talked about being born and raised in a Christian home and about being "saved" when she was 8 years old. Her father, Kenton, was an assistant pastor at a local church in Pennsylvania. She said that when she was growing up, she knew Jesus loved her, but the focus was more on a punishing God.

I did a lot of research, trying to understand what it means to be "saved." The best definition I could find is that being "saved" simply means that you have accepted Jesus into your heart as your savior. I have no idea if something specific happened to Kate when she was 8 years old, but it sounds like she grew up in an atmosphere of fear, being told that God would punish her if she got out of line.

A child living every day in fear and dread is unhealthy and tragic. Just ask the Gosselin children. It makes me wonder how much from Kate's childhood shaped her adult behavior. Certainly, neither Kenton Kreider nor Kate would be happy to engage in a public debate about her real relationship with her parents or what really happened between them. Nobody would win that one, I suspect, so they have both opted to remain silent on the matter.

In *Multiple Blessings*, when talking about how much she loved her grandmother, Kate did take what could be construed as a shot at her father when she said, "Grandma didn't just preach God's word; she lived and breathed it!"

Whenever Kate was asked about her parents in interviews, she would give a very brief, very carefully crafted, very Discovery-approved response: "They changed and had opinions on how to raise the kids."

During the 2009 TLC special, *Kate: Her Story*, Natalie Morales asked Kate about why her parents are no longer part of the children's lives. This is some of that conversation:

"I was one of five kids. I was the middle child. **The forgotten middle child** as they say.

It was definitely; it was a strict upbringing I would say. Um, I went to a Christian school, kindergarten through 12th grade.

NM: so was it a loving home?

Yes, my parents um, did their best um, my mom was the ever present parent who saw to it that our meals were cooked and our you know house was taken care of, um, my parents struggled um, I would say, um, I, I'm famous for telling my mom growing up my whole life, "mom five kids is way too many, there's just, you lose something in the details…"

NM: What is your relationship now with your parents?

My parents email me um, I email them back, they're very different from me, um, nobody's right.

NM: Have you changed or have they changed?

I think both of us have changed, um, there was a lot in my childhood that was not um, happy you know.

NM: Like what?

It would probably take me ten years to figure it out; so to say
that I talk to them on a daily basis is not accurate.

*NM: Are they involved as grandparents in helping with your
children?*

Not so much, and that's probably **more by my choosing at this
point then by theirs.** Is it out of the question forever? No,
probably not
I think the change came after our (6) babies were born. That was
the beginning of me realizing that everybody has an opinion and
um, sometimes those opinions aren't my opinions.

NM: Do they not approve of you putting your children on
television? Was that part of the issue?

No no it was before television, and at that time I felt like it
was just best to step back and take a break.

NM: Do you miss having them in your lives?

There's definitely something missing when you don't have
supportive parents nearby, um, and your kids don't have
supportive grandparents, absolutely.

In March of 2012, despite her earlier words to the contrary, Kate engaged in a
Twitter conversation where she disputed the fact that there's any problem at all
between herself and her parents.

xxxxx @Kateplusmy8 do u ever wonder since u have no relationship w ur
parents what that is teaching them about future relationship w u?

no facts in your question, just your opinion so no I don't wonder...:)

xxxxx @xxxxx @Kateplusmy8 Thank u @xxxxx that is my point. K8 is
choosing to not speak to parents

ha ha you're wrong! Again

xxxxx @Kateplusmy8 The only "fact" @xxxxx assumed was that it was your
decision to not allow your kids to see your family. True?

nope!

Kate's tweets contradicted what she had said in the Natalie Morales interview.
When Natalie asked Kate if her parents were involved as grandparents in helping
with the children, Kate specifically said that it was "probably more by my
choosing at this point then by theirs." So when Kate's tweeties talked about it
being her decision to not speak to her parents, they were just going by the
information she had provided in her interview.

Kenton and Charlene Kreider are the grandparents that took care of Mady and Cara while Kate was in the hospital giving birth to the sextuplets. Beyond that, not very much is publicly known about Kate's relationship, or lack thereof, with her parents, other than what she has stated in interviews. The widely accepted story explaining Kenton and Charlene Kreider's absence from Kate and the children's lives is that Kate's dad asked the members of his church for donations after Jon and Kate had the sextuplets. His church members responded by donating lightly used baby clothes and several cribs. Instead of being appreciative and grateful for the generosity, Kate decided she only wanted new, matching cribs and clothing, not used ones. She told her dad she only wanted cash.

Obviously, Kate's parents couldn't go back to the church members and tell them their daughter had refused their donations and was only interested in cold, hard cash. When Kate said on *Jon & Kate Plus Ei8ht* that her parents "don't know how to help us," what she likely meant was that, since she didn't get the cash she wanted, her parents wouldn't be seeing the family anymore.

The real issue that made Kate furious with her father wasn't about the lovingly donated, "gently used" clothing or the "non-matching" cribs. It was about the money she thought she should receive from her father through his church. More accurately, the issue was the lack of money.

Where was the money!?, Kate demanded. Her money!? She knew that the collection plate was passed for her and her children, so she questioned why the only things she got were some "dirty clothes and used cribs."

Push finally came to shove, and Kate accused her father of stealing *her* money and banished him to the depths of Gosselin Hell. She did the best thing she could do to hurt and punish him and her mother: She vowed to never let them see their grandchildren again.

I don't really know for certain anything different, but in interviewing people in Elizabethtown, PA, where Kate grew up, and more importantly, talking to one of Kate's own siblings, who requested anonymity, I got a little better insight into what makes Kate Gosselin tick.

According to the sibling, "Kate is just like her father. She's driven by power, control and money." This sibling also revealed that Kate and all of her sisters and brother were emotionally and physically abused by their parents. Apparently, Kenton Kreider was the poster boy for Proverbs 23:13-14. He took the phrase "spare the rod, spoil the child" to the extreme. There were daily beatings for any and all disciplinary infractions. "Katie walked around on eggshells, never knowing when or where the next beating would occur." (That sounds hauntingly familiar.) Kate said on an episode of *Jon & Kate Plus Ei8ht* that she was "very, very over disciplined." That would explain where Kate learned how to raise her children, but it's no excuse for abusing them. She also said cryptically on TLC's *Kate: Her Story* that "There was a lot in my childhood that was not happy."

Kate learned another very important lesson (to her) from her father. She learned how to separate good, church-going Christians from their hard-earned money. Kate got to see first-hand, watching her father in church, how easy it was to convince people to give – 'til it hurt. As a young girl, she watched the collection basket being passed around and she wondered how she could get her hands on some of that money. She kept that thought tucked away for a rainy day.

When it rains it pours, and soon enough, Kate had found her own unique way to get her hands on the hard-working Christians' money. She gave birth to six children at once, knowing full well and in advance that there was absolutely no way in Heaven or Hell that she and Jon were going to be able to afford to raise eight children on their own. Kate knew her target audience from doing her own research on the McCaughey septuplets, and she wagered that when she announced to the world that she was dead set against even thinking about "selective reduction," her new flock would hoist her on their shoulders and deliver her to the "promised land."

Kate went to that well of Christian support many, many times with statements such as "We truly believed that if God gave us these babies, He would take care of us."

She played that card over and over again, and it was music to the ears of Christians everywhere.

Here is one last observation. In all of my research, I had never heard Kate speak of or write anything about her father. Whenever she mentioned her parents, it was always in the plural form: "My parents." She never once spoke Kenton's name nor alluded to a single happy memory of her father since the estrangement. Ever.

Kate is afraid of her father and what he might say about her in the media. In March of 2012 Kate got spooked when someone posing as Kate's father on Twitter sent her several very cryptic tweets about things that only Kate, Kenton and the mysterious tweeter would know. Kate was afraid that her father could possibly be the person behind this book and, within days, she blogged about happy memories of her father paying the bills when she was a child:

Kate's Financial Lessons for the Gosselin Kids
Posted on April 30th, 2012 by Kate G

Kate said as a kid, she would watch her father paying the bills on the dining room table. He sometimes let her help by playing mailman and putting the return address labels and stamps on the envelopes. He told Kate how important it is to always pay your bills first to keep a perfect credit score.

I don't believe this was a coincidence.

> "Happy Fathers Day to all great dads out there.
> You are who your kids are likely to become.
> B the best u can b for them today&always!"
> – *Kate Gosselin* 6.17.12

THE LIES AND TIMES OF KATE GOSSELIN

"Once again, if you read something about me
(or most other people in the media) in a tabloid
where information has been provided by an unnamed 'source'
you can assume it to be completely fabricated and totally false."
– Kate Gosselin

Anyone who has ever watched Kate on TV, or has seen or heard or read interviews with her, will probably not be surprised to hear that she lies – a lot. Kate lies to make herself look good and to make others look bad. She lies to get sympathy. She lies to get people to believe she is something she is not. She lies to excuse her bad behavior. She lies to deflect criticism. She lies to blame others for her bad behavior. She lies to make people believe that her children are always happy and are constantly thanking her and singing her praises. In 2013 on *Celebrity Wife Swap* to garner sympathy, Kate said "somewhere around 2011 the world watched Jon and I go through a divorce." 2011? Jon and Kate's divorce was finalized TWO YEARS prior in December 2009.

Kate has lied in every way imaginable. She has lied intentionally. She has lied by mistake. She has told lies of omission. She has denied things that are known to be true. She has lied by saying she does certain things as a matter of routine when, in fact, she has only done those things once or so for filming. She has lied by exaggerating her importance and acting as if she is more experienced, skilled, successful, deserving and important than she is.

In watching Kate on a daily basis and reading Kate's words, both public and private, my opinion is that Kate Gosselin is not only a pathological liar, she is a hypocrite as well. By definition, **hypocrisy** is the state of pretending to have beliefs, opinions, virtues, feelings, qualities, or standards that one does not actually have. Hypocrisy involves the deception of others and is thus a lie. Kate claims to hate bullying, but she bullies others and encourages her fans to do the same.

To prove that Kate is a liar and a hypocrite, I have included some of Kate's blatant lies in this book, and then given the facts. It was a difficult task, choosing only some, because the list of possibilities is so long, and it continues to grow with every television interview Kate gives and every tweet that she tweets.

THE HOUSE

"That's why TLC wants us to continue to be 'normal' ....
Wonder how we will explain the $2M house? :) "
– Kate Gosselin

There has been a great deal of speculation that Jon and Kate didn't actually buy their new million dollar house in Lower Heidelberg Township near Wernersville, PA, but that TLC/Discovery planned on moving them there for filming purposes because Kate complained that their Elizabethtown, PA, home was too small for them.

Kate has always denied this and in 2011 even tweeted in response to a question from a fan about their current house. As in preceding chapters, I have omitted the names of those who tweet Kate in an effort to protect the naive, ignorant or deceived.

> xxxxx @Kateplusmy8 Just read that TLC owns your house. Is it true & do u have to move again?

> **LOL. Not a penny was payed for this house other than what I paid w my hard earned $. Did the company u work for buy ur house?**

Let's dissect Kate's response and provide some history and facts here. Jon's father bought them their first house in Wyomissing, PA. God bought them their second home in Elizabethtown, PA. We know this because Kate told us so when she said, "God had answered our prayer by supplying a house for us that met our every need." (That really means they got it for free.) But Kate's tweet above was intended to make everyone believe that the huge, new million-dollar home was paid for by only Kate and her hard-earned money.

Never mind the fact that Jon and Kate were married at the time they bought that house, so it was Jon's hard-earned money as well, and never mind that the only reason they had that money in the first place was because the eight Gosselin children were made to work like dogs having their every move filmed. So let's look further into Kate's assertion that she bought the house and "not a penny was payed" other than what she paid with her "hard earned $."

In August of 2008, a communication was sent from TLC/Discovery to Jon and Kate Gosselin that lists specific ideas for what would be needed in a new house for the Gosselins. The house was to be "designed with production in mind," have rooms "big enough for film crew to film activities," and have a "separate entrance for crew with room for equipment storage."

The "Overall Goal" was to build a functional and secure home for the Gosselins while filming the ups and downs of the design and building process to share with the viewers.

The focus of the "Draft Plan" was twofold: functionality for the family and to be designed with production in mind.

A few highlights of the plan include:
- No show entrance or foyer

- No dining room. Just a very large kitchen for the family to gather to eat and film
- Family room large enough for the entire family to gather to have their activities filmed
- Separate entrance for the film crew with plenty of storage space for their equipment, the interview set storage and a bathroom for only the crew to use to take stress away from Kate because she freaks out if any of her family, the crew, uses her bathroom
- Area for the kids to have desks and homework area for filming
- Home office for Jon to film the "working from home" angle
- Master suite that would be off limits to cameras
- Of the 7500 sq. ft. planned, the actual space that will be for filming would feel like only 4500 sq. ft. of house.

The "Projected Expenses" highlights of the new house would be:
- The house would be approx.. 7500 sq. ft and the budget would be approx.. $1,275,000 PLUS land costs and furnishings.
- **Jon & Kate are prepared to purchase the land only and to pay all taxes going forward on the house after the initial tax burden.**
- The home is being designed by Jon & Kate to be very "crew/production" friendly in terms of interview set space, storage space for crew equipment, entrance for crew/crew bathroom, etc.
- Lane furnishings will provide furnishings and gross up for taxes.
- For the remaining actual house expenses, they're looking for sponsors like Allstate, Whirlpool, etc. combinations of in-kind and funding will cover both the house and money toward the initial tax burden on the value of the house.
- Lumber is one of the major expenses so they're hopeful a lumber sponsor will step up to reduce that cost.
- Many environmentally friendly "green" product companies would be able to highlight their products on the show (windows, heating, insulation, flooring, etc.)
- Appliances are another large expense so they're hoping that Whirlpool or another sponsor would be interested to provide washers, dryers, ovens and ALL appliances.

Thoughts on Show Creative:
- Picking the land and selecting the finishing touches would give the network countless decisions and great points to cover during filming.
- Jon & Kate are committed to organic foods so they would really be looking forward to learning about green building and making similar choices and sharing with the viewers what they learn. This is a good opportunity to cross-promote TLC experts/hosts and Planet Green hosts/talent.
- The show will appeal to Jon & Kate fans so it will be perfect to run with other TLC programs related to renovations, building, etc. and will migrate viewers to watch other TLC shows as well.

These discussions about the house were a sure sign that TLC/Discovery was prepared to invest in the Gosselins for the long haul. They were also a sure sign that if TLC/Discovery was willing to go to such extremes as to get sponsors to bear the lion's share of expenses for building a new house, and were only asking Jon and Kate to foot the bill for the land and taxes, they would be more than willing to help with the purchase of an existing home. All this points to the high probability that not a whole lot of Kate's "hard-earned $" left her bank account to purchase their current home.

Ever on the lookout to protect her image, and not wanting to jeopardize her speaking engagement source of income, Kate was very aware that they had to be very careful about public perception. When Jon sent her a link to a positive newspaper article about them in June of 2008, Kate said it was a good article and that's why TLC wants us to continue to be "normal". She then gave one of her now-infamous quotes: "Wonder how we will explain the $2M house? :)" Explaining the house was actually not a problem. The easiest way to explain the new "$2M house" to people who thought the Gosselins were struggling financially and had to speak at churches with their hands out to get donations to feed their family, was to simply downplay its size and cost.

> "God had answered our prayer by supplying
> a house for us that met our every need."
> – *Kate Gosselin*

Not God, Kate. TLC/Discovery Communications. Both times.

KATE'S BED REST

> "My kids are the reason that I laid on bed rest for 30 entire weeks."
> – *Kate Gosselin*

When talking about the amount of time she spent on bed rest while she was carrying the sextuplets, Kate has given the number "30 weeks" many times, including when she was a guest on the *Ellen* show on October 28, 2009. Her statement is not true.

While this might be a bit picky on my part, and personally, it is hard to imagine anyone dealing with the physical trauma that it must have taken to carry six babies through to birth, a lie is still a lie. This particular lie is typical of how Kate plays fast and loose with the facts to make herself look like the most selfless, burdened mother who ever lived, and who sacrificed more than any other mother in history. Kate spent a lot of time creating the myth about herself that she was some kind of a superhero for dealing with her "unique situation," as she described it time and time again. This is an example of her bed rest lie:

"Like any mother, um, I laid on bed rest for 30 weeks, um, eaking out every minute of my pregnancy for my little kids. There is nothing I would do to put them in danger."

This is another variation of the lie:

"My kids are the reason I have always done everything. My kids are the reason I laid on bed rest for 30 entire weeks. My kids are the reason that I wrote the books and it's always about them. And, I know that it looks like it's all about me all the time and whatever, but what you don't see is down deep inside it's a desperate desire to provide for my kids."

The truth is, and this was confirmed by Dr. John Botti, Kate's obstetrician, that Kate went on bed rest in her home at 7 weeks, and started bed rest in the hospital at 20 weeks. She gave birth to the sextuplets at 30 weeks. So that's a total of 23 weeks of bed rest. But what's an extra 49 days of suffering here or there? The exaggeration made for a better story though, I guess.

It looks like the passing of a few years has given Kate some newfound clarity. On May 11, 2012, with no *Ellen* talk show television cameras and no millions of home viewers watching and listening, Kate was finally able to tell the truth about her bed rest. This is what she wrote in her "Happy 8th Birthday My Precious 6!" blog on her website, *kateplusmy8.com*:

"I remember the 23 weeks I spent lying on my right side, first at home on bed rest and then in the hospital… Enduring all of the boredom, worry and discomfort."

And the truth will set you free. Better late than never.

MULTIPLE BLESSINGS: THE ENTIRE BOOK

I have interviewed a lot of people who were actually present in the Gosselin's lives during the time period covered in *Multiple Blessings*. All those people told pretty much the same story about how Kate is made to look in the book and how totally nonfactual it is. That's a nice way of saying that the entire book is a lie. It is a rewrite of history to wipe clean Kate Gosselin's very ugly, erratic and narcissistic behavior.

There's not just one passage that can be held up as an example of the falsehoods. If you start from page 1, and read through 193 pages until the end, you will have read a work of almost pure fiction. *Multiple Blessings* took elements of Kate's life that had some basis in reality, and then twisted the reality to fabricate a completely misleading account of her life experiences and actions.

I selected the following excerpt from *Multiple Blessings* about Kate's hospital stay to illustrate this point. Sources have said that Kate's behavior was so over-the-top, that her mental capacity was checked on a regular basis. But here's how she and Beth Carson altered history:

"One morning in the hospital I awoke to two middle-aged men in white coats and clipboards standing over me. Clearing his throat and giving his glasses a nudge, one doctor announced that he and his colleague were there to assess my mental status. I know they were concerned because I probably appeared insanely calm and almost "glazed over" in the light of all of our very real concerns.

I, too, was amazed that I was so calm. What they didn't know or understand was that the peace of God, which even I couldn't describe, had already covered over me like a security blanket. Don't get me wrong; it wasn't as if I was living in denial. I had a bazillion concerns: Would my babies live? Would I live? Would the babies be healthy? How would we all fit into our house? How many diapers a day? A week? A year? How would we ever go anywhere again as a family when our car only fit six passengers? What about clothes, food, and — oh my goodness — college? In spite of this overwhelming list that very well could have consumed me, I had already learned that when doubt and fear began to creep in, it was imperative to redirect my focus immediately. I sang, I prayed, and I read my verses. I repeatedly handed my fears and worries back to God. He in turn rewarded me with an extra dose of peace that enabled me to creep by, minute by minute. It was this exchange that defined my days and bewildered many around me."

More than five people with first-hand knowledge of Kate's hospital stay have gone on record giving me information about how it actually went. Every one of them laughed when they read how Kate was portrayed in her book. Here is a more accurate picture of Kate's time in the hospital, from the people who worked there and had to take care of her.

"Kate was loud, and rude, and demanding, and unapologetic. She was a nightmare patient from the time she got here until the time she left. The nurses all celebrated the day she left."

The following text is from Kate's own pregnancy journal. It sounds like the exact opposite of someone who was "so calm" because the peace of God had covered over her "like a security blanket."

Kate said that she felt very selfish a lot and she wants this pregnancy overwith! She said that she's sooooo miserable and that is an understatement! She said she pees constantly at night and the ridiculous residents wake her up at dawn for stupidity!!!!

There is one last thing that should be mentioned about *Multiple Blessings*. Kate and Beth Carson's *Multiple Blessings* was published and released in 2008. On May 26, 1994, 14 years *before* Kate Gosselin, Beth Carson and Zondervan released *Multiple Blessings: Surviving to Thriving with Twins and Sextuplets*, publisher Harper Perennial released a similar book about raising multiples by author Betty Rothbart. The book was called…wait for it…***Multiple Blessings – From pregnancy through childhood, a guide for parents of twins, triplets, or more.***

Kate Gosselin couldn't even come up with an original title for her book. She had to swipe one from someone else who wrote about the exact same subject.

Kate and Beth's *Multiple Blessings* sold in excess of 523,000 copies. It was a very popular book, just not quite as popular as you might think. Because of Julie May's creativity, the requirement to purchase copies of *Multiple Blessings* was included directly into the contract for Kate's speaking engagements. The sale of 500 books was built in every time Kate went somewhere to speak.

They forced that book on anyone who wanted to book Kate to speak. Now that's how you pad the numbers.

KATE CANCELED CHURCH SPEAKING ENGAGEMENTS BECAUSE SHE WANTED TO SPEND MORE TIME AT HOME WITH HER FAMILY

This lie is a big one. This was a lie not only to us mere mortals, but to God as well. This is text copied from one of Kate's original church speaking engagement solicitation forms. The actual form has a cute photo of the family behind the text. Kate sent these out before she hired her manager, Julie Carson May.

Kate Gosselin's Speaking Engagement Info

Here is some information for you if this is something you are interested in:

We speak for a group of 100 or more. We typically ask that the church/organization cover our travel and accommodations (airfare, hotel, car transport to/from airport on this end and rental car if necessary). As far as a 'speaking fee' goes, we ask for a 'love offering' for church services (which averages around $1800-$2000 just to give you an idea, but is by no means a set 'fee'—we let that up to God to fulfill our needs!!!) and for MOPS groups we set a fee of about $1800. I know that sounds like a lot, but in order to leave our kids and work, this is what we need to cover our time and babysitting! In the past, churches, MOPS groups, organizations have charged admission or provided free tickets and covered our 'fee' in other ways. It is up to you how it should be handled in your situation. We typically use our presentation entitled 'Six (in honor of our 6) Lessons We Have Learned' where we start with a video montage set to music of our family and then do our presentation. We tell our story from the beginning while we weave our points into it — including the pertinent Bible verses that came alive to us during those times and continue to be our guide today! We usually end with about a half hour of questions from the audience, which brings our total presentation time to about 1 ½-2 hours in length. The only other thing we require is a $100 deposit to hold the date you have chosen! I hope this information helps! We enjoy speaking but are still surprised at the demand!

We know it is what God is asking of us!!!!
Thanks and I hope to put your group on our calendar soon!
Because of God's grace!
Kate Gosselin for all ten of us

Here's another pre-Julie May speaking engagement solicitation. Pay attention to the email address Kate used while contacting Christian churches looking for money. It was sixymomma@comcast.net. Get it? "sixy?" Kate's sexy, but she had sextuplets, so now she's "sixy." Cute. Kate somehow thought it was appropriate for churches.

(Cute photos of the family across the top)

Looking for a highly energetic speaker with a very intriguing family... and an amazing story?

Jon and Kate Gosselin were your average couple. After Kate gave birth to
twins Cara & Mady,
they wanted just one more baby.... and ended up with sextuplets!

You have to hear their whole story in person to believe all that has transpired in their family since the addition of the sextuplets. Miracles upon miracles have unfolded before their very eyes...and there is only one way to explain it: God!

This couple has a very inspirational and uplifting message with plenty of real life humor that everyone can benefit from!

Appearances by the entire family or just Kate & Jon are available upon request.
Currently the family is booking speaking engagements in front of audiences of 100+.
Dates are booked on a first come/first serve basis.
A $100 deposit will be collected to confirm your date.
For more information regarding booking and speaking fees contact:
Kate Gosselin by email: **sixymomma@comcast.net**

"Jon and Kate were one of favorite featured speakers. What parent could resist a story like theirs? Although few could relate, no one could deny their genuine love for Christ, each other and the incredible blessings of such a large family. They inspired those of us with far less challenges to rely on a God that is able to meet all our needs. They definitely brought the wow factor and their visit is still a buzz on campus. I would highly recommend this couple for your next event or weekend."

-Lisa Shumacher of the New Covenant Community Church in Fresno, California

(Another cute family photo)

"Jon & Kate Plus Eight" as seen on Discovery Health Channel
www.sixgosselins.com

I've read many of Kate's contracts. There are really too many to include all of them here. In addition to those contracts, I have countless "Speaking Agreement" forms from various churches booking Kate for speaking engagements. To give you a small sampling, I came across 14 speaking agreements that were sent back to Kate with the required deposit in March 2008. They totaled $48,600, and that was BEFORE what happened next, when the real money started pouring in.

As noted earlier, on April 14, 2008, Kate signed a contract for the entire Gosselin family, including Jon, to be represented by Julie Carson May of Media Motion International, LLC.

The contract stated that Julie May needed to make Kate at least $350,000 in the initial term of the contract, and $300,000 per year in any of the option periods, in order to keep Kate as a client. For her time and expertise, Julie May earned a 15% commission on all things Gosselin from that day on. The contract also entitled Julie May to a 15% commission if Kate had Julie help her with any "pre-existing projects" she may have had in the works. This was certainly strong incentive for Julie to work hard to help continue the exploitation of the Gosselin children.

Before Kate hired Julie May, she was asking for and getting $1,800-$2,000 per speaking engagement. Not a bad sum at all. But from that day in April of 2008 forward, Kate began demanding as much as $25,000 per church speaking appearance. Considering this new speaking fee, it certainly would not have been lucrative for Kate to waste her valuable earning time honoring her small-potatoes $1,800- to $2,000-per-appearance deals when she could be making more than ten times that amount.

After negotiating a new contract for *Jon & Kate Plus Ei8ht* with Discovery, Julie May went right to work canceling speaking engagements at Christian churches and conferences Kate had previously booked at the lower fee. Julie May then booked as many new speaking engagements as she possibly could for Jon and Kate at the much higher fee; she even booked some new speaking engagements **on the same days** as the ones she had canceled.

Getting right to the point, Kate decided to throw the Christians under the bus and switch her God to the almighty dollar. When Julie May decided to raise Kate's speaking fee, the moral and ethical thing would have been for Kate to have honored her commitments to the church groups and other organizations who had already booked her at the lower fee. Then, after fulfilling her previous commitments, she could have charged the new speaking fee.

Instead of choosing that path, Julie May emailed the church groups who had previously booked Kate and told them the BIG lie – that Kate could not attend because she needed to be at home with her family, spending more time with her children.

On April 28, 2008, Julie May sent an email to get Kate out of a speaking engagement. She addressed the email to "Judy" and introduced herself as someone working with Kate and Jon Gosselin. She then said that she had some "disappointing news" and proceeded to inform Judy that Jon and Kate "unfortunately" had to "cut back on their upcoming speaking engagements and travel in order to spend more time with their children." Julie May told Judy how really sorry they were that they couldn't make the trip, and they would be happy to return her deposit. She apologized again that they were not able to attend and told Judy that "they were so looking forward to meeting you in person and also meeting your wonderful group!" Julie then said that if Jon and Kate were in her area in the future, there might be a way to work out a future appearance. She left out the part about how much higher the speaking fee would be, however.

There was just one additional little problem with how the cancellations were handled. Kate and Julie May must not have thought that the canceled-on churches would notice the big, fat lie when Kate ended up speaking at a different church on THE SAME DAY on which their event was originally scheduled, but had been canceled. This actually happened. They had the nerve to book speaking dates on the very same days that they had previously canceled other, lower paying bookings, using the excuse that Kate needed to be home with her kids.

Here's one of many speaking engagement lists that I found among Jon and Kate's documents. I have redacted email addresses and telephone numbers. Pay special attention to the last part at the end where it reads "WATCH DATES."

JON & KATE SPEAKING ENGAGEMENTS
Updated August 20, 2008

September 3, 2008   **Little kids first day of school**

September 10, 2008   **Grain Council SMT on Sept. 10 and media either day**
                           before or after (and either Sept. 9 or
11)(Kate and Steve)

September 14, 2008   **Cornerstone Christian Fellowship**
                           Abington, PA (Kate & Jon & Steve)
                                   Contact: Pastor Jason
                                   Phone:
                                   Email: **xxxxxxxx@ccf-ag.org**
                                   Event Specifics: 9:00 and 10:45 am services

September 21, 2008   **Morristown Memorial Hospital**
                           Morristown, NJ (Kate & Jon)
                                   Contact: Heather Colburn (Am. Prog. Bureau)
                                   Phone: 781-878-xxxx
                                   Email: xxxxxxxx@apbspeakers.com
                                   Event Specifics: Afternoon talk (event 1-4
pm)
                                   Car pick up at 10am (req. Brad)

September 30, 2008   **Regis & Kelly (NY—whole family)**

October 2, 2008   **Birmingham - Southern Women's Show**
                           Birmingham, AL (Kate & Jon, same day in and out
                                   from Philly)
                                   Contact: Glenn Rosenbaum (Celebrity Access)

Phone: 818-508-xxxx
Email: xxxxxx@celebrityaccessinc.com
Event Specifics: Airport concierge service.

October 11, 2008   **Orlando - Southern Women's Show**
(Oct. 9-12)   Orlando, FL (Kate, Jon, Cara & Mady)—with Steve,
                     fly from Philly
                     Contact: Glenn Rosenbaum (Celebrity Access)
                     Phone: 818-508-xxxx
                     Email: xxxxxx@celebrityaccessinc.com
                     Event Specifics: Wilderness Lodge (2 nights

paid)

                     Check to Kate for difference in airfares to
go towards Steve

                     payment

October 16, 2008   **GMA/Pre-tape Fox & Friends (NY--whole family)**

October 19, 2008   **First Assembly of God**
                     Waynesburg, PA (Kate & Jon)
                     Contact: Richard Ritenour
                     Phone: 724-627-xxxx (church); 724-852-xxxx

(h)

                     Email: xxxxxxxxx@windstream.net
                     Event Specifics: 10:30 am service, 3:00

ticket event

November 1 OR 2, 2008 **Central Assembly of God**
                     Bossier City, Louisiana (Kate and Steve)
                     Contact: Lori Smith
                     Phone: 318-210-xxxx
                     Email: xxxxxxx@centralonthehill.com
                     Event Specifics: Lori may want to move to
                     Saturday—checking on exp.
                     Sunday evening event (currently, may move to Sat.
Nov. 1st)

November 11-12, 2008 **V-Tech SMT/Media**
                     New York (Kate and Steve)
                     Will be traveling to NY on Nov. 11th for
                     media training, SMT on 12th.

November 14, 2008 **Women of Purpose Conference**
                     Hershey Lodge & Convention Center
                     University Drive & West Chocolate Avenue
                     Hershey, PA 17033
                     Contact: Penny & Jessie
                     Phone: Ruth Puleo 570-460-xxxx
                     Email: xxxxxxx@verizon.net
                     Event Specifics:

December, 2008   **Keep Clear** ☺

LOCATIONS FOR 2009

January 10, 2009   **First Assembly of God**
                     Marcy, New York (Kate and Jon)
                     Contact: Pastor Tim
                     Phone:
                     Email: xxxxxxx@juno.com

Event Specifics: Sat. 2:00 event
Six Lessons with Q&A, signing photo cards
Covering car service

February 4, 2009   **Indianapolis Home Show**
Indianapolis, IN (Kate & Steve, fly in Feb. 4 am,
back Feb. 5 am)
Contact: Brent
Phone: 317-705-xxxx
Email: xxxxxxxx@dmgworldmedia.com
Event Specifics: Cover all Steve expenses
2 talks (likely in afternoon/early evening).

February 7, 2009   **King Street Church**
Chambersburg, PA (just one person, may cancel?)
Contact: Annette Smith
Phone:
Email: xxxxx@kschurch.org
Event Specifics: Julie to discuss security

February 22, 2009   **Gateway Church**
Parkesburg, PA (Kate and Jon)
Contact:
Phone:
Email: xxxx@gcwired.com
Event Specifics:

March 7, 2009   **First Christian Church MOPS**
Elizabethtown, Kentucky
Changed to 1 day event (Kate and Steve?)
Contact: Pastor Stuart or Amanda
Phone: 270-765-xxxx
Email: **xxxxxxx@firstchristianonline.com**

xxxxxxxx@gmail.com

Event Specifics: Change to 1-day event
Call to arrange specifics—Julie to discuss
Kate only and Steve

March 20, 2009   **Roswell United Methodist Church**
Atlanta, Georgia (Kate, Jon, Cara and Mady)
Contact:
Phone:
Email: xxxxxxxx@rumc.com
Event Specifics: 7:30 pm event (?)

April 30, 2009   **Baltimore Washington Medical Center (pending)**
Baltimore, MD (Kate & Jon, evening keynote)
Courtney Conference Center
301 Hospital Drive
Glen Burnie, Maryland 21061
Contact: Adrianne Carroll
Phone: 410-553-xxxx
Email: **xxxxxxxx@bwmc.umms.org**
Event Specifics: 6:00-8:30 pm

May 2, 2009   **PA Women's Conference (awaiting contract, have**
deposit)

Harrisburg, PA 12-2 pm (Kate & Jon)

                    Contact: Chris Lee
                    Phone: 310-822-xxxx
                    Email: xxxxxxxx@cal-entertainment.com
                    Event Specifics: Covering private car
service

                    12:00 Keynote (1 hour) followed by 1 hour
signing

                    (photo cards)

ADDITIONAL POSSIBLE EVENTS:

    Oct. 20, 2008 — North Carolina, Lane Home Furnishing Conference (Jon)
    Nov. 6/7—Sacramento, CA conference (Jon or Kate & Steve)
    November 23/24th—Madison, WI conference event (Kate & Steve)
    Late November—K-Mart SMT/media outreach
    January 22, 2009—Houston, TX, Evening Women's Christian Conference
    event with Lysa Terkeurst (Kate & Steve)
    March 25-30th, 2009—One day in this range, North Carolina, Lane Home
    Furnishings Event (Jon or Jon & Kate and Steve)

"WATCH DATES"—PREVIOUSLY CANCELLED SO WATCH WITH RE-BOOKING:
Sept. 27/28, 2008 -- New Life Church (Louisiana)
Jan. 11, 2009 — First Assembly (moved to 1 day only)
Jan 23-25, 2008 — Mission Viejo CA churches
Sept 12-13, 2009 — Newburgh, IL
Sept. 26, 2009 — Judy DeLoria Michigan conference
Oct. 23-25, 2009 — Ohio

The "WATCH DATES" were written down so Kate and Julie May would make
sure not to contact the same churches they had canceled on…because that might
make Kate look bad.

While the unethical handling of the speaking fee, in itself, is bad enough, if you
take a step back from this big lie, you'll see an even bigger one.

At the same time Kate Gosselin was going from church to church with her hand
out, asking parishioners possibly far less fortunate than herself for "Love
Offerings" to help support her family, because she didn't know how she would be
able to take care of her eight children otherwise, she was actually very quietly
signing those endorsement deals worth hundreds of thousands of dollars that you
read about earlier. She was also moving into that million-dollar home on 23 acres
just outside of Wernersville, PA.

Some of the endorsement deal specifics bear repeating. In September of 2008,
Kate received $50,000 in cash and $35,000 in tax-free merchandise just for
shooting a brief video saying how much they "can't wait to get their new Lane
furniture." On September 15, 2008, again at the very same time Kate was visiting
churches and begging for money, she signed a deal with Kmart for $158,000 cash
for a total of three days of "work."

Deals like these were coming in fast and furiously, and Kate couldn't get enough
of them. But Kate obviously never mentioned any of those deals to the people at
the churches who were passing the collection basket to help a "struggling" mother
of eight. The thought of jeopardizing her now $25,000 per speaking engagement
was the furthest thing from her mind.

In 2008, the same year she was begging for money from church-folk, the Gosselin tax return showed an adjusted gross income of $1,954,414.00. That is the kind of money most people don't see in a lifetime. Despite that, Kate kept on asking and begging and collecting money from less well-off families at churches who believed her lies and wanted to help her feed her children.

What those kind, generous folks were really helping her do was live a life of luxury, going to expensive spas and pampering herself with the finest things money could buy.

Let me be very clear here. The issue was not that Kate was charging a high speaking fee, and that churches and organizations were willing to pay it; the issue was the fact that Kate misrepresented herself and lied about her circumstances as a means to get people to donate more money to her. There is a word for that. It is called fraud.

DOES KATE GOSSELIN REALLY EVEN BELIEVE IN GOD?

Mir-a-cle *noun*
1 : an extraordinary event manifesting divine intervention in human affairs

Miracles to Kate Gosselin include things like getting a good deal on a freezer at Lowes. Call me crazy, but I always thought God would have more important things to worry about than Kate's freezer – like, say, wars, famine, and starving children all around the world, for example. I guess I was wrong. This is a paraphrased excerpt from one of Kate's journal entries:

Another miracle day. Kate said she and Jon got a new freezer for $618 after using a gift card and a rebate and ten percent off. Then Kate's brother Kevin gave her a $100 coupon so Kate sent Jon back to the store for even more savings.

Kate mentions miracles, God, Jesus and Lord several hundred times in her books and journal. Given her actions and willingness to scam others, it makes me suspicious whether she truly even believes in God, or if she just uses God's name as part of the big scam she's been perpetrating on the American public all these years. Kate breaks nine of the Ten Commandments on a regular basis (she hasn't killed anyone yet) and rarely goes to church now that she's rich and famous.

In the beginning, Kate was all about God. God this and God that. She knew early on that by aligning herself with Christians, and speaking about God continuously, she would have a built-in audience to sell her story to, and to buy her books, and to watch her shows – and to believe her lies. But when she got rich and famous, she suddenly stopped going to church. Why would that be?

This is the list of speaking points that Kate delivered to her patrons just before the "Love Offering" basket was passed around for her:

'Six (in honor of our sextuplets) Lessons We Have Learned'
1. God is in control.
2. God is Gracious and Strong.
3. Trust in God.
4. God is love.
5. God will provide.
6. Give God the Glory and Praise.

Kate's testimony: I was born and raised in a Christian home, school and church. I was saved when I was 8 years old on Sept 8, 1983. Growing up, I knew that Jesus loved me and that he saved me, but it was more about how God would punish you when you got out of line. I was never able to see God for who He really is…..It wasn't until He chose to give us our six beautiful children and really put us in a position that we needed to fully rely on Him for EVERYTHING daily and hourly did I realize…. We struggled through the hard times (especially during my pregnancy, and in the first year with 8 kids) and actually asked 'why us?' and were angry with God at times.
Now I can say I am glad that I had to walk through that fire because I now see God-he is amazing! He wants to love me, bless me, forgive me (praise Him for that!!!) and bestow unending grace on me! I am amazed truly by Him everyday! Thank you Lord for loving (even in my multitude of imperfections) and saving ME! Thank you for never changing and never leaving me! I could not do this alone!!!!

Since the day I started reporting on the Gosselins for *US Weekly*, I watched and waited for that beautiful Sunday morning scene where Kate would get the kids all dressed up and take them to church. The girls would have little flowers in their hair, and the boys would be in their matching (of course) Sunday best.
I waited and waited, but I never saw it happen. Not on a Sunday. Not on any Saturday or any other day of the week. And still I waited. Then finally, on Easter Sunday, 2012, Kate tweeted that she would be taking the kids to Easter Sunday services and, sure enough, she actually did it. I saw it for myself. The fact that she tweeted far in advance about going to church was a sure sign that she was angling for a photo op and she would definitely be there.
Since there were no photographers around anymore to prove otherwise, Kate started tweeting about how she takes the kids to church on Sundays. On a personal note, if it was me, and my show (*Kate Plus Ei8ht*) was failing, and my other show (*Twist of Kate*) had been thrown on the scrap heap, I'd be in church too, praying or begging. Whatever it took. So I gave Kate the benefit of the doubt that she was actually going to church, like she tweeted she was, even if it was only to pray for more fame and fortune.
I decided to find out for sure, so I started spending my Sunday mornings once again staking out the Gosselin house, like I had done so many times before, waiting for Kate to load up the kids and take them to church. I wanted to believe Kate Gosselin was telling the truth about going to Sunday services. I really did.
I went to Kate's house early in the morning for eight straight Sundays when I knew she had the kids, since she tweets that she takes them to church on the Sundays when she has custody.
Much to my surprise – OK, not really – the church trips never happened. Not once that I saw, even though on some of the same days that I was there, she tweeted that they had, in fact, gone to church, even as I was there watching and listening to the kids playing in the yard in front of the house.

So how could this be? Isn't church one of the little things that a devout Christian would make time for? Wasn't she breaking the Fourth Commandment and then lying about it?

```
"Remember the Sabbath day, to keep it holy. Six days you shall labor,
and do all your work; but the seventh day is a Sabbath to The Lord
your God; in it you shall not do any work, you, or your son, or your
daughter, your manservant, or your maidservant, or your cattle, or
the sojourner who is within your gates; for in six days The Lord made
heaven and earth, the sea, and all that is in them, and rested the
seventh day; therefore The Lord blessed the Sabbath day and hallowed
it." (Exodus 20:8-11 RSV)
```

OK, after reading that passage, I think it may be a little too strict. Surely Kate should be allowed to have her "manservant or maidservants" working on Sunday. She does have eight children after all.
I've watched Kate spend 10 to 20 hours per week on superficial pampering of herself, and countless hours driving around town without her children shopping and running errands that one of her staffers could easily take care of.
In a journal entry dated December 1, 2006, Kate wrote that she knows that God will provide for them.

Well, God surely provided for Kate, but she must have decided she doesn't need Him anymore. I must have missed the scripture that states that once God provides for you, it is perfectly OK to forsake him. With all of her posturing and holier-than-thou talk of God, it turns out that Kate doesn't have one hour a week to take the kids to church. She mentions the Lord close to 200 times in her journal and in her books, but she can't drag her lazy self out to church to give Him thanks. But no matter. She has fooled her adoring, gullible fans into thinking she goes to church regularly. I'll bet she fooled her Christian life book publisher in the same way as well.
It is actually surprising that she doesn't take the kids to church, at the very least for the rare possibility that it could turn into a photo op. I guess it's just too much of a burden for her to waste that hour on a Sunday when she could be getting her nails done.
So if Kate isn't going to church on Sunday, what is keeping her busy, you ask? These tweets sum up the many far-more-important things she does on Sundays:

I'm up—lots to do! Laundry, baking, fall decorating, running, and more! I'll check in later!!!

Hi all! It's a work day....Just stopping in quick to say 'hi'.....

But Kate...it's Sunday. I know you have no intention of going to church, because I'm standing at your front gate watching. She's not even smart enough to not tweet her day's list, which does not include Sunday mass.

Just back from church... Ate lunch and big surprise... They're riding bikes again! Lol! Georgous day!!!

xxxxx @Kateplusmy8 Yeah..So HAPPY you went to church today! God is awesome and HE loves you and your family soooo much!

agreed! :) we go.. Just don't always remember to mention it lol. When I have kids and am home, we're there!

So Kate doesn't always remember to mention going to church, but she has no trouble mentioning every last detail of her and her kids' lives all day, every day, on Twitter? She mentions and posts photos of the most mundane and inconsequential things, but she forgets to mention church?
Here's an excerpt from Kate's journal about NOT going to church:

Sunday, July 2006
Kate described the day as memorable!!!! They didn't go to church but they cleaned the house and managed not to yell at each other.

This is a paraphrased excerpt from *Multiple Blessings*. Believe it or not, Kate says that God delivered paper towels to her house.

Kate had a list posted around the house of things that she needed so the volunteers knew what they could bring for free. One day she was adding paper towels to the list when she heard someone shuffling around outside the front door. Just as Kate opened the door, she saw one of her evening volunteers wrestling with a large case of paper towels that someone had dropped off. Kate dragged the package inside and smiled to herself. She wasn't at all surprised that God knew exactly what she needed even before she could put in on her needs list. Kate said that she was newly reminded that day that her God delivered…literally>

Here are some more of Kate's "miracles," as documented in her journal:

Kate says that their quote is 'in our lives, it's a miracle a day.' Well today's miracle was more freebies from strangers, including many gift cards to Target, Wal-Mart etc. totaling more than $750. Not a bad day.

Kate called a restaurant and got their seats arranged, which she says took a miracle.

Kate made Jon ask their new dentist for nearly free dental work for eight kids. Put on the spot, the dentist said yes. Kate said she felt like an idiot and she started crying. Free dentistry! Kate said that it was just another miracle from the Lord! Kate also thanked the Dentist while thanking the Lord.

A woman sent Kate shoes for the kids and Kate emailed her to thank her. The woman told Kate that she would continue to send the next size shoes for each child!!!!! She's also sending sneakers for Kate!!!! That was one of today's miracles! The other miracle was free tickets to Dutch Wonderland that someone brought for them!!!!

The miracle of the day today was that Kate found strawberries at Sam's club for only $1.50 a pound! She sent Jon back the next day for three more flats and maybe four!!!! Kate says she is praying for there to be enough to satisfy her need!

The miracle for today was that Kate used up all the milk. She was bummed out but when she went to the store to buy just a half gallon, she found the milk on sale so she bought 15 half gallons and got six rain checks!!! Thank you Lord!!!!!!!!! Another miracle!

Kate Gosselin took everything as a sign from God – when it was convenient and beneficial for her, and when it made her money.

ANOTHER CHRISTMAS "MIRACLE," OR JUST ANOTHER CONVENIENT LIE?

Kate speaks often of her "Christmas Miracle," and after reading about it in *Multiple Blessings*, I'll give her this one. I believe in miracles too.
Kate's "Christmas Miracle," as written in *Multiple Blessings* describes a scare that she and Jon had with the sextuplets early in the pregnancy, and an ultrasound in the hospital a night or two before Christmas, that ended up confirming that all six babies were alive and in good health.
In her third book, *I Just Want You To Know,* Kate wrote about another miraculous Christmas occurrence where God provided for her. This story is on page 66:

Kate said the one of her favorite stores that she mentions frequently, happened on Christmas Eve in 2006. Her brother and sisters and their families were over for dinner and Kate's sister was telling Kate about a family at her church who was struggling financially. Kate said she couldn't stop thinking about this family and she knew God was telling her to write them a check. Kate even got into an argument with God about this that lasted several days. God wanted this and He even put a dollar figure in Kate's head.
Kate couldn't take it anymore and got the family's address and mailed a check on the spot and ran it to the mailbox. Well God works in mysterious ways and when Kate opened the mailbox to mail her check, she found an envelope in there with a bow on it. Kate tore open the envelope and literally almost fell over when she saw a gift card to Sam's Club for the exact same amount that she had just written the check for.

It's very strange that Kate wrote about the exact same story that was told in her first book, *Multiple Blessings*, with a few changes here and there. It's certainly OK to lift from your own body of work, but at least make sure the details are the same.

Kate said this is one of her *favorite* stories that she mentions frequently, so it is obviously a very important part of her life and an example of how God provided for her "perfectly."

And yet, in her journal that she used to write this book specifically, in the entry for Christmas Eve in 2006, there is no mention whatsoever of this new "Christmas miracle" ever occurring. Not a word. Nothing even close. I checked the journal for the following week as well, and it wasn't mentioned there either. The journal is filled with every minor detail of her life, right down to what she ate and what she was thinking, but there was no mention of this "Christmas miracle." How could that be? Could it be that this miracle was a fabrication for the book? A big, fat lie even?

It was a total fabrication. It never happened. It was a lie to sell books.

"WE ONLY FILM A FEW HOURS A WEEK"

Kate always insisted publicly that they were actually doing very little filming. Privately, the truth was an entirely different story. In an email Kate sent to "Crystal" on February 5, 2008, in response to an offer for free hair plugs for Jon, Kate said, "We are filming just about everyday lately....."

Every week and every show had a schedule for the Gosselin family to follow. I have many of those schedules for reference. There was nothing about the family's life that wasn't controlled by a production schedule and pre-planned storylines. (See the chapter, "I WANT MY FAKE TV," for more on this.)

On the Season 3 "Behind the Scenes" episode of *Jon & Kate Plus Ei8ht*, Kate put the rumors about long hours of filming to rest from the interview couch. This is what she said:

```
"And, um, there's also a misconception that we film, you know, like a
whole series in like, some certain timeframe of the year and we're
done for the whole year. No. Um, we've never stopped since we started
in August of 2005. And, it's not glamorous and glorious, and we're
not always smiles and giggles, but we have love in our family, and,
um, that's all that matters."
```

On March 30, 2011, Kate was at it again, telling us, in her own words, that they've never stopped filming. Did she go to *Time* magazine or *People* magazine or *US Weekly* to give this huge interview? Not quite. Kate opted instead for the hard-hitting journalism outlet that is … *cupcakemag.blogspot.com*.

Here's an excerpt from that poignant and hard-hitting interview:

```
Interviewer: 1.) We have to say — we missed YOU and are thrilled
that Kate Plus 8 is back for a 2nd season. What can we expect to
see this season?

Kate: "We've not stopped filming at all so our crazily wonderful
schedule has never missed a beat, but you can expect lots of
travel to amazing places, some helping others, local
history/education... Fun, fun, fun and lots of kid noise and
mom's loud voice, as always! :)"
```

Here are the girls of CupcakeMag wrapping things up. Kate should thank her God for people like this.

"I'M JUST A MOM AND WE'RE JUST A FAMILY, LIVING OUR LIVES"

On August 4, 2008, Kate Gosselin officially turned her "just a family" into a corporation – JKIG, Inc., filing the official paperwork with the Commonwealth of Pennsylvania, Department of State, Corporation Bureau, through her attorney, Paul J. Datte.

Kate hogs up three of the four letters in the corporate name of course.

Katie**I**rene**G**osselin. I hope the J at least stands for Jon. Given Kate's narcissistic tendencies, though, it probably stands for "Just."

This is just a family living their lives?

Here's a quote from Kate, taken from one of her Q&A episodes of *Jon & Kate Plus Ei8ht*:

"First of all, people say that we don't work. That's the hugest misconception, **like they feel like we're just literally living our lives** … which we are … but they don't see like, the background scheduling, the what we have to do to struggle to get down here to do interviews, um, the emails, the conference calls, the phone calls, the phone meetings, the in-person meetings, the magazine article shoots, the phone interviews that we do for all that press stuff. They don't see the background of that and that encompasses, for Jon and I, horrendously more than forty hours a week, besides writing books, traveling and speaking, book signings, I mean, that's all aside from that so to say that we don't work actually makes us laugh because this is beyond words the hardest job we've ever had and um, while it's the most rewarding because we're working from home and we can kind of choose our schedule to a certain degree, it's definitely the hardest."

"MY FAMILY CHOOSES NOT TO BE A PART OF OUR LIVES"

This is an excerpt from a very long email discussing Kate's estrangement from her family that Kate's sister Clairissa sent to Kate on Thursday, June 19, 2008. The subject line was "Hi Sis!!!"

Kate's sister tells Kate that she loves her and that she prays for her everyday. She says she misses Kate terribly and she often thinks of the memories of their childhood together, watching TV, baking and playing in their rooms together, etc. She apologizes over and over to Kate for posting personal information about Kate on her blog, the apparent reason that Kate no longer speaks to her or her family.

She ends the letter by saying that she hopes that all ten of them are doing great and she'd love to hear from Kate, but she knows how busy Kate is. She tells Kate to hug her dear nieces and nephews for her!!

She ends the letter with 'Love you sis'

Does this sound like someone who doesn't want to be a part of Kate's or the kids' lives? It's sad to think that the Gosselin children are missing out on all of this love from their own family.

KATE'S (UN)SOLICITED FREEBIES

In her book, *I Just Want You To Know,* and many times during interviews, Kate always makes sure to say that the free things she received from companies were "unsolicited." Here are a couple of examples:

Kate says that while their schedule got crazier with the show, their financial pressures eased up because of increasing fringe benefits. Kate says thankfully companies unsolicited started sending them products and the kids were happy to open the surprise of the day. She said that so many of the generous people didn't want anything in return – they just wanted to help them through a difficult time.

The reality, however, is that while "helpers" watched the Gosselin children, Kate spent many hours a day writing letters and making phone calls and sending emails to every business under the sun, seeking freebies and handouts, whether she needed them or not. She was, and is, addicted to all things free.
Here's just one of many, many examples of her solicitation letters that I know about and have in my possession. Kate wrote this letter a few months after giving birth to the sextuplets. Notice how enthused she is to begin "marketing" her new babies, or "the six" as she calls them.

Hello Everyone at Gymboree!!!

My name is Kate Gosselin. I recently (05/04) gave birth to sextuplets.
We also have twin 4-year-old girls
!
Since my twins were born, I have been an avid and eager shopper at our local Gymboree (store #467). I was famous for calling all the local Gymborees if two of things were not available! The employees at our local store are awesome, always willing to help me find what I want. Since I found out I was pregnant with **"the six,"** as I get a chance I go to Gymboree. The last time I was

there, Kelly wrote down the customer service phone number and urged me to call — explaining that she feels that Gymboree should hear my story and should donate to our eight children! I held the number for a while and finally called! Kelly was very insistent — she knows my passion for Gymboree and understands that with eight children, times are tough!

If you have a desire to help, please contact me at xxx-xxx-xxxx. **In addition, if there is a way my children could be a help in marketing your clothing lines, we're all for it!** Gymboree's wholesome and hearty clothing is definitely worth our time! Thank you for your style and kindness in my unique situation! Please feel free to visit our website **www.sixgosselins.com.**

Sincerely,
Kate Gosselin

I also found a handwritten list of some of Kate's "Ideas to pitch" from the very early days. She wanted her own product line consisting of umbrella triplet strollers; highchairs that convert to strollers; car seat juice cup holders; her own show on the Travel Channel showcasing large family traveling; and a list of the books that she wanted to write. The cookbook was on there but according to the list, we can look forward to another fake book about the secrets of shopping for ~~ten~~ nine.

There were so many examples of Kate trying to cash in on her babies, I had to devote an entire chapter to it.

I HAVE NO MONEY TO FEED MY KIDS AND PAY MY BILLS

"You've left your children and their mother unable to pay for the roof over their heads…. I need that money to provide for them."
— Kate Gosselin

On October 5, 2009, Kate sat down with Meredith Vieira on the *Today* show and gave a tearful, emotional interview about her tragic financial circumstances. Here's some of the text from that interview, as published on *msnbc.com*:

Kate Gosselin: Jon Took the Money and Ran
Mon., Oct. 5, 2009 7:47 AM PDT by BREANNE L. HELDMAN

The family as a whole may have made major bucks from their hit TLC show, but Kate Gosselin is currently living hand-to-mouth.

Reports that Jon Gosselin removed $230,000 from the family's joint bank account and leaving her with only $1,000 are true, she tells Meredith Vieira on the Today show this morning.

"I have a stack of bills in my purse I can't drop in the mail," she says, choking up. "The last thing I wanted was to do this show and end up not being able to pay our bills."

Given all the drama, the star of Jon & Kate Plus 8 admits, "Every morning, I don't know what I'm going to wake up to…[Jon] has gone way far off the trail."

Kate admits for the first time that she feared Jon might do something like this, and removed $100,000 from the account earlier in the divorce process.

"At some point, I removed it to keep it safe on the suggestion of my lawyer but needed to put it back, according to the arbitrator," she says. "I did that."
She claims she only did this because Jon had already removed funds from the account just before the divorce was filed, and she was afraid.

"I had taken $100,000 and put it aside safely so I could buy my kids food if this occurred," she says. "I was afraid. He was literally buying erratic purchases, randomly purchasing things. The last thing I wanted was to do this show and end up not being able to pay my bills."

When Kate came forward about it, the pair split the change 50/50, and she used it to pay bills, while he "did whatever with it."

As for Jon's claims that the eight kids no longer wish to participate in the reality show, Kate claims the children were "wailing and sobbing" not to be seeing the crew since last week's filming halt.

The octomom feels the show needs to go on, and not just because the income helps keep the family afloat.

"It's something that the kids and I are still enjoying," she says. "The opportunities that they've been provided—I don't say that lightly—we were supposed to be in New York now to see the Statue of Liberty and the kids are having trouble understanding why they're not here and why they're not doing that.

"I don't feel like it's time to end it. If we are all enjoying it, I just feel like Kate Plus 8 going on, the nine of us who want to continue it, should be able to do it."

Jon, however, does have the power to end the show for good.

"He can do it, because TLC has always said if one of us didn't want it to happen anymore, and obviously they're not going to stand in his way. Jon is a parent. He does have that right to say that, but I wish he would think harder about it because it has ended our income and our paychecks and our opportunities."

Despite both parents' claims for desires of peace, Kate doesn't see it as imminent. Nor the three-month delay in the divorce proceedings.

"I do not believe there will be any 90-day stalling of this process," she tells Vieira. "Peace is really far away, and I just have to say again, I never wanted to be sitting here and discussing details. I think in the end, actions speak louder than words…I know that my actions are solely for the kids, to better the kids. I have a lot of peace about this because I know in the end, my actions are appropriate, well thought out and with the kids in mind."

We have to ask, though—if Kate's in New York chatting up the Today show and Jon's in Los Angeles making milkshakes, who is with the eight?

At the time of this interview, as Kate was crying crocodile tears and telling the world that she was worried about being able to buy her kids food, and she had a stack of bills in her purse that she couldn't drop in the mail, she actually had at least ten bank accounts, each containing $200,000 or more, which is the maximum the federal government will insure. In addition, she had many investment accounts. She wanted everyone to focus on the one account that was left with $1,000 in it to give the impression that it was her only money. This would earn her sympathy while at the same time, make Jon look like a monster. When I say she, of course, I mean her and her public relations team at Discovery. That one account in question was just the main account she used to pay the bills, but she actually had access to several million dollars at the time, in other accounts.

As noted earlier, Kate's 2008 tax return showed an adjusted gross income of **$1,954,414.00** for the year. That's one million, nine hundred and fifty-four thousand, four hundred and fourteen dollars. 2009, was an even better year for her financially. She got a huge raise for Season 5 of *Jon & Kate Plus Ei8ht*, clomped around on *Dancing With The Stars* for a lot of money, and filmed *Kate Plus Ei8ht*, for which she reportedly earned $250,000 per episode, just to name a few sources of income.

In the Vieira interview, when Kate said, "At some point, I removed it (the money) to keep it safe on the suggestion of my lawyer…," the "At some point" are the key words. This is Kate's PR team having her telling kind of the truth, while making it appear that Jon removed money first, and Kate took her money as a reaction to him. "At some point" is like saying "I have no recollection of that." It's safe and it holds up in court. But according to the bank statements I've seen, Kate was the first to remove large amounts of money from the couple's joint account.

I came across something very interesting in the Gosselin divorce documents. I know for a fact that Kate had control over all of the family's money. Why would that be a problem when they were happy and working together? It wouldn't be. The problem, though, is that once the marriage was on the rocks, Kate still had total control of the money, and Jon was at her mercy.

Jon's attorney filed a petition that included the following:

```
f. Paragraph 3 — Wife failed to provide a written explanation for
the disposition of withdrawals on the Spreadsheet of Accounts
created by Husband's counsel within twenty (20) days of the date
of the Award. These withdrawals totaled over $1,000,000 between
February 2008 and June 2009.
```

According to this paragraph, **Kate withdrew over one million dollars between February 2008 and June 2009 from the joint accounts without accounting for it to Jon**. That's right about the time that their marriage started to crumble and Kate was moving on with her life.

In December 2011, I found some of Kate's personal bank statements and investment information. Here's a list of some of Kate's investment accounts. These are just the investment accounts that I know about. It is possible there are even more.

LPL FINANCIAL

THORNBURG INVESTMENT MANAGEMENT

OAKMARK

PIMCO FUNDS

BLACKROCK

AMERICAN CENTURY INVESTMENTS

JANUS GLOBAL & INTERNATIONAL FUNDS

OPPENHEIMER FUNDS

MFS INVESTMENT MANAGEMENT

PRINCIPAL FUNDS

IVY FUNDS

J.P. MORGAN

These accounts continue to grow, even as Kate is still accepting gifts from teenagers and Twitter followers who are under the impression that Kate needs financial help to support her children. Kate is a very wealthy woman, yet in 2012, she continued to plead poverty and accept gifts from teenage fans and stay-at-home-moms via Twitter. Here is one of Kate's crying poor tweets from July 17, 2012.

> **Awww yeah. I thought same thing. It IS tough to cover costs of large Fam-I'm struggling- but hoping my decisions are rewarded!:)**

THE HAWAII WAHAHE'E (That means lie)

"You know, I go back very often to our vow renewal in Hawaii.
I think very often of it, and in that moment, I meant those vows.
And there was no option for us other than to be together.
And so much has changed."
– Kate Gosselin

I wonder how it could be so easy for such a lie to spew forth from Kate's lips. The Gosselin's marriage was quietly over for almost a year by the time Jon and Kate traveled with their family, crew and helpers to Hawaii to renew their wedding vows before God (and the TLC audience). Jon and Kate went along with the charade to keep the show going and to keep the money pouring in.
Here is a timeline to help keep matters straight:

August 12, 2008 – Marriage vows renewed in Hawaii; TLC filmed it during the fourth season of *Jon & Kate Plus Ei8ht.*

October 21, 2008 – Jon and Kate move into their new, million-dollar house where Jon immediately begins living in the apartment above the garage.

June 22, 2009 – The divorce papers are filed.

December 18, 2009 – The divorce becomes official.

In the divorce papers, Kate claimed that she and Jon had been living "separate and apart" for at least two years. I've read that part as well, but it has been disputed as a typo or a technicality by Kate's people. I know from conducting interviews and from reading things I probably shouldn't have been reading, that the happy marriage was over long before Kate took her vows before God in Hawaii.
In one of the final episodes of *Jon & Kate Plus Ei8ht*, in June of 2009 while discussing their separation, Kate herself said "We haven't really known where we're going, but we've been dealing with this for a long time.
I found even more evidence that the Gosselin marriage was a sham as early as the summer of 2008. When Kate was filming her "reality" show with her family in North Carolina on Bald Head Island, she took many photos with her camera, as any normal mother would do. But as I was going through those photos, like any normal tabloid reporter would do, it struck me that I found no pictures at all of Jon with the kids taken by Kate. Not one single picture of Jon, Kate's husband and father of her eight, count em', eight children. None. Nada. Zip.
Oddly enough, Kate took many pictures of someone else who was on that family vacation and whom you probably didn't know was there. If you guessed that the someone else was Steve Neild, you would be correct. Kate took lots of pictures of Steve, her bodyguard and rumored love interest, either alone or playing with her kids. That would be unheard of in a happy marriage, especially considering the fact that Kate didn't capture a single image of Jon. Something like that just wouldn't happen in a healthy marriage.
According to an entry in Kate's journal from April 24, 2007, she spoke of having a discussion with Jon in the garage because there were "(important marriage issues that needed to be cleared up!)". It would seem that something serious was going on in the marriage even way back then, two years before the divorce papers were filed.
In November of 2009, when Kate sat down with Natalie Morales for a TLC special called *Kate: Her Story*, Natalie asked Kate, "Who called it quits? Who first said, we can't make this work?"
Kate said, "There was a lot of discussions sometime last year (2008), because we knew at some point something had to give. It was a very mutually agreed upon thing."
According to my sources, the fact is that Kate had unofficially and quietly kicked Jon out of her bed in June of 2007. But a year later, she was standing in Hawaii, lying to the world and, more importantly, to her children and to God, just so she could keep her money train rolling down the track. She and TLC/Discovery were lying to the viewers and laughing all the way to the bank.

Were the vows really necessary though? Couldn't they have just continued to film the show and pretended everything was OK? Nope. This was the ultimate "I'm smarter than you" Kate Gosselin/Discovery lie. How far was Kate prepared to take this lie? What if *US Weekly* had never gotten their hands on that photo of Jon and Deanna Hummel coming out of Legends nightclub in Reading, PA, and exposing potential marital problems? Would we still be watching *Jon & Kate Plus Ei8ht* each week on TLC and thinking everything was all right?

All Jon and Kate ever wanted to do in Hawaii was to go there to visit Jon's family, and get a free vacation out of it. They pitched the idea to TLC several times, but got shot down each time. Kate got more and more insistent that they get to go to Hawaii, and Discovery finally caved.

They could have just filmed a nice, wholesome family reunion show in Hawaii, but TLC/Discovery got greedy and wanted to do something much bigger. They were looking to up the ratings ante, so they devised the plan to do a Jon and Kate wedding vow renewal episode...several episodes actually. Discovery didn't want to spend all that money on travel and only get one episode out of it, so they milked it for all it was worth. They broke the fake trip into four separate episodes: "Hawaii, Here We Come," "Legos & Safaris," "Leis & Luaus," and finally..."For Better or Worse."

In considering the whole Hawaii situation, some nagging questions arise: If Jon had a feeling – even if unwarranted – that Kate was having an affair with Steve Neild (as Jon has said many times in interviews), and if the marriage vow renewal was in fact real and not faked just for filming, then how could Kate disrespect Jon so much by allowing Steve Neild to accompany them on the 2-week trip to San Diego and Hawaii? Knowing of Jon's concerns, how could Kate possibly justify letting Steve stand near her and Jon while they renewed their marriage vows? If Kate truly loved Jon at that time (as she has said over and over on the interview trail), how could she be so inconsiderate of his feelings as to allow Steve to accompany them? If Kate and Steve *were* having an affair, how could she be so crass as to bring Steve along and rub Jon's nose in it? None of it makes any sense. But hold on, you say. There's no evidence that Steve was there, you say. You watched the four Hawaiian trip episodes, and the only person on the trip besides the film crew was Jenny the babysitter, you say. Well I watched those episodes, too, and initially I thought the very same thing. It turns out you and I were wrong. At the very end of the "Leis & Luaus" episode, when they're on the catamaran watching sea turtles and coral, we see Jon laying on his stomach getting some sun. For a split-second, to Jon's right, down the ladder and to the right, leaning backwards and trying to hide from the cameras, you can clearly see none other than Steve Neild and his wife, Gina, in their bathing suits. Having the luxury of watching them on DVD using slow motion and pause makes all the difference in the world when doing investigative research. Oh, and I also have all of Kate's personal photos from the trip, so that made the investigation a little easier.

In reality, this trip wasn't what it appeared to be to the viewing audience. It wasn't a trip planned by Jon and Kate to renew their marriage vows and to look forward to another "90 years" as Kate told Jon during the episode. This was nothing more than a business trip or working vacation, with family friends. Steve and Gina Neild were there along with their own kids, no doubt having the time of their lives.

Another interesting thing I discovered was that there was another TLC reality show couple in Hawaii at the same time as Jon and Kate. It turns out that Matt and Amy Roloff, the married couple from the TLC show "Little People, Big World" were also there.

Was it just a coincidence that they got together for a photo op with Jon and Kate? I'd say no if asked. It sure looks like a TLC-sponsored outing was going on in Hawaii that week. So was this a genuine renewal of marriage vows or a business trip?

Further proof that the vows were a sham can be found throughout the final Hawaii episode just by watching Kate's and Jon's body language. They never really held hands or looked even remotely romantic at all. I know Jon's body language, and he was going through the motions for those episodes, fulfilling his contract like a good soldier.

At the reception, while dancing for the cameras and looking about as passionate as I would look if I were dancing with my mother, Jon and Kate shared a very brief, uncomfortable kiss; it was just a lips-closed peck for the cameras. And even that kiss wasn't genuine. Upon further review using my rewind button, just before the kiss, and knowing the cameras were rolling, Kate can be seen telling Jon to "Kiss me." Kate then said "Thank you for that" to Jon right after the kiss. It was hardly a tender, genuine display of affection.

I've been married twice, to two completely different-minded women. One thing they had in common, however, was the planning of our wedding. A wedding is something women dream about and love, no matter the size. Renewing your vows in front of your children in Hawaii would be just as important.

So why didn't Kate do any of the planning or scheduling herself? After all, according to her, she's an organized, scheduling mastermind. She loves to plan and schedule. For such a self-proclaimed organizer and control freak, it is extremely telling that Kate just didn't care enough to get involved. The vow renewal was nothing more than another episode of the show, and Kate Gosselin couldn't be bothered with it.

The ceremony was organized by Kate's manager, Julie May, along with Jen Stocks from the filming crew. Kate was merely cc'd on emails and sent a schedule and itinerary to follow. She, of course, had the option of making changes, but she did nothing to plan or organize the event in any way.

For the record, if anyone has any doubts about the legitimacy of my information, I have the vow renewal planning emails as well as the trip's itinerary and schedule with Kate's scribbled notes in the margins. I'll be happy to make all that evidence available if asked.

Hawaii was on Kate's radar since day one of her "reality" show. In an email dated September 9, 2007, Kirk Streb, writer/director/editor at Figure 8 Films, summarized a "business meeting" that he had with Jon and Kate to discuss big ideas for them a few days prior to the trip. This was first mentioned in the "I DREAMED A DREAM" chapter. One of those ideas was:

```
- Helping the family go to Hawaii for a family reunion with Jon's
  relatives that live there.
```

Here are some of Kate's remarks during the "Hawaii Here We Come" episode:

"This was the trip. It appeared. The Grand Wailea invited us to be their guests, um, at their resort in Maui and you don't have to ask us twice. We were there!"

So Kate would have us believe that she was just sitting around going about her life when The Grand Wailea decided, out of the blue, to invite her family to be their guests at their resort in Maui.

Here's Kate lying to the "little kids" at home before leaving for Hawaii:

"And you're there this time, which we're gonna tell you, that means we're staying together forever. **Forever. No matter what.**"

Then, on the interview couch, Kate shares these thoughts:

"Once upon a time, like, I thought old people renewed their vows and that was just, like, an old stuffily thing to do, and it was kind of boring and annoying. That's how I used to think about it. But, now, um, that we have eight kids that are, um, with us and, as a part of our family, it made us realize that renewing our vows in front of them was an important thing cause not all moms and dads stay together and we've told them a million times, but it was nice to be able to show them that we'll always be together."

At this point, Kate's eyebrows are raised, which, in addition to her mouth moving, is a telltale sign that she's lying.

"I WAS BY MYSELF"

Kate has been quoted many times telling the same old story. She says often that she was taking care of eight little kids, with very little help. She says that she was by herself all day, every day, though the occasional friend would stop by to play with the kids and sometimes her sister would come over and watch them while Kate ran to the grocery store. She says that Nana Janet came by every week but for the most part she was by herself and exhausted.

Kate was actually only "by herself" from 4 to 6 pm, which was the time after all of her helpers went home, to the time when Jon returned home from work. I'm not disputing that two hours with eight kids in a small house would be nerve-racking, I'm just disputing Kate's statement that she was by herself "all day, every day." I've spoken to many people who were Kate's "helpers" at the time, and they obviously tell a different story. I've been told by people who volunteered their time to help take care of Kate's kids that she pretty much just lounged around all day while she complained of some kind of physical ailment, oversaw the operation and barked orders. That's not too hard to believe.

IF KATE CAN DO IT WITH EIGHT KIDS, I CAN DO IT WITH TWO

Kate shares this story in her book *I Just Want You To Know:*

When she would do speaking engagements, she felt the support and love from the crowd. People would always come to her with tears in their eyes telling her their stories in return. They would say Kate; you're such an inspiration. If you can do it with eight kids, I can do it with two.

Thousands of emails came pouring in, telling Kate how glad they where that she and Jon were so real on TV. Kate says that she has no choice but to be real, and by the way, she's too busy to learn lines or rehearse.

Then and there Kate realized that all moms are the same. They all want the best for their families. She says she's a mom first, like every other mom out there and she still identifies with the unshowered stay-at-home mom wearing a dirty T-shirt and sweatpants with hair that sticks up.

Kate realized that being a mom can be very monotonous and moms need tons of encouragement, but it is the most fulfilling job you can ever have.

So while Kate was being an inspiration to mothers the world over for her tireless efforts in raising eight children by herself while working at the same time – she actually barely saw or spent any quality time with her children at all. Unlike most normal mothers who have to juggle work and multiple responsibilities, Kate has a staff of nannies, babysitters, cleaning people, ironers, laundry folders, personal chefs, bodyguards, handymen, gardeners, pool boys, etc. I'm sure I forgot to mention someone in there, but you get the picture.

Kate masterminds the lists, and her staff carries out the orders. Period.

THE ZONDERVAN BOOK LIES

"We are looking for a Christian publisher for our upcoming book.
If you have any helpful information, please email Kate Gosselin.
Many, many, many people want to read our story.
We would like to put it in print for you!!!"
– *Kate Gosselin*

Scott Bolinder, executive vice president and publisher at Zondervan, said this about the Gosselin family:

"The Gosselins' story is not only unique by nature but also offers an unparalleled set of life experiences that are emotional, inspirational and encouraging."

"Kate and Jon are walking a road that few others have taken, and they consistently show tremendous grace, patience and courage in their daily lives as they seek to provide for their eight children and raise them to honor God in a world where compromise and escape have become all too common."

This is from a publicity release for *Multiple Blessings*:

```
Beth Carson, the couple's friend, offered to help them "capture the
memories on paper" of their unique family situation. "I had told her
(Carson) numerous times that I needed to write this book … for the
kids," Gosselin explained. "I need them to know how much that they
were wanted, loved and know it wasn't the plan we had (to have them.)
It was the plan God had for our family."
```

Now a cynical person like me would wonder aloud why Kate didn't just take the time each day to actually talk to her kids and tell them herself how much she loved and wanted them. That would surely have helped them feel safe and secure at their very tender age, much more so than having those sentiments expressed in a 200-page book that was written by someone else and carefully edited by a team of professionals.

And why Kate feels the need to keep bringing up the fact they she didn't "plan" to have them and that it was all God's idea is really strange.

It's amazing how Kate's own words in her journal were sterilized by Zondervan for *I Just Want You To Know* to suit their own needs and to help exploit the Gosselin children for profit. For example, Kate wrote a journal entry about how she and Jon dealt with an injury to their daughter, Leah. Here are the lowlights:

```
Tuesday, April 24, 2007
```

- Leah had fallen out of bed and there "was BLOOD everywhere!!!!"
- She had a "huge gash on her forehead!!!!!"
- Kate said the gash was about three-quarters of an inch long and gaping open.
- Jon and Kate (the nurse) debated whether to take Leah to the emergency room but because Kate was getting a cold on top of being "exhausted" they decided to skip the trip.
- In the morning the gash was still oozing blood and Kate was still "torn as to what to do about it" so reluctantly made an appointment with the doctor, but then cancelled it and opted to have a neighborhood trauma nurse take a look at it after she got home from work at 11:15 am.
- The nurse of course thought the gash should have been stitched and Kate wrote "Oops." She felt bad about it but just didn't want to take Leah by herself after the rough day she had the day before dealing with one of the twin's teeth.
- Kate wondered if she was being selfish when she made the decision to patch Leah's gaping wound with steristrips rather than taking her to the ER to get stitches.
- Kate wrapped up the entry by praying to God about Leah, saying that she knows that He loves Leah more than she does and asks Him to heal her as 'good as new.' Amen.

This same story appeared in *I Just Want You To Know*, but it had to be toned down so Kate didn't appear to be uncaring and dismissive of the needs of her injured child. In the book version (page 128 if want to read it for yourself), the gash on Leah's head got smaller by a third, and Kate left out the part about her being too exhausted to take Leah to the hospital for treatment (not to mention the added excuse that Kate was "getting a cold!").

So Kate waited until 11:15 the following morning for a trauma nurse friend to come by after work to check out the wound and tell Kate she thought if should have been stitched. "Oops." Kate's 2-year-old daughter had a huge gash in her head that was bleeding through the night, but Kate didn't want to take her to the hospital by herself, and she couldn't deal with more nerve-wracking stuff.

SICK

Here are a few of Kate's paraphrased journal entries where she talked about Leah and Aaden getting sick with pneumonia:

December 2006

Kate said "the six" have been coughing and wheezing for at least a week until she finally decided that she should listen to Leah with her stethoscope. She heard wheezing and other crackly noises that made her nervous so she called the doctor and was upset to hear that they wanted to call in a round of steroids to decrease her inflammation. Kate was not at all happy with that and wanted Leah seen that day because they had a filming weekend coming up and there was no time. She later found out that Leah had pneumonia.

Later, Aaden sounded the same and Kate requested that the doctor call in a prescription of Zithromax without seeing him. The doctor's office called back and Kate said they accused her of being fraudulent and said the doctor would NEVER do something like that. Kate said to herself I guess, that she knew that was a lie because the doctor has done "the same thing in the past!!!!!" Kate said that the office staff was annoyed with her and just wanted to make her life difficult. She went on to add that she'd had enough of the office staff and the entire "area and medical care is quite backwards!"

All wasn't so bad though as she ended the entry by writing about all the free stuff she got because of rushing off to the grocery store and then to the Park City mall for Christmas shopping while being filmed by the camera crew.

December 2006

Aaden didn't get better and in fact, developed "hives of all things!" And now Kate is very annoyed! She called the doctor's office "and talked to 900 people until she got "a jerk of a doctor, Dr. Baker" who according to Kate treated her like she had no brains let alone medical experience as a nurse!!!! *(Remember, this is the nurse who was too tired to take a child to the ER who had a gaping gash in her head that bled through the night.)*

Kate ended the entry by discussing the fun she had doing the narration of their show opening and her five outfit changes for the day.

When Kate included this story about Leah and Aaden's pneumonia in *I Just Want You To Know*, she, or some editors, left out all the parts where she complained about the backwards medical care in her area, and where she mentioned filming. Kate revealed that she hadn't tended to her children's coughs until after the coughing lasted for almost a week, but she made darn sure to get Leah to the doctor when it looked like her illness might jeopardize upcoming filming. After Leah was diagnosed with pneumonia, Kate still made sure to keep her appointment to meet Jen and Scott and Mike for filming at the Giant grocery store. That was on the very same day she had "sick babies to come home to." Kate didn't let anything disrupt filming, not even pesky pneumonia.

Kate continued to sing her own praises in *I Just Want You To Know*. She wrote that she had to work hard to convince the doctor's office staff that when one of the eight got sick, they all did.

Wow. It must have been an amazing revelation to the staff of a pediatrician's office to learn that when one child in a family gets sick, other children in the family get sick as well. Thank goodness Kate worked so hard to convince them of this. She is insufferable when she acts like her family requires special treatment just because it happens to be bigger than other families. She couldn't possibly get any more pompous and ridiculous.

This thought from *I Just Want You To Know* sums up how Kate plays the "I deserve sympathy" card:

> Finding a babysitter last minute for seven kids so I could take one sick child to the doctor was part of my job as a mother of eight little kids.

Part of the job of any mom or dad is to find last-minute babysitters when necessary, whether they have one child or 100. Luckily for Kate, she could call on her sister-in-law Jody for last minute babysitting at the drop of a hat (until Kate banished Jody from her and her kids' lives, that is). Thank goodness Jody was available that day to take care of the sextuplets, including two who were sick with pneumonia, so Jon and Kate could take Mady and Cara to the mall to be filmed Christmas shopping.

THE POOP STORY

Kate got a lot of mileage out of stories that were meant to show how very difficult it was for her to take care of her brood. This is the "Poop Story" as Kate wrote it in her journal.

Friday 2006

Kate said, "Today was a mad day!!!!!!" She was relieved that she had nothing scheduled for the day besides the usual craziness, but during naptime, Kate decided to wake the tups up and noticed that one of the girls was sleeping in poop from head to toe and it was all over her crib. Kate was freaking out. She described the scene vividly as the poop was mashed into the bottoms of both feet and on her sheet, blankets, a book in her crib and some was even flung onto another girl's crib. Ever the loving and compassionate mother, Kate became instantly angry and woke the poor child up with her "angry voice!!!!!" She stood the child in the bathtub to soak her feet and showered her. She said "the poor little thing was shaking with coldness or fear or something!" Kate cleaned everything up and talked about having to spank all six of the little ones the day before for getting into a tissue box. Then she had an ugly incident with another little girl who decided to play in some water in the kitchen and made a water mess for Kate to clean up. Kate said she had had enough and put her in her crib until Jon came home. She told Jon that he could go and "get the little monster and feed her dinner!"

When Kate recounted this same story in *I Just Want You To Know,* she conveniently left out the spanking part and the part where the "poor little thing was shaking with coldness or fear or something." I guess it made for better Christian reading without the violence and neglect.

I don't know about you, but going into parenthood, I knew it would be a difficult and frustrating job sometimes. I spent nine months reading everything I could from every available resource to help prepare myself to become the best parent I could be. Some of the best memories of childhood for a parent are when the little ones get into things and wreak havoc. The funniest photos are when the little ones dump a plate of spaghetti over their heads or get into whatever and are sitting there smiling and laughing, or when they pull out all the tissues from the tissue box and are surrounded by the mess. Most parents run to get the camera to capture precious moments like that.

Kate is not most parents. Kate spanked her children in those moments. She spanked 2-year-old babies for doing exactly what 2-year-old babies do. And she said she put a "soaking and dripping wet" Alexis into her crib and left her there until Jon got home. She doesn't even realize that she makes herself sound like the most uncaring, inept mother of all time.

KATE'S A REGULAR MOM – SHE DOES HER OWN GROCERY SHOPPING

Kate and her handlers worked tirelessly to hone her image as a mom of 8, count 'em, 8 kids who does it all, and does it all far better than any other mediocre mom in the world. These excerpts from a blog Kate wrote in August of 2010 documents how hard it is to be her at the grocery store:

Kate says "the sheer amount of food I buy at the grocery store each week still amazes me!! You're probably thinking, wouldn't she, by now, be accustomed to the fact that she has to wrestle two grocery carts through the store each week (or every other, at least)?"

She says that she's still known to announce her "disbelief at the piled-high carts" as she unloads them onto the weary conveyor belt. She says that she swears that she's heard them pleading for mercy, more than once as she came towards the checkout.

She thinks the other customers must surely hear her inner dialogue become outer dialogue but they know whom she's feeding so they "tend to empathize." They must also feel pity for her as she bags 20 to 25 bags of groceries (and yes, Kate says that she bags them all herself!)

Oh, where to begin with this one? I have followed Kate for more than a year to the Giant grocery store near her home. This also happens to be the grocery store that I've been shopping at several times a week for years, so I know most of the checkout people who work there. I've sat in the parking lot watching Kate exit the grocery store more times than I can count, and I have never, ever, seen Kate with a second shopping cart. Most days she's pushing one of the small, single-serving carts because she's just stopping in to buy a few items on the way home from tanning or the nail salon. I've seen her with a single full cart maybe once or twice around the holidays. I have three kids, not eight, yet I come out of the store with twice the amount of groceries as Kate does for eight kids and herself. How is that possible?

It's possible because Kate has someone to do her bulk shopping for her, and she has meals prepared for her by her personal chef who delivers the food to her house each week, pre-cooked and ready to be heated and served. All Kate has to do is warm the food up in the oven; most days, a paid employee takes care of that chore as well.

I don't begrudge Kate the luxury of having personal shoppers and a chef. If she can afford it, she should enjoy it. I'd do the exact same thing. I hate grocery shopping and I don't enjoy preparing family meals. The problem with this whole grocery shopping thing is that Kate is lying about it and laughing all the way to the kitchen. And her eight little faces are footing the bill and being forced to eat leftovers and rotten food for lunch at school.

To answer her critics who said Kate doesn't do her own grocery shopping, TLC packed up Kate and all eight of her children and took them to Giant for some family grocery shopping. The entire TLC camera crew was there to document it, you know, to prove that Kate was not lying. As was standard procedure, Kate then went on a TV talk show to bore the world with her tales of grocery shopping woe. In February 2011, Kate was a guest on *The George Lopez Show*. She told George that she usually has **three** shopping carts and said, "I warn people. You do not want to be behind me."

In the nearly two years I followed Kate, I never saw her take all eight kids ANYWHERE alone, let alone to the grocery store. It would drive her absolutely insane to be distracted while shopping. And the part about three shopping carts filled with groceries was more nonsense. The only time I ever saw Kate pushing more than one shopping cart was when TLC was filming.

Kate got a lot of mileage out of the grocery shopping stories on Twitter, impressing her fans with her ability to overcome such a difficult chore. Kate tweeted about what a "HUGE" task it was:

> **Ahhh..home sweet home!Groc shopping is a HUGE task! 2carts then all the put away;I'm TIRED!NOT complaining;glad I can put food on r table!;)**

By September, with no television show or tabloid interested in her and her mundane drivel, she continued to take to Twitter to awe her fans with her grocery shopping prowess:

> **I miss u guys! I'll b on later..Put away $700 groc,made dinner, packed lunches, Mady did showers (God bless her) exhausted but I'll b here!**

> **Don't ever let my two heaped up carts intimidate you :)**

Kate gets around her grocery shopping lie like she gets around many of her lies. She leaves out information. She cleverly doesn't say that she actually went grocery shopping, only that she "put away" her groceries. Nobody asked if she physically went and bought the groceries herself though, which of course she didn't, and she certainly wasn't going to volunteer the information that a paid employee did it, as has always been the case since she became a "star."

One day in March 2012, I was grocery shopping at the Giant in Wyomissing, and Kate was there at the same time. As usual, she was pushing only one of the small-sized shopping carts. She wasn't struggling with two or three large carts like she always says she does. I'm a gentleman (believe it or not), and I was with my kids, so I gave Kate plenty of space. I didn't approach her. I didn't try to talk to her. I didn't even smile and wave to her. I just observed her from a distance of 15 to 20 feet away. She came up behind us to get that close, not the other way around.

As we were checking out simultaneously, I took her picture with my iPhone. Kate scowled at me in a way that I had never been scowled at before. She had pure hatred in her eyes. I don't think she even remembers who I am or what I look like. For all she knew, I was an adoring fan simply snapping a quick photo.

MY CHILDREN WERE NOT EXPELLED FROM SCHOOL

"I have eight of the most well-adjusted,
healthy, happy children...that ever were."
– *Kate Gosselin*
10.5.09 Today Show with Meredith Vieira

In late 2010, it was widely reported by the tabloids and most major newsgathering organizations that two of the Gosselin children were expelled from their kindergarten. I had known about the situation for over a month, but out of respect for Jon and the children, I said nothing. After it was reported online, a week went by with no response from Kate or Discovery. I figured the reason for the deafening silence was because they didn't know how to spin it in Kate's favor.

Finally, *People* magazine, the great Kate Gosselin apologist, gave us the first hint of Discovery's spin control, while paying Kate her usual big money:

```
A 'source' tells PEOPLE, "The situation is being grossly
overstated. The kids are going through a challenging time, but
Kate doesn't feel this is something that should be discussed
publicly. It is a private matter."

TLC had no comment, but a 'source close to the situation' says
Kate's number one concern is protecting her children and is
keeping this personal situation as a private matter that she
works out with her kids."
```

A "source." Nice work publicists. If only you would have stopped there, this book would never have been written. But you didn't.

After a full week of thinking until their brains were hurting, Discovery finally came up with the lie, (otherwise known as the legal technicality and navigation around the truth), and they arranged for Kate to take to the airwaves with their spoon-fed story that the kids were not "expelled." They obviously subscribe to the theory that if you say something loud enough and often enough, people start believing it is true.

So, in her earnest efforts to keep the kids' expulsion a "private matter" and not discuss it "publicly," thus "protecting her children during this personal situation," Kate very non-privately talked to *ET*'s Mary Hart about it. Mary asked Kate the pre-approved question of the day: Were two of your children expelled? This was Kate's circumnavigation of the truth:

```
"Two of my children, no, are being tutored at home, with a
teacher who is working closely with our kindergarten teachers in
school, doing the identical curriculum."
"The pressure was getting to them. You have the divorce anger
mixed in with that. The goal is to get them back into school as
soon as possible."
```

Then came the "not discussing it publicly" interview on the *Today* show. On December 1, 2010, Kate sat down with Meredith Vieira to, once again, keep the matter private and set the record straight for us. This is part of that interview:

Meredith Vieira: "Let's separate fact from fiction, beginning with your kids. Two of the sextuplets, Collin and Alexis, reports are that they were expelled from their school. True or false?"

Kate Gosselin: "**That is false.** They were not expelled from school. We have a situation where we are in, my kids are in an academically excelling school, where um, academics are pushed and I fully support it, combined with kids who are having just gone through a divorce of their parents, suffering all of those normal feelings, and the two collided and you know, they just were not doing well with the combination."

"They were having anger issues. They were acting out, having behavior things, um, things that, I felt very alone but once I did the research, talked to other moms, you know that have gone through divorces, very normal, normal stuff in that regard and, so I did what I could do, **we mutually agreed, I brought them home.** I have them with a private tutor um, early education teacher, and she's teaching them one on one. All is well again."

Dealing with the very normal results of a divorce. I think we have done very well, I knew going through a divorce, I knew to watch for stuff. It will happen and this is not abnormal at all."

"Along with weekly therapy. My kids are back. They're happy. They're functioning and all is well again."

Kate also told Vieira, "It was a mutually agreed upon removal until the school figures out how to deal with their needs."

In the most technical sense, Kate was correct when she said the kids were not "expelled." They weren't "expelled" only because the school didn't use the word "expelled" when it requested that the Gosselin kids be removed.

On April 1, 2011, exactly four months to the day after Kate's interview with Meredith Vieira, when the issue should have been long forgotten by the media (which it was since nobody was mentioning it at all), Kate, in promoting the new season of her show *Kate Plus Ei8ht*, went on the *Today* show with Matt Lauer and started it all up again. I say Kate started it up because she was only allowed to be asked specific, pre-approved questions given to the interviewer by her publicist in advance. Her publicist was always standing just off camera watching and waiting to pull the plug if the interview started to go sour. Here's an excerpt from the *Today* show interview:

Matt Lauer discussing the kids who were expelled: " …There were reports that they had been kicked out of school, you actually took them out because they were having some behavior issues (Kate is nodding yes like a bobblehead to Matt) they're still at home, they're not back in school, why?"

Kate: "Um, they're actually starting to integrate, back in, um, within the very immanent future, and, um, there was actual medical issues um, that we dealt with, that um, they're doing wonderfully at home, they're reading at the top level of kindergarten, as well as writing and they're doing amazingly well so I know looking back now, I, I made the right decision, I did the right thing and they're blossoming so …"

Matt: I think you even said at the time, you were open about it, **you said that clearly there is some fallout from a divorce here, there is the emotional strain of that,** so in terms of those two children and the others, are any of them exhibiting some negative behaviors that you think can be attributed to the divorce you went through?

Kate: "Um, every child who's parents um, are you know divorced will go through some negative behaviors, I mean, um, Collin and Alexis's therapist said, you know, a third of the kids will sail through perfectly, a third of the kids will do horribly and a third of the kids will, um, get through it with counseling, so she said you don't ever know which kids will do what but um, the most important thing is for me to have a positive attitude, um, to pick up you know, where our family left off and to continue on with those traditions which is what I'm doing, and, um, we're actually, we're really, we're good now."

Through Kate's TV interviews, it is easy to identify the four stages of Kate's and Discovery's "The Kids Were Not Expelled" lie:

One: No comment. It's a private matter.
Two: The kids are being tutored at home.
Three: The school and Kate mutually agreed and Kate brought them home.
Four: There were some medical issues we were dealing with so I pulled them out.

Now let's examine the truth. In a letter from October 2010, Junior Thiry, business manager for the kids' school, informed Kate that she would be receiving a tuition refund "As a result of the **separation from school** for Alexis & Collin, **at the request of the school**." Thiry explained that, effective October 22, 2010, a prorated tuition refund in the amount of $3,856.27 for each child was going to be processed the next week. He also enclosed a statement for one-on-one support through October 8, 2010, and said that a final invoice for support would be forthcoming soon.

That one-on-one support obviously didn't help the situation, so the school was left with no other choice but to "separate" the children from the school. No matter how Kate/TLC/Discovery tried to spin it, and what words they chose to use, the fact is the children were made to leave the school.

The National Enquirer had it right when they posted the following on their sister website, *radaronline.com*:

One of the expelled Gosselin kids physically harmed an adult at the school TWO TIMES, creating a situation that caused school administrators to believe they had no choice but to remove that child from school.

The nature and extent of the adult's injuries are not known, but the situation was severe enough that it contributed heavily to the school's decision to expel the children.

Both of the Gosselin children were abusive to other children in the school, creating an untenable situation.

Both Jon and Kate were sent a letter from the head of school explaining that despite their best efforts, staff had reached a point at which they had to request the children enroll in another program.

While the teacher was able to achieve some success, it became apparent to the school that the pair needed intensive assistance to help them with their social, emotional and academic needs.

"The demand on the children's classroom teachers -- and the impact on other kids -- was just too great."

When Kate's fans hounded her for more information, Kate did what she does best – she first pleaded ignorance and then she lied:

xxxxx @Kateplusmy8 How r u handling the problem with the kids getting expelled from school? I cant believe a school would to that to 8 ur. Olds

not sure what ur talking about. I have no kids who have been expelled& no 8 ur olds at all. Sure this was for me? :)
2011

xxxxx hey @kateplusmy8, weren't two of your kids expelled from school for bullying? #appledoesntfalltoofarfromthetree #plasticsurgeryhypocrite

nope. Don't believe rumors! Thanks for asking so I could clear it up! Xo

I later found out that the situation was even worse than I originally knew. In 2012, I learned some new details about the expulsion of the Gosselin children and their interactions, or lack of interactions, with certain school employees, as well as Kate's treatment of them at home over the summer. I believe this information will come out soon after this book is published from the people who should be dealing with the situation. This is one part of the story that I can't divulge, because I gave my word that I wouldn't.

"When I speak, um, my yardstick is my kids.
They can pull this up forever. I don't want them to see
anything that's negative that came out of my mouth."
– *Kate Gosselin*
Kate on the Ellen DeGeneres show, 200

YOU'LL NEVER HEAR ME BASHING JON ON TV

On February 15, 2011, Kate told the ladies from *The Talk*, "I didn't want my kids to see me on the *Today* show bashing their father. I won't do it. You will never hear me do it. He will always be their father."

It must have slipped Kate's mind that, while on the *Today* show on December 1, 2010, discussing very private family issues such as two of her 6-year-old children being expelled from kindergarten, she complained to Meredith Vieira about Jon. Showing frustration and anger, Kate said, "I have never personally been apologized to," and added that she doesn't consider "an interview on TV or a tabloid" the appropriate venue to discuss deep-seated family issues.

Kate must have also forgotten what she said on the *Regis & Kelly* show on September 10, 2010, when she told the world that the kids don't like spending time with Jon. Despite starting off the interview by saying "I do try to keep things as peaceful as possible with Jon," Kate immediately commented on how much the kids don't like spending time with him.

Anderson Cooper, filling in for Regis Philbin, asked Kate what she does with her time while the kids are with Jon. Kate responded, "I basically wait for the phone call for how many of them want to come home." She continued by saying, "It's hard to explain to your kids who want to be at home playing with their toys and sleeping in their bed and **spending time with me**." Then she said that when she's able, she brings them home.

This is an excerpt about the situation from my *US Weekly* reporting that week:

```
Jon and Kate Gosselin PA Reporting
Monday, September 13, 2010
        Jon thinks it's strange that the day Kate announces to the
world that the kids would rather be at home with her, the first thing
she does is leave them to go to Mexico with her bodyguard/boyfriend.
They're (Kate and Steve) even dressing alike now in matching colors.
She's making a fool out of herself and embarrassing her children at
the same time. The kids have asked if Steve is going to be their new
daddy and are wondering if they're going to get married. They're very
confused because they know Steve's wife very well and the little kids
ask "what about Gina?"
        Fresh on the heels of Kate announcing on Regis & Kelly that
she sits at home waiting for the phone to ring from the kids wanting
to leave Jon and come back home to her, she added another nanny to
the babysitting staff. This one is a live-in nanny who will be in the
house 24/7. This can only mean that Kate will be spending even less
time at home and with the kids, and even more time out traveling
around with Steve. "If only the world could see what really goes on
behind closed doors at Kate's house instead of listening to the lies
that come out of her mouth on a daily basis. I hope the truth finally
comes out someday and Kate gets what she deserves — a big empty house
with no kids, family or friends."
```

In addition to Kate bashing Jon on TV, she apparently thinks it's also OK to bash Jon on Twitter and to encourage other people to bash Jon on Twitter, which she's been doing now for years.

There is one particularly hateful lunatic posting on Twitter who is one of Kate's biggest supporters. Kate must love having her as a friend…for obvious reasons: Kate doesn't have to bash Jon as much by herself when she's got fans like this doing the dirty work for her. On one single day in August 2012, this person tweeted more than 50 nasty tweets about Jon – which was viewed by Kate's well over 150,000 Twitter followers.

Kate never once asked this tweeter to please stop speaking badly of Jon. Kate has *never* asked any tweeter to stop making nasty, sometimes vicious, comments about Jon, the father of her children. Instead, after all the nasty things this person tweeted, Kate tweeted this back to her on September 14, 2012:

I thank u for your constant FAIR surmising and opinions of situations re me/family! I think ur beautiful too! :) XO

"WE ARE NOT SCRIPTED"

"We're not scripted. You heard me. We are not scripted. We're living. The kids run in and out of the frame and they just live."
– Kate Gosselin

Kate said this in February 2011, when she sat down with some of the ladies on *The Talk*. I say "some" because for some reason, the two most outspoken hosts of the show, Sharon Osbourne and Holly Robinson Peete, found something better to do with their time than to sit on the couch with Kate for 15 minutes. They were there before and after Kate's interview, but not during. Strange.

"We are not scripted."

Whenever you hear Kate make a statement like that, it's a telltale sign that she's lying, and after a little digging, I found a little more proof.

Here are some printed, "scripted," voice-over assignments, written for and given to Kate, telling her exactly what to say for airing on *Jon & Kate Plus Ei8ht*.

KATE

EPISODE #7

"So we thought it might be fun to take them to have their head shots taken."

"But before we left for the photo shoot, we had our Saturday pancake breakfast, which has now become a Gosselin family tradition."

"After pancake breakfast, there was a bit of a potty training party happening in the laundry room."

"After pancake breakfast, a potty training session began, that was somewhat supervised by Mady and Cara."

"Not surprisingly, Joel didn't manage to use the potty that day."

"Aunt Jodi, my brother's wife, is coming over today to get the twins suitcases."

"Uncle Kevin and Aunt Jodi are coming tonight. They're bringing Cara and Mady with them. And our friend Beth will be there as well."

"I had planned the dinner for after the babies went to bed, and a neighbor came over to sit while they were sleeping."

"We had a plane to catch to Florida, and there we were stuck in the snow."

"Jodi and Kevin have 4 kids of their own, and Cara and Mady really love spending time with their cousins." (or something like this)

"So Jodi helped them bake cobweb cookies and meringue puffs" (is that what they were?)

Perhaps they were technically not "scripted" in the strictest sense of the word if the definition of "scripted" is that they were given a "script" of what they were supposed to say throughout the entire show. But even that is a lie, since each episode did, in fact, come with a printed list of "voice-over" narrations for Kate and Jon to read so they could be edited into the show for continuity.

The best way to describe the show is that it was totally scheduled with story lines planned in advance by Discovery and TLC. Kate was given her schedule for the week to let her know where her family would be going, what her family would be doing, and even what her children would be playing with. I have many original "weekly shooting schedules" and itineraries that are detailed, down-to-the-minute instructions for the family to follow with the crew in tow. There was absolutely nothing "organic," normal, or natural about the Gosselin children being filmed.

The "interview" segment of the *Jon & Kate Plus Ei8ht* shows served as a great vehicle to squash any rumors or criticism that may have been present in the media regarding the show. It was mainly during the "Q&A" or "Viewer Emails" segments when they did their best work at "setting the record straight."

During one such segment, a producer asked Jon and Kate this question: "Would you say that the show that we do is realistic?"

Why would they even have to ask that question if not to quell the rumors? Here's Kate's "scripted" response:

Kate: "Yes. It's very realistic. There's no scripting. There's a plan about this is what we want to get." She then added: "Right, that's important for us to let people know we aren't hiding anything. Our goal is to show people how hard this job is." Then Jon said: "Our crew follows us ..."

And Kate quickly interrupted with: "Whatever we do and how we do it."

Kate then continued: "Our goal is to make reality television, so that doesn't mean we're going to guard what we're saying because that wouldn't be real life. If I started to change into this hmm, hmm, hmm (Kate rolls her eyes) person, then why film it cause it's not our life."

HIDE AND SEEK

While reporting for *US Weekly*, a Gosselin nanny told me this:

"Back when TLC was filming the show, it was a filming day and the
kids were playing and they were told by the crew to come outside to
film a staged event. The kids were having fun and didn't want to film
so they all hid at different places in the house and wouldn't come
out. The crew had to go searching for them and the producer was
getting very angry because they were wasting time and Kate became
irate and started screaming at them to "get outside now or else!"

The kids hated having to film and the only time they had any fun was
when they went on special trips and got to do exciting things like
see the battle ship and go to the dude ranch. They hate filming at
home. Kate tries to bribe them to be good for the cameras and when
that doesn't work, she turns to threats. She has no idea how much
damage she's doing to these little kids. She just worries about being
famous."

On April 5, 2011, while on a promotional tour for the new season of *Kate Plus Ei8ht*, Kate sat down with Joy Behar for an interview. It was the same Kate Gosselin, repeating the same scripted talking points. It's funny to watch all of her interviews over the years, and hear her say the exact same thing, with the exact same tone of voice, with the exact same head bobs and mannerisms and fake smiles. How would that be possible unless she had rehearsed it with her "media trainer" over and over and over again?

Joy Behar: "What is it about you that provokes this kind of
        negative attack? What is it?"

Kate: "I don't know, um, I'm still trying to figure that out. I
        know that, um, there's a lot of single moms out there, I
        have more than the average number of kids, um, this is
        something that Jon and I started together, and it was
        working then, um, it's still working for me and the kids
        now, and, um, we're all happy doing it, I'm working,
        they're running in and out of the frame and if they want
        to run off and not do what we're doing, they don't. If
        they don't wanna go along they don't."

Yeah, ask Mady if that's how it worked when she begged to not go on the "amazing adventure" to Alaska.

THE CREW IS PART OF OUR FAMILY

"If someone knocked on your door tomorrow and said, this really great group of dads was gonna come, hang out with your family and film you doing whatever…would they really shut the door and walk away?"

On *The Talk*, which aired in February 2011, Kate and Discovery were in full spin mode doing damage control about the questions that were out there regarding Kate not having any close family around the kids and the kids having to be "working" constantly.

Kate said, "The kids came to me and said mommy, when's our crew coming back? They missed them. I, and I waited for that and I waited, and they came and asked, it was a, it was a normalcy for them. It was a comfort, these guys when the cameras are off, they're dads, they're helping us, they play games with the kids, they read books to em, I mean, this is family to us."

Then the interviewer, Julie Chen, asked Kate, "But then, what happens when that goes away cause there will come a day when that all goes away?"

And Kate responded, "But the people won't go away cause we'll stay in contact with them forever. They have truly, we've made deep, lifelong friendships, I mean you have to remember, these people have traveled with us as well ... they're like a part of us."

I wonder if the crew knows that. From what I've been told by a crewmember that has chosen to remain anonymous, filming Kate Gosselin was one of the most unpleasant experiences of his life. He said, "She treats us like shit. She treats the kids like shit. She's rude to everyone. Nothing surprises me anymore with her."

This love-fest of a family portrait Kate tried to paint contradicts what she told Oprah Winfrey regarding the film crew during an interview in March 2009. Kate said at the time, "The crew changes so often at this point, and, we're seeing a lot of different people, which I once was not comfortable with, but over here you'll see Mike. He's the only one left from the very beginning."

Apparently, the crew really was like Kate's family; none of them are left from the very beginning either.

Kate said she had made deep, lifelong friendships with this great crew of dads, who played games with her kids and read to them. She loved this crew "family" so much, in fact, that she made up a special set of rules just for them. If the crewmembers were such a beloved part of her family, why would Kate treat them any differently than she treated Jon and the kids? Here are Kate's "New House Rules" for the crew.

New House Rules

- This home address is NEVER to be discussed or written down. Directions to this house are not to be discussed either.

- Specific door use- side double doors on left side of house- enters into basement- **no other doors in house to be used by crew members AT ALL please.**

- Absolutely no smoking or drinking alcohol on our entire property (or on the road in front of our house).

- Turn lights off in apt and house every time you leave a room- no exceptions

- **Approved bathroom for crew use is in apartment. This is the ONLY bathroom for crew usage. (do not use bathrooms in house please)**

- No shoes in house or apt at any time. Shoe booties (that have NOT been worn outside!) or no shoes. Period.

- Please leave thermostat in apartment where it is. When leaving, turn down to 66 degrees. Thermostat will be set to a temp- and should not be changed please.

- Use trash cans for all trash. Please remove all trash from apartment and place in outside trash cans everyday and before leaving at the end of each shoot.

- Place all towels (if applicable) in specified area before leaving.

- **Absolutely no eating/ drinking in our house....** All food/ drinks need to remain in apartment.

- **Completely Close doors!!!! Every time and quickly!! No exceptions.**

- Please knock before entering our house-DO NOT just walk in!!!

- Crew equipment storage- all equipment should be stored in crew purchased storage box in first bay of garage. Make all equipment fit and close and lock door before leaving shoot. NO equipment should remain in apartment as we will be using apt for guests between shoots.

- Do not leave trash or any equipment behind in our house. A walk through by a PA should be done at the end of each shoot to ensure that all equipment/ trash was collected.

- **Do not help yourself to tools, our equipment etc. (including product placement items) Please ask before using things that are not yours.**

- Please remember, this is not a 'set' (or a college dorm!)-- its our home!!!! We are very proud of this house, please treat it with care!!!!!!!

Kate sent an email to Wendy Douglas of Discovery telling her that "anytime the film crew is present Jon and or I need to also be present to let them into the house and to oversee. Therefore, I am requesting that the schedule be revised to reflect this."

If the crew was like family and she trusted them to be alone with her children, why wouldn't she also trust them to be at her house without her or Jon there to "oversee" them? Kate trusted contractors to be in her home alone, but not her "family," the crew?

Kate repeated over and over that having the crew around and the constant filming was a "normalcy" for her children. There was another time in history when children were subjected to this same kind of "normalcy." If you Google "Dionne Quintuplets," you will learn how five little girls were exploited and put on display like animals in a zoo. Here is some information about them from Wikipedia (http://en.wikipedia.org/wiki/Dionne_quintuplets):

...The Dionne quintuplets (born May 28, 1934) are the first quintuplets known to survive their infancy. The sisters were born just outside Callander, Ontario, Canada near the village of Corbeil.

...After four months with their family, they were made wards of the King for the next nine years under the Dionne Quintuplets' Guardianship Act, 1935. The government and those around them began to profit by making them a significant tourist attraction in Ontario.

... Across the road from their birthplace, the Dafoe Hospital and Nursery was built for the five girls and their new caregivers. ... The compound had an outdoor playground designed to be a public observation area. It was surrounded by a covered arcade that allowed tourists to observe the sisters behind one-way screens. ...It was a nine-room nursery with a staff house nearby. The staff house held the three nurses and the three policemen in charge of guarding them. A housekeeper and two maids lived in the main building with the quintuplets. The buildings were surrounded by a seven foot barbed wire fence.

Approximately 6,000 people per day visited the observation gallery that surrounded an outdoor playground to view the Dionne sisters. Ample parking was provided and almost 3,000,000 people walked through the gallery between 1936 and 1943. Oliva Dionne ran a souvenir shop and a concession store opposite the nursery and the area acquired the name "Quintland". The souvenirs pictured the five sisters. There were autographs and framed photographs, spoons, cups, plates, plaques, candy bars, books, postcards, dolls, and much more at this shop ... In 1934, the Quintuplets brought in about $1 million, and they attracted in total about $51 million of tourist revenue to Ontario.

This was their normal, too. And they suffered dearly for it their entire lives.

"MY KIDS LOOOOOOOOOVE FILMING THE SHOW!"

In April of 2011, Kate said this to Matt Lauer on the *Today* show: "It is a very positive fixture still in our lives. It's **normal**, it's exciting. They still cheer when the crew comes in the door. **I would not say that if it were not true.**"
There she goes again using the word "normal" to describe the completely abnormal action of selling your children's privacy and childhoods for profit. During that same interview, Lauer expressed disbelief that Kate could put eight children on a 21-hour flight to Australia and avoid a major family meltdown. Kate said even she was surprised by how smoothly it all went. "It was one of the best flights of our lives. **I'm not kidding. I'm shocked to be sitting here saying that.**"

I don't doubt that it was a good flight for Kate. She sat with her handsome, married bodyguard, Steve, in first class, while the suffering children sat in another part of the plane with two babysitters, the film crew and the show's director/producers.

The Season 4 "All You Wanted To Know" episode of *Jon & Kate Plus Ei8ht* was one of those episodes TLC used to respond to the negative criticism in the media regarding the show. Most, if not all, of the questions or comments in those types of episodes were written or "planted" by Kate and the show's producers. This is how they "set the record straight" about how much the kids loved filming:

"Hey, I'm Bonnie, I'm one of the editors on *Jon and Kate Plus Ei8ht*. You know I've gone through tons of footage and it's pretty obvious to me that the kids are pretty comfortable with the cameras. They go from ignoring them completely to sometimes goofing around and wanting to see themselves in it. It's just part of everyday life for them."

We need to give Bonnie, the editor, a big thank you for her input. I'm sure I don't need to say how stupid and contrived her little speech sounds, but I will anyway. It is beyond absurd that the producers would ask someone whose livelihood was so closely tied to the success of the show, to comment on the children's supposed comfort around the cameras. What was Bonnie, the editor, going to say? That she had to edit out footage of the children crying and looking miserable? Yeah, right. That would have been Bonnie's ticket to pink-slipsville.

Kate chimed in with one of my favorite Kate quotes about the kids:

"They're just living. They're not required to do anything. If they don't like being involved in a shoot, they're not. If they don't feel like being around, they're not. If they want to go to a friend's house instead of be present for a shoot, they just are. It's not an issue for the kids.

When talking about the show being put on hold temporarily, pending Jon's complaint, it was pretty impressive that Kate could say the following with a straight face:

"Over the weekend I told the kids that we're not filming at this point. And actually, times eight, there was wailing and sobbing. They love our crew, they love the interaction, they love the events. There is nothing harmful about it. They are angry."

They were angry, all right, but it had nothing to do with the crew not being around. I have seen no signs of any wailing and sobbing and anger from the kids because of the absence of the film crew. In fact, I have seen quite the opposite. From the first day I went to the Gosselin home to begin reporting for *US Weekly*, I've seen the kids react negatively when told they have to film. These are small children who wanted to play and run around. When the crew was at the house, and the kids had to stop what they were doing to be controlled and to film scripted segments of them pretending to do something that they wouldn't normally be doing, their frustration was very evident.

Yes, they were angry. But not for the reason that Kate says. They were angry because they wanted to be left alone to play and do things that other kids do instead of being herded around like cattle on the family farm, from one set-up fake activity to the next.

I've observed the kids while filming and I've spoken to the kids about filming. For every minute of film TLC carefully edits to show the kids looking happy, you can bet there are 30 minutes of unseen film showing the kids being miserable about filming.

KATE DOESN'T HAVE A LOT OF CHILD CARE

Let me be clear from the very start. There is nothing wrong with someone having a nanny or others to help with childcare; however, there is everything wrong with a person who has a nanny and others to help with childcare refusing to acknowledge that those people exist because it would completely contradict a fake image manufactured for a television show.

On *The Talk*, with her publicist standing just off camera, Kate was asked this obviously scripted, pre-approved question: "You don't have a lot of child care, right?" This question was given to the interviewer by Kate's publicist to try and rebuild Kate's tarnished image, in preparation for the upcoming season of *Kate Plus Ei8ht*.

Kate's mind churned for a few seconds trying to pull out the approved, rehearsed answer, and then she said, "I don't. I have a babysitter half the week. Three and a half days, um, and I, when I'm at home, which is most of the time, I'm hands on, I cook every meal. I know people want to say other things about me. I'm doing the math homework. I'm taking care of my kids. That is where my heart is, with my kids."

In this situation, Kate was actually kind of telling the truth while at the same time being very misleading. I'm no genius, so I had my 8-year-old daughter help me with the math on this subject.

Kate made this statement in February, during school, when the kids are out of the house from 7 AM when the bus picks them up, until 4 PM when the bus drops them off.

Here's how Kate's "I have a babysitter half the week" lie breaks down:

There are 168 total hours in a week.
(24 hours in a day x 7 days a week equals 168 hours. So far, so good.)
"Half the week" equals 84 hours.
(168 hours divided by 2 equals 84 hours.)
The kids are away at school for 45 hours a week.
(7AM – 4 PM equals 9 hours a day x 5 days a week equals 45 hours)
The kids are in bed for 56 hours a week.
(8 hours a night x 7 days a week equals 56 hours.)
That leaves a possible 67 hours that the kids could possibly be at home and awake.
Kate has a babysitter for 84 hours a week. At least.

That's not a stretch, believe me, as someone who watched the comings and goings of nannies and babysitters at the house during school and summer vacation for nearly two years. And as someone who's spoken "off the record" to several of the "helpers" since I've been on this job.

There were sometimes up to three babysitters at the house with the kids at any given time during the summer months. Kate also hired a live-in, "overnight" nanny.

And for Kate Gosselin to utter the words, "um, and I, when I'm at the house, **which is most of the time, I'm hands on…**" is laughable. Just read through this book for the real truth about how much time Kate is actually at the house with the kids. Kate looks for any reason to NOT be at the house with the kids. I've seen it, on a regular basis, for nearly two years, seven days a week.

Kate tweeted this in 2011 trying to do damage control regarding a tabloid story about all the help she has:

response2article:nvr had 2bsitters-died laughing@their 'salary',sch tuition$-noteven close.hav nvr pd $ 4 Elysasuzanne clothing

THE KIDS ARE AFRAID OF THE PAPARAZZI

The Gosselin kids are certainly not afraid of the paparazzi. Far from it. I spent several months among the paparazzi that came to Pennsylvania to cover the Gosselin story. For the most part, these were a polite, respectful bunch of guys. Every now and then there would be one or two who stepped over the line and would get too close to the kids while photographing them, or worse, in my opinion, would ask Kate questions about the divorce, etc., in front of the kids. They were doing their job though, which was to engage and get a reaction, so I understood their position. They also didn't have children, like I do, so I'm sure the thought never even occurred to them that what they were doing in front of the kids was even an issue. Your perspective on things changes greatly when you have children.

I support Kate 100% in her resolve to protect her children from strangers, including the paparazzi. I can't even imagine how I would have handled the same situation if I were in her shoes. I'm an overly protective parent when it comes to people being near my kids, and I could never deal with that in a non-aggressive way like Kate did. Kate put up a stone wall to the paps, and I admire her for that. The problem is that Kate told the children lies about the paparazzi and intentionally tried to scare them. Jon's approach was completely different from Kate's. He knew these guys were just doing their jobs and they were going to take pictures regardless of what he or Kate said, so he chose to be civil to them.

In addition to being working paparazzi, one or two of the guys became friends with Jon and, in turn, got up close and friendly with the kids. There were times when a pap or two was allowed inside the fence to hang out while Jon was in the yard with the kids. The kids loved the attention, and as far as I can remember, the paps agreed not to photograph the kids while inside the property. I was a big part of that, and it was fun. We cooked out, had squirt gun battles with the kids, and played games with them. One of the paps even took the time to teach the boys how to ride their two-wheel bicycles without training wheels, and on several occasions, the paps surrendered their cameras to the kids to let them experiment with photography. That's really the only time I ever saw the kids just having fun and being kids – when Jon had custody and they were allowed to run around the property, enjoying their summer. You can do an online search for the video of two of the sextuplets coming down to the fence with their water guns and playing with and squirting the paparazzi. It was fun for them. I was there. I shot the video.

In Kate's defense, there surely are bad paparazzi in the world. But there are also bad doctors, bad lawyers, bad politicians, bad teachers, bad policemen, bad television executives, bad priests and, yes, bad mothers. When you choose to sell your children's privacy to the world, you have to be prepared for the consequences.

I CAN'T RUN WHEN THE KIDS ARE HOME

Kate tweeted often about going out running. She always made sure to inform her devoted fans how many miles she ran. Even Kate's fans would sometimes ask how she could possibly be running when she had eight children at home. Kate, of course, would duck the issue by tweeting that it was a "kidless weekend" or that the kids were at their dad's house. What about the other 95% of the time when they are not at their dad's house, like during the summer months when they're home all day?

xxxxx @Kateplusmy8 the fact that you have time to run for 3+ hours… Hmmm? Mysteriousmommove!

answer= kidless weekend! And I made time! So so so much to do!

xxxxx @Kateplusmy8 Who watches the kids while u run for 3hrs? Not judging just asking I'm a mom of 3 & can't even pee alone

they r at their dads for wkend! And no I can't run when they are home

For two years, Kate has been taking to the streets running while the kids are inside the house…alone. Mady and Cara are in charge of watching them, which isn't a big stretch since the twins entertain the sextuplets most of the time anyway, even when Kate IS at home. The twins also bathe and feed the "little kids" as well. Kate will occasionally run around her driveway while the kids are playing outside, but usually, they're alone in the house, or a high school girl is babysitting them. Either way, the bottom line is that every second Kate spent running around in circles is another second she could have spent with her children…and she chose not to.
Kate tweeted this on a Monday night – a school night – while the kids were in her care:

> **…nothing like screeching bats at dusk to make this girl run faster…Talk about motivation…**

Dusk at Kate's house on that night was around 7:30 pm. So why was Kate outside running in the dark while her kids were home alone, or with helpers, on a school night? Why wasn't she inside with them being a mom – helping them with their homework, playing with them, reading to them, tending to their showers/baths, etc.?

GYMNASTICS

Very little of the money the children earned is being spent on them to give them a normal childhood. They want to play sports and do outside activities, but except for one of the twins playing lacrosse AT SCHOOL, Kate won't allow it – unless it's for filming purposes.
Kate and TLC filmed the kids doing gymnastics, but it was just a single-day experience for the girls, again, for filming only. The problem is that they wanted to do it more and begged Kate to let them. She told them no with no reason given. When a fan asked her on Twitter if the kids still do gymnastics, Kate responded:

> **No.sadly.cost a lot and created per space issues-crowded there.will try to do in future tho. Vry gd for all kids I think.**

THE GOOD BRA

Kate has long denied that she had a boob job. When asked about it in interviews, she has never come out and actually denied it. She just does her usual Kate word dance that allows her to lie without coming out directly with a lie. "I got a good bra" is how she responds to the question.
Does anyone besides her strongest supporters (and no, I don't mean her good bra) believe Kate when she says she didn't have a boob job? Go to 3:52-3:58 of part 2 of the Bald Head Island episode and pause your computer. Kate is bra-less and standing firm and looking fabulously slutty.

Kate is completely hanging out of her shirt. This was during the "Kate's a hot mom' experiment when they were desperate for ratings and she was dressing more and more embarrassingly provocatively. That experiment failed terribly, of course.

RUMOR HAS IT

Even though Kate has been quoted repeatedly as saying that she doesn't pay any attention to the tabloids or the online gossip blogs, in February 2011, she sat down with the ladies on *The Talk* and said, "99% of what you read about me online is not true, um, it's far from true."

If Kate doesn't pay attention to the stories about her online, as she stated, how would she know if what they were saying about her was true or not? Here are some tweets where Kate is, yet again, "clearing up the rumors" for everyone so that, you know, we don't have any misinformation about her:

NOT 1 stitch of truth in radar article, once again... & radar u can't even report my website properly! It's: kateplusmy8.com

Let's play clear up the rumor! Ask me CURRENT rumors and I'll answer instead of letting tabloids write garbage! Ready, set, GO!

xxxxx @Kateplusmy8 I think twitter is great, you finally get a chance to instantly put the record straight – you go girl!

I know. I LOVE it for that... They write, I clear up their dumb lies. The end.
I'm ok 2b held 2higher standards...can expect ppl 2 live up 2 their ind potential. But hate,lies and jealousy r intolerable!

Kate has a special page called Kate + Rumors set up on her personal website just so nobody can get away with telling any lies about her. Here's the text at the top of that page:

Great news! Instead of believing the tabloids, you can come here for the TRUTH about current issues! I'll discuss all rumors that need to be addressed! Imagine that!

Here is a classic Kate tweet from late 2011:

xxxxx @Kateplusmy8 What's the silliest rumor you have ever heard about you...or is that impossible to choose? ;-)

everythingwritten w/o an interv fr me &/or as reported by 'inside sources'(which there r none-inside sources don't giv info)

Well there you have it, everyone. Inside sources don't give info. Kate says so. For someone who insists she doesn't spend time reading the tabloids, she certainly spends a lot of time clearing up their rumors.

Even though Kate Gosselin lies all the time, she has a problem with lies, and the lying liars who tell them. She also has a problem when people tell the truth, but the truth is critical of her. On March 13, 2012, she said as much on Twitter when she announced:

> **And,btw,I've now blocked the Philly paparazzi liar& I encourage ALL to do the same..whether u love or hate me,1 fact remains: he lied to u!**

Kate is very angry, and it appears that she's throwing down the gauntlet and daring someone to prove that she is a liar. The following very beautiful and positive tweet wasn't even sent to Kate. She just saw it and re-tweeted it, and added a little bit of her own personality to it: the venom and hate.

> "For every beauty there is an eye somewhere to see it. For every truth there is an ear somewhere to hear it" — Ivan Panin

> **'....and for every made up lie abt someone, there's a stupid moron to believe and spread it...'(sorry had2add my 2cents)**

CIRCLE THE WAGONS

Kate was able to get away with her constant lying and deceit because her manager and the public relations teams of Discovery/TLC kept her well-insulated from criticism. They circled the wagons to protect Kate lest she stop giving them access to her children. Their approach was illustrated clearly by one situation in particular.

Former child star and current child advocate Paul Petersen spoke out on behalf of the Gosselin children. He talked about the dangers of forcing the children to work filming a reality show. Petersen's involvement made Julie May and Discovery/TLC very nervous, so they quickly got together and came up with a few possible responses, "just in case anyone picks up the story."

The "potential response" that Laurie Goldberg of Discovery Communications sent to Julie May makes their strategy pretty clear. To summarize, this is what she said:

It's ludicrous to equate being a child actor with being in a docuseries about your family; The kids are going about their lives and not working. They're just doing what they do normally but instead of Jon filming their lives, a film crew does; This series allows Kate to stay home and be part of her children's lives; Every decision Jon and Kate make is to better their children's lives; The show made it possible for Jon and Kate to raise and feed their children.

And then the inevitable attack on Paul Petersen: Mr. Petersen is being disingenuous at best in expressing his concern for the Gosselin kids, while he's selling his DVD of the television shows featuring himself as a child actor, and, Mr. Petersen is making a sad attempt to capitalize on the popularity of a well-loved show for his own publicity and financial gain.

It is pathetic how Laurie Goldberg and Julie May could completely disregard the opinion of a well-respected child advocate, and try to discredit him, just so they could protect their investment and continue to exploit the Gosselin children. It is even more pathetic that they would continue to trot out the lie that the kids are just going about their daily lives as they normally would. It is confounding that Kate, who obviously wants her children to work in the entertainment industry, wouldn't want them to be protected physically, psychologically and financially. She took her kids to modeling agencies and auditions; she encouraged strangers on Twitter to send tweets to Ron Howard about using one of the twins in a movie; she mentioned more than once that one of the twins would make a great Disney star, etc. So why then would Kate be so opposed to someone like Paul Petersen looking out for the well-being of her children and defending their rights?
That's a rhetorical question. While Kate would most certainly want laws in place to protect her children's profitability if they were working in a traditional acting environment, she absolutely did not want any restrictions placed on her ability to exploit them herself. Petersen had been pushing for legislation to protect children working in the entertainment industry, and specifically reality TV, at the very same time that Kate Gosselin and TLC/Discovery Communications had been aggressively exploiting the Gosselin children and forcing them to work and "perform" since the day they were born.
When Paul Petersen's name came up on Kate's Twitter again in 2011, it absolutely infuriated her:

Final word: reality kids are NOT acting. They are living&breathing in own environments! Huge difference!Leave them all alone!

SHE WORKS HARD FOR NO MONEY

When the very wealthy Kate Gosselin appeared on the *Wendy Williams Show* in September of 2011, she very predictably played the victim and moaned to the world that she doesn't have enough money. As usual, Kate repeated her overused and stale mantra about how terrible she has it and how hard her life is.

```
Williams: "So a lot of people are under the assumption
          that you made a ton of money doing Kate Plus
          Ei8ht so that you should be ok for a moment."

Kate: "Wouldn't that be nice?
```

As of 2012, Kate was still pleading poverty and looking for the public's sympathy.

"You could offer me every last dollar on the planet.
I don't work for money. I cannot compromise my morals
and standards to get paid a ridiculous amount of money."
– *Kate Gosselin*

NO LIE

What adult do you know who continually has to say "no lie"? Kate says "no lie" in just about every interview she gives and often in her tweets. Does she say "no lie" because she lies so much? Here are some examples of her saying "no lie" in her tweets:

> **GM!I failed 2day!Didn't run bc did not sleep ONE wink-no lie..remem that GREAT coffee@4pm?Yep,it kept wrking all thru nite!:(TOM=game on!**

> **that was a memory filled day! My kids STILL thank me for him EVERY day, no lie. Nearly a year later:)**

> **NO lie. Was talking to a good friend abt that 1 hr ago—her mom was only ch and was shocked too! Lol**

> **I drive the bbb w all 8. The large suv w 6 or less &my little car(2 carts of groceries fit in it- no lie!) when just me!saves gas!**

It is very common to hear Kate say "no lie" because chances are she is, in fact, probably lying.

THE GOOD MOM

*"I'm not out to win any awards.
I'm out to be the best mother I can possibly be."*
– Kate Gosselin

A member of Kate's family told me that Kate had been diagnosed with Bipolar Disorder, but she refused to take medication to control her moods. That diagnosis was confirmed for me because of something I witnessed in November 2009. I couldn't believe my eyes on this one particular day, especially after having watched Kate on a daily basis for six months. Was she taking medication this day? Something was dramatically different about Kate, and I have never seen it again since.

This was one of those days that I wish the Gosselin kids could have had every day. It was Kate, being a good mom and having fun with her beautiful children. I can spot a photo-op a mile away, but this day seemed different. Kate seemed at ease and relaxed, just out enjoying her family. Regrettably, I was the one who called the lone paparazzo to the playground that day. Looking back, I feel bad about that, but at the time, I was just doing my job. In the tabloid world they say, "If there are no pictures, it didn't happen." I wanted a photo-backup of my reporting. Plus, this particular paparazzo was a good friend of mine, and he had always been good around the Gosselin kids.

This is what I saw.

```
Jon and Kate Gosselin PA Reporting
November, 2009
Kate pulled the Sprinter van out of the garage at 10:00 am and loaded
up the sextuplets with Judy's help. This was very unusual and I was
excited to see where they were going. No paps were on the scene yet
as I followed the van along the winding country roads, going 50 in a
40 mph zone. Luckily there was a car in front of them going slow or
Kate may have lost me. She has a lead foot.
They pulled into the Dunkin Donuts parking lot and parked. NO DRIVE
THRU! First time ever. Judy jumped out and helped offload the kids
and they all went inside and sat down. Kate went to the counter to
order donuts and drinks for the group. I waited for Kate to return to
the table and then went inside to order donuts. By this time the pap
that I called got there and he came in to take a few pictures. Kate
started screaming "Get him out of here!!!"and the manager started
yelling at the pap so he left. They got into a shouting match on the
way out the door and the manager got on the phone and called the
police. I went out to my car and we both pulled off the Dunkin Donuts
lot. Kate ordered two dozen assorted donuts and the kids dug in and
had powdered sugar all over their faces and were very happy. Kate
usually makes a point of saying that she only prepares organic,
healthy food for the family. It was so nice to see the kids having
fun with Kate. It's been a long time coming.
```

A few minutes later the police came and went inside and then came out and went across the street to the pap. He told him that the owner is very upset but that he couldn't stop him from taking pictures from across the street. I parked somewhere else to watch in the event that the police tried to detain us while Kate drove off as they've done in the past, just to give her a head start.

After about thirty minutes, they all came outside carrying boxes and a bag with their extra donuts inside to take home.

Instead of going back home, Kate drove to a residential neighborhood in affluent Wyomissing and took the kids to a playground. It was a picture-perfect day. The sun was shining, the leaves were falling. Kate and Judy unloaded the kids and turned them loose on the playground. They went crazy running down the hill to the various swings etc. They were yelling and screaming and having so much fun. They ran straight to the sliding boards and monkey bars. Kate and Judy walked together talking and smiling. They seemed more like friends or sisters than employer/employee. The pap kept a safe distance while shooting so as not to upset Kate while I went and sat on a nearby bench to observe. (Sounds creepy, I know. But everybody there knew who I was and who I was working for. It was business.)

Judy brought her very little dog along for the trip and the kids and Kate took turns holding the leash. At one point Kate got herself all tangled up in the leash and was struggling with it for a few minutes. She jokingly yelled "Judy, you didn't teach me how to operate this!" It was one of those leashes that you push a button and it winds itself up. Kate was having fun like I've never seen before.

Kate had her large Dunkin Donuts coffee in her hand while strolling around between kids. She got on a seesaw with Leah and bounced her up and down. The kids were just having a blast running back and forth between rides.

Joel got himself stuck hanging on the monkey bars and started screaming for help. Oddly or not, he instinctively yelled for Judy instead of Kate and Judy came running and helped him down.

Four kids were riding up and down on two side-by-side seesaws and Kate came over yelling "who wants to go to the moon? Who wants to go to the moon?" The kids were yelling "Me, me, me, me." Then Kate yelled "to the moon!!" and grabbed one end of the seesaw and slammed it down, but it bounced Collin up in the air and he came down hard and slammed his face on the handlebar. I felt so bad for Kate because she hurt her child when she was just trying to have fun with him. She was being a little overzealous, as Jon does sometimes, maybe being aware of the media watching and wanting to be supermom. She quickly scooped him up in her arms and comforted him, wiping away his tears. She gave him TLC (Ha!) and sent him back out to play.

Judy and the girls were on the arm bridge monkey bars, where you hang by your arms and pull yourself across. Judy did it first and Hannah and Alexis tried to follow. They weren't strong enough to make it so they hung there until Judy could help them across. Not nearly as dramatic as when Joel got stuck. When Hannah got to the other side she yelled to Kate "Mommy, Mommy!!" and blew her a kiss. Kate blew two kisses right back to her.

Judy was swinging on the bars now showing Joel how to do it. He was trying his hardest and she yelled "Go Joel you can do it! You're almost done!"

Now Kate was hiding from the boys at the bottom of the tunnel slide and when they came out the bottom she growled like a monster so loud that she could be heard I'm sure for a block. The boys loved it and were laughing hysterically and Kate kept doing it for them.

Kate was alone holding the little dog's leash and she said to him while laughing, "You got a leaf on your face."

Then another little girl came over with her mother and the girl was holding a branch and Kate said loudly "Oh my! I thought you were going to throw that stick at the dog. I almost died!"

Moving across the playground to where Alexis and Hannah were on a little Kiddie seesaw, Kate did a vertical jump up and landed in the middle of the two girls, balancing on the seesaw. She stood there for a few moments and jumped back down. Having watched Kate for six months, this was completely out of character for her. She genuinely looked like she was having the time of her life with her kids and it was so nice to see. Kate and Judy were laughing together and talking across the playground.

Next, all of the kids ran over to the 'diaper swings,' the ones with the built-in seat and the bar that comes down to hold you in. Kate said to them, "you guys are soooooo big. You used to fit in these with no problem. The kids wanted to swing in them so they jammed themselves in and Kate and Judy pushed them. When they were getting them out of the swings, Joel got stuck and it was so funny to see. Kate was holding him stretched out vertically while Judy was trying to untangle his feet from the swing. This went on for two minutes until Judy got him loose. Kate said to him, "say thank you Judy and mommy."

Now for the excitement — A Wyomissing park worker came driving up in his park pickup truck and got out and was walking around picking up branches. When he got close to Kate and the kids he said hello and the kids were talking to him and then Kate joined in and they stood there talking for thirty minutes while the kids played. He was a big guy wearing a neon green shirt with the sleeves chopped off. Very rugged-looking. Kate was very engaged in the conversation and kept it going. Their body language was very flirtatious. Kate was smiling the whole time and was very talkative, kicking leaves around and rocking back and forth. They talked alone for fifteen minutes while the kids played nearby. At one point they both took out their cell phones and appeared to be entering the digits of the other. I was close enough to hear his name and there's no doubt in my mind that this was a potential hookup. Several times he tried to say goodbye and get back to work and Kate kept chatting him up. I thought this was fantastic to see. After everything that she's been dealing with and all the rumors, she very much deserves to meet a new man or at least flirt with a hot guy.

I know the area very well and will try to find him and check into what was said between them.

He was very good with the kids and was talking to them and playing around with them. When he said goodbye, the kids followed him to his truck and one of the boys yelled "By mister man in green!"

After he left, Kate yelled to Judy to "call her and find out her ETA." No idea who they were talking about. Ten minutes later, they packed it up and held hands walking back up the leafy hill to the van where an attractive blonde woman was waiting with her daughter. They loaded up the kids as well as the new little girl and headed back to the Gosselin house for lunch. I heard Kate say to her kids, "wow, first you get donuts, then you go to the playground and now you get to have a friend come home for lunch and to play!"

They went back to the house and everyone went inside and stayed there until 3:30 when it was time for Kate to go to the bus stop and pick up Mady and Cara.

It was a quick stop and the twins jumped in the back and Kate raced back home to finish the play date. The mom came to the house to pick up her daughter just before dark and everyone was inside for the night it looked like. Kate put the Sprinter van back in the garage and Judy left a little after 5 pm. Long day for her but she looked like she had as much fun as Kate did.

A few months later, while still digging for information, I made a new friend, strictly by coincidence. The friend turned out to be the ex-wife of the big, rugged guy that Kate was chatting up at the playground. The man's name is extremely unique and the ex-wife told me the story first, never knowing what I had seen at the playground that day.

She said that her ex got reprimanded at his job with the Wyomissing Borough for bragging about having a sexual relationship with Kate Gosselin.

I would guess that the guy was making the story up to impress his friends but there certainly may have been a date or two with Kate. Who knows? The paps shut it down when it gets dark and I've never been able to catch Kate with another man, even though that was something I had hoped for while working for US. That would have been a big story.

BAD BLOG

*"Nothing that you read on the Internet or in print is true
unless it is approved by us."*
– Kate Gosselin

The Gosselin story has been kicking around the blogosphere for several years now, with some distinct and separate camps of fanatics expressing their opinions – the Kate "haters" and the Kate supporters, or "sheeple." There are also the bloggers who hate Kate, but don't like to be called "haters." It can be a bit confusing at times.

Many people on the blogs claim to be "insiders" or claim to have information that they put out there as fact. Others claim to have "expert opinions." There's even a local blogger from Wernersville who claims to be Kate's "neighbor." That's a bit like saying that Mars is a neighbor of Earth.

Kate Gosselin doesn't really have any neighbors, and she doesn't live in Wernersville, PA. She lives in Lower Heidelberg Township, which is a rural area a couple of miles from the small, time-forgotten town of Wernersville. One day when I was bored, I measured the distance from Kate's driveway to the "Welcome to Wernersville" sign. It is exactly 2.0 miles.

I live 10 miles from Kate's house. I have lived in the area my entire life and I know it well. I drove to the Gosselin house every day for years, so I am also very familiar with the surrounding areas.

There is no question that Jon and Kate had neighbors in Wyomissing and Elizabethtown, PA. However, Kate now lives on a 23-acre property, surrounded by a fence and a few thousand acres of farmland. At the end of her driveway is a metal gate, which is about a football field away from her house. That's as close as you'll ever get to ringing her doorbell and dropping off a pie. Her "neighbor" across the street lives on 600 acres surrounded by cornfields. There's no sign of any entrance to his property, but if you drive past Kate's house, down the street a bit, and look very closely in the winter when the leaves are off the trees, you can see his huge house off in the distance. Kate's "neighbors" are local farmers. The closest living person you may see if you're driving to Kate's house is the little old man and his big dog that live a quarter-mile down the road on the corner.

If you have ever seen tabloid photos of Kate and the kids trick-or-treating at Halloween, it sure as heck wasn't in her "'neighborhood" of Wernersville. You'd have a better chance of seeing the Loch Ness Monster than seeing Kate Gosselin knocking on the door of somebody in Wernersville. In the past, Kate would pack the kids up and drive them three-plus hours to Maryland to trick-or-treat in her bodyguard Steve Neild's neighborhood. I know this because I followed her there while working for *US Weekly*.

As far as the bloggers go, the "haters" and the "sheeple" take things to extremes, but a case can be made for both sides. Both groups are basing their opinions on what they have seen on television and what they have heard coming from Kate's mouth, or from her thumbs via Twitter. They each have fringe members who are prone to wild speculation and who can be unspeakably vile and cruel.

The "Kate lovers" have bought into the television image of Kate as the super-organized, controlling, no-nonsense supermom that was sold to them by Discovery/TLC. That's understandable, I suppose. Lots of people believe what they see on television. Lots of people also believe in little green men. To each his or her own. Some of her fans are young; some are naive; some are simply ignorant. Some of the "sheeple" are probably much like Kate, and see no problem with her words and behavior. I suspect that a lot of Kate's supporters also sympathize with her because they fell hook, line and sinker for the lies that she and Discovery crafted about Jon. The one indisputable fact about her most die-hard fans is that they ALWAYS give excuses and look to lay blame elsewhere for Kate's obvious mistreatment of others, her bad behavior, her lies, and her ignorant and insensitive statements.

It will be interesting to see if any of Kate's fans change their opinion of her after reading Kate's own words and finding out how she really treats her children and dog, and how she makes fools of other people via email. I wonder if they will feel betrayed when they find out how she really feels about her fans, and how fake Kate's "reality" world really is.

The "haters" have taken what they have seen and heard from Kate on television and in interviews and have drawn completely opposite conclusions. They watched her ignore, ridicule and disrespect her children, her husband, and countless others, and saw that something was terribly wrong. They found her detachment from her kids disturbing. They were not blinded by celebrity or a well-crafted persona and, based on Kate's own words and actions, came to understand that Kate is driven by greed and selfishness and an undying desire for fame. They have refused to excuse her blatant lies and are unrelenting in taking her to task.

Before I began writing this book, I had never read any of the blogs. I stuck mainly to the entertainment and tabloid websites to take the temperature of what was being reported about the Gosselins each day. My iPhone was a Godsend early on while I was staked out in front of the Gosselin home, and while I sat alone in my car waiting for something newsworthy to happen on Heffner Road. But once I committed to writing this book, I started reading the blogs from the beginning as part of my research, to see what people were saying and who, if any of them, really knew anything for certain.

There were four Gosselin blogs bookmarked on my computer that I read regularly during this period. By this time, I was privy to most of the details of what I was writing about, so I knew when somebody was posting comments just to give their opinion, or to speculate, or to see their words online, and I knew when somebody with factual knowledge of specific situations was posting. I knew when stories were planted on the blogs by the "players," or by their girlfriends, friends, etc.

I did not, and do not, know everything about what was really going on between Jon and Kate. Only Jon and Kate and the kids know, and that's the way it should always be. So, unless you were in that house, you just don't know. And you never will. Unfortunately, both Jon and Kate have been caught in countless lies, making it very difficult for most people to believe anything they say.

I have read many emails between Kate, her manager Julie Carson May, and Discovery Communications, documenting how Kate would get bothered by something she saw online. She would immediately fire off an email to Discovery requesting that it be taken care of. "Can we sue??" was a question Kate was quick to ask.

Before there were fan sites and bloggers taking sides on the Gosselins, I saw firsthand the power that Kate, through Discovery, wielded. When my wife, Dana, made unflattering comments about Kate on her blog for the *Reading Eagle*, Kate and Discovery had the blog shut down. I worked at the *Reading Eagle* at that time, and I was in the office when the call came in. With one phone call, Kate and company had the world's oldest family-owned newspaper cowering in the corner like a scared child. Dana's blog was shut down within the hour because the people on the newspaper's management team were afraid.

Kate monitored Google News alerts and scoured the Internet and the blogosphere for anyone speaking negatively about her. She kept files on her computer that were filled with material from blogs and tabloids. It consumed her. When ratings were huge, Kate had people to monitor the Internet for her. Once she hit the downside of her reality life, she again became totally consumed with personally scouring the Internet day and night for any mention of her.

Along with keeping tabs on various people and websites, Kate kept a close watch on the "Gwoppers" at *gosselinswithoutpity.blogspot.com*. She had a file on her computer with information from that blog, including who the moderators were. Back in 2005, Kate kept one particular file folder on her computer titled "BAD BLOG." When I looked inside the folder, there was my wife Dana's blog, in all its glory, along with a Word document that contained a single comment from a poster to the blog.

I had forgotten about this era of my life, but there it was, before my eyes. The single comment that Kate Gosselin held up as an example of all things bad ... was something I wrote, several years ago, showing my questionable sense of humor. So, for the sake of full disclosure, here is my comment that Kate Gosselin saved on her computer; it was the only individual comment she saved from Dana's blog:

```
"Tsk, tsk, tsk Dana. Why do you persist in attacking this poor,
helpless woman?
```

Yes, I did tell Kate that she should have many, many children and
yes, I do communicate with the Gosselin family on a daily basis.
Is that so hard for you to comprehend?? I chose her over
thousands of other crazy people to carry this burden. This is all
my fault. I thought she knew it would be a difficult road. The
community needs to get behind this lost soul and raise these
children as if they were their own. Maybe if everyone in Berks
County could just forgo going out to dinner just once a week,
they could give that money directly to Kate to help her on her
journey. After all, put yourself in her shoes. Can you possibly
imagine how exhausting it must be to have to spend every day
watching someone else taking care of eight children?? I know I
wouldn't want to do it — and I'm God."
Posted by: God at May 20, 2005 09:03 AM

Admittedly, it was not my most mature moment. I was just stirring the pot to get
people engaged in conversation. I'm a bit of an antagonist. And, clearly, it
bothered Kate enough to save it. So was this the reason that Kate Gosselin
demanded a PR team a short time later? That comment is still out there in
cyberspace. If you Google "Tsk, tsk, tsk Dana," on the fourth Google search page,
eight items down, you can read the battle being waged even back then, in May of
2005, between the haters and supporters. Those were the pioneers of the Gosselin
blogosphere.

Throughout all the blogging drama, Discovery maintained the power to control
Kate Gosselin's message. The following email samples provide a mere glimpse
into Kate's communications concerning the Internet and its bloggers.

In January of 2008, a concerned viewer sent an email to info@sixgosselins.com to
complain about TLC filming and televising the children being potty trained. The
sender cited the following post from Television Without Pity (TWoP):

You guys should be more careful regarding what you allow to be
shown on tv...the following post from TWoP:

It doesn't matter WHERE the potties were or WHO put them there.

Both the girls and boys were televised, nationwide, sitting on
potties. Kate let that happen for the girls. Even took photos. I
can't believe that Jon/Kate couldn't put their foot/feet down and
say "enough is enough."

So here are little children doing very private things in various
stages of undress...with various non-family adults watching and
filming, perhaps against their will...but as they are so young
they do not have a voice in the matter. **Is this a case to be
reported to Child and Family Protective services? I am a CASA
advocate in Illinois...and I would say yes."**

**I would be inclined to report the behavior...in fact I'm looking
for the appropriate office to contact.**

Instead of considering for a moment that filming the children potty training was a terrible violation of their privacy and extremely dangerous considering that perverted individuals were, no doubt, viewing their images, Kate emailed Wendy from Discovery to ask for help. She told Wendy that they were being reported to child protective services for showing the kids going potty on TV and asked "Can you guys please help?" She also asked Wendy to "please take care of this with the network" and to have Bravo take down the TWOP forum on them because it was "hurting our family in all ways." Since she was on a roll, she asked Wendy to "remove the DHC forum as well." Kate finished by saying "This email is exactly what we don't want to happen."

On May 19, 2009, at 9:43 AM, Julie May sent an email to Kate, with a copy to Laurie Goldberg of Discovery, informing her that she saw a video of an interview with Jodi and Kevin on Radar Online. Laurie Goldberg sent a reply at 12:46 PM that same day, saying that they had gotten a long interview and were clearly "milking" it for all it was worth. She said that they had been the MOST damaging on many levels.

After being alerted that Kevin and Jodi were speaking negatively about her, Kate emailed her three favorite words to Laurie Goldberg: **can we sue?** Kate Gosselin wanted to sue her own brother and sister-in-law.

In another email, Kate gave Jon his hourly instructions about monitoring the Internet. She told Jon to please do a search on Facebook to see who was saying they were going to be in Canada in October. At least she said "please" and "Thx" this time.

There are many other emails just like those.

I spent a lot of time reading the comments on the blogs, mostly the "anti-Kate" blogs. I did so for a very good reason: I was trying to figure out who was on there leaking inside information. Clearly, to me there were, and continue to be, several possible sources.

The one thing you must remember here is that everyone, including immediate family, who ever worked for or had any extended contact with Kate Gosselin and her children had to sign a confidentiality agreement. It was made very clear to each and every one of them that a breach of this agreement would bring down upon them all the legal power that Discovery could muster. They would be left penniless.

So if you were someone who was close to the Gosselin family at one time, maybe inside the house with them or going on trips with them, etc., and you were cast off like Kate's trash, or if you were one of Kate's infertility doctors or nurses, or a doctor's office staffer with access to gossip and information, and you were angry, very angry, but you knew you couldn't utter a peep about what you had seen or heard, how would you get your story out? How would you let people know about the awful things Kate Gosselin was doing to her children and family without losing your career or everything you owned?

You'd become an "anonymous" Internet blogger: a "Gosselin Insider."

So, interspersed among the Kate groupies, the lonely housewives, the grandmothers, the lunatics, the hate-mongers, and all those who sincerely care about the fate of the Gosselin children, there are some real Gosselin insiders on the blogs. I know they are there because I have read the comments back to the start and, armed with the inside story myself, I can see them. I may not know all of them, but I recognize some. I know who the "insiders" are, and I applaud them for doing what they felt comfortable doing in trying to expose Kate's lies while protecting themselves.

The list of possible insiders is long. It includes so many people who Kate purged from her life because they had the nerve to question or criticize her, or to express alarm and concern about her children. Beth, Jodi, Kevin, Carla, Kendra, Christen, Clarissa, Jon, Ashley, Mark, Rhonda, Jacob, Jamie, Ariel, Judy, Kathryn, Clark, Jen, Jeff, Tracy, and Anne are just a few of the many possible choices.

THE HELP

"My day is, make a meal, serve a meal, clean up a meal,
clean up everything."
– Kate Gosselin

"Our church body is 750 people. They're hoping to have 100 people
on the volunteer list. And, actually, we're getting calls and
resumes sent for people that we don't know that want to help."
– Kate Gosselin

Kate was once asked by one of her fans on Twitter if she does everything by herself, or if she hires some help. This was her response:

lol. I DO have help.. But it's my kids! Does that count as help? Lol

Kate Gosselin is notorious for taking credit where credit is not due, from writing a book like, say, *Multiple Blessings*, to more mundane tasks like, perhaps, doing her own grocery shopping. The entire Kate Gosselin "brand" is built on the illusion that one woman is single-handedly raising eight children – on her own – with little to no outside help.
Nothing could be further from the truth.
Not only does Kate Gosselin have more hired help than anyone I have ever met, but she squeezes every last drop of "help" out of the only people she calls friends. This is a paraphrased entry from Kate's journal about her best friend, Jamie, who had come for a visit.

August 2006
We had water fun today! After breakfast we went outside and played in the pool. We went in and dried off the kids and cleaned up their mud and rediapered. Kate told Jamie that it's no wonder that she doesn't do this by herself. She said "it's so hard!!!!!"

This was taken from my online research. It's funny that Angie Krall, the nurse that Kate fought so hard for and whom she wanted to keep around, ended up turning on Kate by speaking to *US Weekly*.

The new issue of US Weekly reports that Jon & Kate mom Kate Gosselin — known for being short with her husband, Jon Gosselin — is even more combative with her family and employees.

Baby nurse Angela Krall, who watched the sextuplets as infants for more than a year, tells US that the **short-fused Kate fired 40 nurses and nurse's aides in the three months before she was hired.** A 2005 AP story reported that a pre-TV Gosselin had petitioned the state to extend payments for Krall, whose fees were first paid by Medicaid (Jon was unemployed; Medicaid provides limited assistance to premature babies). "Kate Gosselin said she feels society has a responsibility to help with the children, since modern medicine promotes the use of fertility drugs, which can lead to multiple births," the AP reported.

While Kate praised Krall in the same story, Krall reveals that Kate posted "demeaning" signs in every room detailing rules, and fired one woman on the spot for washing her hands in the kitchen instead of the bathroom. "Kate flipped," says Krall. "She thought it was cross-contamination."

When Kate sent her now infamous letter begging the State of Pennsylvania to continue to pony up the bucks to pay for Angie Krall to serve her family, she certainly didn't sound like someone who ever had any intention at all of raising her children on her own.

Angie Krall may have technically been a nurse, but to Kate Gosselin, she was nothing but a free helper, plain and simple. Medicaid was paying for Kate Gosselin's full-time babysitter.

CARLA'S LIST

Kate's own personal "to-do" list reads something like this: Go tanning. Get nails done. Get hair done. Get mail. Go to Starbucks. Go tanning. Get nails done... Her "to-do" lists for others look a lot different. Here is an example of Kate's many orders and instructions to Carla Turner, who was her main "helper" at one time. Carla, who is Ashley the babysitter's mother, was considered one of Kate's best "friends."

The recurring theme seems to be that to be a "friend" to Kate Gosselin you have to be doing chores and running errands for her constantly. With a friend like that ... This was part of Carla's chore list for May 3, 2009:

- Fold laundry and put away (check washers and dryers)

- Clean kitchen and appliances/table high chairs, etc. – can't stress this enough!!!

- Pull all hand towels out of all bathrooms and replace (give kids and Jon junky ones and powder rooms nice ones)- check to see if Judy did that

- Take out trash and lock up garage, turn off lights, etc.- if Jon hasn't.

- Straighten up all toys/clothing in rooms etc.. Including kids rooms

- Carry Katherine dishes downstairs.

- Clean windows: front door, side door into family room, and basement sliding door... inside and out.

- Water all plants

- Organize kids movies in rooms... put back in cases etc. and dresser tops etc.

- Straighten dog kitchen and take out their trash.... dumb dogs! :(

- Wipe out cabinet that has coffee mugs in it.... to right of sink

- Throw lily on front porch away (or plant?) and calla lily on mantle in dining room

- Take Easter decorations off table and mantle and store in built in glass cabinet below Christmas dishes... put in cabinets not in glass part!

- Fold table cloth and table pad and put in buffet that is in dining room near kitchen entrance
  (you will see other table cloths - fold Miss Bev style ;)

- Go through kids closets and match up all like things.... there are stray pieces hanging in laundry room and on top of dryers to be put away etc.

- Hang ironing AND dry-cleaning in correct closets.

Kate also told Carla to come as early as possible and "Don't forget to pick up my pig and bring today!!!" She did say "Thanks" and told Carla to call if she had any questions.

THE PHANTOM CHEF

Katherine is/was Kate's personal chef. You know, the one that Kate says doesn't exist. Kate has said that someone will occasionally prepare meals on filming days to make her life easier. That would make sense for her, just as it would make sense for anyone juggling a hectic work schedule. But here's the problem. I checked the shooting schedules, and many of the emails I've seen from Katherine, the personal chef, were about preparing meals on non-filming days.
The fact that Kate doesn't always cook meals by herself for her kids is no big deal, and certainly not cause for criticism. It is an irrelevant issue that most people wouldn't care about in the least. The real issue is Kate's constant need to deceive. She opens herself to criticism over a non-issue because she stubbornly denies the truth. Kate intentionally lies or misleads or leaves out details in an effort to protect her manufactured image of the put-upon mom of eight. She is desperate to hold onto the supermom mantle, but only she and a few rabid and impressionable fans continue to believe the hoax. If she were to just stop lying to try to keep up appearances, she might find that people would respect her honesty. As it stands, the more lies she tells, the worse she makes herself look.

On December 30, 2008, Katherine told Kate she would come by the next day between 3 and 4 to bring her three dinner entrees. She asked if Kate wanted her to call first, and Kate told her, yes, to please call when she was near.

Kate instructed Katherine to "pull and load the refrigerator in the little room to the right" as she walked in the double doors. Kate also told her that her dishes were in the room by the old fridge she would be using.

In another email, Katherine, the phantom chef, gave Kate tips about the food she had prepared and dropped off. She told Kate to put some of the sauerkraut she brought over the slices so they would stay moist when she heated the pork, and that she could freeze the pot pie if she wished.

Reading Katherine's instructions brings up a question: If Kate fancies herself such a great cook, to the point where she is planning to release her own cookbook, and she shares her recipes online on her website on "Menu Mondays," why would Katherine have to explain to Kate how to keep her pork moist or something as basic as freezing her pot pie? Katherine explains things to Kate as if Kate has no idea what to do in the kitchen.

Katherine also said that she told Jon there was ZERO organic produce today so she roasted frozen green beans. She told Kate that she hoped Kate would enjoy the Vietnamese chicken, and to enjoy the "Pewtarex dish and the vino! Happy belated holiday!"

Kate sent Gina Neild an email on January 1, 2009 offering to get Phantom Chef Katherine to make food so they wouldn't have to do it for a farewell party for Gina's parents.

In this tweet from 2011, it seems to have slipped Kate's mind that she also has a personal chef:

> xxxxx @Kateplusmy8 I wish I had your dedication!!! But I am dying to know, how much help do you have? Nanny? Cook? Maid?

> **a babysitter 4 days / week and a weekly cleaning lady&I hav lotsa energy! Wouldn't want a cook if could. This is my job&I love it!**

Kate always plays word games to cover up her lying. Maybe she has decided that a "cook" is not the same thing as a "personal chef."

THE GHOST ARMY OF HELPERS

Here are some examples of Kate giving orders to more people doing her work for her – more people that she said didn't exist. This is a weekly list of household duties Kate sent to one of her "helpers."

Duty:

C&M clean book bags
C&M room cleaned up well!
Keep up with all kids laundry (play clothes)

Wash C&M uniforms & hang (wash shirts/pants together)
Keep running list of foods/products run out

 Water all plants – once per week – Fern-Family Room – Tree & plant on Kit.
 Counter – Plant in front LR – Aloe in DR.

 Check that juice/paper towels/toilet paper/paper plates & bowls/ soap is
 stocked at each location

 Collect All (hand & bath towels) towels, separate according to color (light &
 solid vs. printed & colored and was on normal/warm then dry and fold

 Replace towels (different ones!) in each bathroom.

Laundry has always seemed to be the bane of Kate's existence (next to Jon, that
is). On Season 3 of *Jon & Kate Plus Ei8ht*, "Cooking with the Twins," Kate
complains about how much laundry she has to do, while at the same time telling us
that "Beverly folds all the laundry, Nana Janet irons all the laundry, and Carla
comes and puts all the laundry away." With helpers doing the folding and ironing
and putting away, that only leaves someone actually having to throw the dirty
clothes into the washing machine.

Kate surely must be aware that it is the washing *machines* that actually *do* the
laundry. All she showed us is that she stuffed dirty clothes into the machines while
the cameras were filming her. It is hard to imagine that she would be willing to do
even that small task on non-filming days.

One day, the unthinkable happened, as documented in an email from Kate to
"Amanda" at Media Motion International. Kate started her email with a cry for
"Help!!!!" and told Amanda she had "another wild goose chase" for her. Kate
explained that "Our tempermental ironess (nanna Janet) took her check and quit
today!!!!" (Sorry, Kate, but it's spelled "temperamental".) Anyway, Kate asked
Amanda to "inconspicuously" look around the Berks County- Reading,
Shillington, Sinking Spring, and Wyomissing area to find them a weekly ironer.
Kate whined that she had no luck replacing Janet in the past and told Amanda that
while Janet did an "immaculate job," she was "hard to deal with…"

Always one to point the finger of blame at anyone other than herself, Kate added
that she imagined Jon played a part in causing Janet to quit. She said, "Jon was
busy comissersting with her about me this morning while I was away so I can only
imagine his part in her quitting... Thanks Jon!" (Sorry, Kate, who hates when
others misspell words. It's commiserating, not comissersting.")

Grocery shopping is another particular ordeal for Kate. She even had to go through
the trouble of making up a standard, weekly grocery list for her non-existent
helpers to use as a guideline. She instructed said helpers to please take an
inventory before shopping for the items on the list so they could adjust the
quantities of each item as necessary. These are the items on her list:

- lunch meat- 2 packs natures promise

- cheese sticks/string cheese- check supply and current desire for them by
  kids- get two packs organic if needed.

- eggs- three dozen- organic brown- natures promise

- bagels- everything- 6 fresh from bakery (or current favorite flavor of Mady/Cara)

- cream cheese- one block of Natures promise if needed

- tubs of yogurt for kids- 4 tubs of Stonyfield farms lowfat vanilla or vanilla or fat free vanilla (any combination of flavor)

- bread- natures promise 100% whole grain- 3 loaves

- milk- CHEAPEST fat free organic milk-6 half gallons (can get a combination of fat free, 1%, and 2% to make a total of six)

- crackers- a combination of organic "ritz" crackers, and other types of crackers - get items that are ON SALE- total of four boxes

- cookies- organic cookies that are ON SALE that the kids like- 3 packs

- chips/pretzels- organic/natural pretzels and chips that are ON SALE!- total of four bags

- fruit- apples- one bag if needed, bananas- 2 bunches, pears- 10-12 total, other seasonal organic fruit

- veges- natures promise baby carrots, organic cucumbers,organic celery, organic zucchini etc.-
total of a few of each to cut up for kids

- mac and cheese- 6 boxes ORANGE cheese natures promise mac and cheese- if needed
(check cabinet)

- frozen veges (broccoli, mixed veges, green beans)- check all freezers for need- one bag of each if needed

- cereal- check need- get a total of six boxes of organic cereal that is ON SALE (none if not on sale)

- Please add: one box of earthbound farms baby romaine salad, two pack of cucumbers, three organic tomatoes, stonyfield farms fat free vanilla 6 oz yogurts (if none left at home, get 10. If some at home, make it total 10 altogether please.

- Check supplies of the following: feta cheese, blue diamond smoked almond, bottled water, bare naked granola and Cascadian farms multi grain squares, Barbaras shredded spoonfuls and the other square cereal by

Barbara (can't think of the name!) Please get a bag of granola and a box of cereal if necessary.

- And, check other items we may be running low on (once you open the last of something, it should go on the list immediately).

Kate explained to her ghost grocery shoppers that the quantities she listed could be increased slightly if any of the above items were on sale. (And in the spirit of helpfulness, it's veggies, Kate, not veges.)

This excerpt from my *US Weekly* report details Kate's grueling method of grocery shopping. She must have been exhausted watching yet another ghost helper bringing in the bags:

```
Jon and Kate Gosselin PA Reporting
November 2009
A sign that I've been on the job for awhile came when, ten minutes
after I commented to the paps that I would expect to see about ten to
fifteen grocery bags showing up any time now, a woman in a black
Volvo SUV pulled into the driveway and parked by the front door. Sure
enough, she made five solo trips into the house carrying … white
plastic Giant grocery bags filled with what looked to be everything
for Thanksgiving dinner, for a small army. The third trip she made
was with a giant turkey in white plastic wrapping. She was a blonde
and I've seen her there before but don't know her affiliation to
Kate. Nobody came out of the house to help this poor woman with the
bags. She carried in 16 bags by my count, in the rain.
```

JUDY, JUDY, JUDY

Judy was the Gosselin's absolutely wonderful nanny, and the one constant in the Gosselin children's lives for a long time. She was the best thing that ever happened to the Gosselin kids, and they absolutely adored her. She was loving and caring, and I always maintained that the kids were in great hands with her while Kate was away. Kate apparently didn't seem to care about any of that, though. Kate fired Judy because she remained friends with Jon after the divorce. It didn't matter that Judy was friends with Jon long before Kate ever laid eyes on her, but that's how Kate operates. After she let Judy go, the revolving door of strange nannies and sitters kept spinning, with the kids meeting new strangers to look after them while their mommy was away.

Kate's vengeful nature allowed her to take away her children's long-time, incredible nanny and subject them to being watched by a different high-school-aged girl every week, just to spite Jon. The kids missed Judy and suffered greatly once she was gone.

In addition to Judy's duties as a nanny, which included fixing the kids' hair and dressing them and taking them to and from the school bus stop, Kate also gave Judy some other "nanny jobs." It seems that Judy was more of a mother to the Gosselin kids than Kate was, but anyone close to the family already knew that. Kate was simply the "overseer."

Here's a list of Judy's "jobs" that I found. It was dated April 10, 2009.

- Duty:
- Shoes / jackets swim stuff cleaned up
- Trash if full — emptied & extra cardboard & trash to garage
- C&M lunches packed — healthy stuff
- Basement cleanup!
- Nightlights / TVs & movies turned off
- Each room / bathroom checked & straightened & throw away clutter
- Garage / toys / bike cleaned up
- Turn every light off as you leave rooms
- Empty reload & run & empty dishwasher
- **Help kids make beds (teach, show & help them)**
- **Teach table manners (chew with mouth closed, eat neatly, sitting properly)**
- Sweep kitchen & DR clean bibs, HC & table
- Empty & clean coffee pot
- Empty packages & discard wrappings

So Judy was in charge of teaching the kids how to chew, eat and sit properly? Isn't this something that a mother would/could/should take the time to do personally rather than having the paid help do it for her?

There was a lot of babysitting/nannying going on in the Gosselin house. In this next email, Deanie from Figure 8 Films questions Kate about adjusting an invoice Judy had submitted for her hours. Deanie was concerned about how the charges would affect the budget, especially since they also had to pay Carla and Ashley for their services over the same period:

On April 4, 2009, at 8:42 AM, Deanie wrote to Kate to let her know she had received Judy's hours from the last two weeks. She told Kate that she was a little surprised because she was expecting a flat day rate for the days Judy "slept over." She was concerned there would be a problem ahead if they didn't reach an understanding about Judy's extended hours with the family.

Deanie wrote that for Season 5, the Network had approved four days of babysitting per episode. That would be 40 hours per episode (or it could break out as 40 hours per week if they projected shooting one episode per week. She said it would be challenging to make the charges work because they had to include hours for Carla and Ashley as well over the same time period.

These are the days and hours Judy submitted an invoice for:

Week 1:

Monday, March 23	6:30 am – 12:00 am	17.5 hours
Tuesday, March 24	12:00 am – 12:00 am	24 hours
Wednesday, March 25	12:00 am – 12:00 am	24 hours
Thursday, March 26	12:00 am – 3:15 pm	15.25 hours
Friday, March 27	6:00 am – 6:15 pm	12.25 hours
Saturday, March 28	7:00 am – 8:00 am	1 hour

94 hours

Week 2:

Monday, March 30	6:30 am − 4:30 pm	10 hours
Tuesday, March 31	6:30 am − 2:30 pm	8 hours
Wednesday, April 1	6:30 am – 12:30 pm	6 hours
Thursday, April 2	6:30 am − 4:30 pm	10 hours
	9:00 pm – 10:00 pm	1 hour
Friday, April 3	6:30 am – 12:30pm	6 hours
	6:00 pm – 8:00 pm	2 hours

43 hours

94+43 = 137 hours **X** 25 = \$3425 + ot \$712.5 = \$4137.50

Kate instructed Deanie to pay Judy the day rate for the days Judy invoiced. Kate said she had informed Judy about the day rate when she was hired and she would remind her of it. She also explained to Deanie that the network had recently offered to cover a full-time person in addition to Carla's normal weekly hours. She said they would certainly need that to make Season 5 happen.

THE CARETAKER

Jon Gosselin loves his children and loves taking care of them personally, as this email from Kate's divorce lawyer to Jon's divorce lawyer confirms. Jon didn't want help taking care of his kids while he was at the house with them on his custody time. On June 17, 2009, Cheryl Young sent an email to Charlie Meyer asking him to "Please confirm that Kate should decrease the nanny for Jon's time in the evenings."
It's no wonder and very obvious why Kate Gosselin has absolutely no bond whatsoever with any of her children. Kate has rarely ever done anything with or for her children personally. She either had Jon or a paid "helper" take on the responsibility of raising her children from the time they were babies. She did make time to personally hit her children for minor infractions like climbing out of their cribs.

NOT ENOUGH HELP

From her very first days of being a greedy, money-grubbing wannabe celebrity, Kate Gosselin has been very consistent in a number of areas: buying things for herself, pampering herself, making others do things for her that she doesn't want to do herself, complaining that others who do things for her that she doesn't want to do herself don't do them as well as she could do them herself, and being completely ungrateful for everything anybody has ever done for her that she didn't want to do herself. Here's what she said about her helpers back in 2005:

```
"Volunteers have helped, some, but nowhere near enough."
```

This quote is from the second-to-last episode of *Kate Plus Ei8ht* – in 2011:

```
"I've gotten help, but not the help to the degree that I was hoping
to get."
```

This is a paraphrased excerpt from a blog that Kate wrote for her *kateplusmy8.com* website: Walk a day in my heels and you'll see what life's like in my family's 24/7 fast lane with never a chance for me to finish my list and to remove my load of responsibility that I shoulder mostly alone, or sleep a peaceful night of sleep.

On May 16, 2012, Kate took to Twitter to complain, yet again, about the kind of help she gets, or doesn't get. On that particular day, it happened to be Kate's 8-year-olds doing her wrong by only helping her like...well...8-year-olds. It would be interesting to find out exactly what kind of help Kate expected to get from 8-year-olds.

> **My quote of the day 'I guess if u ask an 8 yr old 4 help,you'll get an 8 yr old kind of help'(re :dog food all over floor after dog is fed)!**

Finally, in this tweet, Kate tells the world, again and for the millionth time, that she is a martyr:

> **lol. As the mom saying goes 'if I didn't do it, who was going to??'**

Who? How about the nanny, the babysitters, the cleaning lady, the laundry girl, the ironness, the cook, the pool boy, the landscapers, the bodyguard, and the manager, for starters?

BETH, A TRUE FRIEND

"KATE IS ONE OF THE MOST ADMIRABLE
AND AMAZING WOMEN I HAVE EVER KNOWN.
KATE SHOULD WIN THE
MOTHER OF THE YEAR AWARD"
– BETH CARSON

Bob and Beth Carson were Jon and Kate's best friends in the world at one time. They watched the Gosselin kids at their house and socialized with the Gosselin family on many occasions. Bob Carson even gave Jon a job at one point. Kate speaks very highly of them in her journal.

During the "Going West" episode of Season 1 of *Jon & Kate Plus Ei8ht*, Jon and Kate sat down at home with their lawyer to draft their first Will. They were preparing an incredibly important document; one that would legally spell out who would raise their eight children in the event of Kate and Jon's death. It is probably the most important decision about their children that any parent will ever make. In the episode, the lawyer asks who will raise the kids, and Kate responds vaguely for the television audience that they chose "a family member and close friends." Well the "family member" part was for the sake of the viewers. There never was a family member in line to be guardian of the children. In researching further, I discovered that in the event of Jon and Kate's untimely death, the Gosselin kids wouldn't go to any member of either side of the family. The kids would be taken in and raised lovingly by ... Beth and Bob Carson. Kate wrote about their decision in her journal.

October 2006
Kate said that their kids would be taken care of by Beth and Bob Carson in the number one position because they have kids who are older and the eight Gosselin kids probably wouldn't be a huge burden on them. Kate also mentioned Beth's wisdom, which will help to cover all situations and she would never hinder any other family members from seeing the kids!

When Jon and Kate started making the big money from their show, they set up a Trust fund. They gave Bob and Beth Carson the high honor of naming them as co-Trustees so they would control the family's money in case Jon and Kate met an untimely demise. Trusting someone to raise your children and putting them in charge of your money is about as close as a person can ever get to you.

In Paragraph 12 of the Gosselin family Trust document, Jonathan K. Gosselin and Katie I. Gosselin were appointed as the initial Trustees of the Trust. It was stipulated that if both Trustees at some point became "ineligible, unable or unwilling to serve as Trustee for any reason," then Robert Carson and Beth Carson would serve as co-Trustees.

To help you further understand the relationship between Kate and Beth, I have included the text of a file that Kate kept on her computer called *Beth a true friend.doc*. The file contains a written exchange between Beth and a blogger who wrote a post critical of Kate. Beth's defense of Kate to the blogger clearly shows Beth had Kate's back. Kate must have been very grateful to have a friend like Beth Carson. Then again, maybe not. I have found no evidence that Kate has ever expressed sincere gratitude to anyone who has helped her; she has simply always expected it.

Here is a partial excerpt of *Beth a true friend.doc* file. Beth's writings are in bold.

Kate Gosselin, Time's Person of the Year?
by Tracee Sioux on November 14th, 2007

(http://archive.blisstree.com/live/kate-gosselin-times-person-of-the-year-28/)

Beth, a friend of Kate Gosselin's, star of Jon & Kate, Plus 8, posted a comment on a post I wrote, of questionable tone, called Sextuplets, My Sympathies. (I am working on the tone, as you can see in Tone Turtle.) The post got a much more extreme response than I expected. I meant no harm to Kate Gosselin, who should win Time Magazine's Person of the Year Award, in my opinion. I felt our exchange was worth it's own post. If only because I feel totally awesome that someone I've seen on TV took the time to write to me.

…**YOU MAY ASK, "HOW DOES SHE HAVE THE RIGHT TO INFORM ME OF THEIR CIRCUMSTANCES?" WELL, YOU SEE, I AM A CLOSE FRIEND OF THE GOSSELINS' (IF YOU DON'T THINK THIS IS LEGITIMATE, YOU CAN WATCH 'JON AND KATE PLUS 8' AND YOU WILL SEE ME PERIODICALLY). I FREQUENTLY CARE FOR ALL EIGHT OF THEIR BEAUTIFUL CHILDREN WHEN THEY ARE UNABLE TO DUE TO APPOINTMENTS, CONFLICTS, OR WHEN THEY JUST NEED A WEEKEND AWAY (WHICH WE ARE ALL ENTITLED TO AT SOME POINT, OF COURSE).**

…**WHY DO YOU THINK JON AND KATE DECIDED TO KEEP ALL SIX OF THEIR SEXTUPLETS, RATHER THAN USING "SELECTIVE REDUCTION" TO LIMIT CHANCES OF HEALTH COMPLICATIONS, BUDGET ISSUES, OR JUST PLAIN INSANITY? THEY KEPT THE BABIES BECAUSE THEY KNEW THAT THOSE TINY GRAY SPOTS ON THE SCREEN WOULD SOON GROW INTO AADEN, ALEXIS, HANNAH, COLLIN, JOEL, AND LEAH.**

…**NO ONE, UNLESS IN KATE'S SHOES, HAS THE RIGHT TO JUDGE OR CRITICIZE THE LIFE OF HER FAMILY.**

…**OBVIOUSLY, KATE GOSSELIN MADE THE CHOICE TO VIEW HER CIRCUMSTANCE AS A BLESSING. SHE HAD ADEQUATE GRACE AND POISE TO**

RECOGNIZE THE REWARDS THAT WOULD COME OF THIS LARGE CHALLENGE SET
BEFORE HER. KATE IS ONE OF THE MOST ADMIRABLE AND AMAZING WOMEN I
HAVE EVER KNOWN.
… AS I'M SURE YOU HAVE SEEN ON THE SHOW, IT TAKES AN AMAZING
WOMAN FOR A JOB LIKE HERS. AND, LIKE YOU SAID, KATE WAS BEST
EQUIPPED FOR IT. NOT WITH MONEY, TIME, SPACE, OR CONVENIENCE, OF
COURSE—BUT WITH FAITH, PATIENCE, KINDNESS, STRENGTH,
GRATEFULNESS, AND DEVOTION. AND THAT'S WHAT MAKES AN INCREDIBLE
MOTHER, RIGHT??! :)

I ALSO WANTED TO THANK YOU FOR YOUR KIND COMMENTS REGARDING MY
RELATIONSHIP WITH THE GOSSELINS. WATCHING EIGHT CHILDREN FOR DAYS
ON END MAY SEEM LIKE A BURDEN, BUT IT IS TRULY A BLESSING,
PLEASURE, AND PRIVILEGE TO BE INVOLVED IN THE LIVES OF THE
GOSSELIN KIDS…

BLESSINGS,
BETH

So what could possibly have caused a rift between such good friends? The answer,
as it so often is, is money, greed and disrespect.

MULTIPLE MESSES

Beth Carson wrote *Multiple Blessings*. She shared the authoring credit with Kate,
of course, because it was Kate's life and because Kate had written down her
thoughts and feelings in a journal, which Beth used for source material. Kate was
also present at the writing sessions, no doubt yammering incoherent thoughts from
her sometimes barely decipherable notes into Beth's ear.
The book project was supposed to be a 50/50 split between Beth and Kate. That
seems fair enough. But Kate found a way to mess up that agreement thanks to her
personal need for greed.
The first problem cropped up when the writing was completed and Kate demanded
that Jon's name be added as an author, thus dividing the profits from the book into
thirds instead of halves. It gave the Gosselins two-thirds of the royalties and
reduced Beth's portion of the profits from 50% to 33 1/3%.
So on the initial book advance of $100,000 they received, Beth lost about $17,000
because of Kate's last-minute change of plan. Having Jon share author credit was
never part of the original deal. The book contract, parts of which appear below,
clearly spells out that the project was to have been a joint effort between Beth and
Kate, not Beth, Kate and Jon. The following text from the agreement with
Zondervan, the publisher, confirms the 50/50 split.
The agreement with Zondervan (Agreement Number 9438-1901) was made on
January 10, 2008. It listed Katie Irene Gosselin (including her address) and Beth
Ann Carson (including her address) as the "AUTHOR" (collectively), and
Zondervan, A HarperCollins Company (including the address), as the
"PUBLISHER". It referenced a work tentatively titled MULTIPLE BLESSINGS
(ISBN 0310289025).

The contract stated: "The AUTHOR agrees that all advances, royalties, and payments shall be divided and paid fifty percent (50%) to Katie Irene Gosselin and fifty percent (50%) to Beth Ann Carson."

The agreement stated that the PUBLISHER would pay an advance to the AUTHOR in the sum of $80,000 against all royalties and payments due to the AUTHOR for the WORK.

Kate's attorney, Paul J. Datte, advised that the proposal should indicate that "the royalty advance is non-refundable regardless of the ultimate sales of the book." He also said, "Kate and Beth will require an advance of $100,000.00."

If you need proof that Beth Carson did, in fact, write *Multiple Blessings*, here is an interview that Beth gave to the local newspaper, the *Reading Eagle*, after her book had become a *New York Times* Bestseller.

Originally Published: 12/12/2008
Slices of life: Author's first book a best seller

Beth Carson of Leesport co-writes a memoir titled "Multiple Blessings: Surviving to Thriving with Twins and Sextuplets" about the events surrounding the births of the Gosselin family's sextuplets.

Beth Carson of Leesport wrote her first book, "Multiple Blessings: Surviving to Thriving with Twins and Sextuplets," about sextuplets being born to Jon and Kate Gosselin. The book is a memoir of the events surrounding the births of the Gosselins' sextuplets, combined with inspirational Christian messages, representing the faith present in their daily lives. Published in October, the book quickly landed on the New York Times best sellers list, where it has been for the last five weeks.

Carson's love of children and desire to want to help out a neighbor led her to the Gosselins just a couple of weeks after their sextuplets arrived home from the hospital.

"I didn't know Kate at all, I just knocked on their door," said Carson, who had read in the newspaper that the babies were born.

At the time, Carson and the Gosselins were both residents of Wyomissing.

After hours and hours of feeding babies together over the course of approximately one year, Carson and Kate Gosselin got well acquainted. One day, they discussed the idea of writing a book. The discussion led to Carson having an epiphany later that evening when she mulled their conversation over and contemplated writing the book.
"I thought wait a minute, I have all of the facts - I have the background - I was there and I took a leap of faith," she said.

While Carson, 42, knew writing a book was something she always wanted to do, there was some initial self-doubt.

"I'm just a mom and I didn't even graduate from college - that planted a seed of doubt and I asked, who am I to write a book," Carson said.

Ultimately, Carson decided not to let her lack of formal training as a writer get in the way of one of her goals, and the next day she shared her thoughts with Kate.

"Kate seemed relieved and happy when I offered to write the book since she knew I was so familiar with her story," she said.

After that conversation they forged ahead with their idea and secured a publisher.

The process of writing the book took about a year, and in order to accomplish the task, Beth and Kate checked themselves into a hotel in Lancaster for a few weekends in order to set uninterrupted time aside.

"Kate and I would literally stay in our room for 72 hours and our husbands would take care of the kids back at home," Carson said.

While Carson is listed as a co-author on the book, she makes each of their contributions clear.

"They lived it and I wrote it," she said.

Their shared Evangelical Christian backgrounds provided the foundation for the religious tone of the book.

"This is a miracle - I felt a responsibility to give God the glory for that," said Carson, referring to the Gosselins' having six healthy children in addition to their twins.

Carson said she felt an overwhelming responsibility to share the Gosselins' story, realizing it was a bit of a "calling" for her to write the book, and she had an objective.

"I hope the book is an honest approach to things you don't hear in the show," she said, referring to "Jon and Kate Plus 8" airing on the TLC.

Now that she has accomplished one of her life goals, being an author makes Carson feel good.

"That's what I'm really proud of," she said. "It's kind of the American dream. Put your mind to it - little by little, day by day and in a year, voila."

Money was never an issue for Beth Carson. All she wanted was to go out on the book tour with Kate to enjoy a little of the glory and great success she had earned through all of her hard work in writing a bestseller. But Kate refused her that reward. She no longer needed Beth Carson, and she wanted the spotlight all to herself. She decided that she alone would be the face of *Multiple Blessings* on the book tour. Once the book became a bestseller, Kate had the opportunity to thrust herself even further into the spotlight, and there was no way she was sharing it with anyone. Not even with Beth Carson, her closest friend in the world and the woman responsible for the success of the book.

In addition to Kate not wanting to share the spotlight with Beth, she very publicly disrespected Beth, as can be seen in this very interesting interview on YouTube.

http://www.youtube.com/watch?v=-vSSoZHDWgY
NBC 8: "More than 1,500 people stood in line for hours last night, to get her (Kate's) autograph in Grandville, MI.

KATE: "In being here in Grand Rapids reading the book this week for CD I am reading through the book again, and it is an amazing story and I still can't believe it's our story."

NBC 8: **"Was it hard to write the book?"**

"Um that process wasn't hard, it was the time to write the book, uh, it took us a year and a half, I started when the little kids were two. Um and uh to relive all of those things that we have been through was probably the most difficult part. **As far as the book went, that was easy.**"

So if you were Beth Carson, who actually wrote *Multiple Blessings* from Kate's hodgepodge notes and experiences, and you were watching the news or saw this on YouTube, and you heard that question put to Kate, "Was it hard to write the book?" and you watched and heard Kate NOT MENTION YOU AT ALL, and then heard her say this about the writing, "As far as the book went, that was easy," wouldn't you be a little bit miffed at your good friend, Katie Irene?

There was one final nail to be driven into the Gosselin-Carson relationship, and that, too, had to do with money. Just as they had done with Aunt Jodi and Uncle Kevin, TLC approached the Carsons about paying them for filming at their house. And in predictable Kate fashion, she reacted in exactly the same way as she had when the offer of payment was made to Aunt Jodi and Uncle Kevin. Kate again went crazy and said, "nobody makes money off my family except me." The Carsons, of course, didn't need Kate's or TLC's money. They were very financially well off on their own. But the idea of Kate showing such disrespect to them ended the relationship for good.

The online community speculated that something must have happened between Beth and Kate during their televised trip to Park City, Utah, because in the middle of the trip, Beth suddenly disappeared. I explored that speculation as best I could through sources close to the family, but they told me that the trip had nothing to do with the falling out, and that Beth flew back home for her daughter's birthday, as was reported.

So that was that. No more Beth and Bob Carson. No televised explanation given. Just gone.

And Kate didn't so much as blink. She had gotten everything she needed out of their relationship and tossed them aside. Kate was now quickly approaching her goal of acquiring every material thing that her "friend" Beth Carson had.

Now it's as if Beth Carson never existed. But she does exist. Everyone saw her on the TLC shows and saw what a huge part of Kate's and the children's everyday lives she and Bob were. Kate's insatiable thirst for wealth and fame caused two more people who loved her children to be ripped away from them.

ARE YOU THERE KATE? IT'S ME, GOD

The events and actions that led to the falling out between Kate and Beth, and ultimately destroyed their personal and business relationships, are pretty cut and dry. Things get a little blurry, however, when trying to understand the role Beth played in developing Kate's image as a devout Christian mother overwhelmingly committed and devoted to God. Remember, it was that image that made Kate a figure to be admired among the church-going faithful; it was an image that helped her sell a lot of books.

In reading through Kate's emails and her journal, and in seeing her up close and personal in real life, it is very hard to believe that Kate really has the deep love of God she claims to have. If she did, she never would have been able to pull off the church scams, and she never would have been as mean and deceitful as we have seen her be. What is more likely, and what I believe, is that Kate modeled her "God complex" after Beth Carson, taking it as her own.

As with most things, Kate overdid the religion angle to the point that it became unbelievable, especially since her words and actions contradicted everything in Christian teachings. (It takes a very special kind of evil to prey upon unsuspecting, generous people who are just trying to make a difference in the life of someone they believe is struggling.) And there are just too many things about Kate's trumpeted relationship with God that don't add up as genuine, starting with this. Kate gave birth to the sextuplets on May 10, 2004. According to *Multiple Blessings*, which chronicles Kate's first date with Jon through the birth of her six, Kate supposedly used phrases like: God will always provide for us; the God I served was loving, kind and generous. He was an almighty God who provided every breath I needed; I trusted God to see all of the details; And my God shall supply all your need according to His riches in glory by Christ Jesus.

Also in *Multiple Blessings*, through Beth Carson's writing, Kate says that she knows her God, and knows how much he has blessed her, and has spoken directly to her, and acted through her. Why then, in November 2006, two-and-a-half years after Kate supposedly used all those phrases about God, and had those beliefs about God, would Kate write this in her journal:

Kate said that Beth told her that God provides and it's right in front of us and sometimes we don't see it. Beth also said that she thinks that God provided Kate and Jon with this series and the amount of money that they made so that Kate can stay home with the kids until they go to school. Kate said that the thought excites her so much, just thinking that she won't have to go to work is soooo amazing!

If Kate's faith in God were so strong, why would she need Beth to tell her that sometimes God provides and we don't realize it? Why would that have not occurred to Kate on her own? If everything Kate said about her trust in God was true, why would Kate need Beth or anyone else to tell her how God operates?

The most obvious answer is that the "trust in God for all things" persona represented in *Multiple Blessings* is Beth Carson's, not Kate's. Beth somehow took the lying, narcissistic, mean-spirited, greedy, selfish, angry and controlling Kate Gosselin, and turned her into a modern day Christian heroine ... to sell books. And once Kate was so viewed among Christians, she no longer needed Beth.

The upside to this sad tale is that Beth and Bob Carson are probably enjoying their beautiful family and thanking God they are no longer involved with Kate Gosselin. I see Beth quite often, playing with her children at the local playground or shopping at the local craft store or at the supermarket. She looks very happy and at peace.

A BLIND EYE

A great, nagging question and, yes, disappointment, for me regarding Beth Carson is that she chose to remain silent and hide in the shadows, rather than speaking up in an effort to protect those beautiful little children that she so lovingly took care of, and was going to raise as her own if anything ever happened to Jon and Kate. *Multiple Blessings* was written in 2008. Kate's journal, which she used to write both *Multiple Blessings* and *I Just Want You To Know*, was written from 2006-2007. Surely Beth had Kate's journal and notes in her possession, and surely she read the same passages Kate wrote about physically harming her children that I read. Even on the outside chance that Beth never personally saw Kate abusing her children, she must have read the words Kate wrote in her journal recounting her verbal and physical ragings against them. So why would Beth ignore what she read, and write a book of lies about Kate being a loving, nurturing, God-fearing woman? If Beth knew what was happening to the children, how could she walk away and do nothing to help them?

It's hard to imagine what Beth Carson, who was in the Gosselin house and around Kate and the children so often, was thinking and how, as a Christian woman, she was able to write a book that was so full of lies.

If you were an outsider reading *Multiple Blessings*, you would have no way of knowing it wasn't an accurate portrayal of Kate. You might even believe that Kate Gosselin was handpicked by God Himself to walk the Earth and spread His word. As it turns out, at the time the sextuplets came home from the hospital, I lived less than 2 miles from Kate's house in Wyomissing, and coincidentally, a close friend of my family was one of Kate's "helpers" and was in that house on a daily basis. She tells quite a different story.

Multiple Blessings was nothing more than propaganda and an excuse for every bad thing that Kate Gosselin ever said or did, and for everything ever written about her in the early days of her pregnancy and life when the sextuplets first came home from the hospital. It was also a vehicle to elevate Kate among Christians by making her appear to have a special or "unique" relationship with God.

Multiple Blessings is filled with references to "miracles" from God, given specifically to Kate Gosselin. Miracles like getting a discount on an appliance at Lowes or saving money on strawberries.

Multiple Blessings is a book filled with lies and mistruths, and Beth Carson wrote it. Did she naively take Kate at her word and write everything she told her without question? Or did she know that much of what Kate wanted her to put on paper was untrue?

THE SOUND OF SILENCE

Kate always plays fast and loose with the facts. Here she is lying on Twitter in December of 2011. Kate's tweets are in bold:

xxxxx @Kateplusmy8 are you still in touch with Beth and other old family friends???

yes... Have amazing supportive friends u may not c but r here :)

This was another Twitter exchange from December 24, 2011:

xxxxx @Kateplusmy8 Are you planning on writing anymore books? Or doing book signings? Would love to meet you! You are such an inspiration!

more books in my head... Looking for literary agent and help organizing onto paper :)

Reading these tweets brings up an obvious question. If Kate was still really good friends with Beth Carson, and she was looking for help organizing her thoughts onto paper to write more books, why would she not collaborate with Beth Carson again? Beth wrote Kate's most successful, *New York Times Bestseller List* book, so why would Kate not turn to her "friend" again for help writing all those other books that were residing in her head?

The answer is: Kate and Beth Carson are no longer friends. This fact was made abundantly clear to me on Saturday, March 24, 2012. That day, I was grocery shopping at the Giant in Wyomissing, PA, where Kate also does her shopping. In the dairy aisle, I came across Beth Carson shopping alone. She didn't see me, and I doubt if she would have even known who I am. In that very same aisle, at the very same time, within sight of Beth, was Kate Gosselin, looking uncomfortable, tense, and as angry as I've ever seen her. There was no contact between the two – no hellos or how are yous – just silence. There was absolutely zero contact between Kate and Beth; they both just looked uncomfortable to be in the same place at the same time. That made three of us. Fortunately, we were all pretty much finished shopping, so the whole encounter lasted only about 10 minutes for me.

No goodbyes were spoken or implied when both ladies left the store separately soon after. If there were still a glimmer of friendship between Kate and Beth Carson, they would have stood in line together, or at the very least, had a goodbye smile or wave as they left the store.

Beth just went about her business. Kate looked like she was ready to explode with rage.

WHERE'S AUNT JODI?

"Aunt Jodi" is Jodi Kreider, Kate's sister-in-law, who is married to Kate's brother, Kevin. Aunt Jodie and Uncle Kevin were featured often on *Jon & Kate plus Eight*. Despite having four children of their own, Jodi frequently babysat for Jon and Kate, and Kevin was on hand to help Jon with various projects. They were presented on the show as kind, loving and protective parents. They were also shown to have some common sense and respect for the Gosselin children. In one particular instance of this, Jodi refused to allow a film crew to keep the bathroom door open when one of the children was going to the bathroom.

In an episode most memorable for Kate's viciousness, Kate called Jodi to admonish her for giving gum to the sextuplets. One of the little boys had gotten gum on his special blanket, and Kate went completely ballistic, screaming at the child and threatening to throw his blanket away. His older sister had to step in to try to help him. It was disturbing and horrible to witness a mother terrorizing her child.

I don't know what happened between Kate and Jodi and Kevin. I know what Jodi and Kevin have said, and I know what Kate has said about them, but only they know what really went on. The following are various sides to the story of what happened and differing versions of why Aunt Jodie and Uncle Kevin are no longer a part of the children's lives. I gave Kate the final word at the end of this chapter because, well, this book is about Kate.

The message below is from Aunt Jodi's sister, Julie. It was taken from the blog, "Gosselin's Without Pity," also known as GWOP (http://gosselinswithoutpity.blogspot.com). To be clear, I have never had a conversation with anyone involved with GWOP, nor have I done any research directly from their site. But in doing a little background research on who Aunt Jodi is, for the people unfamiliar with the Gosselin story, I followed a Google link that led to this posting on GWOP. It would seem to accurately portray Aunt Jodi's side of the story since the author of the message, Jodi's sister Julie, was, at one time, involved with the GWOP website.

A Message to the Group:

****I'm sorry to announce that Aunt Jodi will no longer be part of the show Jon and Kate plus 8. Jodi was not given the option, and although she loved being part of the show, Kate decided it was in her best interest (Kate's) to cut Aunt Jodi from the show. She may still be in a few episodes that have been previously taped, but she will not be in Season 4 which begins filming in May.

I now feel comfortable with letting everyone in on who I am—I am Jodi's sister. Maybe those of you who felt I was being cruel or was taking some things a little too personally will now understand where I am coming from.

Please show your support for Aunt Jodi and let her know how much she'll be missed on the show. This is her actual email address (created for this group).****

This is how Julie describes herself and her purpose on her blog, Truth Breeds Hatred:

"Truth Fears No Questions" — "I am Aunt Jodi's sister, and hopefully what I have to say will open eyes and help raise awareness for the need for laws to protect children in the entertainment industry. This is a tragic example of how money and fame can blind parents, preventing them from making decisions that are best for their children. I urge you to realize that these children were not brought into the world to be used for anyone's entertainment. Just because this is all they know doesn't make it 'normal'. They deserve privacy and protection."

http://truthbreedshatred.blogspot.com/

SISTER JULIE SPEAKS UP

On June 29, 2008, the following was posted on GWOP based on information given to the author of the post by Jodie's sister, Julie:

Aunt Jodi: The Tribe Has Spoken

While the Gosselin children may have many material "blessings", thanks to being exploited by their parents and complicit others, nothing can compare to their Aunt Jodi.

Jodi is married to Kevin Kreider — Kate Gosselin's brother. Jodi and Kevin have four children of their own, but live near Jon and Kate and have been relied upon heavily to babysit the Gosselin children while Jon and Kate tend to the heavy demands on their time that frequently take them away from some or all of their children.

We have seen quite a bit of Jodi and her interaction with the Gosselin children, and although she is wonderful to behold on her own merits, when contrasted with her shrew of a sister-in-law, she seems even better. We've seen Jodi play with the children — actually play with them in a natural, spontaneous way, with no tension about grass stains or melted ice cream. We've enjoyed the children cooking with her in the kitchen, playing dress-up, chilling in front of a video, going for walks around the neighborhood, etc.

Jodi seems to have this refreshing mixture of humor, grace, patience, gentleness, and above all an essential maternal nurturing that we feel starved for when watching the children under Kate's jurisdiction. But we've seen her ability to be stern, too, when Mady needed it, although even that situation she approached (physically) on Mady's level, on her knees and locking eyes with her niece and speaking firmly and directly.

Not only is Jodi a joy to watch, but when the children are in her care, they are like different people… we don't see the tension, the pathologies, the whining, the overall desperation displayed so often when it is only Kate herding them through the day. Many of us will never forget how relieved we felt when we saw sick little Joel finally getting a kind word, a rub on his back, a hug and some reassurance when he was feeling so ill... it helped remove the sting we felt at seeing that same little feverish boy berated for vomiting on his comforter and banished to the laundry room floor lest he add any more to Kate's laundry.

Now for the pale underbelly of this scenario. Before filming began for the Jon & Kate Plus 8 second season, Figure 8 Films wanted to pay Jodi for her role in the series. Not only for her babysitting time, of course, but also for the intrusion of the camera crew and equipment into her home... the disruption to her own home and family.

This never reached Jodi's awareness at the time because of Kate's response — an adamant NO. Her reasoning? In summary and to paraphrase, 'No way! No one gets paid but us!'. The issue of remuneration for the Kreiders was dropped, with Jodi never being aware of it and continuing to help out with the children as she had been doing even back when Jon and Kate were nobodies and the children weren't the nationwide stars they have become; they were simply the nieces and nephews Jodi and Kevin adored.

Fast forward to Season 3, and this time Jodi was approached directly with the offer of a paying contract for continuing to do the show. By now Jodi had seen the scenes in which she was filmed aired on various episodes — footage that included both Jon and Kate badmouthing her to the camera, characterizing her as an irresponsible ditz, saying condescending things about her way of handling the Gosselin children — "She tries, bless her heart!".

To her credit, Jodi cared more about her relationship with her nieces and nephews than she did about what Jon and Kate had to say about her and, even though Kate AGAIN vetoed the idea of compensating Jodi, Jodi said that she loved her nieces and nephews and wanted to be in their lives regardless. She said that it wasn't about the money; as long as she could maintain a relationship with the Gosselin children she wanted to keep doing so.

This wasn't good enough for Kate, who was also suffering from the nagging realization that Jodi made Kate look pretty bad by comparison, so a third party was hired to provide the babysitting (and other) services and Jodi is seemingly no longer of use to Jon and Kate.

You know how they do that little ceremony at the end of each season of Survivor, where the remaining two or three players reminisce about all the players who are no longer in the picture? The list of players voted off of Jon and Kate's island continues to grow, with Jodi being only the most recent fatality.

I hope Jodi's replacement doesn't make Kate look bad or her days may already be numbered. I am 48 years old and I wish I had an Aunt Jodi. As much as I am going to miss seeing her on the show, I'm sure it can't compare to how much the children will miss having her in their lives.

Posted by Serena on 6/29/2008 based upon information granted with permission by Jodi's sister, Julie.

http://gosselinswithoutpity.blogspot.com/2008/06/aunt-jodi-tribe-has-spoken.html

INTERVIEW WITH JODI AND KEVIN

This transcript is from a *CBS Early Show* interview co-anchor Harry Smith conducted with Jodi and Kevin Kreider.

HARRY SMITH, CO-ANCHOR: And joining us now for an exclusive interview are Kate Gosselin's brother and sister-in-law, Kevin and Jodi Kreider. Good morning to you both.

JODI KREIDER, KATE GOSSELIN'S SISTER-IN-LAW: Good morning.

KEVIN KREIDER, KATE GOSSELIN'S YOUNGER BROTHER: Good morning.

SMITH: This is very interesting because over the weekend a lot of people were saying, I don't even know who these people are, and suddenly they have really exploded into the American consciousness. And years ago, when this reality show started, you all were sort of involved in it, weren't you?

K. KREIDER: yes, we were.

J. KREIDER: We were.

SMITH: And what was the idea initially? Here's this family. They have eight children. We'll do a reality show. Was it almost like a — sort of a documentary process?

J. KREIDER: Exactly. It started out that way. And that was a really neat thing to be a part of, thinking that, you know, the children are — a little bit of their life is being captured, but it quickly — we thought it was very innocent at the time.
And it — the first season started, I think, eight episodes. And it quickly turned into more and more demand from Jon and Kate from the network, and it turned into 40 episodes in a six-month span. And also it — there were cameras in the children's bedrooms at one point. And they were filming all year around. And these were very huge concerns for us.

SMITH: Right.

J. KREIDER: We spoke to them about that. And...

SMITH: You talked to Jon and Kate about it?

J. KREIDER: Yes, oh, of course. And their response was, you know, this is our choice, this is what we want to do, just respect that.

SMITH: What do you think changed as those demands grew, as the camera time grew, as the sort of visibility grew? What was the change that concerned you the most?

K. KREIDER: Well, I think we're speaking out now because we want to be the voice of our nieces and nephews. And we're seeing it turn tide that they're being viewed as a commodity, that — I'm sorry. That they...

SMITH: This is clearly an emotional issue for you. Do you want to go ahead?

J. KREIDER: They're being exploited. And it's time for America to see the situation for what it really is, which is unfortunately, there are no laws protecting children in reality TV shows. And it's time for the public to be aware of this.

And that these children are very aware of the cameras in their homes. Their home is their workplace. And this is not a healthy environment for kids to be raised in.

SMITH: When you tried to broach this subject with your sister and her husband, what has their reaction been?

K. KREIDER: We have talked to them many times about, you know, about the subject. And they have often said, you know, hey, you know, this is kind of our lives, this is what we chose, this is how we're going to provide for them. And we feel that they have chosen this path with disregard to their children's safety, security...

J. KREIDER: The effects it's going to have. Now there are effects already being — you know, signs already. And the life...

SMITH: Like what?

J. KREIDER: Like they don't want the cameras around. They have told me personally, I don't like...

SMITH: Your nieces and nephews.

J. KREIDER: Of course, yes. We watched them quite a bit about a year ago and further back. And, you know, they would say, Aunt Jodi, I don't like the cameras on every vacation with us. I don't like them, you know. And, too, you know, kids have bad times, bad moments, they cry, and having the camera zoom in on a crying child. I mean, this is just — this is — this should not be a form of entertainment.

SMITH: Are you estranged now from your sister and her husband?

K. KREIDER: I do talk to Kate and Jon. We haven't seen the kids in a while, which is hard. But, yes, our relationship has definitely been strained now. What we hope is that they will kind of come around, see the effects, see what's most important and...

J. KREIDER: They're very lost right now. They're very blinded by all of this media and this — you know, the fame and the fortune, and...

SMITH: Every time you go to the newsstand, there's another cover and another cover.

J. KREIDER: Of course, of course. And it is time to really put priorities first, which is they say their children, but clearly their actions are showing something completely...

SMITH: You say that they say their children is a top priority.

J. KREIDER: They say their children is their priority, but clearly it is not.

SMITH: This must be so painful for you to have this — what seemed to start so innocently spill over into this kind of national sensation.

J. KREIDER: Yes.

SMITH; And it can't be easy, I imagine, for you to come here and say...

J. KREIDER: No.

SMITH: You're almost begging your family members to walk away from this.

J. KREIDER: It's hard to — yes. As hard...

SMITH: Could they walk — do you think they could walk away?

J. KREIDER: No. No. No.

K. KREIDER: I think our focus is that laws do need to be passed that protect children.

J. KREIDER: Protecting children in reality TV shows because these shows are popping up all over the place.

K. KREIDER: For the future.

SMITH: Yes.

J. KREIDER: And it's time for people to see that.

SMITH: All these subsequent rumors, though, that this has also had an effect on their marriage. Do you have any sense that they're together or not?

J. KREIDER: Well, in their season premiere, you know, it's very clear that they are not. And it is tragic. It is — just about nine months ago, they went to Hawaii and did a vow renewal and that was for ratings. But, you know, the viewers felt that it was, you know, true.

And here, you know, their marriage...

K. KREIDER: You can't imagine as a child realizing that my birthday party, that all the outings that my parents took me on were because, you know, ratings, for ratings, and all organized by production companies.

SMITH: And last but not least, do you think the television company has any responsibility? Does TLC, is that about the cash register, or is there any part of them that is sitting there thinking, what is good for these children?

J. KREIDER: Unfortunately, I think it has come down to all about the ratings. And no one is looking at these children as what they are going through and the life consequences they are going to have as they get older.

SMITH: Kevin and Jodi, we thank you for coming on this morning.

J. KREIDER: Thanks for having us.

THE REBUTTAL

Here is Kate's response to Jodi and Kevin's accusations:

"My brother has made a lot of money off of saying things that are untrue about us. I've not allowed them to see my kids for two years. So I'm not quite sure what information they think they may have."

Nearly 3 years later, Kate still can't let this go. Tweeting in response to a fan, she still sounded as angry as she did back in 2009 when talking about Jodi and Kevin.

xxxxx @Kateplusmy8 i keep seeing the videos abt ur bro n wife...did they ever get paid for appearances? I hope not cuz wow they r mean n tell lies

oh yeah! And sold and bought a big house and went on vacation too... Blood money... Sick.

Kate would do well to learn to say, "That is a private family matter. I'd rather not comment on that."

KATIE & JAMIE: BEST FRIENDS FOREVER?

"A mirror reflects a man's face, but what he is really like
is shown by the kind of friends he chooses."
– Proverbs 27:19

They wore matching diamond solitaire pendant necklaces when they were
together. They had similar hairstyles. They wore matching clothes. A few years
back they were even rumored by the tabloids to be lovers. "They" are Kate and
Jamie Cole Ayers.

So who is Jamie Cole Ayers? She is Kate's best friend in the whole, wide world,
of course.

I saw Jamie a few times with Kate, but I never had the pleasure of a conversation
with her. She's a bit scary and intimidating in my opinion. She appeared to enjoy
the role of being Kate's pseudo bodyguard as they ran around town shopping and
running errands together. The times I saw her with Kate, she gave the appearance
of a person just waiting to get into an altercation with the paparazzi, or anyone
who bothered Kate. I kept a safe distance. This woman can scowl with the best of
them. I found this background information on Jamie online:

    Jamie met Kate 9 years ago at a church in Reading in PA. Also a
    mother of twins, Jamie currently resides in Michigan where she is
    originally from.

    Her husband Mark Ayers filed for divorce from Jamie in July,
    2008. The divorce was finalized in August, 2009.

    Since her divorce Jamie has been flying to PA frequently and
    staying with Kate who trusts her so much, she allows Jamie to
    babysit and discipline the kids.

    Kate doesn't have many friends and is urging Jamie to move to PA.
    She has even offered to help finance her relocation and offered
    her a recurring role on Kate Plus Eight so she'll have a means of
    support.

    Through an associate, reportedly the two are close enough to hold
    hands and take naps together but it's a platonic love.

WITH FRIENDS LIKE KATE . . .

Kate Gosselin presents a holier-than-thou attitude every time she speaks to Jon, or anyone at all for that matter. She and Discovery have done everything in their power to convince the world that she is the good parent and Jon is the bad parent who is to blame for all of the children's behavioral problems.

Kate has made many, many very public accusations about Jon, the father of her children. She has made a big deal to the media, and to Jon, about how concerned she is with his judgment regarding who he lets spend time with the kids, including me; yet, in the next breath, Kate can't say enough good things about Jamie Cole Ayers, her best friend in the world and the only person besides Steve Neild that she can trust and count on. Here are a couple of paraphrased excerpts about Jamie from Kate's journal:

August 2006
Kate said that she had so much fun with Jamie and said that she is such a blessing! Than added, during nap, Jamie mopped the floor and folded the laundry.

August 2006
It was a sad morning because Jamie left!!!!! Kate added that Jamie was the very best helper ever! She made Kate think about how much easier her life would be if they had a part time helper/cook/childcare provider!!!!! And Kate finally added about her 'best friend,' She doesn't annoy me or get in my way.

Based on these journal entries, it would appear that the main prerequisite for being one of Kate's "friends" is that you also have to mop floors, fold laundry and do other chores for Kate.

In her journal, Kate said that she and Jamie care for their kids the same way. Does that mean that Jamie Cole Ayers beats and humiliates her children as well? Maybe she does, because we've seen the tabloid photo of Jamie grabbing and yelling at one of the sextuplets right in front of Kate's garage on Heffner Road – in front of the gawking paparazzi.

Well I would question *your* judgment, Kate, in who *you* allow to be close to your children. I question the steady stream of revolving-door "helpers" and babysitters I have seen entering the children's lives in the short time I've been watching.

I wonder how well Kate *really* knows Jamie Cole Ayers, her best friend in the world. I wonder if Kate ever saw the email or the topless photo that Jamie sent to her husband Jon as she was trying to seduce him – while Kate and Jon were still married.

I've seen them.

I have them.

Here's Katie setting the record straight via Twitter. Why she doesn't just ignore these kinds of tweets instead of feeling the need to tell outright lies is beyond me. This tweet came almost a year after Jamie's comments aired on the final episode of *Kate Plus Ei8ht*.

xxxxx @Kateplusmy8 I was wondering if you ever feel like fame got to you? You changed so much that you seem like a completely other person...

lol SEEM(what u c)& TRUTH r 2different things! I am same albeit I've learned a lot! Friends say 'ur same old Kate' – good2hear!

Kate must not have been paying attention during the final episode of *Kate Plus Ei8ht* when Kate's absolute best friend in the world, Jamie Cole Ayers, took to the interview chair to share a few final thoughts with the viewing audience.

```
"What's funny, one of the last episodes they showed some
flashbacks of Kate. That's the Kate that I met at Reading
Hospital. I saw the softer and the love spark in her eye. Now… I
see her but it's more TV, it's more, what am I wearing? How
skinny can I be? It's not the Kate that I used to know. I always
say to her, you're not Angelina Jolie. And she gets mad."
```

And that did it for Best Friend Forever, Jamie Cole Ayers.

It looks like Jamie was voted off Gosselin Island and banished from Gosselin Land forever after Kate saw Jamie speaking negatively about her during the RV and final episodes of *Kate Plus Ei8ht*. The show was canceled, and so were the paid help/friends, Ashley and Jamie.

But wait! It appears that by July 2012, there was reconciliation between Kate and Jamie. In her never-ending quest to prove to the world that she really, really does have friends, Kate tweeted like a schoolgirl that Jamie was coming to visit. She tried her best to alert the paps that a photo op would be happening, but there were simply no takers.

So Kate tweeted a photo of Jamie doing what Jamie does best for Kate…being a paid employee, cleaning Kate's house for her, and watching her children while Kate runs important errands such as going to the tanning salon and picking up her mail.

This falls under the 'ways your friends offer to help when they visit' category.. http://t.co/0Mni6FUx

The photo Kate tweeted shows Jamie standing barefoot on Kate's kitchen counter, wiping grease and dust off of Kate's giant range hood. What exactly was the point? Yes, Kate, we get it. The only way anyone can be your friend is if they clean your house, or do your laundry, or fix your tractor, or fix your garage door, etc., etc., etc.

Those aren't friends, Kate. Those are paid workers.

Kate also tweeted this while Jamie was staying at the Gosselin house:

All settled back in at home... Let the chaos increase.....my kids plus 3 more at r house w only 2 adults this week!It's A LOT louder here!:)

In case you missed that, Kate just let it slip that there were ONLY TWO adults watching the kids that week, meaning her normal babysitters got a few days off because her "friend" Jamie was in town to do all the work for them. A beautiful friendship, indeed.

———

322

IN STEVE WE TRUST

"Nobody has had the public recognition that Kate has."
– *Steve Neild*

Steve Neild is Kate Gosselin's bodyguard, travel companion, manager and pack mule. This chapter will give you some background information on Steve Neild and discuss his involvement with the Gosselins. The following information was taken directly from his security company's website:

Steve K. Neild
    Executive Vice President
    Prudential Associates

Steve Neild served with the New Zealand Police Department for 19 years, during which time he lead the special operations section and focused on counter-terrorism and dignitary protection.

His special expertise is in VIP protection and major event security planning.

He has been the central point of contact and liaison with marketing and major corporate management operations, local police, various military representatives, and with government and international intelligence agencies.

Mr. Neild also has substantial experience in law enforcement and counter-terrorism operations and management of large critical facilities, such as Auckland International Airport in Auckland, New Zealand.

This resume certainly makes Steve sound like an impressive fellow who has been involved in some high-level security operations. But times change, and today he follows Kate Gosselin around carrying her purse and luggage. If you watch Steve when he is with Kate, he does not exhibit any of the behaviors typical of a bodyguard protecting someone. He comports himself more like a companion. So how does one go from working security assignments of grave import to babysitting Kate Gosselin and doing the extremely dangerous work of carrying her shopping bags?

Perhaps Steve just wanted to retire from the stress of serious security work and opted to go for easy money. A lot of people retire and then take a part-time job pushing shopping carts at the local supermarket to maintain health benefits, etc. Steve Neild was originally hired by Discovery to protect the Gosselin kids while Kate and Jon were traveling for filming. Here's how Kate described it:

Kate said that it came to her attention as a mother thinking if she was going to put kids out there in public, she needed to be responsible and do what she needed to do to keep everyone safe. It was her request that they started traveling with security. Kate said of Steve, "He really has the history, as far as where we've been to now because it's night and day."

Kate's expressed reasoning is completely understandable. We have three kids, and I'm a nervous wreck keeping an eye on them and keeping them safe when we travel, even somewhere local. But somewhere along the line, what began as security for the Gosselin children morphed into Steve becoming a private man-servant and handler for Kate.

TLC provided another bodyguard, named Luke, to Kate Gosselin. Luke looks like an NFL defensive tackle. He's huge. Luke is what a good bodyguard should look like. Luke would make anyone think twice before trying to harm someone he was guarding. Steve Neild on the other hand, not so much. When I see Steve, I just want to run up to him and give him a big hug. I've stood next to Steve Neild and had a pleasant conversation with him. He's very personable and likeable. I'm not a giant guy, but I didn't find Steve to be even a little bit intimidating. He looks like he'd be fun to have a few drinks with.

It made sense to have a bodyguard to look out for the safety of the children, especially when they were traveling so much and were subjected to interactions with strangers, but why, though, does Kate feel that she needs a personal bodyguard when she travels alone, and even to this day, in 2013? I watched her closely for more than 2 years and I never saw an instance of anything remotely threatening happening to her. Nobody in her hometown hassles her at all. If anything, the occasional house mom or some teenage girls would come up to her to say "hi" or to ask to take a picture with her. I have never, EVER, even heard anyone say or yell a nasty word at her. Yet she feels the need to pay a bodyguard $800-plus a day to travel with her.

In 2010, on the "Inside Kate's World" edition of *Kate Plus 8*, Steve Neild said of Kate:

"She has been betrayed by some of the closest people to her."
"I've had threats left in her mailbox, threats left on the front doorstep, so there's a lot of stuff that members of the public don't know. There's stuff Kate doesn't even know, the contents of these emails, that haven't been shared with her. From a security perspective, we look at all that."
"The other side of that now is the media interest. In the last 18 months, it's got to the stage where she can't go to California; she can't go to New York, without 20 or 30 paparazzi following her. It's dangerous."

Steve Neild says he has protected royal families, presidents and elected heads of state during his career. If these claims are true, it makes his statements that none of them have compared to Gosselin and "nobody has had the public recognition that Kate has" simply laughable. He is saying that Kate Gosselin has more public recognition than the British Royal Family and former President Bill Clinton. He is either delusional, or he is just trying to market himself as the protector of the most important woman on earth. In either case, his claim is ridiculous. I find it strange that someone who is supposedly as respected and accomplished as Steve Neild, according to his company's website, would spend the bulk of his time, in the prime of his career, following a mean-spirited, D-list, has-been, former reality TV personality around to the grocery store and to get her hair done.

Discovery paid for Steve's services only when he was traveling with Kate for the show. I have seen, in Kate's own writing, lists of travel dates and details where she makes special notations of when Discovery paid for Steve and the days that she was actually responsible for his salary.

Kate and her manager also included a stipulation for Steve's services into Kate's contracts when traveling for book signings, speaking engagements or various television interviews, etc.

Steve's constant presence has caused much speculation about the nature of his relationship with Kate. I have heard all of the rumors that he and Kate are having an affair, and I have seen them together so I can draw my own conclusions. I don't know anything for certain, however, so I am not going to spend too much time speculating on the subject. All I can do is tell what I know and have observed.

I know that Steve Neild is a liar. I know this because on the first episode of the new season of *Kate Plus Ei8ht*, in yet another desperate attempt to create drama and get ratings, Steve Neild, himself, took to the interview couch to defend Kate's need for personal security. He stated, while looking us right in the eye, that everywhere Kate goes, there are 20 to 30 paparazzi always following her. That was not true.

Having personally followed Kate Gosselin every day for an extended period of time, in Pennsylvania and beyond, as a writer and a working paparazzo, I can tell you that, after the summer of 2009, there was only one dedicated paparazzo who followed Kate every day, or just at times when he felt like it. He lives closer to Kate's house than he does to New York City where the real action is, so it made better financial sense for him to photograph her than to drive 2 hours each way to the city.

At the height of the Jon and Kate media frenzy in the summer of 2009, there were, at most, 10 or 12 paps taking pictures on any given day. Holidays and the kids' birthdays or a special occasion would draw more, even television crews, but just for a single day. I can tell you, again from personal experience, that the paps that came to Pennsylvania to cover the Gosselins are of a different breed than those you see on the streets of Hollywood swarming celebrities. These guys were professional, courteous and for the most part, polite. I found it offensive when one or two first-timers would surround Kate and the kids at the bus stop and get too close, and very offensive when they would ask her rude questions on video in front of the kids. Those paps didn't have kids, so they didn't get why it was such a bad thing. But there certainly was never a threat from any of the paps.

After reading Kate's journal, it is also apparent that Steve is an enabler, and his silence while Kate abuses her little children is unconscionable. In my opinion, he is complicit with Kate and has demonstrated his lack of class and lack of integrity by not coming forward to help those children.

So why would Steve Neild remain silent about Kate's treatment of the kids, and even lie for her on television? Here's a thought: for the money. And not just the $800 a day plus expenses money.

THE TRUST FUND

In the summer of 2009, Kate started removing large amounts of money from the Gosselin's joint bank accounts to protect or hide it during the upcoming divorce battle with Jon. She didn't open a bank account under her name to keep the money safe until things were worked out in the courts. Instead, she did the next most logical thing she could think of, and what most people in her shoes would probably do. She took the family's money and put it into a trust fund, so if something happened to herself or Jon, the children would be taken care of financially. That makes sense.

That is where logic ends and things get interesting when considering whom Kate chose to be the family trustee. The trustee is the person who would make financial decisions for her children about the millions of dollars she had from all their hard work. The person Kate chose for that important duty was Steve Neild. The bodyguard. The family friend who silently stands by Kate hiding her lies and her secrets. The friend who turns a blind eye while she abuses her children.

The trust fund is real. Kate was asked to produce documentation about it during the divorce proceedings. Kate's best friends Beth and Bob Carson were the co-Trustees of the original Gosselin family trust fund, but after they were banished from the Gosselin's lives, the next best choice was, of course, the hired family bodyguard.

Jon's divorce attorney, Charlie Meyer, sent emails about the trust fund to Kate's attorney, Cheryl Young. At the very least, the emails confirm that there is a new trust fund that Jon didn't have access to, and it was a concern to him. After all, it was Jon's money, as well, from those years of filming.

Charlie said that when Kate returns, they were going to need access quickly to the following documents because Jon did not have any of them:

1. Trust Documents and financial records for the trusts
2. Formation documents and records for JKIG
3. Business and personal bank and other account statements
4. All contracts other than the TLC documents they already had.
5. Tax Returns

Charlie sent another email to Cheryl Young confirming their brief call. He reminded Cheryl that she had told him earlier that day that Kate had moved money because she was upset about Jon's spending, including his purchase of a $40,000 car (which really was $32,000). Charlie said it was Jon's understanding that Kate was going out that day to purchase a car, and Charlie could not understand how Kate could rationalize that action.

TRAVELS WITH STEVE

Only time will tell what was really going on between Kate and Steve, and how his presence affected Kate and Jon's marriage. It could have been a cleverly orchestrated ruse by Discovery to keep some interest and mystery alive while the show's ratings continued to plummet. After all, starting with the first episode of *Kate Plus Ei8ht,* there was Steve, front and center on the interview couch yapping away. Then in the "Alaska Episode" of *Kate Plus Ei8ht,* when they were panning for gold with the kids, Steve gave Aaden a gold ring to bring to Kate to tell her that he found it in the stream. It seemed like a shabbily contrived effort to get people talking and wondering about what it meant.

Another thing I found strange about their relationship is the photographic evidence I came across during my research. I have seen hundreds and hundreds of pictures that Kate took with her iPhone and her own camera. During their family beach vacation to the Outer Banks in the summer of 2008, which was documented in the TLC episode, "Gosselins Head South," there is no evidence that Steve Neild was even on that trip. The fact that he was there was well hidden from the viewing audience. But Kate's photos tell a different story. She took many photos of Steve Neild alone, or Steve and the kids. But you know what? I did not find one single photo taken by Kate of Jon. Her husband. This was at a time when they were supposedly happily married.

Also, when Jon took Cara to Utah for a skiing vacation in January 2009, guess who else was there? That's right. Steve Neild. Kate sent Steve along to keep an eye on Cara because she didn't trust Jon. It seems an odd thing to do when Jon and Kate were supposedly still happily married at that time.

I read many, many emails back and forth from Pennsylvania to Utah, and there wasn't one from Kate to Jon. Kate was emailing Cara at Jon's email address, but she never wrote so much as one word to Jon. She did, however, communicate constantly with Steve, asking questions about what he was doing and how Cara was.

On Jan 5, 2009, at 12:03 AM, Steve wrote to Kate that he had dinner with Jon and Cara and the ski guy and his wife. He said that "Cars" was having a good time and was proud to show him all the ski trails she had done. He then told Kate that he had a meeting with Jeff and he would tell her all about it the next day. He signed the email "S".

Kate replied that she couldn't wait to hear about the meeting and that it was killing her that she couldn't see Cara succeeding and enjoying the challenge. She told Steve she would talk to him later and let him know that she would have her phone with her all day to await updates.

Here are some other circumstances involving Steve. I have separated the different occurrences by spaces.

Producer Jen Stocks sent an email on the morning of May 20, 2008, asking Kate about going out to dinner after visiting "The NICU" and, if interested, whether Kate had any ideas where they could go. She told Kate they would like to film it. Early that evening, at 5:57 PM, Kate replied that it was possible, and suggested that they go to Applebees in Hershey, PA, because that restaurant had been very good to them. Kate told Jen to look into it and she would check with Jon. But Kate then added that they would only go "if we have Steve." About 20 minutes later, at 6:18 PM, Jen replied to Kate with the bad news that they didn't have Steve for Friday, just Sunday and Monday, so they would skip shooting dinner.

Kate made a snippy comment about it being an example of "let's do what's easiest!" all because her bodyguard and rumored love interest could not join them. There were several other bodyguards available, but Kate needed Steve there.

On May 12, 2008, Steve sent an email to Jon and Kate to let them know that he would not be sending them a security invoice for being with them the day before. He said that they all had a great time and that his security services should be considered a birthday present for the kids and a Mother's Day present for Kate. Steve thanked them very much for getting lunch and said he appreciated it. The signature line on the email said Steven K. Neild, Executive Vice President Prudential Associates.

Kate was so overwhelmed with gratitude that Steve had so generously waived his exorbitant fee for an evening that she fell all over herself gushing her thanks. "Oh Steve …. Are you sure? Thank you so much." She told him that they had also enjoyed lunch, and that it was the least they could do.

Kate sent a note to Julie May to let her know that the dates for the San Diego trip were March 12-17, not March 13-17. She sounded pretty excited when she told Julie that the "Parkesburg event" had been changed to "Kate and Steve". She told Julie that the contract for the Ontario event was signed, sealed and delivered, and expressed great excitement about going on her first out-of-country event. She did not express a hint of sadness about being away from her family.

Before they left for their trip to Charleston, South Carolina, Kate emailed Steve a list of TEN restaurant options for Asian cuisine and included their phone numbers and web addresses. This sounds like perfectly normal behavior between a bodyguard and his client.

Kate emailed Angela from Zondervan to make sure that Steve would be comfortable on their upcoming trip to Charleston on January 12 to January 17. She asked Angela if the hotel had a conference room where they could write, and she wanted Steve to be able to check in and out, or hang out there if he wanted without feeling uncomfortable.

Kate sent Julie May an email about making a plastic surgery consultation for her "dent leg" sometime in the middle of February. She said she would be in Nyack, New York, an "affluent area" about 45 minutes outside of the city and asked Julie if they should "throw it out to Karen/Angela" about planning a book signing while she was up there. Kate said she would cover the expense of Steve traveling with her the day of her appointment if "they" would cover the hotel and car service home. She asked Julie whether it was worth asking. Kate also told Julie that it would make her feel better about traveling 4 hours by car for a 1-hour doctor's appointment.

NOTES AND OBSERVATIONS

These are partial excerpts taken from my *US Weekly* reporting:

```
Jon & Kate Gosselin PA Reporting
Kate & Steve General Reporting
```
- Kate and Steve spent six days together in Charleston, SC to write book Three.
- Kate and Steve spent six days together in San Diego, CA. Only two of those days was Steve paid for by TLC. Kate paid for the rest.
- Thanksgiving 2008 was the first holiday that Steve spent with the Gosselins.
- Jon never confronted Steve about his suspicions but Steve accused Jon of spreading lies to Gosselin bloggers, Kevin and Jodi Kreider.

This was handwritten by Kate and circled with a big heart on her calendar:

```
Leave for S.D. here
Kate, Mady & Steve
```

An arrow went from March 13-18 of 2009. This text was below that, also in Kate's writing:

```
TLC-SD
2 days of Steve
Part of flights
Part of stay
```

So it was a six-day trip, and TLC only saw fit to cover Steve for two of those days. The rest was vacation time together for Kate and Steve.

Here is more from my *US Weekly* reporting on Kate and Steve. The nature of their relationship was a hot topic back then.

WHAT DO THE KIDS THINK OF STEVE?

The kids love Steve. I think they love him as much or more than they love Kate. Several times when Steve was at the house getting ready to leave on a trip with Kate, when they're saying goodbye in the driveway, I've heard them yelling "bye Steve, by Steve" but no "bye mommy."

When Steve is at the house visiting, the little kids are all over him, wanting him to play with them constantly. He really seems to love them too. He always has time to play with them but Kate usually cuts it short and demands his attention for her own selfish needs, usually asking him to carry something for her or move something for her.

HOW ARE THE KIDS DOING?

Mady and Cara still throw the occasional tantrum or hissy fit, but not nearly as often or as bad as in the past. I think now that Jon has some stability in his life as far as a place to live, they've adjusted to the divorce. They seemed very confused at first by Jon and Kate fighting and living apart but they've adapted and are doing fine. It's obvious that they like spending time with Jon more than Kate because Kate is like a drill sergeant and Jon gives them more space and allows them to act their age. He still disciplines them but they know what they did wrong to get yelled at. A lot of times Kate yells at the kids for no reason and they don't understand why she's so angry at them.

GINA NEILD

I've never spoken to Gina in person or been close enough to her to get a true read on her feelings but I've watched her several times from the fenceline at the property and she strikes me as someone playing the role of the 'good wife,' or the 'obedient wife.' Like most things Gosselin, she started making 'photo op' appearances at the house when the media started focusing on a possible affair between Steve and Kate. She was also photographed having lunch with Kate in Rockville, MD where the Neild's live, right about the time when the affair rumors were going strong. Gina usually stands quietly in the driveway while Kate and Steve are getting ready to leave for a trip and I've never seen any emotion between she and Steve. I've seen Steve hand Kate's bags to Gina to help load into the limo but never any hugs or kisses goodbye. It must really bother her to see the Gosselin kids giving Steve big hugs and kisses and waving goodbye to him and watching him drive off in a stretch limo with Kate while she's left at home to babysit.

DETAILS ON THE JANUARY 2009 CHARLESTON, SC TRIP.

This is what is written on the calendar by Kate:
Charleston, SC to write book #3 (smiley face and four !!!!)
They left at 4:30 am on January 12th for an 8:30 am flight out of Philadelphia and got home sometime after 5 pm. on January 17th.

DETAILS ON THE HOLIDAYS IN 2008

Thanksgiving 2008 was the first time the Neild's came to the Gosselin house for a holiday. Jon thought it was very awkward because by this time, Kate had already decided that their marriage was over and Jon suspected it was because of her having an affair with Steve. Jon said he never confronted Steve about it, but after Kevin and Jodi wrote on their blog that Kate and Steve were having an affair, Steve came and confronted Jon, accusing Jon of telling Kevin and Jodi lies. (Jon wouldn't give any details.)

It was Kate's way of shoving it down Jon's throat that she could do anything she wanted and he was weak. Kate knew that Jon didn't want Steve at the house and especially not at the holidays but Kate went out of her way to plan extended stays with the Neild's and it drove Jon crazy. Jon was in the house but he stayed as far away from Steve and Kate as he could.

After Thanksgiving it became a regular routine. The Neild's would be invited over for Christmas, New Year's, Easter, and every major holiday and Jon hated it and hated the fact that Steve was getting so close to his children. He felt like he was being replaced in his own home.

Kate and Steve took just Mady on a trip to San Diego in March 2009. They left Mady with a babysitter every night while they went out alone. It was just a vacation trip and not a book signing. Mady was very confused, trying to understand why Steve was with Kate and not Jon.

This part was printed by Star Magazine at the time:

"They were riding a four-wheeled cycle. Mady was on one side of her mother, while Kate was nuzzled in close to Steve on the other side — and he had his arm around her! If you didn't know any better, you'd think Kate and Steve were a married couple on a romantic holiday. The way she leaned into him was highly inappropriate for a married woman!"

Kate was later seen "sitting extremely close to Steve on the beach. She had stripped down to her bikini, and Steve had taken his shirt off. They seemed to be ignoring Mady, 8 — but not each other! Kate was laughing and playfully patted his leg. She even put her head on his shoulder at one point."

"On Friday night, we saw Steve leading Kate and Mady into the suite next to ours! It looked to me as if all three of them were spending the weekend together in the same room! I actually felt bad for Mady."

Jon & Kate Gosselin PA Reporting

- Kate went to a reading of Multiple Blessings and Steve went along. That's when Jon first "suspected something was going on and got pissed that they had a nice little vacation date together."

Jon couldn't understand why Steve accompanied Kate alone on a reading of her book, Multiple Blessings. Steve was assigned to the family by TLC to keep the kids safe but Kate decided she needed Steve by her side. Kate wouldn't even explain it to Jon, telling him "you wouldn't understand."

- Jon felt the end of their relationship came when he stopped doing church speaking dates with Kate. In October 2008 Kate said to Jon, "you can live your life. I'm going to live mine."

Kate was totally focused on getting as much money out of people as she possibly could, any way she could. One of her main ways early on was to speak at churches and collect "Love Offerings." Jon never liked doing this and felt bad about it and finally told Kate that he wasn't going to do it anymore. He thought it was hypocritical. It was then that Kate announced the end of their relationship to Jon.

- Kate refused to go to counseling or get couples therapy with Jon. She just decided it was over.

When Kate broke that news to Jon, he was totally caught off guard. He said he never saw it coming and wanted to discuss it and work things out with Kate but she wanted nothing to do with it. She already had her mind made up and had moved on. Jon suggested couple's therapy and marriage counseling for the sake of the kids, but she said no. In Jon's mind, the only explanation for this is that she already had another man in her life and the only person it could have been was Steve Neild. "Kate is smart enough to keep things hidden from the public and will reveal their relationship when it works best for her career.

- Kate was traveling with Steve everywhere in the country and Jon was left at home with the kids. That made him angry and he became suspicious.

The fact that Kate was away with Steve more than she was home and Jon was left at home with all eight kids really started to anger him and get him thinking about them being together and he started asking her more and more questions about it, which made her more and more angry with Jon. Whether or not they're having an affair, the topic of Kate and Steve together was what really drove Jon and Kate apart.

- Kate started inviting Steve to the family's personal holiday celebrations in 2008.

Then, for reasons unknown to Jon, Kate started inviting Steve and his family to their house for holiday celebrations, which really infuriated Jon. Jon thinks she did it to shove it in Jon's face. He also thinks Kate and Steve wanted to show Gina that it was just business and they were just good friends and if Kate and Gina became friends, the rumors wouldn't be as bad in the media.
Kate and Steve were chummy and she drank a lot around him and acted silly, even in front of Gina and he could see Gina's reaction to it and she didn't look happy but Kate didn't seem to care. In Kate's mind, she was the big star and everyone else would just have to fall in line behind her.

- In January 2009, Kate and Steve went to Charleston, SC to write book number three. "Who takes a bodyguard with them to write a book?? They were cooped up the whole time."

Kate didn't even try to explain to Jon why Steve was traveling with her to meet with her publisher and editor and Jon can't understand why she would need a bodyguard to sit in a room working on a book. The only reason he could think of is that it gave them even more time to be together.

- TLC hired Steve and assigned him to the Gosselin family.
- In 2007 Steve became the family's bodyguard. In 2008 Steve became Kate's personal bodyguard.
- TLC protected Kate when she asked for a divorce and threw Jon "under the bus." Jon never wanted a divorce.
- Steve is an executive at his company, yet he spends most of his time out on the road guarding Kate. Why?
- Steve Neild is the trustee of the family money in the event that Jon and Kate should both die.
- On Jon's suspicions, he said 'it's just the way a man looks at a woman."

I pressed Jon further today, telling him that I don't see any real evidence of an affair and I asked him how he could be so sure. He said "it's just the way a man looks at a woman and I've seen them way they look at each other when they're together." He's seen them giving each other playful looks when they thought nobody was looking.

- Xxxxxx the nanny completely agrees that Kate and Steve are having an affair. She "can just tell by how they act around each other. They're like they've been married for ten years but still on their honeymoon."

Xxxxxx doesn't have any concrete proof either except her woman's intuition. She says it's so obvious to her by the way they look at each other and the way they act around each other. They're always very playful with one another, like they're in the early stages of a marriage but also like they've been married for ten years. They bicker back and forth and Steve speaks his mind sometimes like a husband would talk to a wife. Certainly not the way an employee would speak to his employer.

- Jon believes that they've been having an affair since mid 2008 and that it continues to this day. He wouldn't be surprised if they came out with their relationship sometime on one of her new shows.
- Jon never had a conversation with Gina about whether or not she thought Kate and Steve were having an affair but thinks she'd have to be an idiot not to suspect it.

Jon & Kate Gosselin PA Reporting
September 2009
They ended up at ABC Dance Supplies on Kutztown Road in Reading. All the cars and van pulled into their small lot, followed by the paps. It was only then that I realized that Steve Neild was riding in the passenger seat of the van with Kate driving. The crew went ahead to the store and filmed Kate unloading all the kids and the group walking across the parking lot and into the store. It was closed to customers for the shoot and people were being turned away. It's a very small, one-room store filled only with racks of ballet and dance outfits as well as dance shoes. Everyone went inside except for Steve. His job for this day was to stand outside and make sure that the paps didn't interfere and there were no other disturbances. He spent forty minutes standing next to me. I introduced myself and we had small talk but he wouldn't answer any questions for the magazine. He told me he was from Auckland, New Zealand and he speaks with a heavy NZ accent. He was holding an umbrella as the skies were pretty dark and while he was standing there, he was swinging the umbrella like a golf club. We talked a little about golf and local courses and that he doesn't have any time anymore to play as he's always working or with his family. He's very soft-spoken but he looks very confident in his abilities. He's not a bodyguard that comes at you head on like a tough guy but rather just lets you know he's there and looks for mutual respect. He made no demands of us and we respected the boundaries of the shoot and kept at a distance.
As far as Steve not being seen with Kate in awhile he said that he get's a call from TLC when they're doing a shoot and he goes to work. They rotate different people on and off of the job as well.

Kate had no interaction with Steve at all outside of the van until she came out of the store and saw him talking to me. She looked mortified that he was standing there talking to the paps. Her eyes almost bugged out of her head and she did the 'cut' motion with her hand going across her throat at him while making a very scary face with her teeth clinched. She said 'What are you doing??? Don't talk to them — they're the paparazzi!!!" He quickly left us and went back closer to the family.

This looked like much more than a professional relationship to me. Kate seemed to be disciplining him like a boyfriend or a husband. She rolled her eyes at him after telling him not to talk to us. It just seemed like they were way past the point of employer/employee. They looked like lovers trying not to act like lovers.

Jon & Kate Gosselin PA Reporting
October 2009

- Black stretch limo pulled up to the house at Noon. Steve and Kate got in and left town.
- Steve Neild gets Kate's mail at the UPS store in limo.
- Steve gets out of limo at kids school and walks Mady and Cara from school to the car. Kate stays hidden.
- Two paps and I chase limo at high speeds, eventually ending up in Pittsburgh.
- Kate, Steve and kids stopped for dinner at a restaurant in Pittsburgh. Paps left after that.
- Limo driver said Kate and Steve were assholes and they were very rude.

There were two paps and two reporters circling around today, hoping to get comments from Kate about the TLC situation. She stayed in hiding though. There was no sign of her at all until I saw a black limo going up the road toward the house. I quickly drove up in time to see it pull up to the front door and Kate and Steve came out of the house and got into it. The driver got out of the car but Steve beat him to the door and opened it for Kate and got in behind her and closed it himself. They left the property with two paps and me following them. He drove pretty slowly at first because of the winding country roads but when he reached the highway, he sped up to 75 in a 55. They went to Kate's UPS store and Steve got out and went inside and got her mail. He glared at me when he walked back to the car. He wasn't happy about being followed. Once back out on the highway, the driver got back up to high speed again and was weaving in and out of traffic. After thirty minutes, we ended up in Lancaster at Mady and Cara's school. The limo pulled up near one of the buildings and Steve got out and went inside and a few minutes later, he came out with the girls and loaded them into the limo. Kate still hadn't been seen at this point. We drove and chased for another hour at high speeds, going over 95 mph at times and I fell behind the paps in their sports cars. I was driving an older SUV and I got hung up at a traffic light after everyone else ran through it by about eight seconds. After that I never caught back up to them. I was in contact with both paps though the whole time by phone. They got on the PA turnpike heading toward Pittsburgh. I got on about five minutes behind them and headed back. There was no way I could stay with the chase. On the turnpike, they reached speeds over 105 mph according to both paps.

They pulled over at a rest stop halfway between Reading and Pittsburgh and everyone got out to go inside for a break. Steve told the driver to stay with the car while they went inside. He also looked at the paps like "WTF are you still doing following us??"

The driver told the paps that they both (Kate and Steve) were very rude. Steve gave him an address to plug into his GPS and told him "that's where we're going" and then he had the divider put up so they had privacy. The driver said, "these people suck. They're total assholes" Once back in the car, the chase was on again — again going over 100 mph weaving in and out of traffic with two kids in the car. They finally ended up in Pittsburgh at a restaurant. The paps took pictures of them going inside but then decided they'd had enough and began the five-hour trip back home. Both paps were very pissed off that they wasted the trip. They speculated that Kate maybe had a speaking engagement tonight or tomorrow in Pittsburgh or Ohio.

Jon and Kate Gosselin PA Reporting
November 2009
- Steve Neild is the main reason that Kate is happy now. It's him that she's talking to on the cell phone all day. It's like he's there with her she says.

Regarding Steve being at the house for Thanksgiving, the kids told Jon about it and are wondering why Jon won't be there. One of the little girls asked Steve if he was going to be their new daddy. Xxxxxx says that "I think Kate is in love with Steve. Steve is the one Kate is talking to on the cell phone all day long and she's always smiling like a teenager when she's talking to him at home." Kate doesn't talk to her about him but she can hear Kate say Steve this and Steve that while talking to him so she knows it's him. She told me "the kids love him. He's so kind and soft-spoken and smart and everyone is so comfortable around him. Steve's wife comes with him sometimes when he's here and she and Kate are very friendly but it's so obvious that they're having an affair. At the very least they're having an emotional affair. He's good for the kids. He's a strong father figure to them when Jon is not around. They need that in their lives, especially at this age. The twins need to see how a man should really treat a woman and they don't get that from Jon and Kate.

Jon and Kate Gosselin PA Reporting
November 2009
- Steve Neild and his wife were working in the yard for hours. Seemed very distant.

When I was in Maryland watching Steve Neild's house, he was outside with his wife doing yard work for several hours. Now that I think about it, I don't recall seeing them make contact with each other in any way. They acted like strangers. She was raking leaves and he was working on the porch and the cars. They looked like a married couple just going through the motions. When I've seen Kate with Steve, there's more of a natural chemistry about them. They look more like a couple than employer/employee. They look so comfortable with each other and they always look happy to be with each other. I've seen her give Steve a flirtatious glance here and there and he has that confident grin, like the cat that ate the canary.

Jon and Kate Gosselin PA Reporting
November 2009
- Kate didn't come home last night. Left the kids with nannies.
- Nannies stayed at the house with the kids all day.

Kate never came home last night. Nanny stayed with the kids overnight. Nobody had any idea as to where Kate went. I found out later in the day that Kate went to Maryland. Steve lives in Maryland.

Jon & Kate Gosselin PA Reporting
March 2010

- Steve Neild and his wife brought Kate a present for her 35th birthday which is on Sunday 3/28.
- Gina Neild watched the kids today while Kate danced and stayed at the house alone with them after Steve and Kate left in a limo.
- Kate took her Land Cruiser to get detailed. Called police to keep paparazzi away.

Steve and Gina Neild arrived in their Ford Explorer around 8:30 today carrying what looked like a present for Kate. Tomorrow is her 35th birthday. Steve seemed surprised and angry to see the paparazzi camped in front of the house so early. He glared at the group as he was entering through the front gate. Gina didn't even look over at them.

Kate and Tony rehearsed until 12:30 when he and the crew packed up and left the house. Shortly after they left, Kate and Steve left in their own cars, followed closely by the paps. They drove to a local collision/car detailing shop in Wernersville where Kate was met by a Spring Township policeman who made sure to keep the paps away.

Gina Neild brought the kids outside to play and they ran around like they haven't been outside in a month. She stood nearby watching over them as they played with their scooters and bicycles and just generally ran around enjoying the fresh air. They didn't seem bothered by yet another new person watching them while their mom was busy doing something else. It's a normal part of their lives by now. A limo arrived at the house around 1 pm and sat in the driveway waiting for over an hour. Finally Kate, Steve and Gina started bringing their bags out and loading them in the car. They had the limo move across the driveway and up to the front door as close as possible to cut off the view from the paps. Gina gave Steve and Kate a big hug before waving goodbye as the limo drove down the driveway and off the property, followed by the paps.

Jon & Kate Gosselin PA Reporting
April 2010

- Kate and the kids arrived home today after almost a week in LA.
- Kate left with Steve for NYC after 15 minutes at the house.

Kate and the eight kids arrived back home in PA today after almost a week in LA. At 10:15am, two limos arrived at the house. A limo bus was carrying Kate, Steve and Kate's BFF Jaime and the kids. They were followed by a second limo that would take Kate and Steve to NYC a few minutes later. Judy was at the house when they arrived and she came outside to greet them. All the kids ran to her and gave her big hugs like you would expect a mother to get. Judy spends more time with them than Kate so their bond is very strong. Kate went inside the house with Judy while Steve and the limo driver brought the luggage in the house. The kids looked tired from the trip and happy to be back home. After fifteen minutes inside, Kate and Steve came out and got in the second limo and left for NYC. Kate's master schedule says DWTS and I know they're going to be on Regis tomorrow.

Jon & Kate Gosselin PA Reporting
May 2010
- Kate hasn't seen the kids since last Sunday when they left Orlando.

Kate hasn't seen her kids since last Sunday when they left Orlando and returned home. Kate went directly to LA with Steve Neild to prepare for DWTS while a second bodyguard accompanied the kids back to Pennsylvania.

Jon & Kate Gosselin PA Reporting
July 2010
- Kate entertained Steve and Gina Neild, as well as their two sons and a girlfriend at her house on the Fourth of July.
- Kate wore a very small bikini while frolicking at her pool with the Neild's and the kids.

Kate entertained the Neild family at her house today, throwing a picnic and pool party in the back yard, keeping mostly out of sight of the paparazzi at the fence. Steve brought his two sons and one of their girlfriends and they all pitched in playing with the kids and helping with the cookout. They grilled on the back patio behind the house and made a bonfire in the back horse paddock where they roasted marshmallows and hot dogs. The kids were running around laughing and having fun, playing hide and seek in and out of the new trees.
Kate wore a skimpy bikini while they were inside the fence at the pool, but walked to the grill and around the back freely, letting it all hang out in front of Steve and Gina and the two teenage boys. We can't see the pool because of a big wooden fence surrounding it, but we could see a beach ball popping up and down in the pool and hear the music blasting and kids laughing and screaming.

Jon and Kate Gosselin PA Reporting
July 2010
- Kate and Steve went out together at night in Alaska while the kids stayed with another bodyguard.

Kate and Steve went out together every night in Alaska while the kids were left with another bodyguard at the hotel. After they came back to the hotel after a day of filming, Kate and Steve would get cleaned up and into fresh clothes and go out on their own with Steve driving. Steve went to great lengths to avoid being followed.

Jon and Kate Gosselin PA Reporting
August 2010
Xxxxxx is sure Kate and Steve are having an affair but has no proof. She said Kate giggles like a schoolgirl around him and they talk on the phone for hours some nights while xxxxxx is there working and Kate's home. Kate only has one other friend in Jamie, and when she's not on the phone with her, she's on the phone with Steve. Kate get's very annoyed when one of the kids interrupts her while she's on the phone, which is most of the time that she's home. Steve has been at the house more frequently than in the past and not only when Kate is traveling. It's easier for him to go unnoticed by the paps now that all of the new trees have been planted.

Jon and Kate Gosselin PA Reporting
August 2010

- Kate and Steve Neild appeared to be getting romantic on the beach in North Carolina recently.

Kate and Steve went out alone every night for walks on the beach while at Bald Head Island. A bodyguard walked nearby making sure no paps got close enough to photograph them.
Xxxxxx told me that they looked like husband and wife on a family vacation and not like a bodyguard guarding his subject. He said he wouldn't be surprised to hear an announcement soon of Steve leaving his wife and he and Kate being a couple.

Jon and Kate Gosselin PA Reporting
August 2010

- Steve Neild has spent several nights at Kate's house recently — Too tired to drive back to Maryland after filming.

Steve has stayed overnight at Kate's house several times recently, using the excuse that he was too tired to drive all the way back to Maryland at night after filming.

Jon and Kate Gosselin PA Reporting
August 2010

- Steve Neild was at Kate's house again today to 'protect' the family while they went shopping for school clothes at a local department store.
- The only time Kate takes all the kids anywhere together is when the TLC cameras are rolling.
- Steve drove the Sprinter van to the store, then Kate jumped in the driver's seat to make it look like she drove the kids — for filming.
- Steve stayed at Kate's house long after the TLC cameras left for the day.
- With Steve back at the house, Kate went to the tanning salon.

Steve Neild was in town and at Kate's house very early today for a TLC shoot. The crew got to the house at 9 am and readied for a trip to Boscov's department store in the Berkshire Mall in Wyomissing. This was the second of two days of shooting back-to-school shopping scenes. The little kids should love when TLC is filming because it's the only time they get to go anywhere with Kate. They didn't show any signs of having fun though judging by the looks on their faces as they were led from the van to the store. They looked like kids being made to work instead of playing and enjoying themselves.
Steve drove the Sprinter van from the house to the store, and then quickly gave up his seat when they pulled in so Kate could get behind the wheel and give the impression to the cameras that she actually drove the family shopping. There's nothing real about this reality show. Steve got out and made sure nobody approached the family or did anything remotely suspicious. He watches over them like they're his own family.
Once shopping/filming wrapped at the mall, the crew headed back home to get ready for the handover of custody to Jon. Steve stayed at the house while the TLC crew packed up their gear and left for the day.

Jon and Kate Gosselin PA Reporting
August 2010
- Kate and Steve went to NYC this morning and checked into the Essex House.
- Kate wore a low-cut top for her ride to NYC in the back of a limo with Steve.

Steve Neild's car was at Kate's house very early this morning along with Ashley the nanny. Kate and Steve left in a limo and were followed to NYC where they checked into the Essex house. Along the way they stopped at a Dunkin Donuts to grab some coffee. It was raining pretty hard and Steve got out of the limo and came around and opened the door for Kate who climbed out wearing a very low cut blouse with her ample cleavage visible. Pretty casual for a back-seat limo trip with your bodyguard. Kate made a fuss about having to walk in the rain and she yelled at Steve to get her an umbrella but Steve just told her "a little rain won't kill you. Let's go." And they went inside the store for coffee. After that it was straight to the Essex House where they always stay when in the city. Again, Steve held the doors for Kate as they went inside.
Nobody I spoke to knew of any reason for Kate to be there, ie. Talk show appearance etc.
When Kate left the house this morning, the kids were upset that she was leaving them again but all Kate said to the little kids was "Mommy has to work. Have fun while I'm away."

Jon and Kate Gosselin PA Reporting
November 2010
Kate and Steve and all eight kids had a long lunch this past Friday at a restaurant in Wyomissing, PA. They looked like a big family out to eat except the kids were scolded before entering the restaurant. Kate was bent over the little ones yelling at them and pointing her finger in their faces. The kids looked scared and very unhappy. Steve just stood there and let Kate scream at them before going inside. At the table, the kids barely said a word and looked sad. Kate only ordered three meals for the sextuplets to share.

KATE GOSSELIN
Q: Any anecdotal evidence of her bodyguard (Steve Neild) being too present?
When Kate and Steve left the house in the limo for LA on Saturday, the kids were outside to see them off in the driveway, and rather than focus on Kate leaving, the sextuplets were yelling "Bye Steeeeeeve! Bye Steeeeeve!!"
What must Gina have been thinking as she sent her husband off in a limo with the woman he's rumored to be having an affair with, one day before she celebrates her birthday?

At this point, I couldn't be any less interested in finding out if the Kate/Steve pairing is a business relationship or something more. What I do know is that Kate Gosselin has held herself up to be a shining example of a good, Christian woman. It seems that if she gave even the slightest consideration to her Christianity, she wouldn't be prancing around in skimpy clothing with her married "bodyguard." Kate has heard the rumors for years, and her ex-husband has cited the affair rumors as a reason for their marriage failing, yet she continues to flaunt her relationship with Steve Neild in public.

Abstain from all appearance of evil.
– 1 Thessalonians 5:22

WHO LET THE DOGS OUT?

During the summer of 2009, I was at the Gosselin house alone, standing among the trees outside the property, when I watched as Kate drove down the driveway and through the front gate. "Jon's dogs," Shoka and Nala, ran out into the street behind her and chased her down the road, in full view of Kate.

I know she saw them leave the property, because she stopped for a moment in the middle of the road and looked back at them, as if she might actually turn around. I thought she was going to drive back and make sure the family dogs got safely back inside the electric fence, since the gate had closed and they were locked out. She decided against it, however, because she drove away, leaving the dogs to fend for themselves along a very well-traveled (since the Gosselins moved in) country road.

Once the dogs realized they couldn't get back through the gate, they became scared and confused and began behaving erratically. They started running around on the road in front of the Gosselin's property, coming dangerously close to being hit by cars several times. Then, they saw me. They started walking towards me, and I was sure I was going to be mauled by the two police-trained German Shepherds. I stood very still.

Now, I love animals, especially dogs, but I'm sure you will understand my concern when Shoka and Nala headed in my direction. I had spent weeks talking to them through the security fence, but that's like being on the outside of the glass talking to Hannibal Lecter. There's a sense of security there.

But now they were roaming free and coming toward me, tongues out panting and tails-a-wagging. I was on the phone with a pap friend at the time, and he told me to climb a tree. Paps are helpful like that. I hung up, made my peace with God, and tried to get Jon on the phone. He was in a meeting in New York City, so he didn't answer my first call. After my third try, he must have figured it was important, so he answered.

I quickly told Jon my predicament, and he assured me that since I had been standing at the fence every day for months, the dogs knew my voice and my smell and probably wouldn't kill me. (I think he was joking.) Very reassuring. He asked me to please round them up, take off their electric dog collars, and get them back inside the property.

Sure enough, both dogs were very friendly to me, just as Jon had predicted, and they allowed me to remove their collars. Nala, the female, who I'm guessing was the smarter of the two, didn't want to wait around for help getting back inside. A few minutes after I got her collar off, she ran and safely jumped over the fence to relax on the other side. Shoka, on the other hand, was a bit more stubborn. Even after I took his collar off, he didn't want to go anywhere near the fence, so I sat with him in the driveway by the front gate, and we waited for over an hour for Kate to get home.

Shoka and I had a good time together. He let me pet him, and he lounged in my lap as I sat in the shade next to the gate. Shortly before Kate arrived back at the house, Shoka finally allowed me to guide him under a low spot in the fence. He lay down with Nala, and the two probably had a nice discussion about their unsettling adventure.

I'm sure Kate would have enjoyed seeing what happened next. After getting Shoka inside the fence, I decided to walk over to where I had put my backpack. Not even giving it a thought, I walked right up to the fence – still holding the two electric dog collars in my hand. When I got close to the fence, the collars activated and zapped the heck out of me. I didn't know what hit me, and I screamed like a baby. It's too bad Kate missed it.

Kate was stoic but polite when she got back home. I handed her both of the dogs' collars, but she had no idea what I was giving her. One of the twins had to point out what they were.

As a reporter, I had wanted to talk to Kate in person for some time for *US Weekly*, but I wasn't about to start asking her questions in front of the kids. Instead, I handed her a piece of paper with my name and contact information on it, hoping that she would give in and at least answer a question or two – at a time of her choosing – because I had helped her family's dogs. Call me naive.

I found out later that as soon as she got inside the house, she threw my information in the trash and made a joke about me "thinking I was going to get on her good side because I helped her dogs." What was I thinking? It was extremely hot that day. I must have been delusional to even try.

Kate's apparent lack of concern for the safety of Shoka and Nala begs the question: Just how much did Kate like taking care of the family dogs? In short, she didn't. For Kate, the dogs were nothing more than another freebie that made for a few interesting episodes of reality television. After the novelty had worn off, they became a burden to her and she wanted absolutely nothing to do with them. When the divorce proceedings started and Jon was no longer at the house to take care of them, Kate showed her true colors.

Kate made it completely clear to Jon and the entire family that those dogs were "his dogs," and it was his job to take care of them. I'm not exactly sure how she expected Jon to take care of them when it wasn't his custody time and he wasn't allowed on the property, but Kate didn't care about those details.

Kate totally and completely ignored Shoka and Nala and kept them locked inside their cages behind the house. She didn't feed them, and she left them imprisoned, surrounded by their own excrement and vomit until Jon was around to take care of them. I reported this to *US Weekly* and to the local Animal Rescue League, as did several other people with knowledge of the situation. The dogs were so traumatized that they chewed through their metal cages to get out.

Kate finally allowed Mady and Cara to care for the dogs when Jon wasn't at the house. It became their responsibility to feed, clean and entertain the dogs, just as it had become their responsibility to do the same for the sextuplets much of the time. Although I never saw it myself, I was told that Kate also physically abused Shoka. She did the same to Nala, but Nala growled at her and threatened to bite her. That's probably the real reason Nala was permanently banished from the family.

For anyone who doesn't believe that Kate could beat a dog, please remember that she was capable of hitting her children when they were just toddlers in diapers. It should be no stretch at all, then, to believe that she would be OK with beating a dog, especially one who had been trained to not bite her.

Kate finally had enough and made Jon get rid of "his dogs." I was there with Jon the day they were taken away. Jon was sad, and the kids were very, very sad. Kate couldn't have cared any less. When asked about the dogs at the Southern Women's Show in Charlotte, NC, in September 2009, Kate said that she just needed a break from them and they would be back. She said that the breeder "took them back for a short period of time." She also said, "I'm feeling like I have not enough time to take care of my kids, let alone give the dogs what they need, and the kids surprisingly weren't that upset about it. They'll come back I'm sure at some point. But for now, I just needed a break." Kate also told a "joke" about how crazy the dogs are. "They sleep in a metal crate... a huge metal crate. They bent the bars and got out. I think in the winter I'm going to have them pull the kids in a sleigh."

Kate's handlers should have told her that there is nothing funny whatsoever about the dogs being confined for so long and becoming so desperate to be free that they bent the metal bars of a cage.

Fast-forward a year, and Discovery/TLC was looking for episode ideas to rehab/rebuild Kate's tarnished image, so they decided to bring the dogs back to the kids...for filming, of course. Kate was initially dead-set against the idea, but she went along with it on one condition - that only Shoka be allowed to return to the family. Nala would now be left alone without her family or her brother.

The rumors regarding her cruelty to the dogs continued to plague Kate, so in 2011, she decided to do what she had done so successfully for all those years when she lied about how much her kids loooooooved filming their reality show: she denied, deflected and called her critics bullies. And in true Kate Gosselin form, she also started to totally overcompensate in her tweeting and blogging. To prove how wrong everyone was, she started blogging about Shoka on her website. Oh, correction. Shoka started writing blogs about himself (http://www.kateplusmy8.com/category/shoka-diaries/).

You heard right. Shoka was now blogging and telling us how much he is loved and cherished by Kate, and how he is such a big part of the Gosselin family. The "family" angle is still sad and telling because Nala was also part of the Gosselin family, and she was permanently banished...like all of Kate's human family: her parents, brothers and sisters, nieces and nephews, aunts and uncles. All banished. Shoka made sure to tell us that those horrible rumors about Kate not loving him and even abusing him were all just a terrible pack of lies. Surely Shoka the dog wouldn't lie, now would he? I've spent a lot of quality one-on-one time with him, and he seems like a pretty straight shooter.

But Kate needed to assure everyone that she really, really loves Shoka and she takes absolutely amazing care of him. You don't have to take Kate's word for it. You can hear it directly from Shoka's mouth.

Kate posted a blog - which she, no doubt, thought was clever and cute - about Shoka getting into and eating loaves of bread that she said she had baked herself and had wrapped in plastic for the trash men as a Christmas present:

As if that wasn't bad enough, Kate got herself in even more trouble when she tweeted this:

worried? He's in the dog house tonight. Ate baked goods for trash men... Plastic and all!!! Bad dog!

Within hours, the anti-Kate blogs were up in arms about Kate's carelessness in leaving dangerous plastic-wrapped items where Shoka could get his paws on them and swallow them. Dog owners and pet lovers lambasted her for being so cavalier about Shoka eating the plastic wrap, which could have caused choking or serious intestinal damage. That thought, of course, would never have occurred to Kate Gosselin because she doesn't have the slightest clue about how to properly care for anything, especially a dog.

Kate was so panicked by the outcry over her latest blunder that she, I mean, Shoka, was forced to write another blog within days to tell everyone that he was fine and there was nothing to worry about. So on December 21, 2011, Shoka blogged that "NO WAY" did he eat any wrappers; this despite the fact that "he" had blogged that he had "eaten some doggone plastic wrap" and Kate had tweeted that he had eaten "Plastic and all!!!"

Kate is also guilty of leaving Shoka outside in the cold and rain all night, most times as a "punishment" for his misbehaving, or acting like a dog. She leaves him alone in the dark, howling to come inside. I've heard it, and I've heard about it. And so has Kate. In fact, she was hearing so much criticism about it that Shoka wrote two blogs on this topic – just a few months apart. It's a regular thing with Kate, letting us know that Shoka really, really loves being locked out of the house alone on cold, dark, rainy nights.

No matter how many blogs Kate writes pretending to be Shoka, and how many lies she puts into Shoka's mouth about how really happy he is, the fact is that Kate Gosselin simply does not care enough about Shoka to take proper care of him. Here is just one more of the many examples of this. On Easter Sunday, 2012 – four months after Kate blogged about dogs choking on certain toys and plastic bread wrappers – Shoka was allowed to run free with "1,400" filled, plastic Easter eggs laying all over her property. He ate as many sharp, plastic eggs as he could, while Kate was in the house drinking wine. (She tweeted the photo of the wine telling everyone what she was doing.)

At one point, Shoka was even eating the plastic eggs directly out of the garbage bag being used to carry them by a stranger who was placing them around the yard for the kids. Shoka's entire head was in the plastic bag eating the plastic Easter eggs, and Kate never once set foot outside to check on him. It's a miracle poor Shoka is still alive.

On July 8, 2012, in her never-ending need to tweet everything, Kate gave us a hint as to her relationship with Shoka. A young fan tweeted Kate about Shoka and said, "Have fun when he comes to give you his big ole good night kiss!!" Kate proudly announced this in reply:

he knows he's not allowed to give me any kisses ever so no worries there! Lol

Sadly, Shoka is never allowed to give Kate a kiss, and yet she would have us believe that he's the most loved dog ever and a huge part of her family. What's even sadder is that I have never seen Kate kiss any of her children either, not in person and not in any of the thousands of family photos I found.

THE PAPARAZZI

"They're all sort of bald and fattish, aren't they?
They have a look."
– *Kate Gosselin*

I had my first up-close and personal meeting with the Gosselin kids in the summer of 2009, on their turf, in their driveway up by the garage as they were playing outside. Here are my *US Weekly* notes about that first meeting:

```
5 pm - Jon had seen a dirt bike along the highway for sale and he
asked me yesterday if I could stop by on my way home and check it
out. I did and after a visit and a few phone calls, I successfully
purchased it for Jon and had the guy bring it to the house. I didn't
mention Jon's name until we got to the property and he seemed pretty
happy to meet Jon and he watches the show all the time. They had a
mutual friend or two in common and Jon invited him to ride sometime
at the property.
Jon brought the bike over behind the white minivan that's always
sitting in front of the garage so the paparazzi couldn't see it but
he let one guy (me) photograph the purchase.
The kids were all over me up there asking excitedly "are you a
paparazzi?" I told them I was a good guy, and they were just so
friendly and talking to me and asking me questions. They loved the
dirt bike and one of the little girls said, "Daddy always gets cool
things!"
```

This is what I observed about the kids interacting with the paps:

```
Jon & Kate Gosselin PA Reporting
April 2010
Despite what Kate says to the contrary, and despite her efforts to
make the kids afraid of the paparazzi, the kids love them. It's
pretty much the same people every day and Jon says that since they
grew up with cameras in their faces, it's a natural part of their
lives. I play with the kids all the time and they love it. They know
us as their daddy's friends and they feel at ease around us. It's sad
that Kate scares them and yells at them to the point that when she's
with them and they see us nearby, they're afraid to even look in our
direction. Collin is such a sweet little boy and he smiled and waved
to one of the paps in the parking lot at the bus stop a few weeks
back and that turned into the infamous photo of Kate slapping him and
covering his mouth. She's a horrible mother.
```

These are some more of my notes. Reading all this now, years later, I feel like a total idiot. But at the time, I was desperately trying to be the best reporter I could be, so I could keep my job and feed my own children. Some of the stories are hilarious, though, even to me. We did manage to have some fun while working.

Jon and Kate Gosselin PA Reporting
November 2009

Got to the Gosselin house this morning at 8 am. There was a gold car sitting in the driveway (Kate's chef preparing her meals) along with Kate's Land Cruiser and the Sprinter van.

Kate went out at 10:05 in the Land Cruiser followed by me and the paps. She took a different route today and ended up at Performance Toyota. She pulled all the way around the back out of sight. The paps stayed away because they said they'd been thrown off the lot before. I drove to the back and as I was going around behind the building, I almost drove into Kate sitting in the car and two employees who were standing in front of her door talking to her. She quickly pointed me out and they told me to get off the lot. I went off the lot and next door to a gas station and parked in the back and climbed a hill and could watch her from the tree line. I called a pap over to take pictures as well. She was allowed to wait in a new car in the back of the lot while her car was taken inside for work/service. She unloaded a box and some other personal belongings out of the Land Cruiser and into the car. She sat in the passenger seat of a silver Toyota making calls on her cell for an hour. When her car was finished, they pulled it out and drove it over right behind the car she was in and she got out and jumped in after talking to an employee for a few minutes.

After the Toyota dealership, she drove to a different Dunkin Donuts and went through the drive thru, getting a large coffee of some kind. I couldn't hear the order. The pap was behind her taking pictures. From there she headed to the UPS store and like she usually does, she parked on the wrong side facing the wrong direction right underneath a sign that reads 'No Parking Fire Lane'. Must be nice being Kate Gosselin. After five minutes inside she came out with her mail and was greeted by the pap right in her face videotaping her and asking her questions. Today's questions were about Jon's televised apology last night, her speeding ticket, how she spent Halloween and who she liked in the World Series. Her responses were blank stare, blank stare, blank stare and blank stare. Her usual. She has never uttered a syllable to the paps with video cameras.

After UPS she drove to her bank branch in Shillington, PA. She was inside for forty-five minutes. We waited by her car in the lot out front. While I was standing there I couldn't help but notice some of the things she had on her front seat. She was leaving town today and I guess she doesn't like leaving them at home. She had a box with files in it and four big binders. The labels on the binders were: LHOTP, LLC, JKIG, Inc., K8,INC., BC/BS. This is all of her personal and financial information. After coming out of the bank and getting in her car, she sat for a few minutes and got out and went inside again for another twenty minutes. I had already jumped in my car getting ready for the next phase of the chase so I didn't see if she was going through papers etc. She stayed inside the bank for an additional twenty minutes.

After the bank she got on the highway at high speed and got off in West Reading where she stopped by the dry cleaners. She went to the drive-thru and picked up several shirt bags.

The FedEx/Kinkos store was next. She parked in a parking space this time and went inside. She took in four or five large envelopes from her box on the front seat. She got there at 1:11 pm and literally stayed inside for over an hour, coming out at 2:27 pm. We can't go in or see what's happening inside because she hides behind large signs that the employees move into place to block our view. I could see her making a lot of copies and filling out FedEx mailing labels.

Four high school girls were at Starbucks next door and saw her go
inside and were waiting for forty-five minutes for her to come out
but they finally gave up. I asked what they would say to her and they
just wanted to take a photo with her on their cell phones.
(Wyomissing school district had a half day today.)
I was parked right next to her while she was inside and when she came
out, the paps were right in her face again and she looked very
annoyed but kept her composure as usual. She's unflappable. When she
got back in her car she leaned over towards the passenger side to put
things back in the box and looked at me through the window. I smiled
and waved and she rolled her eyes and looked away. That's as much of
a reaction as you'll get from Kate.
She left the FedEx lot and sped back up State Hill Road toward home.
The speed limit is 40 mph and she was going 55 mph approaching the
blind hill at the State Hill boat launch parking lot. A pickup
pulling a boat pulled out in front of her crossing her lane and she
barely avoided hitting him. She swerved to the right and just got
around him and kept going. I was following — not chasing. She drives
erratically all the time. It's going to end badly one of these days.
I hope I'm not there when it happens.
On the winding country road leading to her house, she drives into the
other lane going around S turns. Very dangerous.
Kate got back to the house at 2:45 pm. The gold car was gone by now.
Just the Sprinter van was there. I was the only one at the house and
it was dead quiet and I could hear Kate yelling when she got inside
the house. From the street to the house is a football field away and
I could hear her all the way down at my car. I originally thought she
was just venting from spending the past four and a half hours being
followed and grilled by the paps, but I later learned that she was
yelling at Jon when he told her that he would be late getting home.
She would now have to go pick up the kids at the bus instead of him.
I waited in my car out in front of the house. No police came by to
chase me this time. Kate went out again in the Land Cruiser instead
of the big blue Sprinter van at 3:30 pm. This was odd because there
were no nannies there and Jon wasn't home and the bus drop off is at
4 pm, fifteen minutes from her house. I followed her and she went
back to the FedEx store of all places. I called the paps that were
waiting at the bus stop and they came and took even more shots of her
coming out. She was inside from 3:40 to 3:55 making more copies and
she came out with something that looked like a large calendar folded
over. It was on heavy paper and looked glossy but I couldn't see what
it was. Kate could be heard saying "Goodbye, thank you!" coming out
of FedEx.
At this point we were all wondering who if anyone was picking up the
kids because eight kids can't fit in the Land Cruiser safely and no
nannies were there.
As it turns out, Kate had to call Judy to come to the bus stop to
help her with the kids. I'm not sure why she didn't just bring the
Sprinter down and do it herself but Judy was at the bus stop in her
white car when we pulled in. Kate pulled in front of her and they
were having a nice conversation, and then Judy went in the back of
her car and pulled out a tiny little baby and brought it over to Kate
who jumped out of her car and took the baby from Judy and was making
goofy faces etc. at it. It was cute. I'd never seen Kate appear happy
when not in front of the TLC cameras. She looked genuinely happy now.
I never saw any kind of friendly interaction between Kate and Judy.
I'm guessing it's because Kate called Judy at the last minute to help
her out with the kids. She only worked from 3:30 to 4:30 and then
went home.

When the bus arrived, Kate went over and escorted all the kids off and they went over and waited with Judy in between the two cars. Judy put the baby in the back of her car and loaded the twins in the back of her car while Kate rounded up the sextuplets and she and Judy got them all jammed into the Land Cruiser — somehow. Kate had them all gathered up and had to scold them a bit because they weren't standing still like she told them too. She told them that five-year-olds should be able to listen better than they were doing. Kate told the kids "Daddy will be at home when we get there!" She talked about Jon to them with a smile on her face. That was nice to see.

Judy was on one side and Kate on the other side of the Land Cruiser and they took fifteen minutes getting them all strapped in. I'm not sure how many seats Kate's car has back there and it didn't seem safe to have them all back in there no matter how short the drive is.

Jon and Kate Gosselin PA Reporting
November 2009
The Gosselin family chef was at the house today preparing the meals for the week. She was there from 8 to 11:30. A few minutes after she left, Kate went to the garage and got her Land Cruiser and came flying out of the front gate trying to lose the paparazzi from the start. She went way over the speed limit along the winding country roads around her house and ran two stop signs along the way.

She bypassed her usual first stop at Dunkin Donuts and got on the highway and sped to the UPS store. She parked beneath the sign that reads No Parking Fire Lane, facing the wrong direction. I parked right behind her. It seemed like the thing to do at the time.

She came back outside to her car three separate times to get things. She even mumbled out loud "I left my brain at home today."

While we waited outside for her to come out, various store owners and customers took the time to call us losers and told us to get lives. When she finally came out, she sat in the car for about ten minutes reading some of her mail and talking on the phone.

Next stop was her bank branch in Shillington. Again, she sat in the car for fifteen minutes reading her mail while a pap stood right outside her window waiting to video her. She got out and the first question was "Kate, are you sad that the TLC show is almost over?" Kate had no response.

After the bank, Kate led us on a high-speed chase on the highway and through town and we ended up at the Old Navy store in Wyomissing. She went inside for about fifteen minutes and bought some shirts for the girls and shirts and pants for the boys. She brought her bags out and put them in the car and then went next door to Toys R Us. I fed today's question to Kate to the pap that was filming her. "Kate, do you think all of this could have been avoided if you'd just put a dog collar on Jon in the very beginning?" No reaction. I was hoping for a chuckle, after all, it was her comment from the TLC show tonight.

I went inside Toys R Us behind her and told the paps where she was so they could run in quickly and shoot her. She was in the boys department going up and down the isles looking for presents for the boys I overheard her say to an employee. I put myself in the next isle on her route and I was holding a GI Joe doll and browsing when she came around the corner and nearly ran into me. She rolled her eyes and turned right around and went to the next isle where the pap was waiting to take her picture. At this point I headed to the front to checkout because I could see she was about to lose it. I could hear her yelling about the pap and several employees yelled at him to get out saying "that's not necessary." Kate told them about me too but I was already gone. Kate was now at the register next to mine and she was watching me angrily as I pretended to be a customer. I got some early Christmas shopping done. She didn't want us to see what she bought. She put the store circular overtop of her cart to hide her gifts. Perhaps the boys read the tabloids at school and might find out what she bought them for Christmas. She got some cars and trucks and a monster that roared and growled. It activated while she was at the register and everyone laughed, including Kate. As Kate was pushing her cart to her car, being filmed and shot by the paps, a woman who saw her said "I love you Kate" and Kate turned to her and smiled. It should be noted that at all the stores she visited today, she made it a point to walk her shopping cart back to the store rather than just leave it in the lot like a lot of people do, even if it meant another round of questions and pictures.

Next we went to the Target shopping center but went next door to Bed Bath & Beyond instead. I had a 20% off coupon that I offered to her but she must not have seen or heard me and kept walking inside. I have a terrible invisibility complex after spending hours with Kate everyday. I went inside and watched her browsing the dinnerware section. Either she's gearing up for a fancy party or she's buying gifts. She spent $200 on a fancy china table setting and cloth napkins and tablecloth. She saw me watching her but didn't seem to mind as I wasn't taking her picture and I had a comforter in my hand holding my store coupon. She knew she didn't have a chance of having me removed. As it turned out, Kate had her own BB&B 20% off coupon that she used on her purchase. She's a thrifty shopper.

It was now almost 3 pm and she had to get back to the house to get the van to pickup the kids. We raced out of the shopping center and headed toward her house, when she made a very dangerous U Turn across four lanes and headed in the opposite direction. Three miles of aggressive driving later and we were at the Dunkin Donuts drive thru getting coffee. I waited for her at the exit and followed her the rest of the way back to the house. She unloaded all of the bags and took everything inside, then got the Sprinter van and headed to the bus stop to pick up the kids.

I had tipped off a pap to something she did last Monday when I followed her back from the bus stop. She thought she was alone as I came circling back by the house and she was stopped at the gate with the back doors to the big van open and she was struggling to lift these two giant trash cans into the back of the van while the kids were inside, saving her a long walk down and back up the driveway. Today a pap was hiding across the street in the bushes, out of sight, when she got to the house. I stayed well behind to let him get his shots. Kate did the same thing and stopped to load up the cans. He told me that he scared her when he started shooting. He did video as well. I haven't seen the shots online yet but if it's what I saw last week, it will be great for your 'Stars, they're just like us' page.

Jon and Kate Gosselin PA Reporting
November 2009
After FedEx, it was on the highway for a chase to pick up her mail at
the UPS store. Kate is so predictable that I can drive ahead of her
and meet her at her destination. She really is a creature of habit as
Jon once told me. She was parked illegally again, right under the
sign that read 'No Parking Fire Lane.' Pap firing away with the
questions as she walked to the car.
Some of the favorite questions of the day:
"Kate, did you ever consider trying yoga like Jon to smooth yourself
out a little bit?"
Kate's response — Vacant stare.
"Kate, can you comment on why you never make a comment on my videos?"
Kate's response — Vacant stare.

Jon and Kate Gosselin PA Reporting
April 2010
All the pap agencies got word *somehow* that both Jon and Kate would
be together at the house today because there were as many here as
during the summer at the height of the story. They didn't get the
shot they were hoping for though because Kate left the house early,
at 8:45 am to go run errands, leaving Jon alone with the kids. No
nannies. In fairness to Kate, it is Jon's custody day so she didn't
need to be there.
She left the property followed by a host of paps and went to Dunkin
Donuts first for a coffee drink. After coffee, she went to Planet
Nails and tans for a two-hour manicure/pedicure session. The paps
were fighting with each other outside in the parking lot while they
waited. On the way inside Planet Nails, the pap who's here every day
videotaped Kate and said to Kate "You know Kate, if we didn't have
such a complicated relationship, I'd give you a big hug right now."
Kate responded, "don't bother."

This is a funny story that is so very typical of Kate's behavior.
Back in December of 2010, Kate had not been photographed locally for more than
ten days because her pap was out of the country shooting a couple of A-List
celebrities. Kate had gotten used to coming and going unnoticed for a few days, so
she was out and about running errands, looking a hot mess – no makeup, hair
unkempt, shabby-chic clothes. Not her best look. But on this day, the pap was
back in town and he surprised her by showing up at the tanning salon where she
was taking care of some important Kate business. When she came outside and saw
him there, she seemed horrified that she looked, well, like a mother of eight from
Berks County, Pennsylvania, which was something of an atrocity to Kate
Gosselin, though. She quickly jumped in her car and made a bee-line back to her
house, a 20-minute drive, where she stayed for 30 minutes, only to come right
back out and drive to approximately the same location she had just come from.
She went to Planet Nails to get her nails done.
So what was so important that she had to race back home? The pap was back in
town. Kate had rushed home to fix her hair, put on makeup, change her clothes
into something glamorous, and put on high heels – just for him. And you. Kate is
so consumed by her public image and appearance that she wasted an hour driving
back home to change, just so she would look good for the tabloids – the ones she
says she doesn't pay attention to. Meanwhile, Collin and Alexis were sitting at
home with a babysitter.

After leaving the nail salon, she went straight back home for the day.

By the end of the summer of 2009, the Gosselin frenzy had died down and the hordes of paparazzi had gone away. For more than 2 years after that, except for a day in April 2010, and on a special occasion here and there, there was only one lone paparazzo who would come by to photograph Kate. But Kate needed to keep up the illusion that she was in demand. She continued to give her fans the impression that she was still being hounded constantly by throngs of photographers.

It was usually one pap, once a month. Maybe.

As of this printing in 2012, having been off of television for over a year, Kate has taken to posting photos and videos of her children on Twitter and her own Kate + My 8 website for all the world to see. She is so desperate to get herself and her children back on television that she tweets every detail of their private lives to strangers, trying to keep interest in them alive. Kate Gosselin has become her own paparazzi. While other celebrity mothers go to great lengths to ensure their children's privacy, Kate Gosselin does the exact opposite. She shares their thoughts, their secrets, their words and, worst of all, their private photos, with the world.

In June of 2011, rock singer, Pink, posted this on her website:

> "Here's the bottom line: we don't want you to take our little girl's picture. We don't want you to one day follow our little girl home from school. We don't want our little girl's picture in a magazine or on a blog. If you take or publish her picture, it is against our wishes, and without our consent as parents, as people."

Pink sounds like a normal parent trying to protect her child.

Recently, Halle Berry and Jennifer Garner successfully lobbied for and got into law an anti-paparazzi bill 606, making it illegal in California for paparazzi to photograph celebrity's children without their consent. "We're moms here who are just trying to protect our children," Berry told the legislators. "These are little innocent children who didn't ask to be celebrities. They didn't ask to be thrown into this game and they don't have the wherewithal to process what's happening. We don't have a law in place to protect them from this."

Kate has obviously never felt the need to protect her children from the prying eyes of strangers, nor has she ever respected their privacy. On the contrary, she has done everything in her power to prevent her children from having any privacy. She has purposefully trotted her kids out in front of the cameras to entertain others, thus inviting the attention of the paparazzi. So, when Pink tweeted that "Paparazzi stalking children should be illegal," Kate had the absolute nerve to tweet this in response:

@Pink I totally agree! My kids (or any kids stalked) shouldn't even have a word ('P-ppl') for paparazzi or know they exist!

Kate is the only one stalking her children. She is the one putting them at risk and constantly tweeting and posting photographs of them online to the world of strangers, stalkers and pedophiles.

KATIE'S MEN IN BLUE

Kate Gosselin acts as if she is above the law. I have seen her use the local police force as her own personal security company and sometimes as her bellhops/baggage handlers as well. The officers never appeared to mind. It is perfectly understandable that when there was a media circus surrounding the family, the police would need to be involved to make sure the family and community were protected. But their involvement sometimes extended far beyond protection. What is most troubling is that I have witnessed local police officers allowing Kate to break the law, right in front of them without any repercussions. Here are some examples of Kate's personal relationship with the local men in blue.

- Kate almost always parks the wrong way, on the wrong side of the street at her UPS store, directly beneath a sign that reads "NO PARKING FIRE LANE" – sometimes while having a conversation with the local police who stop by to say hello and make small talk.
- While the police drove the speed limit next to me and the paps to detain us (back when the paparazzi/paparazzo were still interested in Kate), they watched as Kate sped off at speeds over 80 mph.
- Kate called the police to carry her bags and escort her from a hotel to her car.

Here are my notes detailing a few instances of Kate interacting with the local police.

Jon and Kate Gosselin PA Reporting
August 2009
1 am — On the way home I drove by the Days Inn where Kate had been spotted earlier in the day. Her car is in the parking lot so I decided to park nearby and hopefully get a look at she and Steve leaving the hotel together. (Just wishful thinking. I had no idea if Steve was with her or not.)
2:20 am — A Wyomissing policeman knocks on my window and asks what I'm doing and takes my license and runs my plates. I told him the truth about what I was doing there. He asked who I was following and I said Kate Gosselin and he said "That poor family." I said that she's not really a great person and he said "so I've heard." He was ok with me being there and recognized that I was just doing my job and I thanked him.
15 minutes later he came up to me again and told me that the hotel doesn't want me anywhere on the property. I went across the street, which was ok with him.
3 am — There are now 4 police cars patrolling the small hotel parking lot shining their spotlights in car windows etc. looking for any other paparazzi. Two of the cars stay parked on either end of the row where Kate's car is. I continue to watch the front door through binoculars.

4 am — Both police cars go around to the lobby and the officers get out and go inside. The one officer is standing in the doorway and keeps looking out into the lot.

4:05 am — Kate emerges alone from the hotel followed by the police officer **who was pulling her suitcase across the lot for her**, believe it or not. She is wearing her pink newsboy hat and is aware of my presence from the officers. She stares at me across the lot. I stare back through high-powered binoculars.

Right at the moment that Kate gets into her car, another police car pulls up along side of me, across the street from the hotel and up in the Olive Garden parking lot. He approaches me and tells me that he knows who I am and there aren't any problems. He just has to detain me while Kate gets escorted out of their jurisdiction.

You're kidding me, right? I ask, and he tells me he just doing his job.

The police give her an escort out of the lot and up onto the highway where I begin to follow. She immediately gave it everything she had and was off to the races.

Jon and Kate Gosselin PA Reporting
August 2009
…1:30 pm — Kate and the two oldest come out of the house and walk to the garage where they get into the black Land Cruiser and start down the driveway. Paps are running for their cars and fans are all abuzz. Kate sits at the top of the driveway as a police cruiser pulls up to the gate and clears the area for her, yelling at people to move back. Kate now slowly drives down the driveway, pushing buttons on her phone or some other device while she's driving. She stops next to the policeman and I can hear her yell "Thank You" out the window to him and then they chat for about 30 seconds. He follows her down the road and then comes back and now he's screaming mad. Apparently a new paparazzo was taking his picture helping Kate out of the gate and he caught him and he was livid and screaming at the 'senior' pap. He yells "I don't mean to take it out on you but this is getting very old!!!" The officer gets in his car and sits in the driveway for awhile. I went to talk to him and he was fuming that this guy was sneaking pictures of him.

Jon and Kate Gosselin PA Reporting
November 2009
… At 7:20 am, Steve left the property in his SUV. He just looked at me. He didn't say anything. I wasn't sure if Kate was stuffed in the back somewhere and they were sneaking out to hit the Black Friday sales but I didn't think Kate would let herself be seen out shopping locally banging elbows with the large crowds of regular people.

A nanny came to the house at 8:55 am to start her crossover shift as Kate is leaving and Jon is set to return sometime today.

Kate loaded up her bags and left the house in her Land Cruiser at 9:30 am. The Neilds were still inside minus Steve who was out somewhere.

… Kate went to Dunkin Donuts first and then drove to the UPS store. When she got into the parking lot, there was a police car parked near where she parks at the store. She rolled up to him and they talked out of the window for a few minutes, then went around the side of the building in their cars and talked for a few minutes more. The paps backed off and watched from across the parking lot and across the street. Kate started leaving the lot — she didn't go in UPS — and the police car was following her. When she got out of the lot to the intersection, the police car stopped and held up traffic including the paps while a second police car had traffic to the on ramp blocked from the other direction. The paps were held back for about two minutes before they were allowed to follow.

The paps drove all the way to the Park City Mall in Lancaster and looked for her there but couldn't find her. That's the direction that she goes when she leaves town but we haven't been able to figure out where she stays when not at home.

Steve came back to the house at 9:45 am, fifteen minutes after Kate left, and picked up his family and loaded up their things and left. That was it for the visit. It was a very well organized getaway for Kate. Well planned.

Jon and Kate Gosselin PA Reporting
December 2009
… We slowly crept along the country roads until we got to the main roads where she was free to be herself and speed. She led me into the shopping center with the UPS store and she parked out front, illegally under the no parking sign and facing in the wrong direction. I stopped close by to observe. I could see that the UPS store was closed and I could also see that she was turned completely around in her seat staring at me through the back window as she was talking on the phone. I knew what was coming and I was on the phone with the pap at the time, and within ten minutes a Spring Township police officer pulled into the parking lot and parked right behind her. Kate got out and walked back to talk to him. This was a repeat of the last time she left town mysteriously and had the police block the paps in the lot so she could escape. I anticipated her next move and drove out of the lot and across the highway and got on Rt. 222 heading toward Lancaster. As I was leaving the lot I could see in my rearview mirror that Kate was driving now with the policeman following right behind her.

I just started driving and within a minute I saw Kate and the officer coming behind me. I stayed at the speed limit because I knew this guy would be looking for any reason to pull me over. As Kate passed me, she kept her eyes straight ahead. She didn't look at me or smile or anything like that. Just drove past. The policeman looked me up and down as he passed me and all I could do was follow now. The policeman drove 55 with me behind him but Kate was allowed to pull away at high speed. He stayed on the highway for about two miles till he was well past his jurisdiction, and then he pulled onto the center divider and headed back. By this time Kate was about a mile ahead of me and I knew I had my work cut out for me. She's almost impossible for me to follow if I start out right behind her but with a mile head start forget it. I went the next thirty-five miles on the highway going between 85 and 95 mph and never was able to catch up to her. The only place she could have gone that would allow me to find her would be the Park City Mall but I drove the parking lot three times and couldn't find her. The mall was the end of the line for the chase and Kate successfully got away from us again with the help of the police.

Jon and Kate Gosselin PA Reporting
February 2010

… She left the property and again was driving very fast over the highway and toward her UPS store. When she pulled in there was already a Spring Township policeman sitting there waiting for her so the paps took off across the highway. She stayed there for about ten minutes talking to the policeman before getting on 222 heading toward Lancaster. The policeman drove next to me so I wasn't able to follow Kate but the paps were up ahead waiting for her. Kate sped off at blinding speed, right in front of the police as I was left behind. When the policeman got to the end of his jurisdiction he pulled off and I joined in the chase, already several miles behind.

No wonder Kate acts like she's above the law. Apparently, she is.

HIGH-SPEED PURSUIT

"When it is my time, the time that God has chosen to take me,
I will go no matter what!!!! There is no changing His plans for me.
It all comes back to the fact that He is in charge and in control, not
me!!!! And actually, that is comforting to me!"
– *Kate Gosselin*

Kate Gosselin is a dangerous driver. I know this because I have witnessed her doing all of these dangerous things:

- Driving the wrong way on a one-way street through a residential neighborhood.

- Driving with no headlights at night.

- Driving at very high speeds.

- Swerving across three lanes of traffic to exit…at high speeds.

- Making U-turns across two lanes of traffic.

- Speeding through residential neighborhoods.

- Running stop signs.

- Running red lights.

- Driving while talking on the phone and drinking coffee. With her kids in car.

Some will excuse Kate's dangerous driving by blaming it on the horrible paparazzi that were following her to see where she was going or to photograph what she was doing. That is a terrible excuse. The paparazzi's presence may have annoyed her, but being irritated was no reason to put herself or her children in danger. There was nothing forcing her to drive so carelessly. Also, Kate's dangerous driving did not only occur when she was being followed.

One of my greatest fears for the Gosselins is that this story is going to end in tragedy – for one or more of the kids – because of Kate's driving and her belief that God has a time in mind for her and everyone else to die, and that time and place is predetermined. If she believes she can do nothing to alter that plan, she will continue to think nothing of driving erratically at speeds over 100 mph – with kids in the car – while talking on her cell phone. The phone is always in her hand when she's driving, as is her coffee cup. I have seen her driving at very high speeds while talking on her phone with her left hand and holding a coffee and the steering wheel with her right hand.

100 MPH + Cell Phone + Coffee + Children screaming = DISASTER

Kate drives in and out of traffic at high speeds, switching lanes and cutting other drivers off without signaling. She has driven at night without headlights to lose the paparazzi. Worst of all, she speeds through residential neighborhoods where other people's children are outside playing, sometimes driving the wrong way on a tight one-way street. I have seen it many times. Back when there was still interest in Kate Gosselin, that maneuver was always her sure-fire way to lose anyone following her because she knew that the paps would back off when she hit the neighborhoods. Nobody wanted to be responsible for helping Kate injure or kill herself, her children, or anyone else.

I have taken photos and video through the windshield of my car, and the paps have done so as well, showing the speedometer along with Kate's car in view in front of me – driving in excess of 100 mph, often just to get to the post office or tanning salon.

The paparazzi, which she says she hates so much, were even concerned about her driving habits and couldn't understand why she would take such risks. When I was in Las Vegas with Jon, one of the paps called to tell me to please pass on to Jon that **they had followed Kate at 110 mph that day with three of the sextuplets in the car**. They didn't report her or release their video. They only wanted me to tell Jon so that maybe he could talk to her about it. When even the aggressive, low-life paparazzi are concerned for you, you have a problem. Even they know when to back off and be safe.

It doesn't matter if you have Mario Andretti driving your car for you, you can't control what other, less-careful drivers will do on the road, and all it takes is one miscue for you to lose everything. So why would Kate increase the probability that something tragic could happen by driving so recklessly? It isn't worth risking the lives of your children.

I have followed Kate many times, but one early-morning experience sticks out in my mind as an example of Kate's evasive tactics. I was out looking for Kate one night and into the early morning. Jon was at the house with the kids, and Kate's whereabouts were unknown. It was a big deal back then to try and pinpoint where exactly Kate would go when she was not at the house with the kids during Jon's custody time. I had pretty much given up and called it a night when, at 1 AM, I spotted Kate's Land Cruiser in a local hotel parking lot on the way back to my house. I decided to wait and see what was going on and, sure enough, at 4 AM, Kate left the hotel with a police escort. The rest of this story is in the "Men in Blue" chapter, but this is an excerpt dealing with Kate's driving.

August 16, 2009
… The police gave her an escort out of the lot and up onto the
highway where I began to follow. She immediately gave it everything
she had and was off to the races. Two other vehicles were in pursuit
at high speeds. At least one of them had a New York plate. I was way
behind going 85mph and losing ground. I could see Kate putting her
turn signal on as though she was getting off at an exit and then
turning off her headlights to try and fool the paps. She must be
crazy to be driving like this at high speeds, in the dark. I kept
with them as far as I could before she lost me around Premise Made
Candies which is very, very close to I78 so I'm concluding that she
was headed to NYC. It takes about 2 and a half hours from here which
would get her there around 7 am. She may be taping another interview
or something else today.

Here are some more excerpts from my notes on Kate's driving:

Jon and Kate Gosselin PA Reporting
October 2009
… There were two paps and two reporters circling around today, hoping
to get comments from Kate about the TLC situation. She stayed in
hiding though. There was no sign of her at all until I saw a black
limo going up the road toward the house. I quickly drove up in time
to see it pull up to the front door and Kate and Steve came out of
the house. The driver got out of the car but Steve beat him to the
door and opened it for Kate and got in behind her and closed it
himself. They left the property with two paps and me following them.
He drove pretty slowly at first because of the winding country roads
but when he reached the highway, he sped up to 75 in a 55. They went
to Kate's UPS store and Steve got out and went inside and got her
mail. He glared at me when he walked back to the car. He wasn't happy
about being followed. Once back out on the highway, the driver got
back up to high speed again and was weaving in and out of traffic.
After thirty minutes, we ended up at xxxxxxxxx School where Mady and
Cara go. The limo pulled up near one of the buildings and Steve got
out and went inside and a few minutes later, he came out with the
girls and loaded them into the limo. Kate still hadn't been seen at
this point. We drove and chased for another hour at high speeds,
going over 100 mph at times and I fell behind the paps in their
sports cars. I was driving an older SUV and I got hung up at a
traffic light after everyone else ran through it by about eight
seconds. After that I never caught back up to them. I was in contact
with both paps though the whole time by phone. They got on the PA
turnpike heading toward Pittsburgh. I got on about five minutes
behind them and headed back. There was no way I could stay with the
chase. On the turnpike, they reached speeds over 105 mph according to
both paps.
They pulled over at a rest stop halfway between Reading and
Pittsburgh and everyone got out to go inside for a break. Steve told
the driver to stay with the car while they went inside. He also
looked at the paps like "WTF are you still doing following us??"
The driver told the paps that both Kate and Steve were very rude.
Steve gave him an address to plug into his GPS and told him that's
where we're going and then he had the divider put up so they had
privacy. The driver said, "these people suck. They're total assholes"
Once back in the car, the chase was on again — again going over 100
mph weaving in and out of traffic with two kids in the car.

They finally ended up in Pittsburgh at a restaurant. The paps took pictures of them going inside but then decided they'd had enough and began the five-hour trip back home. Both paps were very pissed off that they wasted the trip. They speculated that Kate maybe had a speaking engagement tonight or tomorrow in Pittsburgh or Ohio.

Jon and Kate Gosselin PA Reporting
October 2009
… Next stop was the dry cleaners in Wyomissing. It was very brief and no pictures were taken because of the location and it being a drive-thru dry cleaners. Now is when the fun began though. After doing a U-turn on the busy street, Kate got on the gas and began her quest to lose the paps so she could leave Reading for wherever she goes when she's away from home. The paps were on her as she went 60 in a 35 speed limit until Kate went into a residential neighborhood and was racing around corners and up and down tight, tree-lined streets where children were playing. The three-car paparazzi caravan backed off at this point and Kate made her getaway.

Jon and Kate Gosselin PA Reporting
October 2009
… More aggressive driving at high speeds, going 80 in a 55 mph zone and she led me to Pier 1 Imports for shopping of all things. She stayed inside for an hour shopping.

Jon and Kate Gosselin PA Reporting
October 2009
…After ten minutes at the gas station, Kate made a dangerous move out of the parking lot and across two lanes of traffic to try to lose the paps. Horns blew as she drove through, nearly getting into an accident. There was no reason for the erratic driving because she just drove the ten minutes straight home after that.

Jon and Kate Gosselin PA Reporting
October 2009
… At a little before 8:30am, a woman in a white van showed up at the house and went inside. About twenty minutes later Kate left the property in her Land Cruiser followed by the paps. Kate took off at high speeds on the highway driving in and out of cars and getting off and on various exits. The paps were still on her until she started speeding through a residential neighborhood and running stop signs. They backed off of her a bit and she ended up losing them.

Jon and Kate Gosselin PA Reporting
November 2009
… She left the FedEx lot and sped back up State Hill Road toward home. The speed limit is 40 mph and she was going 55 mph approaching the blind hill at the State Hill boat launch parking lot. A pickup pulling a boat pulled out in front of her crossing her lane and she barely avoided hitting him. She swerved to the right and just got around him and kept going. I was following — not chasing. She drives erratically all the time. It's going to end badly one of these days. I hope I'm not there when it happens.
On the winding country road leading to her house, she drives into the other lane going around S turns. Very dangerous.

Jon and Kate Gosselin PA Reporting
November 2009
… A few minutes after she left, Kate went to the garage and got her
Land Cruiser and came flying out of the front gate trying to lose the
paparazzi from the start. She went way over the speed limit along the
winding country roads around her house and ran two stop signs along
the way.
She bypassed her usual first stop at Dunkin Donuts and got on the
highway and sped to the UPS store. She parked beneath the sign that
reads No Parking Fire Lane, facing the wrong direction. I parked
right behind her. It seemed like the thing to do at the time.
… It was now almost 3 pm and she had to get back to the house to get
the van to pickup the kids. We raced out of the shopping center and
headed toward her house, when she made a very dangerous U Turn across
four lanes and headed in the opposite direction. Three miles of
aggressive driving later and we were at the Dunkin Donuts drive thru
getting coffee. I waited for her at the exit and followed her the
rest of the way back to the house. She unloaded all of the bags and
took everything inside. Then got the Sprinter van and headed to the
bus stop to pick up the kids.

Jon and Kate Gosselin PA Reporting
November 2009
Kate left the house at 8:15 this morning hoping to go undetected. I
just happened to be rolling by the house in a different vehicle that
she's used to seeing so she didn't see it was me initially. She sat
inside the gate until I passed and I kept going, anticipating the
direction she would be driving. In a rare change, Kate was driving
behind me for several miles. I was going ten miles an hour over the
speed limit and she was right up my butt, talking on the phone the
entire time. When we got to the highway entrance I let her pass me
and then proceeded to follow her at speeds reaching 95 mph for the
next ninety minutes. You can't imagine what it's like to follow Kate
Gosselin for ninety minutes. You need to pretty much strap in and
pray. I broke more traffic laws and some laws of physics trying to
stay with her. She is an extremely aggressive driver and goes from
zero to 80 as fast as her Land Cruiser will allow. She did everything
she could to lose me, weaving in and out of traffic and getting off
at exits at the last second.
When we got to the Harrisburg area she was especially aggressive. She
pulled into a realtor's office and parked and then quickly drove over
a curb and back out onto the street and took off. Fortunately I
guessed right at her direction and caught up to her as she was
parking at her hairstylist — Diane's Hair Design at 3853 Derry St.
… The chase began again with more of the same evasive measures and we
ended up in Hershey Pa, driving through the attractions and up to the
Hotel Hershey. Kate drove around to the left side of the hotel where
the spa is located and stopped by the doorman/valet and talked to him
for a few seconds, then preceded to her parking space. The man
instantly started walking toward me and I knew she ratted me out so I
peeled off and drove around the building and parked in a different
lot where I could still see her car.

Jon and Kate Gosselin PA Reporting
November 2009
It was now ten minutes to bus drop off and Kate pulled out of
Starbucks and turned right to head towards home. I didn't know what
she was doing and I guess, neither did she because she drove a
hundred feet and then suddenly made a U-Turn across four lanes of
traffic and went to the bus stop. I had to wait a few minutes to turn
around and I don't know why she would make such a dangerous turn but
that's Kate. She's a very aggressive driver.

Jon and Kate Gosselin PA Reporting
December 2009
The paps shot her as she was coming out of the nail salon and into
her car. Then she made another trip to Dunkin Donuts for a large
coffee. She was gesturing to the person at the drive thru window
about the pap who was standing right in front of her car. He got the
hint and backed off. When leaving the Dunkin Donuts lot, she pulled a
very dangerous move, cutting into oncoming traffic so the paps and I
couldn't get right out behind her. Horns were blowing but we kept up
pursuit. She got on the highway heading toward Lancaster and after a
very speedy 80-95 mph chase, we ended up at the kids school in
Lancaster.
… Repeat the 90 mph car chase home, but this time with a child in the
car.

Jon and Kate Gosselin PA Reporting
December 2009
… A few minutes after Noon, Kate went flying out of the gate and sped
down the road toward Wyomissing shopping area. She was going 70 in a
40 mph zone and passed a car illegally on a single-lane road with
dangerous curves. All of that crazy driving and she ended up at her
bank in Shillington.. The bank branch closed at Noon but a woman from
the bank came outside and met her at her car and gave her a large
envelope. Kate opened it in the car and looked at some papers for a
few minutes, then got on her cell phone and talked for five minutes
before driving away.

Jon and Kate Gosselin PA Reporting
December 2009
…A second nanny and a housekeeper were all at the house early today.
The kids are off from school for Christmas vacation. Kate got in her
Land Cruiser and left the house at 8 am this morning and headed
toward Lancaster. She drove at speeds reaching 90 mph on Rt. 222,
even though there were patches of ice on the roads. She didn't call
the police so I'm guessing this was just a routine trip somewhere but
I couldn't keep up with her and lost her near the Park City Mall. I
drove through the mall lot several times looking for her with no
luck.

...A nanny arrived at the house at 1 pm and went inside. Kate left the house thirty minutes later by herself, driving very fast along the winding country roads near her home. As she got closer to town, she was driving 70 mph in a 40 mph zone trying to lose the paparazzi (or just being Kate.) Her high-speed chase ended back at Planet Nails in Wyomissing where she stopped briefly the day before. This time however she was inside for over an hour getting extensive work done on her fingernails. She came out looking fabulous and ran to her car and jumped in and sped home. When she got there she went to the garage and pulled out the Sprinter van and pulled it right up to the front door where she normally parks it to block the paps view of the entrance to the house. She then went inside and came out a few minutes later with the boys. It looked like she was trying to sneak them into her car. She left the property and again was driving very fast over the highway and toward her UPS store.

From the Paps: "Kate came flying by at excessive speed and reached speeds over 100 mph in traffic heading toward Lancaster. She continued past Lancaster and got off at the Elizabethtown exit, trying to lose the paps the entire time. She pulled into a residential neighborhood and into a driveway to a house and quickly jumped out and shuttled the boys inside."

Since October 2009, Kate has been cited four times for traffic violations. This article provides details about those citations.

Kate Gosselin Cited Twice Since July

Updated: Wednesday, 14 Sep 2011, 3:37 PM EDT Published: Wednesday, 14 Sep 2011, 3:29 PM EDT

Fox 29 has learned that Reading, Pa.-area reality TV mom Kate Gosselin has been cited twice since July for traffic offenses, including an incident where she was driving 88 miles per hour.

Traffic court dockets show Gosselin, cited under her legal name Katie I. Gosselin, was pulled over by Pennsylvania state police on Sept. 11, 2011 in South Londonderry Township in Lebanon County.

She was charged under a statute regulating roadways. That case is still pending and Gosselin received a traffic citation.

On August 9th, Katie I. Gosselin was pulled over by state police in Brecknock Township in Lancaster County. She was charged with driving 88 miles per hour in a 65 mile per hour zone.

That case was settled with a guilty plea in court and Gosselin was not present at the hearing. She paid fines of about $164.00.

There were no details on passengers in Gosselin's vehicle in the two recent incidents.

Gosselin has two other traffic citations since 2009.

On Feb. 26, 2010, Katie I. Gosselin was pulled over by state police based in Gettysburg after she was speeding at 73 miles per hour in a 55-mph zone.

That case was also settled with a fine of about $155.

On Oct. 30, 2009, Katie I. Gosselin was cited for an incident related to obedience to traffic control devices in Adams County. She pled guilty and paid another fine.

The last two incidents were documented on Web sites like TMZ. In the 2009 incident, TMZ said Gosselin was reportedly doing 70 miles per hour in a 55 miles per hour zone. TMZ said her eight children were in the SUV at the time.

Under Pennsylvania's points system for traffic violations, speeding tickets can give a violator between 2 and 5 points for each offense. After a driver compiles 6 points, the state requires testing and other remedial measures.

Gosselin should be under the 6-point threshold.

Kate can't blame her dangerous driving on the paparazzi anymore. They no longer follow her, but her reckless driving habits continue. Given Kate's driving record, it is completely hypocritical for her to dispense driving advice to others such as she does in this Twitter exchange:

xxxxx @Kateplusmy8 night Kate :-). Driving myself to school in the morning for the first time since passing my test on Friday :D wish me luck xD x

omg Ellie. Drive carefully... I remember those days. Cars are weapons! Always remember that! Be safe;) xo

Another fan tweeted:

xxxxx @Kateplusmy8 U should have had a "tweet twaffic" party w/us while U waited! We could have entertained U! :)

while driving? Oh never!

Kate needs to follow her own advice.

UNDER THE INFLUENCE

Sources of mine who are very close to the family, and who have been inside the house with Kate, have told me that Kate is a big drinker. I have been told things like:

"Wine is her drink of choice to take the edge off."

> "She drinks the cheap stuff. She regularly drinks an entire bottle of wine herself at night before going to bed. She also drinks wine during the day."

> "Kate has staffers buy the wine for her and bring it to the house in bags so nobody would know about it."

> "Kate was a big drinker at the height of her fame during the show. She was often blurry-eyed drunk."

I have seen pictures of an obviously drunk Kate Gosselin. I have never personally seen Kate drinking, but I have seen her recycling bin, and there have always been plenty of discarded wine bottles in it. In fairness to Kate, many parents have a drink or more at the end of the day to calm their nerves. If I were in Kate's shoes, I'd probably drink myself to sleep at night, too. But here's the difference: we other parents have not lied about drinking in order to market ourselves to a Christian fan base; we have not branded ourselves publicly as an example of great parenting; and we have not been interviewed stating over and over again that we are selfless and everything we do is for our kids. The fact of the matter is that no one would care much at all whether Kate likes to drink if she, herself, hadn't lied about it, and if she drinks responsibly.

Kate's drinking is only relevant because, given her volatile nature, there is concern about what would happen if she were drinking while being angry with the children or, possibly more worrisome, while driving with the kids in the car at her usual very high speeds.

Kate has said in the past that she doesn't drink at all. On March 19, 2011, while she was in New York City for a "pre-birthday celebration," a paparazzo that was shooting video asked Kate if he could buy her a shot for her birthday. She replied, "I don't do shots." (And yet, I have a photo of Kate pounding shots.) The pap asked her what she drinks, and she answered, "wine." So it just begs the question: Why all the lying about drinking? Oh, right. Image is everything.

The subject of drinking also comes up in some of Kate's emails. Once again, these are only interesting because of Kate's insistence early on that she doesn't drink or that she just drinks wine.

In December of 2008, Kate emailed Gina Neild and told her she was "Still not sleeping." She said she was listening to her music and still couldn't get over "those delish choc martinis". Kate said, "oh baby, keep those away from me! :)"

On Thursday, January 1, 2009, at 8:31 AM, Kate sent an email to Gina assuring her that she was going to "totally behave on this occasion!" Kate continued by saying, "No more drinking" and she had "drank my fill for a long while…" She told Gina that her New Year's resolution was "no more drinking!"

Later that same morning, Gina responded to Kate, saying that she had a chocolate martini waiting for her. Kate replied: "Oh man don't tempt me!!!! … But you know my new years resolution…..I wonder how long that will last?! :)"

Here are a couple of other things Kate said about drinks and drinking in emails: Actually ate yesterday…. And not planning to eat much on Sunday…. So darn yummy! Just drinking… Lightly!" and "We tried out our pom martini recipe last night… It's perfection!"

And here are a couple of examples of Kate tweeting to people who have mentioned something about wine to her:

> xxxxx @Kateplusmy8 and I've heard red wine is good for u n moderation; Awesome!

> **My rare treat... Merlots lately. I'm a light weight so a bottle lasts a looonggg time lol**

> xxxxx @Kateplusmy8 We are joining you for movie night. "Hugo" at our house. A glass of wine in place of popcorn. Enjoy your night.

> **hey! Me too! A very rare glass here.. Had to wonder if wine was spoiled, lol! I think it's ok... Loving movie so far!**

These are both examples of Kate-speak. She often says the exact opposite of the truth, even if nobody asks. She makes a point of acting like she doesn't drink much by saying things such as, "My rare treat," and "a bottle lasts a looonggg time." In the same way she often says, "No lie," her use of the word "rare" in both these tweets tells us that it isn't a rare occurrence at all. But Kate did have a professional "Media Trainer" and publicist for years feeding her the EXACT wording to use in any given situation. She must think that if you repeat a lie often enough, it becomes the truth.

RACISM

"I dont c color"
– Kate Gosselin

Kate Gosselin is, at best, ignorant, and, at worst, a racist. She would disagree with this assessment, of course, because she believes she can do no wrong. She is either too self-engrossed as to be completely unaware of her intolerant and judgmental behavior, or she just doesn't care. Neither of these reasons excuses her behavior. In June of 2012, Kate put any accusations that she is racist to rest through this Twitter exchange:

you beter retweet me.. I've tweeted you twice & you keep ignoring! #racistpeoplethesedays

REALLY??!Wow!A busy mom misses tweet& I'm accused of being racist?Harsh! I dont c color–God made us all! Have a fun day!

Kate claims she doesn't "c" color. If this is true, why then does she always feel compelled to describe people based on their ethnic appearance, even when such descriptions are completely unnecessary? These are some examples of Kate's less than stellar moments as they pertain to the differences among us.

"BLACK MAN"

This is a paraphrased excerpt from Kate's journal:

October 2006
The Gosselins were in New York City on their way to the American Girl store and they were in a hurry. Unfortunately there was a Hispanic parade right outside the store and the streets were barricaded!!!!
Then, when they got to the store, they had to wait in a long line with everyone else waiting for their reservations. Kate said there was a big bodyguard (black man) who told them they would have to go to the end of the line and Kate said she wishes she could have seen his face when they were waved to the front of the line past everyone else!!!!

I'm not sure how calling the bodyguard out as a "black man" had any relevance here. But it is true to form. Kate Gosselin has a habit of identifying people by their color or nationality, even when it is irrelevant to the story. She did this on page 35 of her first book, *Multiple Blessings*, when she talked about her second infertility doctor and said she saw "the concentration in the deep dark eyes of my African doctor as he himself tried to remain calm as the images unfolded."
Why did Kate have to call him her "African" doctor? He's a doctor in Wyomissing, Pennsylvania. She didn't travel to Cape Town, South Africa, to see him. Does she refer to everyone in her life by their color or country of origin?
The following exchange on Twitter pretty much sums up Kate's ignorant nature. This tweeter is the only black woman I can remember Kate ever responding too. Perhaps Kate feels that black people need to be singled out and spoken to in a different manner.

I am most grateful for my babies Jacob12Austin12Jayden10Kayla10Isaac9Gavin8Hannah8Abraham7Liam2 & my husband Brandon soblessed.

you a supa momma! :) I think we could be friends who reallllly understand each other lol

"you a supa momma?" I'm not usually nitpicky, and I tried to read this several different ways to give Kate the benefit of the doubt, but I can only see this as being very racist. If you look at this woman's Twitter feed from the same time as Kate's response to her, you'll see how articulate she is and how she actually spells out her words and uses complete sentences, unlike Kate. This woman sounds like a very well-spoken, thoughtful, intelligent person. Yet Kate responds to her like she's talking to some hip-hop or rap person. I don't recall ever seeing Kate respond to anyone like that.

Kate Gosselin just can't put a filter on her mouth, or in this case, her fingers. This is what happens when Discovery's Laurie Goldberg is no longer around to put words into Kate's mouth for her.

"MR CHOCOLATE"

Besides Steve Neild, the Gosselins had another bodyguard who accompanied them on trips for filming. I met him and spoke to him several times while working for *US Weekly*. (I never talked to him for this book or for my *US Weekly* reporting. He was always completely professional and loyal to the family.) To give you a physical description, this bodyguard is a very large, athletic-looking black man whose muscular build actually makes him look like a bodyguard - unlike Steve. Thanks to Kate, the Gosselin children referred to him as "Mr. Chocolate." She must have thought that it would be cute to have her kids calling him that name. It would have been interesting to find out how he felt about it.

"ASIAN BOYS AND GIRLS"

Kate Gosselin has eight part-Asian children. Her ex-husband Jon is half Korean. What would ever possess her to think that her being photographed making a "slant-eye" pose with a big smile on her face could look anything other than disrespectful? This is an excerpt taken from my *US Weekly* reporting. Kate tells the kids that they are Asian boys and girls? Not just boys and girls? There is a big difference between celebrating your child's cultural and ethnic heritage and making fun of it.

```
Jon and Kate Gosselin PA Reporting
November 2009
        Jon got back home just in time to get the girls loaded up to
take them to a movie this afternoon with Judy the nanny. Judy had the
girl's hair done in pigtails and they looked so cute and were very
excited about seeing the movie. The boys had seen it a week earlier
they told me. They were seeing Cloudy with a Chance of Meatballs in
3D.
```

The paps followed Jon and were waiting at the theater entrance when Jon walked in with Hannah and Alexis. They walked inside and the girls were hamming it up for the paps videotaping them. Jon bought the tickets and gave the girls their 3D glasses and told them not to open them until they got inside the theater. Hannah opened hers right away and put them on and they were imitating Joel from a week ago saying **in a very Asian accent, "Mommy says I'm an Asian boyyyyy. I'm an Asian Girlllll!" over and over.**

"MY OWN PERSONAL SWEATSHOP"

Upon giving birth to the sextuplets and raising her total of offspring to eight, Kate joked, "Now I can open my own personal sweatshop some day."

"CHINA DOLLS"

When discussing her children's Asian genetics in an FAQ episode of *Jon & Kate Plus Ei8ht*, the interviewer asked Kate about the kids looking more like Jon. Kate went a bit overboard, as is typical for Kate.

> Producer's Question: "Oh, this is a good one. All eight of your children have the Korean characteristics. Is that common?"
>
> Kate: "Um, I don't know cause my kids are my kids, but I do know that when I was pregnant with Cara and Mady, Jon's mom said to me one time, I hope you don't expect your kids to look like you and I said, well no, actually I was hoping that they would look like Jon, picturing the little China doll babies, and um, because she said that the Korean, the Asian gene is very dominant, and she was right.
>
> Producer's Question: "Everyone in the family is Asian except for you. Does that bother you?"
>
> Kate: "Not at all. I love it. The more Asian they can look, the better, **and I actually wish I was Korean. And we all know that."** "I don't know. I think they're beautiful, and my kids are gorgeous and I don't care how they look, they're my kids and, I've never once cared that they didn't look like me."

Let's forget for a moment Kate's crass "little China doll babies" comment, and focus on her answer to the producer's question of whether it bothers her that everyone in the family is Asian except her. First, Kate says that it doesn't bother her at all, but in the very next breath she contradicts herself and overcompensates by saying, "I actually wish I was Korean." Then she flips back to saying that she has "never once cared that they didn't look like me." Her flip-flopping shows either a complete lack of genuineness (which is entirely consistent with her past words and actions), or a complete lack of cognitive ability.

Before leaving this topic, we should also examine Kate's comment that the "more Asian they can look, the better." Given her track record, it would not be a stretch to think she means that the kids looking more Asian would make them more interesting and marketable for television. As much as Kate likes to engage in verbal gymnastics, the meanings behind her words are usually completely transparent.

THE NANNY & PLANET NAILS

This entry from my *US Weekly* reporting speaks to how Kate stereotypes people based on their race:

```
Jon and Kate Gosselin PA Reporting
September 2009
        A source tells me that Jon hired the main nanny, but Kate
likes her a lot because "she's Asian and she works 24/7 and she knows
how to do hair and nails. Kate loves having Asians working for her.
That's why she goes to Planet Nails. It's owned by Asians and she
thinks they don't get involved in other people's business and they
wouldn't talk to reporters about her."
```

"OUR KOREAN FOOD MAKER"

In the "Sextuplets Turn 3" episode of *Jon & Kate Plus Ei8ht*, Jon proudly introduces his grandmother to the TLC audience.

"This is my grandmother, Gammy," Jon says.

And, of course, the words that spring from Kate's mouth when introducing Jon's sweet little grandma to the TLC viewing audience is this:

"This is our Korean food maker."

Kate is always so very nice and respectful.

"RETARDED"

Some people believe we have gone overboard in trying to be politically correct. While this may be true, it is still always best to avoid speaking words that could hurt someone's feelings. It is probably pretty safe to say that using the word "retarded" in a derogatory manner is not acceptable and is thought to be particularly insensitive. Was Kate's use of this word in her following journal entry, then, just an uncharacteristic slip, or is it a word that she throws around without consideration?

January 2007
Kate was talking about making an appointment with the doctor but she wasn't happy with them so she referred to them as a retarded practice.

Kate has also used the word "retarded" to describe people who get on her nerves or annoy her in some way. She did this in an email mentioned earlier.
In April of 2012, Kate accepted a paid speaking job at Camp Barnabas, which is a Christian camp that provides life-changing opportunities to people with special needs. Her cavalier and insensitive use of the word "retarded" calls into question her motivation for taking this job. Was her heart truly in the right place, understanding the particular challenges of special needs individuals, or was she just interested in padding her wallet? Her words and actions make everything she does suspect.
Someone who has known Kate for most of her life, who wishes to remain anonymous, said this about Kate:

"If you don't look like her, Kate considers you a second-class citizen."

WORK PERMITS AND THE 85/15 SPLIT

In 2010, Pennsylvania State Representative Thomas Murt formally complained to then State Attorney General Tom Corbett and officials in the Department of Labor & Industry (L&I) that the Gosselin children lacked the proper work permits to appear on television in Pennsylvania, and couldn't do so until they turned seven. This came about in response to rising concern and criticism that the Gosselin children were being exploited and working illegally. The L&I conducted an investigation into the matter, and their findings are summarized in the following Associated Press article.

Pennsylvania opts for no legal action against 'Jon & Kate Plus 8' producers over child-labor issue.
Published: Wednesday, April 14, 2010, 3:46 PM

The Associated Press/file
HORSHAM — Child-labor permits should have been obtained for the children appearing on the TLC television show "Jon & Kate Plus 8," but the state will not take legal action against the producers, Pennsylvania regulators have concluded.
No action will be taken provided a portion of the proceeds from the now-canceled reality show is put into a trust fund for Jon and Kate Gosselin's children and child-labor permits are obtained for future filming, the state Department of Labor and Industry said in a five-page letter obtained Wednesday by The Associated Press. The letter was signed by a government attorney and sent to Figure 8 Films and Discovery Talent Services last month.

It's important to not that we did an investigation and we made sure the children were not in any danger or endangered as a result of the work they were doing," said Labor and Industry press secretary Troy Thompson.

The agency ruled that the children were employed under the state's Child Labor Law because of the direction they sometimes received, because of their continued participation in the series and because the Gosselins and others were paid for the show.

It said that at least 15 percent of the gross proceeds, due to the children, must be placed in trust funds until they reach the age of 18 or unless needed for their safety, education, welfare or health. **Laurie Goldberg, a spokeswoman for Discovery Talent Services and TLC, said Wednesday the trust was established in November** and that the amount placed in trust exceeds the 15 percent level. Thompson said the new stipulations must be met or labor regulators may prosecute in the future. The letter said that **Figure 8 Films, TLC, Discovery Talent Services, the Gosselins and other affiliated parties all deny there were violations of the child-labor law or that permits were required.**

Laurie Goldberg said Discovery Talent Services and TLC have complied with state labor regulations and continue to do so. **She said they agreed to get the permits even though they maintain they are not required under state law.** "These allegations are either completely inaccurate or a distorted representation for maximum attention," she said.

After the ruling came down, Laurie Goldberg, spokeswoman for Discovery/TLC, continued to argue the company line that they were not required to get work permits for the children; this, despite the fact that the agency had determined and ruled that the children were, indeed, working.

Although they were found to be in violation of Pennsylvania Child Labor Law, Discovery/TLC and Figure 8 Films got off scot-free, with no fines imposed. That gave the appearance that the great Commonwealth of Pennsylvania didn't want to ruffle any feathers or jeopardize future filming projects. Film and television industry projects bring in big bucks to states; therefore, many states work very hard to provide tax breaks and other incentives to attract production companies. It certainly wouldn't look very inviting if Pennsylvania had decided to take legal action against Discovery.

There is a question about whether it had ever occurred to anyone that the kids needed permits to film *Jon & Kate Plus Ei8ht*. Discovery/TLC continued to hide behind their excuse that they were filming "reality." Kate pleaded ignorance and said she "didn't know they needed them" in the first place.

It is important to understand that Kate Gosselin was not only controlling, but was in total control of anything and everything having to do with the family business. She did the talking and the negotiating and the deciding. She gave the orders, and Jon went along and did what he was told – or else. So when it came time to sign the family's first big contract with Discovery, Kate was in her glory. Contrary to Kate's statements that she didn't know she needed to obtain work permits, and that nobody ever told her to get them, and she "thought Discovery would take care of them…," the bottom line is that Discovery did, in fact, tell Kate and Jon that they were responsible for obtaining any necessary permits and/or licenses. Discovery went so far as to build specific wording into the contract with the Gosselins – which Kate signed.

I have all of the Gosselin family contracts. The exact wording regarding the work permits, from the contract dated October 4, 2006, is: "Family has obtained and will maintain at all times during the service term (and any extension thereof) any and all work permits, immigration clearances necessary to enable family to perform services hereunder." It is wording that was designed to protect Discovery in case any legal issues arose from the Gosselin sweatshop, which was about to open for business

Kate Gosselin decided to thumb her nose at the legal system and forgo fulfilling her obligation to the Network to obtain work permits for the kids, as contracted, because she was arrogant, and she wanted to give the illusion that her children weren't working at all, and were "just going about their daily lives, doing what they would normally do in a day."

Discovery, of course, knew better. They knew the kids would be working. They knew that "reality" television required more than reality. When they installed permanent studio lighting in the Gosselin's house for filming, it was one of many telltale signs that the house had become a fully functional television studio. There would be schedules; direction; takes and retakes; lines to be read; and coaching, prodding and trickery to get the kids to do what the producers wanted. There would be product placement and cameo appearances, and a host of manufactured storylines. Yes, Discovery knew the kids would be working and that they would need permits to do so. Their crack legal team would surely have researched Pennsylvania's child labor laws, including age restrictions on filming, so it worked out well that they could place the responsibility for the permits elsewhere.

In addition to addressing the work permits, the L&I ruling specified that a trust fund had to be established for the kids. Kate had never set aside any money AT ALL for the children to get from seven seasons of giving up their childhoods and being forced to work. She was legally forced to do so when the Murt investigation began, but she did it very reluctantly. The trust fund was set up just two months before the Murt hearing. I have a statement from the trust fund account. Here is some basic information about it, including the name of the account:

"THE CHILDREN'S HOUSEHOLD" at Kate's P.O. Box in Sinking Spring, PA.
LPL Financial
Brown Funds

Gosselin Childrens IRREV Trust – Conception Date: February 17, 2010

Read that carefully. Conception Date: February 17, 2010. So it would appear that one hundred and sixteen (116) episodes of *Jon & Kate Plus Ei8ht* were filmed with absolutely zero money being put aside for the children. Only twenty-seven (27) episodes of *Kate Plus Ei8ht* were filmed after February 17, 2010.
Now look more carefully at this part of the L&I ruling:

> "...at least 15 percent of the gross proceeds, due to the children, must be placed in trust funds until they reach the age of 18 or **unless needed for their safety, education, welfare or health.**"

Guess who gets to decide on the "need" to withdraw the kids' money for "safety, education, welfare or health" necessities. That would be Kate Gosselin, and there is no system in place to question her as to why she's removing the children's money. Just her word. It is like the fox guarding the hen house.

The only reason Kate Gosselin has her wealth today is because she was paid handsomely for allowing her eight children to be filmed and exploited for our entertainment. She couldn't, and can't, earn a living from TV herself because she has no talent and is supremely unmarketable. Her spinoff solo show, *Twist of Kate*, never even made it out of the testing stages. A TLC employee told me off the record "It was a total failure from the get-go because she is terribly boring and annoying and nobody wanted to see just Kate Gosselin. They want to see the kids."

And yet those kids have almost nothing to show, financially, for their years of work. Even though Kate was forced to set up a trust fund, the sad truth is that, if only 15% was put aside for the kids, it means that out of every $1,000 dollars the kids earned from filming, Kate got $850, while each Gosselin child got $18.75…even less if Kate decided to take any of it to fulfill their "needs."

Kate got $850 per $1,000.

Each Gosselin child possibly got $18.75. If they were lucky.

DANCING WITH THE STARS . . . AND KATE

When Kate signed on to do *Dancing With The Stars* (DWTS for short), there was a lot of talk in the media and on the blogs about Kate being away from her children for extended periods of time while practicing and flying back and forth to Los Angeles to film the show.

Kate nipped that talk right in the bud and declared in television interviews that she would only be away from the kids for three days a week **at the most**. She would rehearse at home, with the kids there to support her, and then she would leave on Sunday night to fly to Los Angeles and return home on a late flight after the Tuesday filming. Three days. Not a bad gig for a single working mother of eight, who would be banking about $300,000-$500,000 for the short-term job.

While the plan sounded good on paper, it never even came close to happening the way Kate spelled it out. I was at the Gosselin house all day, every day during the DWTS period, and I kept close tabs and detailed notes on Kate's comings and goings. It wasn't pretty if you were one of the Gosselin kids hoping to spend time with your mother, that's for sure.

The Sunday to Tuesday trips quickly turned into Saturday to Wednesday excursions, and sometimes the flight back home from Los Angeles would skip Pennsylvania all together and take Kate straight to New York City for rehearsing, or for stylist to the stars Ted Gibson to spend an entire day working on her hair for several thousand dollars. It seemed evident to me that Kate was looking for any excuse she could find to not be with her kids.

The saddest part was the obligatory photo op in the front yard, in front of the paps, where Kate would appear to be playing with and spending quality time with her children. I say photo op because the fun romps in the front yard, in front of the cameras, where the pictures turned up in every tabloid and entertainment website, lasted about three or four minutes – which was just about long enough for Kate to pat the kids on the head like dogs and have photos taken to show the world that she was, indeed, home with them like she promised she would be. Those photos, like Kate, lied.

These are my notes from all day, every day, during the *Dancing With The Stars* days at the Gosselin house.

```
Jon & Kate Gosselin PA Reporting
March 4 & 5, 2010
```
- Kate has been away from her kids for two weeks.
- After Jon left on Sunday, the kids have been with nannies and sitters all week while Kate is seeking fame.

Kate hasn't seen her kids since Saturday, February 20th. She left the house at 6 am on Sunday morning. Jon took over custody at 7:30 am that day. Jon left the house and kids on Sunday, February 28th so the kids have been without either parent all week. They've been with Judy and various babysitters and helpers.

Jon & Kate Gosselin PA Reporting
March 6, 2010

- Kate arrived home sometime overnight on Friday night. She and Steve went to Maryland from NYC in a limo.
- Judy the nanny arrived at 11:15 on Saturday morning to relieve Kate of her parental duties.
- Two DWTS people arrived at the Gosselin house just before 11:30.
- Tony the dance partner arrived at 11:35, driving himself in his Porsche Carrera.
- The kids played outside most of the day with nannies while Kate and Tony rehearsed in the basement.
- The two DWTS staffers left the house at 6:30 pm. Tony and a second nanny where still there at 8:45 pm when I got removed from the street by police.
- Tony is staying at the Homewood Suites where Kate stayed often — not in the apartment above the garage.
- Dance rehearsal resumed at 8 am today (Sunday) with Judy at the house taking care of the kids.

Kate arrived back home sometime overnight on Friday night. She left NYC with Steve Neild in a limo at 11:30 am on Friday and I'm speculating that they had to go to Maryland first to drop Steve off and for Kate to pick up her car. I don't know what they did between NYC and Kate arriving back home.
The kids would normally be in bed at 9 pm on a Friday night so I'm guessing that Kate didn't see them until they woke up on Saturday morning, usually around 7 am. That gave Kate only a few hours to get reacquainted with them before handing them over to Judy who arrived at the house at 11:15 am.
A few minutes before 11:30 am, a white rental car with Mass. plates came to the house with two people in it. A twenty-something blonde got out of the driver's side and went to the front door to ring the bell while a dark-haired twenty-something guy stayed in the passenger seat waiting. Kate came to the front door wearing a skin-tight, light blue tank top and directed them to go around the house and enter through the basement entrance. The blonde went back to the car to grab her things and the guy and they went inside through the back door. I'm guessing one was a DWTS staffer who brought music and the other, probably the guy since he stayed inside the car and acted like a primadonna was perhaps a dance instructor or choreographer. They brought a few bags with them and a rolling suitcase. Inside the bags I could see (through binoculars) a box of triscuits, some Starbucks bottled coffee drinks and some iHome products. iHome is audio equipment for plugging an iPod into. They went inside and weren't seen again until they left at 6:30 p.m.
Ten minutes later at 11:35 am, Tony the dance partner arrived in his black Porsche Carrera. He went to the front door and Kate welcomed him inside the house with a hug and a huge smile. (the other two got sent around the outside of the house. Kate must think they're not important to her.)

A minute later Tony came back outside to grab a bag from his trunk. He was wearing a long sleeve, skin-tight white shirt and tight black pants with bright white socks. He had no shoes on. (Kate made him take off his shoes) He hurried to the car and back in the house with his cargo.

Just before Noon, all eight kids and Judy came outside to play. They were allowed to play in front of the house where they could be seen and photographed. This was strange because Kate has been going out of her way to make sure the kids were hidden around back, out of the view of the paparazzi. For the next three and a half hours, the kids were outside playing in the cold. They didn't seem to mind though. Half of them had their coats off and Judy was carrying them around. They played lacrosse, rode bikes, scooters and played various other games with each other.

At 3 pm, a new nanny that I don't know came to the house to take over for Judy. They both stayed outside with the kids for twenty minutes and then Judy tried to get them to come inside by announcing "snack time, come inside". That got six of the eight running but Aaden and Joel wanted nothing to do with it. They just stopped and stared back at Judy as she was trying to get them to go in. Their defiance lasted another two minutes until Judy yelled "your mom said to get in the house." That did the trick. They ran inside.

The kids were inside for 45 minutes and then back out to play until dark. None of the dance group made an appearance outside all day. The two staffers left the property at 6:30 pm. Tony and the other nanny stayed at the house until well into the darkness. At 8:45 pm the police finally told me to leave the front of the property and that made it impossible for me to know when anyone else left because there are several ways to exit. I kept driving by the house but Kate had all the lights off up by the front door and garage and it's 100 yards from the fence to the house so you couldn't see anything.

I checked Austin's several times throughout the night to see if they ducked out for a bite to eat and I also drove by the house to make sure that Tony wasn't staying in the apartment above the garage. I was pretty sure he wouldn't be up there because I was in there a week ago with Jon and it's filled with Jon's crap and it's a mess.

I found Tony's car in the parking lot of the Homewood Suites at Midnight so we know where he's staying.

Jon & Kate Gosselin PA Reporting
March 7, 2010

- The nanny arrived at 6:30 am to help Kate with the kids.
- Tony and the crew arrived at 7:30 am to begin rehearsal.
- Rehearsal wrapped at Noon and Tony left town.
- Kate left the kids crying with a new, mean nanny at 12:20 to go tanning.
- Kate came home an hour later for five minutes and left again with Leah and Colin to go to Dick's Sporting Goods.
- Kate left the kids again to go to Target — which is connected to Dick's where she was a short time ago.
- Kids totally ignored new, mean nanny when she gave them instructions.
- Kate got home at 4:45 but the nanny stayed until 6 pm.
- Kate spoke to pap she hates for first time in 8 months. I'm sure it's in her DWTS contract to be affable.

Judy the nanny arrived at the house at 6:30 am to help Kate get the kids up and ready for the day. Tony was at the Homewood Suites until he left for Kate's house at 7:15am. He and the crew arrived at 7:30 am to begin rehearsing for the day.

Judy had the kids outside playing — in front of the house again for most of the morning. They sporadically ducked inside for potty breaks but were outside the rest of the time. At Noon, rehearsal wrapped and Tony and the crew left for the day and Judy was relieved by the new, mean nanny. She even looks mean and the kids hate her.

Kate came outside at 12:20, having not spent any time with the kids all morning, and she was about to get in her car when the little girls started yelling and crying for her to stay. I'm a good distance from the house but it's dead quiet out there and it was very easy to here the conversation. The little girls yelled "Mommy, why do you have to gooooooo?!! When will we see yoooooooou?!" And Kate said "I'll be back soon" and she got in the car and drove off.

I was certain that she was leaving her kids at home for a DWTS emergency or something very important but guess where she went? Wait for it. TANNING! She saw her kids for a few minutes today and left them with a new nanny to go tanning.

The minute Kate drove down the driveway, the mean nanny yelled at the kids to get in the house. They wanted to stay outside playing and she yelled at them again to get in the house. After a second refusal, she started counting to 5. I have no idea what happens when you get to five but the kids obviously do because that made them jump and she gathered them up in a group on the front steps and marched them inside. After that, I went and joined the pap at the tanning salon where Kate stayed inside for an extra fifteen minutes. She usually does a half hour but today it was forty-five minutes. For the first time in eight months, Kate responded to the paparazzi (that she hates with a passion) when he asked her a question. I told him before hand that I thought she would say something if he asked a DWTS question, guessing that it's built into her contract in some way. Sure enough, when he asked her something about how well she thinks she'll do, her response was "you'll have to wait and see." And with that, the pap was so thrown by her uttering a syllable that he backed himself right into the tanning salon in front of her while walking and taking pictures and video. Funny.

After tanning, Kate drove the twenty minutes back to the house where she stayed for less than five minutes as she picked up Leah and Colin and drove right back down the same way she came and went to the Target shopping center and went into Dick's Sporting Goods. She was inside for about 15 minutes looking at Under Armour brand workout clothing. Tony was wearing Under Armour yesterday and he may have recommended it to her to keep her muscles warm and loose. I couldn't see what she ended up buying but that's all she looked at and came out with a bag.

On the way to the car the kids were looking at the pap taking their picture and Kate said to them "Don't worry. They know who you are but you're safe with me."

After they got in the car, Kate sat in the parking space for fifteen minutes reading something she had in her lap.

They drove back to the house and Kate went inside and five minutes later, the new, mean nanny came back out with all eight kids. After playing for about an hour, the nanny told the kids to put their bikes in the garage. She told them again and then a third time, getting absolutely no response at all from the kids. They were within twenty feet of her and just completely ignored her. That made her mad but Kate was in the house so she just went and got the bikes herself and put them away while the kids continued to play in their Crooked Houses. The kids all went inside with the nanny at 3.

Sure enough, at 3:15, Kate came out and got in the car and left —
AGAIN. This time she drove to the exact same place as before and went
into Target — which is right next to Dick's in the strip mall. She
spent forty-five minutes inside shopping and came out pushing her
shopping cart, looking fabulous in tight white pants, high heels, a
bright blue top and crazy, white-framed sunglasses. She had several
bags and I could see that she bought a bunch of bottles of some kind
of juice and she put them in a cooler in the back of the Land
Cruiser. She also bought a toaster oven. After loading the car, the
ass-kissing pap took her shopping cart for her so she wouldn't have
to walk it twenty feet to the cart rack.
I'm trying not to judge her, but it looks like she's looking for any
excuse at all to leave the house and get away from her kids.
She got back to the house around 4:45 and went inside. The kids were
all inside when she got home. All was quiet but the nanny stayed at
the house until 6 pm when I guess Kate finally called it a day.

Jon & Kate Gosselin PA Reporting
Wednesday, March 10, 2010
- Kate left for NYC at 7am
- Nannies watched the kids while Kate was away — Again
- Kate and Steve Neild arrived at the Essex House hotel
- Kate and Steve took a taxi to Ted Gibson's for Kate's new
  hairdo
- Tony joined Kate and Steve at Ted Gibson's before going out
  to dinner with Kate at Nobu
- After Nobu, Kate and Steve returned to the Essex House.

Judy arrived at the house at 6 am to take over parenting duties for
Kate who was preparing to leave for an overnight trip to New York.
Judy and the new, mean nanny would be rotating with a third nanny
while Kate was away.
Kate and Steve arrived at the Essex House around 10 am and checked
in. Steve helped Kate with her bags and followed her into the hotel.
They stayed inside until 12:30pm when they came out and jumped into a
taxi and drove to Ted Gibson's salon on 5th ave. Steve escorted Kate
inside for her extension-removal appointment with Ted's team.
While Kate was upstairs in the salon getting worked on by a team of
stylists, Steve came outside and stood watch over the paparazzi who
were nearby trying to get pictures. All they could see from across
the street was the top of Kate's head and several people working on
her. Steve stood around the building and paced back and forth, taking
the time to have small talk with the paps.
At 6:30 pm, Tony arrived at Ted Gibson's to meet Kate. He was inside
for an hour waiting before the group of Kate, Tony, Ted, Steve and
another guy came outside at 7:30 and got into a taxi van to head to
Nobu for an 8:00 dinner reservation.
The group was in Nobu for two hours and fifteen minutes and came out
smiling at 10:15 pm.
The pap asked Kate what she was doing in New York and she responded
with a smile, "working."
Meanwhile, back in PA, Judy was watching the kids all day and they
played outside for most of the day with the usual assortment of
bikes, scooters and lacrosse sticks and balls. The new, mean nanny
took over for Judy at 3 pm and she was scheduled to stay until 9 pm
when she would be relieved by a third nanny for the overnight shift.

Jon & Kate Gosselin PA Reporting
Thursday, March 11, 2010

- Kate was supposed to get her hair extensions put back in at Ted Gibson's today but was a no-show.
- Kate's whereabouts today were unknown by all of my contacts including three photo agencies who were searching for her.
- Back in PA, same nanny rotation as yesterday.
- The kids are sad/mad at Kate. She was supposed to take the kids on a trip during their Spring Break but canceled because of DWTS.

Kate was rumored to be spending the day again today at Ted Gibson's to get her hair extensions put back in but she didn't show up and wasn't spotted anywhere in New York or anywhere else by any of the paps and agencies that I spoke to. She gave everyone the slip today leaving the paps speculating as to where she was. LA?
According to xxxxxx, the nannies were all scheduled the same as on Wednesday with no word of Kate coming home tonight.
She said that the kids told her that Kate had planned on taking them on a special trip while they were home for Spring Break but she had to cancel because of DWTS. "The little kids are sad and disappointed but they're used to that by now from both Jon and Kate. Mady and Cara are mad at Kate though and are giving her the silent treatment"
"They think she cares more about her career than them."
Judy and the kids played outside all day and the kids took a long nap around lunchtime. The mean nanny arrived at 3:15pm for her 3 pm shift and the kids begged Judy not to go. "They hate the new nanny because she's mean to them and yells at them."

Jon & Kate Gosselin PA Reporting
March 12&13, 2010

- Kate was away from the kids again from Wednesday before they woke up to Saturday night after they were asleep.

Kate left town and the kids again at 6:30 am on Wednesday (3/10) morning before the kids woke up, and returned sometime overnight on Saturday (3/13.) She's supposedly starting dance rehearsals again on Sunday at her house with Tony.
The kids spent their Spring Break cooped up in the house with nannies instead of taking a trip with Kate as promised.

Jon & Kate Gosselin PA Reporting
Monday, March 15, 2010

- Tension and diva tendencies being displayed by Kate and Tony.
- Tony was an hour late to rehearsal yesterday so Kate kept him waiting today while she ran errands. When she got home, he left a few minutes later for almost an hour.
- Kate used the boys as props today for photos to prove she's a great mom. Paps missed her.
- Tony was followed by a pap when he left the house and he stopped to talk to him. The paps love Tony saying what a great guy he is.
- Tony said he spoke to Kate about being nicer to the paps, telling her "they're just doing their job."
- Two nannies at the house today with the kids who are still on Spring break.
- Second nanny loaded up Mady and Cara and took them somewhere.

Two nannies were at the house this morning when I arrived. Judy and a new nanny in a Jeep Grand Cherokee. The DWTS people got to the house at 10:30 am and entered through the basement entrance around the back of the house. Tony arrived at 10:55 am, closely followed by the paps that shot him early at his hotel.

Kate was bothered by Tony being late yesterday. She's very anal about time and being on time. You can set your watch by Kate's schedule and when Tony kept her standing around waiting for him to show up, she became very annoyed. Rehearsal was supposed to start at 11 am today but Kate decided to give a little payback and she went out shopping at 10:30, saying "let's see how he likes standing around waiting."

She took the three boys along with her as props for the waiting paps to show that she's a great mother. Kate has been reading the tabloids and a sitter told me that the US Weekly stories the past two weeks have her pissed.

Kate took the boys with her to run errands while her dance team waited at the house. They went to UPS for mail, the bank in Shillington, Target and the Giant grocery store before finally returning to the house at 12:15 pm. Aaden, Colin and Joel each carried a small bag inside while Kate had two large, white plastic bags in each hand. Kate came out a second time to the car to get her mail, which included several boxes and two bags of letters, etc. A new nanny came out and brought the rest of her things in the house. At 12:45 Tony came outside alone and left the property in his white Porsche. The DWTS crew stayed at the house. A pap followed him into Wernersville where Tony finally pulled over and got out and talked to the pap and answered his questions on video. The pap couldn't stop gushing about what a wonderful guy Tony is, saying how polite and professional he is. Tony offered that he has spoken to Kate about how she deals with the local paparazzi, telling her that they're just doing their jobs. He said that she'd be happy to talk to them on camera now. He also asked the paps to please not write anything scandalous because he's a happily married man.

Tony arrived back at the house at 1:45 pm, waving to me and the paps as he pulled in the front gate. He parked the car and went inside and they've all been inside presumably dancing since then.

Jon & Kate Gosselin PA Reporting
Wednesday, March 24, 2010
Reporting by Robert Hoffman

- Kate's sister from Ohio is staying with her at the house to help with the kids.
- Judy is at the house helping out today even though all eight kids are in school.
- Kate and Tony were dancing at the house today.
- Judy dropped the kids off and picked them up at the bus stop.
- Kate was livid and could barely control her temper as the judges were speaking to her after her poor performance.
- Kate thinks the judges know nothing and she did much better than they said.

Kate's sister from Ohio is staying at the house with Kate, helping with the kids and with the chores. She got here on Tuesday morning in her pickup truck. She's pretty rugged and told xxxxxxx that "the paparazzi better not even think about asking me any questions." Kate has hardly spent any time with the kids at all since she's been home. Kate's sister and two nannies have been at the house with them since Kate returned from LA.

Kate stayed inside all day today and didn't run any errands. Tony arrived at the house at 1:30 pm carrying a tray of Starbucks coffee for himself, Kate and crew. Kate kept them waiting in the basement until 2:15 pm while she stayed upstairs in her room doing God knows what. Tony is losing patience with Kate and her attitude and doesn't seem as happy as he was when he first came to the house. There weren't many smiles or much small talk today between Kate and Tony. They kept it strictly professional. Kate's very nervous now after seeing how good the other dancers were compared to her and she's determined to work even harder than she has been. She was livid and could barely control her temper as the judges were speaking to her after her first dance. She wanted to go right back at them like they do sometimes on American Idol with Simon but Tony sensed it and was squeezing her hand to calm her down.

Kate now hates the two male judges and thinks they don't know what the Hell they're talking about. She thinks they tried to humiliate her with that 'shopping cart' remark and can't wait to blow them away and put them in their place with her next dance. She said she was just nervous and can dance so much better than she did. She's also a little bit pissed off at Tony for giving her a false sense of how well she was doing. He's always so positive about Kate's dancing. Maybe he should keep it a little more real with her and let her know what she's doing wrong and fix it for next time.

Tony was still at the house at 9 pm tonight, along with a nanny and Kate's sister. The basement lights were still on so it looks like they're stepping it up to longer days of rehearsing.

Jon & Kate Gosselin PA Reporting
Thursday, March 25, 2010

- Kate left the house before the kids woke up today while Judy and a second nanny stayed with them. Mady and Cara didn't go to school today.
- Kids forced to stay inside all day because Kate doesn't want them photographed without her — so she looks like she's with them when she's home.
- Tony wasted his morning at his hotel. Kate scheduled dance rehearsal today from 3-6 pm. Tony suggested they dance all day and they got into an argument!
- DWTS crew arrived at 2:41 pm. Tony arrived at 3:07.
- TLC person at the house meeting with Kate this afternoon.
- Kate had the pool man at the house today to clean and open the pool.

Kate left the house this morning at 6:15 am before the kids woke up. She didn't say where she was going and nobody was here that early to follow her. She was away from home until 1:40 pm when she finally pulled in the driveway followed by the paparazzi that were waiting for her nearby.

The tups don't have school on Thursdays but Kate kept Maddie and Cara home today too for some reason. Kate gave strict instructions to the nannies to keep them inside all day. "Under no circumstances are they to go outside and have their picture taken!" xxxxx told me that Kate wants to make sure that the kids aren't photographed without her so it looks like she's always with them when she's at home. She's mad at Kate because "the kids were begging to go out all day and when Kate came home, all she had to do was to go outside for five minutes with them and be photographed and then they could stay out and play." "She's such a f-ing bitch!"

Tony was at his hotel until he left to go to the Gosselin house at 2:45 pm. He arrived at 3:07 pm.

A twenty-something guy in a gold car with New Jersey plates came to the house at 1:55 and went in through the basement. One of the paps says he's a PA (production assistant) from TLC. He stayed for an hour and left just before 3 pm.

Jon & Kate Gosselin PA Reporting
Friday, March 26, 2010

- Tony and crew arrived at the Gosselin house for a 10 am start time.
- Kate left the house within five minutes of Tony leaving and went to have a mani/pedi at Planet Nails in Wyomissing.
- Kate smiled and talked to the paps today after her hour-and-a-half pampering session.
- Judy dropped kids off at the bus stop and picked them up and stayed at the house all day.

The ladies at Kate's supermarket know me pretty well and when I checked in today for an update, they told me that they've taken to calling the shopping carts Kate Gosselins, after the judges remarks when scoring Kate's first dance last week. They yell to the cart boys "go bring in the Kate Gosselins" and everybody gets a big laugh.
Tony and the DWTS crew arrived at the house within minutes of each other this morning for a 10 am start time. Tony brought his usual tray of Starbucks drinks to give everybody an energy jolt.
Tony's a high-energy guy who wants to dance all day and night to prepare for the next show and he's getting frustrated with Kate's schedule of pampering and only dancing for three or four hours at a time.
Tony and crew left the house a few minutes before two and Kate was right out the door behind them. She drove like a bat out of Hell through the winding country roads and down into town to go to Planet Nails & Tans for an hour-and-a-half manicure and pedicure. She was drinking water and eating an apple when she arrived wearing her workout clothes and black hat. She looked very happy and upbeat and actually smiled and interacted with the three paparazzi who were shooting and videotaping her as she walked from the salon to her car. One of the paps told her that it's been reported that she's lost a lot of weight from dancing and she replied "I'll take that!"
I spoke to a woman who was in Planet Nails while Kate was inside and she said she was laughing and having a great time in there talking about DWTS and how hard it is for her and how hard she's working. "Kate sure loves to talk about herself. I didn't hear her mention the eight kids though. That's sad."
Judy once again took the kids to school in the morning and picked them up afterward. Kate was at the house both in the morning and afternoon but had other things going on that were obviously more important than her kids.

Jon & Kate Gosselin PA Reporting
Saturday, March 27th, 2010

- Steve Neild and his wife brought Kate a present for her 35th birthday which is on Sunday 3/28.
- Kate and Tony rehearsed from 9:30 to 12:30 today before heading to LA.
- Gina Neild watched the kids today while Kate danced and stayed at the house alone with them after Steve and Kate left in a limo.
- Kate took her Land Cruiser to get detailed. Called police to keep paparazzi away.

- Jon is due at the house tomorrow for three days of custody while Kate's in LA.

Tony and the DWTS people arrived at the house just before 9:30 this morning. Judy was at the house helping Kate with the kids in the morning but kept them in the house the entire time.

Steve and Gina Neild arrived in their Ford Explorer around 8:30 today carrying what looked like a present for Kate. Tomorrow is her 35th birthday. Steve seemed surprised and angry to see the paparazzi camped in front of the house so early. He glared at the group as he was entering through the front gate. Gina didn't even look over at them.

Kate and Tony rehearsed until 12:30 when he and the crew packed up and left the house. Shortly after they left, Kate and Steve left in their own cars, followed closely by the paps. They drove to a local collision/car detailing shop in Wernersville where Kate was met by a Spring Township policeman who made sure to keep the paps away. They took pictures and were quickly removed. The officer told them it was private property and they had to leave immediately. A man from the Toyota dealership where Kate gets her Land Cruiser serviced was there at the shop to meet Kate and get her squared away. Kate left her car and drove back to the house with Steve.

Gina Neild brought the kids outside to play and they ran around like they haven't been outside in a month. She stood nearby watching over them as they played with their scooters and bicycles and just generally ran around enjoying the fresh air. They didn't seem bothered by yet another person watching them while their mom was busy doing something else. It's a normal part of their lives by now.

A limo arrived at the house around 1 pm and sat in the driveway waiting for over an hour. Finally Kate, Steve and Gina started bringing their bags out and loading them in the car. They had the limo move across the driveway and up to the front door as close as possible to cut off the view from the paps. Gina gave Steve and Kate a big hug before waving goodbye as the limo drove down the driveway and off the property, followed by the paps.

As of 10 pm tonight, Gina was still at the house alone with the kids. A nanny will probably take over in the morning and then hand them off to Jon when he arrives.

Jon & Kate Gosselin PA Reporting
Monday, March 29th, 2010
Reporting by Robert Hoffman

- Jon plans to watch Kate on DWTS at home with the kids, "to cheer her on."
- Kate winning or doing well on DWTS would be great for the family, says Jon.
- Jon shopped at Kate's Giant for snacks for the show tonight. Was papped pushing a shopping cart in the store.
- Judy is at the house tonight helping Jon with the kids.
- If there was any doubt that there's tension between Kate and Tony, the show tonight put that to rest.
- Kate's performance tonight was horrendous.

Jon took the kids to school this morning in the Sprinter van and then had an early breakfast with a friend at local diner, Gianotti's in Wyomissing. Jon is trying to eat healthier so he had an egg white omelet and coffee while his friend showed no sympathy and had a Western omelet, bacon, hash browns and pancakes drenched in syrup.

Jon wanted to stay out of sight today so he got back to the house
before 8 am and laid low inside where he took a nap and caught up on
some paperwork for several projects that he says he has in the works.
He snuck out of the house around Noon and went to visit a friend who
lives in West Reading. He said he plans to watch DWTS tonight at home
with the kids and have a "Go Mommy Party." They're going to have
snacks and junk food and they will vote for mommy as many times as
they can from the house phone, the apartment phone and Jon's two cell
phones. Jon says it would be great for the family for Kate to go far
or even win on DWTS. He's totally supportive of her career and wishes
he could be there to cheer her on in person, be he knows that's not
possible. "She'd see me in the audience and probably trip and fall."
Jon left the friends house in the Sprinter van around 3:40 and went
to the bus stop to get the kids, where the paps were waiting for him.
He talked with them for a few minutes until the bus pulled in. Jon
opened up the back of the van and the side door before going to get
them at the bus. The kids were all excited to see him there, with the
little ones yelling "daddyyyyyyyy" as they came down the steps, gave
him a hug or high-five and went to the van. After he got them all, he
put their backpacks in the back of the van, strapped them in and
headed back home. Cara was on the late bus, having a sports activity
at school so she got picked up at 6 while Judy watched the rest of
the kids at the house.
On the way to get Cara at the late bus, Jon stopped at Kate's Giant
supermarket and did some shopping for tonight. He was photographed in
the frozen food isle buying Weight Watchers dinners and JiffyPop
Popcorn. He already had ice cream and other snacks at the house for
tonight for the party.
If there was any doubt in anyone's mind that there's tension between
Kate and Tony, tonight's DWTS show sure put that to rest. Tony quit
and walked out at one point, leaving Kate in tears.
Tony said "I've never been questioned about my teaching before. I've
taught world champions. I teach teachers.
If that's how Kate and Tony act with the DWTS cameras rolling, just
imagine what goes on in Kate's basement. It's nasty.
When Tony came back to Kate after walking out, Kate said "thank you
for coming back. A lot of people quit on me in life.

Jon & Kate Gosselin PA Reporting
Wednesday, March 31, 2010
- Dance practice at the house from 10am — 4pm today.
- After rehearsal, Tony gave Kate a ride to the Toyota
  dealership in his Porsche convertible — top down of course.
- Judy dropped kids off and picked them up at the bus stop.

Tony arrived at the Gosselin house a few minutes before 10 am
carrying his usual assortment of Starbucks coffee drinks for himself,
Kate and DWTS crew, who arrived 15 minutes before him. He waved down
to the fence to a few well-wishers who were standing outside the
house and yelled to him when he arrived.
Judy took the kids to the bus stop this morning in the Sprinter van
and gave them all hugs and kisses as she helped them up the steps to
the bus. She stood outside the bus waving to the tups that were
waving and smiling back through the window as it pulled away.

A few minutes after 4 pm, Tony came outside to leave, looking good as always. He put the top down on his Porsche convertible and got it and started it up but then just sat there for five minutes. Kate came out of the house and got in the car and they left the property together, looking like Ken and Barbie. They were both all smiles for the paps that were waiting at the gate to photograph them as they left. Tony even offered one an extra Starbucks drink he had in the car but the pap was caught off-guard by his kindness and didn't know how to react.

They sped off down the country road and wound around through the hills and arrived ten minutes later at Kate's Toyota dealership where she had left her Land Cruiser a few days earlier. Tony was just giving her a ride to her car before heading back to his hotel.

Jon & Kate Gosselin PA Reporting
Thursday, April 1, 2010

- Kate and Tony practiced today for six hours.
- Kate and Tony were alone in the house for the first time today.

Today is Jon's 33rd birthday and he celebrated it away from his kids. He wanted to be at the house spending his birthday with his kids but because of the custody arrangement, he can't, so he's spending the day with his immediate family and will be cooking dinner and staying in with them tonight. He'll be coming back home to be with the kids this weekend while Kate is dancing in the house with Tony and will be staying in the apartment above the garage while she is in the main house.

Judy was at the Gosselin house at 6:30 am to help with the kids and to get Mady and Cara to the bus stop. Kate stayed behind with the sextuplets.

The DWTS crew arrived at the house at 9:40 and went straight to the basement entrance behind the house. Tony was running a little late today and arrived in his white Porsche Carrera convertible at 10:10. He was dressed in a white, tight, short-sleeve t-shirt, black pants and white sneakers and was carrying his usual tray of Starbucks coffee drinks and a white plastic bag. As he was walking from his car to the house, the tups came rushing out the front door yelling "Tony's here! Tony's here!" Tony walked right by them and around the house to the basement entrance. I'm sure he must have said something to them in the form of a greeting but from where I was standing, I couldn't hear anything. He was probably late and wanted to get in there before Kate got mad at him.

Judy came outside with the kids and stayed out with them for an hour as they played on their scooters and bikes and did the usual running around enjoying themselves. After that they stayed inside the rest of the day.

Judy was the first to come outside at 3:05 pm when she took the Sprinter van to get Mady and Cara at the bus. She brought the sextuplets along with her so they wouldn't disturb dance practice. They left very early for the bus and sat at the bus stop for 45 minutes. Judy climbed in the back with the kids while they waited.

Back at the house, dance rehearsal was wrapping up and the crew left the house at 3:50 pm, leaving Tony and Kate inside alone for the first time since they've been together. They were alone until Tony came outside to leave at 4:30 pm. Judy was just getting back to the house with the kids. She stayed around until 5 pm when she handed over total custody of the 8 to Kate. Kate used the remaining daylight as a photo-op and played with the kids out front in the yard in front of the paps. I say photo-op because this is maybe the third time she's been in front of the house playing with the kids since this story broke. The kids had a great time playing with Kate. It was a rare moment for them and they made the most of it. They showed off their bike-riding skills to her yelling "mommy, mommy look at me." They also circled the driveway on their scooters and even had Kate get out the four-wheel-drive toy car that they love to race around in.

Kate stayed outside with the kids for over an hour playing. The paps wrapped up at 6 pm and oddly enough, Kate took the kids inside minutes later.

They stayed inside until dark with no visitors.

Jon & Kate Gosselin PA Reporting
Friday, April 2, 2010
Highlights: Kate Gosselin is a Diva

- Kate told Tony after last week's show that she's the reason people know his name, reminding him who the star is.
- Kate wishes she would have gotten Maks as her partner instead of Tony.
- Kate has gotten so frustrated with Tony that she walked out on him and the crew to go shopping.
- Kate blames Tony for her poor dancing performances saying, "I thought he could teach me but I guess he can't."
- Kate makes Tony use the basement entrance to the house now instead of coming through the front door.
- Kate avoids the line at UPS when she gets her mail. Has employees bring it to her while she waits in car — parked illegally.
- Kate also gets special service at the hospital. She waits outside in the car while a staffer brings her files out to her.
- Kate asks for and gets personal security while shopping at Target.
- Kate gets a new mani/pedi each week to match her dress on DWTS.

Kate told Tony in the heat of the moment while arguing last week that "I'm the reason anyone knows your name so give me a break please", reminding Tony of who the star really is. Tony just stood there with his arms folded and his head down trying not to get angrier.

Kate confided in xxxxxxx that she wishes she had partnered with Maks instead of Tony because "Maks is a stronger personality and would be able to deal with her better. Kate likes a man who takes charge and Tony's a pushover."

Kate got so frustrated with Tony last week during rehearsal that she stormed out saying "I need to get out of this house!" and she went and ran errands while Tony and the crew sat in the basement waiting for her to come back. She came back with a Target bag and a Dunkin Donuts coffee in hand.

Kate blames Tony for her poor dancing performances, telling xxxxxx "I thought he could teach me but I guess he can't. He knew I couldn't dance at all but he promised me he would turn me into a good dancer and I wouldn't embarrass myself. So much for that." xxxxxx says Kate takes little jabs at Tony which get under his skin, saying things like "here comes the great dance instructor!" when he arrives. She says she's just kidding and Tony laughs it off but you can tell he get's pissed at her. "Tony takes this very seriously."
"Kate makes Tony use the basement entrance to the house now instead of coming through the front door. She says it's quicker for everyone that way but she's really just trying to show him that she's the boss and he's just part of the crew."

Jon & Kate Gosselin PA Reporting
Saturday, April 3, 2010

- Kate blew off dance rehearsal this morning for an Easter egg hunt photo op to trump Jon.
- Tony left the property frustrated because of another wasted day with no rehearsal.
- Steve and Gina Neild and their sons helped Kate with the egg hunt.
- Kate left in a limo with Steve while the kids were stuck inside with the mean nanny the rest of the day.

Kate blew off dance rehearsal this morning to have an egg hunt for the kids and to trump Jon. Jon had called her on Friday to discuss custody arrangements and he told Kate that he was planning to have an egg hunt for the kids in the yard. Kate didn't have anything planned and was just going to bring the kids something "Eastery" from LA but when she found out about Jon's egg hunt, she decided that she'd beat him to it and she went to Target last night to pick up supplies. She went all out, buying plastic eggs filled with candy, pretty baskets for the kids and baskets full of candy and toys for prizes.
Tony stayed in town last night because they were scheduled to dance this morning before leaving together for LA. Instead, when he got there, Kate told him that she decided to have an egg hunt for the kids and they would make up the missed dance practice when they got to LA. Tony was pissed and sped off in his convertible, rather than staying and riding together in the limo to the airport with Kate and Steve like they did last week. Kate was overheard saying "He'll get over it" after Tony left.
Steve and Gina and their two boys were at the house early and the boys came outside and hid all the eggs in the yard while the kids were kept under wraps in the house. Kate wanted to get the egg hunt over early so she could prepare for the trip but the paparazzi weren't at the house yet so she delayed the hunt for an hour until the paps arrived. Kate had the tups all dressed up in matching outfits — obviously for a photo op to make herself look like a good mother since she went nowhere else with the kids today.
Kate's rule is to always have the kids play behind the house when she doesn't want them photographed by the paps. The back yard would have been a much better place to have the hunt but the paps can't see back there. Kate treats the kids like pawns or worse yet, pets, playing with them only for the cameras. Once the pictures are taken, she turns them back over to the nannies.

Kate wanted the kids in matching outfits to look good for the magazines. It took almost an hour to get the kids ready because Kate wanted ribbons in the little girl's hair and they had to look "perfect." The little girls wore matching pink dresses while the boys wore brown shirts and shorts. Mady and Cara picked out their own outfits, with Cara wearing a blue t-shirt over jean shorts and Mady wearing a pink sleeveless shirt over jean shorts. The kids were whining about wanting to go out and find eggs but Kate kept making excuses as to why they had to wait. Finally, the paparazzi arrived and coincidentally, the egg hunt started a few minutes later.

Kate gathered all the kids together up by the front door and gave them instructions before counting to three and saying go! The kids scattered in all directions searching for eggs, laughing and screaming as they ran from egg to egg, filling their baskets. There were eggs everywhere. Kate went all out for this photo op. She pretended to be having as much fun as the kids were, pumping her fist forcefully in the air every time one of the kids yelled "Mommy I found one, I found one!!" As soon as the kids found their eggs and plenty of pictures had been taken by the paps, the kids were shuffled back into the house where they stayed for the rest of the day.

Kate had pre-made 'prize baskets' for the kids that she bought at Target, sealed coldly in shrink wrap and containing a few wrapped pieces of candy and a stuffed toy. The kids were excited about them though so that's all that matters.

Steve stayed out of sight for most of the time at the house, coming out to the car only once to bring something inside. Instead, Gina and the boys made more of an appearance with the kids and Kate, helping out with the hunt.

When the limo arrived at 12:30, Kate and Steve loaded up their bags and said goodbye to their families. Kate must have done her goodbyes inside because she came out alone and left without the kids in the yard this time. Gina and the boys stayed behind but left an hour later, leaving Judy alone at the house with the kids. The mean nanny came at 3 pm to relieve Judy and the kids were kept inside the rest of the day.

Jon & Kate Gosselin PA Reporting
Wednesday, April 7, 2010

- Kate didn't return home to her children today, opting to go straight to New York for a TLC promo filming session on Thursday. Another day without parents for the kids.
- Paps and reporters ambush the kids at the bus stop this afternoon. Kids scared and hiding their faces.

Even though Kate was due back at the house today after being away from the kids since Saturday, Xxxxxxx said that she (Kate) was going to be in NYC on Thursday to film promo spots for TLC, along with the other stars of their shows for the upcoming season, and that there was a chance that she would go directly to New York, rather than return home. Well that's exactly what Kate did. Went straight to NYC. The only movement at the house today was Judy taking the kids to the bus stop in the morning and then returning in the afternoon to pick them up. Kate's cleaning lady was also at the house for most of the morning, leaving several bags of trash out by the garage before leaving.

Jon & Kate Gosselin PA Reporting
Thursday, April 8, 2010

- Kate spent the day in NYC — day 5 1/2 away from the kids this week.

- Two nannies sharing custody at the Gosselin house today and overnight tonight.
- DWTS judge Bruno Tonioli had tough words for Kate.

Kate opted to go from LA to New York, rather than go home and spend time with the kids yesterday. She was supposedly in New York at a secret location filming promo spots for TLC for her new shows next season, along with other TLC stars.

The last time she was at the house with the kids was Saturday afternoon before Easter.

The mean nanny stayed with the kids overnight and Judy came this morning to drive Mady and Cara to the bus stop. When she got back to the house at 7:20 am, she took over custody of the sextuplets and stayed with them at the house all day. They played outside on their bikes and scooters and took turns in the new big red ball. They miss Kate and keep asking when she's coming home. They tried to call Kate for most of the day but Kate didn't pick up. Kate finally called them at 5:30 pm to talk.

Judy left at 6:30 pm tonight, handing over custody once again to the mean nanny who will stay overnight.

(Source — online)

Dancing With the Stars judge Bruno Tonioli didn't hold back when discussing Kate Gosselin's less-than-graceful moves on Wednesday's Lopez Tonight: "Kate is pretty dreadful. She's crap," he told host George Lopez.

Tough reviews aside, the outspoken Italian admitted the mom of eight is "a tough cookie" for facing all the criticism. "She gets it in the face, she comes back and she tries to get better," he said. "[But] it doesn't really work."

Tonioli also said Gosselin, who has squabbled with partner Tony Dovolani, turns the show into "our own disaster movie" on a daily basis. "2012 is nothing compared to the catastrophe she produces," he said.

Jon & Kate Gosselin PA Reporting
Friday, April 9, 2010

- Kate hasn't seen the kids since last Saturday, but rather than picking them up at the bus this afternoon, she went ......TANNING with Tony.
- Kate is leaving again for LA tomorrow late morning. Not exactly the Sunday to Tuesday night that she told the world before DWTS started.

Kate has been away from home and the kids since last Saturday afternoon and she got home sometime overnight last night but didn't take them to the bus stop this morning, which means she probably slept in and didn't see them this morning. Judy took the kids to the bus stop this morning so Kate could get some rest before dance rehearsal. So after six days away from the kids, you'd think that Kate would be anxious to see them and do anything to be with them, right? Well at the very same time that Judy was waiting at the bus stop to pick up the kids this afternoon, Kate opted instead to ......GO TANNING! She and Tony jumped in his Porsche SUV and went to Kate's salon for a thirty-minute session. Tony didn't tan today. He just waited patiently in the lobby for her while she went in the back for a spray tan.

Kate is leaving again for LA early tomorrow so hopefully she'll manage to squeeze in some quality time with her kids before then. Before DWTS started, she came out and told the world she would be with them all the time while practicing at the house and only be away from them from Sunday night to Wednesday morning — taking the redeye back from LA on Tuesday night. It certainly hasn't worked out that way.

Kate didn't even bother picking up her car at the Toyota dealership where she has it stored because she's leaving again so soon tomorrow. Jon is due back at the house for custody around 3 pm Saturday.

Tony stopped at Starbucks to pick up some coffee for the group at 10:45 am and was at the house at 11:05 — going in through the basement entrance. The paps jokingly call it the service entrance now.

Two male DWTS crew guys were at the house in a gold car at 10:50 and went inside carrying some equipment bags.

Judy left the house at 3:19 pm for the bus stop in the Sprinter van to get the kids. I figured Kate and Tony would use the extra time to practice but the DWTS crew left the house fifteen minutes later, which means the dancing had stopped for the day. At 3:45, Tony and Kate came out and jumped in Tony's black Porsche SUV and headed down toward the bus stop. I was sure that they were going to give us an elaborate photo op of the two of them being so happy together and getting the kids and big, dramatic hugs and kisses etc. which would have been the smart, fake, Kate Gosselin thing to do. Instead they chose to go tanning. Kate has become so totally consumed with her career that she thought tanning would be a better choice than seeing her kids home from school.

When they got to the tanning salon, the paps were there shooting and they both put on their happy faces but they ran from the car to the salon. Kate even tried to cover her face.

After thirty minutes inside, Kate came out of the back, grabbed Tony and they literally ran back to the car, both smiling once again and Kate looking into the video camera and saying "I'm late! I'm late!" to the pap.

They got back to the house at 4:45 and Tony just dropped her off and left. He waved to the paps as he drove out of the front gate. Judy stayed for another 30 minutes and left Kate alone with her kids at 5:15 pm. That should give them about four hours of quality time for the week before Kate jumps back into dance mode Saturday morning.

Jon & Kate Gosselin PA Reporting
Saturday, April 10, 2010

- Kate and Tony rehearsed today at the house, and Tony left immediately after they were finished, looking like he was happy to get out of there.
- Steve arrived at the house in the limo today and left with Kate soon after.
- Kate saw the kids briefly before leaving once again for LA.
- Kate leaves an itinerary for Jon when she lets him have custody, making him handle the doctor's appointments and shoe shopping while she jets off to LA.

Kate emails an itinerary to Jon of what he has to do with the kids when he's there. She always has him take the kids to the doctor and for haircuts when he's at the house because she's too busy to do it herself. This weekend's list: Mady and Cara have an appointment with the dermatologist on Monday and The "little kids" need shoes.

Tony and the DWTS crew arrived early today to start dancing at 6:30 am. Carla was at the house with the kids and I'm guessing Kate was dancing before they even woke up today, as they usually sleep late on Saturday and Sunday, usually til 7 or 7:30am.

Carla brought the kids outside to play at 9:30 and parked herself in a chair up by the garage while the kids rode their bikes, scooters and just generally ran around. The kids were having a great time playing but Carla got too cold and ended playtime after only fifteen minutes. The kids were visibly upset and yelling that they wanted to stay outside but she made them go in. Cries of "we want to stay outside!" could be heard down at the fence.

In the short time that they were outside, Carla sat in a chair reading Kate's new book. She made sure it was visible to the paparazzi. Every moment of these people's lives are carefully orchestrated for maximum media exposure. It's all an illusion.

At 10:15, Carla loaded up Mady and Cara in her white minivan (that Jon and Kate gave her) and they left the property. They were brought back to the house by a hulking lady I haven't seen before. They had their lacrosse sticks so we thought they had a practice but Jon later told me that they had a lacrosse game today.

DWTS rehearsal wrapped at 11 am and Tony got right out of there, unlike the first week when he stayed around to talk and they all left for the airport together. He looked like he was happy that they were finished. This may have been the last time Tony has to put up with Kate's crap on her home turf. According to the paps it was very unusual for Tony to leave so abruptly. He always takes the time to interact with the paps on the way out of the property. He totally blew them off today which was strange because they were yelling "Good luck Tony" and things like that. He just wanted to be done with this it looked like.

Kate was in the house with the tups and the mean nanny. Jon also refers to her as the 'spy nanny' because she reports his every move back to Kate and makes sure Jon knows this. She's very confrontational with him.

At exactly 1 pm, Kate came out with her wash basket in hand followed by the little girls who were yelling at her not to go. Leah yelled "where are you going mommyyyyyyy?!" and Kate kept walking and simply responded coldly but loudly, "I'll be right back." Kate's important reason for walking out on her children today after seeing them so briefly? Planet Nails & Tans for her weekly mani/pedi. To be fair, today it was only an hour instead of her usual ninety minutes.

She came out of Planet Nails at 2:15 and raced back to the house and got there at 2:30, just a few minutes before a blue Neon was pulling in with Mady and Cara in the back seat, returning from the lacrosse game. Kate jumped out of the Sprinter and went straight in the house, leaving the kids outside with the spy nanny. She came back out five minutes later to talk to the lacrosse lady and pretend to give a shit about her kids, knowing the paps were there shooting.

While she was standing outside talking, the kids were just aimlessly wandering around the driveway. One of the little girls walked over to Kate and wrapped her arms around Kate's legs to give her a big hug and she didn't want to let go. It's so quiet on that property and the wind was blowing toward us and it was easy to hear her say "I don't want you to go mommy."

At 2:49, the black limo SUV arrived at the house and Steve Neild got out and carried a black duffle bag into the house. Kate followed him inside and a minute later he came back out carrying Kate's red suitcases. He really does do everything for her. Strangely, after loading Kate's bags into the limo, Steve went back in the house and brought the same black duffle bag back out and put it in the limo. Not sure what that's about.

Kate stood by the limo talking to the spy nanny and Steve, and the kids came to her to say goodbye — not the other way around. Mady was down by the Crooked Houses and Cara yelled to her "Mady, mommy's leaving!" and Mady walked back up to Kate to say goodbye. Kate leaned down to give all the little kids a group hug — to save time I guess — when she noticed Colin standing there crying. It was heartbreaking. She picked him up and gave him a big, long hug. I couldn't hear what she said to him but she was talking quietly to him. He hugged her very tightly and only let go when she put him back down with the other kids.

With that, Kate and Steve got in the limo and drove off at exactly 2:58 pm, leaving the kids behind once again, wandering around the yard looking sad. If I did the math correctly, Kate had a little over two hours today that she could have spent doing anything with the kids, but in that time, I'm sure she needed to do some packing for the trip.

KATE'S DWTS LIES

Kate takes breaks from dancing rehearsals to spend time with the kids.
Kate never stops dancing to play with or spend any time at all with the kids. The only time she stops dancing for the kids' sake is when she has to go upstairs to yell at them for yelling down to the basement to get her attention.

Kate has been working hard and practicing her heart out for DWTS.
Kate has devoted less and less time to rehearsing since week one and it certainly shows in her performances. Tony has become totally frustrated with her and has pretty much given up any hope of teaching Kate to dance. He just wants this nightmare to be over. As for Kate? She was just in it for the paycheck and seems to have lost interest now that she has her two new shows to focus on. She got a large bonus for making it through as far as she did and that's all she wanted.

Kate told the world that when she's away from the kids, Jon is at home with them.
Jon is only allowed at the house on certain days and if he can't make it to the house at exactly the time when he's scheduled to be there, Kate punishes him by canceling his custody all together. He flew from Utah to Pennsylvania and his flight was delayed and he told Kate over the phone that he would be late getting there and she told him "if you can't be here when it's your custody time, don't bother coming at all."

Kate will only be away from the kids doing DWTS from Sunday to Tuesday.
The reality is that Kate leaves the house on Saturday, early afternoons and doesn't return, sometimes for six days.

Kate says the kids are thrilled to be filming again but Xxxxxxx says otherwise. She told me Friday that Kate spun it to the kids so that it sounds exciting and not like work. She told them that they would be taking great vacations and going on exciting adventures. What kid wouldn't be happy to hear that news? Mady and Cara unfortunately don't share in the tup's excitement. They both threw a fit and were yelling and crying. They don't want to film again. They hate the idea of having their private lives on television for their friends and everyone else to see. They're at the age where they get embarrassed easily and worry about what their friends at school will say.

Jon & Kate Gosselin PA Reporting
Thursday, April 22, 2010
- Kate and the kids arrived home today after almost a week in LA.
- Kate left with Steve for NYC after 15 minutes at the house.

Kate and the eight kids arrived back home in PA today after almost a week in LA. At 10:15am, two limos arrived at the house. A limo bus was carrying Kate, Steve and Kate's BFF Jaime and the kids. They were followed by a second limo that would take Kate and Steve to NYC a few minutes later. Judy was at the house when they arrived and she came outside to greet them. All the kids ran to her and gave her big hugs like you would expect a mother to get. Judy spends more time with them than Kate so their bond is very strong. Kate went inside the house with Judy while Steve and the limo driver brought the luggage in the house. The kids looked tired from the trip and happy to be back home. After fifteen minutes inside, Kate and Steve came out and got in the second limo and left for NYC. Kate's master schedule says DWTS and I know they're going to be on Regis tomorrow.

Jon & Kate Gosselin PA Reporting
Friday, May 21, 2010
- Kate hasn't seen the kids since last Sunday when they left Orlando.

Kate hasn't seen her kids since last Sunday when they left Orlando and returned home. Kate went directly to LA with Steve Neild to prepare for DWTS while a second bodyguard accompanied the kids back to Pennsylvania.

Kate tried to dispel any rumors of her being hated by the cast and crew of *Dancing With The Stars* every chance she got, in print and in television interviews. She was always quick to tell everyone how much she and Tony liked each other and how they got along so wonderfully. She told the *Today* show's Meredith Vieira that she "loved" her cast mates. She said, "Most of them I will stay in touch with, from the hair, to make-up, to cast, crew and dancers. It's like a big family unit."
Kate's dancing partner Tony Dovolani appears to be one of the nicest, classiest, most mellow persons on Earth, who wouldn't say a bad word about anyone. Or almost anyone. Even Tony couldn't stand to be around Kate Gosselin for one second longer than he had to.
On March 29, 2012, Tony Dovolani and his partner from Season 14, Martina Navratilova, were being interviewed by Anderson Cooper when Anderson brought up Kate and all of her drama on DWTS. Here's what Tony had to say:

Cooper: "I remember watching her dance, I'm still traumatized by that experience."

Dovolani: "Wait, wait wait. Anderson, did you just call it dance? We didn't dance."

Cooper: "It's true. I don't know what it was. Did you have to take a long vacation after that experience Tony?"

Dovolani: "There was a lot of therapy involved."

That was it – a few seconds of cute little banter. No harm done. Tony was responding to Anderson Cooper by stating the obvious and making a joke. But Kate is starved for attention, so instead of laughing it off, she created a mountain out of a molehill and felt compelled to respond. She took advantage of her position as a blogger on a coupon website – a site intended to help people save money – to "set the record straight" by posting an inappropriate and thin-skinned rebuttal:

Kate Responds to Anderson Cooper & Tony Dovolani
Posted on April 2nd, 2012 by Kate G

Oh, geez. Tony was joking around. It was a cute exchange that lasted about 10 seconds, and then it was over. Kate is so very thin-skinned at arbitrary times. It seems that she is only willing to laugh at herself when there are cameras around to capture her image.

There were reports that Brad Garrett said terrible things about Kate in jest during his comedy routine in Las Vegas in March 2012, and Kate was seated in the front row just a few feet away. The photo online shows Kate and Steve Neild laughing hysterically, and Kate tweeted several times about how funny the show and Brad, in particular, was.

So why the hurt feelings and righteous indignation regarding Tony Dovolani, Kate's former dance instructor, who is a two-time World Champion dancer, and who, by all accounts, is one of the most humble, personable, classy and obviously gifted dance instructors on the planet?

Kate's number one obsessed fan, who often deletes her tweets immediately so people can't discuss them, told Kate that she would have done better on DWTS with a different partner than Tony, and said that if she had the right teacher, she would have gone much farther on the show. This is how Kate responded:

@lol! I've been told that a few times. So funny...

Please forgive this personal note to Kate: We all saw you "dance," Kate. Jesus, himself, could have been your dance instructor and you still would have sucked. In August of 2012, Tony Dovolani was being interviewed by Fox 5 Las Vegas and had even more uncharacteristically critical words to say about Kate. When the interviewer asked Tony if he and Kate were still besties, Tony rolled his eyes and head, looked to be in pain, and said, "Oh Yeeeeaaaaaahhhhhh!"

```
Interviewer: I always feel sorry for you because of all
the seasons, I feel you got the all-time hardest partner
in Kate Gosselin.

Tony: Well I can tell you how they paired me up, I mean
whoever fails the psychiatric evaluation I tend to get
them or physical evaluation and every once in awhile
someone slips through like Melissa or Stacy.

Tony went on to add, "I wasn't her husband, I was her
teacher and you have to be nice to me and she wasn't."
```

It looks like Kate lied about her "wonderful" relationship with Tony. It also looks like Kate can no longer blame her abysmal failure at dancing on Tony being a bad teacher. On November 27, 2012, in Season 15 of *Dancing With The Stars*, Tony Dovolani finally captured the coveted mirror ball trophy with his hard-working, pleasant and appreciative partner, Melissa Rycroft.

HOLIDAYS, STAYCATION AND CRUISE, OH MY

"I need to look at, 'what's best for the kids?
What's best for the kids?'
That is what I say to myself constantly."
– Kate Gosselin

If you are looking for evidence that Kate Gosselin is a devoted mother whose primary focus in life is on making her children happy, you will not find it among these pages. You will also not find evidence that Kate has any genuine desire to provide her kids with memorable and joyful holidays or vacations. Anything that might have been construed as such in the past was fueled by the presence of a film crew and cameras capturing those golden moments of her children's lives to make money for her. Contrary to everything Kate says and tweets about "traditions" and making memories, and how she does everything for her kids, the truth is that Kate does everything for herself first, then gives her children whatever sloppy seconds are left over. Kate Gosselin's world revolves around her own wishes and comfort. Kate treats holidays not as special moments in time to share with her children, but as chores that must be completed as quickly and effortlessly as possible for her. It is understandable how anyone just reading her tweets about how hard she works to give her children wonderful memories would never know this. She seems to get far more enjoyment out of tweeting about how wonderful she is, and how she is doing all these amazing and fabulous things to prepare for a holiday, and how exhausted she is from all that preparing, than out of spending special, uninterrupted time with her kids. Kate spends more time conversing with her tweetie friends and her so-called "haters" than she does being immersed in the joy of watching her children delight in the experience of the holiday. And she is oblivious to all she is missing.

In this chapter, you will not only learn about Kate's methods for heaping holiday happiness upon her ever-appreciative and gushingly thankful children, you will also find out about Kate's strategy to save money on vacations (abridged version: she gets one; her kids do not) and about the fiasco that was her failed attempt at a "celebrity" cruise.

I'M DREAMING OF A BLACK CHRISTMAS

"Peace on earth, good will toward men." Those words, spoken by angels on the first Christmas, still resonate in our hearts. We long for peace – in our hearts, in our homes, and in our world.

At 1:15 pm on December 25, 2011 – Christmas Day – Kate "the Christian" Gosselin expressed what "Peace on earth" means to her when she tweeted the following:

'Peace on earth' really refers2those hours after all the toys r unwrapped&the kids scatter to play w/ them... Ahhhh, listen.. I hear peace!

It is worth noting here that, in all her tweeting that day, Kate never once mentioned the true meaning of Christmas. Not once. She said nothing about the birth of the Lord, Jesus Christ. Nothing, that is, until she was prompted to do so by her faithful tweeties who pointed out her rather egregious oversight.

Leading up to Christmas 2011, there was information leaked to the tabloids that, because Kate was "out of work" due to the cancellation of her show, she had told the kids they would be getting only one Christmas present each that year. That was true.

Kate, of course, read that tabloid story and set in motion her plan to prove to the world that it was a lie and that she truly was the "bestest" mom in the whole, wide world.

So on Christmas Eve, with eight beautiful children in her house who, undoubtedly, would have loved for their mom to give them her undivided attention, Mother-of-the-Year nominee Kate Gosselin did what any loving, devoted mother would do – she hosted a tweet party.

HEY! My gift 2u.... A TWEET PARTY... NOW 4 the next ?? til my kids stop playing peacefully :) ... Tell ur friends! Whatcha wanna ask me?

That Christmas of 2011 was my third Christmas being involved in the Gosselin saga. Still working for *US Weekly*, I was pretty relentless and left no stone – or trashcan – unturned in digging for information. My seven-day-a-week job was based solely on me being able to provide *US Weekly* with juicy, "insider" information. That wasn't always easy. There were many times when I had to get my hands dirty. Really dirty.

Starting with Christmas 2009, I and a pap friend of mine filled my old SUV with pretty much all of Kate's after-Christmas trash bags, to bring home to my lab for analysis. Well. It wasn't really a lab. The first year, my lab, otherwise known as the Gosselin trash repository, was in my kitchen. When my wife walked in and saw what I was doing, I thought she was going to kill me, right there on the kitchen floor. I see her point now, of course, but at the time, I was on an adrenaline high, working to support our kids.

Anyway, my main interest the first year was to see what the Gosselin kids got for Christmas. *US Weekly* wanted to know, and I didn't want to ask anyone point blank, so I found out the answer the nasty way. I learned many things about Kate's Christmas with the kids as a result of my trash picking, and I reported a lot of it to my employer. They chose what to print and what not to, of course.

This is what I discovered. Kate's online descriptions of a "Norman Rockwell" type Christmas inside the Gosselin house just didn't match up with the evidence and "insider information" I gathered from combing through all of her trash. Not even a little bit. The evidence proved something entirely different.

I'll start with Christmas 2011, because that's when Kate was on Twitter and her website lying about it. I still have every piece of that trash in my garage and basement. That sounds kind of twisted, I know, but I wanted to be able to prove my statements if called upon to do so. Of course, I also took pictures every step of the way, from the trash pickup at her house to the individual items displayed on a table in my lab, which I had relocated from my kitchen to my basement by then.

I know a lot of what the kids got for Christmas because I have all of Kate's online ordering receipts and the packaging that the items came in. They got some nice presents, for sure. So even if Kate's original intent was to give them only one present each, that didn't end up being the case. Perhaps the leaked tabloid story gave the kids a better Christmas.

It is not my place, nor anyone else's, to judge the number or quality of gifts a child should receive for Christmas. To me, that is a personal and private matter, and none of my business. It remains so until someone makes the matter not personal and private, and tries to deceive others in the process. What Kate does or does not give her children for Christmas would be a complete non-issue if she simply kept those matters private and didn't constantly go on record saying things like her kids deserve everything on a "golden platter," all the while moaning about how financially strapped she is. We then find out that she short-changes them to provide goodies for herself. All bets are off at that point.

Now on to specifics. I will dispel one of Kate's Christmas lies right away. This one is about Kate's gift-wrapping, which she tweeted about non-stop for several weeks. In all of the bags that I brought home from Kate's house – two trash pickups after Christmas day just so I wouldn't miss anything – the ONLY colorful wrapping paper that I found was in a single bag, and the pieces were torn up into very small sizes. Kate mentioned that she wraps stocking gifts individually, so these pieces would fit with that story.

Other trash bags were packed with what I know to be blank or unprinted newspaper. The local paper gives away "end of rolls" to anyone who wants it, and that is what Kate used to wrap her presents for her children. Blank, plain, discarded, FREE, unused newsprint. (Having worked at the local newspaper, I've used it once or twice in the past. But I put in the effort to hand-decorate the paper, and I always added ribbons, bows and tags for a festive look.)

For Kate's kids, though, there were no colorful bows. No ribbons. No fancy tags. Nothing. Just blank, off-white paper with a child's name written very small with a black pen. That name was for Kate to keep track of each child's presents as she put them in their own pile in their own designated spot on the floor.

In previous years, I found colorful post-it notes used as nametags for the children's gifts. Not fancy tags, but at least someone took a second to write a name on them. I guess there was no room in the 2011 budget to buy colorful post-it notes for the kids' Christmas presents after Kate purchased two new vehicles for herself that year.

The blank paper only matters because it is just another example of how Kate scrimps on the kids. Kate posted several photos online showing some of the kids sitting in front of colorfully wrapped presents, and she posted a photo of the kids at the table with the tree and many colorful presents around it. Those presents, however, were gifts that Kate wrapped for other people, including Steve and Gina Neild and their two boys. Most of the colorful presents around the tree were for Kate herself, from her tweeties. There were also wrapped presents for the kids from Kate's tweeties, but Kate didn't let them open them on Christmas day. She chose to put them away and use them later as incentives for good behavior.

The kids weren't even allowed to open their presents in the "family" room near the tree because Kate didn't want them to make a mess. Instead, they sat on the floor near the front steps, so that Kate could more easily put the paper in the trash and get it out of the house. The whole process was conducted like everything else that goes on in that house – with military precision and an exact adherence to orders. Kate wrote a blog about the "HUGE Success" that was her Christmas Day celebration. She puts these things out there online for one reason – to create the illusion for her fans that she is the greatest mom who ever lived, and no one else could possibly measure up. You probably know by now that the reality of the situation is almost always the exact opposite of what Kate says, or tweets, or blogs that it is.

Kate had tweeted about a "last minute Christmas miracle" several times leading up to the big day. Tweeties the world over were speculating about what this miracle could be. A miracle is defined as:

`1:` an extraordinary event manifesting divine intervention in human affairs
`2:` an extremely outstanding or unusual event, thing, or accomplishment

So you would think that this last-minute miracle present was going to be the present of all presents, right? As it turned out, Kate's "last minute Christmas miracle" present to the kids was … a $2.00 beta fish from the local pet store … for Mady only. According to Kate, "**Mady has been asking for a pet fish for as long as she could talk.**"

Mady had wanted a $2.00 beta fish since she was about 2 years old, and she had to wait for 9 years and a Christmas miracle to get one. Kate didn't even buy the fish bowl. As a matter of fact, she needed assistance just to think of this miracle. Someone had sent her flowers in a fishbowl as a gift, and she said that was what "spurred" her idea.

On a brighter note, Cara and Mady had a little Christmas treasure hunt around the house for the kids, leaving them hand-written clues on their personal note paper at each location. Now that's fun! My parents used to do that for my sister and me growing up and I, in turn, do it for our children. And they love it! It doesn't take a lot of money, but it does take effort – something Kate somehow finds impossible to give. It's too bad that the sextuplets' memories of those treasure hunts will be that their older sisters did it for them instead of their mother.

Interestingly, one of the treasure hunt clues read, "Where do the babysitters sleep?" This should leave no doubt in the minds of even Kate's most ardent supporters that strangers sleep over to watch the kids, even though Kate insists she does everything herself.

I found something else in the Gosselin trash that is the saddest thing I've read so far from the children. It was written in black marker by one of the Gosselin twins, and Kate, of course, threw it in the garbage. I have the original document in my office as a reminder of why I'm doing this.

> I've been hoping for a black Christmas
> Just like the ones I never knew
> Where the bush bottoms glisten
> And A-dults ignore
> To hear sleigh bells in the rain
> I've been hoping for a black Christmas
> With every Christmas card I receive
> My your days be sa-ad and dark
> And may all your Christmases be black.

This same child said on *Celebrity Wife Swap*. All I've ever known is work.

VIVA STAYCATION

For years, while filming *Jon & Kate Plus Ei8ht*, then *Kate Plus Ei8ht*, Discovery Communications/ TLC and Kate had always taken the kids on a working/filming vacation over spring break. Although the kids had to work on these trips, at least they got a chance to see new sights and maybe enjoy themselves for a bit.

A few years ago when they were filming on Bald Head Island in North Carolina, Kate said this would be a "tradition" that she would always continue for the kids. Not surprisingly, after the TV shows were canceled and the filming ended, the Bald Head Island vacation "tradition" ended as well. Kate failed to specify that a tradition would only remain a tradition if someone else were footing the bill.

In 2011, Kate told us that she didn't take the kids to Bald Head Island to continue the 1-year-old tradition because she couldn't rent the exact same house. Having rented summer beach houses before, I can tell you from personal experience that if you rented the house the previous year, you automatically get right of first refusal to rent it again the next year. Realtors do business this way to get the house locked up as far in advance as possible for their clients. So when Kate said that the house was booked, what she was really saying was that Discovery was no longer paying for her trips, so the "traditions" had to stop and the kids would lose out – as usual.

As 2012 rolled around, it proved to be another not-so-great year for vacationing for the eight Gosselin children. Kate once again came up with excuses as to why she was not taking her children on vacation. For the first time in several years (since TLC canceled Kate's show and, with it, all of her free trips), Kate "decided it would be fun" to take a "staycation!" What that meant was that the kids didn't get to reap the rewards of their hard work by going somewhere they might enjoy during their spring break from school.

A staycation can be a fun, affordable way to do family-friendly activities and entertain children during spring break or vacation time. This was a golden opportunity for Kate to finally do some things with, and entirely for, her kids. She had the chance to find out what they would like to do for a change; then actually do it. Instead, according to Kate's tweets and blog, the kids played school in the basement all week and did some work around the house.

"Staycations are a great way to save money! Check out our Spring Break plans on my Coupon blog!

`Spring Break at the Gosselins`
`Posted on March 5`[th]`, 2012`

> Typically during our very long ten day spring break, we have a fun trip planned. This year, I must admit it has crept up on me and I just realized the other day that I had planned absolutely nothing exciting. After my panic attack subsided, I decided that a rather relaxing home based 'staycation' may not be so bad after all. By staying home, we will not only save money, but we will truly be able to relax and that may turn out to be a different kind of fun. So, for our staycation, I decided the following things are a must in order to make it memorable for the whole family...

Kate then listed a few "musts" that they would be doing on their staycation. These fun and exciting events included:

> "At least one (if not two or three) movie nights with popcorn with a 'surprise.' I'm known for burying a small candy treat in the bottom of each of my kids' popcorn cups, so it has become an expected tradition (God help me if I should forget the surprise!)

> "A picnic lunch at a local playground – weather permitting, of course."

> "Reorganizing the garage and moving the kids' toys to the large shed I recently relocated to the right of our garage."

It's kind of funny that Kate said, "I'm known for burying a small candy treat in the bottom of each of my kids' popcorn cups..." She did that one time because they were filming. Also, those fun and exciting staycation events sound suspiciously like activities kids would ordinarily do even when not on break from school.

This is part of a blog Kate posted the next day, March 6, on her own website, *kateplusmy8.com*:

School During Spring Break…?!
March 6, 2012

> Our spring break comes really early each year. Usually, we have plans to travel somewhere. This year, it snuck up on me and with other obligations, doctor appointments and whatever else, I realized we would be spending time at home, playing… Oh and did I mention sleeping in? I made some mental plans for fun things to carry out this week but the kids have suddenly developed an amazing plan all on their own!

A few days later, Kate tweeted about their amazing, fun and exciting trip to the playground:

Good morning! Playground and picnic day! http://t.co/vX3w0blx

RT @xxxx @Kateplusmy8 **RT? Kate Gosselin's Kids Spend Spring Break in "School"! http://t.co/JPwqvYGw** via @babbleeditors **NICE ARTICLE:)**

A mere 30 minutes after Kate tweeted that picture of her kids at the playground, a "Kate approved" article appeared online about Kate's spring break, using Kate's own photo. The photo shows six freezing sextuplets by a picnic table eating their snacks. In Kate's own blog, she wrote: "A picnic lunch at a local playground – weather permitting, of course."

The kids were taken to the playground by somebody, maybe a babysitter, on Friday, when the weather was 40 degrees and very windy. The kids looked very cold. Thursday, the day before, was 70 degrees and sunny. That day would have been the perfect day for a picnic at the playground. The forecast had those days called perfectly all week, so the weather wasn't a surprise to the rest of us. How could the "most organized person on the planet" and the ultimate "masterminder" mess that up?

What was lost in the midst of Kate's excited tweeting and blogging about a staycation for the kids was the fact that Kate had no intention of settling for a staycation herself. Instead, she snuck away to Las Vegas with her handler, Steve, to attend a comedy club opening. She wasn't even smart enough to continue tweeting to her fans at least once or twice a day to give the impression that she was at home. It was only after a few photos of Kate and Steve at the comedy club turned up online, and a designer/dressmaker outed her on Twitter by telling her she looked "amazing" in his dress, that she came out of hiding and admitted what we already knew – that she was away from her kids once again having a grand old time on a lavish trip for herself.

With Steve accompanying her, the question arose yet again about Steve's role in her life. A tweet from one of her superfans gave Kate the chance to explain why Steve has to accompany her on her travels. Apparently, this 38-year-old mother of eight, former reality star who is now fading away into obscurity, desperately needs a bodyguard. She tweeted that having a bodyguard was "Important for my safety. :)" (Somehow, the story, "The Ransom of Red Chief," by O. Henry springs to mind.) Kate said just a few short months ago that Steve was now her "road manager," so it remains foggy what it is he actually does.

The bottom line is, while the kids got to do absolutely nothing but work around the house and play school in the basement on their spring break, Kate treated herself to a four-day birthday present away from them, to Sin City. Then, in true Kate fashion, she returned home and tapped out these "Look, I'm a regular mom, just like you all" tweets:

> **Good day!This morning sure came fast! We had egg, ham and cheese burritos for breakfast then quickly out the door..grouchy Monday morning..**

> **...sitting at the bus stop eating dry organic 'Cheerios'... So hungry!!The life of a mom, I guess??! :)**

HOPPY EASTER, GOSSELIN KIDS

As Easter approached in 2012, Kate posted her "much-anticipated" coupon blog about her plans to save money for the holiday. Any guesses on where she planned to cut corners once again? If you said, "on the kids," you would be correct. That question was too easy, I know.

While their friends were probably getting Easter baskets filled with fresh chocolate, assorted candies and maybe a few toys, the Gosselin children's mother planned to fill their baskets with … "toothbrushes, socks and batteries." And if we are to believe what Kate wrote in her blog, the kids were also going to be lucky enough to get year-old, non-Easter-themed candy that she kept in the freezer all year because she got it at half-price the day after last Easter. Her advice: "Don't waste money on Easter-themed candy."

Kate also informed us that her kids were not getting any special Easter outfits that year. She wrote that, instead of buying said Easter outfits, she would be buying the kids one pastel-colored item of clothing, like a polo shirt or skirt, so they could wear it year round. Her frugality would not be the object of anyone's scorn if she worked just as hard trying to save money on purchases for herself.

The disgrace of this is that Kate actually described how she would be saving on buying things for her children just two days after returning home from that expensive, first-class trip to Las Vegas with her married "friend." Kate was comped two tickets to the comedy club opening in Vegas, but her first-class travel, including limousine to and from her MGM Grand hotel suite, her expensive meals, and her Vegas shopping spree all came out of the family money. Money the kids earned.

Kate got a luxurious trip to Las Vegas with a handsome, married man. The Gosselin kids got a working staycation and year-old Easter candy.

But a new twist was about to impact Kate's Easter plans.

On Friday, April 6, 2012, Kate "found out" via Twitter that Jon might possibly be going to court the following week to fight for more custody time with his kids. Kate pretended not to be aware of the impending court appearance. Whether she knew or not, the fact that it became public knowledge might be why she suddenly did a 180-degree turn from her previous Easter plans, where the kids would be getting year-old candy and batteries, socks and toothbrushes, and they would not be coloring eggs. These were Kate's Easter tweets *before* the court news reached her:

xxxxx @Kateplusmy8 how many dozen eggs do you color?

> **kids get bored of it so I'll probably HB a few dozen (were overrun remember) and see how they go...**
>
> xxxxx @Kateplusmy8 mine only wanted 2draw on them w/clear crayon.I ended up coloring.Ran out of gloves (see bike tweet) so now my fingers r awful
>
> **yep. Happened to me last year. Make a mess then run off... Ugh!**

But in the span of three days, after news broke of Jon possibly going to court for more custody, Kate suddenly changed her tune about her Easter plans:

> **GM everyone! Busy day here! 800+ eggs&8 baskets to fill, cooking, baking and Easter outfits to lay out! I better get going...!! Yikes!**

xxxxx @Kateplusmy8 Do you still hide hundreds of Easter eggs around outside for the kids to find?

> **yes.. Stuffing is on the list for today and tomorrow. 6-800 this year!**
>
> **just counted my supply.. Actually 1100-12—eggs this year... We have 2 little friends joining us :)**

According to Kate's tweets, the number of eggs she filled went from 600-800 one minute to 1100-1200 the next. How is it possible that Kate "just counted" her supply and she didn't know exactly how many eggs she had? Keep reading for the answer to that question. ;) Here are some more of her pre-Easter tweets:

xxxxx @Kateplusmy8 Please tell me @Kateplusmy you're not really hiding 800 eggs. It seems like the kids would get burnt out trying to find all of them

> **my kids dash like its an Olympic sport! Gotta hide that many (or more!) to make it last more than a blink of an eye!**
>
> **Kids in bed,dog in bed,house is cleaned up so I'm saying GN! Lots of cooking,easter basket preparing&egg filling tomorrow,oh my!Need sleep!**

....settling into another four days with my kids....plan to over Easter egg,candy and toy them..So excited to see hoppy faces all around! :)

xxxxx @Kateplusmy8 I'm betting this is a custody hearing. Explains why you are going overboard with Easter celebrations. You will never learn.

lol. Overboard? I'm actually scaling back this year...I go overboard for every holiday and birthday... The nature of a mom!

xxxxx @Kateplusmy8 Still filling eggs Kate?:)

yes. Then onto Easter baskets... Almost done!:) yay!

xxxxx @Kateplusmy8 I have just read that you have 1100/1200 eggs ...that will keep the ADULTS occupy for a while haha xx kids can chill out xx

oh yeah- always takes way longer to hide than to find. Why is that? :)

....and with that, good night to all! What a long fun day! As for tomorrow, I better rest quick! Hoppy Easter! http://t.co/ybmYOl94

The link Kate posted in this last tweet was to a photo of her Easter baskets on the dining room table. Kate had made it sound like she had created the most incredible baskets in the history of Easter basket making. The photo showed them to be nothing special; really very mediocre at best for a woman nearing 40 who claims to be super at everything she does. Her tweeties were absolutely amazed, though, and gave her an A++++ grade for her effort. Well, at least the kids got baskets. Things got far more interesting on Easter Sunday. This is Kate's version of how Easter day went:

4.8.12   (Easter Sunday)

Home fr church (wonderful Easter celebration!) now let the candy,lunch&egg hunting begin! Excitement in air- Feels like Christmas here....;)

And so the eggs were filled (well, last night) hidden, hunted, emptied and returned to the bin within two hours! http://t.co/Wd2NnQXp

...it's all over!The last of r guests hav gone, house is still in partial disarray,all r well fed,very well candied (includingmommy!)& happy

Now that you've read Kate's version of Easter, I will tell you what really happened on the Gosselin's 2012 Easter Sunday. I can do this because I was there, at Kate Gosselin's house, watching the events unfold.

Just as she had promoted on Twitter for a week, Kate did take the kids to church on Easter Sunday. I watched and photographed them as they entered and exited the building. Despite online rumors that they left church early, the Gosselins stayed inside the church through the entire service and exited with the rest of the huge crowd.

As she was leaving the parking lot, Kate stopped her van to take a photo of a donkey that was tied up behind the church. She posted the photo to prove to the Twitter world that she actually did make it to Easter services. One thing strikes me as very funny about her Twitter photo of the donkey. If you look in Kate's side mirror, you can see my car directly behind hers. At the time I couldn't figure out why she was stopping and holding up traffic. I thought she saw me and was coming back to confront me. Nope. Just a routine snapshot of a jackass.

After Easter mass and the donkey photography, Kate drove straight back home. I had fully expected to see the Gosselin yard covered in Easter eggs placed there by a "helper" while Kate and the kids were at church. I just knew that Kate wouldn't be doing the menial job of placing the eggs in the yard herself. She's just too lazy. But when we got back to the house, the yard was bare. Where were the 1100-1200 Easter eggs? And if they weren't there now, how long would it take for Kate to scatter them around?

This was a real bummer to me because here I was, wasting my Easter Sunday watching Kate Gosselin while my own family was at home enjoying their day without me. I did break away at 11:45 to head home so I could help my wife put eggs in our yard for our own egg hunt. The kids had a great time. Each of our three kids got 27 eggs and that seemed more than enough to make them happy. I took tons of photos and video of the great fun my kids were having, but I just had to see for myself what 1200 colored eggs looked like for ten children, so I raced back to Kate's house and took my place among the trees with the pap. And there we sat – the pap and I. Sitting in the bushes in the chilly air, waiting for something to happen. Anything. On Easter Sunday. Lame, I know.

Up to this point, all we got to see were the three boys walking down to the barn to take care of the chickens. Their chore. They walked down at exactly 11 AM and stayed until 11:30. They looked so happy to be out of the house and doing what little boys should be doing – playing around the outside of the barn and just enjoying being outside.

Meanwhile, back at the house, Kate had company. I photographed a happy couple wandering around outside. I didn't recognize them, but I later identified them as Kate's stylist Deanna from New York City and Deanna's boyfriend/husband/companion? Take your pick.

Several hours went by, and the only activity we saw was what appeared to be a family portrait sitting being set up by the front of the house. Deanna's boyfriend/husband/companion spent 30 minutes moving several potted plants around so they were "just right" for the photos. Pretty boring stuff. This took place between 3 and 4 PM. After the photo shoot, the kids were allowed to play outside for a bit for the first time that day. They rode their scooters for a few minutes, and then the excitement started.

At 4:15 PM, two SUVs arrived at the Gosselin compound. Within minutes, two strangers – an Asian man and a Caucasian woman – emerged from the vehicles with a large storage tub filled with plastic Easter eggs. (Apparently, the Easter Bunny drives an SUV. Who knew?) The strangers transferred the eggs from the tub into white garbage bags, then carried the garbage bags around the property, scattering the eggs for the upcoming egg hunt.

I showed Jon some photos that I took of the two strangers, thinking that the Asian man was a family member or friend of the family, but he had no idea who they were. He had never seen them before.

The fact that strangers delivered and scattered Easter eggs around the yard meant that Kate never even had the plastic Easter eggs at her house, so her entire week's worth of tweets about filling Easter eggs was yet another whopper of a Kate Gosselin lie. Once again, Kate did nothing…yet she had spent a week on Twitter telling everyone how hard she was working to prepare for the holiday.

Kate tweets photos of every minor thing she and her kids are doing during the day. She once tweeted photos of a bag of flour that she bought, and she tweeted a photo of a bunch of towels that she folded. She thinks these photos prove to everyone what a wonderful mother she is and how hard she works. With all of her photo sharing, how is it possible that she failed to tweet one single photo of the actual stuffing of the 1200 Easter eggs that she said she herself filled full of candy and other surprises? Was it that she couldn't take pictures because the eggs were filled elsewhere and brought to the house at 4:15 PM on Easter Sunday by complete strangers?

During the hour that the two strangers were meticulously placing the eggs, Kate tweeted a photo of a glass of red wine from inside the house, while the kids were once again being entertained by strangers. So Kate's exhausting Easter preparations consisted of her hiring a company to set up and orchestrate an Easter egg hunt for her children while she stayed inside and drank wine? Kate never once set foot outside of the house to watch the kids during the egg hunt. Not once. The strangers even took pictures of the Gosselin kids collecting the Easter eggs, so that was another annoyance Kate didn't have to bother with either. I guess that was part of the "egg hunt package."

If you were following along at home via Twitter, you would probably have assumed that the egg hunt took place right after church and that Kate was unwinding with a glass of wine later in the day after all of her hard work. In reality, the egg hunt didn't start until 5:15 PM, and it was over by 5:45 PM. It took 30 minutes for the kids to pick up 1200 eggs scattered around 23 acres. By 6:00 PM, Kate put a photo on Twitter of the Easter eggs packed up back in the storage tub.

Meanwhile, questions arose on Twitter about the pap pictures from the Easter egg hunt. Deanna, the newest self-appointed defender of Kate, decided to 'clear things up' about who took the photos. She tweeted:

> I was there on Easter &there was a pap that drove by and took pics during hunt

> Um,yes,1camera was mine.The guy in the pap photo is a family member of a kid at EEhunt--he has a short lens-not pap

When Deanna mentioned "The guy in the pap photo," she was talking about the stranger who placed the eggs in the yard and who was also taking pictures of the kids. If we are to believe Deanna that "The guy in the pap photo is a family member of a kid at EEhunt-," here is a question to ponder. If you brought a child to an Easter egg hunt at a "friend's" house, would your friend expect you to volunteer to spend an entire hour walking around a 23-acre property individually hand-placing more than 1000 plastic eggs, while your friend sat inside the house drinking wine? No friend of mine would.

As I said, I was there. And I took pictures. I photographed this so-called "friend" and his partner placing the eggs around the yard for more than an hour while Deanna was inside with Kate. I took several hundred photos with a 500-mm lens, so I was very much up close up and personal to the action.

Kate claimed on Twitter that she had absolutely no idea that a pap was there taking pictures. Someone tweeted Deanna asking her about this:

> xxxxx @deannatweeting @xxxxx @xxxxx @xxxxx @kateplusmy8 How were you able to see the pap & Kate couldn't? Said she didn't notice a pap.

Deanna answered:

> I didn't see the pap,but can tell where he was on the road based on pics.He drove by

That was a lie. Deanna was outright lying when she said "I didn't see the pap." I took a nice, clear photo of Deanna and her man smiling and pointing DIRECTLY INTO MY LENS as I stood across the street. Someone sent this tweet calling her out and questioning her story:

> xxxxx @deannatweeting @xxxxx @kateplusmy8 this is why ppl call BS. You say a pap drove by then u say u didn't see one. Sounds fishy.

Deanna then tried to extricate herself from her lies by responding that there's a single spot on the road where the paps can drive by and see in the yard only for a second:

> There is a curve of the road where the paps drive by &can c into the yard 4 a second.im not a fan of paps:(

I was not driving back and forth on the road shooting from a single spot. There were no trees in front of me. The Easter eggs were placed in the only area of the property where the paps actually CAN just stand there and take as many pictures as they want. It doesn't take a genius to figure out why the Easter eggs were placed in that exact area. Kate had tweeted about the Easter egg hunt for an entire week, basically inviting the paps to show up to take pictures of her kids enjoying the fabulous egg hunt she was putting together.

If Kate wanted to protect her children from the lone paparazzo and me, she wouldn't have had the eggs placed around the only part of her property that gives a crystal-clear view of the action. She would have had the eggs placed only on the right side of the house, behind the house, or better yet, in the HUGE horse paddock behind the house where nobody could ever see. I was back in that area many times before the divorce, riding motorcycles, cooking out and walking in the woods. It's completely private. But that's not what Kate wanted. Sorry, Deanna. We're not buying your lies.

Of all Kate's lies and misdirections about her Easter preparations, one particular Twitter exchange sums up the most important part of this Easter story. In the span of two weeks of tweeting about the Easter holiday – the absolute most important day on the Christian calendar – Kate never once mentioned one word about the true meaning of Easter or expressed any sentiment about the solemn days leading up to Easter Sunday. This tweet (in bold) is Kate Gosselin's only mention of Good Friday, the day on which Christians believe Jesus carried his cross, was crucified and died for our sins:

xxxxx @Kateplusmy8 Good Friday to u Kate & Kids & to all the world!!!

aww. You too. I was born on Good Friday... 37 long years ago lol..

It's nice to know that Good Friday is so important because it was the day Kate was born. Happy Easter, Gosselin kids.

CRUISE CONTROL

Just sit right back and you'll hear a tale, a tale of a fateful trip ... Actually, no you won't because this floating, would-be disaster never got the chance to leave port, as many suspected from the day it was announced. It is impossible to imagine anyone, anywhere, ever thinking there would be enough people on Earth foolish enough to spend their hard-earned money to go on The Kate Gosselin Celebrity Cruise – especially in August during hurricane season. But here was the pitch, in black and white:

Sail with Kate!
Join reality star KATE GOSSELIN on a spectacular ship
Join reality TV star Kate Gosselin, full time mother (of Eight) and author of several books including her latest, I just Want You To Know, Letters To My Kids On Love, Faith and Family, aboard the Allure of the Seas, the newest ship in Royal Caribbean's awe-inspiring Oasis class.

Highlights & Extras
- Private Events and Highlights
- Please check back often as more details become available.
- Meet Kate Gosselin at our private welcome cocktail party
- A commemorative personalized gift from Kate (one per family)
- Capture your memories onboard with a personal photo with Kate Gosselin

- Join Kate for a private BBQ on deck with a fabulous band
  - Join Kate for a morning brunch
  - Fun fun family games with Kate and staff
  - Charity dinner with Kate (optional)
  - Got questions for Kate? Attend her Q & A session
- Check out Kate's latest book and bring it onboard for a book signing
- Doesn't Kate always have the best ideas! Learn a new craft from the professional herself
  - Let's explore! Shore excursion with Kate
- Let's talk about our fabulous cruise experience! Private group farewell dinner

Events subject to change.

This cruise had nothing to do with Kate wanting to meet or please her fans. Kate wouldn't give her fans the time of day if there wasn't something in it for her. No, this cruise was just one more shameless attempt for Kate to make money by taking advantage of her fans, and for her manager, Julie May, to earn a commission. This was obvious because of the extremely inflated price of the "Sail with Kate!" cruise and because they scheduled it during hurricane season, which meant they could make the greatest profit since there would normally be plenty of cabins available to sell.

Kate is uncomfortable around people in general, and her "annoying" fans in particular. She had to change her tune, though, to seem warm, welcoming and excited as she tried to convince her "followers" to plunk down their hard-earned money to cruise with her. These are some of her tweets about the cruise:

Here's a big announcement that will have an Allure for you and your kids http://t.co/KbJBKi0c Come hang out! Can't wait to meet you!

I would love to have a chance to meet you. . We are gonna have SO much F.U.N. http://t.co/KbJBKi0c

Hey guys, have you booked your cruise with me yet? I cannot wait to get crazy and have fun with YOU! http://t.co/KbJBKi0c

I can't wait to meet you all!Pls don't miss it! I'm getting all teary eyed hoping2meet so many of u in 1 place! http://t.co/KbJBKi0c

That sure sounds like a person who really, really, really wants to meet her fans, doesn't it? But was she being truthful? Read on, then you make the call.

In January of 2012, Kate was in Los Angeles doing an interview at The Grove, whatever that is. There was video footage of her and Steve Neild outside after her interview ended, and she was surrounded by her "fans." You know, the ones who she says over and over and over that she would loooooove to meet.

So there was Kate, at ten o'clock in the morning, standing up on a platform being interviewed, all dressed up in a shiny silver mini-dress right out of Star Trek Deep Space Nine, smiling and surrounded by her adoring fans and curious onlookers. Yet the moment the interview ended, the fake smile left Kate's face and she stepped down from the platform to get the Hell out of there and away from her admiring fans (or "friends" as she likes to call them on Twitter) as fast as she could. Steve, bodyguard/road manager extraordinaire, had the presence of mind to make her come back for a minute to interact with some of the people who had waited patiently for a chance to see her. Google "Kate Gosselin at The Grove." If you watch and listen to the clip closely, you will hear Kate say to Steve, "That wasn't part of it."

"That," meaning interacting with her fans, might not have been "part of it," but it sure as heck is something that a person in Kate's position should be smart enough to do if she is serious about maintaining the false appearance that she gives a crap about her fans.

Kate pitched the cruise on Twitter relentlessly. She didn't provide any helpful details about it, she just begged and cajoled and gushed over her fans to try to convince them to pony up the big bucks for the cruise. It's disgusting that Kate was on Twitter badgering her fans who couldn't afford to go on her cruise, to go on her cruise, just 2 months before she wrote a blog where she told people how they could save money by taking a staycation. As usual, Kate's tweets are in bold.

xxxxx @Kateplusmy8 we r planning Disney cruise for ths summr. Maybe I change it 2 ths one :)

seriously, Sarah? Please DO!!!!

you signing up? I'll die if so!!! Say yes! And bring the tweenie...:)

xxxxx @Kateplusmy8 So happy for you! I'd love 2 go-have to wait and see...

omg!!!!! Say yes... to the cruise! :)

ours is outta ft Lauderdale... Do it do it do it! ;)

xxxxx @Kateplusmy8 OMGosh!!! I cannot believe it. I am so excited and pray I can do this. May have to sell an organ, but by golly I want to go! :)

I'll cry tears of joy if you can do it and especially if you bring all your organs (and pianos!) along lol!

xxxxx @Kateplusmy8 Me too. I think it would be a blast. Gonna try and go.

yay! Please do! Omg I'm getting so excited- already!

xxxxx @Kateplusmy8 Kate...would U wheel around in wheelchair? LOL

I'll wheel you anywhere u want to go... I'll give the lights out man a break, no problem! Don't let wheels stop u! Please?!

xxxxx @Kateplusmy8 Just read about your Cruise...then I got a text on my phone saying "Needs some extra funds for the New Year" ...Sho-do!

oh Leigh we'd laugh til we cried... Get moving lady...;)

xxxxx @Kateplusmy8 just got brochure 4 "Katecruise" u r making it tough to say no! Thx 4 info!!!

please say yes, Rhonda! So want to meet you!!!;)

xxxxx @Kateplusmy8 Researching cruise,airfare,hotel w/DH this afternoon. Anything you can say to convince him to sign on? ;-)

puuuulllleeassse? I so wanna meet you! (for real!)

yay!!! This is so amazing... Getting to meet some great tweety friend! :) so so exciting!

ahhhhh! I'm so excited!!!!! Cannot wait to meet you!!! Who else is going??! Please tell!

xxxxx @Kateplusmy8 So adorbs..Every year me+a circle of friends take cruise every year+my bf for over 30yrs is a travel agent..very tempting.. ☺

DO IT DO IT DO IT DO IT..Lolo

In these next tweets, rather than telling this very impressionable and fragile girl who has been idolizing Kate for many months, not to worry about missing the cruise because she's doing the right thing by saving for college, Kate responds with only a sad face. What a perfect way to make this poor girl feel guilty and bad.

xxxxx @Kateplusmy8 I have to save up for college!

Sad face :(

In this next Twitter exchange, a woman tweets to Kate telling her that she can't afford to go on Kate's cruise because she is already going on a cruise one month before. Not seeming to consider this woman's financial circumstances, Kate continues to beg her to go:

xxxxx @Kateplusmy8 I still want to go on cruise in August but since we are going to Alaska in July not sure finances can handle both

please please sign up! Dying to meet you!We will all have so much fun! Can't wait!Will spend lotsa X w my friends! :)

Some of Kate's followers finally dared to mention the expense of the trip, which by all accounts was priced much higher than it should have been. To give you an idea of how much higher, the exact same cruise without the Kate Gosselin events could be booked on *expedia.com* for $824 per person. The price range for the cruise including the "Sail With Kate" experience came in at a whopping $1,900 to $3,175 per person. But in her tweets, Kate denied all responsibility for the expense. The bold tweets are Kate's answers to questions and comments about the cost of the cruise on Twitter:

> xxxxx @Kateplusmy8 I've been unemployed for 2 years. OMG....who can AFFORD this? I'm soooooooo sad now......

> xxxxx @Kateplusmy8 Not that many people can afford to join you. Why so expensive?

> **I have nothing to do with that... I'm just going to meet greet and have fun with everyone! :)**

> xxxxx @Kateplusmy8 Are you paying?

> **I so wish I could pay for all of you... I wish $ didn't stop vacations/family memories. Don't you?**

> xxxxx @Kateplusmy8 need to lower the prices.

> **I'm not in charge of that or it would be free for ALL! :)**

The prices for celebrity events such as this are not arrived at arbitrarily. You can bet your bottom dollar that Kate's manager, Julie May, negotiated and settled on Kate's compensation for the cruise long before it was ever announced. And as Kate's representative, Julie May would have been obligated to inform Kate about the negotiated price. That's the way it works. There's no way Kate's manager would let a cruise line dictate dollar figures to her. So when Kate told her followers that she had nothing to do with the price of the cruise, she was telling them yet another BIG, FAT LIE.

For weeks, Kate avoided answering the many questions she received on Twitter regarding whether her kids were going on the cruise.

> xxxxx @Kateplusmy8 are the kids going?! :)

> xxxxx @Kateplusmy8 Your cruise sounds so fun...wish I could go! :(Are the kids going with? Your first cruise?

These tweets elicited no response from Kate, the ultimate responder to all tweets great and small. But rather than just saying "Nope. It'll just be me. My kids won't be joining us," she kept hope alive that they were going. You could sense that it was only a matter of time until the kids were drawn into this lie and exploitation.

So after almost a month of shameless promotion and lies to try to get people to sign up, and despite all of Alice Travel's marketing nonsense that people were going crazy for the Kate cruise, sales were dismal. The response was totally underwhelming. It was time to bring out the ace in the hole.

Believe it or not, even though she wishes it were not so, and often deludes herself into believing it's not so, and tries her darndest to do things to make it not so, Kate Gosselin is smart enough to realize that the only reason anyone cares about her is because of her kids. So what to do? What to do? Oh, wait. She would do the same thing she always does to salvage a moneymaking plan:

Yep. It's true! Mady and Cara are sailing too! Can't wait to have a big girls week with our fans! Join US!

Alice Travel even revised the itinerary to add the very creepy sales pitch that said something like, "Watch Kate play with her children on the beach!" Nothing screams vacation fun like putting children on display like trained monkeys.

But not even dangling the kids as bait could save this stinker of a non-event. So after more than three months of guerilla marketing and promotion, and Kate's shameless begging, the Kate portion of the cruise was quietly laid to rest. It was simply destined to fail, like everything else Kate Gosselin touches.

And after her hundreds and hundreds of tweets about the cruise, you are probably curious about how Kate notified her 90+ thousand Twitter followers of its cancellation. In true Kate Gosselin fashion, she didn't. It was as if Kate's involvement in the cruise had never been announced. The Alice Travel website disappeared, and Kate never mentioned it again, or gave any public explanation at all. The organizers were kind enough to release this brief statement on May 9, 2012:

```
Kate Gosselin Cruise Canceled: 'We Didn't Get The Turnout We
Desired,' Says Organizer

"Yes, that event has been canceled. We just didn't get the
turnout that we desired and mutually we agreed that if we didn't
get it, we would cancel," President of Luxury Cruises, who merged
with the company originally organizing the event, Alice Travel,
exclusively told RadarOnline.com.
"All ticket purchasers have been notified and everyone has been
refunded. Some have chosen to continue on with the cruise, but
everyone was given the choice."
"Kate asked for everybody's names, addresses and phone numbers
and reached out to each one personally," the spokeswoman said.
"It was nothing to do with her. We needed to hit certain numbers
and they just weren't where they needed to be."
```

That apparition you see in the distance is the rapidly fading form of a has-been reality show participant disappearing from the consciousness of people who were once fooled by her.

THE BEST DAY

"I have an excellent father
His strength is making me stronger
God smiles on my little brother
Inside and out
He's better than I am
I grew up in a pretty house
And I had space to run
And I had the best days with you."
– *Taylor Swift*

I have had the distinct good fortune of spending time with the Gosselin kids on many, many occasions during Jon's custody time. Here is a snapshot of what the Gosselin kids' lives are like when they are with their dad.
On a random night in 2012, I visited for a few hours with Jon and the kids. This is their "normal" when they are with Jon.

- They cooked a nice dinner and ate as a family with some guests.

- They had Dunkin' Donuts after dinner and couldn't eat them fast enough.

- They played games and made crafts.

- Jon sat with the girls and made beaded jewelry with them, and he seemed to really enjoy it.

- Two of the little girls made me beaded bracelets.

- Jon made a campfire outside and roasted marshmallows with the kids. The kids loved it and gobbled them up as fast as he could make them.

- The little kids took turns reading books to me and showing me their toys.

- Jon handed out animal masks for all the kids to play with and pretend to be wild animals.

- A friend of Jon's was showing the kids card tricks. They were captivated.

- The Disney channel was playing on the big TV in the background, but nobody was paying attention to it. They were having too much fun.

- Jon's girlfriend, her three kids, and her mom were also there, having fun and playing with the kids as well. It was great to see the kids playing with other children in an unstructured, healthy environment.

- The kids were allowed to be just kids. There was nobody barking orders, and there wasn't a minute-by-minute schedule for them to follow … like there is when they are at home with their mother.

I have never seen the kids so happy and relaxed.

There is a beautiful photograph taken long ago of Hannah running into Jon's arms, with her own arms wide open and a huge smile on her face. She jumped up into his grasp and gave him the biggest hug I have ever seen her or any of her siblings give.
Kate Gosselin has been photographed by the paparazzi about fifty times more than Jon, but I have never seen a photo like the one taken of Hannah running into Jon's arms. I have never seen a photo of any of the Gosselin kids showing any kind of happiness or affection towards Kate, ever.
If anyone on Earth can produce a single photo of Kate Gosselin with any of her children showing this much genuine love and emotion, I would love to see it.
These kids are truly happy when they're with their dad. When the kids are photographed with Kate, they almost always look sad or scared.
Pictures don't lie.

THE REBRANDING OF KATE GOSSELIN

If Kate Gosselin dislikes her ex-husband Jon as much as it would appear to the world, since she verbally bashes him every chance she gets in interviews and online tweeting, and continues to do so years after the divorce, why then does she keep his last name? In 2013, why is Kate Gosselin not Katie Kreider?

The answer is quite simple really – it is because "Kate Gosselin" is a "brand." Kate Gosselin, mom of eight. Kate Gosselin, mother of sextuplets and twins. Kate Gosselin…Supermom!

Kate Gosselin wants us to forget everything ugly we have ever seen of her on television for the past 8 years; every bad thing we have read about her in the press (tabloids and otherwise); and every bit of nastiness we have heard from her own lips. Kate wants everyone to believe that all of the bad parenting and horrendous behavior we witnessed during seven seasons of her "most realistic reality shows" was a product of TLC's careful editing to make her look bad – even though Kate always had final approval of the show before it aired, as demonstrated in her emails back and forth with the Network.

Kate had total control over the final product, and yet she chose to show the world the mostly nasty moments of her life? If that was the best they could come up with, it is scary to think about what was left on the cutting-room floor.

As the end of her contract with Discovery Communications was drawing near in March of 2012, desperation was setting in for Kate. It became very noticeable via Twitter, her own website, and her few-and-far-between television interviews that she felt the need to change her ways and the public's increasingly bad perception of her.

A lot of people were fooled by this tactic, and Kate and her manager, Julie Carson May, must be very thankful for each and every one of Kate's fans who refuse to believe she can do anything wrong. Without the undying and unwavering cluelessness, ignorance and support of those fans, Kate and Julie Carson May would not be able to continue their scam/charade/web of lies. Kate is so deeply appreciative, she wrote the following sincere words on Twitter:

thank u. I am always so grateful 2those of u who continue 2 stand by my side, knowing the truth and fighting the despicable 1s

You need look no further than Julie Carson May's company website for the answer to how Kate Gosselin, a complete failure as a mother, housewife, cook, businesswoman and human being, started transforming before our very eyes into a fitness expert, nutrition expert, motivational speaker, supermom, chef, etc.

MEDIA MOTION INTERNATIONAL specializes in building and developing expert and celebrity **brands.**

In 2005 Julie Carson May founded media Motion International to focus on building brands and platforms for talented experts, celebrities, hosts, and corporations. **Her expertise is in working with talent and companies in the life improvement field including fitness, nutrition, health and wellness, design, and many other areas.**

It is interesting, or maybe just an incredible coincidence, that those are the exact areas that Kate Gosselin began to pretend she was an expert in, once Discovery pulled the plug on both her reality shows. Kate Gosselin is a product being "marketed" to the viewing audience.

Despite the fact that she has failed at everything she has ever touched, Kate continues to try to rebrand and reinvent herself over and over in the hopes that she will finally find a character/persona that people will want to watch on television and whose books people would want to buy.

Here are just a few of Kate's past and present attempts at finding a "brand":

- The happily married, exhausted, God-fearing Christian mother of eight
- The exhausted, single mother of eight
- The exhausted, single, happy homemaker mother of eight
- The exhausted, organized mother of eight
- The exhausted, dating mother of eight
- The world-traveling mother of eight
- The hot and sexy mother of eight
- The marathon-running, fitness expert mother of eight
- The coupon-cutting, money-saving expert mother of eight
- The speaking out against bullying mother of eight
- The "giving back" and helping other mothers, inspirational mother of eight

The world is still waiting for one that will stick.

After Kate lost her TV show, and no other viable TV opportunities arose through which she could rebrand herself, she was forced to take to social media to retain some kind of public presence. She became a Twitter-holic, desperately trying to keep her brand alive while simultaneously trying to create new brands in the process. Since Kate's primary, and usually only, means of interaction with the public is through Twitter, the rest of this chapter contains heavy doses of tweets to and from Kate.

After having read Kate's own words in this book, and having seen her in action throughout seven seasons of reality television, you can decide for yourself if Kate Gosselin is being genuine or just following the next set of instructions laid out for her by her manager.

ONE IS THE LONELIEST NUMBER

Do you remember hearing about an upcoming new TLC show called *Twist of Kate*? It was going to be a show where Kate alone, no eight, would travel the country trading places with people and doing their job for a day. A pilot episode was reportedly filmed, but the show never saw the light of day.

In dissecting what caused *Twist of Kate* to flop before it ever aired, you need think no harder than to notice what was missing from the idea for the show: the eight. The eight children made Kate famous, and both Kate and Julie Carson May know it. This is why they will continue to exploit those kids for their own monetary gain as much and as often as they possibly can until somebody finally puts a stop to it. Eight kids. Every time Kate Gosselin opens her mouth, she works in the fact that she has eight kids. That's her entire shtick. She is nothing without her eight children. In honor of Kate's favorite number, here is a selection of eight of her tweets from the scores of tweets where Kate mentions the number 8:

> **GM all! It's another nice sunny one! Looking forward 2 more pool time and movie night including popcorn w a surprise tonight with my gr8 8!**

> **Went 2 church this am,then we dashed out 2 r pool! 80ish degrees, pure sun w/ my 8 little fish swimming!Ahh!How every Mothers day should be!**

> **Happy Mothers Day everyone! I am reminded today of how blessed I am to be a mom....8 times!!! Hope your day is filled w/ overwhelming love!**

> **I stood at utility sink for 8 hours straight once... 8 sets of sheets w chunks... Agreed.. Wasn't fun! :(**

> **My six of EIGHT will be EIGHT in EIGHT days... Omg!All the 8's... That's so cool! I'm so elated I have 8 healthy smart happy healthy kids!XO**

> **I am getting ever closer to 88,888 followers.... Isn't that SO cool? My favorite number, of course, is the number '8'...**

> **...just heard I hit 88,888 followers at 1:08am! How cool is that? Just like I tell my 8 kids..'I love you all..as if you were my only 1'! XO**

> **there's many reall Kate's I'm sure...I'm the one w/ 8 kids**

Kate Gosselin has eight children. Who knew?

TWITTER REBRAND: THE POSITIVE KATE GOSSELIN

In all her years on television, Kate has rarely shown herself to be a pleasant person to be around. She has usually been seen barking orders, or yelling at someone, or hitting someone, or criticizing someone, or making fun of someone, or making snide remarks about someone, or being negative, or complaining about how put upon she is, or whining about how awful her children and husband are and how difficult her life is. But as she began her descent into obscurity, something miraculous happened. The Kate Gosselin from TV suddenly transformed from a shrew into little Suzie Sunshine. Or at least her tweets would have us believe that miracle occurred. Here are eight of Kate's remarkably positive tweets:

I don't have X 4 people who hate others 4 working hard,staying pos,&trying 2 make a diff! Do you?

xxxxx @Kateplusmy8 Loved seeing you on Dr. Drew! Wish you had another show.. Any chance? xoxo

that would be great! I never rule out any chances of greatness in my life... You shouldn't either! :)

GN all! It is time to 'get flat' I've been told.... So catch u when Mr Sun comes up again... Another day2make a + difference in our world!

GM! Today I'm reminding myself that only thing that matters are the 8 people that call me mom! Don't care how it LOOKS, we know what's REAL!

Night night! Have pleasant dreams all! I dream of peace and harmony,hard work, honesty,kindness&positivity for all! ☺

GM all... Failure is NOT an option; it's a cop out! Remind yourselves of that (as I am) as often as is necessary! Keep on keeping on....o

I prefer positivity over negativity...helps motivate me 2keep going! I c the glass half full Bc that's better than empty,right!:)

GM all!Remember this:Don't focus on negativity,find the positive in every situation...It's always there,u just have 2 look harder someXs!:)

THE HAPPY HOMEMAKER

Kate is forever going on and on about how making elaborate homemade meals, her fantastic baking accomplishments, and all the chores she does. She makes doing normal, everyday household chores sound like Herculean tasks. She then brags about how her children gush over her meals and praise her and thank her incessantly. No normal child does this unless they feel forced to do so in some way. If what she says is true, they have clearly learned the art of self-preservation by heaping praise upon her. The following tweets document some of Kate's great homemaking accomplishments.

xxxxx @Kateplusmy8 what did you guys have for dinner tonight?

funny u ask..I made chicken pot pie soup&home made bread that took until 6:30 2 bake! I made amaz ham/Swiss paninis from it!Yum!

Back from church,fed lunch,cleaned up & about 2 attack the spring clothing switch overX8...Yikes! It's a huge job! Not so sure I'm ready!

I made meatloaf and invented a sweet/sour BBQ sauce2serve over it! Mash pot, steamed carrots &spinach!

Since you asked- baking egg custard pies (big surprise!), lemon squares, nest cookies and angel food cake. Then on to cooking...

Ha ha ha... Multi tasking..conditioning hair treatment while baking! My kids got quite a laugh! http://t.co/W5B1EFbS

GM all... Getting up to feed my little army breakfast...followed by laundry and all that other stuff.. Have a good day...

THE LOVING, DOTING MOTHER

It seems that Kate's idea of being a good mother is to send out massive numbers of tweets about how wonderful she is, and include staged photos of her children or blab about what they are doing.

Go to http://t.co/J4Q4wUXz **To read my newest posting 'Love Is...' Check it out! Lotsa heart pictures included! :)**

This next tweet contained a link to a photo of five of the sextuplets sitting on the sofa holding up their books, in exactly the same way. This photo couldn't look more staged, and I found out later that it, in fact, was:

http://t.co/yx3FdlqU A doctors office waiting room? I think not... Just lotsa kids waiting in a room for dinner.. I found them this way.

This tweet includes another totally staged photo to prove to complete strangers that she is a good mother with happy children:

> http://t.co/oLynBasD I just can't get enough of this...it is SO cute! They are reading Joel's book 'Zombie in Love'—such a cute book!

This is a photo of the kids dancing in the living room. It should have remained a private moment for the kids:

> http://t.co/6jEOi8U4 ...dancing to Madonna during halftime show... Making Super Bowl memories..even if we have no clue about football..lol

> It's late again! Just helped 11ur olds finish video 4 sch project and now X2 sleep! GN all my tweetie friends! I'm so thankful for ea of u!

> I'm measuring eggs with rulers and discussing exclamatory versus interrogative sentences... How can you tell I'm doing homework??;)

> ...laying in my bed...doing mad lib book with Cara and Mady... Ahh life is good! :) I love this kinda good ole fashion fun! :)

Kate can't even spend a few minutes of quiet time with her daughters without exploiting it for all to see. This is her way of proving to strangers that she really is a good mother:

> Line from mad libs: 'then have a cup of delicious hot spit w/ a spoonful of liverwurst in it & you are all ready to go off 2 school!' LOL!

> ...now they are double teaming me... Hurling out the parts of speech requests so fast, I can't think straight! oh my!

> I DID hav a great day. Got 8/8 perfectly amaz sch reports!Kids r in top of classes-Must b doing sumthing right!;)

THE EXHAUSTED, OVERWORKED MOTHER OF EIGHT

It's hard to imagine how a person who has no job and 9 hours of alone time every day can be so exhausted. But Kate sure wants you to believe her life is a struggle.

> My motto today:'I will make it thru this day...' (repeat often) A determined attitude helps remind me that I CAN DO ANYTHING...u can too!:)

> xxxxx @Kateplusmy8 MSD to Kate, come in!

> oh msdtake me away... I need a vacation!

This was tweeted while the kids were home for Spring Break. Poor Katie Irene was forced to be with her children for a few days…with babysitters.

xxxxx @Kateplusmy8 you're a MACHINE! Where do you get your drive?

I force myself-theres just no option for me!:(

xxxxx @Kateplusmy8 Remember when they were little and the bus didn't take them – you were exhausted by dinnertime. I don't know how you did it.

I'm still exhausted by dinner time but don't feel so stifled.. Those days were SO hard!

Just finished working. Non stop day. When do my days slow down???

I just finished working and now I'm tired... Am comes too fast here... Gotta sleep!

I had to stop running to enjoy this amazing blue sky and white puffy clouds..1 of my favorite things in life! http://t.co/V3TEpFaq

This was taken in the middle of a work/school day while most moms were hard at work at their full-time jobs. Kate can't seem to get it through her head that it's not a good idea to tweet things like this telling the world how exhausted you are from all of the work you do all day long while you're home alone for 9 hours.

What a day! PT conferences, 5.3 mi run, shopping w my tweenies..they out shopped me FOR SURE! I'm very tired!:(How are u all?

GN all. I just finished up what I needed2get done today&I'm really tired! Thanks2each of my steadfast tweety supporters&friends! XO to u!

xxxxx @Kateplusmy8 seriously you are a machine!! I don't know how you do it!

I'm a machine because I have to be! Who else will keep up if I don't?? ;) yes, moms ARE machines! :)

...there are no words to describe my pace 2day...the amount I accomplished is mind boggling...great to be feeling better! How's everybody?

And so now that I've finally stopped moving, I've noticed that I'm tired...Catch u tomorrow between the fast moving madness around here!GN!

I think I need a break.... :) someXs I wish I could beam me2the sand &sun..4just a few hrs (oh & w a Lites out man)

GN tweeties.A crazy busy insanely impossibly logistical wk coming up!Hoping 2 get a run or 2 in 2... Yikes.Sleep is an impossible dream..

Did Kate copy and paste the beginning of this tweet from the preceding one, or was this her talking point for the day?

So we survived r crazy busy insanely impossibly logistical day&although I didn't accomplish EVERYTHING,I did fit an 8.5 mi run in+all good!GN!

The great thing about Katie Irene is that in the middle of telling everyone how exhausted she is and how hard her life is (for someone home alone for 9 hours every day), she'll mix in a tweet like this:

xxxxx @Kateplusmy8 That's the spirit!! Any fun plans 4 2day??

I'm running, meeting a friend and doing errands! Yay!:)

And then there's this tweet, where Kate obviously forgets that almost all moms have to work for a living while helping to support their family, unlike Kate who is home alone all day long going shopping and tanning and getting her nails and hair done:

..ohhh I just giggled out loud as I set my alarm clock for crack of dawn for the FINAL time until next school year! Now THAT makes me happy!

In case you missed that, Kate just told you that rather than having only 9 hours to herself all day at home while you and I are working, she'll now have the next 3 months off as well.

THE FASHION & BEAUTY EXPERT

This tweet gives you an idea of the extent of Kate's expertise on beauty:

Beauty blog #2 just posted! Go read more helpful tips at: kateplusmy8.com

When you go to Kate's website and click on the Fashion & Beauty tab, you will see a couple of blog entries from Kate's professional makeup artist, Deanna Bell. If Kate were being honest, her personal fashion and beauty tips would read like this:

Go to a posh salon in New York to get a professional to do your hair.
Get freebies from cosmetic companies.
Get freebies from clothing companies.
Get your makeup artist friend to write your blog posts about beauty tips.

THE HEALTH & FITNESS EXPERT

Kate fancies herself a fitness expert because she runs many miles. But all of my research and observations strongly suggest that the biggest reason that Kate runs is because she wants to get away from her kids as much as possible. The welcome side effect of all that running for her is that it also helps her remain as skinny as possible. Unfortunately, neither of these reasons for running has anything to do with being fit and healthy. And much of Kate's "expert" fitness advice is not only incorrect, it is often dangerous.

Just got back from my 7.16 mile in 1hr 12min...1ˢᵗ run outside in awhile..was georgous&reminded me why I am a runner!Renewed hope in life!:)

Holy cow! I just ran 18 miles! I'm amazed... And very hungry and extremely tired! :) but very happy! :)

Fitness blog: 'What I'm Eating' is now posted on my site! Kateplusmy8.com Go read it and learn my secrets to fitness success!

xxxxx @Kateplusmy8 The fans are hoping for perhaps a fitness show for 2012? Maybe something where you can also teach your healthy eating to fans?

a fitness show would be a dream come true- not for me only but a way to reach ALL moms who desire fitness but don't know how!

THE HOT, FIT MOM

Every woman likes to feel attractive and fit. Not every woman constantly proclaims how attractive and fit and "hot" she is. Kate has raised praising herself to an art form.

xxxxx @Kateplusmy8 How can u have a body so toned and fab after 8 kids?! X

running, healthy eating& determination! It's possible for anyone!:)

Awkward:When a woman tells me in groc store:'my husband saw you in ppl mag&sd 'Kate is smokin' hot!' That never gets easier...what2say?!

THE NOT MEDIOCRE COUPON BLOGGER

Before her first online coupon blog even posted, she was already tweeting about how hard she was working.

Sorry guys! I'm working—and loving it! :) busy!

Another day, another city! I love my job! Coupons and saving excite me!! Yay!!!

What Kate was referring to here was simply her visit to Coupon Cabin's office in Whiting, Indiana. Hiring Kate appeared to be little more than a publicity stunt to get their name out. If not a publicity stunt, then Coupon Cabin did not do their research to find out exactly what they would be getting, or not getting, from Kate Gosselin. The old adage that "no publicity is bad publicity" does not apply in the case of Kate Gosselin, as I'm sure they have found out by now.

Good news! Over time I've learned a lot about how 2 stretch a budget!Excited 2 share my tips as a blogger @CouponCabin!

Educating the world about how to save money isn't really working too well for Kate, given the fact that she drives three cars costing a total of around $200,000, including a Mercedes, a Toyota Sequoia and an Audi sports car. She was supposed to be giving us mediocre people advice on how to save money, but that is pretty difficult to do for someone who takes a limo to New York City every 6 weeks to get her hair cut and colored at one of the most expensive salons in the country; who follows her salon visits with trips to a very expensive restaurant in the city; who says she buys and eats only organic foods, shopping regularly at Whole Foods, one of the most expensive grocery stores; and who pays a small army to maintain a 23-acre compound in the country.
Here she takes a stab at helping her loyal followers on her blog:

> "This is a really quick idea for breakfast that I recently thrilled my kids with! I bought a "pancake pen" at Williams-Sonoma and made pancakes shaped into hearts and my kids first letters of their names! ..."

Within minutes of this blog being posted on Kate's website, her tweeties began to point out that rather than going to a high-end store like Williams Sonoma and buying their pancake pen for 10 dollars, Kate could have purchased her pancake pen at her local craft store for under 2 dollars. Kate then returned to her website to post a "Money Saving Tip."

The following article by Jen Chaney of the Washington post sums up Kate Gosselin's "not mediocre" job as a coupon blogger.

`Kate Gosselin, coupon blogger: What she's taught us so far`
`By Jen Chaney`

`Kate Gosselin: setting new standards in coupon blogging.`

Earlier this month, in a watershed moment for coupon blogging, Kate Gosselin was named coupon blogger at CouponCabin.com.

"We look forward to sharing the unique insight she has gained over the years," the president of CouponCabin said in the press release that touted the announcement, a comment that suggested that, as a mother of eight, Gosselin would impart important lessons about finding deals and saving money.

Well, we're now 10 days and four posts into Gosselin's new gig. And here's what we've learned about shopping and family budgeting from Kate Gosselin.

1. Kate Gosselin did not have a face-lift.

In an item posted yesterday, Gosselin confirmed that she has had no work done on her face. "With all of the buzz about me having had a facelift, I will confirm that I have not had one (I am only 36!!!)," she wrote.
I am grateful for this blog post because the buzz about the former "Kate Plus 8" star's possible face-lift was so deafening that I could barely have conversations with people. "So what happened at work today? I said — WHAT HAPPENED AT WORK TODAY? I'M SORRY FOR YELLING BUT IT'S OBVIOUSLY HARD FOR YOU TO HEAR ME OVER THE INCREDIBLE BUZZ ABOUT KATE GOSSELIN'S POSSIBLE FACE-LIFT." Yes, that's exactly how nightly dinner discussions with my husband had been going until now. Thanks to Gosselin, peace has been restored to our home.

2. Cyber Monday is much, much better than Black Friday.

Gosselin made this point in a blog post about Black Friday as well as one on Cyber Monday. This observation was in no way influenced by the fact that Gosselin is working for a Web-based enterprise that specializes in online shopping discounts.

3. In 2004, it was possible to get a really good deal on stockings at Pottery Barn.

This was a key point in that Cyber Monday post; the former "Dancing With the Stars" contestant recalled how, shortly after the birth of her sextuplets, she opted to shop online rather than drag all six babies and her two older children to the mall. As a result, "on that Monday following the Thanksgiving weekend, I was able to find a great deal on Pottery Barn monogrammed stockings for each of'' the kids, she wrote.

Hey, that's useful information. All you need to do is purchase a time machine (I understand Amazon.com is offering a sweet deal on those right now), set it for 2004, then immediately get online and buy those monogrammed stockings. Assuming, of course, that Gosselin's purchase didn't deplete the entire stock.

4. There actually are some useful coupon codes in Gosselin's post.

Links to discounts at stores ranging from Kohl's to Bath & Bodyworks can be found in Gosselin's blog. However, I am guessing those links are coming from a CouponCabin staffer who (again, guessing) probably dumps embed code into the posts Gosselin writes.

Is that useful for those trying to save money this holiday season? Absolutely. Are those discounts evidence of unique insight that only Gosselin can provide?
Uh, no. But the holiday season is still young, my friends. And Gosselin still has time to wow us with gift ideas and cash-saving suggestions that only she — a woman who, again, just to be crystal clear here, has never had a face-lift — can provide.

THE ORGANIZING MASTERMIND

Kate has always represented herself to the world as some kind of organizational genius. Somehow, she came to believe that plastering post-it notes everywhere and making lists of instructions for others to carry out was all that was required to be labeled as an organizing guru. Just like her other manufactured personas, this one is false. It is a much easier task to keep a household organized when you have nannies and housekeepers and a personal chef and laundry people and lots of worker bees at your beck and call.

GM twitter world! In organization mode here! Thrilled w/ sale at Gymboree outlet (3.99 shirts for boys!) so led2closet organization..!

RT @borderlinewow Can u come over & organize my house like yours? **Haha! I'D BE GLAD TO..WOULD B FUN! :)**

xxxxx @Kateplusmy8 Now that would be something to watch! Hello organization show?

totally agree—Org house, then sched,etc to allow for exercising and healty cooking 2! Would be so much fun!

Back from church,fed lunch,cleanedup & about 2 attack the spring clothing switch overX8...Yikes! It's a huge job! Not so sure I'm ready!

I had a huge 2do list 2day...Some got done &also some extras:I organized my desk 2 day&my bathroom yesterday!Exciting, huh?Ah,I love order!

xxxxx @Kateplusmy8 do the 3 little girls and 3 little boys wear the same size clothes?

nope! It's all so confusing and I have to think hard to organize it all!

In the next tweet, Kate tweeted and posted a photo of a small shelf with folded towels and swimsuits on it. She was very proud of being able to accomplish this daunting task all by herself.

> http://t.co/mpLf02ec **My top of the morning project.. Organizing swim suits and towels inside near the pool! Oh how I love organization! :)**

THE INSPIRATIONAL SPEAKER

When you're down, and troubled, and you need a helping hand, just follow Kate Gosselin on Twitter and you, too, can be uplifted by her positive attitude and sunny disposition. It's strange that her Twitter personality completely contradicts everything she has ever shown herself to be.

> **GM all.. New day, new ideas and determination! I love the open of a fresh new day with new hopes, dreams, paths and plans! Make this 1 count!**

> **Good morning all! Make every minute count today... Do something nice for someone today- it'll make YOU happy! :)**

> **Waking up to birds chirping...Making me long for spring!Best sound EVER! C'mon spring...I'm waiting! Have a great day all! Choose happiness!**

> **Hi guys! Run hard and make every minute count in everything you do today! You'll never get this 'today' back to do again,so do it right!:)**

This next tweet came in right about the time that Kate's TLC/Discovery contract was finished and she was feeling abandoned.

> **...when life throws u hurtful lemons,make lemonade drink it&smile&try2find it in u 2 thnk the 1s who tried2hurt u but acid made u stronger!**

> **GM all! Lots planned here at home today.. Will tell you all about it.... Later :) Have a great day! Keep smiling...I know I will!**

> **Happy Sunday 2u!Have a great day! Choose a smile,not a frown!Choose a + response instead of a negative one!Start w a deep breath if nec! :)**

> **Night night! Have pleasant dreams all! I dream of peace and harmony,hard work, honesty,kindness&positivity for all! :)**

> **GM! Another day full of promise and possibility! Live it fully... We will never get another chance at this today! Have a good one!**

> xxxxx @Kateplusmy8 My best friend tells her kids – Make someone smile today who isn't smiling – then asks them abt it when they get home!

I do too! I'm going to use that!teach my kids to help make the world a better place,1smile at a X! LOVE IT!

RT @xxxx "you can find happiness in any situation if you look hard enough" <3 - @Kateplusmy8 **YES,I'LL RT MY OWN QUOTE—BC IT'S SO TRUE!**

xxxxx @Kateplusmy8 Feel like sharing some of your strength for adversity? I could really use some help right now..

My motto:Failure is NOT an option. Give self permission 2 'crumble' 4 a min, then pick back up&keep going. Push thru! Hugs!XO

SUPERMOM!!

Kate always tweets things that are intended to make people admire and/or marvel at her for being so very busy. She doesn't seem to grasp the fact that most moms and dads or caregivers are doing all these things AND working full-time jobs as well. Her tweets about doing laundry or teaching others how to do laundry are particularly amusing since she doesn't do her own laundry. She has people to do it for her.

GM all!My 8 r successfully off2 school&I've got tons 2do..Lots coming up &I hav deadlines! Working fast&furious 2day-just the way I lik it!

Goodnight my tweeties... Another long and tiring day here.. SO glad to see my bed! :) Anyone feel the same way?? :) Catch you tomorrow..XO
2.9.12

Good am! Attack The Laundry post is freshly posted! Check it out now at kateplusmy8.com Enjoy reading! Hope my process helps U!

Dinner done, doing showers, the to play for awhile... Then kids bedtime... Then MY bed time! Ahhh, this mommy is tiiiiired!
2.25.12

I just fed an army of really hungry 7yr olds...12 over easy eggs&2scr eggs,10 pcs of toast... Made me think of teenage yrs! I'm in trouble!
2.27.12

Bfast,trip2pick up easter ham,play at park (while I squeezed in a quick run),picnic lunch, grab mail,8 hair cuts,stop@pharmacy-all by 2pm!
3.9.12

....just ran an enjoyable 11.5 miles,made dinner,now on my way to late bus pick up..That was AFTER pet store, consignment shop, FedEx stops!
4.5.12

...there are no words to describe my pace 2day...the amount I accomplished is mind boggling...great to be feeling better! How's everybody?

4.25.12

This poor woman seems to have bought into Kate's supermom act, but her reaction is probably not what Kate was expecting:

xxxxx @Kateplusmy8 Thanks for bragging. You just made the rest of us moms feel like losers. :(

no way! If you're a mom, you're an automatic super woman! We all are:) moms job is never done! Keep plugging away!:)

AUTHOR

This tweeter wants Kate to write a book. It isn't clear whether the tweeter realizes that Kate already has her name on three books. It is also not clear why, with so much free time on her hands, Kate has not gotten "a chance" to write more books.

xxxxx @Kateplusmy8 I AGREE!! LOVED WHAT U WROTE! U SHD WRITE A BOOK ;) Love ya and miss seeing your kids faces! My 3yr old also loved watching!

great to hear! More books coming hopefully once I have a chance to write them :)

ALL OF THE ABOVE

Kate takes every opportunity on Twitter to talk about all the great things she thinks she is qualified to do, to proclaim what a great mom she is, and to whine about the "rif raf" that goes alone with her line of work (whatever that work may be at this point).

xxxxx @Kateplusmy8 if you could decide what your next step in your career would be...what would it be!? Never say never. Remember all is possible!

public speaking/talk show/helping moms get into shape/organize etc..

xxxxx @Kateplusmy8 are u addicted to fame?

nope. Addicted2my kids, life,&enjoying my job. I lov adventure and challenge!Hate the rif raf that goes w this line of work

xxxxx @Kateplusmy8 loved her interview in runners mag. I have three kids and can barely find the time to run...how she does it with 8 is amazing!

thx 4 encouragement:)... It takes some fancy schedule dancing 2b a runner/mom of 8! I'm determined-it can happen!;)

xxxxx @Kateplusmy8 you seriously need your own daytime tlk show!! Fashion, healthy living, family...you know it all ;) we miss you on TV!!!

and I miss tv... Match made in heaven lol

KATE'S SELF-GLORIFYING RESPONSES AND RETWEETS

Here is a sampling of some of the complimentary tweets Kate receives. She liked some of them so much she felt compelled to retweet them. A "retweet" is marked by the letters RT at the beginning of the line. Kate's reply to a retweet appears at the end of the line in bold. The tweeter's name has been removed to protect the naive.

RT @xxxx @Kateplusmy8
You motivate all ages Kate..definitely need ur own exercise show. **WOULD LOVE2 MOTIVATE ON BIGGER SCALE LIKE SHOW!**

RT @xxxx @Kateplusmy8
I continue to find it amazing that Kate carries on alone as a strong and loving mother :O) **AWW SWEET. THANKS!**

RT @xxxx @Kateplusmy8
Her books are fab! I loved them&couldn't put them down.Read both in1day. **THX 4 great review!:)**

xxxxx @Kateplusmy8 it's amazing what you have done for your kids some people may judge u but u wouldn't be able to provide half as much as a nurse

correct! Thx for recognizing that I am doing BEST I can 4 my kids. They have a wonderful life..it's my greatest accomplishment!:)

RT @xxxx wow! I just re-fell in love w/you!You are amazing,strong and just wow!And looking gorgeous!! Get it! **AW SWEET!**

A RADICAL IDEA

Kate Gosselin is a wealthy woman nearing forty. She has the luxury of being able to stay home and spend some real quality time with her children before they leave home for good. They made her all that money. She could stop the constant tweeting that always seems to be at its heaviest when the children are at home with her. They would probably appreciate it if she were to give them back what fleeting moments of their childhood they may still have left. There may still be time for her to set things right by putting their needs ahead of her own for a change.

TWEET TWEET

Join us&ignore the lies of haters.Have a ?, get answers from me!;)
– Kate Gosselin

Kate has been tweeting like a maniac ever since the tabloid industry finally decided she was no longer newsworthy, and the lone paparazzo no longer waited breathlessly outside her front gate to follow her and take her picture on a daily basis. I say paparazzo (singular) because the paparazzi (plural) had long since vanished. They were only there for a few months during the summer of 2009. After that, except on a few occasions, it was just the lone pap – Kate's very own personal stalker – giving the illusion to Kate's few remaining fans that she was still being followed and photographed. She did nothing, of course, to dispel the rumors that the paps had gone. She still spoke about how much she was being followed and how much she hated the paparazzi, even when they were no longer interested in her.

Kate dreaded the day when she would leave her property along her quiet country road … alone. No paparazzo. Desperation mode had set in, and Kate realized that the media frenzy was over and she would soon be all alone with her eight children. And how was she going to spread her lies now that the interview circuit had all but closed its doors on her?

Anyone who knows Kate knows that she despises regular people. She mocks and belittles and talks down to and makes fun of everyone, including her children. She has nobody left in her life that isn't paid to be there or who doesn't fulfill her narcissistic needs. Go back and re-read "The World According to Kate" if you need a reminder about how Kate feels about people. This includes her fans and those who tweet her incessantly.

So the thought of Kate Gosselin lowering herself to share her innermost thoughts and feelings with complete strangers via Twitter is absolutely bizarre. But she's doing it. Why?

One reason is that Kate needs constant attention and adoration. She is a textbook narcissist, and the thought of being alone without anyone telling her how wonderful she is on a daily basis is frightening to her. Kate had gotten so used to having people treat her like a celebrity that she didn't know how to act when that was taken away from her by TLC canceling her show. So she took to Twitter to tell her followers how wonderful she is and they, in turn, tell her back how wonderful she is. Log on to Kate's Twitter sometime and listen to the narcissistic love fest.

Another reason Kate put all her energy into tweeting about herself, possibly more than any other "celebrity" in the history of Twitter, is because she read online about celebrities like Kim Kardashian making money by tweeting to their large followings. Kate thought this would be an easy way to make money while sitting at home doing nothing. She also read online that her ex-husband, Jon, was also pocketing some easy money doing the same, but on a much, much smaller scale than Kate.

So not to be outdone, Kate set out to conquer the Twitter universe. She envisioned herself easily collecting several million followers, like Kim Kardashian. You see, in Kate's mind, she's a much bigger celebrity than Kim, and if Kim can do it, so can Kate, times 8.

The beauty of Twitter for Kate is that she is free to say anything, whether it is true or not. She expected that since the lone, lazy paparazzo had gone long ago, or stopped by only rarely, nobody would be around to call bullshit on her lying tweets. Well, almost nobody.

I included this chapter about Kate's addiction to Twitter because it provides some perspective about her thought processes and behavior. Her tweets provide a fascinating look into how she continues to exploit her children and disregard their safety by broadcasting their words, activities and photos to strangers; how she uses her fans to satisfy her craving for attention and adulation; how she tells tales to make herself look special or to gain sympathy; how she successfully gets people and companies to send her free things; and how she uses Twitter as a platform in her never-ending campaign to smear the father of her children.

In this chapter, as in those previous, I have removed the Twitter names of those tweeting with Kate in an effort to protect the "haters," the ignorant, and those blinded by the pinpoint of light reflecting off a has-been reality "star." I would also rather not give any of her rabid, hate-filled, or creepy fans that clamor for her time and attention and information about her kids the satisfaction of seeing their names in print. Welcome to Kate's life on Twitter. Her tweets appear in bold type.

THE BUS STOP LIE

Early on, when Kate first started tweeting, the Kate-hate blogs were abuzz with questions about whether Kate was actually doing the tweeting herself. It was a legitimate question considering that Kate has someone to do everything else for her. Why would she actually do the tweeting herself?

I was a bit curious myself, having followed her on her daily travels for so long, so I checked in on Kate every now and then to see what she was tweeting. I wasn't buying that someone was doing her tweeting for her, but I was suspicious about whether she was actually doing the things she said she was doing in her tweets.

On a day when Kate was tweeting about going to pick up the kids at the bus stop, I hopped in my car and made the 5-minute trip there myself – on a hunch. I sat in my car, staring at the big blue bus at the school bus stop, reading on my iPhone Kate's constant tweeting in real time about her being there – at the bus stop – anxiously waiting for the bus to arrive and return her beautiful babies to her. But my mind was blown, because sitting in the big blue bus, at the bus stop, just a few feet away from me was, not Kate Gosselin, but a college-age babysitter. I kept watching, expecting to see Kate jump out of the back of the van to meet her babies and run to them with open arms. Surely Kate wouldn't lie about a thing like that, would she? And why?

Alas, the young babysitter rounded up the kids, loaded them into the van and drove them home, without Kate Gosselin anywhere near. To be fair, I have seen Kate picking the kids up at the same bus stop many, many times. I'm not sure why she felt the need to lie about it that day. Personally, I don't believe anything anyone says to me or tweets anyway, and I know that television and the entertainment industry in general is all a fabricated illusion.

It must somehow make Kate happy to spend all day tweeting lies to complete strangers. But a grown woman with eight small children in her house while she's tweeting non-stop, day in and day out, has a problem. Every second she spends staring at her computer or tweeting on her smart phone while her children are at home is a second she could have spent with them. And she chooses not to.

KATE'S HARROWING EXPERIENCE

We had our one and only snowstorm of 2011 just before Halloween. To everyone else in Berks County, it was just another snowstorm. But to Kate Gosselin, it was a harrowing experience that she barely survived.

When Kate described the scene at her house to her Twitter followers, she made it sound like she and the kids were snowed in like Jack Nicholson and the Torrence family in the movie *The Shining*. It made for great drama to buy into if you were at home in another state.

Except that I was at my house, 10 minutes away from Kate's house, reading her tweets and looking out my front window, and wondering just what the heck she could have been drinking at the time to be tweeting such nonsense. Everyone believed her tweets, though, because there was no reason not to.

It was an early snowstorm, with wet snow, so it stuck to tree branches and knocked down the weaker branches from the trees. It was nothing special for this part of the country. But to Kate Gosselin? Well, that's quite a different story, as always. Kate's situation is always unique, and always harder and more important than yours or mine. She always has it worse than everyone else.

I drove to Kate's house three times during her "harrowing experience" to document what was actually going on during the day and night. I took many photographs of the roads leading to Kate's house, of Kate's plowed driveway, and of Kate's completely plowed at all times roads, not only in front of her house, but all the way into town and to the highways.

The TOTAL accumulation of snow on Kate Gosselin's property was 5.5 INCHES. Just under the 6 inches that was forecast for her area. I photographed myself standing in the snow in her front yard (on the other side of her fence, of course), and I photographed a measuring stick next to my boots in her front yard. I did this twice – at the height of the snow and her tweeting, and at 7 AM the next morning after the snow had stopped.

At 3 pm on Saturday, there were just under 1.5 inches of snow on Kate's property. But here's how Kate described the mild snowstorm on Twitter during that time:

> **Um instead of painting pumpkins today, we are shoveling our 6 inches of snow.. And counting. Not cool**

> **And did I mention we lost power? Cold lunch and uh cereal for dinner?**

Kate must have forgotten that she has a huge grill under her covered back porch right outside her basement doors, protected from the snowfall, that she could have used for cooking. But her situation started getting more desperate:

> **I've lost most of my driveway trees to the heavy snow. We are stuck bc of branches. 8+ inches of snow now.**

Did you hear that? She said "8+ inches of snow" had fallen. At 4:00 in the afternoon. She said she lost most of her driveway trees. Neither was true.

Here's the truth of the matter. There was actually about 2.5 to 3 inches of snow, maybe, around that time in the late afternoon. I was there at her house by then, and Kate's driveway had already been plowed by her snow-removal company; a few very small branches were pushed off to the side all along the driveway. This was in stark contrast to the many, many houses I passed on the way to Kate's that actually had sustained significant tree damage and whose homeowners were outside cleaning up the mess.

Kate said, "I've lost most of my driveway trees to the heavy snow."

She, in fact, lost only one tree, up close to her front door. It split in half. The other 30 trees were in perfect condition, until the following week when she had them pruned way back to prevent any future snow damage like what had happened to the single damaged tree. "Most of my driveway trees" was one tree out of 30. A big fat lie.

Just then, one of Kate's favorite tweeties threw a monkey-wrench into Kate's plans to create this incredible drama around herself. She asked to see a picture of the damage.

> xxxxx @Kateplusmy8 Yes take pic, im trying 2 visualize all the damage done to the trees!

For those unfamiliar with Kate Gosselin, you should know that she takes, and posts to Twitter, pictures of anything and everything under the sun. Posting a picture of the damaged trees would have been a simple, no-brainerish thing for Kate to do, if she had wanted to. But a picture would have proven that Kate was lying. So…Kate waited a little while and then tweeted this excuse:

I cant it's too upsetting. Trunks left along driveway. Branches everywhere... I am so upset

She said there were trunks and branches EVERYWHERE! But she was too upset to take a picture? I took some pictures. Besides the one tree right up by her front door, the rest were fine. They had some thin, weak little branches neatly pruned off by the heavy snow, but otherwise, all were in good shape.

A tweetie threw another common sense question at Kate, the self-proclaimed "most organized person on the planet" who never hesitates to give the rest of the world advice on how to run a household:

xxxxx @Kateplusmy8 You do have a generator don't ya?

no :(

Kate lives in a giant house out in the country, with eight kids inside, with multiple refrigerators and freezers filled with food, and she doesn't have a backup generator? I live almost in the city and I have a backup everything. Just in case. Kate tweeted more updates:

Driveway is now plowed, branches pushed2the side&still no power/heat.Cereal &fruit salad 4 dinner.Kids ea have flashlight/playing in dark!

The house was completely dark, so I'll say Kate was being honest about the power being out.

I'm literally sick abt my tree loss. Too expensive2replace trees&they were my favorite part of property!;(Worried abt cold temps overnight

Did she make that comment about her trees being too expensive to replace in order to get people to send money, or just to get sympathy because things are so incredibly difficult and sad for Kate? Who knows? Her track record of lying and embellishing and scheming and taking advantage of people is the justification for this question.

Kate finally posted a picture of the one seriously damaged tree to prove that she had lost "most" of her driveway trees. It was not surprising that she was this stupid. If the lazy paparazzo had been interested, he could have easily driven an hour to take the same photos I did to prove her wrong.

A tweetie, no doubt trying to lift Kate's spirits, tweeted that things could be a lot worse; that at least "you are all together! :)" Kate responded in her usual upbeat, can-do way:

I know but feel helpless

This was at 7 pm. I drove home and went back out again, just to see what was going on around town. This was a normal snowy Saturday night in Berks County. The roads were plowed and fine. All of the restaurants near Kate's house and her Target shopping center were open and bustling with crowds.

If Kate truly felt helpless, and was worried about her children being cold, or eating cold food, she could have SIMPLY driven her very large SUV down her plowed driveway, through her open front gate, and down her completely plowed road to any one of the many hotels in the area, including the Homewood Suites, where Kate used to stay when Jon would come to the house for his custody time. It was the same hotel where Tony and the *Dancing With The Stars* crew stayed, and it's a stone's throw from about 12 restaurants, one of which, The Texas Roadhouse, is in the same parking lot.

At the very same time of night that Kate was describing her harrowing experience being "snowed in," my wife and kids were hosting a Halloween party at our house – 10 minutes from Kate's house on Heffner Road – with many of the kids' friends and parents there having a great time, so life was going on as usual. People were out and about.

This tweetie tried to make the clearly distraught and traumatized Kate feel better:

> xxxxx @Kateplusmy8 aww so sorry Kate, I know your disappointed, but it's the material things u can replace LATER. As long as ur fam isn't hurt.

I know that well but the trees gives usprivacy :)

Kate also tweeted about what was really important:

U hav NO idea what Id do4a HOT coffee! I'm freezing2the core(I'm always cold even in summer)!

Kate could have used her cell phone (you know, that device that is permanently attached to her hand) to call one of the 20 restaurants within 10 minutes of her house to order takeout. The roads were clear. And yes, she could have had coffee delivered, too.

Kate made sure to keep her tweeties apprised of everything her kids were up to during the storm:

Kids were playing haunted house in basement.Now playing a flashlight game ie lights click on as quick as poss aft Mady names what 2shine on

Thank God the twins were there to take care of and entertain the sextuplets while Kate complained and tweeted to strangers the entire time. One of her tweeties gave her some good information:

> xxxxx @Kateplusmy8 "I just bought a portable batt pack, u charge it + can plug stuff ie: coffee maker,lamp,ph chargers if pwr

And to that, Kate Gosselin, "the most organized person on the planet," said:

really? Were do I get such a miraculous invention?

Ummm, how about Target, Dick's Sporting Goods or any other nearby store? And now here is another of the many, many lies she told during this ordeal. It's hilarious how even her Twitter followers, most of whom are teenage girls, can figure out what to do, but Kate can't.

> xxxxx @Kateplusmy8 use your grill to cook. Don't you have a fireplace? Go to Wally world & get a couple heaters. Close off all rooms but one.

roads not plowed. Can't go anywhere

And I repeat: The roads were perfectly clear and safe to drive on, even with kids in the SUV or BBB.

> xxxxx @Kateplusmy8 awfully quiet Kate how u holding up?

lack of caffeine is making me sluggish. Kids still going strong. Humming twinkle twinkle in stereo w flash light clicks 4 beat

> xxxxx @Kateplusmy8 theres always starbucks ! Our Target has one in the entrance ! :-)

snowed in

Going2charge my phone in car now...B back later..Don't panic! We r fine :) (as fine as we can b w/o lights,heat,hot food&coffee that is lol)

> xxxxx @Kateplusmy8 How much snow did you guys get?

10-12 inches

> xxxxx @Kateplusmy8 -almost lost our trees and bushes 2,I went out several times during storms with baseball, knocking off snow!

I shook branches too... Couldn't get to them fast enough. Branches broke on treed next to me as I furiously worked

Does anyone reading that tweet truly believe that Kate Gosselin went out in the snow and "furiously worked" shaking tree branches? Kate stole that idea from her tweetie, as she so often does. The only thing Kate "furiously worked" at during her snowstorm ordeal was tweeting:

> xxxxx @Kateplusmy8 Oh, okay, the older trees...all of them? From the weight of the snow?We had snowstorms twice last spring-

yes, lost at least half of each tree and one is now just a trunk :(

> xxxxx @Kateplusmy8 Hopefully there's some insurance coverage that can help with (tree) replacement. You haven't had them that long, have you?

the trees along driveway (lining the entire driveway) fell. They were planted when house was built-before us!

And still her incessant, desperate tweeting continued. Even her teenaged fans and otherwise unoccupied moms seemed surprised at how stupid and helpless she is:

xxxxx @Kateplusmy8 u do not need the electric light for stove. You can light it with match. Boil water. Been there Kate tryin 2 help

I don't have any matches—they scare me! But I would have tried a candle lighter thingee had I known! :)

xxxxx @Kateplusmy8 I'm surprised u don't have a backup generator. Has this ever happened before?

not this long

xxxxx @Kateplusmy8 See isn't twitter really grand...here U go thru this ordeal & U have ur tweeties 2 stand w/ya...encourage ya!

YES! My phone is charging in car while I tweet on iPad using its 17%power remaining! I don't feel alone w just a flashlight now!

Kate's eight children were in the house with her during the power outage yet she was glad that she didn't feel alone because Twitter strangers were there to comfort and encourage her. I guess the little kids were comforting and encouraging themselves as usual. Pathetic.

Dear PP&L: My 8kids want pancakes 4bkfast&I NEED coffee2function as a momof8. If u can fix r wires b4 am I'll b 4ever grateful.Luv,gosselins

It would be such a treat to hear Kate speak or give an interview without constantly reminding everyone that she has eight children. Yes, Kate, we get it. You have eight kids. You're a mom of eight. Kateplusmy8. We get it! What else can you do?

I am warm and so r my kids. I need2go2sleep now.It's been a long harrowing day! Good night all&thx for keeping me company tonight!xoxo

Too bad Kate couldn't enjoy the company of her eight children who were in the house the entire time she was tweeting away to strangers.

AUSTRALIA "BUSINESS" TRIP

In November of 2011, Kate and bodyguard Steve Neild flew halfway around the world to Australia for Steve Irwin Day where Kate was taking part in a charity auction to raise money for the Australia Zoo. One of the items being auctioned off was a luncheon with Kate. I will refrain from commenting about that amazing prize and instead wonder aloud how Kate somehow equates this luxurious trip and time away from her children as "working." Here's Kate getting just a bit defensive with a tweetie:

RT It's always all about you, isn't it Kate?
NOPE.ALL ABOUT MY KIDS & BEING THEIR MOM! IF IT LOOKS LIKE@ME, LOOK AGAIN!

First, how was being away from her children, all about her kids? Next, how it "looked" was that Kate was given a free trip to Australia for herself and Steve, where she got to spend even more time away from her children, for no reason that was of benefit to them. How it also looked is that, once again, when she was away from her children, she went on several days of Twitter silence. Quite the opposite of the hours-long "Twitter Parties" she hosts while her children are with her in the house. Here is a tweet about the trip:

GM from sunny and warm Aus!!I am looking forward 2 Steve Irwin Day tomorrow! Always amazed by the beauty of this, my 2nd favorite country!:)

And here are some tweets with Kate setting the record straight about the trip:

X2 set the record straight! Jon did NOT keep kids during recent trip&esp not so I could save $& all holidays r shared& happily agreed upon.

Sick of all the fables &fairytales..Don't believe wut u read! Sick how tabloids prey on ppl esp moms trying2support their kids! Move on ppl

xxxxx @Kateplusmy8 Just curious...why do you care what anyone thinks when it comes to your kids and Jon...you don't owe anyone an explaination

except that people listen and believe and I'm way better than that and it gets 2 every1 after awhile! Thx 4 ur support!

xxxxx @Kateplusmy8 Who did have the kids while u were on vaca if not their dad

first off, I wasn't on vacation lol, and second, my babysitter, as usual when I travel...

When Kate says "my babysitter, as usual," what she means is a high school/college-age girl she has hired to be her babysitter du jour. After Kate fired Judy, the kids' wonderful nanny, there was no consistent babysitter in the Gosselin kids' lives. Kate's eight young children were left with new strangers on a regular basis while she traveled the world with a married man.

IN SICKNESS AND IN TWEETS

This is an example of how Kate tweeted non-stop to strangers, including "haters" and possible pedophiles, while she should have been taking care of her sick children. This reminds me of the epic *Kate Plus Ei8ht* "Gosselin vomit fest." Nothing has changed since then. Throughout this entire Twitter saga where Kate gave a play-by-play of her sick children vomiting, she never once tweeted anything sympathetic or caring or loving towards her children. She didn't tweet one kind or compassionate word. It was only me, me, me, me, me, I'm exhausted!

Got a 'no thank u' @ dinnerx from a child..knew all 2 soon what that meant..Yep, tis the season2clean up vomit!If it hits all, wish me luck!

xxxxx @Kateplusmy8 Lol do u still have the yellow basins?? :)

we do but my babysitter misplaced them so I'm trying to find them... Not good!

Kate is the "most organized person on the planet," but she can't find her yellow basins for when her kids are sick? And then she has the nerve to blame the babysitter.
The mass tweeting about vomit had only just begun. This is just part of it:

xxxxx @Kateplusmy8 What did U feed this child 2day? LOL 4 times! U sure he/she hasn't been outside grazing? Mine used 2 eat dandelions! 4real!

nothing unusual. Has a temp now...

I know but I'm bracing myself! Not to give a play by play but we are up to 3X's by now... Ugh. I'll be up all night!

xxxxx @Kateplusmy8 Let's hope we don't do the vomeria fest X 8 for sure! One child is enuf...one adult is enuf...ask my hubby! LOL.

Oh make that four times.... (Vomit)

xxxxx @Kateplusmy8 Oh no...same child...or 3 different ones! Put them out there w/Shoka! LOL

same child- one so far...

nope no L rm floor- its further away here, so wouldn't help!But standard is comfy bed on the floor – all washable,near mom!

xxxxx @Kateplusmy8 Well....this makes 4 great advertisement 4 eligible bachelors! Guys r thinking...vomit..one kid 4 times...8 kids 32 times LOL!

and then it starts all over again! Yay!

xxxxx @Kateplusmy8 I'm cleaming up vomit too – 9 year old vomited in the car and I've been told it's in my hair (she sits behind me)! YUCK!.

oh ewwwww and I thought a bed and pj change was bad!

xxxxx @Kateplusmy8 Me thinks Kate is in clean-up mode again! Hope it doesn't get her sick as well! Not good 4mommy 2b sick!

oh no! I will it away...

xxxxx @Kateplusmy8 I hate it when everyone is vomiting, and staying up all night, urgghhh nasty! That's REAL talk from a REAL MUM....

uhhuh. It's the lowest it gets being a mom.. I remember 1 yr Jon stripped as I rinsed chunks&washed..ALL pm long.1after other sick

Child is snoring now. Think I may sign off to get some sleep before next round of vomit! Good night all!

Perhaps Kate should do this in reverse order next time. Take care of the sick children first, then after they're sleeping peacefully, tweet to the online strangers about every detail of what took place.

Never one to pass up an opportunity to talk about herself and tell everyone how hard she works and how difficult her life is, her tweeting took a turn for the pitiful:

xxxxx @Kateplusmy8 how did you survive the night? How are the kids?

Two are now in the sick bay... And I'm dead exhausted from the events of the night :(

2 down; 6 to go... It's going to b a fun day here, not! Hopefully they all get it over w at 1X... I'm exhausted from being nurse all night!

This is Kate doing what she does best: making it all about her and making everything seem like such hard work. She forgot to mention the babysitter who was there with her actually taking care of the kids.

Heat is off.. Bundled up and airing out.. Old time trick to ward sickness off! ☺ I believe fully in it! Fingers crossed...

xxxxx @Kateplusmy8 Good morning kate, I hope u got a little rest last night, did anyone else end up sick? Hope today looks better.;-)

two are sick and I was up all night... Needing gatoraide and goldfish by the truck load here...

Can't tell u how thankful I am for my friend John who brought Gatorade/goldfish for my slew of sick kids! His momma taught him well!

How is it possible that this one-time nurse and self-anointed most organized person on the planet, who has eight children who could potentially get sick at any time, does not have any Gatorade or goldfish crackers in her house if that is what she gives her children when they are sick?

NURSE ~~RATCHET~~ KATE

Kate Gosselin is a registered nurse and she's been dispensing her own brand of medical advice online for over a year. If she approached nursing the way she approaches everything else in her life, with laziness and disregard for the welfare of others, than I should be very wary of seeking out advice from this person.

Heat is off.. Bundled up and airing out.. Old time trick to ward sickness off! :) I believe fully in it! Fingers crossed...

xxxxx @Kateplusmy8 Just ran 15 miles in 14 degree windchill & took my 1st 20 minute ice bath. Wowzers!!!have u done an ice bath post run?

uh... Ice bath? What's that do?

Not only is Kate a registered nurse, but she also claims to be an accomplished runner. Yet she's never heard of an ice bath? At the very least, she should have been smart enough to Google it before making herself look stupid. But Kate never thinks before she tweets.

xxxxx @Kateplusmy8 Avoiding flu bug but have a nasty cough.2day is a run day tho so it better go away!tricks 4 getting rid of a deep chest cough?

they say to put Vicks rub on your feet and wear socks to bed.... Have done it. It worked... Good luck!

xxxxx @Kateplusmy8 If by omg you mean Oh My Groin. Actually I'm fine!! I stretched before I got in the car!

ok that is funny! Didn't mean that but always good to stretch before exercising lol

Kate's suggestion to slather Vicks on your feet and wear socks to bed to cure a deep chest cough is too ridiculous to comment further on. It speaks for itself. And no, Kate, it's certainly not "always good to stretch before exercising lol". In fact, there's a big debate about whether runners should stretch before, after, or at all. Since Kate has so many tweeties that can't decide what to put on their toast in the morning without asking her, she should be more responsible when dispensing training advice so she doesn't get one of her tweeties seriously injured.

All it would have taken for her to dispense accurate and helpful information would have been a quick Google search about stretching before running or working out. She would have found numerous articles indicating that many fitness experts now agree that static stretching before a workout is potentially harmful, and many now recommend to not stretch before a workout when muscles are cold.

Kate should just stick to telling everyone over and over again how tired and exhausted she is and that her children are thrilled to be living with her. Maybe no one will get hurt that way. Here is some more solid medical advice from Nurse Katie:

> **wait2hrs after vomit. Then giv CLEAR:)Gatorade-1 sip@a X.increase gradually.when stops vom,goldfish/Gatorade 4 1-2days Gd luck!**

> xxxxx @Kateplusmy8 hey kate :) What do goldfish do for sick kids ?

> **goldfish and Gatorade.... This moms choice for rehabbing sick bellies :)**

Kate Gosselin is/was a nurse and is the self-proclaimed "most organized person on the planet" who knows better than us all. Her go-to remedy for "sick bellies" is goldfish crackers and Gatorade, yet she doesn't have a supply of goldfish and Gatorade on hand just in case any of her kids get sick? She had to put it out on Twitter for someone to bring her the necessary supplies to help her sick children. And then she got upset when someone on Twitter questioned her. Kate is the one putting every personal detail of her and her children's lives online for all the world to see, and then she gets irate when people criticize her and call her out on how ridiculous she sounds. She should just ignore her critics, but she always responds to them.

> xxxxx @Kateplusmy8 You need help getting Christmas lights you need help getting fish and a drink??Really??

> **help getting Goldfish&Gatorade 4 sickkids?Yes!Don't think u would take 8 kids2grocstore, 2 that r vomiting? Think b4 tweeting pls.**

JESUS – THE REASON FOR THE SEASON

Since Kate never mentions Jesus or her faith anymore, her fans feel the need to point it out to her, especially at Christmas, this very important time of year for all Christians. Then, when she is reminded that she should mention Jesus, she gets defensive and spouts her BS. By the way, years after Kate's website went live, the "inspiration" page still says "COMING SOON." It must just be an oversight, I guess. She's far too busy tweeting all day and night to strangers and writing blogs by Shoka the dog.

xxxxx @Kateplusmy8 Jesus Christ is the reason 4 the season- Christ-mas! Never played up the Santa bit – my sons weren't traumatized by it.

Same here!Kids know it's a day of giving2 ea other for the happiness of 1s we love! :) Jesus was our gift so it's symbol!

xxxxx @Kateplusmy8 Hope this Christmas allows for time to be w/ family & friends...as well as focus on Jesus the Christ that came for you & I ?

has and will.. I love the holidays for just those reasons!

xxxxx @Kateplusmy8 Don't feel attacked.many r probably wondering because in the past you have made a point of how strong your faith was

and still is... Oh my... Conquered dark days triumphantly bc of my faith, wo a doubt!

xxxxx @Kateplusmy8 what about church & a relationship with Christ??I don't ever HEAR you mention anything about it.

not sure what and why you ask? I sorta feel attacked w that ? Altho I don't think u meant it? :)Jesus is the reason4season4sure!

Kate tweeted that she wasn't sure why she was asked about her relationship with Christ. The tweetie asked that question because Kate doesn't speak, tweet, blog or live like she currently has any belief in God whatsoever, but during her early days traveling around the country and speaking at churches with her hand out collecting "Love Offerings," and in her book, *Multiple Blessings*, "God" was every other word out of her mouth. Why is it so hard to keep up the lie? Why did Kate stop talking about the Lord once she became a millionaire and a celebrity?

To put all the rumblings to rest about her not going to church, Kate pulled quite a publicity stunt. She was so desperate to convince her tweeties that she actually believes in God, and goes to church, that she dressed the kids up and took them to church on Christmas Eve...and took a photo of them to post on Twitter. They arrived late to the service and left early, but Kate accomplished her mission. During the candlelight service on one of the holiest days on the Christian calendar, Kate Gosselin whipped out her camera and started taking pictures of her kids, totally disregarding everyone else at the service and never once giving any thought to the distraction she was causing.

That total disregard for the sanctity of the church underscores just how little respect she has for her religion. Even Kate's own father, Kenton Kreider, felt the need to remind Kate of the reason for the season. He sent her a Christmas card, and on the back of the envelope, he personally wrote in all caps: "KEEP **CHRIST** IN **CHRISTMAS**".

THERE IS NO SANTA CLAUS. BUT THERE IS A MS CLAUS*E?*

Kate sounds like a broken record in her tweets here about Santa Claus. These "results are the same" sound like canned responses from a PR person:

xxxxx @Kateplusmy8 Do ur kids still believe in Santa?

no never did here :) result is the same tho ;)

xxxxx @Kateplusmy8 Merry Christmas ! Do your kids still believe in Santa ?? If they don't, did u tell them ? Or did they find out themselves ?? :)

we never did Santa! :) results are the same tho :)
12.24.11

xxxxx @Kateplusmy8 do your kids buy gifts for each other? And do they still believe in santa?

cara and Mady do (w their own $..so cute) and no Santa here but result is the same so no big deal! :)
12.24.11

Kate decided to deprive her children of all the wonder and magic that is the tradition of believing in Santa Claus. That's fine. She's the parent. But if allowing the children to believe in Santa is against her religious beliefs, why does she get to pretend that she is "Ms Clause" (and spell it incorrectly to boot)?

Silly tweeties... I see you calling me! I'm eyeball deep in wrapping and (shh) presents...I'm playin Ms Clause tonight... No run again 2day!

xxxxx @Kateplusmy8 MSD having a few drinks in your honor tonight. :O)

cool thanks. Ms clause is too busy to party

And on her own website, one of the things she listed in her December 24, 2011, blog, "8 things that tell me it's Christmastime," was this:

My bedroom is no longer anything but Ms Claus' Workshop – I cannot walk in any direction without fear of colliding with a wrapped package!

I guess Santa doesn't exist to her just like her children's father doesn't exist to her.

CHRISTMISC TWEETS AND "FEATS"

Here is a compilation of miscellaneous tweets from Kate in the month leading up to Christmas and on Christmas Eve and Christmas Day:

xxxxx @Kateplusmy8 Did u get your Christmas decorations up?

no. lights don't work& ..... got frustrated&ran 10 mi instead. Tgiving is away&Christmas this wk bef I leave next wkend

Ok,seriously,why is EVERY store out of white Christmas lights???!Only ONE strand of ours works &I promised lights on tree yesterday! Oh no..

That tweet was at 6:00 PM. Kate left the kids alone in the house to go out shopping for more lights. She never had to do this by herself before in her life and she had no idea how to string tree lights. I found out that rather than splitting the strands of lights up over several extension cords or the special cord with several different outlets, Kate plugged them all in together, overloading the small fuse. The twins pointed it out to her.

This is a tweet from Kate answering a question about Christmas shopping:

xxxxx @Kateplusmy8 do your kids still draw names for each other?

not this year...So far. Didn't have a chance to go shopping for them... may do it last minute with the crowds, yikes!

TLC and paid employees helped Kate take care of that Christmas shopping in the past. Now she says she didn't have a chance to go shopping? She's home alone for eight and a half hours all day, every day, with no job and nothing to do except go to the tanning salon and get her hair and nails done, but she didn't have a chance to go Christmas shopping for her kids as of December 15th?

This next series of tweets is all about stress and gift wrapping.

Okay, back to wrapping now.... And running etc... Day is too short, I can tell you that already...;)

xxxxx @Kateplusmy8 how do you guys do Xmas now? Separate or together? Hope you finish ur wrapping! :)

def seperate. We do Christmas at home, same as always and they do Christmas at their dads after. It's the way kids requested

xxxxx @Kateplusmy8 When you're don't wrapping you can come help me!! :) will seem like a little job compared to your stack, I'm sure!!

I won't be done til Christmas eve/wee hours of Christmas am I don't think. Want help then, lol?

GM all.Woke up as if it was a sch am today!!?!!:/ I'm just about2attack the wrapping again... Amongst many othr things 2day! Have a gd 1!

xxxxx @Kateplusmy8 u are all excited about wrapping, thats why u woke up early. lol ;-) have a gr8 day!

um, more like stressed about it... But close, lol!

xxxxx @Kateplusmy8 I struggle w/ 3kids, 1DIL & 1grand... Does Santa leave his gifts wrapped or unwrapped at ur house? Santa leaves our unwrapped.

nope, everything including stocking gifts are wrapped here... This santa is a glutton for punishment I know! Lol

xxxxx @Kateplusmy8 you must need a lot of wrapping paper lol.

rolls and rolls and rolls and rolls

Kate said "rolls and rolls and rolls and rolls." How about one big roll of blank, off-white newsprint?

Another of Kate's Christmas illusions that I can personally call BS on is her claim that she always leaves baked goods outside for the trash men. Again, I was on Gosselin Christmas and holiday trash patrol starting in 2009, and I only wish she would have left a nice snack out for the trash men. I probably would have eaten it. It got lonely out there on Heffner Road. I photographed, observed and removed Kate's holiday trash for 3 years. She never once left anything for the trash men...except trash.

xxxxx @Kateplusmy8 I heard on the radio that you leave cookies out for the garbage men because there is soooo much of it after Christmas. Funny!

I do &candy etc. they r some of THE kindest garbage men ever! So patient when I'm late putting it out or have tons (weekly)!

xxxxx @Kateplusmy8 why did u make 121 loaves of bread?

teachers, trash men, bank lady, nail girl, friends who help out, bus drivers, etc and so on

I'm not sure exactly why Kate goes to such great lengths to create an alternate personality and universe for herself. Oh wait, yes I do. She has to lie to try to make people think she is a supermom. Here is an example of Kate getting caught in one of her lies/embellishments:

Merry Christmas Eve all... I have sixteen LOUD excited feet stomping above me.. Better go get them and feed them breakfast! Have a good one!

xxxxx @Kateplusmy8 You'd think 4 bigger feet could try to keep the 12 smaller ones quiet.

you'd think.But they r on other side of house..&asleep (they are tweens) so its just 12 loud feet now that I think abt it!

Kate's Twitter fans can't see inside of her house. She didn't have to backpedal on her bullshit there. She could have gotten away with that tweet about the "sixteen LOUD excited feet."

It just wouldn't be A Very Gosselin Christmas without Kate talking about doing everything alone and her children's screams of joy:

xxxxx @Kateplusmy8 Whats the hardest part about Christmas with 8 kids??? My 1 just about does me in!

honestly? Doing it alone. Wish I had someone to share the shrieks, smiles&excitement w! Overwhelming to orchestrate alone!

W/ 1hr&1min 2go til Christmas,I'm grabbing sum sleep be4 r Christmas am madness begins!I can't wait2hear ripping/tearing/screams of joy!!

Merry Christmas all..Let the Gosselin stampede begin... Can't wait 2thrill the kids!It's the happiest day of the year for 8 marvelous kids!

TO VALENTINE'S DAY AND BEYOND!

Kate was tweeting her own horn talking about all her pre-Valentine's Day preparations. Of course, just as she did at Christmas, Kate had to throw out there that she was "home alone doing this."

It's all about love today... Making my kids valentines and getting all their treats ready today just in time for Tuesday!!

Preparing to make our valentine boxes... This mom is home alone doing this...so we are all ready... http://t.co/Y7KakpUv

GM!Beginning to pack 8 V day lunches full of surprises 4 tomorrow..all abt LOVE here.. Kids get SO excited! Next, pre prepping ? breakfast!

Decorated V day boxes successfully..I was so into it,I 4got 2take a pic!Sorry guys! It was an enjoyable peaceful experience 4 all=amazing!

Kate's tweeties were begging for a photo of her "amazing" "V day" boxes even before she started making them, but Kate somehow forgot to take the picture. Kate also "forgot" to take a picture of her "amazing" all-night Easter egg stuffing session and her "amazing" Thanksgiving Day dinner that she prepared for so many people because she "lost track."

Even though Kate's fans didn't get to see a photo of the amazing "V Day" boxes she decorated, Kate did post a photo on Valentine's Day showing the surprises that awaited her "8" at the table. The surprises were cute and mediocre and normal. She didn't need to keep trumpeting how what she was doing was all about love, which is kind of the point of the day. They probably love anything nice that she does for them.

> **http://t.co/v8rHHZ3q St. Valentine(me- no, I'm not a saint!)is ready...?Surprises await my 8 at their places at the table..I'm SO excited!!**

> **Wishing u the Happiest of Happy Valentines Days today...may urs b filled w/love&contentment..Our am was a huge success!We r loved&blessed!**

Here comes trouble. Everything Kate does is so special and great that she thinks she needs to present it to the world. Kate made the mistake of tweeting a photo of the "heart-y" breakfast she made. The photo showed what appeared to be a simple breakfast that would have required about 10 minutes to prepare. The portions on the kids' plates looked like she was feeding 2-year-olds, and her fans and critics alike took notice and commented – which set Kate off. Her tweeties should have known that they can only tweet about how awesome Kate is at everything and never question her mothering.

> **Here was our 'heart-y' breakfast... http://t.co/1oGXiQ4X I LOVE doing this stuff for my kids!**

> xxxxx @Kateplusmy8 .... That's all your kids have for the most important meal of the day? Wow..

> **and a bus snack already packed daily for the bus ride... They eat me outta house and home.. 6 am is light breakfast!**

> xxxxx @Kateplusmy8 Turkey bacon, one slice: 31Kcal. Mini-muffin: 50 Kcal. 81 calories, plus a couple of kids got half an egg, another 40 kcal.

> **that was a cream cheesepoundcake muffin w/ abt 200 cal each... + a 100 calorie bus snack after. Don't ? my mothering – thx!**

And that right there folks is why there are no friends or family members involved in Kate's or the Gosselin children's lives. Because EVERYBODY questioned her mothering and they were all cast off.

This next tweet from Kate was posted at 2:47 pm on Wednesday, February 15, 2012. The kids were dropped off at the school bus EIGHT hours before, and Kate said she was still cleaning up the "fall out" from Valentine's Day. She must have forgotten that she showed us pictures of what she did for the kids. Even if she cleaned up everything by herself, it was maybe 30 minutes of work. Kate knows her 15 legitimate Twitter followers are easily fooled.

> **..I'm here. Trying2 straighten up all the Valentines 'fall out'.It was like a little Christmas here, I think! Not ignoring u tweeties!XO**
> 2:47 pm on 2.15.12

> **I've been trying to post a tweet all day... Twitter not letting me... Ugh, I hate 'twitter jail'... Sorry, guys. I'm not ignoring you.. :)**

In fact, Kate *is* ignoring you. Whenever she wants to ignore her tweeties, which is usually when she's doing something without the kids and she's enjoying herself, meaning she's with Steve, she always tells them that she is in "Twitter jail." She has used this excuse many, many times. "Twitter Jail" actually exists, and it's a sanction put on someone who tweets TOO OFTEN in a given day.
"All day" in Kate time equals 3 hours, because her first tweet was posted exactly 3 hours earlier.

DEAR SUPERMOM

Here's a Twitter fan that obviously hasn't watched a single episode of *Jon & Kate Plus Ei8ht* or *Kate Plus Ei8ht.* If she had, she probably wouldn't have been asking Kate for advice about crying babies. At least Kate gave this tweetie an honest response:

> xxxxx @Kateplusmy8 Did your rock babies to sleep or let them cry them self 2 sleep??

> **must let them cry and learn to soothe themselves...Rocking triplets=you'll never get2bed! I promise, Crying gets shorter ea pm!**

Of course she never rocked her babies. Of course they had to learn to soothe themselves. She barely had any contact at all with her babies except for what was filmed for profit. Obviously, Kate Gosselin doesn't have the first clue how to take care of eight children, or do anything on her own for that matter.
It is difficult to view Kate as the "supermom" she tries to portray herself as after reading her answer to a tweet such as this:

> xxxxx@Kateplusmy8 Don't you feel Blessed you have those memories on tape :) They are for sure treasures into the past for you and your kids.

> **I DO—now more than ever! I was physically present back then, but also phys/emotionally exhausted so I don't remember a lot!**

So Kate just said in her tweet that in all the time she was filming with her family –
their entire lives from after the sextuplets were born up until 2011 – she was only
"physically present" and she doesn't remember a lot. That's not exactly the picture
of a "supermom." She missed the most fragile, developmentally significant years
of her children's lives. But hey, at least she has professional "home movies" of
herself being a narcissistic, rude, angry monster to her family and everyone she
has ever come in contact with.

Kate is oblivious to the needs of young children. Why on Earth would anyone
who's trying to convince the world that her kids have wonderful, happy, carefree
lives, tweet about how structured and inflexible their lives are? She is so proud of
her rigidity that she brags about it to the world:

> **My motto on way home EVERYDAY: 'routine, chickens, dinner, chores,
> homework, showers then bed. Time to play if you hurry!' :)
> play..repeat..**

She sounds like a drill sergeant running a boot camp. Kids need some structure
and routine in their lives, but they also need spontaneity and flexibility. Her tweet
makes it sound like she is pounding that "motto" of routine into her kids' heads
every single day. Constantly hearing that and never straying from the daily script
must be an absolute nightmare for her children.

MOVIE NIGHT

Kate promised her followers that she would be having a "movie night" at home
with her kids. Family movie nights should be a special time where Kate can share
a relaxing and pleasant experience with her kids. But she makes it sound anything
but pleasant. The children must sit in a certain order on the floor a few feet in front
of the television –on the stripe of the rug so they can't spill popcorn on said
precious rug – and Kate sits behind them on a comfy sofa throwing a "Tweet
Party" for complete strangers. Kate tweeted photos of her DVD and popcorn and
of the kids sitting all lined up on the floor:

> **http://t.co/Kde2b5RR Our family night tonight...we can't wait.**

> **...moments til movie start..Sitting on 'the stripe'(of the rug-2 avoid
> extra mess) w/buttery popcorn, munching&ready!
> http://t.co/4UcWMDwy**

The Twitter "party" started out innocently enough, but as usual, things went sour
pretty quickly:

> xxxxx @Kateplusmy8 Great movie! Sounds like fun nght planned. But I don't
> get why u don't take kids to movie theatre? U have money.

...we all have money. It's in our personal choices on how to spend it that counts... Have a good day!

xxxxx @Kateplusmy8 Wow sorry that I hit a nerve by asking.But how much does it cost for a tanning session as compared to a movie?

comparing apples2oranges now? How I spend my per $ is also none of your business. Inspect your own finances,not mine!

xxxxx @Kateplusmy8 Kate pls calm down.I didn't mean to get you so upset.Just asking why deny kids movies at theatre.Still dn't understand.

1st takes more2make me 'uncalm';2nd: not deny I CHOOSE not 2go into public&cause panic&spend $ 4same movie we can watch @ home!

In that last tweet, Kate is saying she can't go out in public with the kids because it causes a panic. Not true. I've been out with Jon and the kids in public many times and guess what? There has never been a panic. At best, some teenage girls would politely stare for a minute or so. We've been to movies, fast-food places, arcades, playgrounds. No panic. The panic only occurs when Kate is with the kids in public and someone looks at her because she is screaming and flailing her arms in the air shouting, "They're taking unauthorized pictures of us!!! They're taking our picture!!! THEY'RE LOOKING AT US!!!!!!!!"
People would stare at anyone carrying on with such histrionics.
And now, back to the movie.

xxxxx @Kateplusmy8 Don't ur kids ask 2 C new movies tht their friends saw & R talking abt?Most kids don't want 2 be left out.

seriously? Theres a lot more2life than seeing latest movie...Like getting good grades&playing outside!geesh!

xxxxx @Kateplusmy8 Geesh like I don't know that? There are some movies kids should see in the theatres like 3D etc.

no; still don't agree.Movies r never 'shoulds' in life!Good experience? Sure. But no one would die w/o them!

xxxxx @Kateplusmy8 There R many movies that my kids would nvr wait to C months later on DVD. Harry PotterStar WarsTwilight...

that's ur kids..Mine prefer 2 play tog,read&play outside! C how it's dangerous2judge based on ur exp alone?

btw we have a 3D tv and glasses so all 3d movies can be viewed at home too;)

Could somebody PLEASE inform Kate that she doesn't HAVE TO respond to everybody who tweets something she doesn't want to hear? She always ends up making herself look bad. At the very least, she could try to be smart enough to think about what she's tweeting. Minutes after tweeting that they have a 3D TV and glasses so they can view 3D movies at home, Kate felt compelled to tweet this:

> **except xtra glasses r $100 ea so we don't actually have a pair 4 each person!Too many in Fam!**

> xxxxx @Kateplusmy8 By that logic than neither is owning 3 cars, tanning, nails, NYC, coloring hair, Iphone, Should I go on?

> **again.My choices,my $.Have I told u once how2spend Urs? 1 word: jealousy. Blocking u now.Sorry!**

After blocking this tweeter, an uber-fan of Kate's chimed in with the following:

> xxxxx @Kateplusmy8 Well...U were patient w/that one 4quite a while! U tried ur best 2b reasonable. Was time 2move on! Next? LOL

> **yep! My kids have been clear across the world—I'll never agree that movie in theatre is the 'end all' experience of life!**

It looks like Kate missed the point once again. Her kids "have been clear across the world" while working on their reality show to make money for Kate. Now that the reality show has been canceled, Kate is not spending their hard-earned money on them – she is spending it on herself. She is maintaining her extravagant lifestyle by continuing to travel three hours each way to New York City to get her hair done every six weeks; tanning three times a week; manicures; pedicures; a two-seat, $50,000 sports car on top of two other over-$50,000 vehicles...and on and on.

KATE GOSSELIN'S TWITTER "FRIENDS"

Since anyone who has ever attempted to be Kate Gosselin's friend in real life has been cast off because they didn't know how to help her, Kate has taken to Twitter for friendship.

> **Woo hoo! I now have 79,000 wonderful supporting followers and friends! I'm a lucky girl to have each of you! :) xoxo**

> xxxxx @Kateplusmy8 I am so glad that you take the time to talk with all your fans, and try to make them feel more like friends:) xox

> **you are friends! :) and you probably get more time than my non virtual friends ... Sadly. Just not enough time in life!!!**

Kate is very quick to call anyone and everyone on Twitter her friend. She says she loves all her Twitter friends and, as you can see by reading her tweets, Kate readily shares everything about her children's private lives with them. She gives these people very personal information about her children, including intimate details of their whereabouts at any given time. Kate Gosselin just doesn't think and doesn't consider that, out in Twitter land, there are pedophiles and unbalanced people who could harm her and/or her family. Let's take a quick look at just who Kate's newest "friends" are.

Kate responded to a "close friend" named AdmiringDxxxxxx probably because he/she mentioned Lady Gaga's Twitter account and Kate wanted to somehow be connected to a true celebrity. If she had bothered to look at what her "friend" AdmiringDxxxxxx was tweeting to others at the same time she was tweeting to him/her, she would have seen tweets where he/she wrote "I'm sending a bomb," "I hate black people," "you're both fucking retards," and "shut up fat bitch."

Kate responding to this next tweet from SADIEMAEGLUTZZ is a disturbing example of her complete ignorance and disregard for her children's safety.

> SADIEMAEGLUTZZ @Kateplusmy8 I'm so tempted to follow @Kateplusmy8..
> they need their show back.

please do and I agree...

I had a special interest in Charles Manson at one time, so the name Sadie Mae Glutz hit me like a sledgehammer when I read that tweet. Sadie Mae Glutz, whose real name was Susan Denise Atkins, was a member of the Charles Manson "Family" and was convicted of participating in eight murders, including those of five people at the Beverly Hills home of Roman Polanski and Sharon Tate, who was 8 months pregnant at the time. In her testimony, Atkins (Glutz) described how she held Sharon Tate down as she pleaded for her and her unborn baby's life. To cause more suffering, they held off killing Tate until all the others were dead, then they stabbed her repeatedly while she called out for her mother.

I'm not implying that the person who chose this name for a Twitter handle is crazy or a murderer, but how can Kate possibly know? This Twitter "friend" showed a stunning lack of decency by choosing such a name. Kate is just exceedingly stupid to engage with anyone who would give themselves a name that is synonymous with brutality and murder. None of that seems to matter, however, as long as SADIEMAEGLUTZZ is feeding Kate's enormous ego.

Whenever someone compliments or is supportive of Kate, she has a habit of never looking at them deeper. If she had, she would have seen that other tweets from @SADIEMAEGLUTZZ's to his/her friends from the same day that Kate Gosselin befriended him/her were filled with profanity and sexually explicit images.

Instead of delivering information about her children to foul-mouthed tweeters just because they compliment her, Kate should be thinking about how she can best keep her children safe. I've been on Kate's property many, many times with Jon, and I know the area around her property very well. It's very dark at night and it's secluded, and her house is a football field away from the road. Anyone could easily gain access to her property. It is very scary to think she has put out a welcome mat for possible danger.

Obviously Kate doesn't care who or what tweets to her, and she certainly doesn't care enough about anyone (other than celebrities) to know their names. She doesn't even look at your name unless you tweet a message that Kate likes.

Does anybody remember Hailey Glassman, the daughter of Kate's tummy-tuck doctor? When she was college age, Hailey ended up having a globetrotting, very public affair with Kate's husband, Jon. The tabloids called her "Hailey the Homewrecker."

The next tweet is proof positive that Kate couldn't care less who is tweeting her as long as they are stroking her ego. Someone calling herself "Hailey Glassman" tweeted Kate to ask if she would share her "Monkey Munch" recipe, and Kate was happy to jump right in with an answer:

hAiLeYgLaSsMaN1 Hey @kateplusmy8 can u share the recipe for the "Monkey Munch". It's so yummy, my mom & I never seem to make it as tasty as you did.

go to the chex website... It should be there..not my recipe but love it! Called 'muddy buddies' there! Enjoy! :)
3.25.12

The next tweet was Kate's response to her "number one fan" who asked Kate a personal question about who was at Kate's house for her big Christmas party. Of course, Kate gave her the information she wanted. Sorry "number one fan." You won't see your name in print here. This was Kate's response:

kids friends and their parents (my friends)

Kate and her manager/PR people have gone to great lengths to try to convince everybody what almost nobody believes…that Kate Gosselin really, really does have friends. Kate just can't stop telling us that she has friends. Here is how she described a visit from two of her "friends" that came to town for a "girl's weekend."

xxxxx @Kateplusmy8 Happy Saturday!! Whatcha doing this weekend?

my marathon girls are coming to visit!!!! :) yay!

Gotta go get rdy 4my wkend w/ my marathon friends!We ran the Las Vegas marathon together in Dec&are spending some girl X tog this wkend!YAY!

Just finished a fun run/major gab session w my marathon girls! Was so wonderful to run between them again! Off 2 enjoy dinner/drinks later!

Aww the girls and I ready for dinner.... http://t.co/Z2vR6Sbx

So,I'm home&ready4 bed..latest night out in a LONG time!We had a great dinner at Green Hills Inn&nonstop girl talk!Up2run again in am! GN!

xxxxx @Kateplusmy8 So another "fun run" this mornin I see! U must really be in good shape 2do that back2back runs! How far have U been going?

only 6 each day yesterday and today. We talk the whole time. So fun and great to be able to talk while running a good pace!

xxxxx @Kateplusmy8 are you & ladies planning pool side relaxation today? On my list after late lunch with my dad.

why yes, we are... While we wait for my kids to get home! :) can't wait to meet each other!

xxxxx @Kateplusmy8 hey kate, just droppin in to say hi! any special plans for today!

marathon girls for relax then dinner when my kids get home! Ran this am with them so a good weekend overall

xxxxx @kateplusmy8 Did you have a fun day as I relaxed like it was going out of fashion!

well, here relaxing IS long out of fashion lol. Yes we had a great day visiting with wonderful friends!

We had such a wonderful visit w gracious friends!My kids loved meeting &playing w my marathon girls! :) It was a 'must do again weekend'!

Wow. All of that tweeting just because her two "marathon girls" came to visit and stay for the weekend. As it turns out, the two "friends" in question were the same two ladies who just happened to show up at one of Kate's speaking engagements, and then just happened to convince Kate that she could run a 26.2-mile full marathon just one month prior to the marathon in Las Vegas.

It has been suggested on the blogs that this "friendship" is nothing more than a business relationship set up by Kate's manager, who just so happens to specialize in fitness and nutrition.

According to her tweets, Kate was without her kids that weekend in June 2012, left alone in a very, very large home that is equipped with guest rooms and an apartment above the garage. I witnessed Gina Neild's parents staying there when they visited Kate for the holidays.

The point is, the house is large enough and comfortable enough to have accommodated Kate, her eight children, Steve and Gina Neild and their two teenage sons, plus Gina's parents in the apartment above the garage.

So here is the question: If these two ladies who visited Kate are really and truly Kate's "wonderful friends," like the above Twitter love-fest would suggest, and not simply business associates, and Kate had the house all to herself because her children were away for the weekend as she tweeted, why then would Kate have them stay 7.26 miles away at the Homewood Suites in Wyomissing, PA?

As soon as I saw the photo that Kate posted, I knew they were at the Homewood Suites, which has been Kate's favorite local hotel for years. The TLC crew sometimes stayed there on overnights, and Tony Dovolani stayed there during the *Dancing With The Stars* days.

Just out of curiosity, I drove there because I thought I recognized the hotel, having been there many times over the past several years. Sure enough, Kate's photo was taken right outside the lobby to the right of the front doors.

The restaurant they went to was another 15 minutes away from the Homewood Suites, so it would appear that Kate stopped by the hotel to pick up her "friends" and then continued on down the highway for dinner. I wonder if the "friends" even got to visit the Gosselin homestead because Kate posted the following tweet, which included a link to a photo on Kate's website:

New picture is up! Oh so cute! We had a great picnic/swim with friends on Sunday! Check out http://t.co/J4PZZkWF **to see the gr8 shot!**

It's curious that the "friends" weren't even in Kate's photo.

So Kate spent the weekend alone in her giant, empty house while her "friends" stayed miles away at a hotel.

POOR LITTLE RICH GIRL?

On February 8, 2012, with millions of dollars in the bank, a million-dollar home, $200,000 worth of cars sitting in her garage, nannies, a cook, gardeners, a pool service, an $800- to $1,000-a-day bodyguard/road manager on call, etc., believe it or not, Kate tweeted that she was sewing a sock for one of her girls. It sounded like a scene right out of *Les Miserables*. Woe is you, Katie Irene. Woe is you.

How can u tell I'm tired?   I'm sewing cara's sock that has a hole in it.She is 1 sock on&1sock off&I asked her if her foot is still 'bald'?

And alas, the sock sewing momma is done and she's going to sleep.. Lots of variables here so haven't been getting sleep....& I am going now!

Now listen to this "super" mother first complaining about how much money caring for her children's eyesight is costing her, and then making a joke about their "blurry eyes" to strangers on Twitter:

...6 eye dr)ophthalmologist) appointments & $650 later,it's dinnertime w 6 sets of blurry eyes!;) I could feed them ANYTHING tonight lol!

xxxxx @Kateplusmy8 Ha...imagine all the kids in glasses...cute? 2 know whose is whose....designer frames? $$$$ LOL!

no!!!! I hold my breath each year... Too expensive and constant repairs! 1 in glasses is PLENTY!

This next tweet sums up the maddening contradiction that is Kate Gosselin. She moaned about how eye doctor visits for her kids are so expensive, but she thinks $130 earbuds for herself are "Expensive but totally worth it!"

xxxxx @Kateplusmy8 I need new earbuds the standard issue just aren't cutting it on the treadmill. What do you use?

I use bose earbuds! Expensive but totally worth it! Stereo right into your ears! :)

Kate, the multi-millionaire, is forever complaining about how expensive it is to raise her eight children, while at the same time bragging about her lavish lifestyle. I'd love to get a line-item breakdown of how much her hair appointments in New York City, her weekly manicures/pedicures, her three-times-a-week tanning sessions, her luxurious trips around the globe (without her kids), etc., etc., etc., actually cost her.

As if the horrible tragedy of the expensive eye care was not enough, there was an even greater tragedy Kate had to endure and cry about on Twitter. These tweets document her months of sadness because she can't afford to take her kids on vacation:

xxxxx @Kateplusmy8 My friend at work just made reserv. This summer @ outerbanks. Made me think of your trips. :)

oh I so so wish we could go this summer... Kids need sand&sun!

Aww Cara&Mady&I are reminiscing abt r trip 2 Aus and NZ..the flight there etc..Great memories!Kids say a lot 'When are we traveling again?'

xxxxx @Kateplusmy8 If they want to go back & r asking why not take them all back?

flight costs!!!!

xxxxx @Kateplusmy8 memorizing the fast fleeting sound of the waves crashing and the sound of the ocean-my peace and serenity

hey lady, I saw your tweet yesterday. Did you have to rub it in? :) my kids are BEGGING for a beach get away :)

It sure sounds like Kate is, as well. Begging that is. But be warned. This is what happens if you question Kate, even if you're a fan of hers:

xxxxx @Kateplusmy8 I don't get how she says the kids miss traveling.well then use YOUR money n takethe kids on vaca likethe rest ofus do

I'm sorry but I detect much bitterness in you. I gotta keep my life positive so I need to block you. Sorry you're so negative :(

Here's Kate the millionaire responding to a tweetie who asked Kate if she had any plans to take the kids to the beach this year:

lol...I'd give anything to go to the beach with my tribe...but no, don't have any sorry!

Kate would "give anything to go to the beach" with her "tribe"? So why doesn't she? I'm broke and I live ten minutes from Kate and I take my kids to the beach all the time. It doesn't cost a lot. Simply pack a cooler with sandwiches and other snacks and drinks, or take a Coleman grill and cook hamburgers and hot dogs under a pavilion by the playground while the kids play. We go to Stone Harbor and Cape May, which are both less than three hours from Kate's driveway. Both have quiet beaches where nobody would bother her, or even notice her if she didn't stand around waving her arms and screaming for attention. She would have to pay for her own gas though.

Everyone will be relieved to know that in August of 2012, Kate got her grifting wish! A company named @RelaxOnTheBeach stepped up to the plate to save Kate and the Gosselin eight from a dreary summer by giving her the use of a beautiful beach house...for free.

Leading up to that point, Kate had proudly tweeted to the world in June of 2012 about her monthly luxurious trip to New York City to be styled by celebrity stylist Ted Gibson, then wined and dined at one of the city's finest restaurants, Fig & Olive:

Thank you @JasonHueman and @tedgibson for making me beautiful and for sharing an amazing dinner @fig&olive with me! Fun day w friends! XO

Kate was still talking about her financial struggles in July of 2012:

Awww yeah. I thought same thing. It IS tough to cover costs of large Fam-I'm struggling- but hoping my decisions are rewarded!:)

She is struggling to cover the costs of having a large family, but she is clearly not struggling so much that she has to forego her trips to NYC so Ted Gibson can make her beautiful.

ME, ME, ME, ME, ME, ME, ME

Besides the fact that Kate shouldn't be tweeting every tiny detail of her children's lives to strangers, she always manages to make EVERYTHING about herself. She also takes cues and ideas from her tweeties and makes them her own.

Here's a girl who randomly tweeted to Kate that she was watching a specific episode of *Jon & Kate Plus Ei8ht*, and, miraculously, Kate and her boys happened to be watching the EXACT SAME episode.

xxxxx @Kateplusmy8 I'm watching the episode of J&K+8 when the twins get there instruments! Me and my twin also played those same exact instruments.

oh my! The boys are watching that now! I watched too! They were little and toothless playing instruments! So cute!

What are the odds of that happening? Does Kate ever realize how foolish and full of crap she sounds? There are close to 150 episodes of *Jon & Kate Plus Ei8ht* and *Kate Plus Ei8ht*, and Kate said she was watching the exact same episode at the exact same time as her tweetie.

After reading her Twitter feed for so long, I have seen that it is impossible for Kate to receive a tweet and not end up making it about herself. Read these tweets to see how Kate turns everything back to her:

xxxxx @Kateplusmy8 Been crying my eyes out..just received a call that my great aunt passed away :*(...can I get a RT?

my great aunt passed away as well last week. I'm sad too... Hang in there; I know how you are feeling :(

xxxxx @Kateplusmy8 My twins Kaylin & Carye turn 4 today!!!!

happy 4ᵗʰ! When I turned 4, I asked my mom all day 'can't u believe I'm 4 mom?' I guess I couldn't believe it, lol!

xxxxx @Kateplusmy8 Busy week here at home and tchng 3rd grade too:) Coursework due, mileage to get in and girl scout leader stuff-Motivate!

that's exactly how I'm feeling today.. The list is so long, I can't see the bottom of it.. Good luck!

xxxxx @Kateplusmy8 HEY KATE MY GRANDMA DIED SATURDAY AT 1 AM I AM SO SAD I NEED SOMEONE TO TALK TO

oh no!!! I remember how I felt! It's devastating! Are you ok? I'm so sorry...

This poor girl in the following tweet was just trying to ask Terri Irwin a simple question. She didn't include Kate Gosselin in her tweet, but because Kate follows Terri Irwin on Twitter, and Kate is on Twitter most of the day, every day (except when she is out and about pampering herself), she decided to insert herself into the conversation and make it about herself, as always:

xxxxx @TerriIrwin How long is a Rhino pregnant for? :-)

I thought same thing... But,must say,however long it is,I'm SURE I was also pregnant same X..Felt that way anyway!Lol/

MARATHON MOMMA

Kate gave a speech at Penn State University on November 3, 2011. She tweeted later that that was the day she decided to run her first full marathon…which just happened to be only one month later. She certainly didn't give herself a lot of time to prepare.

Julie May, Kate's brilliant manager, decided that after Kate failed miserably at everything else, she would try to rebrand her once again into a fitness expert and have her become a "runner" to inspire moms the world over to get in shape. Since Julie May is the brain behind the operation, Kate nodded her head up and down and went along with the plan. Kate sees only dollar signs.

So when Kate got the following tweet, a light bulb –albeit a dim one –went off above her head.

Oooooooh. So that's why she wanted to run a marathon. For her kids. It sounds like a random tweeter gave Kate the idea that running a marathon would be a good example for her kids.

So Kate was setting a good example for her kids by flying off to Las Vegas with a married man for nine days to participate in a race that was going to take mere hours? If Kate's motivation for running really was about setting a goal, working hard and teaching her kids a lesson, then why did she need to leave them for so long and travel to an adult playground in the desert? She could have driven an hour to Philadelphia for their marathon or competed in one of the many marathons near her house.

The Philadelphia Marathon was held on November 20, 2011. I'm betting that since it was an actual, sanctioned race in a blue-collar town, the thought of competing there never even crossed Kate's mind.

If her running was truly about the kids, she would have taken them to Philly in the van and had them there at the finish line "cheering her on." They could have brought the signs they made for her, watched her cross the finish line, and had an all-around great day. They would have been back home before dark.

As it turned out, Kate taught them the lesson that being a mom means spending hundreds of hours away from them training for and competing in a marathon on the other side of the country. For most parents who put their children's needs ahead of their own, the last thing they would ever want to do is spend so much time AWAY from them. Actions speak louder than words, and Kate doesn't seem to realize that her kids have been watching and internalizing her actions their entire lives. And they won't ever forget them.

To be fair to Kate, there are countless parents in the world who couldn't care less about their children and who do things to their children even worse than what Kate ever did to hers. Some people's children are less important to them than others. For me? My world revolves around my children. Kate's world revolves around Kate.

Here are some of Kate's tweets about running:

@runnersworld no!I'm running the las Vegas rock n roll marathon on Dec 4!Omg!I can't believe I'm doing it! Scared2death!0 prof training!EEK!

So Kate tweets to *Runners World* and she just happens to land an interview in *Runners World* a few months later? No. This connection was set up by Kate's manager well in advance as part of Kate's rebranding. It was meant to appear "organic," as Julie May says on her website.

This is a question from the interview with Kate in *Runners World:*

Q: What do your kids think about your running? Do they understand it?

Yes, I think the best part of running and the best part of running this marathon is the fact that my kids see me pick a goal and they see me complete it…

Kate has her priorities a bit backwards She should be helping her children achieve THEIR goals.

Q: Are you bringing them with you?

I'm not. And I'm sad. I have promised them I will run one that they can be at the finish line. I would like to see no other eight people more than them at the finish line. I'm sad that they're not going to be there…

Kate also talked about the t-shirt she wore:

"…my marathon t-shirt, and a new Inspirational t-shirt I had made for this day. The front said "finishing is winning" and the back said "my first 26.2 is for all the nonbelievers."

Kate explained the sentiment on the back of her shirt by saying that she dedicated the first marathon to "anyone who doubted me!" "I have to say, I really love to prove people wrong!" But Kate has always said that she ignores her haters. She even tweeted that "To me, they don't even exist."

So rather than dedicating her marathon to her children, Kate dedicated it to complete strangers who don't believe in her and who criticize her and call her out on her lies. Those are the same people she says she ignores. For someone who claims to not care at all about what her "haters" or "nonbelievers" think or say about her, she sure went to a lot of trouble to prove them wrong. The only people even talking about Kate at this point were online bloggers who don't like her. You'd have to actually go to their blogs to even know this. And just what kind of lesson, exactly, was she teaching her children by wearing a t-shirt with that spiteful and completely unnecessary message?

Kate also talked about "how proud my eight little cheerleader are!?" Kate is too self-absorbed to see that it should be the other way around. She should be the cheerleader for her children. She is so wrapped up in herself, that she has reversed the roles of parent and child.

Meanwhile, the Gosselin children have never been involved in any activity outside of school. Her 7-year-old sextuplets at the time of this writing had never done a sport, in a league, with other little children. TLC took the kids to a single gymnastics lesson to film an episode, but after that, Kate told the kids and the world that it was too expensive to continue doing gymnastics.

Everything you do as a good parent should be for your children, rather than looking at your children as your **"eight little cheerleaders!"** If ever there was single statement from Kate telling us exactly where her children fit into her life, it's that one right there. "My eight little cheerleaders." It is now and always has been, all about Kate Gosselin.

Here are some tweets from Kate talking about the race after the fact:

xxxxx @Kateplusmy8 Hey Kate...Was that Rod Dixon U met at the finish line?

yes- met him Friday night and he surprised me at finish line!

xxxxx @Kateplusmy8 U were very fortunate 2have opportunity 2meet up w/Rod Dixon...2 get personal advice from him! A proven winner himself!

and we shall stay in touch... He's amazing!

xxxxx @Kateplusmy8 That was such an accomplishment, I bet you are still on cloud 9. I know I would be.

and looking forward to next with help of rod Dixon! :) can't wait!

Knowing how manufactured Kate's every move is, it doesn't seem likely that Rod Dixon just happened to "surprise" her at the finish line. More likely, it was a meeting set up in advance by her manager, Julie May, who, by the way, just happened to be standing there with Rod Dixon waiting for Kate to arrive at the finish line. Julie probably had to point Kate out to him so he could fulfill his end of the contract.

Rod Dixon is over 60 years old and a very accomplished athlete. Kate expects us to believe that he took time out of his life to "surprise" her at the finish line just because he wanted to.

There has been much online speculation about whether or not Kate Gosselin even finished the marathon on her own. People who say they were actually there, running in the race themselves, saw Kate walking, being driven on a scooter by her bodyguard from check point to check point, etc. I can't verify these reports. What I do know is that Kate's word is suspect, given that I've caught her lying about 500 times.

This is what I know as fact. Kate does run. I have seen her running near her home. Whenever I've seen her running though, she looks more like a donkey plodding along the street. She looks to be in pain and near death. So when I watched the video online of Kate crossing the finish line of her first 26.2 mile marathon, fresh-faced, smiling and not looking even a little bit exhausted, it was hard not to believe there's truth to the rumors of her cheating.

The other think I know as fact is that Kate Gosselin takes every shortcut there is in life. Are we to believe that this time she actually accomplished something on her own...without help? I sure don't.

Kate addressed the cheating rumor in this tweet:

xxxxx @Kateplusmy8 Some runners are saying you were seen riding on a scooter and did not run the entire race. Please correct this inaccuracy.

a scooter? No cheating is tolerated.R They Jealous much? Can't accept I did it—I'm still in shock, and pain!:)

I wasn't there and I really couldn't care less if Kate ran a marathon or not. You decide, after having read this book, if you believe Kate Gosselin actually trained and completed a grueling 26.2 mile marathon, or if she took a few shortcuts presented to her.

What I do care about is the constant lying, self-promotion and extreme ignoring of her children's needs and the toll it will eventually take on them. All I know is that Kate left her kids in the hands of babysitters beginning on the morning of November 29, and didn't return home until the evening of December 8, all so she could spend a day running, or pretending to run, a marathon.

Once Kate finally returned home to her children, she was suddenly completely exhausted. She had been filled with energy and enthusiasm for nine days while she was away from them in Las Vegas, but the minute she got home, she became exhausted.

I'm taking the day off...other than taking care of my kids of course. Just letting the work build up..feeling exhausted&feels good to rest!

Looks like the Marathon Mama was another one-off, failed experiment. Kate now completely ignores Tweets like this.

xxxxx @Kateplusmy8 Do you have any races planned this summer? How's the running going?

BATTLING THE "HATERS"

Kate considers anyone who disagrees with her about anything, or criticizes her at all, a "hater." But instead of ignoring the people who criticize her, she argues with them.

xxxxx @Kateplusmy8 why do you have so many haters? I think you are great

I think because the fiercest hate comes from jealousy, boredom, and hate for oneself...

xxxxx @Kateplusmy8 Kate how dare you presume to speak for "real moms" You are a cheat, a liar, and an abuser

ALL real moms work hard@whatever makes kids happy and provides best for them, including me!:) Have a gd day!:)

xxxxx @Kateplusmy8 How can you stand all these people who seem to have nothing better to do with their lives than direct their misery at you?

I just block them. To me, they don't even exist ;) my rule: ignore annoying ppl in life- you'll succeed, they'll crumble :)

xxxxx @Kateplusmy8 Omg your haters make me not want to tweet you! Ergh!! Keep on rockin Kate, our home loves you & your kids!

no! Don't go away! Just block liberally! That's what I do and my screen is ALLL positive! Yay!:)

Kate said above that her Twitter "screen is ALLL positive! Yay!" Yet she spends the majority of her time interacting with haters. Instead of just simply and quietly blocking them, she feels compelled to engage them first, for the attention. Kate constantly tweets about positivity and love, but her Twitter timeline shows nothing but negative and hateful comments, bullying and threats. She is very critical, but she can't take criticism. She bullies others, but she complains that she is bullied when others criticize her or express a differing opinion.

xxxxx @Kateplusmy8 Jealous? I don't keep company with people that are beneath me!

then stop following me since I'm 'beneath you'. I'll help you, I'll block you now.... Have a nice day!

xxxxx @Kateplusmy8 Spend some time with your kids before they get taken away

seriously? If u can't stand reading about our awesome and happy lives,unfollow. U are now blocked. Negativity doesn't fly here!

nope. Can't have people bullying, name calling, and telling UNTRUTHS... So, yes, you are now blocked.

xxxxx @Kateplusmy8 Those kids are thought of as a commodity & always have been.

Your comment disgusts me. Consider yourself blocked.

xxxxx @Kateplusmy8 Good for you Kate

I know, really, 'commodities'?They r reason I live&breath& meaning of my life! Yes, they belong 2 me&blessed2b their mom! Geesh!

I think that tweeter made a good point there. The definition of "Commodity" is: 1. A basic good used in commerce. Let's not forget Kate's letter to Gymboree when the sextuplets were born where she wrote "…if there is a way my children could be a help in marketing your clothing lines, we're all for it!"

STUPIDITY

"Think b4 tweeting pls."

From watching Kate in action on "reality" television, listening to her interviews, and reading her Twitter words, it is clear that she has demonstrated stunning ignorance and a complete lack of interest in the world around her whenever it isn't about her. She is also intellectually challenged. Kate was once quoted during the Australia/New Zealand episodes as saying of the Kiwi bird… "Whenever you say Kiwi, I do not think of the bird with no arms. I think of a fruit. I'm sorry."
I'm sorry, too, Kate, that you think birds have arms and you say things like that in front of your young children who are learning from you.
Normally, I wouldn't even think to point out someone's grammatical errors, since I make enough of my own all the time. Kate, however, very condescendingly tells us over and over again how important education is, and always talks about how important grammar and spelling are to her; she says she "despises" misspelled words. She was shown correcting Jon's grammar, even though she is guilty of some of the most idiotic and repetitive spelling and grammar mistakes I have ever seen.
Having studied Kate's journal and Twitter feed, and having watched her on television for several years analyzing her words, I can say one thing for certain: Kate Gosselin is ignorant and lacking in intelligence and common sense. She puts other people down to hide the fact that she's shallow and uneducated.

we were so this year, last year at this time… In Sidney for the new year! Wish we were there now! :(

xxxxx @Kateplusmy8 but you can't spell it??

oh crap… Spell check must have gotten me?! Oops!

Kate always blames spell check whenever she is called out on her atrocious spelling. Spell check is not the culprit. Spell check wouldn't have automatically changed Sydney to Sidney. The only way it would have changed the spelling of that word is if she wasn't even close to the correct spelling, and spell check picked a spelling for her.

> xxxxx @Kateplusmy8 that's ok – us Aussies get offended when our cities are misspelt :))

I get offended when anything is misspelled lol!

> xxxxx @Kateplusmy8 I'm not hating but do you intently spell things wrong? Gorgeous btw. Just saying and I do love your show and miss it!

no just lots to say on twitter & cut corners. In 'real' life, I despise misspelled words! :) thanks..

Kate's excuse about cutting corners would be understandable, except that many of her misspelled words actually have too many letters in them, so the cutting corners excuse doesn't fly. She types more letters than she needs. She also consistently spells certain words wrong, like "gorgeous," as the tweeter pointed out. Kate always spells it "georgous."

When she traveled to Connecticut to exploit her children further by making them run in a "kidsmarathon" that they clearly didn't want to run in, as evidenced by videos posted on YouTube, she thanked her host town repeatedly via Twitter after the race. It obviously wasn't important enough for her to spell the name of the town correctly.

What a wonderful wkend!The Lichtfield road race was HARD but fun&running w Rod Dixon was a wonderful honor! Thx Lichtfield! We love u all!

And, I must add much thanks2the town of Lichtfield,Ct 4 ur hospitality,&4welcoming our family!We were honored2b a part of a ur trad events!

thank you for your kind words! We SO loved being a part of such a wonderful Lichtfield tradition! Such kind wonderful ppl!

I enjoyed ur 'neck of the (beautiful) woods' so much that we'd love 2 make it a tradition 2 visit Lichtfield each yr 4 events!:)

Kate had four cracks at spelling correctly the name of the "beautiful" Connecticut town she ran in. She got it wrong all four times. For the next time, just in case she's reading this, it's Litchfield. Litchfield, Connecticut. This tweetie spelled it correctly:

> xxxxx @Kateplusmy8 **Litchfield** race times are always determined by the weather and it's .9 longer than a 10k so a 1:08 is a great time!

The more Kate tries to use words that make her sound intelligent, the more they highlight her ignorance:

> xxxxx @Kateplusmy8 Rain here on the sunshine coast near Australia Zoo too!!

I find 'rain on the sunshine coast' to be an Oxy moron? Is it just me?? Lol!

Yes. It is just you, Kate. The rest of us know that oxymoron is one word. You also didn't need to capitalize the "O" either. You actually added a corner to your corner cutting.

you can't see good when it's raining outside? Don't let surroundings determine your attitude! :) have a good rainy am! :)

You can't see WELL when it's raining either.

> xxxxx @Kateplusmy8 big 'G' on God! (:

I know. Twitter has done it to me—pet peeve of mine too. Sorry..So disrespectful :(bad me.

She somehow managed to capitalize four letters in that tweet, though. Just not the "G" in God.

Kate isn't just a poor speller, she's plain lazy. With her iPhone in her hand 24/7, she has access to a world of information. Any question she has can be answered with the press of a button or two. On March 19, 2012, Kate was tweeting about the new season of *Dancing With The Stars*, which was starting that night. She had to insert herself into the story to remind everyone that SHE, you know, was on DWTS.

I woke up feeling NERVES.. For all DWTS contestants!!! First dance is tonight! Eeek! Good luck all! Have FUN!!!

....getting my pjs on &ready2watch @dwts! SO happy 2b sitting on my sofa w/ my girls watching&not vomiting from nerves back stage!:)

I'm loving the dancing on @DWTS this season already! So glad I don't have to dance tho! Happy on my sofa! Lol #dwts

But then, Kate's ignorance and laziness reared their ugly heads once again. One of her tweeties had to point out to her that she was using an incorrect Twitter name for *Dancing With The Stars*.

> xxxxx @Kateplusmy8 Kate, just so you know, when you tweet"@DWTS" it's not an account that has anything to do with Dancing With The Stars!

what is their @ thingy then?

Kate can't be bothered to look up the official Twitter account for DWTS, so she asked her tweetie to do it for her. It turns out that Kate was actually tweeting to an account called DeathWalksTheStreets, which included some offensive tweets containing profanity.

THE SKINNY ON PLAGIARISM

Plagiarism is defined in dictionaries as the "wrongful appropriation," "close imitation," or "purloining and publication" of another author's "language, thoughts, ideas, or expressions," and the representation of them as one's own original work.

In February of 2012, having no publicist to control her words for her, Kate once again put her foot in her mouth when she made a potentially dangerous tweet to her many impressionable teenage "tweeties."

> xxxxx @Kateplusmy8 Man! I wish! Getting ther but not quite there yet. But I don't know what you're talking about; you look AMAZING!!!
>
> **I'd agree with u if I was on your profile pic :) keep working...'Nothing tastes as good as thin feels' :) 1 of my many mottos!**

Not only is Kate ignorant and unintelligent, she has never had a single original thought of her own and has been plagiarizing other people's thoughts and works for years. This plagiarized comment by Kate – who has five impressionable daughters and mostly young teenage girls as Twitter followers – was one that even she should have known to keep to herself. Not Kate. She was so proud of it too; until the online backlash hit her. Again.

The quote, "Nothing tastes as good as thin feels," is a slight variation on an actual quote from supermodel Kate Moss, who was also criticized for it a few years ago. If Kate had researched the quote before blurting it out to the world, she would have found this:

> "Kate Moss, the model, has been accused of encouraging teenage girls to become anorexic after claiming she lives by the motto: "Nothing tastes as good as skinny feels."
>
> Critics condemned Moss's comments, saying that, as a role model to millions of girls and young women, they could lead to more instances of eating disorders."

Kate changed the word "skinny" to "thin" and made the quote her own. While telling us that she's not into plagiarism, she of course, took someone else's quote without attributing it to that person.

THANK YOU, MOMMY!

Kate is constantly putting words in her kid's mouths in an effort to make complete strangers, whom she doesn't and really shouldn't even care about, think she's a great mother. She is always talking about how much her children thank her for absolutely EVERYTHING and they're constantly "SHRIEKING" for joy about everything Kate does! Oh, mommy, thank you for that grape! Oh, mommy, thank you for making me sit on the rug stripe to watch a movie! Baloney.

When Kate bought the kids new bikes, she wrote on her web blog that they were "Such thankful amazing kids!" She said she received "four thousand thank-you's" "every hour on the hour for two days from all 8."

In a *Couponcabin.com* blog that Kate wrote about her Thanksgiving meal, she said "a chorus of eight 'Yummy, mommy!' makes it totally worth it."

Here is Kate tweeting about how thankful the kids are that she brought Shoka back from the breeder after she had vanquished him:

> **that was a memory filled day! My kids STILL thank me for him EVERY day, no lie. Nearly a year later:)**

("No lie"? Hmmm. Again with that? And does anyone truly believe that the kids thank her *every single day* for bringing Shoka back?)

In this tweet, Kate just can't help but throw Jon under the bus again:

> xxxxx @Kateplusmy8 Latest rumor that kids says they want to live with their daddy! Because..U are mean! LOL I know U want to address that one!

> **we all wish hewould tak them more than 4d/mo but doesn't.they have fun there but def love living w me/here. So happy here!**

I have watched every television show Kate Gosselin has ever been involved in, and I know the kids personally. I know she's a horrible mother. Her tweeting and blogging to the contrary isn't going to change that fact. She can't rewrite history. She may have gotten used to reality being written for her, but she can't change reality to suit her, no matter how hard she tries. And she sure does continue to try. Now in addition to eight children, one dog and every single person who has ever met her being absolutely head over heals in love with her, Kate Gosselin has now brought home a pet bird named Zorro who just can't get enough of her.

> **In the last few days, I SWEAR I've heard Zorro repeat 'love you' & just now I said 'thank you (bc he kissed my cheek) &he repeated me! #WOW**

TMI

The Gosselin children have absolutely zero privacy in their lives. Their mother blogs and tweets intimate details of their lives to anyone who's interested. In addition to her intrusive fans who clamor for every tidbit of information about her and her children, this audience of Twitter strangers almost certainly includes possible pedophiles, mentally unbalanced persons, or others who might do her family harm.

Kate has no boundaries when it comes to what she will tweet or say about her kids during interviews. She must never consider that her children will most surely be teased at school because of the personal information she offers to the world. Setting aside the fact that it's disrespectful and intrusive, it is just plain stupid and dangerous for a parent to be telling complete strangers where she will be taking her very famous children at any given time of the day. It is even worse when she tweets that she is out somewhere and her children are home alone.

There are hundreds of examples of Kate tweeting about what she and/or her kids are doing. These just scratch the surface:

Good eve! Kids and I are going out 2 dinner! Rare treat! Every1 is excited—including me=no clean up!Yay! Rarely eat out unless traveling!

...a lovely revelation from my kids amaz dentist:all 6 need 2c @readingorthodontics UM,life is abt2get REAL crazy Omg! Dr Nat,here we come!

Shuttling Mady back &forth to final weekend of play practice...She has her 1st part in school play 'Alice in Wonderland' SO proud mom here!

...GM all...I'm heading to pediatrician later 2day w/ a sick child instead of 2church... They r all upset that we aren't going! Me 2! :(:(

Mady is using word 'tragic' repeatedly in Mad Libs..Says 'tragic- its my favorite word!' ..... I would have guessed 'dramatic' was her fave!

....headed back home w/ my Hannah&her double ear infections...quick stop at pharmacy 1st &we will b all fixed up!

Busy day!Hannag is on the mend,ran 10mi, made it meatball subs w/ ground chicken(of course!) & homemade rolls, played,showered&2 bed we go...

GM all! Up early for play practice & densist appts...mommy shuttle bus is on duty! Gotta get every1 fed& out the door! ...catch u later!

Hannah is great!Ear infections didn't slow her playing down at all;just 'mom my ear hurts' every once in awhile!She's all good!

Mady is ?'ing my antibiotic knowledge-Me:'I'm a nurse u no' Mady:'yeah,but u haven't been in the dr industry 4awhile so I'm just checking!'

Bliss is..Sitting in a movie theatre w my 11 yr olds on either side of me,munching away on popcorn waiting 4 the HungerGames 2 begin....

Mady is putting on a quick 'one woman show' and then we are all going to sleep... Long weekend of fun! Monday is on its way... Zzzzzzzz..GN!

I just said 2 kids:'We have surprise guests again tomorrow!' Kids started guessing..Aadens 1st guess, excitedly: 'THE (film) CREW!!':(

C, M & I had a sleepover in my rm last pm...I've been awake for 3hrs now..they r STILL sleeping soundly..the word 'preteen' comes 2 mind..

Just back from running,in kitchen making protein shake.Joel walks in 'So,how was the run?'Do I suddenly hav adult children? Aw,he's so old!

...&just said GN 2 my cara on the phone..She gives great big sis care 2her bros/sisters while they r visiting their dads..warms my heart!

Kate doesn't just give a blow-by-blow of what the children are doing, she tweets pictures of what they are doing. Here are some examples:

Ok. This is one cute sight! They are thrilled to 'snap' peas! And I am thrilled to have the help! http://t.co/BwtcTYxD

http://t.co/J4PZZkWF Check out K8s Kids... New artwork posted that is too darn cute to miss! Can't wait to hear what you think!

Posting first VIDEO ever! Leah's hidden talent that even I didn't know about!!! She can snap her toes! Can you? http://t.co/C50bNS2y

go to my website http://t.co/QzYScyU8 lots of recent pics there! Enjoy!

Here was our afternoon entertainment...girls pedicures! Mady cleaned&I clipped&painted! So fun! http://t.co/70CuEkWB

Even some of Kate's fans/followers/haters are smart enough to see the danger in Kate tweeting every detail of the family's lives to complete strangers.

xxxxx @Kateplusmy8 Not a good idea that you tweet about when u r going to be away from your house. It's not safe to inform fans & nonfans.

On June 8, 2012, Kate tweeted that her children were going to be in Litchfield, Connecticut, for a running event that coming weekend. She posted a link to a website that provided every detail of where and when she and her children would be in public so anyone with good or bad intentions could find them.

So excited!My kids and I are running TOGETHER this weekend in a KIDSMARATHON run! Starting to pack! We are ready2run! http://t.co/kf3BFLeE

Kate sharing this information about her children's whereabouts is in stark contrast to what she does when she travels with her bodyguard and without the kids. In those situations, she remains silent about her plans and destination until AFTER the event is over, for her own safety. Here's a tweet that Kate responded to on the subject of safety:

xxxxx @Kateplusmy8 Was ample media on the opening. People have learned 2 help Kate stay under radar until she gets where's she's going.

yep. You're correct. Important for my safety. :)

KATE'S TWITTER GUARDIAN

Well, what do you know? Right on the heels of the online Gosselin critics discussing the fact that Kate has no friends who aren't paid to deal/work with her, guess who suddenly jumped into the Twitter fracas? Why, it's Deanna, the Stylist. Deanna inserted herself into the forefront of a great war being waged by Kate's fans to defend her against the "haters." How Deanna got tangled in Kate's web is anyone's guess. Maybe she was excited to rub elbows with a D-list celebrity. Or maybe she is just as intellectually challenged as Kate. Whatever the reason, Deanna has become Kate's new best friend, and her vocal protector on Twitter. The obvious question for Deanna that keeps playing over and over is, "WHY DO YOU SPEND SO MUCH TIME ONLINE ENGAGING THE HATERS ON TWITTER?"

Not only does Deanna defend Kate, she lies while doing it. Either she has more in common with Kate than I thought, or she is truly naïve and ignorant about what Kate does. I skimmed Deanna's 24-hour tweet-fest and found a couple of lies without really even trying, so I'm going to assume that much of what Deanna says on Twitter about the Gosselins are either big, fat lies, or misunderstanding of fact. All these next tweets are from Deanna.

When a tweeter asked Deanna if Kate is happy, Deanna replied:

@xxxxx @xxxxx @kateplusmy8 Yes, Kate is happy& she is sweet! I don't get all of the hate at all!!

@xxxxx @xxxxx @kateplusmy8 No lies here! Why don't you want people to know that Kate is nice and the kids r happy???

(Apparently, Deanna is afflicted with the same "No lies" syndrome as Kate, where she lies but says she's not lying.)

@ xxxxx @ xxxxx @kateplusmy8 are you angry bc I am crushing your tabloid view of the family? Y so mean?

@xxxxx @ xxxxx @kateplusmy8 Reality shows are created situations that can show a persons worst moments.

What? Reality shows are "created situations?" Not Kate's reality shows, Deanna! Kate said her shows were the most realist reality shows out there, remember?! There just happened to be a great bunch of dads with cameras taking home movies of Kate and the kids, who just happened to be going about their daily business, running in and out of frame, living their lives. REMEMBER?

If Deanna is going to defend Kate, she'd better brush up on Kate's history.

Amongst all Deanna's tweets defending Kate, I found this bizarre statement:

@xxxxx @xxxxx the kids tell me they love Kate and talk lovingly about her. How do you know them???

Why would 7-year-old kids tell a friend, a stranger, or anyone, that they love their mom and they "talk lovingly about her?" Oh, that's right. THEY WOULDN'T! Kids don't think like that. Kids are self-involved creatures who are trying to figure life out for themselves. I've been around the Gosselin kids a lot and, oddly enough, they've never come close to articulating anything remotely similar to those thoughts. They have, however, voiced many, many, many complaints about their mother.

Deanna was undaunted in her quest to protect Kate's good name. When someone tweeted to Deanna saying that she needed to accept that "KATE went on national TV and was a rude nasty person," Deanna responded:

@xxxxx @xxxxx So you saw her on a TV show and I see her carry in 20 bags of groceries and hug her kids. We base opinions on different things.

Deanna said she has seen Kate carry in 20 bags of groceries. Deanna said she has seen Kate hug her kids. Well, there you go. Color me corrected. Those are clearly signs that Kate is a great mother. Those things obviously prove beyond any doubt that Kate is not a rude and nasty person. Right.

I have never seen Kate carry 20 bags of groceries into the house. I can't remember a single instance in all the time that I followed and watched Kate, and in all the pap photos I have seen of Kate, where she has *ever* carried more than a few bags of groceries. I've also never seen Kate hug any of her kids, except when she had to for her fake reality shows.

Deanna lives on the Upper East Side of Manhattan; I live 10 minutes from Kate's house and have shopped at the same grocery store as Kate. I've seen Deanna at Kate's house twice. She's definitely not a fixture at the Gosselin compound, so I don't know what she is basing her observations on.

Deanna continued to battle with the worst of the Kate haters on Twitter for hours over a two-day period. She doggedly responded to EVERYONE…well, everyone except me, that is. She must have gotten the memo from Kate that anything that says "Gosselinbook" is to be ignored so it will go away.

Although it is a fool's errand, Deanna made a valiant effort in trying to defend Kate. She will just need to take a lot more lessons in the art of lying from Kate, who is a master of the art.

THE FINE ART OF GRIFTING

Since filming began in 2006, Kate has been given EVERYTHING she's asked for on a silver platter. TLC/Discovery either just bought her everything she wanted straight up, or for the larger items, they incorporated product placement deals with sponsors, where the product would be worked into the show "organically," to make it appear that Kate and the kids had actually purchased the product. Kate Gosselin *has* never and *will* never, spend any of "her" money on her children if she doesn't absolutely have too.

Kate Gosselin knows EXACTLY what she's doing when she mentions or tweets about loving something, or wanting something, or needing something. She's been doing it since her very first television special and it has always worked for her. She became accustomed to asking for anything and everything and having it delivered to her by Discovery/TLC or companies who like the exposure even a washed-up reality star can give them. A polarizing figure such as Kate is always good for a few extra views on a website.

After her shows were canceled and her contract had expired, Kate had to find a new way to ask for and get freebies. The Christians were onto her game by now, which made it impossible for Kate to tap that well again, so she found and began to worship in a new place to fulfill her grifting needs. That place was the Church of Twitter. And she found that it was good.

Twitter has given Kate a platform to mention something she needs or wants, and have her fans fall all over themselves to get it for her. Since she is still considered a "celebrity," even in the most generous sense of the word, Twitter has also allowed her to get products from companies that are looking for publicity.

Kate gets gifts from fans, but most importantly, she gets gift cards. That's what she's really looking for. She also knows how to work businesses to get free stuff. She just includes their name in her tweets and before she knows it, the company sends her their product.

Kate's usual method of manipulation is to throw something out there on Twitter about something she is looking for. This is one such instance:

Any1 know where to find a cute 'what's on the menu this week' chef chalkboard (think sidewalk café type but smaller& hangs on wall) online?

Now Kate knows good and well that she can find anything she wants through a quick and easy Google search. Or, she could just type in www.amazon.com **and she would find a mother lode of products to meet her every desire**. But if she did that, her fans wouldn't send her stuff for free.

It doesn't appear that anyone took the bait this time on the chalkboard grift:

xxxxx @Kateplusmy8 Did u get ur menu chalk board yet? Cant wait to see it :)

oh there is SO many online, I can't decide... Still deciding lol!

Here she is dropping major hints that she'd like eight new laptops delivered to her front door by someone...anyone. She needs those laptops because she has 8 kids, you know, and she had to scrounge around for laptops to use. What does that even mean? Does she have multiple laptops laying around the house? This tweet sure made it sound that way:

http://t.co/J9GqOdg3 ...The scene at r house last pm...Scrounged around4any laptop we could find2speed the homework process! Still not enuf!

xxxxx @Kateplusmy8 Well lots of families have made it w one computer so I'm sure you'll suffice

one hour to complete six math homework assignments each night? Um, not happening... ;(

xxxxx @Kateplusmy8 I wish you had spoken sooner. I just donated some office laptops. I would have sent them your way. :(

oh crap! That sucks,huh?We could used ur old laptops but lotsa others can 2 I guess! Thanks for thought! Good of u 2 donate!

xxxxx @Kateplusmy8 looks like it's about time to invest in laptops (MacBooks!!) for everyone :D

agreed... Birthdays are coming... But then again, wow, that's a lot to take on... I'm not a computer specialist lol

xxxxx @Kateplusmy8 I'm a fan of u and ur cute family....I just don't like complaining when lots of families have far less than u #stayblessed

...&far less kids 2! Wasn't complaining.. Was marveling @ another growing up milestone,read my tweets thru + lenses,not neg 1s!

PERSONAL GRIFTING

xxxxx @Kateplusmy8 Hey K8, I'm being a pest tonite, sorry. If I wnted to snd smthing-what addr.?? Could snd to hme addr, but not sur y'd wnt that

email me through my website...:)

xxxxx @Kateplusmy8 Do you have any other books out apart from Multiple Blessings and Eight Little Faces?? Read them in one day loved them ☺

yes! My very favorite and most recent 'I Just Want You to Know' can get it here: http://t.co/jP1YBjpK

Now if Kate really gave a crap about her Twitter fans, like she claims to, and if Kate was really interested in helping people save money, like she preached on her *couponcabin.com* blog, then why would she direct her fans to purchase her book from the Zondervan website for the full retail price of $22.99 plus tax, shipping and handling? Maybe it's because Kate is not at all interested in helping her fans save money when that money could be hers. She still gets a percentage of book sales from Zondervan's site, so that is where she will send them.

A simple search of the internet shows that Kate's book, *I Just Want You To Know*, can be purchased through *Amazon.com*, the most popular site on Earth to make purchases, for $0.01, plus shipping and handling. It is also available in pretty much all dollar stores and discount book stores for the same price or lower. So why not tell her fans that?

Why, indeed. The answer is obvious. In its simplest, purest form, it all boils down to everything that Kate is about: money. If you buy her book at her former publisher's website for full retail price, she will earn more royalties from the sale.

BIRTHDAY GRIFTING

Kate always preemptively tweets hints to her fans about upcoming birthdays, sometimes weeks in advance, to give her fans plenty of time to go shopping and send gifts to her or her kids. She knows that most of her fans that send her presents and gift cards are teenage girls and stay-at-home moms with limited incomes, yet she does absolutely nothing to discourage them. She has never asked anyone to please donate items or gift cards to others who are truly in need instead. In 2011, Kate started tweeting hints about the twins' upcoming birthday a full two weeks ahead of the big day.

Getting ready for 2 very loved kids' birthdays... They have everything all planned out and so do I :) Can't wait to help them celebrate 11!

xxxxx @Kateplusmy8 Hey MamaG! I still need to know what I should get M&C. Im getting a few things for them for a late birthday present.. lol(:

aww sweet. If u want 2, anything thrills them, really and truly. Very grateful girls,even a card will make them happy!:)thx!

xxxxx @Kateplusmy8 What color is your and your kids favorites? I like to knit socks and mittens in their favorite colors if you like ? :)

oh great! Thanks!Email me and I'll answer! :)

xxxxx @Kateplusmy8 KATE- I want to send u a package for u and the kids......where do I address it to?!?!? I hope u rspond. <3 u!!!!!!

email me at my website...and I'll tell you :) thanks

xxxxx @Kateplusmy8 I thought Icoudnt go wrong getting u something frm 1 of ur fav stores! I loved"shopping for u!"I'll have to do it again soon;)

got it. Love it. SO thoughtful and kind of you and your book will go in the mail tomorrow! When were u in paris, lucky girl?

xxxxx @Kateplusmy8 Hi- how do we send gifts w/o ur address? I would love to send a surprise!

aww lol. Ask @BarbGilmer for my address. She will give it to you! So sweet of you. :) thx! U guys make me smile- thanks for that!

xxxxx @Kateplusmy8 I was wondering if you have got the gift yet. For your B-Day If not soon it might go out of date+we wouldn't want that! X ;)

YES! You naughty girl! Lol I'm going to eat some chocolate right now! Thank you! Yum!!It's been a chocolate needing day here!

omg! Delicious can't even describe this Cadbury 'bubbly' choc!It's dangerous..I'm giving it2my kids-they can eat it b4 I do!

Kate has often talked about eating, and allowing her children to eat, candy and food sent to her by complete strangers. It doesn't matter how many times she has tweeted these people, they are still strangers she knows nothing about. Kate is always talking about how she must have security with her because it is important for her safety, but she is oblivious to where the real threats are likely to come from.

Kate receives these gifts but very often doesn't acknowledge them or even take the time to tweet a personal "thank you" to the gift giver. Here, after not hearing a peep from Kate, one of her young fans is forced to ask Kate if she received the presents she sent:

xxxxx @Kateplusmy8 Um it had some English chocolate a message two cards two bracelets... I sent it 3-4 weeks ago :) thnks for replying ur the bestx

I'll keep eyes peeled...

And if the gift givers are really lucky, they will see a mass thank you tweet like this:

Dear every1 who sent M&C bday cards/gifts(if I missed u personally): none were necessary,all appreciated&each made us all smile! Thanku XO

Kate Gosselin is a multi-millionaire. To this day, she is still hinting for and accepting gifts from fans via Twitter.

Do yourself a favor and block those idiots... I'm not asking for gifts??!
It's a haters ploy!
— Kate Gosselin
2.28.12 on Twitter

CORPORATE GRIFTING

Kate is an equal opportunity grifter. She will grift from her lowly little fans and from small and large corporations alike. Here she is putting the word out to her fans in Australia and New Zealand that she could really use some Nutrigrain cereal:

> **...sadly,this am, we opened our LAST box of Nutrigrain cereal that we brought back from Aus/NZ...a sad day here!:(Wish we had it in the US!**

For most people and families, a "sad day" is when the power gets turned off because they cannot afford to pay the bill and your family has to spend two days living in the dark. A sad day for Kate is running out of her special cereal from an exotic FREE vacation.

Here she is singing the praises of Bell & Evans chicken.

> **...it's chicken(200 lbs of it!)food saving day! Thx @bell&evans chicken outlet4great prices&2my food saver 2! ..sorry, pic won't load :(**

> **http://t.co/4QwhsVH2 ...the final case of chicken..I'm food saving it now and then I'm done! Wow! What a job! @bell&evans @foodsaver**

In case you missed that little Kate trick/lie, here it is in slow motion. Kate told us about her 200 lbs of chicken that she bought/got from Bell & Evans. She took a picture of it all, but oddly enough, she said the picture wouldn't load :(. Kate did manage to successfully load a picture of only one 20-lb box of chicken. It's a shame we didn't get to see the other nine boxes. I'm sure she had them. Kate would never lie about something to make it look like she had to work harder than she actually did.

> **http://t.co/9ADT4tOT These were for dinner! They r new & we tested them courtesy of @bell&evans w/ sw pot fries& baked beans! Huge hit!**

Kate included the @bell&evans in her tweet, but Bell & Evans isn't even on Twitter. Kate should do her homework to make sure her target will see her tweets before grifting for free products.

K8TY KEURIG!

Thanks to a sharp-eyed poster at *realitytvkids.com* for noticing Kate responding to Keurig. And abracadabra…it appears to have worked for Katie.

> xxxxx @Kateplusmy8 Keurig Did you know that the new Vue brewer allows you to brew bigger? Enjoy up to an 18 oz. travel mug of your beverage of choice. #KeurigVue

> **@Keurig WOW! Sounds like my kind of coffee maker :) good job, keurig! It's 1 reason I love you so much! :)**

> xxxxx @Kateplusmy8 GM K8ty Keurig! Rainy here and was dragging but feeling more awake now after my run! Have a good one!

> **aww I smiled again at my new name—K8ty Keurig! That is SO me today on this dark day! Need Xtra coffee! Yum! @Keurig**

> **…still thanking @Keurig and now @coffeemate and @Starbucks too for taking care of a caffeine needing mom of 8's needs! Thanks all! Xoxo**

> xxxxx @Kateplusmy8 Lazy Katie did it again. She's Tweeting to @coffeemate when the Coffee-Mate brand Twitter name is actually @Coffee_mate. It took me all of five seconds Kate to look it up on my iPhone, just like the one that you have.

HOLY GUACAMOLE!

While representing CouponCabin at the March 2012 BlogHer Conference in New York City, Kate made the rounds visiting various exhibitors and collecting lots of freebies. Kate the millionaire was apparently in desperate need of some guacamole dip, so she grifted some free "Wholly Guacamole" product from their booth. After Kate returned home from the conference, she did what any appreciative guacamole lover would do with the free guacamole she had scored.

In a unique and innovative marketing move, Kate thought it would be amusing to dump "Wholly Guacamole" guacamole over her daughter Leah's head and take a picture of Leah smiling cutely for the camera. Kate then tweeted the photo to the world. Most significantly, she also tweeted it to @eatwholly, who no doubt must have been overcome with joy to see their product being used in such a "wholly" unappetizing and wasteful way. Kate is always looking for new and exciting ways to exploit her children to bring attention to herself. Maybe Kate actually thought this stunt would cause Wholly Guacamole to consider hiring her as a spokeswoman. The exploitation of the Gosselin children has come to this.

> **Wholly Guacamole, Leah! She wears it well! (and smiles while wearing it!!!) @eatwholly** http://t.co/hUvkDONr

BELLA, BOOKS AND PANHANDLE

Kate does not hesitate to lure her Twitter "friends" into her seemingly endless "not mediocre" money-making schemes. They are so enamored of her, they make easy marks for her begging and scamming.

On July 10, 2012, Kate started subtly selling vegan/candy/energy/protein bars just by mentioning that she likes them and that she eats them all the time. Smart bloggers at *realitytvkids.com* quickly sniffed out via the Bella Bar website that this was nothing more than a way for Kate to make a quick and easy buck. And there would be absolutely nothing wrong with that if only Kate would just be upfront with her fans and tell them that this is a way for her to make a few bucks, instead of pretending that she just randomly fell in love with Bella Bars and felt compelled to tell her fans how much she loves them. Maybe Kate should have paced herself a bit and not tweeted four consecutive tweets about Bella Bars in a matter of minutes. How quickly a big "star" has fallen.

WOW,have you tried the Bella Bar? It is so healthy and delicious! I'm eating one right now......I'm totally addicted! https://t.co/v9QDDgG8

A FREE box of Bella bars goes to a lucky new fan of their Facebook Page! Click this link to enter for your chance>> https://t.co/v9QDDgG8

The Bella Bar folks also have a special for all of my followers: FREE shipping on any order during the contest! Use coupon code "Kate"!

I've tried every bar in the world, I think... I cannot get anough of Bella bars... I'm in love! :) Go enter to win.. https://t.co/v9QDDgG8

Some people, even millionares, are just addicted to free stuff and easy money. No matter how much they have, they will always want more and will do anything to get what they want, even if it means taking advantage of their loyal fans. And Kate's loyal fans can't buy those bars fast enough to help her line her pockets even further.

xxxxx @Kateplusmy8 My Bella bars arrived today! Already tried the chocolate nut. So good! Thanks Kate! @Bellabars

and now you must order the Athena bar! Omg that Bella bar makes me screech! ;)

BIRDS OF A FEATHER

There is one particularly worrisome Kate fan who for years has tweeted, and continues to tweet, awful things about Jon, encouraging Kate to further alienate the children from their father. She tweets to Kate advising her to tell the children to keep things from Jon, and to tell them their father is "HER ENEMY." She tells Kate to THREATEN them and punish them with the "SPOON." In other words, this fan is telling Kate to smack the heck out of those kids if they dare speak to their father.

These are the people Kate surrounds herself with. And Kate never, NEVER, asks her fans who tweet terrible things about Jon to stop. But she is the first to cry "bully" when someone says something critical about her.

Here are just some of the *hundreds* of horrible and twisted tweets about Jon from this one person. I did not include her Twitter name here because everyone who follows Kate Gosselin knows who she is.

> xxxxx @deannatweeting @xxxxx @kateplusmy8 Kate needs to tell her kids to NOT tell Jon anything about he*r* home or what she's doing.

> xxxxx @deannatweeting @xxxxx @kateplusmy8 If the kids do tell Jon or anyone her business or what goes on in their home, I would get SPOON

> xxxxx @deannatweeting @xxxxx @kateplusmy8 Kate should tell her children their father is HER ENEMY.

> xxxxx @xxxxx @Kateplusmy8 Kate doesn't have to isolate her kids but she better threaten them about telling Jon or anybody HER business

> xxxxx @xxxxx @Kateplusmy8 Kate, w/ exception of sexual/physical abuse THREATEN ur children if they reveal YOUR business 2Jon. Tell kids Jon is YOUR enemy

Very, very scary. A lot can be learned about a person from the company she keeps.

LAST "WRITES"

It seems only fitting to regurgitate a couple of Kate's Twitter writings as the final words in this chapter. I want to give her every opportunity to set the record straight and put the truth out there. Too bad she is telling untruths as she states "only the facts."

> **Ok, I'm saying GN now. Great2put the truth out there so these morons who make stuff up look&feel stupid! I feel better now! Until next X....**

> xxxxx @Kateplusmy8 you're a bad mom

I'm sorry you feel that way. Have u ever met me or spent time in our home? Yeah, I didn't think so! Have a nice evening..

xxxxx @Kateplusmy8 Twitter, Facebook, google is here for eternity. What goes on here, is a diary to your children – remember that.

I do! That's why I state only the facts :)&only when needed. Talk abt Only things that make it to the public--& then only2correct!

People don't have to have ever met Kate or spent time in her home because she invited them all inside for seven seasons of filming. She showed us all what kind of mother she is. It's not a secret.

HELL ON WHEELS: THE END OF AN "ERROR"

"I have always dreamed of taking the kids
on an RV trip to see this country."
– *Kate Gosselin*

The final two episodes of *Kate Plus Ei8ht* aired on August 29th and September 5th of 2011. Those episodes, officially titled "RV Trip" and "RV Breakdown," tell an illuminating story about the final relationship between Kate and TLC. I am recapping these episodes in detail because so much happened that explains why TLC, Ashley Turner and Jamie Cole Ayers had finally had enough of Kate Gosselin.

Anyone truly interested in the Gosselin story will take the time to watch these episodes. They clearly illustrate and epitomize why TLC had finally decided to part ways with Kate for good. TLC did not attempt to hide, disguise, excuse or sugarcoat Kate's entitled, demanding, lying, sadistic and narcissistic behavior, as they had done so often in the past.

In the first of the RV episodes, Kate was shown tearing the tags off all the brand new clothes she was given for the trip. Kate always demanded new clothes for everyone whenever they filmed an episode. She seemed very annoyed that she had to remove the tags by herself, though. Usually a production assistant did that tedious work (you know, the normal, everyday mom things) for her.

When she was outside packing her SUV, she yelled at Mady for not helping her quickly enough and scolded her in an irritated tone, saying, "You should know by now whenever you're helping me you should be running at all times!"

The crew loaded everything into the RVs in her front yard except for one or two bags so they could get footage of Kate working hard packing up the RVs. Now packing a vehicle is a task that normal people do every single day in preparing for a trip, but Kate couldn't even handle that job without drama. She made it look so hard and exhausting. She struggled by herself to push a couple of bags into the outside storage compartment of one of the RVs, got frustrated and snapped at the film crew saying, "At some point we're going to have to stop playing 'we're filming a TV show' and really work because I'm really done!" She was standing there all flustered, with her hands on her head acting like the typical lazy, demanding, put-upon Kate Gosselin we have seen so often. It's interesting that her comment about filming a TV show wasn't edited out.

After this dramatic display of poor, overworked Kate packing up the RVs, something strange and entirely non-RV-trip-like happened. Kate and her children and security guards and babysitters set off on the "dream" RV trip two days later by getting on an airplane and jetting off to South Dakota to meet up with their packed RVs. I wonder if their luggage at least enjoyed the road trip.

They flew to South Dakota on an RV vacation because it is a fake reality show, and they had already scripted which scenes they were going to be filming out west. TLC didn't want to waste anyone's precious time by having them actually driving to their destination in an RV while on an RV trip.

One of the scripted "scenes" in this realist of reality shows that they had planned ahead of time was "Kate drives the RV." Kate said, "I actually wanted to try to drive for the first part of the trip to see what it would be like if I took this on myself. (She actually drove less than a mile, just for fake filming.) Here are some highlights from the RV trip. Ours has always been the realist reality show.

At a rest stop, Kate and the kids were playing by the water in what looked like mud. They were throwing it at each other and having a grand old "spontaneous" time. Then Kate yelled, "That could be totally sewage, you do realize!" She then said, "It smells like sewage so I wouldn't say put it on her face!" so of course Kate was shown with the sewage or mud or whatever it was splattered on her own face. Kate continued, "Oh my word, this is so raunchy! It's in Mady's mouth. It's probably not good. It's sewage!" while laughing and having a good time.

Then Kate ran around smearing the "sewage" in Jamie's son's face, and he smeared it in Kate's. Kate was still laughing as she got "sewage" in her mouth. A few minutes later, with all of the kids laughing and running around playing and having a great time, Kate announced, "I'm done! Let's call it quits! Let's go!!" Cut! Filming was done, so the kids' fun was over, too.

It was nice to see the kids having fun, but Kate's participation was confusing. Were we to believe that Kate, who called herself a "manic germophobe" in *Multiple Blessings*, and who has always been portrayed as an OCD clean freak, was OK with getting "raw sewage" in her mouth? This is the same woman who later in the trip wouldn't go in the huge river during the rafting excursion because she was afraid there might have been pee in there; her own kids' pee for that matter.

So which is it Kate? Are you a germophobe, or are you a complete faker and liar, pretending to have fun while "raw sewage" is being thrown in your face? Of course the mud wasn't raw sewage, but they had to create a little fake drama for filming.

In another scene, the RVs pulled over for a few minutes to let the kids out for some fresh air and exercise. Once again, the kids were having a wonderful time running around and playing, but Kate said, "They're sick of the RVs already and we haven't really ridden in them yet, so we're inventing fun … evidently," as she looked on in disgust. It is astonishing how she can take the pleasure out of most normal childhood experiences. Most parents who see their children thoroughly enjoying themselves would allow their fun to continue for as long as possible. Kate is not most parents.

There was nothing that was pleasing to Kate about this trip. While complaining about her seat being uncomfortable, Kate said, "I'm sure there's RVs that are convenient in the world. This is not one of them."

I'll bet the company that let TLC use their RVs was really happy about their vehicle being bad-mouthed like that on television.

Kate has completely forgotten who she is and where she came from. She's a hillbilly from a cow pasture in rural Pennsylvania. She is not a star. She has no marketable skills or talent that anyone can see. Where did she get this false sense of entitlement? She gave birth to six babies at one time. That's the only reason anyone knows her name.

NEXT STOP, MOUNT RUSHMORE

"Traveling is knowledge. Traveling is learning.
Traveling is life experience. I'm a huge advocate of traveling."
– Kate Gosselin

Kate Gosselin is a huge advocate of traveling when someone else is paying for it. When the traveling Gosselin side-show reached Mount Rushmore in South Dakota, Cara started to tell us about the Presidents on the national memorial, specifically pointing out Teddy Roosevelt. Kate quickly interrupted her daughter's moment to correct her and tell us all that it is not, in fact, Teddy, it's Franklin Delano Roosevelt. Kate informed us, "And that is FDR. Do you see it?"

Not only is Kate blindingly, shockingly stupid, she just couldn't let Cara have her moment, and she wouldn't let go. When her mistake was corrected on camera by a member of the crew, Kate looked angry and outraged. She said, "It's Teddy Roosevelt, OK, correct me, whatever (rolling her eyes.) It's one of those Roosevelt people. Ok, I think we can cut it. Wave it goodbye."

Cut! Kate is not happy. Filming is done. The kids' fun is done. And they drove away from this "educational" stop on their road trip. Move on to the next shot.

GRAND CANYON NATIONAL PARK
(One of the Seven Natural Wonders of the World)

"Grand Canyon, that's where we're going.
A huge missing chunk of Earth, deep crevicy thing."
– Kate Gosselin

Kate was so awed by the sight of the Grand Canyon she just couldn't find the words to adequately express her appreciation of it. Well, that really means she said the first stupid thing that came to her mind. As she stood at the edge of one of the most breathtaking sights in nature anyone will ever see, Kate uttered these inspired words:

"Whew, this is freaky! Wouldn't wanna be here when an earthquake strikes."

"Oh, I am just so like, freakazoided. It's like wasted land, I mean, like what could you ever do besides come and gawk at it?"

Her friend Jamie, who does not pretend to know everything about everything like Kate does, appeared to understand this was supposed to be an educational trip, so she said, "I wonder how far it stretches."

Kate, looking at the cameraman for approval, answered: "Like ten thousand miles or something!?"

(Educational note to Kate: The Grand Canyon is actually 277 miles long. Not 10,000. Close enough for Kate, though.)

Earlier, Kate had sent Cara and Mady back to the RV with Ashley due to bad behavior. Her family was at the Grand Canyon filming a television show, and Kate sucked all that joy out of it for her girls, and once again, made everything about her. "They came to take a picture and they're gone! I will not take it!" she said.

As Jamie and Kate were staring out at the wondrous scene before them, Jamie said, "It's too bad Ashley, Mady and Cara aren't going to see all this."

Kate nonchalantly remarked: "I know!"

THE FACTS OF REALITY LIFE

For these "unscripted" RV trip episodes, each of the kids was given facts to inform us about various things so they could pretend to know about them and seem well-educated. When they visited Old Faithful, Hannah spoke out of turn and Mady snapped, "Hannah! That was my fact! I'm starting over!" That prompted this exchange between Kate and Mady:

Kate: "Do you want to go sit on the end of the bench?"

Mady: "No, I want to start over!"

Kate: "No. Nobody's listening twice!!"

Then to make sure everyone knew how difficult everything was for her, Kate announced, "I'm about to spew like that thing. I'm getting really close."

The kids were loving watching Old Faithful shoot boiling water and steam into the air. They wanted to stay, but the crew had gotten their shot and that's all that mattered to Kate. As soon as she had had enough of watching "that thing" and putting up with a few people taking pictures, she was ready to leave.

"Let's get outta here before we're photographed to pieces. Let's go!"

CAMPFIRE COOKING

The best part of this whole fake, scripted episode is when it was decided that Kate was going to cook dinner over a "campfire." Kate made a big deal about never having cooked over a "campfire," and the kids were shown gathering rocks and wood and brush. Kate disappeared with Steve in an SUV for several hours to go shopping for organic chicken.

Later, we saw a campfire being started with the wood the kids had gathered, and we were given the impression that Kate was cooking the chicken over the campfire. There was just one minor detail. The producers/editors at TLC made the mistake (or was it a mistake?) of showing a close-up of Kate cooking the chicken, not over the wood-burning campfire they had shown us moments earlier, but on a grill rack placed over charcoals exactly like the charcoals Kate has in her grill at her house, the one she claims she cooks on very often. She looked surprised that the chicken got burned as it sat unattended for too long on that grill in extreme heat, dripping fat onto the hot coals just inches below.

Then, during the scene, Kate threw a fit saying, "These kids have like no clue what this takes!"

(I'm pretty sure that 7-year-olds don't really need to know basic grilling skills.)

She later said, "It's shocking, um, (Kate wide-eyed) I mean I enjoyed it actually. I've never cooked over a campfire and I grill all the time, but that doesn't count. I nearly burned it, but it was still edible so we're good."

PIZZA PARTY

While standing outside of a luxury RV being angry and put off...Kate said, "I've never stood next to an RV in flip flops on gravelly stones and ordered takeout. It's really odd. It's time to go home." That summed up her mood and things continued to spiral downward from there.

Kate threw a tantrum and had a total meltdown on camera because Jamie and Ashley had the nerve to allow the children to eat some of the last four remaining slices of pizza. Kate flipped out because the pizza was supposed to be for the adults for lunch and Steve had "reserved" a slice the night before. There was one slice left and Mady, Kate's own flesh and blood, handed it to Steve without wrapping it in foil or putting it on a plate. Kate blew her top. Judging from her over-reaction, you would have thought that Mady had contaminated the pizza with nuclear waste. Kate screamed about how disgusting it was. Poor Mady, clearly upset, said, "Mommy, I'm sorry. I didn't know, Okay?" Kate's comforting words to her were, "It's not your fault. The adults in there should tell you to stay out of the fridge."

Kate went on to talk about her "masterminding the meals" and "foraging for food." She made it sound like she was trapped in the wilderness and forced to scrounge for seeds and berries to keep her family alive instead of, horrors, having them eat macaroni and cheese instead of pizza.

Kate's meltdown over Mady touching a slice of pizza is even more bizarre considering that earlier in the trip Kate was laughing and having a jolly good time while she and the kids threw RV "raw sewage" on each other, with some of the kids even getting it in their mouths.

A TEARFUL GOODBYE

Kate's "best friend," Jamie, and her other longtime "friend" and babysitter, Ashley, were along on the trip to help watch the kids. Kate called them what the rest of us already knew they were...paid help. Kate made it clear that Ashley and Jamie were not doing the work they were being paid to do. She said, "I can't do it all myself and I have asked for help, and I've gotten it. I've gotten help, but not the help to the degree that I was hoping I would get." That's Kate-speak meaning Jamie and Ashley were being paid to do everything, but Kate actually had to pitch in a little bit, and it was more than she could bear.

"I'm not happy and I shouldn't be happy," Kate continued. I have always had what we needed. I am masterminding for 15 people. I am not along as help. Naturally, I'm a little busy. The funny thing is we pull out 25 minutes late and it's always my fault cause they're in there watching a movie. I went in yesterday, they're all in the air conditioning on the HDTV and I just went... not one adult came and asked if they could...is there anything I can do? I mean, that's not **paid help** in my opinion, I'm sorry. I feel very bad saying bad things about two of the people I like the most. I'm not trying to say it about them, I just, I don't know what happened to them. I don't know if this is like posh trip that they're usually used to going on, I, I don't know what it is. **We don't go on posh trips. I struggle from the beginning to the end. I get very little sleep."**

Kate blamed everyone else for the reason they pulled out late, but Ashley exposed what really happened. She said, "The two hours yesterday that she's talking about that she was 'getting ready,' she was putting on her makeup and taking a shower, and we had all the kids over here. It's just BS. It's just a joke to me and if she really...if that's what she thinks, I'm over it. It's bullcrap. It's such a joke. It's enough. I've had it." With tears in her eyes, Ashley said, "It just sucks because I'd die for these kids, but I just can't spend one more minute with her. Please send me home."

A voice off camera told her, "Yep. We'll do it. We'll start working on it." Then, with the blurred images of the two RVs side by side in the background, these words appeared on the screen: "DURING A PRIVATE CONVERSATION, ASHLEY TOLD KATE THAT SHE WAS LEAVING."

We next saw Ashley standing outside the RV with the kids, who were all crying and obviously distraught. Ashley said goodbye to them with these words: "Look at me. I will see you again. Alright? I love you with all my heart and don't let anybody ever tell you differently."

Her choice of words was very telling...and very sad. Over the years, Ashley has probably seen and heard Kate lie to the kids about all of the family members and friends who are no longer in their lives because of Kate's horrible behavior. Ashley was, no doubt, worried that Kate would lie to them about *her* reasons for leaving, so she made sure to tell them not to believe *anyone* who might tell them she doesn't love them. So because of Kate's mean, disrespectful, selfish behavior on this trip, and probably due to an accumulation of mean, disrespectful, and selfish behavior over the years, the Gosselin children lost their beloved babysitter and friend.

Kate was completely perplexed about Ashley's negative comments and her quitting. She said she had absolutely no idea what could have made Ashley want to leave. That right there sums up Kate Gosselin's cluelessness or straight up lack of caring about how badly she treats others. Everyone in her life leaves her and she says has no idea why.

With the same stunning lack of awareness she has always displayed, Kate said, "The funny thing about Ashley is that we've never even had a small disagreement in our lives." She also said, "I've never had a run-in with Ashley, ever, 'til this trip, cause she has always said to me, 'I used to think that you were, ya know, mean and yelling at me when you were stressed, but then I realized you were just yelling cause you were stressed'."

Kate contradicted herself in one sentence. First she said that she and Ashley had never had a small disagreement in their lives, but then she quoted Ashley as saying that Kate was mean and yelled at her. Ashley said she had put up with Kate treating her badly and with terrible disrespect, for five years.

So how could Kate stand before the TLC viewing audience and tell such a blatant lie? Either she is too stupid to realize that she contradicted herself, or her mind is so warped and self-absorbed that she is unaware of how badly she treated Ashley. In the five years that Ashley cared for the eight Gosselin children, Kate was plenty mean and disrespectful to her. Given how things played out on the RV trip, it is logical to think that Ashley only put up with the earlier abuse and didn't speak up to defend herself or fight back for the sake of the children. But everyone has a breaking point. For Ashley, Kate's behavior on the RV trip pushed her over the edge.

At the end of the episode, Kate wrapped up the situation and tied it with a big bow of self-pity, saying, "People leave my life and I keep on going. Pretty much everyone leaves me eventually, and, most people can't take it, but I have to take it. I can't leave so, I wouldn't leave if I could."

She also said, "This has been the greatest organizational challenge of my life, and other than the exhaustion, the fact that my back hurts, my kids are screaming, my babysitter quit and all that, I actually still strangely enjoy the organization factor. I don't know why." What Kate doesn't understand is that her obsession with organization is precisely why things go so badly so often. She has shown herself to be incapable of being flexible, so when something doesn't go exactly as planned, she lashes out at those around her and makes things worse.

In the show's finale, Kate, Steve, Jamie and Ashley each sat down separately to answer some final questions about the RV trip. When asked about Ashley leaving, Kate said this: "I think she was very angry with me, but quite honestly I think it was a little over dramatic. It's a little dramatic – I thought." "Jamie and I hashed it out. Steve and I hashed it out. Ashley and I hashed it out, and everybody's fine." But when Ashley was asked if she and Kate had spoken, Ashley said, "We have, um, a few times. Nothing deep. Small talk. Nothing really, um, to, to fix it."

Jamie said: "You can blame it on stress; you can blame that you treat people badly because of stress, but it's no excuse to treat the people that love you the most and are closest to you, so poorly, because we're the ones that support you and love you."

That doesn't sound like much was hashed out at all.

THE BLAME GAME

The RV episodes were painful to watch. There was constant complaining and whining, and people acting spoiled and unappreciative of everything they were seeing and doing, and everything they have. The ugly moments I have described are just the tip of the iceberg of terrible behavior that took place on that trip and were captured on film forever. You need to watch the episodes for yourselves to see all the disturbing things that occurred.

Kate had heavily promoted these episodes on Twitter, and she answered questions from her fans on Twitter while watching the RV episodes "together" with them. In reading her tweets, she just doesn't see that anything she does is wrong, or she sees it and doesn't care. Here is a tweet, which is also a lie, from Kate:

Ashley left without telling me :(that's why I'm not there...

According to TLC, in capital letters across our television screens, Ashley told Kate in private that she was leaving. In her continued tweeting, Kate bad-mouthed and blamed Ashley for what transpired:

underminded, like I said! And made kids cry but u won't see that! :(

not sure! This really perplexed me! I've known and loved Ashley for a LONG time! Not sure what the real issue was?!?

It was another rough one...bad attitudes got the best of some... Watch next week... For more drama... And some fun too, I hope!

Watching this, yes it looks harsh.. But you're only seeing parts of all of it..

xxxxx @Kateplusmy8 Is everything okay between u & Ashley?

no matter what,I love her despite it all.Shes family2me&she will come@fully..I **hav no doubt&either does Carla,her mom,my friend!**

Kate's tweeting of blatant untruths caused Ashley to finally break her silence and check in on a Gosselin blog – *realitytvkids.com* – to set the record straight.

```
Hi everyone- as THE Ashley that you all are talking about I just
have to say when I stumbled across this overview of the episode I
was DYING laughing because the admin has what happen down pat.
Obviously there a lot more arguments and bad behavior that they
didn't show but I truly enjoyed reading this. I appreciate the
kind words as I have struggled with leaving the kids ever since
it happened . . . I would ask that everyone continue to pray for
the family as we can see they need it.

— Ashley Dawn Turner
```

During her Twitter party, Kate also tried to justify her horrible behavior on the rafting trip when EVERYONE else was having a great time splashing in the water.

I had camped for so long and had been filthy for so long, I just couldn't get wet that day! No siree!

There were eleven or so other people on this trip, not counting the film crew, who had also "camped" for "so long." None of them whined and complained and acted so immature – not even young children. Why was it that everyone else could have a great time except for Kate? Then because nothing is ever her fault, Kate went off on the river raft guide:

Omg this guy sent me directly over the edge! I was rude to him and he underminded my parental authority often.. UGH!

"This guy," the river raft guide, couldn't have been better mannered or more even-tempered. He sent Kate over the edge because he may have been the first person on the trip to not be totally intimidated, controlled and directed by Kate, and she had no idea how to react to him. (Petty Author's Note: This was the second tweet in which Kate wrote the word "underminded" instead of "undermined." This wouldn't matter at all if she didn't hold herself up as the perfect speller and grammarian and correct others when they are wrong.) Kate tweeted more about the drama of the trip:

I felt ganged up upon by all of them and felt like I had the organizational job of 1,000 ppl!

Seriously the drama was not ME!

Then someone tweeted Kate that it sure looked like it was her, and Kate responded:

oh sure but over the top drama wasn't me.

Finally, a particularly vocal tweeter really got under Kate's skin with several critical tweets. The tweetie told Kate that it made her sick to her stomach to hear Kate talk about not having help, and that she was "appalled" at what she saw. Kate jumped in to set the record straight:

nope. Ur only seeing edited footage.

And she tweeted this to another fan:

Hard to watch and see that ppl don't understand due to editing etc.

And here again on March 12, 2012, Kate tweeted with the viewers in the United Kingdom, who were just getting to see the final episodes of *Kate Plus Ei8ht*. A tweeter told her they were just seeing the RV episode; another tweeted that Kate "seemed very hard to please." This is how Kate responded:

> **oh, my, remember: drama and editing work magic :) we are all still friends lol**

> **lol. Remember editing &drama gets ratings.Sad u didn't c the many good Xs we had :(I'm not hard2pls,lots of planning on my mind**

Either Kate does not understand the concept of editing, she is stupid, or she is simply delusional. Or, she is all of the above. Anything captured on film can definitely be changed through omission or rearrangement. But the funny thing about film is that you can't edit IN behavior that did not occur. Viewers saw Kate saying and doing all kinds of horrible, nasty, mean-spirited, narcissistic things to her family, friends and paid workers. This wasn't some CGI-generated or special-effects-laden movie. This was the real Kate Gosselin exposed for all the world to see. She can't deny that she said and did ALL of those terrible things, yet she still blames "bad editing." If TLC did edit OUT Kate's good behavior, any reasonable person would have to ask themselves "why?"

Kate continued to tell everyone over and over again on Twitter that TLC's editing showed only the bad moments, and focused only on the times when Kate was complaining and miserable. Even if that were true, Kate Gosselin still showed more ugly, mean moments on that family trip than any normal person would display in a lifetime. It was horrible and embarrassing. Words cannot do it justice. This was Kate unplugged and unhinged. TLC finally showed the world the real Kate Gosselin.

As stated previously, Kate had final say in the editing of her show. She got a preview copy sent to her a week or more in advance to make final edits, then she spent a week hyping the episodes on her Twitter page. She gave final approval to everything the viewers saw, good and bad, because she had absolutely no idea that anything was abnormal about her behavior. This was very much like her keeping a daily journal documenting her abuse of her children to be included in her book about letters of love to her children.

Over the years, Kate has told us, ad nauseam, that her "...*Kate Plus*..." shows are the realist reality we will ever see. She assured us that they were just a family living their lives and being filmed. If that was true, then who was to blame for the disastrous RV trip? Whose idea was it? Did TLC force her to go on this trip? Was it a coincidence that Kate suddenly blamed all her outrageous behavior on bad editing at the same time that TLC decided to ditch her and stop protecting her? Even while watching the RV episodes and seeing how horrible Kate Gosselin is as a person, a mother, and a human being, some people continued to give her a pass, buying into her mantra that the editing was at fault. During her Twitter party, Kate played the victim, as always. Someone tweeted that they felt sad for Kate because "She's accustomed to people leaving, but doesn't connect it to her actions." Kate responded with this tweet:

I sure do but they don't connect my actions to my unusually stressful life either..Not justifying but St goes both ways! Gnight!:)

Gnight, Kate. Everyone knows nothing is ever your fault.

Doron Ofir, who's cast several reality shows, including Jersey Shore and RuPaul's Drag Race, also insists that however contrived the situations are, people are behaving in an authentic way.
"Something that makes me crazy is when cast members say, 'The edited me to be this character,' like Omarosa's famous line," he says. "Ten years later, you know Omarosa is what she is."
http://www.businessweek.com/articles/2013-05-23/the-reality-tv-dissident-dave-hester-of-storage-wars

THE END?

IT MIGHT BE A CRAZY LIFE …
BUT IT'S THEIR LIFE.

Some of the following information was known by me at the time of the original book being released but withheld to protect the source(s), and some information came to light more recently.

Kate Gosselin is completely obsessed with getting back on television because of the high salaries that she sees other reality 'stars' being paid. She wants desperately to get a new show on a different network so that she can rub it in TLCs face that they made a terrible mistake when they canceled her and 'abandoned' her. She refuses to accept the fact that she was a novelty act and the television-viewing audience has lost interest in her antics and has moved on. She believes in her heart that she is more talented than anyone else on television and she becomes enraged just talking about it. She believes that she would be the best host The View has ever had and having her as a permanent member of the panel would garner the highest ratings ever for the show. In Kate's mind, people are just too blind or too stupid to give her a chance. When Jenny McCarthy was recently given the permanent slot, Kate went into a weeks-long depression filled with binge drinking and violent outbursts toward her children. The children were very quiet and careful in that house during that time, in an attempt to protect themselves from Kate's wrath.

Kate's drinking though is something that the children are accustomed to. They've been dodging her and quietly cleaning up after her for several years. Kate once fell down several stairs while drunk in front of the children and the oldest girls helped her up and cleaned up the broken glass from her drink.

A college-age babysitter once tried to stop Kate from going out to run errands in the afternoon after seeing Kate finishing a drink and witnessing her slurred speech. The sitter confronted Kate politely at the front door and told her that she didn't think it would be a good idea for her to drive in her condition and offered to run Kate's errands for her. Kate snapped at her and told her not to ever question her again and to worry about watching children and doing her job and left. The sitter was fired when Kate returned later the same day.

Kate no longer identifies with Katie Kreider. She doesn't know who she is or who she was. In Kate's mind, there is only Kate Gosselin, television star. She can't enjoy her children because she is so focused and consumed with trying to get another show so she can go back to the pampered lifestyle that she's become accustomed to. She has completely lost touch with reality.

500

The emotional abuse and physical beatings of the Gosselin children continue to this day. Many of Kate Gosselin's supporters refused to believe that she would ever lay hands on her children, especially babies in diapers, but the fact remains that it wasn't an isolated period of time documented in her private journal. That journal was merely a snapshot of the Gosselin children's permanent reality. That journal was filled with Kate's stories of 'loving' her children, not the reality of their situation. The world won't hear the true story of the children's horror until they're old enough to tell it for themselves.

After her divorce from Jon, Kate was caught on video violently spanking two of the boys in the driveway of their home, the moment they got out of the van from returning from an overnight with Jon. The other children just watched in fear as the spanking took place, perhaps not knowing if they were next. I later found out the reason for the beating was because the boys told Kate they wanted to stay longer at Jon's house because they were having too much fun. Kate now promises the children presents and trips to Toys R Us for toys if they tell Jon that they don't want to go to his house.

The paparazzo who shot the video didn't release it because he shot it from private property. He was there at the time hoping to snap what would have been a very valuable photo of Kate with her bodyguard Steve Neild in a romantic moment, but that didn't materialize.

Kate Gosselin had one babysitter who would actually administer her own beatings to the Gosselin children at Kate's direction when she was away. The sitter was given the authority by Kate to carry out Kate's way of 'teaching' the children for even the smallest of infractions. This included spanking the children, withholding meals from the children and locking the children in a room for hours at a time. This same sitter was told by Kate to lock one of the boys in the bathroom for her entire shift because he left splashes of water on the sink and floor without toweling it off.

Beating or spanking her children isn't the only way Kate gets her message across to them. Kate recently pushed one of the boys outside in below-freezing temperatures without his coat, gloves or hat for fifteen minutes because the boy didn't close the door all the way when he came inside from playing in the snow. The child was screaming and crying and banging on the doors all around the house. His face was bright red from being so cold when Kate finally allowed him to come back into the house.

On one occasion, one of the boys was punished for having Shoka in the basement when he was supposed to be outside. Shoka had an accident by the door and Kate was so enraged that she brought the boy down to the basement and screamed at him while showing him the mess. To show her complete domination of the child, she grabbed him by the back of his neck and forced his face down to within inches of the mess, trying to rub his face in it. He struggled and resisted and ended up with only a spanking instead of a face-full of dog feces.

This is the Gosselin children's normal.

The Gosselin dog's normal wasn't much better. In fact, it was very similar to the children's normal. That's why they were sent away after only a short time as being 'part of the family.'

Both Gosselin dogs, Shoka and Nala, were abused by Kate during the separation and divorce when Jon was away from the house. Kate treated the dogs and the kids in the same manner but the dogs resisted and 'fought back.' Kate would use a stick, a spoon, a tube or whatever else she had handy to discipline the dogs for minor infractions that dogs commit, like tracking mud into the basement after being brought in from being outside in the pouring rain and…mud. If Kate got growled at by one of the dogs for hitting them for minor animal infractions, she would banish them to the outdoors overnight. She talked to them like people and thought she could reason with them. She locked them outside in the freezing rain and snow and left them to watch the family through the basement windows. One freezing cold night, she sadistically went to the glass door where the female dog Nala was howling to come inside and she smiled and waved to her and told her how warm it was inside and that maybe she'll think about her actions so she could come back in the following morning. She got down on the floor to pet Shoka who was laying by the door looking out at poor Nala. Kate Gosselin is cruel and she seems to enjoy the power that she has over children, animals and adults.

This is Kate Gosselin's normal.

As strange as this may sound, Kate Gosselin possesses some qualities of character that could have been extremely useful in putting her on a path to becoming a very successful businesswoman. She is tenacious and determined and goal-oriented. As distasteful as it is, it took a great deal of planning and single-minded focus for her to achieve her goal of having and exploiting a gaggle of children to gain wealth and fame.

Unfortunately, Kate Gosselin also possesses qualities of character (more accurately, character flaws) that have prevented her, and will always prevent her, from being successful on her own without her children. She has shown herself to be incredibly lazy, intellectually challenged, developmentally stunted, completely lacking in self-awareness, ignorant of the world around her, conceited, selfish, hypocritical, ungrateful, socially awkward and abusive. I could go on and on, but you get the picture.

When Kate had the backing of Discovery/TLC, she was presented with more opportunities than the vast majority of the mediocre masses will ever see in a lifetime, and she squandered each and every one. She can try to blame every person under the sun for her failures, and eliminate every person who has not agreed with her from her life, but in the end she only has to look at the image staring back at her from a mirror to know where the fault lies.

In reviewing the events that created and fueled the Gosselin Family phenomenon, and ultimately turned it into a tragedy of epic proportions, one thing is very clear. The desire for money and power, on the part of Discovery/TLC/Figure 8 Films and their associates, and on the part of the Gosselin parents, caused eight innocent children to be exploited and, yes, abused, in the most despicable ways. We will never know how great a part the pressure of filming the TV show played and contributed to Kate Gosselin's admitted anger and violent outbursts towards her children. It is inconceivable to think it was not a major factor, and the network and producers should be held accountable for their role in allowing it to happen.
The Gosselin saga should be viewed as a cautionary tale by anyone even considering putting his or her children's lives on display to the world. There is no monetary value that can be placed on privacy, dignity and respect, but the price of *denying* children those basic human rights is without measure.
Alexis, Leah, Hannah, Joel, Aaden, Collin, Cara and Mady Gosselin will be paying that price for the rest of their lives. That is the tragedy.

TLC INTERVIEWER QUESTION:
"Would you say that the show that we do is realistic?"

KATE GOSSELIN:
"What you see is what you get. We aren't hiding anything."

Kate was once asked, if she "had a crystal ball, would she have taken the fertility drugs?" It is heartbreaking to imagine how Kate's beautiful children will feel when they one day read their mother's answer to that question:

"If I could have looked into the future,
I would not have done it."
– *Kate Gosselin*

EPILOGUE

On October 16, 2012, Kate Gosselin was fired from her job as a "blogger" for CouponCabin, an online coupon service. In a scathing letter that appeared on the company's website, Scott Kluth, founder and CEO, made it very clear that Kate was not a good fit for the company. The firing led to immediate speculation about what would have caused Kluth to issue such a public rebuke. Was it Kate's lack of professionalism? Was it that she misrepresented herself as a struggling mom who has to cut coupons, instead of acknowledging that she is a millionaire? Was it that she failed to promote CouponCabin, and its charitable endeavors, in her appearances? Was it that she used her blog to showcase personal issues and dissatisfaction with others, instead of providing information and suggestions to help people save money? I suspect it was all of the above and, quite possibly, some things we have yet to hear about. Here is the letter in its entirety.

To all our Kate blog readers:

Some nine-plus years ago, I started CouponCabin with the thought of creating a single website that had all the best coupons… no gimmicks, no fluff, just a site that was easy to use and that had great deals. Along the way, we've helped our users collectively save hundreds of millions of dollars.

A series of recent events have made it clear to me that Kate Gosselin and her contributions do not align with the authenticity which we set out to build almost a decade ago, and that Ms. Gosselin is simply not a good fit with the wonderful team and culture at CouponCabin.

It's with this that I am writing to inform you of our decision to discontinue Ms. Gosselin's feature blog on CouponCabin.com. Ms. Gosselin's contributions garnered both positive attention and criticism, but as always, I respect and appreciate your candid opinions, which often encourage us not to lose sight of our mission — to help YOU save money.

We wish Kate, her family and her support staff all the best.

Scott Kluth
Founder and CEO of CouponCabin.com

Kate's October 16, 2012 did not get any better. That day, Legislation authored by Representative Thomas Murt (R-Montgomery) to address inadequate child labor laws in Pennsylvania passed the House and Senate. Murt began an investigation in 2009 in response to concerns about the working conditions and lack of work permits for the Gosselin children. House Bill 1548 is meant to protect the rights and well-being of children working in TV and film, and to ensure that children working in reality TV have the same protections. Governor Tom Corbett signed the bill on October 25, 2012.

As a personal note: Kate, if you are the subject of Congressional hearings, and a law has been passed based on your failure to protect your children, you may want to rethink what you are doing.

Murt Child Labor Bill Goes to Governor
10/16/2012

HARRISBURG—Legislation to reform the state's laws regulating children in entertainment is on its way to the governor's desk, said Rep. Tom Murt (R-Montgomery), author of the measure, after the House joined the Senate in passing Murt's reforms.

"This is a major victory for the state's children," Murt said. "The entire General Assembly has stated emphatically that those employed in film and television are indeed working and must have rights and protections."

After an extensive investigation into children in films and television programs shot in Pennsylvania that began in 2009, Murt introduced House Bill 1548 to reform the state's antiquated laws to address the changes in the industry.

"This legislation was designed to mimic the child labor laws of California," Murt said. "I wanted to protect the health and financial wellbeing of child performers, but also wanted to provide reasonable guidelines that film and television producers could follow."

The bill was crafted after meetings with representatives of the Motion Picture Association of America and Paul Petersen, the former child actor whose organization, A Minor Consideration, helps legislatures write their labor laws to protect child performers.

While film and TV production has nearly doubled over the last decade, the state's child labor laws regulating entertainment were written years before color television, HBO and reality TV.

Murt's investigation into child labor in reality TV revealed that the state laws regulating entertainment were so antiquated that children under 7 could not legally appear on a television series filmed in the state.

House Bill 1548 allows children on television, but limits the hours a child can work. The bill also makes sure a studio teacher is on set so a child actor's education is provided for.

Under the reforms in House Bill 1548, children under 16 on a film set must be accompanied by a parent or guardian at all times. They can work no more than eight hours a day or 48 hours per week, and minors must finish work by 10 p.m. on school nights.

The bill also requires that trust accounts be established for minor actors, in which the employer must deposit 15 percent of the child's gross earnings. "It's the only way to make sure a portion of the child's earnings are there for them when they reach adulthood," Murt said.

The bill also defines the term "reality program" to make sure the children who appear on reality TV have the same protections as the children on a movie set.

"By updating the state's child labor laws, I believe we will encourage more TV and film production," Murt said. "We have created the clear legal guidelines the industry asked for and ensured child performers are paid and their health is protected."

State Representative Thomas Murt
152nd District, Pennsylvania House of Representatives
Contact:
Rep. Murt's Office
215-744-2600

ACKNOWLEDGMENT

Thank you, Dana Hoffman,
for being a loving, dedicated mother to our children,
and for being the first person
to publicly shine a light
on Kate Gosselin's web of deceit.

Thank you Madeleine, Alexandra and Nickolas
for making us so proud!!!

Thank you to all of the 'Inside Sources.'
Without you speaking out against the fraud, lies and abuse,
there would be no story to tell.

Special thank you to B.C., A.T., J.A., C.T., J.G., M.G., K.K.